D1215265

DOMESDAY BOOK

Index of Places

History from the Sources

DOMESDAY BOOK

A Survey of the Counties of England

LIBER DE WINTONIA

Compiled by direction of

KING WILLIAM I

Winchester
1086

DOMESDAY BOOK

36
Index of Places

J. McN. Dodgson and J. J. N. Palmer

PHILLIMORE
Chichester
1992

1992

Published by

PHILLIMORE & CO. LTD.
Shopwyke Hall, Chichester, Sussex

© J. McN. Dodgson and J. J. N. Palmer, 1992

ISBN 0 85033 702 X

Printed and bound in Great Britain by
Bookcraft (Bath) Ltd.

Publisher's Note

Medieval cathedrals often took so long to build that their completion ceremonies looked back not only to the long-departed original architect but to one or two of his successors who also failed to survive until the 'topping out'. Dr. John Morris approached Phillimore, in 1969, with a proposal that the entire text of Domesday Book should be translated afresh into modern English to provide the first ever uniform English version, free from the inconsistencies and transliterations of the mainly Victorian translations that impeded research and comparative study. With the help of such scholars as Herbert Finberg, W. G. Hoskins, Vivian Galbraith and John Dodgson, the work was begun in 1970 but, seven years later, with only half a dozen counties completed, Dr. Morris tragically died at the early age of sixty. Professor Dodgson took over and saw the whole translation – and the rapidly growing apparatus of notes – through to completion, co-ordinating what had now become a team of around forty scholars engaged on the project. The county-by-county edition was finished in time for the Domesday Ninth Centenary celebrations of 1986, and Dodgson turned his attention to the 'cumulative' index and analysis that had been discussed since 1970 but could now begin in earnest with considerable input from Dr. John Palmer of the Hull University Domesday Project. John Dodgson died, sadly, in 1990 with the Persons and Places parts just completed in respect of his personal input. J. D. Foy, working independently, had by then finalised his great subject index in typescript.

The magnitude of their achievement earns increasing recognition with every year that passes and for decades to come historians and students will have cause to recall Morris's inspiration and Dodgson's industry. Like most pioneers they suffered from critics and detractors, ranging from the first question asked by the then chairman of Phillimore, in 1969, 'but surely anyone working on Domesday is able to cope with medieval calligraphy and abbreviated Latin?' to 'why are they wanting to change the translation on which I've based my lectures for the past 30 years?'. But they persisted and, in the end, prevailed. They made our greatest public record reliably and cheaply available for the first time since 1986 and, with their unique three-part Index, provided the first comprehensive apparatus to meet the needs of serious study and historical research. Their publisher is proud to have worked with them and to have seen their scholarly edifice constructed to stand as an enduring monument to their memory.

INDEX of Places and Place-names mentioned in the Phillimore translation of Domesday Book

The Phillimore edition of Domesday Book was published over a twelve-year period during which both the annotation of the text and the indexing became more elaborate. The present index is a revised version of the county indices in a common format, arranged in single alphabetical sequence for the whole of Domesday England, incorporating corrections to the county indices and additional identifications. All references to places named in the major Domesday texts are collected in the main index, together with references to discussions of the identification of many places in the notes to the county volumes; anonymous entries identified in these notes are also included. All other places which are discussed in the notes but which are nowhere named in either Domesday Book itself or in the major satellite texts are indexed in the Supplementary index. In the main, these are subholdings of Domesday manors identified from later sources.

In the first column of the index, place-names are given the modern form found on Ordnance Survey maps, all affixes and suffixes which are not part of the Domesday name-form being indicated by the use of square brackets. Unidentified or conjectural place-names are printed in italics, in their Domesday spelling if no modern equivalent is known. Alternative spellings are indicated by an oblique stroke (*Merestone/Merestun*) or conflation (*E(le)stolf*) for either *Estolf* or *Elestolf*. Where Domesday does not differentiate between what are now distinct settlements with the same root name (e.g., Great and Little Abington), separate grid references for each are supplied. Where possible, the references for such distinct settlements are distinguished by separate entries in the index.

The index is sorted on a word-by-word basis according to rules implemented in the following sequence:

(1) the root place-name: [King's] Langley is therefore sorted under **Langley**, and [Chew] Stoke under **Stoke**.

(2) The 'surname' (if any) is the second element on which names are sorted, irrespective of whether this occurs before or after the root name. Hence Appleton, [East] Appleton, and Appleton [le Moors] are sorted in that order, [East] Appleton being treated as though its name were Appleton East for sorting purposes.

(3) the third sort key is the county, in the alphabetical order of its name and not of the abbreviation used.

(4) the final element for sorting purposes is the parish named in parentheses as an aid to identification, ignoring 'by', 'in', 'near' or other such words accompanying the parish name.

The county named in the second column of the index is the county in which the place-name occurs in Domesday Book. Where a place is named in more than one county or in a county other than that to which it traditionally belonged, both the ancient county and the Domesday county are indicated, only the grid reference for the historic county being supplied, as in these two instances:

Acton [Beauchamp] HEF	HEF	SO6750	EW1
Acton [Beauchamp] HEF	WOR		11,1
Amesbury WIL	HAM		1,31.EW1
Amesbury WIL	WIL	SU1541	1,3.24,16-17

The sections into which the Domesday scribe has subdivided the text of some counties is indicated by the addition of abbreviations for Cumberland, Westmorland, Lancashire, the Isle of Wight, Flintshire, Wales, and the Ridings of Yorkshire. The full list of abbreviations used to identify the counties or parts thereof is:

BDF	Bedfordshire	LIN	Lincolnshire
BRK	Berkshire	MDX	Middlesex
BKM	Buckingham	NFK	Norfolk
CAM	Cambridgeshire	NR	North Riding: see YKS
CHS	Cheshire	NTH	Northamptonshire
CON	Cornwall	NTT	Nottinghamshire
CUM	Cumberland: see YKS	OXF	Oxfordshire
DBY	Derbyshire	RUT	Rutland
DEV	Devonshire	SFK	Suffolk
ER	East Riding: see YKS	SHR	Shropshire
ESS	Essex	SOM	Somerset
FLN	Flintshire: see CHS	SRY	Surrey
GLS	Gloucestershire	SSX	Sussex
HAM	Hampshire	STS	Staffordshire
HEF	Herefordshire	WAR	Warwickshire
HRT	Hertfordshire	WES	Westmorland: see YKS
HUN	Huntingdonshire	WIL	Wiltshire
IOW	Isle of Wight: see HAM	WOR	Worcestershire
KEN	Kent	WR	West Riding: see YKS
LAN	Lancashire: see CHS, YKS	YKS	Yorkshire
LEC	Leicestershire		

The grid references given in the third column of the index use the National Grid system of the Ordnance Survey. Grid references are supplied for all places whose location is reasonably certain, unidentified places being indicated by a double-query in the grid column. In such cases the notes to the county volumes often supply possible identifications, together with their respective Ordnance Survey co-ordinates. Where no precise location for the seat of a manor can be ascertained, that of the parish church has been used.

The fourth column of the index supplies the references to the text, citing chapter and paragraph in the form introduced by the Phillimore edition which has since become standard. In the case of Cornwall and Shropshire some chapters are subdivided, giving three figure references. Unless the form of the reference itself reveals its origin (eg, WoA1 or EvQ1), sources are distinguished by the use of Roman and italic type, according to the following conventions:

(a) 1,25   Place named in Domesday Book
(b) *1,25*   Place named in satellite text
(c) 1,29 *note*   Place named in Domesday and discussed in notes
(d) 1,29 note   Place named only in note
(e) 1,25 *and note*   Place named in Domesday; satellite cited in note
(f) 1,29 *in note*   Unnamed manor identified in note

Satellite sources are only normally noted if they supply place-name information not given in the Domesday text.

J. McN. Dodgson, University College, London.

J. J. N. Palmer, University of Hull.

On the Feast of St Willibrord of Utrecht, 1988.

PART ONE

Places

A

Abberley	WOR	SO7567	15,8
Abberton	ESS	TL9919	20,20. 24,51. 34,16
Abberton	WOR	SO9953	9,1a
Abbotsbury	DOR	SY5785	13,1
Abbotsham	DEV	SS4226	5,6
Abbotskerswell	DEV	SX8568	7,2
Abbotskerswell: see Kerswell DEV			
Abbotstone	HAM	SU5634	2,23
Abdon	SHR	SO5786	4,3,7
Abedestone IOW	HAM	??	1,W6
Abegrave: see *Prestgrave* LEC			
Abingdon	BRK	SU4997	7,38
Abinger	SRY	TQ1145	21,6
Abington	NTH	SP7761	59,3
[Great and Little] Abington	CAM	TL5348	1,16. 14,14. 29,10;12
		TL5349	
Abington [Pigotts]	CAM	TL3044	1,19-20. 2,3. 13,5. 26,24. 32,13
Abla IOW	HAM	??	1,W21
Ablington	GLS	SP1007	WoA1
Ablington	WIL	SU1546	23,4
Abney	DBY	SK1979	7,11
Aby	LIN	TF4178	4,59;60. 13,4
Acaster [Malbis] WR	YKS	SE5845	11W3. SW,An3
Acaster [Selby] WR	YKS	SE5740	6W3. 11W4. 24W3. 29W28-29. CW40. SW,An3-4
Aceshille	NTH	??	35,11
Achebi (in Snape) NR	YKS	??	6N120 *note*. SN,CtA35
Achelie (in Boldre Hundred)	HAM	??	NF9,15
Achelie (in Redbridge Hundred)	HAM	??	NF1,1
Achurch	NTH	TL0282	6a,22
Ackhill (Wales)	SHR	SO2865	5,7
Acklam ER	YKS	SE7861	5E63. 29E29. SE,Ac4
Acklam NR	YKS	NZ4817	1N28 *note*. 4N3. 11N9. 31N5. SN,L32-33
Ackley (Wales)	SHR	SJ2501	4,1,36
Ackton WR	YKS	SE4121	9W95. SW,Ag2
Ackworth WR	YKS	SE4418	9W52 *note*. SW,010
Acle	NFK	TG4010	1,151
Acleta	ESS	??	25,10
Acomb WR	YKS	SE5751	2W3. 29W13. SW,An15
[Castle and West] Acre	NFK	TF8015	8,22;88. 15,5. 22,15-16;20
		TF7815	
[South] Acre	NFK	TF8014	1,71;75. 8,95. 12,2
Acrise	KEN	TR1942	5,224
Acton (near Nantwich)	CHS	SJ6253	8,16. S1
Acton	DOR	SY9878	55,41
Acton	SFK	TL8945	34,2
Acton [Beauchamp] HEF	HEF	SO6750	EW1
Acton [Beauchamp] HEF	WOR		11,1
Acton [Burnell]	SHR	SJ5302	4,4,3
Acton [Ilger]	GLS	ST6783	6,1
[Iron] Acton	GLS	ST6783	69,6;7
Acton [Piggott]	SHR	SJ5402	4,3,18
Acton [Reynald]	SHR	SJ5323	4,3,59

Acton [Round]	SHR	SO6395	4,3,6
Acton [Scott]	SHR	SO4589	4,27,33
Acton [Trussell]	STS	SJ9318	2,3
Acton [Turville]	GLS	ST8080	60,6
Adbaston	STS	SJ7627	2,20
Adber DOR	DOR	ST5920	ES4;7;9
Adber DOR	SOM		19,74. 24,37. 47,11
Adbolton	NTT	SK6038	10,12;56
Adderbury	OXF	SP4635	1,7a. 3,2. 27,6
Adderley	SHR	SJ6639	4,24,1
Addestone	WIL	SU0643	10,4
Addingham WR	YKS	SE0849	1W46 note. 1W73. 21W5.
			SW,Bu32. SW,Cr3
Addingrove	BKM	SP6611	14,6
Addington	BKM	SP7428	4,40. 23,30
Addington	KEN	TQ6558	5,51
Addington	SRY	TQ3764	34,1. 36,7
[Great and Little] Addington	NTH	SP9575	4,21-22. 6a,29. 11,4
		SP9573	
Addlethorpe	LIN	TF5569	2,19. 3,46. 12,79-80;81-82. 24,51.
			29,17;19;23. 38,8. 68,10
Addlethorpe WR	YKS	SE3448	1W49. 28W21. SW,Bu37
Adel WR	YKS	SE2740	5W2 note. SW,Sk18
Adewelle (near Careby)	LIN	??	8,5
Adforton HEF	HEF	SO4071	ES6
Adforton HEF	SHR		6,13
Adgestone IOW	HAM	SZ5986	7,15. 9,6
Adisham	KEN	TR2254	3,18
Adlach	OXF	??	58,38
Adlestrop	GLS	SP2426	12,2. EvO8
Adley HEF	HEF	SO3774	ES3;19-20
Adley HEF	SHR		4,20,26. 6,27-28
Adlingfleet WR	YKS	SE8421	17W1. SW,St2
Adlington	CHS	SJ9180	1,26
Admington WAR	GLS		11,11
Admington WAR	WAR	SP2046	EG4
Adsborough	SOM	ST2729	25,3
Adstock	BKM	SP7330	16,8
Adstone	NTH	SP5951	1,6. 17,1. 18,73
Adwell	OXF	SU6999	35,21
Adwick [le Street] WR	YKS	SE5408	5W30-31. 10W39. CW22. SW,Sf9
			note. SW,Sf34. SW,02
Adwick [upon Dearne] WR	YKS	SE4701	10W14. SW,Sf9 note
Adworthy	DEV	SS7715	34,42
Afettune	KEN	??	5,176
Afflington	DOR	SY9780	28,6-7. 37,7. 41,1. 57,20
Affpuddle	DOR	SY8093	11,5
Afton	DEV	SX8462	34,49
Afton IOW	HAM	SZ3486	1,3
Agardsley	STS	SK1327	10,4
Agglethorpe NR	YKS	SE0886	6N96. SN,CtA29
Aia	KEN	??	9,47
Aighton LAN	YKS	SD6739	1L1 note. See also CHS Y2
Aike ER	YKS	TA0445	2B14. 5E33. SE,Sn4
Ailby	LIN	TF4377	2,20. 4,63
Ailey HEF	HEF	SO3448	25,9
Ailstone	WAR	SP2051	40,1
Ailsworth	NTH	TL1199	6,5. 6a,3
Ailwood	DOR	SY9981	56,58
Ainderby [Mires] NR	YKS	SE2592	6N52-53 note. SN, CtA19-20
Ainderby [Quernhow] NR	YKS	SE3480	6N157. SN,CtA43

Ainderby [Steeple] NR	YKS	SE3392	1Y2. 6N34. SN,A1. SN,CtA14
Ainsdale LAN	CHS	SD3112	R1,24
[Little] Airmyn WR	YKS	SE7225	16W1. SW,BA9
Airton WR	YKS	SD9059	30W28
Airy [Holme] NR	YKS	NZ5711	1N16. SN,L27
Aisby	LIN	SK8792	1,39;47
Aisby	LIN	TF0138	26,47
Aisholt	SOM	ST1935	21,31
Aiskew NR	YKS	SE2788	6N123. SN,CtA36
Aislaby (near Pickering) NR	YKS	SE7785	1N53. SN, D18
Aislaby (near Whitby) NR	YKS	NZ8508	5N9. SN,L10
Aismunderby WR	YKS	SE3068	2W13 note. 13W21 note. SW,Bu19
Aisthorpe	LIN	SK9480	24,7. 68,27-28
Aitone	SHR	??	4,3,34
Akeley	BKM	SP7037	14,26
Akenham	SFK	TM1448	1,117. 8,68;71. 38,11. 14,5;16
Akethorpe	SFK	TM5493	1,56
Alac	HEF	??	1;5;34
Alalei IOW	HAM	??	9,4
Alberbury	SHR	SJ3514	4,1,9
Albright [Hussey]	SHR	SJ5017	4,3,51;57
Albrightlee	SHR	SJ5216	3g,7
Albrighton (near Shifnal)	SHR	SJ8004	4,25,6
Albrighton (in Shrewsbury St Mary)	SHR	SJ4918	4,3,71
Alburgh NFK	NFK	TM2787	1,129;221. 4,48. 29,7
Alburgh NFK	SFK		ENf2
Albury	HRT	TL4324	4,11
Albury OXF	BRK		B3;?8 note
Albury OXF	OXF	SP6505	59,22. EBe2
Albury	SRY	TQ0547	19,36
Alby	NFK	TG1934	9,87;174
Alcamestune	HEF	??	29,10
Alcaston	SHR	SO4587	4,21,19
Alchin (in Buxted)	SSX	TQ5028	2,1g
Alciston	SSX	TQ5005	8,1. 9,63;65;81;99-100
Alcmuntona	NFK	??	9,68 note. 12,25 note;26
Alcombe	SOM	SS9745	25,11
Alconbury	HUN	TL1875	1,6. 5,2. 19,15;17-20. D22
Aldborough	NFK	TG1834	8,130. 9,87;146;151
Aldborough WR	YKS	SE4066	1Y18. 1W30. 21W3. 24W10. 25W27. 28W36. SW,Bu13
Aldbourne	WIL	SU2675	1,10
Aldbrough ER	YKS	TA2438	14E11. SE,Hol14
Aldbrough NR	YKS	NZ2011	6N13-14. SN,CtA10
Aldbury	HRT	SP9612	15,3
Aldcliffe LAN	YKS	SD4660	1L2. See also CHS Y3
Aldeburgh	SFK	TM4656	6,130. 21,105
Aldeby	NFK	TM4593	20,36
Aldenham (in Cashio Hundred)	HRT	TL1400	10,17
Aldenham (in Dacorum Hundred)	HRT	TQ1398	9,4
Alderbury	WIL	SU1826	19,2-3. 37,14. 68,33
Alderford	ESS	TL7633	23,11
Alderley	GLS	ST7690	64,3
[Nether] Alderley	CHS	SJ8476	14,6
[Over] Alderley	CHS	SJ8676	9,28
Aldermaston	BRK	SU5965	B5. 1,44-45
Alderminster WAR	WAR	SP2348	EW5
Alderminster WAR	WOR		9,3
Alderstone	WIL	SU2424	67,35
Alderton	GLS	SP0033	1,43. 11,5
Alderton	NTH	SP7446	18,9;91

Alderton	SFK	TM3441	6,152;159;162;164;240. 21,77
Alderton	WIL	ST8382	41,9. 49,3
Alderton [Hall]	ESS	TQ4296	8,7
Aldfield WR	YKS	SE2669	1W40. 2W8. 28W38. SW,Bu20
Aldglose	KEN	TR0844	5,171
Aldham	ESS	TL9125	18,24
Aldham	SFK	TM0444	14,112. 35,6. 1,105
Aldingbourne	SSX	SU9205	3,3
Aldingham LAN	YKS	SD2871	1L8. See also CHS Y9
Aldington (near Hythe)	KEN	TR0736	2,23;25
Aldington (in Thurnham)	KEN	TQ8157	5,68
Aldington	WOR	SP0644	10,5
Aldon	SHR	SO4379	7,6
Aldredelie (in Kingsley)	CHS	??	1,10
Aldridge	STS	SK0600	12,24
Aldringham	SFK	TM4460	6,70;74
Aldrington	SSX	TQ2705	12,20-21
Aldsworth	GLS	SP1510	3,4 note. 10,5. 78,11
Aldwark NR	YKS	SE4663	5N70. SN,B26
Aldwick	SOM	ST4961	37,5
Aldwincle	NTH	TL0081	6a,27. 41,6
Aldworth	BRK	SU5579	63,1
Alethorpe	NFK	TF9431	1,16
Aley	SOM	ST1838	25,4
Alfildestuna	SFK	??	16,45. 36,5
Alford	LIN	TF4576	24,70. 66,2
Alford	SOM	ST6032	19,65
Alfoxton	SOM	ST1441	35,13
Alfreton	DBY	SK4055	16,7
Alfriston	SSX	TQ5103	10,57-58
Algamundestuna	NFK	??	9,52 *note*;68 note
Algar[kirk] Hundred	LIN	—	12,73
Algar[kirk]	LIN	TF2935	11,7
Alhampton	SOM	ST6234	8,30
Alkborough	LIN	SE8821	8,29. 14,29
Alkerton	GLS	SO7705	78,16
Alkerton	OXF	SP3742	7,50. 35,32
Alkington	GLS	ST6998	1,15
Alkington	SHR	SJ5339	4,14,8
Alkmonton	DBY	SK1838	6,35
Aller (in Abbotskerswell)	DEV	SX8768	48,11
Aller (in Kentisbeare)	DEV	ST0506	16,103. 32,3
Aller (in South Molton)	DEV	SS6927	3,57. 42,12
Aller (in Carhampton)	SOM	ST0042	21,63
Aller (near Langport)	SOM	ST4029	32,8
Aller (in Sampford Brett)	SOM	ST0739	18,3
Allercott	SOM	SS9539	25,23
Allerford	SOM	SS9046	32,4
Allerston NR	YKS	SE8782	1Y4. 1N46. SN,D12;14
Allerthorpe ER	YKS	SE7844	1Y10. SE,P3
Allerthorpe [Hall] NR	YKS	SE3386	6N153 *note*. SN, CtA43
Allerton LAN	CHS	SJ4187	R1,15
Allerton WR	YKS	SE1133	9W131 *note*. 9W144. SW,M7
Allerton [Bywater] WR	YKS	SE4127	9W1. SW,Sk4 *note*
[Chapel] Allerton WR	YKS	SE3037	9W14. SW,Sk4 *note*. SW,Sk9
[Chapel and Stone] Allerton	SOM	ST4050	24,11
		ST4051	
Allerton [Mauleverer] WR	YKS	SE4157	1W37 *note*. 28W3. 29W16; 31W1. SW,Bu10 -11
[North]allerton: see Northallerton YKS			
Allestree	DBY	SK3439	4,2

Allexton	LEC	SK8100	1,3. 40,27;39
Allington FLN	CHS	SJ3857	16,1
Allington	DOR	SY4693	33,4
Allington	HAM	SU4717	49,1
Allington (in Hollingbourne)	KEN	TQ8456	5,70
Allington (near Maidstone)	KEN	TQ7457	5,41
Allington	LIN	SK8540	18,31. 19,1. 58,8
Allington	SSX	TQ3813	10,103. 12,50-52
Allington (in All Cannings)	WIL	SU0663	26,1
Allington (near Amesbury)	WIL	SU2039	16,3. 23,7
[East] Allington	DEV	SX7748	30,3
[South] Allington	DEV	SX7938	17,53
Allisland	DEV	SS4811	52,6
Allum	HAM	SU2707	NF7,1
Almeley	HEF	SO3351	6,8
Almington	STS	SJ7034	8,22
Alminstone	DEV	SS3420	42,3
Almondbury WR	YKS	SE1615	9W105. SW,Ag7
Almondsbury	GLS	ST6084	1,15
Almshoe	HRT	TL2025	5,5
Almsworthy	SOM	SS8441	21,56
Almundestune	HEF	??	29,9
Alne NR	YKS	SE4965	2N24. SN,B23
[Great] Alne	WAR	SP1159	10,1
Alnesbourn	SFK	TM1940	8,13
Alneterne	SFK	??	21,47
Alphamstone	ESS	TL8735	11,4. 23,19. 90,60
Alphington	DEV	SX9189	1,43
Alpington	NFK	TG2901	9,?52 note;?68 *note*. 12,?17 *note*;?25-26 note
Alpraham	CHS	SJ5859	17,2
Alreford	DEV	??	16,167
Alresford	ESS	TM0620	4,4. 18,44. 20,65. 23,33
Alresford	HAM	SU5833	2,1
Alretone (in Utkinton and Delamere)	CHS	??	1,20
Alretunstall (in Timperley)	CHS	??	13,7
Alrewas	STS	SK1615	1,11
Alsager	CHS	SJ7955	1,32
Alsop [en-le-Dale]	DBY	SK1655	1,15
Alspath	WAR	SP2682	15,1
Alston (in Malborough)	DEV	SX7140	17,40
Alston (in Trimley)	SFK	TM2737	2,19. 7,96;101;113
Alston [Sutton]	SOM	ST4151	24,14
Alstone	SOM	ST3146	24,33
Alstone	STS	SJ8618	11,6
Alstonfield	STS	SK1355	8,28
Alswick	HRT	TL3729	24,1
Altcar LAN	CHS	SD3206	R1,36
Althorp	NTH	SP6865	18,23. 35,3b
Althorpe	LIN	SE8309	63,14
Alton	HAM	SU7139	6,1
Alton	HAM	??	23,28
Alton	HEF	SO4253	10,52
Alton	LEC	SK3914	13,66
Alton	STS	SK0742	1,54
Alton (in Figheldean)	WIL	SU1546	68,18
Alton	WOR	SO7374	15,4
Alton [Barnes]	WIL	SU1062	24,2
Alton [Pancras]	DOR	ST6902	2,2
Alton [Priors]	WIL	SU1162	2,4
Aluredestuna	SFK	??	39,12

Alvacott	CON	SX3195	5,8,2
Alvanley	CHS	SJ4973	26,7
Alvaston	DBY	SK3933	9,1
Alvechurch	WOR	SP0272	2,84
Alveley SHR	SHR	SO7684	ES5
Alveley SHR	STS		8,3
Alverdiscott	DEV	SS5125	15,39
Alverstoke	HAM	SZ6098	3,12
Alverston	GLS	ST5999	31,2-3
Alverstone IOW	HAM	SZ5785	6,22
Alverton (in Penzance)	CON	SW4630	5,1,11
Alverton	NTT	SK7942	11,3. 20,2. 22,1
Alvescot	OXF	SP2704	58,21
Alveston	GLS	ST6388	1,14
Alveston	WAR	SP2356	3,3-4
Alvestone	WIL	??	12,4
Alvingham	LIN	TF3691	1,88. 4,58. 27,22. 40,25
Alvington GLS	GLS	SO6000	E8
Alvington GLS	HEF		17,1
Alvington IOW	HAM	SZ4788	1,15
[West] Alvington	DEV	SX7243	1,16
Alwalton	HUN	TL1395	8,2
Alwineclancavele	DEV	??	34,4
Alwinestone	DEV	??	15,57
Alwington	DEV	SS4023	15,8
Alwin's Land	SOM	??	21,22
Alwoldesberie	OXF	??	45,3
Alwoldestorp	NTT	SK6865	18,6
Alwoodley WR	YKS	SE3141	1W16 *note*. SW,Sk15
Amaston	SHR	SJ3711	4,27,17
Ambaston	DBY	SK4332	9,1
Amberden [Hall]	ESS	TL5530	34,19
Amberley	HEF	SO5447	21,5
Amberley	SSX	TQ0213	3,5
[Chapel and Lower] Amble	CON	SW9975	5,4,10
		SW9874	
Amblecote	STS	SO9085	12,14
Ambrosden	OXF	SP6019	26,1
Amcotts	LIN	SE8514	63,16-18. CW,17
Amersham	BKM	SU9698	4,11. 12,4. 21,1. 26,2. 36,2. 38,1. 44,1
Amerton	STS	SJ9927	8,13
Amesbury WIL	HAM		1,31. EW1
Amesbury WIL	WIL	SU1541	1,3. 24,16-17
Amington	WAR	SK2305	28,1
Amotherby NR	YKS	SE7573	1N62. 5N36 note. 23N24. 31N8. SN,Ma3-4
Ampleforth NR	YKS	SE5878	2N10;14. 23N1.SN,Ma22
Ampney	GLS	??	45,5
Ampney [Crucis]	GLS	SP0601	67,1-2. 69,2. 77,1
[Down] Ampney	GLS	SU0996	1,65
Ampney [St Mary]	GLS	SP0802	26,1
Ampney [*St Nicholas*]	GLS	SP0801	60,3
Ampney [St Peter]	GLS	SP0801	10,12
Amport	HAM	SU2944	23,44. 29,15
Ampthill	BDF	TL0338	24,10
Ampton	SFK	TL8671	14,64
Amwell HRT	ESS		1,3
Amwell HRT	HRT	TL3712	23,4. 34,13
Andersey (now Nyland)	SOM	ST4550	8,1
Anderson: see *Winterborne* (Eastern Winterborne) DOR			

Andover	HAM	SU3645	1,41
Andrebi (in Roos) ER	YKS	??	14E4 *note*. CE46. SE,Hol7
Andret	HAM	??	17,4
Angmering	SSX	TQ0604	11,65-66. 13,57
Anlaby ER	YKS	TA0328	1E1. 5E2. 15E2. 21E3. 29E1. SE,He2-3
Anley WR	YKS	SD8161	1W73. 30W6. SW,Cr4
Anmer	NFK	TF7329	5,2. 8,31
[Abbotts] Ann	HAM	SU3243	6,11
[Little] Ann	HAM	SU3343	16,4
Anne: see Amport, Monxton, Thruxton HAM			
Annesley	NTT	SK5052	13,11
Annington	SSX	TQ1809	13,8
Ansford	SOM	ST6333	24,19
Ansley	WAR	SP2992	15,3
Anstey	HAM	SU7240	1,4
Anstey	HRT	TL4032	17,3. 37,20
Anstey	LEC	SK5508	C11. 13,22
[East and West] Anstey	DEV	SS8626 SS8527	3,62. 14,1-2. 16,78
Anstie	SRY	TQ1644	21,5
[North] Anston WR	YKS	SK5184	10W1. 12W1;20. SW, Sf2
[South] Anston WR	YKS	SK5183	10W1. SW,Sf2 *note*
Ansty	WAR	SP4083	15,5
Ansty	WIL	ST9526	37,2. 67,37
Antingham	NFK	TG2532	9,149-150;180. 17,8
Antony	CON	SX3954	3,2
Antrobus	CHS	SJ6480	1,1. 1,36
Anwick	LIN	TF1150	30,34. 64,2
Apethorpe	NTH	TL0295	1,23
Apeton	STS	SJ8518	11,6
Aplestede	HAM	??	23,34
Apley	LIN	TF1075	22,18-20. CS,31-32
Appethorp	NFK	??	4,15. 54,1
Appleby LEC	DBY		3,2. E1. E4
Appleby LEC	LEC	SK3109	11,2. 14,22. E5
Appleby	LIN	SE9515	8,27. 17,2. 24,10
Appledore	CON	SX3268	5,2,25
Appledore (in Burlescombe)	DEV	ST0614	24,14
Appledore (in Clannaborough)	DEV	SS7401	16,49
Appledore	KEN	TQ9529	3,20
Appleford	BRK	SU5293	7,28
[Great, North and Upper] Appleford IOW	HAM	SZ5080 SZ5081 SZ4980	6,3. 9,12;24
Applesham	SSX	TQ1907	13,20
Appleton	BRK	SP4401	33,6. 65,19
Appleton	CHS	SJ6383	24,8
Appleton	KEN	TR3447	5,194
Appleton	NFK	TF7027	9,7. 34,3
[East] Appleton NR	YKS	SE2395	6N63 *note*. SN,CtA22
Appleton [le Moors] NR	YKS	SE7388	SN,D21 *note*. SN,Ma14
Appleton [le Street] NR	YKS	SE7373	1N69. SN,Ma7
Appleton [Roebuck] WR	YKS	SE5542	25W2. CW36. SW,An4
Appleton [Wiske] NR	YKS	NZ3904	1N119. 31N1. SN,A4
Appletona/-tuna	NFK	??	9,68 *note*. 12,17 note
Appletreewick WR	YKS	SE0560	29W41;45
Appley	SOM	ST0721	19,22. 20,2
Apps	SRY	TQ1168	19,27-28
Ardeley	HRT	TL3027	13,3
Arden [Hall] NR	YKS	SE5290	23N8

Ardington	BRK	SU4388	41,4;5
Ardleigh ESS	ESS	TM0529	30,20. 32,40. 39,8;12. 47,2. B31
Ardleigh ESS	SFK		EE3
Ardley	OXF	SP5427	15,5
[East] Ardsley WR	YKS	SE3025	9W120 note. SW,M1
[West] Ardsley WR	YKS	SE2825	9W120 note. SW,M13 note
Argam ER	YKS	TA1171	1E26 note. SE,Tu5
Argameles LAN	CHS	SD3318	R1,29
Arkendale WR	YKS	SE3861	1W38. 24W11. SW,Bu12
Arkesden	ESS	TL4834	25,26. 26,3-4. 32,43. 90,28
Arkholme LAN	YKS	SD5872	1L3. See also CHS Y4
Arksey WR	YKS	SE5706	10W37. SW,Sf34 note. SW,O1
Arlescote	WAR	SP3948	16,56
Arlesey	BDF	TL1936	5,2. 18,6. 24,30. 56,9
Arleston	DBY	SK3429	6,85
Arley	WAR	SP2890	42,2
[Upper] Arley WOR	STS		7,1
[Upper] Arley WOR	WOR	SO7680	ESt1
Arlingham	GLS	SO7010	1,15
Arlington	DEV	SS6140	38,1
Arlington	GLS	SP1106	1,58
Arlington	SSX	TQ5407	9,39
Armingford Hundred	CAM	—	Appx J
Arminghall	NFK	TG2504	1,218
Armley WR	YKS	SE2733	9W121. SW,M3
Armston	NTH	TL0685	6a,14
Armthorpe NR	YKS	SE6204	29W9. SW,Sf22
Arncliffe WR	YKS	SD9371	30W35
Arncliffe [Hall] NR	YKS	NZ4500	1N128 note. 31N5 note. SN,A7
Arncott	OXF	SP6117	9,10. 47,1
Arnesby	LEC	SP6192	4,1. 25,2
Arnestorp (in Hatfield) ER	YKS	??	14E5 note. SE,Hol10
Arnewood	HAM	SZ2797	NF10,3
Arnford WR	YKS	SD8356	30W10
Arnodestorp (in Hinderwell) NR	YKS	??	13N3 note. SN,L11
Arnold	NTT	SK5845	1,45. 30,49
Arnolton	KEN	TQ9755	D18. 5,147
Arrallas	CON	SW8853	5,4,12
Arram ER	YKS	TA1649	14E30 note. SE,Hol22
Arreton IOW	HAM	SZ5486	1,W4
Arrington	CAM	TL3250	13,11. 14,45
Arrow	WAR	SP0856	4,1
Arthington WR	YKS	SE2744	5W1. SW,Sk19
Arthingworth	NTH	SP7581	1,15e. 8,3. 18,15. 35,13
Arundel	SSX	TQ0107	11,2
Asc(h)am (in East Wilton) NR	YKS	??	6N111 note, SN,Ct A32
Aschebi (in Myerscough) LAN	YKS	??	1L1 note. See also CHS Y2
Aschelesmersc/Aschilesmares (in Pickering Marishes) NR	YKS	??	1Y4 note. SN,D12 note
Ascot [d'Oyley]	OXF	SP3018	28,25
Ascot [Earl]	OXF	SP2918	7,61
Asebi (in Baldersby) NR	YKS	??	6N160 note. SN, CtA44
Asenby NR	YKS	SE3975	13N17
Asfordby	LEC	SK7019	1,3. 42,9
Asgarby	LIN	TF3366	14,69
Ash	DBY	SK2632	6,37
Ash (in Bradworthy)	DEV	SS3216	34,5
Ash (in Braunton)	DEV	SS5137	19,14
Ash (in Petrockstow)	DEV	SS5108	6,2
Ash (in South Tawton)	DEV	SX6891	1,29
Ash (in Stourpaine)	DOR	ST8610	37,4

Ash	KEN	TQ6064	5,7
Ash	OXF	??	24,6
Ash	SFK	TM3355	6,282;290
[Abbots] Ash	DEV	??	6,7
[One] Ash	DBY	SK1765	1,27
Ash [Priors]	SOM	ST1529	6,19. 22,20
[Rose] Ash	DEV	SS7821	16,143
Ash [Street]	SFK	TM0146	2,14
Ash [Thomas]	DEV	ST0010	25,20
Ashbocking	SFK	TM1654	1,73. 21,25. 25.59. 52,6
Ashborough	WOR	SO9772	1,1a
Ashbourne	DBY	SK1846	1,14-15
Ashbrittle	SOM	ST0521	19,20;36
Ashbrook	GLS	SP0802	53,2. 69,8
Ashburnham	SSX	TQ6814	9,7
Ashburton	DEV	SX7569	2,19
Ashbury	BRK	SU2685	8,1
Ashbury	DEV	SX5097	39,7
Ashby	LIN	TA2500	4,65-68. 12,23. 57,1-3
Ashby	LIN	SE8908	1,39;54;59. 8,26
Ashby (near Eccles)	NFK	TM0090	1,140
Ashby (near Repps)	NFK	TG4115	10,84. 17,11. 19,30
Ashby [by Partney]	LIN	TF4266	3,44. 13,6. CS,35
[Canons] Ashby	NTH	SP5750	39,9
[Castle] Ashby	NTH	SP8659	56,45
[Cold] Ashby	NTH	SP6576	12,2. 18,50-51. 35,19e. 47,1b
Ashby [de la Launde]	LIN	TF0555	26,49. 35,15
Ashby [de la Zouch]	LEC	SK3516	13,65
Ashby [Folville]	LEC	SK7012	14,17. 40,32
Ashby [Magna]	LEC	SP5690	25,5. 34,1
[Mears] Ashby	NTH	SP8366	56,18
Ashby [Parva]	LEC	SP5288	17,5
Ashby [Puerorum]	LIN	TF3271	4,65. 28,39
Ashby [St Ledgers]	NTH	SP5768	23,4
Ashby [St Mary]	NFK	TG3202	9,57;61;65;69. 12,19;22
[West] Ashby	LIN	TF2672	1,105. 24,72. 66,1. 68,7
Ashclyst	DEV	SY0198	16,89
Ashcombe	DEV	SX9179	34,10
Ashcombe	SOM	ST3361	5,13
Ashcombe	SSX	TQ3809	12,56
Ashcott	SOM	ST4337	8,11;14
Ashden	BRK	SU5281	21,3
Ashdon	ESS	TL5841	33,20
Ashe	HAM	SU5349	30,1
Ashe [Ingen]	HEF	SO5826	1,8;57
Asheldham	ESS	TL9701	24,43;55
Ashen	ESS	TL7442	23,12
Ashendon	BKM	SP7014	14,11. 23,9
Ashenfield	KEN	TR0947	7,13
Ashfield	SFK	TM2162	3,65. 4,6. 6,20;22. 16,29;3421,32. 52,10. 67,4
[Great] Ashfield	SFK	TL9967	14,93. 66,3;17. *14,92*
Ashford	DBY	SK1969	1,28
Ashford (near Barnstaple)	DEV	SS5335	16,66;85
Ashford	KEN	TR0142	9,6
Ashford	MDX	TQ0771	8,2
Ashford [Carbonell]	SHR	SO5270	5,3
[South] Ashford	KEN	TR0041	9,4
Ashill	NFK	TF8804	21,17. 15,5
Ashill	SOM	ST3217	10,6. 19,18
Ashingdon	ESS	TQ8693	24,38

Ashington	SOM	ST5621	21,94
Ashington	SSX	TQ1316	13,47
Ashleigh	DEV	SX3983	17,9
Ashleworth	GLS	SO8125	1,15
Ashley	CAM	TL6961	29,1
Ashley	CHS	SJ7784	13,6
Ashley GLS	GLS	ST9394	E15
Ashley GLS	WIL		30,5
Ashley	HAM	SZ2595	NF3,11. NF9,36
Ashley	NTH	SP7990	26,10-11. 30,1;8. 56,2
Ashley	STS	SJ7636	8,25
Ashmansworthy	DEV	SS3318	16,31
Ashmore	DOR	ST9117	1,17
Ashover	DBY	SK3463	10,9
Ashow	WAR	SP3170	17,49
Ashperton	HEF	SO6441	8,9. 15,8. 22,1. 36,1
Ashprington	DEV	SX8157	1,71
Ashreigney	DEV	SS6213	1,65
Ashtead	SRY	TQ1858	5,20
Ashton (near Tarvin)	CHS	SJ5069	5,1
Ashton	CON	SX3868	5,2,27
Ashton	DEV	SX8584	6,6. 44,1
Ashton (in Winterborne St Martin)	DOR	SY6687	S5,1 note
Ashton	HEF	SO5164	1,10a
Ashton (near Polebrook)	NTH	TL0588	6,12. 6a,34
Ashton (near Towcester)	NTH	SP7649	40,4-5
[Cold] Ashton	GLS	ST7472	7,2
Ashton [Gifford]	WIL	ST9639	27,14
Ashton [Hall] LAN	YKS	SD4657	30W39 note. See also CHS Y12
Ashton [Keynes]	WIL	SU0494	11,1
[Long] Ashton	SOM	ST5470	5,34
Ashton [on Ribble] LAN	YKS	SD5230	1L1. See also CHS Y2
[Steeple and West] Ashton	WIL	ST9056 ST8775	15,2
Ashton [under Hill] (in Tewkesbury Hundred) WOR	GLS		1,40
Ashton [under Hill] (in Tibblestone Hundred) WOR	GLS		1,60. EvL
Ashton [under Hill] WOR	WOR	SO9938	EG2;5
Ashton [under-Lyne] (St Michael's Church) LAN	CHS	SJ9399	R5,2
Ashwater	DEV	SX3895	3,4
Ashway	SOM	SS8631	21,50
Ashwell	HRT	TL2639	9,10. 33,7. 36,14-15. 37,9
Ashwell RUT	LIN		13,38
Ashwell RUT	RUT	SK8613	R16. ELc4
Ashwell [Hall]	ESS	TL7030	67,2
Ashwellthorpe: see [Ashwell] Thorpe NFK			
Ashwick	SOM	ST6348	7,15
Ashwicken: see [Ash] Wicken NFK			
Ashwood	STS	SO8788	7,6
Aske [Hall] NR	YKS	NZ1703	6N57 note. SN,Ct A20 note
Askerswell	DOR	SY5292	16,1
Askham	NTT	SK7474	5,4
Askham [Bryan] WR	YKS	SE5548	6W1. CW42. SW,An11 note. SW,An18
Askham [Richard] WR	YKS	SE5348	25W15. CW28. SW, An11 note
Askrigg NR	YKS	SD9491	6N79. SN,CtA25
Askwith WR	YKS	SE1648	8W2. 13W25. 28W28. SW,Bu32-33

Aslackby	LIN	TF0830	18,19;22. 24,97. 42,10. CK,9
Aslacton	NFK	TM1591	4,56. 9,98;211;223
Aslockton	NTT	SK7440	1,57. 11,22. 17,18. 20,6. 30,37
Aspall	SFK	TM1664	6,201;206;221. 16,48. 34,18. 77,4
Aspenden	HRT	TL3528	31,6
Aspley	STS	SJ8133	2,13
Aspley [Guise]	BDF	SP9436	23,17
Assecote	DEV	??	21,11
Asselby ER	YKS	SE7128	3Y4. 5E25. SE,How4;7
Assington	SFK	TL9338	34,3
Astcote	NTH	SP6753	39,15
Asterby	LIN	TF2679	14,53
Asthall	OXF	SP2811	29,3
Astley (near Hadnell)	SHR	SJ5218	3d,2
Astley	WAR	SP3189	16,42
Astley	WOR	SO7867	15,9
Aston FLN	CHS	SJ3067	FD7,1
Aston (in Newhall)	CHS	SJ6147	8,17
Aton (near Runcorn)	CHS	SJ5578	A17
Aston (near Hope)	DBY	SK1883	1,29
Aston (near Sudbury)	DBY	SK1631	6,28
Aston (near Wigmore)	HEF	SO4671	9,4
Aston	HRT	TL2722	5,8
Aston (in Oswestry)	SHR	SJ3227	4,6,6
Aston (Wales)	SHR	SO2991	4,1,35
Aston (in Wem)	SHR	SJ5328	4,14,11
Aston [near Stafford]	STS	SJ8923	2,21
Aston (near Birmingham)	WAR	SP0889	27,1
Aston WR	YKS	SK4685	5W22. 12W1;11. SW, Sk2 note. SW,Sf33
Aston [Abbots]	BKM	SP8420	8,2
Aston [Blank] (alias Cold Ashton)	GLS	SP1219	3,5. WoA2. WoB18
Aston [Botterell]	SHR	SO6384	4,3,66
Aston [by Budworth]	CHS	SJ6880	9,24
Aston [by Stone]	STS	SJ9131	1,47. 11,9;23
Aston [by Sutton]	CHS	SJ5578	A17. 9,19
Aston [Cantlow]	WAR	SP1359	37,1
Aston [Clinton]	BKM	SP8712	24,1
[Coal] Aston	DBY	SK3679	17,5
Aston [Eyre]	SHR	SO6594	4,3,60
Aston [Fields]	WOR	SO9669	2,81
Aston in Munslow: see Munslow [Aston] SHR			
Aston [Ingham]	HEF	SO6823	21,3
[Ivinghoe] Aston	BKM	SP9518	12,20. 21,5
Aston [Juxta Mondrem]	CHS	SJ6556	8,44
Aston [le Walls]	NTH	SP4950	45,5
[Middle] Aston	OXF	SP4727	27,9-10. 58,22
[North] Aston	OXF	SP4729	41,1
Aston [on Carrant]	GLS	SO9434	1,24
Aston [Rowant]	OXF	SU7299	35,3
Aston [Sandford]	BKM	SP7507	4,23. 23,6. 43,3
Aston [Somerville] WOR	GLS		66,4
Aston [Somerville] WOR	WOR	SP0438	EG16
[Steeple] Aston	OXF	SP4725	7,45
Aston [Subedge]	GLS	SP1341	21,1
Aston [Tirrold]	BRK	SU5585	1,6. 19,1
Aston [upon-Trent]	DBY	SK4129	1,38. 6,93
Aston [Upthorpe]	BRK	SU5586	61,2
[White Ladies] Aston	WOR	SO9252	2,53;55
Astrop	OXF	SP3008	59,10

Astwell	NTH	SP6044	43,9
Astwick	BDF	TL2138	23,45-47. 32,12
Aswarby	LIN	TF0639	24,79;103. 57,32
Atcham	SHR	SJ5409	3g,6
Ateleia	ESS	??	28,1
Athelhampton	DOR	SY7794	3,16
Athelney	SOM	ST3429	10,6
Atherfield and [Little] Atherfield IOW	HAM	SZ4679 SZ4680	1,13. 6,8
Atherstone	WAR	SP3097	15,2
Atherstone (on Stour)	WAR	SP2050	4,2
Atlow	DBY	SK2348	6,13
Atrim	DOR	SY4495	13,8
Attercliffe WR	YKS	SK3788	10W42. SW,Sf35
Atterton	KEN	TR3042	9,9
Attleborough and Attleborough [Minor]	NFK	TM0495 TM0694	50,6-7. 59,1
Attlebridge	NFK	TG1216	4,34. 10,37. 19.33. 25,9
Aubourn	LIN	SK9262	18,29;30
Auburn ER	YKS	TA1762	1E13 *note*. SE,Hu5
Auckley WR	YKS	SE6501	5W8. SW,Sf21 *note*
Auckley, another WR	YKS	SE6501	SW,Sf21
Audby (in North Thoresby)	LIN	TF2897	4,24;42. 25,12. 27,16. 44,6;14
Audleby	LIN	TA1104	4,17-22. 16,35
Audlem	CHS	SJ6543	5,12
Audley	STS	SJ7950	17,13
Aughton LAN	CHS	SD3905	R1,2;22
Aughton ER	YKS	SE7038	5E7;24. CE18. SE,C8
Aughton [Hall] WR	YKS	SK4586	5W21 *note*. 5W24. 12W1;16. SW,Sf32
Aunk	DEV	ST0400	34,18;34
Aunsby	LIN	TF0438	39,2
Aust	GLS	ST5789	3,1. WoB15
Austerfield WR	YKS	SK6694	5W8. SW,Sf21
Austerson	CHS	SJ6649	8,31
Austhorpe WR	YKS	SE3733	9W1. SW,Sk4
Austonley WR	YKS	SE1107	1Y15. SW,Ag12
Austrey	WAR	SK2906	8,1. 19,6. 41,1
Austwick WR	YKS	SD7668	1L4
Authorpe	LIN	TF4080	55,2
Avebury	WIL	SU1069	1,23d
Aveley	ESS	TQ5680	18,27. 40,9. 75,1
Aveley	SFK	TL9439	27,7
Avenbury	HEF	SO6553	7,9
Avening	GLS	ST8898	1,49
Averham	NTT	SK7654	18,1
Avethorpe (in Aslackby)	LIN	TF0629	18,20. 27,56. 42,10. 57,42
Aveton [Gifford]	DEV	SX6947	35,26
Avill	SOM	SS9743	25,17
Avington	BRK	SU3768	43,2
Avington	HAM	SU5332	3,4
Avon	HAM	SZ1498	21,4. 23,49
Avon Dassett: see [Avon] Dassett WAR			
Awbridge	HAM	SU3323	23,16. 39,1
Awliscombe	DEV	ST1301	19,25-26;32;36;43. 25,14. 34,23;26;45
Awre	GLS	SO7008	1,13
Awsthorp	RUT	SK8912	R14
Awsworth	NTT	SK4844	10,48. 30,33
Axbridge	SOM	ST4354	1,2;31
Axminster	DEV	SY2998	1,11. 19,45

Axmouth	DEV	SY2591	1,14
Axton FLN	CHS	SJ1080	FT1,9
Aycote GLS: see Eycot GLS			
Aylesbeare	DEV	SY0391	16,136
Aylesbury	BKM	SP8113	1,1. 3a,1
Aylesby	LIN	TA2007	3,39. 12,14-16. 27,4
Aylescott	DEV	SS5241	3,40
Aylesford	KEN	TQ7258	1,2
Aylestone	LEC	SK5701	9,1. 12,1. 44,1-2
Aylmerton	NFK	TG1840	8,132. 9,145-146
Aylsham	NFK	TG1927	1,91;149;192;194-195. 8,8
Aylworth	GLS	SP1022	34,6. 52,6
Aymestrey	HEF	SO4265	1,10a;10c
Aynho	NTH	SP5133	45,1
Ayot [St Lawrence]	HRT	TL1916	9,9. 42,12
Ayot [St Peter]	HRT	TL2115	20,2
Aysgarth NR	YKS	SE0088	6N82. SN,CtA26
Ayshford	DEV	ST0415	24,13
[East] Ayton NR	YKS	SE9984	8N11. 13N12. SN,L27 note. SN,D7
[Great] Ayton NR	YKS	NZ5610	11N5. SN,L29
[Little] Ayton NR	YKS	NZ5710	1N17-18;22. 5N27. 11N4. SN,L27-29 note. SN,L29
[West] Ayton NR	YKS	SE9884	1Y3. SN,D7
Azerley WR	YKS	SE2574	28W14. 29W23. 31W3. SW,Bu23-24

B

Babcary	SOM	ST5628	19,66. 45,3
Babingley	NFK	TF6626	29,3. 34,1
Babington	SOM	ST7051	5,49
Babraham	CAM	TL5050	1,15. 5,17. 14,15-16. 25,1. 26,11;54. 29,11. 38,1. 41,5. EE1
Babthorpe ER	YKS	SE6929	3Y4. SE,How5
Babworth	NTT	SK6880	1,12. 9,33
Baccamoor	DEV	SX5859	17,92
Backstone	DEV	SS8319	29,1
Backwell	SOM	ST4968	5,30
Baconsthorpe (in Attleborough)	NFK	TM0495	4,46
Baconsthorpe (in Holt): see [Bacons] Thorpe NFK			
Bacton	HEF	SO3732	10,16
Bacton	NFK	TG3333	7,18
Bacton	SFK	TM0567	41,7-8
Badbury	WIL	SU1980	7,6
Badby	NTH	SP5658	11,6
Baddesley [Ensor]	WAR	SP2798	17,16
[North] Baddesley	HAM	SU3920	29,7
[South] Baddesley	HAM	SZ3596	NF3,4
Baddiley	CHS	SJ6050	8,40
Baddington (in Stoke Prior)	WOR	SO9568	2,81
[Great] Baddow	ESS	TL7204	15,2. 72,3
[Little] Baddow	ESS	TL7707	20,52. 33,13
Baden [Hall]	STS	SJ8431	2,11
Badgemore	OXF	SU7483	24,1
Badger	SHR	SO7699	4,17,1
Badgeworth	GLS	SO9019	31,11
Badgworth	SOM	ST3952	24,10
Badgworthy	DEV	SS7943	19,18
Badingham	SFK	TM3068	6,55;306
Badlesmere	KEN	TR0155	5,149. 7,30
Badley (= Clare Park)	HAM	SU8047	3,8
Badley	SFK	TM0655	1,70. 21,20. 25,53
Badlingham	CAM	TL6770	14,67. Appx A
Badminton	GLS	ST8082	60,5
Badmondisfield	SFK	TL7457	1,121. 65,1
Badsey	WOR	SP0743	10,7
Badsworth WR	YKS	SE4614	9W45. SW,O7
[West] Bagborough	SOM	ST1733	2,3. 25,51. 31,4
Bagburrow	HEF	SO7545	2,28
Bagby NR	YKS	SE4680	23N7-8
[The] Bage	HEF	SO2943	25,4
Bagendon	GLS	SP0106	63,4
Baggrave	LEC	SK6908	1,3
Bagillt FLN	CHS	SJ2175	FD2,5
Baginton	WAR	SP3474	17,51
Bagley (near Stoke Pero)	SOM	SS8842	21,61
?Bagley (in Wedmore): see Bodeslege SOM			
Bagnor	BRK	SU4569	53,1
Bagshot WIL	BRK		21,6

14

Bagshot WIL	WIL	SU3165	E2
Bagthorpe	NFK	TF7932	8,108
Bagton	DEV	SX7041	17,34
Bagtor	DEV	SX7675	48,7
Baguley	CHS	SJ8190	27,2
Bagwich IOW	HAM	SZ5182	9,8
Bagworth	LEC	SK4408	44,10-11
Baildon WR	YKS	SE1539	2W4. 24W1 *note*. SW, Sk1;18
Bainton	OXF	SP5826	37,1
Bainton ER	YKS	SE9652	5E42. 23E9. SE,D5
Bakewell	DBY	SK2168	1,27
Balby WR	YKS	SE5601	5W8. 10W23. SW,Sf15-16;21
Baldebi (in Whitby) NR	YKS	NZ9010	4N1 *note*. SN,L4
Baldenhall (in Guarlford) WOR	HEF		1,42
Baldenhall (in Guarlford) WOR	WOR	??	EH1
Baldersby NR	YKS	SE3578	6N159. SN,CtA44
Balderton	NTT	SK8151	6,1-2
[Little and Marsh] Baldon	OXF	SU5698	6,17. *note*
		SU5699	
[Marsh] Baldon	OXF	SU5699	35,17
[Toot] Baldon	OXF	SP5600	7,19;28. 17,2. 42,1
Bale	NFK	TG0136	1,21. 4,19
Balham	SRY	TQ2873	26,1
Ballidon	DBY	SK2054	10,22
Ballingdon SFK	ESS	TL8640	36,8
Balmer	SSX	TQ3509	10,110. 12,16
Balscott	OXF	SP3841	7,65
[East and West] Balsdon	CON	SX2898	5,7,5
		SX2798	
Balsham	CAM	TL5850	5,6-7. 14,82. 26,52. Appx D
Balterley	STS	SJ7650	17,11-12
Baltonsborough	SOM	ST5434	8,22
Bamford	DBY	SK2083	10,17
Bampton	DEV	SS9522	1,24. 23,5
Bampton	OXF	SP3103	1,6. 5,1. 7,33. 28,21
Banbury	OXF	SP4540	6,4;12
Banham	NFK	TM0688	8,61. 9,79. 11,1. 15,11. 19,13
Banningham	NFK	TG2129	8,136. 17,31. 21,35
Banstead	SRY	TQ2559	5,8
Banthorpe (in Braceborough)	LIN	TF0611	18,14. 24,30. 59,5-6
Banwell	SOM	ST3959	6,9
Barbon WES	YKS	SD6282	1L3. See also CHS Y4
Barby	NTH	SP5470	35,8
Barcheston	WAR	SP2639	28,10. 44,9
Barcombe	SSX	TQ4214	12,48
Barcote (in Buckland)	BRK	SU3197	65,7
Barden NR	YKS	SE1493	6N105. SN,CtA31
[Great and Little] Bardfield	ESS	TL6730	20,79. 23,39;42
		TL6530	90,65
Bardney	LIN	TF1169	24,17-18;45-53. CS,36-37
Bardolfeston	DOR	SY7694	3,15
Bardsea LAN	YKS	SD3074	1L6. See also CHS Y7
Bardsey WR	YKS	SE3643	1W4. SW,Sk12
Bardwell	SFK	TL9473	14,72;82. 25,21. 76,10-12
Bare LAN	YKS	SD4565	1L2. See also CHS Y3
Barethorn (Nachededorne)	BRK	??	1,24
Barford	NFK	TG1007	4,9. 17,4. 20,12
Barford	NTH	SP8582	1,21-22
Barford	WAR	SP2760	28,15. 37,4
Barford (near Downton)	WIL	SU1822	37,9
[Great] Barford	BDF	TL1352	23,36-37;39-40

[Little] Barford	BDF	TL1756	8,5. 45,1
Barford [St John and St Michael]	OXF	SP4433	7,49. 9,6. 48,1
		SP4332	
Barford [St Martin]	WIL	SU0531	47,2. 67,81. 68,19
Barforth [Hall] NR	YKS	NZ1616	6N1 *note*. SN,CtA3;5
Barfreston	KEN	TR2650	5,132
Barham	CAM	TL5746	5,16. 14,8-10
Barham	KEN	TR2050	*3,18.* 5,138
Barham	SFK	TM1350	6,10. 8,66;78;*81.* 21,*22*;24;26;27
Barholm	LIN	TF0911	8,35-36. 24,29;35. 51,4 -5. CK,3
Barholm Hundred	LIN	—	CK,4
Barkby	LEC	SK6309	15,10. 41,3
Barkestone	LEC	SK7734	15,4
Barkestone	SFK	TM2746	40,4
Barkham	BRK	SU7867	1,20
Barkham	SSX	TQ4321	10,114-115
Barking	ESS	TQ4483	9,5;7
Barking	SFK	TM0753	21,14;16;18;20. *25,53*
Barkston	LIN	SK9341	1,15;23. 14,90.. 54,2. 67,15-16.
			CK,64
Barkston WR	YKS	SE4936	9W22. SW,BA5
Barkway	HRT	TL3835	31,4. 33,9. 37,12. 38,1
Barkwith	LIN	TF1681	2,2;4. 4,49. 16,17. 34,17. 40,7;8
Barlaston	STS	SJ8939	11,24
Barlavington	SSX	SU9716	11,23
Barlborough	DBY	SK4777	10,4
Barlby ER	YKS	SE6334	3Y4. 16E3. SE,How6;10
Barlestone	LEC	SK4205	13,46. 17,10
Barley	HRT	TL4038	5,18. 12,1. 29,1. 31,3. 34,9. 37,11
Barley (in South Wraxhall)	WIL	ST8262	67,28
Barley	WOR	SO8537	2,37
Barling	ESS	TQ9389	5,12. 18,16
Barlings	LIN	TF0774	3,3. 22,17;19. 26,7-8;21. CS,30-31
Barlington	DEV	SS5616	3,15;19
Barlow	DBY	SK3474	12,1. 17,1
Barlow	SHR	SO3883	4,20,10
Barlow WR	YKS	SE6428	16W1. SW,BA9
Barmby [Moor] ER	YKS	SE7748	1Y10 *note*. 2B13. SE,P9
Barmby [on the Marsh] ER	YKS	SE6928	3Y4. SE,How5
Barmer	NFK	TF8033	8,108
[East] Barming	KEN	TQ7254	11,2
[West] Barming	KEN	TQ7154	5,101
Barmston ER	YKS	TA1558	14E26. SE,Hol21
Barn [Hall]	ESS	TL9214	33,8
Barnaby NR	YKS	NZ5716	5N26 *note*. SN,L26
Barnack	NTH	TF0704	36,2
Barnacle	WAR	SP3884	16,48
?Barnacott	CON	SS2409	5,5,22
Barnbrough WR	YKS	SE4803	10W15. 12W1;5. CW9-10. SW,Sf9
Barnby	SFK	TM4789	1,30. 4,39
Barnby [Dun] WR	YKS	SE6109	5W10 *note*. 10W30. 13W8.
			SW,Sf23
[East and West] Barnby NR	YKS	NZ8212	SN,L7 *note*
		NZ8112	
Barnby [Hall] WR	YKS	SE2908	9W64 *note*. SW,St1
Barnby [House] NR	YKS	SE7260	23N32 *note*
Barnby [in the Willows]	NTT	SK8552	6,3. 7,2
Barnby [Moor]	NTT	SK6684	1,16. 9,54
Barnes	SRY	TQ2176	2,3 note. 13,1
Barnetby [le Wold]	LIN	TA0609	13,17-19. 22,6. 34,4
Barney	NFK	TF9932	34,13;17

Barnham	SFK	TL8679	4,10. 7,1. 14,89. 26,8. 31,1
Barnham	SSX	SU9604	11,82
Barnham [Broom]	NFK	TG0807	8,72. 61,4. 62,1
Barnhill [Hall] ER	YKS	SE7328	3Y4 *note.* SE,How3
Barningham	SFK	TL9676	10,1. 14,81. 37,4
Barningham NR	YKS	NZ0810	6N1;6. SN,CtA7;9
[Little] Barningham	NFK	TG1433	1,194. 8,8. 10,39. 35,12
[North] Barningham	NFK	TG1537	8,133. 9,146;149;154;156. 10,64. 25,24. 30,3. 66,99
Barnoldby [le Beck]	LIN	TA2303	12,24
Barnoldswick (in Burton in Lonsdale) WR	YKS	SD6671	1L3
Barnoldswick (near Gisburn) WR	YKS	SD8746	30W3
Barnsley	GLS	SP0705	3,4. WoA1. WoB17
Barnsley IOW	HAM	SZ6090	1,W16. 7,12
Barnsley WR	YKS	SE3406	9W80. SW,St15
Barnstaple	DEV	SS5533	C6. 1,1;2. 3,3;6;45. 16,2;65. 17,1. 28,17
Barnston	CHS	SJ2783	9,9
Barnston	ESS	TL6419	30,29
Barnstone	NTT	SK7335	10,61. 11,27
Barnwell	NTH	TL0484	1,25. 9,5
Barnwood	GLS	SO8518	10,1
[Great] Barr	STS	SP0495	12,25;28
[Perry] Barr: see Perry [Barr] STS			
Barrington	CAM	TL3949	11,3. 14,39. 17,5. 21,5. 32,18. Appx H
Barrington	SOM	ST3818	21,97
[Great] Barrington	GLS	SP2013	1,66–67. 56,1
[Little] Barrington	GLS	SP2012	34,11
Barrow	CHS	SJ4668	9,5
Barrow	SFK	TL7664	1,120
Barrow [Guerney]	SOM	ST5367	5,32
Barrow [Hall]	ESS	TQ9288	23,43
Barrow [on Humber]	LIN	TA0721	30,1-2;5
Barrow [on-Soar]	LEC	SK5717	C8. 43,1
Barrow [upon-Trent]	DBY	SK3528	1,19. 6,82. 10,26
[North and South] Barrow	SOM	ST6029 ST6027	19,62. 24,20
Barrowby	LIN	SK8736	14,88–89;95. 58,2-5
Barrowby [Grange] WR	YKS	SE3347	13W29 *note.* 24W20. SW,Bu35
Barrowden RUT	NTH		1,2a. 26,3
Barrowden RUT	RUT	SK9400	EN2;11
Barsby	LEC	SK6911	1,3. 32,2
Barsham	SFK	TM3989	6,296. 7,40;45. 18,5. 19,18
[East and West] Barsham	NFK	TF9133 TF9033	1,16. 8,99;117
[North] Barsham	NFK	TF9138	8,138
Barstable [Hall]	ESS	TQ7089	18,4
Barston	WAR	SP2078	17,15. 23,4. 44,15
Bartestree	HEF	SO5640	7,1
Barthomley	CHS	SJ7652	8,30
Barthorpe [Grange] ER	YKS	SE7759	5E64 *note.* 26E2. SE,Ac8
Bartington	CHS	SJ6076	26,3-4
Bartley	HAM	SU7253	69,5
Bartley [Green] WAR	WAR	SP0081	EBW3
Bartley [Green] WAR	WOR		23,1
Barton	BRK	SU5097	7,6;9
Barton	CAM	TL4055	12,2. 31,3. 37,2. Appx K
Barton (near Halsall) LAN	CHS	SD3509	R1,37
Barton (in Hereford)	HEF	SO5039	2,11

Barton (in Kington)	HEF	SO2957	1,69
Barton (in Bradley)	STS	SJ8718	11,6
Barton	WAR	SP2532	22,12
Barton NR	YKS	NZ2308	6N1. SN,CtA4
Barton (near Preston) LAN	YKS	SD5137	1L1. See also CHS Y2
[Abbots] Barton	GLS	SO8418	10,1
Barton [Bendish]	NFK	TF7105	13,3. 21,2. 31,21. 66,2;36
Barton [Blount]	DBY	SK2034	6,34
[Earls] Barton	NTH	SP8563	56,15
Barton [-Ede, Steeple-, and -Westcot]	OXF	SP4424	7,46-47. 8,4. 29,19
		SP4225	
		SP4425	
[Great] Barton	SFK	TL8967	14,48
Barton [Hartshorn]	BKM	SP6431	4,37
Barton [in Fabis]	NTT	SK5232	10,7. 13,1-2. 13,1-4. 30,23
Barton [in-the-Beans]	LEC	SK3906	13,73
Barton [in-the-Clay]	BDF	TL0830	8,2
[Kings] Barton	GLS	SO8418	1,2. EvQ29 note
Barton [le Street] NR	YKS	SE7274	1Y4. 5N45. SN,D11;19.
			SN,Ma14
Barton [le Willows] NR	YKS	SE7163	5N63. SN,B10
Barton [Mills]	SFK	TL7173	25,33;38. 54,3
Barton [on Sea]	HAM	SZ2393	NF3,12-13
Barton [Regis]	GLS	ST5973	1,21. EvK7
Barton [St David]	SOM	ST5431	21,92. 46,21
Barton [Seagrave]	NTH	SP8977	4,17
Barton [Stacey]	HAM	SU4341	1,17. 29,2. 47,1
Barton [Turf]	NFK	TG3421	8,12. 17,42;46;50. 31,4
Barton [under-Needwood]	STS	SK1818	1,20
Barton [upon Humber]	LIN	TA0322	13,18. 24,13-15. CN,1
Barugh WR	YKS	SE3108	9W72. SW,St5
[Great] Barugh NR	YKS	SE7479	1N70. 2N4. 23N21. SN,Ma8
[Little] Barugh NR	YKS	SE7679	1N71. 2N4. 23N21. SN,Ma8-9
Barwell	LEC	SP4496	6,3-4
Barwick	NFK	TF8035	8,33
Barwick: see *Englebi* YKS			
Barwick [in Elmet] WR	YKS	SE3937	9W1.SW,Sk4
Barwythe BDF	BDF	TL0214	E4
Barwythe BDF	HRT		21,2
Basche(s)bi (in Lastingham) NR	YKS	??	1N57 note. SN,D20
Baschurch	SHR	SJ4221	4,1,3
Basford	CHS	SJ7152	8,27
Basford	NTT	SK5443	10,22-23;51-52. 30,28;34
Basford	STS	SJ9851	8,31
Bashall [Eaves] WR	YKS	SD7142	30W37 note
Bashley	HAM	SZ2497	17,3
Basildon	ESS	TQ7189	24,7-8
[Lower] Basildon	BRK	SU6178	1,8
Basing	HAM	SU6652	23,6
Basingstoke	HAM	SU6352	1,42-44. 5a,1
Baskenea	NFK	??	4,15
Baslow	DBY	SK2572	1,28
Bassetts	ESS	TL7908	4,18
Bassingbourn	CAM	TL3344	2,4. 14,27. 26,25
Bassingfield	NTT	SK6137	9,81. 10,13
Bassingham	LIN	SK9059	1,26-27
Bassingham	SSX	??	9,131
Baston	LIN	TF1113	11,4. 24,27
Bastwick	NFK	TG4217	4,27. 9,21. 10,88. 17,15. 64,5
[Wood] Bastwick	NFK	TG3315	1,44;158. 17,2-3. 20,19. 66,91;93
Bastwood (in Eastham)	WOR	SO6767	15,12

Baswich	STS	SJ9422	2,2;4
Batcombe	SOM	ST6939	8,24
Bath SOM	GLS		E9
Bath SOM	SOM	ST7565	1,28-31. 5,20;30;66. 7,1. 40,1. 41,1. EW1
Bath SOM	WIL		B4
Bathampton	SOM	ST7766	7,11
Bathampton	WIL	SU0138	27,15-16
Bathealton	SOM	ST0724	25,43
Batheaston	SOM	ST7867	1,30-31. 7,10. 45,10
Batherton	CHS	SJ6549	8,28
Bathford	SOM	ST7866	7,6
Bathingbourne IOW	HAM	SZ5483	1,W2
Bathley	NTT	SK7759	24,3
Bathurst	SSX	TQ7615	8,5
Bathwick	SOM	ST7565	5,37
Batley WR	YKS	SE2424	9W139. SW,M9
Batsford	GLS	SP1833	68,4
Batson	DEV	SX7339	15,74
Battersby NR	YKS	NZ5907	1N24. SN,L30
Battersby [Barn] WR	YKS	SD7052	30W37 note
Battersea	SRY	TQ2676	5,13. 6,1
Battisborough	DEV	SX5948	6,7-8 notes. 39,14
Battisford	DEV	SX5754	21,17
Battisford	SFK	TM0554	2,11. 7,57. 31,56. 53,3. 74,3
Battishill	DEV	SX5085	*16,7*
Battle	SSX	TQ7415	8
Battleford	DEV	SX8364	39,11
Battlesden	BDF	SP9628	16,2. 40,2. 55,1
Battramsley	HAM	SZ3099	NF9,24
Baumber	LIN	TF2274	22,23. 24,20. CS,23;33
Baunton	GLS	SP0204	51,1. 78,5
Bausley (Wales)	SHR	SJ3315	4,4,8
Baveney	SHR	SO6979	4,11,13
Baverstock	WIL	SU0231	13,17
Bawburgh	NFK	TG1508	4,9
Bawdeswell	NFK	TG0420	4,29;31
Bawdrip	SOM	ST3439	24,23
Bawdsey	SFK	TM3440	6,154;157;161. 11,1. 21,76;79;80
Bawsey	NFK	TF6519	4,45. 7,2
Baxby NR	YKS	SE5175	2N13 *note*. 2N14. 23N1. SN,Bi2
Baycliff	WIL	ST8139	24,26
Bayfield	NFK	TG0540	1,25. 25,18
Bayford	HRT	TL3108	1,18
Baylham	SFK	TM1051	7,55;58;61;63;65. 76,15
Baysham	HEF	SO5727	1,54
Bayston	SHR	SJ4808	4,14,12
Baythorn [End]	ESS	TL7242	37,12
Bayton	WOR	SO6973	15,6
Bayworth	BRK	SP5001	7,10
Beachampton	BKM	SP7736	14,31. 41,5. 57,4
Beachendon	BKM	SP7513	4,24. 23,13
Beadlam NR	YKS	SE6584	5N41;52. SN,Ma19
Beaford	DEV	SS5514	1,51
Beal WR	YKS	SE5325	9W59. SW,O13
[Great] Bealings	SFK	TM2348	6,121. 67,11;15
[Little] Bealings	SFK	TM2248	*3,33*. 16,3. 21,59. 31,16. 67,12
Beaminster	DOR	ST4701	3,10
Beamonston	KEN	TR0148	5,166
Beamsley WR	YKS	SE0752	1W45;73. 21W4. 24W14. SW,Bu31. SW,Cr3

Beara [Charter]	DEV	SS5238	3,31
Beare (? in Worlington)	DEV	??	20,5
Bearley	WAR	SP1860	22,27. 28,18
Bearstone	SHR	SJ7239	4,19,7
Bearwardcote	DBY	SK2833	3,1. 6,94
Beauchamps	HRT	TL3831	17,10
Beaumont	ESS	TM1724	35,11
Beausale	WAR	SP2470	4,3
Beauworth	HAM	SU5726	2,1
Beauxfield	KEN	TR3045	7,19
Beaworthy	DEV	SX4699	21,4
Beccles SFK	NFK		1,63
Beccles SFK	SFK	TM4290	1,39-40;43. 14,120
Becclinga	SFK	??	7,72
Beceslei	HAM	??	NF8,2
Bechenehilde	WIL	??	25,18
Bechetuna: see *Beketun* SFK			
Bechington (in Friston)	SSX	TV5498	10,66
Beck	NFK	TG0220	4,30
Beckbury	SHR	SJ7601	4,26,5
Beckenham	KEN	TQ3769	5,39
Beckering	LIN	TF1280	2,15. 16,18. 22,12. 28,30. 32,12
Beckett	BRK	SU2489	17,6
Beckford WOR	GLS		1,59-60. EvL1
Beckford WOR	WOR	SO9735	EG4
[East] Beckham	NFK	TG1539	1,149. 9,155. 10,8;65
[West] Beckham	NFK	TG1439	25,13
Beckhampton	WIL	SU0868	29,8
Beckingham	NTT	SK7790	5,4. 9,119
Beckington	SOM	ST8051	22,24
Beckley	HAM	SZ2296	NF3,15
Beckley	KEN	TQ7074	5,107
Beckley	OXF	SP5611	29,2
Beckney	ESS	TQ8495	18,15
Beckwith [House] WR	YKS	SE2852	21W9 *note*. SW,Bu38
Bedale NR	YKS	SE2688	6N122. SN,CtA35
Beddingham	SSX	TQ4407	9,35-37. 10,3;14
Beddington	SRY	TQ3065	19,15. 29,1-2
Bedecote	HAM	??	1,34
Bedfield	SFK	TM2266	6,307
[East] Bedfont	MDX	TQ0873	8,3. 11,2
[West] Bedfont	MDX	TQ0673	11,3
Bedford	BDF	TL0449	B. 4,9. 6,1. 13. 53,32;56. 57,14
Bedgrove	BKM	SP8412	4,6
Bedhampton	HAM	SU7006	6,4
Bedingfield	SFK	TM1768	6,12;68;75-77;232;319. 14,104.
			19,10. 31,5-6. 43,5. 75,5. 77,3
Bedingham	NFK	TM2893	1,182;184. 9,168
Bedminster (in Bristol) GLS	SOM	ST5871	1,7
Bednall	STS	SJ9517	2,4
Bedstone	SHR	SO3675	4,20,25
Bedworth	WAR	SP3586	16,44
[Great and Little] Bedwyn	WIL	SU2764	1,2;23j. 39,1
		SU2966	
Beeby	LEC	SK6608	7,2
Beech	SSX	TQ7216	8,4. 9,25
Beechamwell	NFK	TF7505	4,43. 9,233. 21,8. 31,29
Beechingstoke	WIL	SU0859	12,1
Beeding	SSX	TQ1910	12,20;47. 13,1
Beedon	BRK	SU4878	7,15
Beeford ER	YKS	TA1254	14E24. SE,Hol20

Beeley	DBY	SK2667	1,31
Beelsby	LIN	TA2002	12,36. 47,7. 48,10. 68,45
Beenleigh	DEV	SX7556	28,12
Beer (in Offwell)	DEV	SY2098	16,174
Beer (near Seaton)	DEV	SY2289	7,4
Beercrocombe	SOM	ST3220	19,28
Beere [Crocombe]	SOM	ST2441	16,8
[Great] Beere	DEV	SS6903	16,47
Beesby	LIN	TF4680	12,85. 24,63. 28,32
Beesby	LIN	TF2696	12,28-29
Beeston	BDF	TL1648	21,12-14. 25,14. 47,3. 56,7. 57,11
Beeston	CHS	SJ5358	2,24
Beeston	NTT	SK5236	10,34
Beeston WR	YKS	SE2830	9W124-125. SW,M1
Beeston [Regis]	NFK	TG1743	19,21-22. 23,18
Beeston [St Andrew]	NFK	TG2513	1,189;191. 7,17. 12,29. 20,25
Beeston [St Lawrence]	NFK	TG3221	17,44
Beetham WES	YKS	SD4979	30W40. See also CHS Y13
Beetley	NFK	TF9718	10,5
Beetor	DEV	SX7184	16,60
Beffcote	STS	SJ8019	1,7
Begbroke	OXF	SP4613	59,11
Beighterton	STS	SJ8011	14,1
Beighton	DBY	SK4483	5,2. 10,3. 16,3
Beighton	NFK	TG3808	10,25. 47,2
Bekesbourne	KEN	TR1955	5,122. 7,3
Beketuna/Bechetuna	SFK	??	1,29. 31,26
Belaugh	NFK	TG2818	1,194;235. 17,33. 20,31
Belbroughton	WOR	SO9176	26,13
Belby [House] ER	YKS	SE7728	1E2 *note*. 3Y4-5. CE12;17. SE,How4;7
Belchamp [Otten, St Paul and Walter]	ESS	TL8041 TL7942 TL8240	5,3. 20,26;28. 43,4
Belchamp [Walter]	ESS	TL8240	35,6
Belchford	LIN	TF2975	11,9. 14,46-57
Belenei	SFK	??	16,43
Belgrave	LEC	SK5907	C11. 13,20. 41,1
Belice (in Hayne Hundred)	KEN	??	9,18-19
Belice (in Rolvenden Hundred)	KEN	??	5,130
Bell [Hall]	WOR	SO9377	23,8
Belleau	LIN	TF4078	13,3
Bellerby NR	YKS	SE1192	6N104. SN,CtA31
Bellhurst	SSX	TQ8625	9,124
Bellington	WOR	SO8876	23,14
Belluton	SOM	ST6164	1,28. 17,6
Belmesthorpe RUT	LIN		56,4. CK,2
Belmesthorpe RUT	NTH		56,1. ELc2-3
Belmesthorpe RUT	RUT	TF0410	EN16. ELc10;18
Belstead	SFK	TM1241	6,26. 16,42. 32,5. 35,3. 46,3. 71,2
Belstead [Hall]	ESS	TL7210	22,18. 78,1
Belstone	DEV	SX6193	16,15
Belswardyne	SHR	SJ6003	4,21,9
Belthorpe ER	YKS	SE7854	2N16 *note*. SE,P9
Beltoft	LIN	SE8006	63,13
Belton	LIN	SE7806	63,10;12;25. CW,17
Belton	LIN	SK9339	1,15;19. 31,1. 39,4. 57,25. 67,13-14;16-17. CK,59-61
Belton	SFK	TG4802	1,35;59
Beltrou	HEF	??	29,6
Bemerton	WIL	SU1230	55,2. 67,34

Bempton ER	YKS	TA1972	5E52. SE,Hu6
Benacre	SFK	TM5184	14,165
Bendish	HRT	TL1621	10,20
Bendysh [Hall]	ESS	TL6039	20,77. 90,64
Benefeld (in Twineham)	SSX	TQ2519	12,54-55
Benefield	NTH	SP9888	59,2
Benehale	SHR	SJ3004	4,1,35
Benenden	KEN	TQ8032	5,180; *181*
Benfield	SSX	TQ2607	12,22
[North and South] Benfleet	ESS	TQ7690	1,1;14. 6,1. 24,13
		TQ7786	
Bengeo	HRT	TL3213	16,12. 27,1. 33,15. 34,15-19.
			36,18
Bengeworth WOR	GLS		E34
Bengeworth WOR	WOR	SP0443	2,75. 10,12
Benhall	SFK	TM3761	3,101. 6,47;53-54. 7,140;149-150
Benham	BRK	SU4367	7,16. 54,3. 65,11
Beningbrough NR	YKS	SE5257	23N28
Benningholme [Hall] ER	YKS	TA1239	14E11 *note*. SE, Hol16
Bennington	HRT	TL2923	36,6-7
[Long] Bennington	LIN	SK8444	12,50. 15,2. CK,38
[Long] Bennington two Hundreds	LIN	—	12,49
Benniworth	LIN	TF2081	2,16. 14,59
Benson OXF	BRK		B1
Benson OXF	OXF	SU6191	1,1. 58,14;19
Bensted	ESS	TL7403	27,14. 41,9
Bensted	KEN	TQ7049	5,100
Bentfield [Bury]	ESS	TL4926	32,19
Benthall (in Alberbury with Cardeston)	SHR	SJ3913	4,27,20
[High] Bentham WR	YKS	SD6669	1L5 *note*
Bentley (near Farnham)	HAM	SU7844	2,25. ESr
Bentley (in Montisford)	HAM	SU3129	53,1. 69,15
Bentley	SFK	TM1138	1,101;103-104. 3,71;75
Bentley	SRY	SU7844	3,1 *in note*.
Bentley	WAR	SP2895	31,8
[Lower and Upper] Bentley	WOR	SO9865	26,4
		SO9966	
Bentley ER	YKS	TA0135	2E17. 5N1a. SE,Wel5
Bentley WR	YKS	SE5605	5W30. 10W38. SW,Sf34 *note*.
			SW,O1
[Fenny] Bentley	DBY	SK1750	1,14
[Great] Bentley	ESS	TM1021	35,9
[Hungry] Bentley	DBY	SK1738	6,36
[Little] Bentley	ESS	TM1224	21,9. 23,31
Benton	DEV	SS6536	2,10
Benton [Hall]	ESS	TL8213	11,1
Beoley WOR	WAR		EB W2
Beoley WOR	WOR	SP0669	9,2
Bepton	SSX	SU8518	11,15
Berden	ESS	TL4629	24,54
Bere	DEV	??	24,17
Bere [Ferrers]	DEV	SX4563	15,46
Bere [Regis]	DOR	SY8494	1,2. 24,1. 55,15
Berewic	ESS	??	18,37
Berg(h)ebi (in Topcliffe) NR	YKS	??	13N16 *note*. SN,Bi5 *note*
Bergestorp	LIN	??	8,7
Bergh [Apton]	NFK	TM3199	*12,17.* 15,28 *note*
[East] Bergholt	SFK	TM0734	1,100-101;102 note;103-105;119.
			3,68;70;80-82. 5,6-8. 16,35-
			37;41;46-47. 25,65-67;69-70;72-
			73;75;77. 28,5. 32,5;8. 35,3-4.
			38,21. 40,3-4. 58,1. 61,1. 71,1-2

[West] Bergholt	ESS	TL9528	23,36. 46,2. 90,70;73
Bergolbi/Berguluesbi (in Seamer) NR	YKS	??	1N31 *note*. 31N5. SN, L38
Beria	SFK	??	3,69
Bericote	WAR	SP3169	17,62
Berkeley	GLS	ST6899	1,15-19;63
Berkesden	HRT	TL3328	17,8. 37,19
Berkhamsted	HRT	SP9907	15,1;5;12
[Little] Berkhamsted	HRT	TL2907	37,21
Berkley	SOM	ST8149	22,25
Berkswell WAR	NTH		19,2
Berkswell WAR	WAR	SP2479	16,27. EN2
Bermesdena	SFK	??	52,11
Bermondsey	SRY	TQ3379	1,4. 17,2
Bernaldeston	HEF	SO2861	29,16
Bernardsmoor	DEV	??	16,105
Bernebi (in Birdforth) NR	YKS	??	11N18 *note*, SN,Bi3
Berrick [Salome]	OXF	SU6293	35,24
Berrington	SHR	SJ5306	4,3,14
Berrington	WOR	SO5767	57,6. 19,1
Berry [Pomeroy]	DEV	SX8261	34,48
Berrynarbor	DEV	SS5646	23,2
Berth	SSX	TQ3320	13,3
Bertuna	ESS	??	90,35
Berwick	KEN	TR1235	2,42
Berwick (in Atcham)	SHR	SJ5410	4,3,25
Berwick (in Shrewsbury St Mary)	SHR	SJ4714	4,1,20
Berwick	SSX	TQ5105	9,89;94
Bescot	STS	SP0097	1,5
Besford	SHR	SJ5524	4,23,14
Besford	WOR	SO9144	8,8
Beslow SHR	SHR	SJ5808	4,14,16
Beslow SHR	WIL		68,24 note
Bessete	HAM	??	35,3
Bessingby ER	YKS	TA1565	1Y11. SE,Hu4
Bessingham	NFK	TG1637	30,2
Bestha(i)m (in Fewston) WR	YKS	??	1Y19 *note*. SW,Bu28
Besthorpe	NFK	TM0695	9,126;129
Besthorpe (near Caunton)	NTT	SK7360	1,21;24. 12,9
Bestwall	DOR	SY9287	26,49
Beswick ER	YKS	TA0148	1Y9. 5E31. SE,Sn3
Betchworth	SRY	TQ2150	19,39;47
Betley	STS	SJ7549	17,10
Betterton	BRK	SU4386	1,12. 33,5
Betteshanger	KEN	TR3152	5,200
Bettisfield FLN	CHS	SJ4737	B13. 2,1
Betton (in Norton in Hales)	SHR	SJ6936	4,23,9
Betton (in Shrewsbury St Chad)	SHR	SJ5009	1,6
Bevendean	SSX	TQ3406	10,107. 12,18
Beverington (in Eastbourne)	SSX	TQ5900	10,5;7
Beverley ER	YKS	TA0339	2E1;3;17. CE33. SE, Sn10
Beversbrook and [Lower] Beversbrook	WIL	SU0073	32,4. 56,5
		ST9972	
Beversham	SFK	TM3558	67,6
Beverstone	GLS	SO8693	1,15
Bevington WAR	WAR	SP0353	EW7
Bevington WAR	WOR		10,15
Bewerley WR	YKS	SE1565	24W15. SW,Bu28
Bewholme ER	YKS	TA1650	14E29. SE,Hol22
Bewick [Hall] ER	YKS	TA2339	14E11 *note*. SE,Hol17
Bexhill	SSX	TQ7407	9,11
Bexington	DOR	SY5386	47,5
Bexley	KEN	TQ4973	2,6

Bexwell	NFK	TF6303	9,231. 15,2. 66,9;48
Beyton	SFK	TL9362	31,54
Bhompston	DOR	SY7290	26,6;12
Bibury	GLS	SP1106	3,3;4. EvK80. WoA1. WoB16-17
Bicester	OXF	SP5822	28,3
Bichenehilde	WIL	??	25,12
Bicher(t)un (in Newhall with Clifton) WR	YKS	??	2W4 *note*. SW,Sk2
Bickenhall	SOM	ST2818	19,27
Bickenhill	WAR	SP1882	17,2
[Middle] Bickenhill	WAR	SP2083	17,3
Bicker LIN	LIN	TF2237	2,30. 12,75;89. 56,22. 57,44. 67,19
Bicker LIN	RUT		ELc17
Bicker Hundred	LIN	—	CK,66
Bickerston	NFK	TG0808	66,31
Bickerton	CHS	SJ5052	2,20
Bickerton	HEF	SO6530	15,5
Bickerton WR	YKS	SE4550	28W37. SW,An17
Bickford	DEV	SX5758	29,8. 52,28
Bickford	STS	SJ8814	17,3
Bickham	DEV	SS8620	28,10
Bickham	SOM	SS9541	25,15
[Abbots] Bickington	DEV	SS3813	45,2
[High] Bickington	DEV	SS5920	1,40;67
Bickleigh (near Plymouth)	DEV	SX5262	21,19
Bickleigh (near Silverton)	DEV	SS9407	15,61
Bickleton	DEV	SS5031	36,8
Bickley	CHS	SJ5448	2,19
Bickmarsh WOR	GLS		78,7
Bickmarsh WOR	WAR		43,2
Bickmarsh WOR	WOR	SP1049	EG17. EW2
[English] Bicknor	GLS	SO5815	37,2
Bickton	HAM	SU1412	22,1
Bicton	CON	SX3169	5,2,26
Bicton	DEV	SY0785	51,1
Bicton (near Montford)	SHR	SJ4414	3f,3
Biddenham	BDF	TL0250	4,4. 6,1. 13,1-2. 23,28. 25,4. 56,1-4
Biddesden	WIL	SU2950	42,4
Biddestone	WIL	ST8673	27,21
Biddlesden	BKM	SP6339	1,7. 12,27
Biddulph	STS	SJ8960	1,33
Bideford	DEV	SS4526	1,60
Bidford [on-Avon]	WAR	SP1051	1,3. 4,5
Bielby WR	YKS	SE7843	1Y10. 1E11a. SE,P1
[North] Bierley WR	YKS	SE1729	9W134 *note*. SW,M8
Bierton	BKM	SP8315	4,7
Bigbury	DEV	SX6646	15,44
Bigby	LIN	TA0507	7,18. 13,18. 25,14
Biggin (formerly Holme)	WAR	SP5378	17,44-45
Biggleswade	BDF	TL1844	51,2. 51,4
Bighton	HAM	SU6134	6,3
Bignor	SSX	SU9814	11,78
Bigods	ESS	TL6224	30,31
Bilborough	NTT	SK5241	1,50. 10,39
Bilbrook	STS	SJ8703	7,5
Bilbrough WR	YKS	SE5346	22W2. SW,An8
Bilby	NTT	SK6383	9,45
Bildeston	SFK	TL9949	41,1
Bile	HAM	??	NF8,1
Bilham [House] WR	YKS	SE4806	5W14 *note*. 10W15. 12W1;7. SW,Sf9

Billesdon	LEC	SK7202	28,4
Billesley	WAR	SP1456	18,14
[Great and Little] Billing	NTH	SP8162	18,2;4. 48,3. 57,1
		SP8062	
Billingborough	LIN	TF1134	2,32. 24,94. 26,36. 27,58. CK,51
Billingborough Hundred	LIN	—	12,55
Billingford (formerly *Pyrleston*)	NFK	TM1679	1,226 *and note*. 15,25. 43,2
Billingford (near North Elmham) NFK	NFK	TG0120	4,31. 32,1. 39,2. ESf7
Billingford (near North Elmham) NFK	SFK		56,6
Billinghay	LIN	TF1554	2,40-41
Billingley WR	YKS	SE4304	10W25. 29W8. SW,Sf17;19
Billington	STS	SJ8820	11,6
Billockby	NFK	TG4213	9,19. 10,90. 17,14. 64,6
[West] Bilney	NFK	TF7115	23,12-13. 66,96
Bilsby	LIN	TF4676	13,8
Bilsham	SSX	SU9702	11,86
Bilsington	KEN	TR0434	5,175
Bilsthorpe	NTT	SK6560	17,5
Bilston	STS	SO9596	1,4
Bilstone	LEC	SK3605	11,3
Bilton	WAR	SP4873	12,6. 17,36
Bilton ER	YKS	TA1532	2E27. 14E47. SE,Mid1. SE,Hol25
Bilton (near Harrogate) WR	YKS	SE3157	21W11. 29W38. SW,Bu39
Bilton (near Wetherby) WR	YKS	SE4750	25W10. SW,An10
Binbrook	LIN	TF2193	18,7-8. 53,2. 57,6
Bincknoll	WIL	SU1079	29,2-4
Bincombe	DOR	SY6884	17,2
Binderton	SSX	SU8410	11,4
Bing	SFK	TM2853	6,187;245
Bingham	NTT	SK7039	9,97-99
Bingley WR	YKS	SE1039	24W1 *note*. SW,Sk18
Binham	NFK	TF9839	34,14-15. 66,89
Binley	WAR	SP3778	6,5. 17,52
Binnerton	CON	SW6033	1,16
Binnington ER	YKS	SE9978	5E57. SE,Bt9
Binsley	ESS	TL8438	23,10. 36,9
Binstead	HAM	SU6015	3,9
Binstead IOW	HAM	SZ5792	6,17
Binsted	HAM	SU7741	23,56
Binsted	SSX	SU9806	11,80
Binton	WAR	SP1454	28,14. 34,1. 35,2. 37,5
Bintree	NFK	TG0123	12,28. 25,1. 56,1
[Little and Much] Birch	HEF	SO5031	1,58
		SO5030	
[Great] Birch	ESS	TL9419	20,39
Birch [Hall]	ESS	TM2122	20,67
[Little] Birch	ESS	TL9420	32,26. 60,3
[Great] Bircham	NFK	TF7732	19,9-10. 20,2
Bircham [Newton]	NFK	TF7633	20,1
Bircham [Tofts]	NFK	TF7732	2,5
Birchanger	ESS	TL5022	1,10. 14,4. 30,48
Birchgrove	SSX	TQ4029	10,110
Birchill	DBY	SK2270	1,28
Birchover	DBY	SK2362	6,74
[Ing]birchworth: see Ingbirchworth YKS			
[Rough]birchworth: see			
Roughbirchworth YKS			
Birdbrook	ESS	TL7041	37,11
Birdham	SSX	SU8200	11,44
Birdingbury	WAR	SP4368	6,4. 17,27
Birdsall ER	YKS	SE8164	2B18 *note*. 5E58. 29E15. 31E6.
			SE.Sc1

Birkby NR	YKS	NZ3302	1Y2 *note*. SN,A1
Birkby [Hall] (near Cartmel) LAN	YKS	SD3777	23N22 *note*. See also CHS Y10
Birkby [Hill] WR	YKS	SE3539	9W13 *note*. SW,Sk8
Birkin WR	YKS	SE5326	9W26. CW4. SW,BA7
Birley	HEF	SO4553	9,16-17. 10,51
Birling	KEN	TQ6860	5,57
Birlingham	WOR	SO9343	8,4
Birmingham	WAR	SP0786	27,5
Birstall	LEC	SK5908	C11. 13,21;61
Birstwith WR	YKS	SE2359	1W43. 28W23. SW,Bu30
Birthorpe	LIN	TF1033	24,95
Bisbrooke RUT	NTH		1,2e. 56,25
Bisbrooke RUT	RUT	SP8899	EN2;17
Biscathorpe	LIN	TF2384	3,41
Biscot	BDF	TL0823	1,5
Bisham	BRK	SU8585	21,7
Bishampton	WOR	SO9951	2,21
Bishopsbourne	KEN	TR1852	2,17
Bishopsgate	MDX	TQ3381	3,27
Bishopsteignton	DEV	SX9173	2,4
Bishopsteignton: see Teignton DEV			
Bishopstoke	HAM	SU4619	2,6
Bishopstone (formerly *Mansell*)	HEF	SO4143	2,46
Bishopstone (in Montacute)	SOM	ST4917	19,86
Bishopstone	SSX	TQ4700	3,1
Bishopstrow	WIL	ST8943	24,28
Bishopsworth SOM	GLS		E9
Bishopsworth SOM	SOM	ST5768	5,20-21
Bishopthorpe WR	YKS	SE5947	1W29 *note*. 23E19. 29W12;27.
			SW,An1
Bishton	SHR	SJ8001	4,25,7
Bishton	STS	SK0220	17,6
Bisley	GLS	SO9006	28,1
Bispesdone	OXF	??	51,1
Bispham (near Blackpool) LAN	YKS	SD3140	1L1. See also CHS Y2
Bisterne	HAM	SU1401	NF9,38
Bistre FLN	CHS	SJ2762	FT3,1;6-7
Bitchfield	LIN	SK9828	7,40. 26,48. 59,11
Bithen (in Middlethorpe) WR	YKS	??	SW,An17 *note*
Bittadon	DEV	SS5441	3,60
Bittering	NFK	TF9317	1,80;213
Bitterley	SHR	SO5677	4,8,13
Bittesby	LEC	SP5086	1,12
Bitteswell	LEC	SP5385	10,9. 29,7
Bitton	GLS	ST6869	1,9. 78,13
Bix	OXF	SU7285	20,8. 58,12
Bixley	NFK	TG2504	9,32;42;45;114. 66,81
Bixley	SFK	TM2044	3,17. 21,68. 31,14
Blaby	LEC	SP5797	44,3
Blachford	DEV	SX6160	17,66. 29,5
Blackawton	DEV	SX8050	1,24
Blackborough	DEV	ST0909	16,101. 34,20. 51,7
Blackburn LAN	CHS	SD6828	R4,1
Blackford	SOM	ST6526	8,9. 36,8
Blackmanston	DOR	SY9180	56,52;65
Blackmanstone	KEN	TR0729	9,12
Blackmore	SOM	ST2438	21,35
Blackpool	DEV	SS6825	1,41
Blackslade	DEV	SX7375	34,46
Blacksworth	GLS	ST6273	75,3 *in note*
Blackwell	DBY	SK1272	1,28

Name	County	Grid	Ref
Blackwell WAR	WAR	SP2443	EW2
Blackwell WAR	WOR		2,46
Blacon	CHS	SJ3767	20,1
Bladon	OXF	SP4414	7,22
Blagdon	SOM	ST5058	37,1
Blagrove	DEV	SS7716	21,9;11
Blakeney	NFK	TG0343	1,19. 10,56. 25,20
Blakenhall	CHS	SJ7247	18,6
[Great] Blakenham	SFK	TM1150	1,3;67. 8,57. 9,1
[Little] Blakenham	SFK	TM1048	21,21. 29,6
Blakesley	NTH	SP6250	1,6. 18,95. 22,7. 35,24
[Little] Blakesley (now Woodend)	NTH	SP6149	1,6 note. 35,24 note
Blakewell	DEV	SS5536	16,74
[Langton Long] Blandford	DOR	ST8905	26,37. 47,4. 56,31
Blandford [St Mary]	DOR	ST8805	26,29. 34,6. 49,1. 56,14
[High] Blandsby NR	YKS	SE8287	1Y4 note. SN,D11
Blankney two Hundreds	LIN	TF0659	31,16
Blaston	LEC	SP8095	1,4. 15,2. 40,20
Blatchams	ESS	TL8610	20,61
Blaten [Carr] NR	YKS	??	5N29 note. SN,L44
Blatherwycke	NTH	SP9795	30,10
Blaxhall	SFK	TM3556	3,87;89;92. 6,29;33–34;37;39;41. 7,136. 8,80. 16,6. 21,36. 45,1
Blaxhold	SOM	ST2234	21,77
Blaxton	DEV	SX4762	39,20
Bleadon SOM	BDF		3,8;10–11
Bleadon SOM	BKM		5,10 note;18
Bleadon SOM	SOM	ST3456	2,11. EBe1-3;EBu1-2
Blean	KEN	TR1260	12,4
Bleasby	LIN	TF1384	16,15. 28,29. 48,9;11
Blechingley	SRY	TQ3250	19,2
Bledington	GLS	SP2422	11,2
Bledisloe	GLS	SO6808	1,13
Bledlow	BKM	SP7702	12,3
Bledone BDF, BKM: see Bleadon SOM			
Bletchingdon	OXF	SP5017	B9. 28,19. 58,27
Bletsoe	BDF	TL0258	23,27. 53,8
Blewbury	BRK	SU5385	B1. 1,5. 17,7
Blickling	NFK	TG1728	1,57. 10,38–39;65
Blidworth	NTT	SK5855	5,9;11
Blidworth Hundred	NTT	—	18,6
Blingsby	DBY	SK4664	5,5
Blisland	CON	SX1073	1,6
Blisworth	NTH	SP7253	35,7
Blithfield	STS	SK0424	8,27
Blo Norton: see [Blo] Norton NFK			
Blockley GLS	GLS	SP1634	E23. EvA117;119 note. EvC38;40. WoB7. WoC6
Blockley GLS	WOR		2,38
Blofield	NFK	TG3309	10,28. 20,21
Blorant FLN	CHS	SJ1173	FT1,3
Blore	STS	SK1349	11,40
Bloxham	OXF	SP4235	B5. 1,7a-7b
Bloxholm	LIN	TF0653	16,46. 27,46
Bloxwich	STS	SJ9901	1,6
Bloxworth	DOR	SY8894	11,4
Blundeston	SFK	TM5197	3,54. 7,54
Blunham	BDF	TL1551	6,3. 21,11. 53,35
[Broad] Blunsdon and Blunsdon [St Andrew]	WIL	SU1590 / SU1389	24,21. 27,12. 67,100
Bluntisham	HUN	TL3674	4,2. 6,10

Blunt's [Hall]	ESS	TL8014	20,10. 34,5
Blyborough	LIN	SK9394	3,4. 14,16. 28,1. 63,1
Blyford	SFK	TM4276	13,2
Blymhill	STS	SJ8012	11,56
Blyth	NTT	SK6287	9,49
Blythburgh	SFK	TM4575	1,10;12. 1,10. 6,82;89b–89c. 7,5. 26,12a. 33,10
Blyton	LIN	SK8594	1,39;51. 16,31. 57,8
Boarhunt and [North] Boarhunt	HAM	SU6008 SU6010	3,23. 21,1. 23,33
Boarscroft	HRT	SP8717	15,8
Boasley	DEV	SX4992	16,6
Bobbington	STS	SO8090	11,43
Bobbingworth	ESS	TL5305	37,15
Bochelande	KEN	??	5,131
Bockhampton	BRK	SU3481	48,1. 65,12
Bockhampton	DOR	SY7292	58,1
Bocking	ESS	TL7523	2,2
Bockingham	ESS	TL9321	90,18
Bockleton	WOR	SO5961	3,1
Bocolt	HAM	??	NF9,3
Boconnoc	CON	SX1460	5,13,2
Bodardle	CON	SX0960	5,4,13
Bodbrane	CON	SX2359	5,12,1
Boddington	GLS	SO8925	1,41. 19,2
[Lower and Upper] Boddington	NTH	SP4852 SP4853	18,96. 22,2
Bodebi	LIN	??	36,2
[Higher] Boden and Boden [Vean]	CON	SW7723 SW7724	1,1
Bodenham	HEF	SO5351	10,9. 24,9
Bodeslege (?Bagley in Wedmore, ?Butleigh)	SOM	??	8,12 note
Bodeugan FLN	CHS	SJ0574	FT1,2
Bodham	NFK	TG1238	23,18. 25,21. 66,97
Bodiam	SSX	TQ7825	9,120
Bodicote	OXF	SP4637	17,6. ?20,7. 34,3
Bodigga	CON	SX2754	1,7
Bodiggo	CON	SX0458	5,3,9
Bodmin	CON	SX0767	4,3
Bodney	NFK	TL8398	8,96. 22,8. 23,1
Bodrugan	CON	SX0143	5,3,10
Bodsham	KEN	TR1145	7,26
Boduel	CON	SX2263	5,24,15
Boehill	DEV	ST0315	24,11–12
Bogeuurde WR	YKS	??	30W37 *note*
Bojorrow	CON	SW7023	1,1
Bolberry	DEV	SX6939	15,38;73
Bolderford	HAM	SU2904	NF9,16
Boldre	HAM	SZ3298	NF9,19
Bole	NTT	SK7987	5,4. 9,118;125
Bolebec	SHR	??	4,1,32
Bolham (in Tiverton)	DEV	SS9514	51,8
Bolham [Water] (in Clayhidon)	DEV	ST1612	16,121
Bolingbroke	LIN	TF3465	14,66–83. CS,38
Bollingham	HEF	SO3052	1,69
Bollington [Hall]	ESS	TL5027	32,20. 90,35;41
Bolney	OXF	SU7780	59,1
Bolnhurst	BDF	TL0859	2,4–5. 3,8. 10,1. 53,6
Bolsover	DBY	SK4770	7,1
Boltby NR	YKS	SE4986	23N13–14

Bolton ER	YKS	SE7752	2B11. 29E5. SE,P7
Bolton WR	YKS	SE1635	9W131 *note*. SW,M6 *note*
Bolton [Abbey] WR	YKS	SE0753	1W73. SW,Cr1;5
Bolton [by Bowland] WR	YKS	SD7849	13W40
[Castle] Bolton NR	YKS	SE0391	6N87 *note*. SN,CtA27
Bolton [Farm] (in Urswick) LAN	YKS	SD2572	1L8 *note*. See also CHS Y9
Bolton [le Sands] LAN	YKS	SD4867	1L2. See also CHS Y3
Bolton [Percy] WR	YKS	SE5341	13W7 note. 13W12. CW33;35;40. SW,An4
Bolton [upon Dearne] WR	YKS	SE4502	10W26. 13W7 *note*. SW,Sf19
Bolton [upon Swale] NR	YKS	SE2599	6N24 *note*. SN,CtA12
[West] Bolton NR	YKS	SE0290	6N88. SN,CtA27
Bolun	DBY	??	6,18
Bonby	LIN	TA0015	25,1. 36,3
Bonchurch and [Upper] Bonchurch IOW	HAM	SZ5777 SZ5778	7,1
Bondleigh	DEV	SS6504	3,20
Bonhunt	ESS	TL5133	57,6
Bonington: see Sutton NTT			
Bonnington	KEN	TR0534	9,48
Bonsall	DBY	SK2758	1,12
Bonthorpe	LIN	TF4872	3,51
Bonyalva	CON	SX3059	1,7
Boode	DEV	SS5038	*3,32*
[Great] Bookham	SRY	TQ1354	8,17
[Little] Bookham	SRY	TQ1254	20,2
Boothby	LIN	TF4868	14,101. 24,60. 28,43
Boothby [Graffoe]	LIN	SK9858	1,5. 27,59
Boothby [Pagnell]	LIN	SK9730	24,81. 57,55
Boothorpe	LEC	SK3117	14,21
Bootle (near Liverpool) LAN	CHS	SJ3494	R1,20
Bootle CUM	YKS	SD1088	1L6. See also CHS Y7
Booton	NFK	TG1222	37,3
Bordelby (now Mount Grace) NR	YKS	SE4498	1N129 *note*. 31N5. SN,A7
Bordley WR	YKS	SD9464	30W34
Boreham	ESS	TL7509	20,56. 22,17. 24,58
Boreton	SHR	SJ5106	3b,5
Borham	SSX	??	11,90
Borley	ESS	TL8443	54,1. 90,55
?Borough (in Bridgerule) DEV	CON		5,11,6
Borough (in Bridgerule) DEV	DEV	SS2602	EC1
Borrowby (near Loftus) NR	YKS	NZ7715	5N8. SN,L9
Borrowby (near Northallerton) NR	YKS	SE4289	1Y2. SN,Bi5 note. SN, A1
Borstal	KEN	TQ7366	4,14-15
Borthwood IOW	HAM	SZ5784	7,8
Borwick LAN	YKS	SD5273	30W40. See also CHS Y10
Bosbury	HEF	SO6943	2,29
Boscombe	WIL	SU2038	16,2. 32,7
Bosent	CON	SX2163	5,3,4
Bosham SSX	HAM		5,1
Bosham SSX	SSX	SU8004	1,1. 6,1;5. 12,33
Bosle	SHR	??	4,21,11
Bosley	CHS	SJ9165	11,5
Bosley DOR	HAM	SZ1495	17,2
Bosmere	SFK	TM0954	21,*16*;47
Bossall NR	YKS	SE7160	23N32 *note*. SN,B27
Bossiney	CON	SX0688	4,13
Bossington	HAM	SU3331	28,5
Bossington	SOM	SS8947	10,6. 32,5
Bostock	CHS	SJ6769	5,11
?Bosvisack	CON	SW7846	5,24,8

Boswell [Banks]	KEN	TR2643	5,195;221-*222*
[Husbands] Bosworth	LEC	SP6484	16,7. 17,15. 23,4;6. 33,1
[Market] Bosworth	LEC	SK4003	9,5. 13,72
Botelet	CON	SX1860	5,14,1
Boteuuarul FLN	CHS	??	FT2,2
Bothamsall	NTT	SK6773	1,8-9. 1,30. 9,48
Bothelford (in Helsington) WES	YKS	??	1L7 *note*. See also CHS Y8
Botley	HAM	SU5113	29,6
Botolph [Bridge]	HUN	TL1797	1,2. 19,9
Bottesford	LEC	SK8039	15,5-7;15-16
Bottesford	LIN	SE8907	1,39;60. 28,17-18
Bottisham	CAM	TL5460	17,1. Appx C
Boughton	CHS	SJ4265	A5
Boughton	HUN	TL1964	19,31
Boughton	NFK	TF7002	21,6. 31,25
Boughton (near Northampton)	NTH	SP7565	17,5. 30,15. 56,19;60-62
Boughton (in Weekley)	NTH	SP9081	8,1. 48,1
Boughton	NTT	SK6768	9,16. 17,1
Boughton [Aluph]	KEN	TR0348	10,2
Boughton [Malherbe]	KEN	TQ8849	2,33. 5,79
Boughton [under Blean]	KEN	TR0458	2,18
[Old] Boulby NR	YKS	NZ7618	1N4. 4N2. SN,L12
Bouldon	SHR	SO5485	4,21,18
Boulge	SFK	TM2552	3,33. 6,181;244. 8,18. 26,17.
			32,11. 39,15. 46,11. 67,25
Boultham	LIN	SK9669	59,3
Boulton	DBY	SK3833	10,19
Bourn	CAM	TL3256	7,1. 14,49. 32,23. 33,1
Bourne	LIN	TF0920	14,87. 27,51-52. 42,1-3;7. 59,7.
			67,9. CK,40
[East?] Bourne	SSX	??	9,88;90
[East?] Bourne: see also Eastbourne SSX			
Bourton	BKM	SP7033	B1. 14,32
Bourton	SHR	SO5996	3c,8
Bourton	WAR	SP4370	16,30
[Black] Bourton	OXF	SP2804	40,1. 59,12-13
Bourton [on-the-Hill]	GLS	SP1732	19,2
Bourton [on-the-Water]	GLS	SP1620	12,3 EvO10
Boveney	BKM	SU9377	11,1. 51,2
Boveridge	DOR	SU0614	10,2
[Little] Bovey	DEV	SX8376	3,8
[North] Bovey	DEV	SX7383	17,22
Bovey [Tracey]	DEV	SX8278	3,8
Bovington	DOR	SY8288	56,59
Bow: see Nymet [Tracey] DEV			
Bowcombe	DEV	SX6655	15,75
Bowcombe IOW	HAM	SZ4686	1,7. EW1
Bowcombe IOW	WIL		1,3
[Great] Bowden	LEC	SP7488	1,4. 27,2. 40,18
[Little] Bowden LEC	LEC	SP7487	E12
[Little] Bowden LEC	NTH		18,19
Bowdon	CHS	SJ7586	13,3
[East and West] Bower	SOM	ST3137	24,8. 35,2. 46,5
		ST2636	
Bowers [Gifford]	ESS	TQ7587	6,3. 34,1. 42,1. 83,1
Bowithick	CON	SX1882	5,13,6
Bowley	DEV	SS9004	9,1 note. 21,8
Bowley	HEF	SO5353	7,2
Bowley	KEN	TQ9049	5,74
Bowley	SSX	TQ6008	10,83
Bowling WR	YKS	SE1732	9W132. SW,M6

Bowood	DOR	SY4499	3,17
Bowthorpe	NFK	TG1709	1,82;206
Bowthorpe ER	YKS	SE6933	SE,How5 note
Box	HRT	TL2726	5,7. 28,5. 36,6
Boxford	BRK	SU4271	7,14. 54,2
Boxgrove	SSX	SU9007	11,102
Boxley	KEN	TQ7758	5,102
Boxted ESS	ESS	TL9933	20,37. 25,17. EHu
Boxted ESS	HUN		D7
Boxted	SFK	TL8250	8,46
Boxwell	GLS	ST8192	10,3
Boxworth	CAM	TL3464	7,6. 14,54. 21,8. 23,4. 26,47
Boyatt	HAM	SU4520	58,1
Boycott BKM	BKM	SP6537	E4
Boycott BKM	OXF		49,1
Boyland	NFK	TM2294	31,7
Boyleston	DBY	SK1835	6,55
Boynton	SFK	TM0937	3,81. 16,44. 25,72. 71,1
Boynton ER	YKS	TA1367	1Y11. 1E15. 5E49. SE,Hu5
Boynton [Hall] ER	YKS	TA1367	1Y11
Boythorpe	DBY	SK3870	1,1
Boythorpe ER	YKS	SE9972	1Y14. SE,Bt8
Boyton	CON	SX3191	3,7. 5,5,4
Boyton (in Caple St Andrew; in Plomesgate Hundred)	SFK	TM3747	6,132;134;138;140
Boyton (in Caple St Andrew; in Wilford Hundred)	SFK	TM3747	6,172
Boyton (near Clare)	SFK	TL7144	25,16;88-89
Boyton	WIL	ST9539	24,25
Boyton [Hall]	ESS	TL7133	23,28-29
Bozeat	NTH	SP9059	35,14. 56,39;54
Bozen	HRT	TL4127	17,12. 20,12. 33,11
Brabourne	KEN	TR1041	5,171. 9,42
Braceborough	LIN	TF0813	18,14. 24,30. 59,5-6
Bracebridge	LIN	SK9667	6,1. 16,47-48
Braceby	LIN	TF0135	1,15;17. 14,88
Braceby Hundred	LIN	—	3,34
Bracewell WR	YKS	SD8648	30W15
Bracken ER	YKS	SE9850	SE,Sn2 note
Brackenborough	LIN	TF3390	27,23-24
Brackenholme ER	YKS	SE7030	SE,How5 note. SE, How7;9
Brackley	NTH	SP5937	21,1-2
Bracon [Ash]	NFK	TG1700	9,186;189
Bradaford	DEV	SX3994	17,11
Bradbourne	DBY	SK2052	6,6
Bradden	NTH	SP6448	30,17;19. 58,2
Braddock	CON	SX1662	5,2,5
Bradeley	STS	SJ8851	11,28
Bradenham	BKM	SU8297	57,15
[East and West] Bradenham	NFK	TF9308 TF9109	8,93. 22,2. 31,34; 40. 66,64
Bradenstoke	WIL	SU0079	24,19. 68,23;31
Bradeston	NFK	TG3408	10,76-77
Bradfield	BRK	SU6072	22,2
Bradfield	ESS	TM1430	39,7. 46,2-3
Bradfield	WIL	ST8982	41,3
Bradfield [Combust, St Clare, and St George]	SFK	TL8957 TL9057 TL9059	2,3. 14,52;59
Bradford (near Cookbury)	DEV	SS4207	16,21
Bradford (in Pyworthy)	DEV	SS2801	17,19

Bradford (in Witheridge)	DEV	SS8216	19,40. 20,8
Bradford WR	YKS	SE1633	9W130 *note*. SW,M6 *note*
Bradford [Abbas]	DOR	ST5814	3,4
Bradford [on-Avon]	WIL	ST8261	12,4
Bradford [on-Tone]	SOM	ST1722	2,3. 19,39
Bradford [Peverell]	DOR	SY6593	34,2
[West] Bradford WR	YKS	SD7444	30W37
Brading IOW	HAM	SZ6086	7,7
Bradle	DOR	SY9380	49,9
Bradley (near Ashbourne)	DBY	SK2245	6,44
Bradley (Belper)	DBY	SK3547	6,66
Bradley	DEV	SS9013	3,79;82. 50,5
Bradley	HAM	SU6341	2,10
Bradley	HEF	SO3261	24,3
Bradley	LIN	TA2406	4,69
Bradley (near Bilston)	STS	SO9595	12,23
Bradley (near Stafford)	STS	SJ8818	B6. 11,6;67
Bradley (in Huddersfield) WR	YKS	SE1720	9W110 *note*. SW,Ag15
[Great and Little] Bradley	SFK	TL6753	14,157. 25,92;103. 44,
		TL6852	1. 76,1
Bradley [Green]	WOR	SO9860	2,20
[High and Low] Bradley WR	YKS	SE0049	1W59 *note*
		SE0048	
Bradley [-in-the-Moors]	STS	SK0541	15,1
[Maiden] Bradley	WIL	ST8038	31,1
Bradmore	NTT	SK5831	25,1-2
Bradney	SOM	ST3338	24,24
Bradninch	DEV	SS9904	19,31
[Goose, North and South] Bradon	SOM	ST3820	19,17;23;25. 47,4
		ST3620	
		ST3618	
Bradpole	DOR	SY4894	1,2
Bradstone	DEV	SX3880	1,36
Bradwell	BKM	SP8339	14,40. 17,20. 23,31
Bradwell	DBY	SK1781	7,8
Bradwell	DEV	SS4942	31,2
Bradwell [Quay]	ESS	TL9907	18,23
Bradworthy	DEV	SS3214	*19,3.* 34,6
Brafferton NR	YKS	SE4370	1N105-106 *note*. 5N74. 28W34.
			SN,B26
Brafield [on-the-Green]	NTH	SP8258	2,3. 9,6. 56,20h;56
[Great] Braham WR	YKS	SE3552	13W32 *note*. 21W14;17. SW,Bu41
[Little] Braham WR	YKS	SE3552	13W32 note. 24W16-17. SW,Bu40
Brailes	WAR	SP3139	1,1
Brailsford DBY	DBY	SK2541	6,40. S
Brailsford	DBY	NTT	S5
Braintree	ESS	TL7523	90,48;76
Braiseworth	SFK	TM1371	6,198;205;225-226;228
Braithwell WR	YKS	SK5394	12W1;4. 13W9. SW, Sf25
Bramber	SSX	TQ1810	13,9
Brambletye	SSX	TQ4135	10,105
Bramcote	NTT	SK5037	1,46. 10,37. 29,1
Bramcote	WAR	SP4188	14,4. 22,10. 44,2
Bramdean	HAM	SU6128	68,7. 69,3
Bramerton	NFK	TG2904	1,120. 2,9. 9,28;45;161e. 12,13.
			66,80
Bramfield	HRT	TL2915	37,22
Bramfield	SFK	TM3973	3,3-4;7 note
Bramford	SFK	TM1246	1,2;7;119. 25,52. 74,7
Bramford [Speke]	DEV	SX9298	3,67. 16,123;129. 24,2
Bramhall	CHS	SJ8984	13,5

Bramham WR	YKS	SE4242	5W7. CW2. SW,BA3
Bramhope WR	YKS	SE2443	21W1. SW,Sk16
Bramley	DBY	SK6465	16,8
Bramley	HAM	SU6559	23,5
Bramley	SRY	TQ0044	1,1d–e;11. 5,1;3;30. 8,29
Bramley (near Leeds) WR	YKS	SE2435	9W123 note. SW,M3
Bramley (near Rotherham) WR	YKS	SK4992	12W1;15
Bramley [Grange] WR	YKS	SE2076	28W15 note. SW,Bu24
Brampton	DBY	SK3471	8,2. 12,3-4
Brampton	HUN	TL2070	1,8. 29,4. D24
Brampton	LIN	SK8479	7,10;12
Brampton	NFK	TG2124	8,8. 20,30-31
Brampton	SFK	TM4381	1,107. 7,7. 33,4
Brampton [Abbotts]	HEF	SO6026	5,1. 6,1
Brampton [Ash]	NTH	SP7987	26,8. 30,5;9. 56,6
Brampton [Bierlow] WR	YKS	SE4101	29W7. SW,Sf16 note. SW,Sf17
Brampton [Bryan] HEF	HEF	SO3772	ES15
Brampton [Bryan] HEF	SHR		4,20,18-27 notes. 6,23
[Church] Brampton	NTH	SP7165	18,7;99
Brampton [en le Morthen] WR	YKS	SK4888	5W25. SW,Sf16 note. SW,Sf33
Brampton [Hall] WR	YKS	SE3666	1W55 note. 5W38. SW,H7-8
[Little] Brampton	HEF	SO3061	24,3
Bramshall	STS	SK0633	11,38
Bramshaw HAM	WIL	SU2715	67,55;78
Bramshill	HAM	SU7461	23,37. 43,4
Bramshott	HAM	SU8432	27,1
[Kirk] Bramwith WR	YKS	SE6211	10W29. 12W1;22. CW12.
			SW,Sf22
[South] Bramwith WR	YKS	SE6211	10W29 note
Brancaster	NFK	TF7743	15,4
Brandesburton ER	YKS	TA1147	2E40. 14E31. CE35. SE,No2.
			SE,Hol7 note. SE,Hol22
Brandeston (near Cretingham)	SFK	TM2460	21,96. 47,3
Brandeston (near Waldingfield)	SFK	TL9146	16,10
Brandiston	NFK	TG1421	1,54
Brandon	LIN	SK9048	24,100. 37,3
Brandon	SFK	TL7886	21,5. 28,2
Brandon	WAR	SP4076	17,54
Brandon [Parva]	NFK	TG0708	4,11
Brandsby NR	YKS	SE5971	23N27
Brannel	CON	SW9551	5,1,8
Bransbury	HAM	SU4242	3,15
Bransby	LIN	SK8979	18,4-5
Branscombe	DEV	SY1988	2,22
Bransford	WOR	SO7952	8,10a note. 9,5c
(?) *Branshill* SSX	SRY	TQ7615	11,1
Branston	LEC	SK8129.	3,14
Branston	LIN	TF0267	31,12;16;18. CK,14
Branston	STS	SK2221	4,2
Branston Hundred	LIN	—	31,11
Branstone IOW	HAM	SZ5583	7,8
Brant	NFK	??	19,31
Brantham	SFK	TM1134	3,73;82;83 note;85. 6,27. 16,43.
			36,3;7;11. 39,17
Brantingham ER	YKS	SE9429	3Y1. 5E9 note. 31E4. CE13.
			SE,Wel1. SE, Wel2 note.
			SE,Wel6
Branton WR	YKS	SE6401	18W1. SW,Sf16 note. SW,Sf21
Branton [Green] WR	YKS	SE4462	1W32. 24W5. 29W31. 31W3.
			SW,Bu4
Branzuic	LIN	??	16,48

Brascote	LEC	SK4402	13,11
Brassington	DBY	SK2354	6,5
Brasted	KEN	TQ4655	2,31
Bratoft	LIN	TF4765	13,6. 68,9
Brattleby	LIN	SK9480	3,1. 24,6. 26,1
Bratton	SHR	SJ6314	4,14,19
Bratton	SOM	SS9446	25,25
Bratton [Clovelly]	DEV	SX4691	16,5
Bratton [Fleming]	DEV	SS6537	2,9;10. 15,40
Bratton [Seymour]	SOM	ST6729	24,15
Braughing	HRT	TL3925	17,15
Brauncewell	LIN	TF0452	27,45-46. 64,6
Braunston	NTH	SP5466	2,5. 38,1
Braunstone	LEC	SK5502	13,5;41
Braunton	DEV	SS4836	1,5. 3,31. 13a,3. 16,74;80
Brawby NR	YKS	SE7378	2N3. SN,Ma8
Brawn	GLS	SO8224	1,2. 64,1
[Great] Braxted	ESS	TL8515	25,1
[Little] Braxted	ESS	TL8314	4,14. 28,5
Bray	BRK	SU9079	B2. 1,22. 65,6
Bray (in South Molton)	DEV	SS6726	1,41 note. 3,45. 52,36
[High] Bray	DEV	SS6934	3,30
Braybrooke	NTH	SP7684	8,7. 14,2. 29,1. 30,11-12. 56,10;31
Brayley	DEV	SS6830	42,15
Brayton WR	YKS	SE6030	9W20. SW,BA5
Brea	CON	SW3728	5,12,3
Breadsall	DBY	SK3739	6,69-70
Breadward	HEF	SO2855	1,69
Breamore	HAM	SU1518	1,37
Brean	SOM	ST2956	24,29
Brearton WR	YKS	SE3261	1Y19. SW,Bu18
Breaston	DBY	SK4633	6,65. 9,5. 13,1. 16,1
Breck (in Whitby) NR	YKS	NZ9010	4N1 *note*. SN,L4
Breckenbrough NR	YKS	SE3883	5N71 *note*. SN,Bi6
Breckles	NFK	TL9594	1,5;7;9-10;137. 9,123. 22,22
Bredbury	CHS	SJ9292	5,14
Bredenbury	HEF	SO6056	10,69
Bredestorp	LIN	??	30,28
Bredfield	SFK	TM2652	3,27;31. 6,169;182;246;258. 7,129. 21,75;79;84-85;87. 25,23. 26,20. 67,19;23
Bredicot	WOR	SO9054	2,60
Bredon WOR	GLS		E19. EvA103. EvC22. WoB5. WoC4
Bredon WOR	WOR	SO9236	2,22
Bredons Norton: see [Bredons] Norton WOR			
Bredwardine	HEF	SO3344	19,5
Bredy	DOR	SY5089	43,1
[Little] Bredy: see Littlebredy DOR			
[Long] Bredy	DOR	SY5690	11,12
Breighton ER	YKS	SE7033	15E4-6. 21E7. SE,He8
Bremhill	WIL	ST9773	8,12
Bremridge	DEV	SS6929	3,56
Brendon	DEV	SS7648	34,14
Brenscombe	DOR	SY9782	55,46
[East] Brent and Brent [Knoll]	SOM	ST3451 ST3350	8,33
[South] Brent	DEV	SX6960	6,11-12
Brenzett	KEN	TR0027	P5-6;18
Brereton	CHS	SJ7864	18,2

Bressingham	NFK	TM0780	1,179. 14,24-25;34. 66,41
Bretby	DBY	SK2923	1,18
Bretforton	WOR	SP0943	10,5-6
Brettenham	NFK	TL9383	9,131. 15,10. 24,4 *and note*. 49,6
Brettenham	SFK	TL9653	2,13. 14,115. 25,109
[Monk] Bretton WR	YKS	SE3607	9W90. SW,St13 *note*
[West] Bretton WR	YKS	SE2813	1Y15 *note*. SW,St13 note. SW,Ag10
[North and South] Brewham	SOM	ST7237 ST7236	21,90. 25,55
Brewood	STS	SJ8808	2,1
Brexworthy	DEV	SS2813	34,6 note. 52,2
Briantspuddle	DOR	SY8193	56,48
[Great and Little] Bricett	SFK	TM0350 TM0549	25,56. 29,8. 30,3. 34,8. 38,8. 76,14
Bricewolde	HRT	??	37,23. 42,9
Brickendon	HRT	TL3310	14,2. 33,14. 34,14. 42,8
[Bow] Brickhill	BKM	SP9034	6,2. 14,48-9
[Great] Brickhill	BKM	SP9030	13,4
[Little] Brickhill	BKM	SP9032	4,43
Bricklehampton	WOR	SO9842	8,5
Bricticeshaga	SFK	??	52,8
[Great] Briddlesford IOW	HAM	SZ5490	7,4
Bridestowe	DEV	SX5189	16,7
Bridford	DEV	SX8186	16,128. 17,21
Bridge	DOR	SY6577	49,13. 55,18. 56,41
Bridge	SFK	TM4770	7,6;52
Bridge [Sollers]	HEF	SO4142	2,48;50
Bridgeford	STS	SJ8827	2,21
Bridgerule	DEV	SS2702	35,2
[East] Bridgford	NTT	SK6943	9,100-101
[West] Bridgford	NTT	SK5837	10,9
Bridgham	NFK	TL9585	15,10;29. 49,6
Bridgwater	SOM	ST3037	24,21
Bridlington ER	YKS	TA1767	1Y11. 1E12. 5E47. SE,Hu2-3
Bridport	DOR	SY4692	B2. 3,12. 18,1
Bridwick	DEV	SS6442	3,47
Brierley	HEF	SO4955	1,10a
Brierley WR	YKS	SE4111	9W67. SW,St3
[West] Briggs	NFK	TF6510	13,5. 66,4
Brigham ER	YKS	TA0753	5E53. SE,Tu5-6
Brighthampton	OXF	SP3803	7,29. 59,25
Brightling	SSX	TQ6820	9,31
Brightlingsea ESS	ESS	TM0718	1,26. ESf 1
Brightlingsea ESS	SFK		1,96. EE1
Brighton	SSX	TQ3105	12,13-15
Brightston	DEV	??	2,17
Brightwalton	BRK	SU4279	15,1
Brightwell	BRK	SU5790	B2. 2,3
Brightwell	SFK	TM2443	21,54
Brightwell-cum-Sotwell: see Brightwell, Sotwell BRK			
Brightwell [Baldwin]	OXF	SU6595	7,8. 58,7
Brigmerston	WIL	SU1645	42,5
Brignall NR	YKS	NZ0712	6N1 *note*. SN,CtA6
Brigsley	LIN	TA2501	4,68. 12,39. 57,3
Brigstock	NTH	SP9485	1,13a
Brihtoluestuna	SFK	??	31,9;14
Brill	BKM	SP6513	1,6
Brimblecombe	DEV	SS5609	40,3
Brime	NTH	SP5446	43,6

Brimfield	HEF	SO5267	1,10a;20
Brimham [Hall] WR	YKS	SE2262	21W7 *note*. 24W13. 28W20.
			SW,Bu26
Brimington	DBY	SK4073	1,1
Brimpsfield	GLS	SO9312	50,3
Brimpton	BRK	SU5564	40,1. 46,1
Brineton	STS	SJ8013	11,55
Brington	HUN	TL0875	6,23
[Great and Little] Brington	NTH	SP6665	18,44. 35,3c
		SP6663	
Briningham	NFK	TG0334	4,18. 10,57;59
Brinkhill	LIN	TF3773	13,9
Brinkworth	WIL	SU0184	8,4. 28,8
Brinsley	NTT	SK4548	10,31
Brinsop	HEF	SO4444	19,3
Brinsworth WR	YKS	SK4189	10W7. 13W6. SW,Sf5-6
Brinton	NFK	TG0335	10,8
Briseuuei	KEN	??	D24
Bristitune	WOR	??	1,2
Bristol GLS	GLS	ST5873	1,21. 3,1. 75,1. E9. EvK7
Bristol GLS	SOM		5,20
Briston	NFK	TG0632	1,22. 8,116
Britford	WIL	SU1628	1,6. 67,58;70;91
Britwell [Salome]	OXF	SU6793	35,22-23
Brixham	DEV	SX9256	17,29
Brixton (in Broadwood Kelly)	DEV	SS6005	16,29
Brixton (in Shaugh Prior)	DEV	SX5460	17,91
Brixton (near Yealmpton)	DEV	SX5552	17,86-87
Brixworth	NTH	SP7471	1,16
Brize Norton: see [Brize] Norton OXF			
Broadaford	DEV	SX6555	1,23. 15,69
Broadclyst	DEV	SX9897	1,56
Broadclyst: see Clyst DEV			
Broadfield and [Lower] Broadfield	HEF	SO5453	1,21
		SO5452	
Broadfield	HRT	TL3231	7,3. 18,1. 37,5. 41,2
Broadhembury	DEV	ST1004	23,20. 42,16
Broadhembury: see Hembury DEV			
Broadhempston	DEV	SX8066	15,43
Broadhempston: see Hempston DEV			
Broadholme	NTT	SK8974	9,5. 21,3
Broadley	DEV	SX7254	17,45
Broadlowash	DBY	SK1650	1,14
Broadmayne: see Mayne DOR			
Broadnymett	DEV	SS7000	16,48
Broadward	HEF	SO4957	1,28. 14,3
Broadwas	WOR	SO7655	2,68
Broadwater SSX	HAM		69,40
Broadwater SSX	SSX	TQ1404	12,22. 13,30
Broadway	SOM	ST3215	19,19
Broadway	WOR	SP0937	9,4
Broadwell (near Stow on the Wold)	GLS	SP2027	12,4. EvO7
Broadwell	OXF	SP2504	54,1
Broadwey	DOR	SY6683	
Broadwey: see Wey DOR			
Broadwindsor	DOR	ST4302	57,15-16
Broadwood	SOM	SS9841	25,16
Broadwood [Kelly]	DEV	SS6105	16,26
Broadwoodwidger	DEV	SX4189	*1,25*. 17.5
Brobury	HEF	SO3444	10,54
Broc	WOR	SO7772	16,3

Broch (= Brooks's Copse)	BKM	??	26,5 *note*
Brockdish	NFK	TM2179	1,226. 14,18
Brockenhurst	HAM	SU3002	NF9,44
Brockford	SFK	TM1265	14,47
Brockhall	NTH	SP6362	18,45
Brockhampton	HAM	SU7106	3,26. 23,35
Brockhampton	HEF	SO5931	2,15
Brockhurst	STS	SJ8211	11,56
Brockhurst	SSX	TQ4037	10,104
Brockington	DOR	SU0110	26,47
Brocklesby	LIN	TA1411	3,5. 14,38. 27,64. 32,2. 34,9-10. CN,8
Brockley	SOM	ST4666	45,16
Brockley (near Kedington)	SFK	TL7247	25,14
Brockley (near Manston)	SFK	TL8255	8,45. 14,14. 40,1
Brockmanton	HEF	SO5459	1,10c
Brockton (in Longford)	SHR	SJ7216	4,12,1. 4,27,30
Brockton (in Stanton Long)	SHR	SO5793	4,3,13
Brockton (in Sutton Maddock)	SHR	SJ7203	4,17,2. 4,23,16 note. 4,27,26 note
Brockton (in Eccleshall)	STS	SJ8131	2,11
Brockton [Grange] (in Sheriffhales) STS	SHR		ES9
Brockton [Grange] (in Sheriffhales) STS	STS	SJ8013	14,1
Brockworth	GLS	SO8916	63,1
Brocton	STS	SJ9619	2,4
Brodertuna	SFK	??	3,41. 6,278
Brodsworth WR	YKS	SE5007	5W15. 10W34;43. SW, Sf29
Broford	SOM	SS9131	21,51-52
Brokenborough	WIL	ST9189	8,6
Brome	SFK	TM1476	1,9. 6,63-64;203. 7,75. 11,5. 14,141. 19,20
Bromeswell	SFK	TM3050	3,23;53. 6,168;180;185;190. 6,235;249. 21,74;83;86;88
Bromfeld	KEN	??	7,2
Bromfield	SHR	SO4876	3d,6-7
Bromham	BDF	TL0151	15,1. 23,29. 53,9. 57,18. 23,28
Bromham	WIL	ST9665	1,14
Bromkinsthorpe	LEC	SK5802	C11. 13,5. 25,3
Bromley	KEN	TQ4069	4,5
[Abbot's] Bromley	STS	SK0824	4,5
[Gerrard's] Bromley	STS	SJ7734	2,20
[Great] Bromley	ESS	TM0826	77,1
[King's] Bromley	STS	SK1216	1,12
[Little] Bromley	ESS	TM0927	23,32. 42,8
Brompton	SHR	SJ5407	4,5,5. 4,20,1
Brompton (near Northallerton) NR	YKS	SE3796	1Y2. 3Y15. SN,A1;6
Brompton (near Scarborough) NR	YKS	SE9482	1Y4. 1N44. 8N6. 31N8 *note*. SN,D10
Brompton [on Swale] NR	YKS	SE2199	6N21. SN,CtA12 *note*
[Patrick] Brompton NR	YKS	SE2190	6N137. SN,CtA12 note. SN,CtA38
[Potter] Brompton ER	YKS	SE9777	1Y14. SE,Bt8
Brompton [Ralph]	SOM	ST0832	25,7
Brompton [Regis]	SOM	SS9531	1,11. 19,35
Bromsberrow	GLS	SO7434	45,3
Bromscott	OXF	SP2607	27,3
Bromsgrove WOR	WAR		EB W1
Bromsgrove WOR	WOR	SO9570	1,1a
[? Castle] Bromwich	WAR	SP1489	EN5 note
[West] Bromwich STS	NTH		36,3

[West] Bromwich STS	STS	SO9992	EN3
Bromyard	HEF	SO6554	2,49
Brook IOW	HAM	SZ3983	1,1
Brook	KEN	TR0644	*3,21*
Brooke	NFK	TM2999	14,16-17;38
Brookhampton	OXF	SU6097	29,13
Brookley	HAM	SU2902	NF9,30
Brooksby	LEC	SK6716	40,36. 43,1
Brooks's Copse: see *Broch* BKM			
Brookthorpe	GLS	SO8312	1,5
Broom	BDF	TL1743	24,11
Broom	SHR	SJ3731	4,26,2
Broom	WAR	SP0953	4,6
Broome	NFK	TM3591	9,172. 14,35. 35,10
Broome (in Cardington)	SHR	SO5298	4,28,1
Broomfield	ESS	TL7010	30,9
Broomfield	KEN	TQ8452	5,85
Broomfield	SOM	ST2232	25,49
Broomhall	CHS	SJ6346	8,36
Broomham	SSX	TQ7213	9,26
Broomsthorpe	NFK	TF8528	15,23
Brotton NR	YKS	NZ6919	5N17. SN,L17
Brough [Hall]	STS	SJ8322	11,5
Brough [Hall] (near Aldbrough) NR	YKS	SE2197	6N64 *note*. SN,CtA22 *note*
Brough [Hill] (in Bainbridge) NR	YKS	SD9390	6N77 *note*. SN,CtA22 note. SN,CtA25
[Sprot]brough: see Sprotbrough YKS			
Broughton (in Aylesbury)	BKM	SP8413	15,1
Broughton (near Moulsoe)	BKM	SP8940	14,46. 53,10
Broughton FLN	CHS	SJ3363	FD2,1-2. FD5,1. FD8,1
Broughton	HAM	SU3032	1,21;37. 4,1
Broughton	HUN	TL2877	B21. 6,3. D4
Broughton	LIN	SE9608	35,1-2. 44,4. CW,10
Broughton	NTH	SP8375	1,15k. 56,12
Broughton (near Banbury)	OXF	SP4238	34,1
Broughton (near Myddle)	SHR	SJ4924	3d,1. 3f,5
Broughton	STS	SJ7633	2,12
Broughton	SSX	TQ5502	9,51
Broughton WR	YKS	SD9451	8W3. 30W17
Broughton (near Malton) NR	YKS	SE7673	1N67. 8N17. 23N24. SN,L41 note. SN,Ma6
Broughton (near Preston) LAN	YKS	SD5234	1L1. See also CHS Y2
Broughton [Astley]	LEC	SP5292	C11. 10,7. 13,38. 40,8
[Brant] Broughton	LIN	SK9153	12,47
[Church] Broughton	DBY	SK2033	6,31
[Drakes] Broughton	WOR	SO9248	9,1a;1c
Broughton [Gifford]	WIL	ST8763	27,1. 67,97
[Great] Broughton NR	YKS	NZ5406	1N36 *note*. 5N30. 23N18. SN,L41-42 *note*
Broughton [Hackett]	WOR	SO9254	8,24
Broughton [House] (in Newsham) NR	YKS	NZ1009	6N45 *note*. SN,CtA17
Broughton [in Furness] LAN	YKS	SD2087	1L6 *note*. See also CHS Y7
[Little] Broughton NR	YKS	NZ5606	29N9 *note*. SN,L41 *note*
[Nether] Broughton	LEC	SK6926	1,2
Broughton [Poggs]	OXF	SP2303	50,1
[Upper] Broughton	NTT	SK6826	1,59
Brown	SOM	SS9936	25,12
Brownsover	WAR	SP5077	31,9
Brownsover: see also *Over* WAR			
Brownwich	HAM	SU5103	2,24
Browston	SFK	TG4901	1,53

Broxbourne	HRT	TL3607	43,1
Broxhead	HAM	SU8037	63,1
Broxholme	LIN	SK9177	18,2
Broxted	ESS	TL5726	10,1. 25,12
Broxton	CHS	SJ4853	2,14
Broxtow	NTT	SK5341	1,49. 10,41. 28,3
Bruckland	DEV	SY2893	16,164 note. 34,53. 35,4
Bruisyard	SFK	TM3266	3,98. 7,73;145
Brumby	LIN	SE8909	1,39;58
Brumstead	NFK	TG3626	9,88;183
Brundall	NFK	TG3208	1,192. 10,80. 52,3
Brundon SFK	ESS	TL8642	49,1;4
Brungarstone	DEV	??	3,8
Bruntingthorpe	LEC	SP6089	13,26. 44,6
Bruntuna	SFK	??	41,15
Brushford	DEV	SS6707	16,53-54. 25,7. 47,3
Brushford	SOM	SS9225	1,12. 19,16
Brutge	SFK	??	6,28. 67,5
Bruton	SOM	ST6834	1,9;31. 21,91. 24,17. 36,1
Bryanston	DOR	ST8706	26,46. 56,34
Bryanston: see Blandford DOR			
Brympton	SOM	ST5115	21,96
Bryn FLN	CHS	SJ0379	FT1,1. FT2,1
Bryncoed FLN	CHS	SJ2362	FT3,3
Brynford FLN	CHS	SJ1774	FT1,6. FT2,7
Bryngwyn FLN	CHS	SJ1073	FT1,3
Brynhedydd FLN	CHS	SJ1076	FT1,1
Bubbenhall	WAR	SP3672	22,11
Bubnell	DBY	SK2472	1,28
Bubwith ER	YKS	SE7136	21E7. SE,He9-10
Buchehale	SHR	??	4,14,29
[Long] Buckby	NTH	SP6267	18,72. 48,6 note
Buckden	HUN	TL1967	2,4
Buckenham (near Attleborough)	NFK	TM0691	1,139. 4,46. 6,1. 8,55-58. 9,126-127;129-131. 14,6. 19,12. 20,5. 24,1-4. 49,6. 52,1. 58,1. 59,1. 66,24;74-75;90
Buckenham (near Hassingham)	NFK	TG3505	1,103. 10,79. 14,14
Buckenham [Tofts]	NFK	TL8394	23,15. 50,2
Buckfast	DEV	SX7467	6,13
Buckham	DOR	ST4703	3,18
Buckingham	BKM	SP6933	B1-13
Buckland	BRK	SU3498	5,1. 7,47. 17,12-13
Buckland	BKM	SP8812	3a,2
Buckland (in Braunton)	DEV	SS4837	19,13
Buckland (in Dolton)	DEV	SS5613	42,7
Buckland (in Haccombe)	DEV	SX8871	19,41
Buckland (in Thurlestone)	DEV	SX6743	15,38. 17,36 note
Buckland	GLS	SP0835	10,6
Buckland	HAM	SU6501	23,32
Buckland	HRT	TL3533	5,20
Buckland (near Dover)	KEN	TR3042	D18. M4. 5,223
Buckland (in Luddenham)	KEN	TQ9761	D18. 5,152;157
Buckland	SRY	TQ2250	19,14
Buckland: see *Torp* LIN			
Buckland [Brewer]	DEV	SS4120	15,12
Buckland [Dinham]	SOM	ST7551	47,19
[East] Buckland	DEV	SS6731	3,54-55;63
[Egg] Buckland: see Eggbuckland DEV			
Buckland [Filleigh]	DEV	SS4609	3,13
Buckland [in the Moor]	DEV	SX7273	48,10

Buckland [Monachorum]	DEV	SX4968	21,20
Buckland [Newton]	DOR	ST6905	8,3
[North] Buckland	DEV	SS4740	19,12
Buckland [Ripers]	DOR	SY6582	55,4
Buckland [St Mary]	SOM	ST2713	47,1;7
Buckland [Tout Saints]	DEV	SX7546	24,18. 25,25
[West] Buckland	DEV	SS6531	16,73
Bucklawren	CON	SX2755	1,7
Bucklebury	BRK	SU5570	1,23. 17,3. 31,3. 58,3
Bucklesham	SFK	TM2442	2,16. 21,61
Buckminster	LEC	SK8823	3,15
Bucknall	LIN	TF1668	11,9. 13,23. 25,16
Bucknall	STS	SJ9047	1,34
Bucknell	OXF	SP5625	28,13
Bucknell	SHR	SO3573	4,20,26 note. 6,29
Buckton HEF	HEF	SO3873	ES14
Buckton HEF	SHR		6,21
Buckton (near Flamborough) ER	YKS	TA1872	1Y11. 5E51. SE,Hu7-8 note
Buckton [Holms] (near Settrington) ER	YKS	SE8469	8E1 note. 23E16. SE, Hu8 note. SE,Sc5
Buckwell	KEN	TR0448	5,164
Buckworth	HUN	TL1476	10,1. D23
Budbrooke	WAR	SP2565	26,1
Budbury	WIL	ST8261	67,64
Budby	NTT	SK6170	1,24
Buddington	SSX	SU8823	11,13
[East] Budleigh	DEV	SY0684	1,9
Budshead	DEV	SX4560	39,18
[Great] Budworth	CHS	SJ6677	9,25
[Little] Budworth	CHS	SJ5965	1,19
Buerton (near Audlem)	CHS	SJ6843	8,24
Bugbrooke	NTH	SP6757	18,3;41;83-84
Buglawton: see [Bug] Lawton CHS			
Bugthorpe ER	YKS	SE7757	2B19. 26E1. SE,Ac6
Buildwas	SHR	SJ6304	1,7
Bulby	LIN	TF0526	27,41. 57,57
Bulcamp	SFK	TM4376	7,19. 13,5
Bulcote	NTT	SK6544	11,10
Bulford	WIL	SU1643	16,1
Bulkington	WAR	SP3986	16,41
Bulkworthy	DEV	SS3914	15,14. and note
Bulley	GLS	SO7619	58,1
Bullingham: see Bullinghope HEF			
Bullinghope and [Lower] Bullinghope	HEF	SO5137	10,19. 21,6. 25,2
Bullington	LIN	TF0977	3,8. 13,26. 14,58. 22,20. CS,32
Bullington	SSX	SU7609	8,12. 9,13
[Lower and Upper] Bullington	HAM	SU4541 SU4641	16,6
Bulmer	ESS	TL8440	23,14
Bulmer NR	YKS	SE6967	5N53;61. SN,B3
Bulphan	ESS	TQ6385	9,2
Bulwell	NTT	SK5445	10,46;50;66
Bulworthy	DEV	SS8617	52,20
[Helions] Bumpstead	ESS	TL6541	35,12. 38,4. 90,83
[Steeple] Bumpstead	ESS	TL6741	20,27. 21,5. 22,12. 23,21. 38,5. 90,61
Bunbury	CHS	SJ5658	2,25
Buncton	SSX	TQ1413	13,56
Bungay	SFK	TM3389	1,108 note;110-111. 4,19;25
Bunny	NTT	SK5829	13,6;14
Bunshill	HEF	SO4342	31,3

Buntingford (including Layston)	HRT	TL3629	5,23, *note.* 17,6-7. 31,5. 36,12. 37,17
Bupton	DBY	SK2237	2,3. 6,52;60
Burbage	LEC	SP4492	6,1
Burbage	WIL	SU2361	1,23b. 27,4. 68,4;11
Burch	SFK	??	6,145
Burcombe	WIL	SU0730	13,16. 22,4
Burcot	WOR	SO9871	1,1a
Burcstanestune	HEF	??	23,3
Burdale ER	YKS	SE8762	1E42 *note.* 23E14. SE,Sc7
Burden [Head] WR	YKS	SE2943	5W4 *note.* SW,Sk20
Bures	ESS	TL9034	23,16;29. 40,5
Bures	SFK	TL9034	14,30. 25,42. 38,1. 55,1
[Mount] Bures	ESS	TL9032	39,6. 46,1
Burford	OXF	SP2512	B6. 7,36
Burford	SHR	SO5868	5,1
Burg	LIN	TA1046	67,3;5-6. 68,26
[Lower and Upper] Burgate	HAM	SU1515 SU1516	1,37-38. 69,35
Burgate	SFK	TM2936	7,77;108
Burgate	SFK	TM0875	35,5;7
Burgelstaltone	SSX	??	9,79
Burgericestune	KEN	??	*2,11*
Burgesgata	SFK	??	6,144
Burgh	SFK	TM2351	3,20. 4,17. 6,119;123-124. 8,10. 21,67. 26,16. 31,15. 32,22;28. 46,8. 52,4
Burgh	SFK	TM2934	7,80. 39,1
Burgh [Castle]	SFK	TG4704	69,1
[Great] Burgh	SRY	TQ2358	5,24
Burgh [le Marsh]	LIN	TF5065	12,78. 24,50. 29,14;18-21;25-26. 38,9
Burgh [next Aylsham]	NFK	TG2125	9,175. 30,5
Burgh [on Bain]	LIN	TF2286	34,22
Burgh [St Margaret]	NFK	TG4414	1,165. 9,18;157. 10,87. 17,14. 64,1
[South] Burgh	NFK	TG0004	8,81-84 *and note.* 66,34
[The] Burgh	LEC	??	1,7
Burgham	SSX	TQ7028	9,93
Burghfield	BRK	SU6668	21,20. 46,4
Burghill	HEF	SO4744	19,2
Burghley	NTH	TF0406	6a,5
Burghwallis WR	YKS	SE5312	9W37. SW,O4
Burham	KEN	TQ7262	5,58
Burland [House] ER	YKS	SE7730	CE16 *note.* SE,How2
Burleigh	SSX	TQ3537	10,99
Burlescombe	DEV	ST0716	24,30
Burleston	DOR	SY7794	12,5
Burley	BRK	??	21,21 *note.* 65,16;17
Burley	DBY	SK2864	1,11
Burley RUT	LIN		24,80
Burley RUT	RUT	SK8810	R15. ELc5
Burley [in Wharfedale] WR	YKS	SE1646	2W4 *note.* SW,Sk1
[North] Burlingham	NFK	TG3610	1,99. 10,68;73. 19,23;28
[South] Burlingham	NFK	TG3707	10,74;77
Burlingjobb (Wales)	HEF	SO2558	1,64
Burmarsh	KEN	TR1032	7,28-29
Burmington	WAR	SP2637	22,3
Burn (in Silverton)	DEV	SS9405	47,9
Burn [Hall] (near Thornton le Fylde) LAN	YKS	SD3344	1L1 *note.* See also CHS Y2
[Kirk]burn: see Kirkburn YKS			

[South]burn: see Southburn YKS			
Burna	ESS	??	20,63
Burnaston	DBY	SK2832	6,94
Burnby ER	YKS	SE8346	1Y10. 2A3. 11E9. 13E10-11.
			SE,P2
Burneston NR	YKS	SE3084	6N151. SN,CtA41
Burnett	SOM	ST6665	*1,28*
Burnham	BKM	SU9282	29,3
Burnham	ESS	TQ9496	33,12. 90,6
Burnham	LIN	TA0517	22,38. 34,5
Burnham [Deepdale]	NFK	TF8044	9,138
[East] Burnham	BKM	SU9583	7,2
[High and Low] Burnham	LIN	SE7801	63,11
		SE7802	
Burnham [Norton, Sutton, Ulph and	NFK	TF8243	8,118. 9,84;136.
Westgate]		TF8341	16,6. 23,4
		TF8342	
Burnham [on-Sea]	SOM	ST3049	24,27
Burnham [Overy]	NFK	TF8442	1,147
Burnham [Thorpe]	NFK	TF8541	8,105. 38,2
[Nun]burnholme:			
see Nunburnholme YKS			
Burniere	CON	SW9873	2,5
Burniston NR	YKS	TA0192	1Y3. SN,D2
Burnsall WR	YKS	SE0361	25W33. 29W42
Burntown	DEV	SX5078	*17,13*
Burpham	SRY	TQ0152	18,2
Burpham	SSX	TQ0408	11,68
Burreth (in Tupholme)	LIN	TF1569	4,45. 14,57. 43,4
Burrill NR	YKS	SE2387	6N124. SN,CtA36
Burrington (near Chulmleigh)	DEV	SS6316	5,8
Burrington (in Weston Peverell)	DEV	SX4757	17,74
Burrington	HEF	SO4472	9,3
Burrough [Green]	CAM	TL6355	14,78
Burrough [on-the-Hill]	LEC	SK7510	14,32. 29,12. 42,1;4
[Nether and Over] Burrow LAN	YKS	SD6175	1W72 note. IL3. See also CHS
			Y1;4
Burslem	STS	SJ8749	11,22
Burstall	SFK	TM0944	16,18;35. 25,71;77. 34,7
[Great] Burstead	ESS	TQ6892	18,2
[Little] Burstead	ESS	TQ6691	4,8
Burstock	DOR	ST4202	27,11
Burston	BKM	SP8318	12,12-13. 14,18. 23,25. 35,3
Burston	DEV	SS7102	16,55
Burston	NFK	TM1383	1,151;170;176;178-179. 7,8;10;14.
			14,32
Burstwick ER	YKS	TA2227	14E1. SE,Hol1
Burthy	CON	SW9155	5,3,16
Burtoft	LIN	TF2635	11,8
Burton (near Tarvin)	CHS	SJ5063	B9
Burton	DBY	SK2167	1,27
Burton	LIN	SK9674	7,9. 18,5. 24,3. 60,1. 68,1. CW,1
Burton	STS	??	10,2;10
Burton (in Castle Church)	STS	SJ9120	11,6
Burton	SSX	SU9617	11,27
Burton (near Kendal) WES	YKS	SD5376	1L4 *note*. 1L7. See also CHS Y8
Burton [Agnes] ER	YKS	TA1063	1Y14. 31E1. SE,Tu4 note. SE,Bt1
[Bishop] Burton ER	YKS	SE9939	2E1. SE.Wei7
Burton [Bradstock]	DOR	SY4889	1,2. 18,1
[Cherry] Burton ER	YKS	SE9941	2E8. 5E37. CE11. SE.Sn7
Burton [Coggles]	LIN	SK9825	14,95. 26,48. 31,9. 35,13

Burton [Coggles] Hundred	LIN	—	12,52. CK,5
Burton [Constable] ER	YKS	TA1836	2E28 note. SE,Mid1
[Constable] Burton NR	YKS	SE1690	6N109. SN,CtA32
	YKS	??	1Y3 note. SN,D5
Burton [Dale] (near Scarborough) NR			
Burton [Dassett]: see [Burton] Dassett WAR			
Burton [Fleming] ER	YKS	TA0872	1E23-24 note. 1E26 note. SE,Tu4 note
[Gate] Burton	LIN	SK8382	12,1-2. CW,10
Burton [Hall] (in Gateforth) WR	YKS	SE5829	9W20 note. SW,BA5 note
Burton [Hastings]	WAR	SP4189	19,2
[High] Burton (in Burton on Ure) NR	YKS	SE2282	6N120 note. SN,CtA27 note. SN,CtA35
[Hornsea] Burton ER	YKS	TA2046	14E7. SE,Hol7 note. SE,Hol12
Burton [in Lonsdale] WR	YKS	SD6572	1L3
Burton [Joyce]	NTT	SK6443	9,75. 12,18
[Kirk]burton: see Kirkburton YKS			
Burton [Latimer]	NTH	SP8974	4,9;12. 41,1-2
Burton [Lazars]	LEC	SK7616	14,29. 18,5. 29,3
Burton [Leonard] WR	YKS	SE3263	1Y18. SW,Bu15
Burton [on-the-Wolds]	LEC	SK5921	29,14. 35,1. 43,3-4;7
Burton [Overy]	LEC	SP6798	C11. 13,16
Burton [Pedwardine]	LIN	TF1142	24,105. 57,30
Burton [Pidsea] ER	YKS	TA2531	14E4. SE,Hol7 note
Burton [upon Stather]	LIN	SE8717	1,64
Burton [upon-Trent]	STS	SK2423	4B3. ED1-2
[West] Burton	NTT	SK8085	5,4. 9,116
[West] Burton (in Friston)	SSX	TV5497	10,28
[West] Burton NR	YKS	SE0186	6N85. SN,CtA27 note
Burtone	SHR	??	4,27,31
Burwardsley	CHS	SJ5156	2,21
Burwarton	SHR	SO6185	4,11,9
Burwell	CAM	TL5866	7,9. 11,2. 14,69-70. 26,2. Appx A
Burwell	LIN	TF3579	55,1-2
Burwell Hundred	LIN	—	CS,6
Burweston (near Welford)	STS	??	2,22
Bury	DEV	SS7307	2,3
Bury	SSX	TQ0113	5,3
Bury [St Edmund's]	SFK	TL8564	14,167
Burythorpe ER	YKS	SE7964	1E49. 8E6. 31E8. SE, Ac2
[Great] Busby NR	YKS	NZ5205	1N37. 11N13. 29N9. SN,L43
[Little] Busby NR	YKS	NZ5104	29N9 note. 31N5. SN, L43
Buscombe	DEV	SS6839	3,35
Buscot	BRK	SU2397	18,2
Bushbury STS	STS	SJ9202	7,3. 12,19;22
Bushbury STS	WAR		27,6
Bushey	HRT	TQ1395	33,2;4
Bushley WOR	GLS		WoC4
Bushley WOR	HEF		1,44
Bushley WOR	WOR	SO8734	2,30. E4
Bushton	WIL	SU0678	2,8
Butcombe	SOM	ST5161	5,31
Butleigh	SOM	ST5233	8,12;18;40
? Butleigh: see Bodeslege SOM			
Butley	CHS	SJ9177	2,30. 26,8
Butley	SFK	TM3651	3,40;50. 6,292. 8,25
Buttercrambe NR	YKS	SE7358	23N29;32-33
Butterford	DEV	SX7056	17,61-62
Butterleigh	DEV	SS9708	52,38

Butterley	HEF	SO6157	1,13. 10,70
Buttermere	WIL	SU3461	25,10. 37,3. 68,17
Butterwick	LIN	TF3844	57,38-39
Butterwick NR	YKS	SE9971	23N24. SE,Bt7 *note*
[West] Butterwick	LIN	SE8305	63,22
Buttery	SHR	SJ6817	4,14,17
Buttsbear	CON	SS2604	5,11,3
Buttsbury	ESS	TQ6698	29,5
Butyate (in Bardney)	LIN	TF1371	38,10
Buxhall	SFK	TM0057	5,5. 7,55. 8,49. 12,7. 21,11. 26,5
Buxton	NFK	TG2322	20,29;32
Bycarr's Dike	NTT	SK7896	1,44
Bychton FLN	CHS	SJ1580	FT2,8
Byfield	NTH	SP5153	22,1. 23,12
Byfleet	SRY	TQ0661	8,28
Byford	HEF	SO3942	10,60
Bygrave	HRT	TL2636	7,2;4
[Old] Byland NR	YKS	SE5585	11N17. SN,Bi3
Bylaugh	NFK	TG0318	4,30
Byley	CHS	SJ7269	11,3
Byrton	ESS	TL9324	62,3
Bytham	LIN	TF0118	8,7. 51,8. 59,10. CK,8
Bytham Hundred	LIN	—	30,31. CK,7
[Castle] Bytham: see [West] Bytham LIN			
[West] Bytham	LIN	SK9918	3,28-30. 51,9
Bythorn	HUN	TL0575	6,22
Byton	HEF	SO3663	24,2
Bywood	DEV	ST1608	24,1

C

[Higher] Cabilla	CON	SX1469	5,22,1
Cabourn	LIN	TA1401	14,39. 22,8-9. 25,4;9;12. 27,13;18. 44,13
Cadbury (near Thorverton)	DEV	SS9104	21,7
[North] Cadbury	SOM	ST6327	36,5
[South] Cadbury	SOM	ST6325	36,7
Caddington BDF	BDF	TL0619	12,1
Caddington BDF	HRT		13,2
Cadeby	LEC	SK4202	13,44
Cadeby WR	YKS	SE5100	10W22. 27W2. SW,Sf14-15
[North] Cadeby	LIN	TF2796	12,27
[South] *Cadeby* (in Grimblethorpe)	LIN	TF2487	3,48-49. 16,36-8. 27,27-30;32. 49,5-6
Cadenham	WIL	ST9877	22,5
Cadleigh	DEV	SS9107	19,24. 51,5
Cadney	LIN	TA0103	1,66. 12,11;13. 16,34
Cadretone (in Allerton Mauleverer) WR	YKS	??	28W2 *note*
Cadwell	OXF	SU6495	14,4
Caenby	LIN	TF0089	7,3
Caerlon (Wales) GLS	GLS	ST3390	S2. W2. E36
Caerleon (Wales)	HEF		14,1
Caerwent (Wales)	GLS	ST4690	W2 *note*; 7 *note*; 12;15
Caerwys FLN	CHS	SJ1272	FT2,5
Cainhoe	BDF	TL1036	24,15. 55,3
Caisne(i)d	SFK	??	*34,15*
Caister	NFK	TG5112	1,164-165;201. 17,63
Caistor	LIN	TA1101	1,65-80. 27,10. CN,2;6
Caistor [St Edmunds]	NFK	TG2303	14,15. 20,22
Calbourne IOW	HAM	SZ4286	2,1. 6,6
Calceby	LIN	TF3875	3,50. 13,4;7
Calcot	BRK	SU3370	17,5
Calcot FLN	CHS	SJ1775	FT1,8
Calcot	GLS	SP0810	20,1
Calcote	LIN	TF1483	34,14
Calcutt	WAR	SP4764	17,19-20;37
Calcutt	WIL	SU1193	67,1
Caldbergh NR	YKS	SE0985	6N97. SN,CtA30
Caldicot (Wales)	GLS	ST4888	W2;15
Caldecota(n)/Caldecoten/Kaldecotes	SFK	??	6,212. 14,136;149. 31,37;39. 41,8
Caldecote	BKM	SP8842	12,30. 17,18. 57,17
Caldecote	CAM	TL3456	14,50. 26,40. 39,1
Caldecote	HRT	TL2338	23,2
Caldecote	HUN	TL1488	19,2
Caldecote	NFK	TF7403	21,13. 22,*1*
Caldecote	WAR	SP3495	2,2
Caldecott	CHS	SJ4352	12,2
Caldecott	NTH	SP9869	35,1c
Caldecott RUT	NTH		5,2
Caldecott RUT	RUT	SP8693	EN7
Caldecott	SFK	TG4701	69,2
Caldenesche (in Huby) NR	YKS	??	1N97 *note*
Caldeuuelle (in Marton le Moor) NR	YKS	??	5W38 *note*. SW,Bu42 note. SW,H9

Caldeuuelle/Cradeuuelle (in Spofforth) WR	YKS	??	13W34 note. SW,Bu42 note
Caldicott	GLS	SP0821	34,5
Caldwell	DBY	SK2517	3,6
Caldwell NR	YKS	NZ1613	6N12. SN,CtA10
[Great] Caldy	CHS	SJ2285	10,4
[Little] Caldy	CHS	SJ2385	3,8
Callestick, [Higher] Callestick and Callestick [Vean]	CON	SW7750 SW7649 SW7749	4,9
Callington	CON	SX3569	1,10
Callow	DBY	SK2751	1,13
Calme	NTH	??	8,11
Calne	WIL	ST9971	1,1. 3,2. 25,5. 58,1
Calow	DBY	SK4071	17,9
Calstock	CON	SX4368	5,2,12
Calstone [Wellington]	WIL	SU0268	25,5. 53,1. 58,1
Calthorpe	NFK	TG1831	9,87. 17,26. 37,2
Calton WR	YKS	SD9059	30W30
Calvely	NFK	TG0105	15,18
Calver	DBY	SK2374	1,28
Calverhall	SHR	SJ6037	4,24,4
Calverleigh	DEV	SS9214	52,21
Calverley WR	YKS	SE2037	9W126 *note.* SW,M4
Calverton	BKM	SP7939	26,8
Calverton	NTT	SK6149	5,10. 16,3. 30,13
Calvintone	CHS	??	6,2
Cam	GLS	ST7599	1,15
Camberwell	SRY	TQ3276	30,2
Camblesforth WR	YKS	SE6426	16W1. 29W2. 31W5. SW,BA7;9
Cambridge	CAM	TL4458	B. 14,12. 1,17
Camden Town: see Rug [Moor] MDX			
[Queen] Camel	SOM	ST5924	1,22
[West] Camel	SOM	ST5724	9,7
Cameley	SOM	ST6157	5,62
Camerton	SOM	ST6857	8,31
Camerton [Hall] ER	YKS	TA2126	14E1 *note.* SE,Hol2
Camisedale (in Ingleby Greenhow) NR	YKS	??	1N35 *note.* 23N18;35. SN,L40-41
Cammeringham	LIN	SK9482	26,10. 44,1
[Chipping] Campden	GLS	SP1539	28,4
[Castle and Shudy] Camps	CAM	TL6343 TL6244	21,1. 29,7
Campsall WR	YKS	SE5414	9W36;38. SW,O3
Campsey [Ash]	SFK	TM3255	*3,21*;38. 6,279;288. 22,2. 67,28
Campton	BDF	TL1238	16,9. 18,7. 47,4
Canap(p)etuna/Canepetuna	SFK	??	1,106. 3,80. 35,4
Candlesby	LIN	TF4567	12,81. 24,49. 29,22. 68,8
Candlet	SFK	TM2936	7,95
[Brown] Candover	HAM	SU5739	6,13
[Chilton] Candover	HAM	SU5940	2,19
[Preston] Candover	HAM	SU6041	21,2. 23,30. 29,13. 35,7. 69,6;8
Canewdon	ESS	TQ8994	24,24
[Great and Little] Canfield	ESS	TL5918 TL5821	21,3. 22,6. 30,38. 35,1. 90,21
Canford [Magna]	DOR	SZ0398	31,1
[All] Cannings	WIL	SU0761	14,2
[Bishops] Cannings	WIL	SU0364	3,2
Cannington	SOM	ST2539	1,6;13. 16,3. 46,9. 47,25
Cannock	STS	SJ9810	1,25. 17,5
Canonsleigh	DEV	ST0617	24,15
Canonteign	DEV	SX8382	3,97

Canterbury	KEN	TR1557	C. D22;24. 1,4. 2,1;24. 3,9. 5,76;78;81;124–125;127;144–145;147;151;155;160;220. 7,4;11. 13,1
Canterton and [Upper] Canterton	HAM	SU2713 SU2612	NF10,4
Cantley	NFK	TG3804	1,94
Cantley WR	YKS	SE6202	18W1-2. CW15. SW,Sf21
Cantlop	SHR	SJ5205	4,25,1
Cantsfield LAN	YKS	SD6272	1L3. See also CHS Y4
Canwick	LIN	SK9869	4,80. 6,1. 7,51. 16,47 -48. 33,2. 67,26-27. CK,18
Capel [St Andrew]	SFK	TM3748	3,21. 5,150;166;183. 7,126. 21,72;79
Capenhurst	CHS	SJ3673	9,8
Capesthorne	CHS	SJ8472	1,31
Capland	SOM	ST3018	47,5
[How] Caple	HEF	SO6030	2,14
[Kings] Caple	HEF	SO5628	1,8 note;55
Capton	SOM	ST0839	1,15
Caradon	CON	SX2971	1,8. 5,4,11
Carbrooke	NFK	TF9402	22,10. 49,3;5
[West] Carbrooke	NFK	TF9501	49,5
Carburton	NTT	SK6173	1,24
Cardeston	SHR	SJ3912	4,4,18
Cardington	BDF	TL0847	23,10. 53,33
Cardington	SHR	SO5095	4,3,44
Caretorp (in Wigglesworth) WR	YKS	??	30W10 *note*
Cargoll	CON	SW8156	4,10
Carhampton	SOM	ST0042	1,6;13. 16,6. 30,2. 32,4
Carlby	LIN	TF0514	7,38. 24,33. 59,4
Carlesmoor WR	YKS	SE1973	28W16. SW,Bu24
Carleton LAN	YKS	SD3339	1L1. See also CHS Y2
Carleton (near Skipton) WR	YKS	SD9749	30W14
[East] Carleton	NFK	TG1702	9,96;184. 20,34. 32,3. 65,11
Carleton [Forehoe]	NFK	TG0805	1,81. 4,11. 17,4
Carleton [Rode]	NFK	TM1192	1,207. 4,56. 8,14. 9,207;209;222. 29,11
Carleton [St Peter]	NFK	TG3302	9,59;66;173. 12,23. 21,26. 31,45
Carlingcott	SOM	ST6958	19,60
Carlton	BDF	SP9555	2,7. 24,20-21. 46,2. 57,6
Carlton	CAM	TL6453	14,79. 18,1-2. 26,5. 41,4
Carlton	SFK	TM3864	3,49;94. 6,69
Carlton (near Barnsley) WR	YKS	SE3610	9W76 *note*. SW,St7
Carlton (in Lofthouse) WR	YKS	SE3327	9W.119 *note*. SW,M2
Carlton (near Middleham) NR	YKS	SE0684	6N93 *note*. SN,CtA29
Carlton (near Snaith) WR	YKS	SE6424	29W1. 31W5. SW,Sk16 note. SW,BA7
Carlton (in Stanwick) NR	YKS	NZ1912	6N1 *note*. 6N14. SN, CtA4;10
Carlton (near Stokesley) NR	YKS	NZ5004	5N28. SN,L43
Carlton [by Nottingham]	NTT	SK6141	12,17
Carlton [Colville]	SFK	TM5190	4,38. 31,32
Carlton [Curlieu]	LEC	SP6997	1,4. 13,17
[East] Carlton	NTH	SP8389	18,13. 31,1 note
[East] Carlton (near Guiseley) WR	YKS	SE2243	11W1 *note*. SW,Sk16 *note*
Carlton [Farm] (in Stockton on the Forest) NR	YKS	SE6756	2N19 *note*. SN,B14
[Little] Carlton Hundred	LIN	—	CS,7
Carlton [Husthwaite] NR	YKS	SE4976	2N14. SN,Bi2 *note*
Carlton [in-Lindrick]	NTT	SK5883	1,24;30. 9,50
Carlton [le Moorland]	LIN	SK9057	30,27

[Little] Carlton	LIN	TF4085	22,29
[Middle] Carlton (in North Carlton)	LIN	SK9477	24,4. 33,1. CW,3
Carlton [Miniott] NR	YKS	SE3981	1N109. 23N8. SN,Bi2 note. SN,Bi6
[North] Carlton	LIN	SK9477	68,3
Carlton [on-Trent]	NTT	SK7963	1,21;24. 2,5. 5,5. 9,61. 12,10;14;23. 30,2
Carlton [Scroop]	LIN	SK9445	12,46. 15,1-2. CK,37-38
[South] Carlton	LIN	SK9576	4,1. 26,20. 68,2
[West] Carlton ER	YKS	TA2138	14E50. SE,Hol26
Carnaby ER	YKS	TA1465	29E28. SE,Bt5
Carnforth LAN	YKS	SD4970	1L2. See also CHS Y3
Carnychan FLN	CHS	SJ0980	FT2,12
Carperby NR	YKS	SE0089	6N86. SN,CtA27
Carsella	CON	SW9457	5,24,9
Carshalton	SRY	TQ2764	25,2
Carsington	DBY	SK2553	1,13
Carswall	GLS	SO7427	39,3
Carswell (in Buckland)	BRK	??	65,15
Carthorpe NR	YKS	SE3083	6N150. SN,CtA41
Cartmel: see *Cherchebi* YKS			
Carton	WOR	SO7173	19,10
Cartuther	CON	SX2663	5,3,5
Cartworth WR	YKS	SE1407	1Y15 *note*. SW,Ag14
?Carvean	CON	SW8847	5,24,23
Carworgie	CON	SW9060	1,18
[Castle] Cary	SOM	ST6332	24,17
Cary [Fitzpaine]	SOM	ST5427	22,18
[Lytes] Cary	SOM	ST5326	45,1-2
Cascob (Wales) HEF	HEF	SO2366	24,3
Cascob (Wales) HEF	SHR		5,6. E4
Casewick	LIN	TF0709	24,35. 27,37. 52,1. CK,1
Cassington	OXF	SP4510	7,32;37;64
Cassio	HRT	TQ1096	10,16. 33,4
Casterton WES	YKS	SD6279	1L3 *note*. See also CHS Y4
[Great and Little] Casterton RUT	NTH		1,4. 58,1
[Great and Little] Casterton RUT	RUT	TF0008 TF0109	EN4;21
Casthorpe (in Barrowby)	LIN	SK8635	4,78. 57,47. 58,4. 59,2. CK,20
Castle Bromwich WAR: see [? Castle] Bromwich WAR			
Castlethorpe	LIN	SE9807	44,4
Castlett	GLS	SP0925	34,9
Castlewright (Wales)	SHR	SO2689	4,1,35
Castley WR	YKS	SE2645	1W53. SW,Bu49
Caston	NFK	TL9597	1,4;8;16;135. 8,51
Castor	NTH	TL1298	6,4. 6a,1
Castweazel	KEN	TQ8337	*3,22*
Catcott	SOM	ST3939	8,5
Catesby	NTH	SP5259	35,10
Catesfella	SFK	??	8,29
Catfield	NFK	TG3821	4,51. 9,88
Catfoss [Hall] ER	YKS	TA1446	14E33 *note*. CE38. SE,Hol22
Cathanger	SOM	ST3422	9,8
Catherston [Leweston]	DOR	SY3694	26,64
Catmore	BRK	SU4580	21,1
Caton LAN	YKS	SD5364	1L4. See also CHS Y5
Catsfield	SSX	TQ7213	8,11. 9,2
Catsley	DOR	ST5203	27,10
Catsley	SHR	SO7279	4,11,15
Cattal WR	YKS	SE4554	25W27. SW,Bu6

[Little] Cattal (= Old Thornville Hall) WR	YKS	SE4554	24W6 *note.* SW,Bu7
Catterall LAN	YKS	SD4942	1L1. See also CHS Y2
Catterick NR	YKS	SE2497	6N52. SN,CtA19
Catterton WR	YKS	SE5145	25W6. CW24. SW,An8
Catthorpe	LEC	SP5578	37,3
Cattistock	DOR	SY5999	12,4
Catton	DBY	SK2015	6,17
Catton (near Norwich)	NFK	TG2312	1,188;233
Catton (near Postwick)	NFK	TG2907	10,78-79. 24,6
Catton NR	YKS	SE3778	13N19. SN,Bi5
[High and Low] Catton ER	YKS	SE7153 SE7053	4E2 *note.* SE,P4
Catwick ER	YKS	TA1345	2E39. 14E34. CE40. SE,No1. SE,Hol23
Catworth HUN	HUN	TL0873	13,4. 19,12;32. 29,3. D17
Catworth HUN	NTH		6a,26
[Little] Catworth	HUN	TL1072	4,5. 13,5. D18
Cauldon	STS	SK0749	11,4
[Purse] Caundle DOR	DOR	ST6917	15,1. 56,55. E1
[Purse] Caundle DOR	SOM		19,86
[Stourton] Caundle	DOR	ST7115	26,70-71. 34,15. 38,2. 39,2. 54,2. 56,54
Caunton	NTT	SK7460	5,16. 12,8
Caurtune	SHR	??	4,20,19
[North] Cave ER	YKS	SE8932	2B5. 5E1. 11E2. 23E3. 31E4 *note.* CE13. SE,C1-2
[South] Cave ER	YKS	SE9231	11E1. SE,C1
Cavendish	SFK	TL8046	8,46. 25,47. 43,2. 76,3;6-7;20
Cavenham	SFK	TL7669	25,35. 28,4
Caversfield OXF	BKM		15,2
Caversfield OXF	OXF	SP5825	EBu1
Caversham BRK	BRK	SU7175	B9
Caversham BRK	OXF		20,1. EBe3
Caverswall	STS	SJ9542	11,36
Cavil ER	YKS	SE7730	3Y4 *note.* SE,How2
Cawkwell	LIN	TF2879	14,50. 32,11
Cawston	NFK	TG1323	1,30;53-55;57;195. 8,8-9. 10,17. 21,34-35. 37,3. 64,1
Cawston	WAR	SP4773	17,22;26
Cawthorn NR	YKS	SE7789	1N55. 31N8. SN,D19
Cawthorne WR	YKS	SE2807	9W70. SW,St4
Cawthorpe	LIN	TF0922	42,4-6
Cawton NR	YKS	SE6476	5N43. 23N4. SN,Ma23
Caxton	CAM	TL3058	26,42
Caynham	SHR	SO5573	4,11,4
Caythorpe	LIN	SK9348	37,2-3;7
Caythorpe: see *Alwoldestorp* NTT			
Caythorpe Hundred	LIN	—	CK,36
[Low] Caythorpe ER	YKS	TA1167	1E32 *note.* 2B15. SE,Bt5
Cayton NR	YKS	TA0583	1N42. 31N9. SN,D5
Cayton WR	YKS	SE2963	1Y19. SW,Bu19
Cefn Du FLN	CHS	SJ0180	FT1,1
Celdewelle	WIL	??	36,1
Cellesdene	DBY	??	17,18
Celverdescote	NTH	??	18,11
Celvertesberie	DEV	??	3,76
Cerne	DOR	??	3,14. 12,16. 17,1 note. 24,5. 26,64
Cerne [Abbas]	DOR	ST6601	11,1
[Up] Cerne	DOR	ST6502	2,3
[North] Cerney	GLS	SP0207	2,12. 52,3

[South] Cerney	GLS	SU0497	56,2
Cerney [Wick]	GLS	SU0796	45,5
Cestersover	WAR	SP5081	31,10
Cestersover: see also *Over* WAR			
Chaceley	GLS	SO8530	E32 note. EvA55. EvC106
Chacombe	NTH	SP4943	5,4
Chadacre	SFK	TL8552	46,2
Chaddesden	DBY	SK3836	6,68
Chaddesley [Corbett]	WOR	SO8973	28,1
Chaddleworth	BRK	SU4177	10,1. 41,1
Chadlington	OXF	SP3221	58,3;23
Chadnor and [Lower] Chadnor	HEF	SO4352	8,5
		SO4252	
Chadshunt	WAR	SP3452	6,16
Chadstone	NTH	SP8558	53,1
Chadwell	ESS	TQ6478	4,11. 18,11. 83,2
Chadwell	LEC	SK7824	1,3
Chadwich (in Bromsgrove)	WOR	SO9776	1,1c (erroneously Chadwick)
Chaffcombe	DEV	SS7503	*2,2*
Chaffcombe	SOM	ST3510	5,2
Chagford	DEV	SX7087	3,65. 32,5
Chainhalle	BDF	??	23,5-6
Chalcroft IOW	HAM	??	9,7
Chaldean	HRT	TL4220	4,5
Chaldon	SRY	TQ3055	5,9
Chaldon [Herring] and [West] Chaldon	DOR	SY7983	1,12. 24,3. 55,33
		SY7782	
Chale IOW	HAM	SZ4877	6,1. 9,19
[Great and Little] Chalfield	WIL	ST8563	25,8-9
		ST8463	
Chalfont [St Giles]	BKM	SU9893	43,2
Chalfont [St Peter]	BKM	TQ0090	4,10
Chalford	OXF	SP3425	24,2;5
Chalgrave	BDF	TL0027	20,2. 49,1
Chalgrove OXF	BRK		B2
Chalgrove OXF	OXF	SU6396	35,6. EBe1
Chalk KEN	ESS		EKt
Chalk KEN	KEN	TQ6872	5,104
[Bower]chalke and [Brood] Chalke	WIL	SU0325	13,9
		SU0223	
Challacombe	DEV	SS6940	3,33
Challonsleigh	DEV	SX5955	21,16
[West] Challow	BRK	SU3688	16,2
Chalton	BDF	TL1450	54,3
Chalton	HAM	SU7316	1,13. 21,6-7;10
Chalvington	SSX	TQ5109	9,61;115. 10,90-91
Chamberlain's [Hall]	SFK	TL7477	28,1b
Chancton	SSX	TQ1314	13,17-18
Chapmonswiche (in Peover Superior)	CHS	SJ7974	20,7
Charborough	DOR	SY9297	1,9
Chard	SOM	ST3208	6,4
Chardstock DEV	DEV	ST3004	ED1
Chardstock DEV	DOR		3,13
Chardwell	ESS	TL4734	22,20
Charfield	GLS	ST7292	74,1
Charford	DEV	SX7258	6,10
[North] Charford	HAM	SU1719	27,2. ?69,29
[South] Charford	HAM	SU1618	23,1;53. 23,3. 43,6. ?69,29
Charing	KEN	TQ9549	2,19
Charingworth	GLS	SP2039	45,1
Charlcombe	SOM	ST7467	7,8

Charlcotte	SHR	SO6386	4,21,13
Charlecote	WAR	SP2656	16,12
Charles	DEV	SS6832	16,71
Charleston	SSX	TQ4906	10,15
Charlesworth	DBY	SK0092	1,30
Charleton	DEV	SX7542	17,49
Charley	LEC	SK4814	43,1
Charlinch	SOM	ST2337	21,12
Charlston	SSX	TQ5200	10,30
Charlton	BRK	SU4088	1,11. 20,2. 21,10. 27,3. 47,1
Charlton (? in Upottery)	DEV	??	1,11. 3,96
Charlton	HRT	TL1728	1,8
Charlton (near Dover)	KEN	TR3142	M2-3
Charlton (near Greenwich)	KEN	TQ4177	5,33
Charlton	MDX	TQ0869	18,1
Charlton	NTH	SP5236	2,11. 18,38
Charlton (in Shawbury)	SHR	SJ5622	3g,9
Charlton (in Shepton Mallet)	SOM	ST6343	8,23
Charlton (in Hungerford) BRK	WIL	SU3368	32,5
Charlton (near Malmesbury)	WIL	ST9688	8,9
Charlton [Abbots]	GLS	SP0324	11,8
Charlton [Adam]	SOM	ST5328	19,43
Charlton [Mackrell]	SOM	ST5228	22,19
Charlton [Marshall]	DOR	ST9003	1,5
Charlton [Musgrove]	SOM	ST7231	33,1
Charlton [on-Otmoor] OXF	NTH		23,17
Charlton [on-Otmoor] OXF	OXF	SP5615	EN9
Charminster	DOR	SY6792	2,1
Charmouth	DOR	SY3693	26,67
Charnage	WIL	ST8331	3,5
Charndon	BKM	SP6724	37,2
Charnes	STS	SJ7833	2,11
Charney [Bassett]	BRK	SU3894	7,40-41
Charsfield	SFK	TM2556	3,26;36. 6,179. 7,133. 16,5-6. 21,78; 104. 31,18-19. 32,9. 46,12
[Little] Charsfield	SFK	TM2556	3,28
[Great] Chart	KEN	TQ9741	3,14
[Little] Chart	KEN	TQ9445	3,15
Chart [Sutton]	KEN	TQ8049	5,72
Chartham	KEN	TR1055	3,12
Chartley	STS	SK0028	1,14
Charwelton	NTH	SP5355	10,2. 18,36;66. 23,15
Chasepool	STS	SO8589	12,3
Chastleton	OXF	SP2529	7,54-58. 11,2. 24,7. 58,36
Chatcull	STS	SJ7934	2,11
Chatham	ESS	TL7013	30,7
Chatham	KEN	TQ7568	5,89
Chatsall (in Stoke on Tern)	SHR	SJ6331	1,9. 4,23,5
Chatsworth	DBY	SK2670	1,32
Chatteris	CAM	TL3985	5,46. 7,11
Chattisham	SFK	TM0942	1,106
Chaureth	ESS	TL5828	90,77-78
Chawleigh	DEV	SS7112	16,43
Chawson WOR	SHR		4,1,5
Chawson WOR	WOR	SO8862	25,1. E8
Chawston	BDF	TL1556	21,3. 23,34. 25,7-8
Chawton	HAM	SU7037	23,25
Cheadle	CHS	SJ8788	26,9
Cheadle	STS	SK0043	1,57. 11,42
Cheal	LIN	TF2228	7,34-35
Cheam	SRY	TQ2462	2,2

Chearsley	BKM	SP7110	14,12. 23,10
Cheaveley	CHS	SJ4261	A3
Chebsey	STS	SJ8628	10,9
Checkendon	OXF	SU6683	43,2
Checkley	STS	SK0237	17,19
Chedburgh	SFK	TL7957	21,40
Cheddar	SOM	ST4553	1,2. 21,78
Cheddington	BKM	SP9217	12,21-22. 17,13. 18,2. 19,5. 26,6.
			57,16
Cheddleton	STS	SJ9752	8,30
[Upper] Cheddon and Cheddon	SOM	ST2328	2,3. 22,22
[Fitzpaine]		ST2427	
Chedglow	WIL	ST9493	25,20-21. 26,19. 28,10. 67,51
Chedgrave	NFK	TM3699	31,43-44
Chediston	SFK	TM3577	3,13. 7,14-15. 68,2-3
Chedworth	GLS	SP0512	1,57
Chelborough	DOR	ST5405	36,8. 47,3
Chelchis/Cheldis (in Glusburn) WR	YKS	??	13W45 *note.* 21W16
Cheldon	DEV	SS7313	16,147. 40,4
Cheletuna: see *Keletuna* SFK			
Chelford	CHS	SJ8174	1,30
Chellaston	DBY	SK3830	1,19. 6,84
Chellington	BDF	SP9555	3,10 note
Chellow [Grange] WR	YKS	SE1235	9W131 *note.* 9W144. SW,M7
Chells	HRT	TL2625	20,4. 34,6. 36,4
Chelmarsh	SHR	SO7287	4,11,6
Chelmick	SHR	SO4691	4,22,1
Chelmsford	ESS	TL7006	3,12
Chelsea	MDX	TQ2778	20,1
Chelsfield	KEN	TQ4763	5,23
Chelsham	SRY	TQ3759	19,3;7
Chelsworth	SFK	TL9847	14,109
Cheltenham	GLS	SO9422	1,1
Chelveston	NTH	SP9969	35,1c
Chelvey	SOM	ST4668	44,2
Chelwood	SOM	ST6361	17,5. 34,1
Chelworth (near Chedglow)	WIL	ST9794	8,7
Chelworth (near Cricklade)	WIL	SU0892	68,30
Cheneboltuna	ESS	??	23,25
Chenebuild	WIL	??	25,19
Chenecol/Chenucol/Chenuthesholm (in	YKS	??	14E35 *note.* CE37 *note.* SE,Hol23
Long Riston) ER			
Cheneltone	SHR	??	4,25,5
Chenenolle	SSX	??	10,69
Chepstow (Wales)	GLS	ST5394	S1;W2 note;14;16-17
Cherchebi (= Cartmel) LAN	YKS	SD3778	1L8 *note.* See also CHS Y9
Cherington	GLS	ST9098	64,2
Cheriton (in Brendon)	DEV	SS7346	34,15
Cheriton (in Payhembury)	DEV	ST1001	15,63
Cheriton [Bishop]	DEV	SX7793	52,11
Cheriton [Fitzpaine]	DEV	SS8606	36,19
[North and South] Cheriton	SOM	ST6925	25,56. 28,2. 36,14
		ST6924	
Cherrington	SHR	SJ6620	4,4,25. 4,23,4
Chertsey	SRY	TQ0466	6,1. 8,18
Cheselbourne	DOR	SY7699	19,14
[Little] Cheselbourne	DOR	SY7796	55,3
Chesfield	HRT	TL2427	Appx
Chesham	BKM	SP9601	4,12-13. 26,3. 36,3. 56,1
Cheshunt	HRT	TL3502	16,9-11
Chespuic FLN	CHS	??	27,3

Chessington	SRY	TQ1863	19,24. 29,2
Chester	CHS	SJ4066	C. A. FD1,1
[Little] Chester	DBY	SK3537	B1
Chesterfield	DBY	SK3871	1,1
[Great] Chesterford ESS	CAM		1,10;15;22. EE1
[Great] Chesterford ESS	ESS	TL5042	1,9
[Little] Chesterford	ESS	TL5141	42,9
Chesterton	CAM	TL4660	1,9. Appx O
Chesterton	HUN	TL1295	9,2. 19,8
Chesterton	OXF	SP5621	35,18
Chesterton	WAR	SP3558	6,17. 17,67-68. 19,5. 44,8
Chesterton Hundred	CAM	—	Appx O
Cheswardine SHR	SHR	SJ7129	ES8
Cheswardine SHR	STS		11,13
Chetelescote	DEV	??	24,27
Chetelestorp (in Storwood) ER	YKS	??	15E7 *note*
Chetelstorp (in Escrick) ER	YKS	??	6E1 *note*. SE,P6
Chetestor	HEF	??	25,8
Chettiscombe	DEV	SS9614	16,159
Chettle	DOR	ST9513	49,7
Chetton	SHR	SO6690	4,1,31
Chetwode	BKM	SP6429	4,36
Chetwynd	SHR	SJ7321	4,19,2
Cheveley	CAM	TL6860	1,4. 14,62. 28,2. Appx B
Cheveley Hundred	CAM	—	Appx B
[Great and Little] Cheverell	WIL	ST9854	1,3. 25,3
		ST9953	
Cheverton IOW	HAM	SZ4584	6,9;10
Chevet WR	YKS	SE3415	19W83 *note*. SW,St15
Chevington	SFK	TL7860	14,5
Chevithorne	DEV	SS9715	16,158. 34,43
Chew [Magna]	SOM	ST5763	6,13
Chewton [Mendip]	SOM	ST5953	1,29
Chichacott	DEV	SX6096	16,4
Chicheley	BKM	SP9045	17,24-26
Chichester	SSX	SU8604	1,1. 2,5-6. 3,7. 6,4. 7,2. 8a,1. 11,1;3;5-6;8-12;14-15;18-19; 21;25;30-34;36-37;39;104–105;107
Chickerell	DOR	SY6480	1,4 note. 56,8
Chickering	SFK	TM2076	6,318. 8,40. 19,7;9
Chickney	ESS	TL5728	34,9
Chicksands	BDF	TL1239	4,8. 55,11-12
Chickward	HEF	SO2853	1,69. 29,18
Chiddingly	SSX	TQ5414	10,95
Chideock	DOR	SY4292	1,2
Chieveley	BRK	SU4773	7,12
Chignall	ESS	TL6610	30,10-12;15. 32,32
Chigogemers/Chigomersc/Ghigogesmersc (in Thornton Dale) NR	YKS	??	1Y4 *note*. 5N34. SN, D15
Chigwell	ESS	TQ4493	49,3;5
Chilbolton	HAM	SU3939	3,3. 41,1 (erroneously Cholbolton)
Chilbourne	SFK	TL7248	1,91. 25,86
Chilcomb	HAM	SU5028	3,1
Chilcombe	DOR	SY5291	56,35
Chilcompton	SOM	ST6451	3,2. 24,30
Chilcote LEC	DBY		1,25
Chilcote LEC	LEC	SK2811	E4
Chilcote	NTH	SP6574	18,68
Childerditch	ESS	TQ6089	1,23. 24,4. 57,5

Childerley	CAM	TL3561	3,6. 32,44. 41,16. Appx O
Childrey	BRK	SU3687	28,2. 45,2-3. 55,3
Childs Wickham: see			
Childswickham WOR			
Childswickham WOR	GLS		47,1. EvN13
Childswickham WOR	WOR	SP0738	EG13
Childwall LAN	CHS	SJ4289	R1,17
Chiletuna: see *Keletuna* SFK			
Chilford Hundred	CAM	—	Appx F
Chilfrome	DOR	SY5898	36,6
Chilham	KEN	TR0653	5,144
Chillenden	KEN	TR2653	5,207
Chillerton IOW	HAM	SZ4884	7,23. 8,7
Chillesford	SFK	TM3852	3,93
Chillington	DEV	SX7942	1,34
Chillington STS	STS	SJ8606	EW5
Chillington STS	WAR		28,19
Chillyhill	SOM	ST5662	37,4
Chilmark	WIL	ST9632	13,5
Chilsworthy	DEV	SS3206	52,1
Chilthorne [Domer and Vagg]	SOM	ST5219	19,79-80
		ST5218	
[East] Chiltington	SSX	TQ3615	12,43-44
[West] Chiltington	SSX	TQ0918	11,57. 13,48
Chiltlee	HAM	SU8431	1,6
Chilton	BRK	SU4885	7,34. 31.2
Chilton	BKM	SP6811	14,7
Chilton (in Cheriton Fitzpaine)	DEV	SS8604	42,22. 44,2
Chilton IOW	HAM	SZ4182	7,20. 8,12
Chilton	SFK	TL8842	6,2
Chilton	SFK	TM0459	21,12. 31,49
Chilton [Cantelo]	SOM	ST5722	26,7
Chilton [Foliat]	WIL	SU3270	28,2
Chilton [Polden]	SOM	ST3739	8,5
Chilton [Trinity]	SOM	ST2939	21,10. 46,12
Chilton [Trivett]	SOM	ST2538	21,23-24
Chiluesmares/Chiluesmersc (in Pickering	YKS	??	1Y4 *note*. SN,D12 *note*
Marishes) NR			
Chilvers [Coton]	WAR	SP3590	38,1
Chilwell	NTT	SK5135	10,26. 13,1;4-5
[East] Chilwell	NTT	SK5236	13,1;4. 30,52
Chilworth	HAM	SU4018	39,4
Chilworth	OXF	SP6303	29,11. 56,1
Chilworth	SRY	TQ0247	5,1b
Chinbaldescote	SHR	??	4,20,21
Chineham	HAM	SU6554	23,10
Chingescamp	HAM	??	2,16
Chingford	ESS	TQ3894	5,2. 32,7
[East, Middle and West] Chinnock	SOM	ST4913	19,44;48-49
		ST4713	
		ST4613	
Chinnor	OXF	SP7500	58,24
Chipnall SHR	SHR	SJ7231	ES8
Chipnall SHR	STS		11,13
Chippenhall	SFK	TM2875	6,311. 14,105;145. 67,7
Chippenham	CAM	TL6669	22,6. Appx A
Chippenham WIL	GLS		E16
Chippenham WIL	WIL	ST9173	1,5. 45,2. 62,1
Chipping LAN	YKS	SD6243	1L1. See also CHS Y2
Chipping Warden: see [Chipping]			
Warden NTH			

Chippinghurst	OXF	SP6001	17,1
Chipstable	SOM	ST0427	9,2
Chipstead	SRY	TQ2757	8,27. 19,12
Chirbury (near Montgomery)	SHR	SO2698	4,1,10
Chirton	WIL	SU0757	30,1
Chisbury	WIL	SU2766	29,1
Chiselborough	SOM	ST4614	19,47
Chiseldon	WIL	SU1879	10,5
[East and West] Chisenbury	WIL	SU1452	56,2
		SU1532	
[Great and Little] Chishill CAM	ESS	TL4238	20,72-73. 22,21. 26,5. 30,46.
		TL4137	90,34;86
Chislet	KEN	TR2264	7,9
Chiswick	ESS	TL4437	50,1
Chisworth	DBY	SJ9992	1,30
Chithurst	SSX	SU8423	11,9
Chitterley	DEV	SS9404	15,60
Chitterne	WIL	ST9943	23,5. 24,22-24
Chittleburn	DEV	SX5452	17,84
Chittlehampton	DEV	SS6325	52,10
Chivelstone	DEV	SX7838	17,57
Chivington	SRY	TQ3351	19,1
Chivington	WOR	SO9147	9,1a
Chobham	SRY	SU9761	8,22
Cholbolton: see Chilbolton HAM			
Cholderton	WIL	SU2242	25,15-17. 32,8
[East] Cholderton	HAM	SU2945	23,46. 43,1. 50,2. 68,10
Chollington	SSX	TV6097	10,6
Cholmondeley	CHS	SJ5351	2,7
Cholmondeston	CHS	SJ6359	8,45
Cholsey	BRK	SU5886	1,7. 43,1
Cholstrey	HEF	SO4659	1,10a
Chorley (near Nantwich)	CHS	SJ5650	8,39
Chorlton (near Nantwich)	CHS	SJ7250	8,20
[Chapel] Chorlton	STS	SJ8137	2,11
[Hill] Chorlton	STS	SJ7939	2,11
Choulston	WIL	SU1548	16,4
Choulton	SHR	SO3788	4,5,6
Chowley	CHS	SJ4756	2,13
Chrachetorp/Crachetorp (in Hessle) ER	YKS	??	21E4 *note*. SE,He1
Chrishall	ESS	TL4538	20,71
Christchurch: see Twynham HAM			
Christian Malford	WIL	ST9678	7,4-5
Christleton	CHS	SJ4365	2,6
Chubworthy	SOM	ST0326	25,40
Chulmleigh	DEV	SS6814	16,140
Chunal	DBY	SK0391	1,30
Churcham	GLS	SO7618	10,11
Churchdown	GLS	SO8720	2,1
Churchford	SFK	TM0838	36,1;16
Churchill	DEV	SS5940	20,4
Churchill	OXF	SP2824	15,4
Churchill (near Kidderminster)	WOR	SO8879	23,7
Churchill (near Worcester)	WOR	SO9253	2,59
Churchover	WAR	SP5180	14,5. 17,56. 22,1
Churchover: see also *Over* WAR			
Churchstanton SOM	DEV		37,1
Churchstanton SOM	SOM	ST1914	EDe1
Churchstoke (Wales)	SHR	SO2794	4,27,25
Churston [Ferrers]	DEV	SX9056	17,30
Chute [Wood]	WIL	SU3151	1,19

Ciclet	DEV	??	24,31
Cildeest	HAM	??	NF9,20
Cildresham: see also *Schildriceham*	KEN	??	5,146
Cilowen FLN	CHS	SJ0573	FT1,2
Cippemore (in Kinver)	STS	??	12,11
Cirencester GLS	BRK		61,1-2
Cirencester GLS	GLS	SP0201	1,7;8. 32,1
Cirencester [Rectory]	GLS	SP0201	25,1 *in note*
Clachestorp	SFK	??	6,274;284
[Great and Little] Clacton	ESS	TM1716	3,15
		TM1618	
Clactone (in Oxspring) WR	YKS	??	9W70 *note*
[East] Clandon	SRY	TQ0551	8,29 *note*
[West] Clandon	SRY	TQ0452	27,3
Clanfield	OXF	SP2802	29,18
Clannaborough	DEV	SS7402	16,51
Clanville	HAM	SU3148	23,48
Clapcot	BRK	SP6091	33,3;4
Clapham	BDF	TL0352	19,1. 19,2
Clapham	SRY	TQ2975	25,1
Clapham	SSX	TQ0906	13,15
Clapham WR	YKS	SD7469	1L4
Clapton (in Cucklington)	SOM	ST7529	19,68
Clapton and [Higher] Clapton	SOM	ST6727	36,7
Clapton [in Gordano]	SOM	ST4774	5,27
Clarborough	NTT	SK7383	1,41. 5,8. 9,127-128. 30,39;54
Clare	SFK	TL7645	25,1
Clare [Park]: see Badley HAM			
Clareia	NFK	??	3,2
Claret [Hall]	ESS	TL7643	20,25
Clareton WR	YKS	SE3959	1Y18 *note*. 28W8. SW,Bu11-12
Clatford	WIL	SU1568	41,5
[Upper] Clatford	HAM	SU3543	1,25
Clatinges	HAM	??	23,2;54
Clatterbrune (Wales)	HEF	SO3164	24,3
Clatworthy	SOM	ST0530	25,8
Claughton (near Garstang) LAN	YKS	SD5342	1L1. See also CHS Y2
Claughton (near Lancaster) LAN	YKS	SD5666	1L4. See also CHS Y5
Claverdon	WAR	SP1964	16,16
Claverham	SOM	ST4466	5,17
Claverham	SSX	TQ5309	9,94;114. 10,87-88
Clavering	ESS	TL4731	24,52-53;56
Claverley SHR	SHR	SO7993	ES3
Claverley SHR	STS		8,1
Claverton	CHS	SJ4063	FD5,2
Claverton	SOM	ST7864	45,11
[Long] Clawson	LEC	SK7227	15,12. 20,3-4. 43,11
Clawton	DEV	SX3499	17,15
Claxby	LIN	TF4571	12,94. 14,86. 24,61-62. 25,19-20
Claxby	LIN	TF1194	14,8-11. 28,23. 30,36. 32,8. 44,15. CN,19
Claxby [Pluckacre]	LIN	TF3064	13,9. 28,42-43
Claxton	NFK	TG3203	9,53;56;59.;12,20;22
Claxton NR	YKS	SE6960	1N94. 5N61. SN,B11
Claybrooke	LEC	SP4988	44,7
Claydon	SFK	TM1349	8,54. 74,10
[East] Claydon	BKM	SP7325	16,7. 21,3. 23,15-16
[Middle] Claydon	BKM	SP7225	16,5
[Steeple] Claydon	BKM	SP6926	55,1
Claygate	SRY	TQ1563	6,3
Clayhanger	DEV	ST0222	18,1

Clayhidon	DEV	ST1615	16,111
Clayhill	SOM	ST2637	21,7
Claypole	LIN	SK8448	4,77. 64,17
Claythorpe	LIN	TF4179	13,3. CS,12
Clayton FLN	CHS	SJ3166	FD3,1
Clayton	STS	SJ8543	13,6
Clayton	SSX	TQ2913	12,37
Clayton (near Bradford) WR	YKS	SE1132	9W131;144. SW,M7
Clayton (near Thurnscoe) WR	YKS	SE4507	5W18 *note*. SW,Sf30
Clayton [West] WR	YKS	SE2510	9W89. SW,St12
Clayworth	NTT	SK7288	1,40. 9,126
Cleasby NR	YKS	NZ2513	6N15. SN,CtA11
Cleatham	LIN	SE9301	4,14. 8,19;21;24. 28,18. 68,32
Cleaving [Grange] ER	YKS	SE8546	1E3-4 *note*. SE,Wei6
Cleckheaton WR	YKS	SE1925	9W136. SW,M8
Clee	LIN	TA2908	2,7. 4,32;36-37;71. 14,5
Clee [St Margaret]	SHR	SO5684	4,21,2
Cleestanton	SHR	SO5779	3c,13
Cleeton ER	YKS	TA1855	14E8 *note*. 14E54. SE,Hol13
Cleeve and [Lower] Cleeve	HEF	SO5923	1,8
		SO5823	
[Bishops] Cleeve	GLS	SO9627	3,7. WoA3. WoB19
[Old] Cleeve	SOM	ST0341	1,13
Cleeve [Prior]	WOR	SP0849	2,76
Clehonger	HEF	SO4637	21,7. 26,2
Clenchwarton	NFK	TF5820	19,2
Clent	WOR	SO9279	1,4;6
Cleobury [Mortimer]	SHR	SO6775	4,11,13. 6,2-4
Cleobury [North]	SHR	SO6286	7,1-2
Cle'pham	SFK	??	6,142
[Burgh]clere	HAM	SU4761	50,1
[High] Clere	HAM	SU4360	3,7
[Kings] Clere	HAM	SU5258	1,43-44. 6,9. 23,22. 69,42-43
Cleu	SHR	??	9,2
Clevancy	WIL	SU0575	26,16
Clevedon	SOM	ST4071	44,1
Clewer	BRK	SU9475	49,1
Clewer	SOM	ST4451	5,19
[Cockley] Cley	NFK	TF7904	1,73. 8,92. 66,65
Cley [next the Sea]	NFK	TG0443	1,19
Cleythorpe	NFK	TF7903	21,14
Cliddesden	HAM	SU6349	37,1
Cliff	ESS	TM1130	39,11
Cliffe	KEN	TQ7376	3,6. 5,110
Cliffe ER	YKS	SE6631	5E14. CE1 note. CE21. SE,C5 note. SE,How7
Cliffe [Hall] NR	YKS	NZ2015	6N1 *note*. SN,CtA4
[Kings] Cliffe	NTH	TL0097	B3b. 1,26
[North] Cliffe ER	YKS	SE8737	1Y6. 29E25. SE,C5 note SE,Wei1;3
[South] Cliffe ER	YKS	SE8736	3Y1. 31E5. CE1 *note*. SE,C5 *note*
[West] Cliffe	KEN	TR3544	5,186
Clifford	DEV	SX7890	16,110. 47,11
Clifford WR	YKS	SE4244	5W6. SW,BA3
Clifford [Castle]	HEF	SO2445	8,1. 10,3
Clifford [Chambers] WAR	GLS		1,37
Clifford [Chambers] WAR	WAR	SP1952	EG2
[Ruin] Clifford	WAR	SP2052	22,21
Clifton	BDF	TL1639	4,7. 8,6. 21,17. 24,28. 53,36
Clifton	CHS	SJ5280	A18
Clifton	DBY	SK1644	10,24

Clifton	GLS	ST5673	75,1;2 note
Clifton (near Fledborough)	NTT	SK8171	6,8;10-12. 9,3;5
Clifton (near Nottingham)	NTT	SK5434	S6. 10,5-6;10. 13,3. 30,25
Clifton (in Conisbrough) WR	YKS	SK5196	12W1;3. CW7-8
Clifton (near Lytham) LAN	YKS	SD4630	1L1. See also CHS Y2
Clifton (near Morley) WR	YKS	SE1622	9W137. SW,M9
Clifton (in Newall with Clifton) WR	YKS	SE1948	2W4 note. SW,Sk2
Clifton (in Norwood) WR	YKS	SE2053	1Y18 note. SW,Bu29
Clifton (near York) NR	YKS	SE5953	C30. 6W6. 6E1. 13E6 note. CE30. SN,Y5
Clifton [Campville] STS	DBY		1,25
Clifton [Campville]	STS	SK2510	1,29. 16,1
Clifton [Maybank]	DOR	ST5713	27,6
Clifton [on Ure] NR	YKS	SE2184	6N119 note. SN,CtA34
Clifton [upon Teme] WOR	GLS		1,11. EvK10
Clifton [upon Teme] WOR	WOR	SO7161	19,3. E35
Clifton [Reynes]	BKM	SP9051	5,18-19. 18,3. 53,6-7
Clifton [upon-Dunsmore]	WAR	SP5376	6,9. 14,2
Climping	SSX	TQ0002	11,75-76
Climsom	CON	SX3674	1,9
Clingre	GLS	ST7299	1,17
?Clinnick CON: see Kilminorth CON			
Clippesby	NFK	TG4214	1,46-47;166. 9,16. 10,91. 17,15. 64,4
Clipston	NTH	SP7181	1,15i. 4,10. 8,10. 35,2
Clipston	NTT	SK6334	9,104
Clipstone	NFK	TF9730	8,101
Clipstone	NTT	SK6064	9,39
Clive	CHS	SJ6765	1,33
Clixby	LIN	TA1004	1,70
Cloford	SOM	ST7243	19,53
Clophill	BDF	TL0838	24,14
Clopton	CAM	TL3048	2,2. 25,4. 32,9
Clopton	NTH	TL0680	6a,24. 55,6
Clopton (near Thistleton)	SFK	TM2252	6,127. 8,7;43. 31,17. 34,15-16. 46,6-7;9. 47,1-2. 52,2
Clopton (near Wickhambrook)	SFK	TL7654	21,41. 25,5-5a;80;91. 26,11
Clopton (near Stratford upon Avon)	WAR	SP2056	22,22
Clopton (in St John in Bredwardine)	WOR	??	2,10
[Lower] Clopton WAR	GLS		34,3
[Lower] Clopton WAR	WAR	SP1645	EG11
[Upper] Clopton WAR	GLS		1,12
[Upper] Clopton WAR	WAR	SP1744	EG1 (erroneously identified as Longborough)
Closworth	SOM	ST5610	19,52
Clothall	HRT	TL2731	5,14. 16,3. 28,6. 37,3
Clotherholme WR	YKS	SE2872	13W23. SW,Bu20
Clotton	CHS	SJ5263	23,3
Cloughton NR	YKS	TA0094	1Y3. 5N31. 13N7. SN,D3
Clovelly	DEV	SS3124	1,59
Clown	NTT	SK5773	1,24
Clowne	DBY	SK4975	10,4. 17,10
Clumber	NTT	SK6274	1,24. 9,41-42
Clun	SHR	SO3080	4,20,8
Clunbury	SHR	SO3780	4,20,4
Clungunford	SHR	SO3978	4,3,46. 4,20,24
Clunton	SHR	SO3381	4,20,3
Clutton	CHS	SJ4654	9,4
Clutton	SOM	ST6259	5,14
Clyffe	DOR	SY7791	12,6

Clyffe [Pypard]	WIL	SU0776	20,3-4. 25,11. 26,17. 27,9. 28,3-4. 29,5. 39,2. 50,3. 67,75. 68,23-24;26
Clyst Fomison: see Sowton DEV			
Clyst [Gerred]	DEV	SY0298	43,2
Clyst [Hydon]	DEV	ST0301	16,86
Clyst [St George]	DEV	SX9888	34,30
Clyst [St Lawrence]	DEV	ST0200	15,58
Clyst [St Mary]	DEV	SX9790	44 note. 3,7
[West] Clyst	DEV	SX9795	16,92
Clyst [William]	DEV	ST0602	52,39
Coaley	GLS	SO7701	1,15
Coates	LIN	SK9183	4,6. 7,15. 16,42. 26,12. 28,8-9
[Cold] Coates	NTT	??	9,35
[Great] Coates	LIN	TA2309	4,35. 12,16. 27,3-4. 32,5. 44,8. CN,12
[South] Coates	LIN	TA2409	4,34-35. 30,13
Coberley	GLS	SO9616	42,1
[Upper] Coberley	GLS	SO9715	2,8. EvK103. EvM3
Cobhall	HEF	SO4535	10,20
Cobham	SRY	TQ1060	8,6
Cockerham LAN	YKS	SD4652	30W38. See also CHS Y10
[South] Cockerington	LIN	TF3888	3,30. 4,57-58. 26,21. 27,25. 40,18;23
Cockfield	SFK	TL9054	14,24
Cockhampstead	HRT	TL4125	17,13
Cocking	SSX	SU8717	11,11
Cockington	DEV	SX8963	20,10
Cockthorpe: see [Cock] Thorpe NFK			
Cocle (? in Kelsall)	CHS	??	15,1
Coddenham (near Aveley)	SFK	TL9539	43,2. 76,22
Coddenham (near Hemingstone)	SFK	TM1354	1,74. 3,60. 6,6. 7,67;69. 8,63;77. 16,20. 21,24. 34,9. 38,5;10;17; 20. 53,4. 56,2;5-6. 74,16
Coddiford	DEV	SS8607	52,23
Coddington	CHS	SJ4455	1,15
Coddington	HEF	SO7142	2,32
Coddington	NTT	SK8354	6,3;6-7. 7,3-4
Codford [St Mary and St Peter]	WIL	ST9739 ST9640	32,10. 37,1. 48,6
Codicote	HRT	TL2118	10,6
Codnor	DBY	SK4249	7,6
Codsall	STS	SJ8604	17,1
Coffinswell	DEV	SX8968	5,13
Cofton [Hackett]	WOR	SP0075	2,84. 26,3
Cogenhoe	NTH	SP8260	41,9. 56,58
Cogges	OXF	SP3609	7,27
[Great and Little] Coggeshall	ESS	TL8522 TL8521	2,1. 20,7. 71,3. 90,8
Cogshall	CHS	SJ6377	5,4. 20,10
Coiwen FLN	CHS	??	FT2,6
Cokeham	SSX	TQ1705	13,41;45
Cokenach	HRT	TL3936	34,10
[East, North and West] Coker	SOM	ST5312 ST5313 ST5113	1,23
Colaton [Raleigh]	DEV	SY0787	1,46
Colber	DOR	ST7714	1,2. 8,1 note
Colburn NR	YKS	SE1999	6N65. SN,CtA23

Colby	NFK	TG2231	1,57
Colchester	ESS	TL9925	B. 3,16. 6,8.. 9,8. 17,1. 20,8;36;39. 34,6
Coldborough	HEF	SO6328	22,4
Coldcotes WR	YKS	SE3334	9W1 note. SW,Sk4
Coldeaton	DBY	SK1456	1,15
Coldmeece	STS	SJ8532	2,11
Coldmeece: see also Millmeece STS			
Coldred	KEN	TR2747	5,191
Coldridge	DEV	SS6907	3,22
Coldstone	DEV	SX5561	17,97
Colebrook (in Collompton)	DEV	ST0005	5 note. 19,23
Coleby	LIN	SE8919	13,13. 34,24–25
Coleby LIN	LIN	SK9760	1;7–8. 32,35. 56,19
Coleby LIN	RUT		ELc16
Coleford	SOM	ST1133	21,42. 25,35
Colemere	SHR	SJ4332	4,25,3
Colemore	HAM	SU7030	57,2
Coleorton	LEC	SK4017	14,18;28. 17,28
Coleridge (in Eggbuckland)	DEV	SX4958	17,77
Coleridge (in Stokenham)	DEV	SX7943	23,23;25
Colerne	WIL	ST8271	27,17
Colesbourne	GLS	SP0013	3,2. 68,9. WoB16
[Little] Colesbourne	GLS	SP0013	3,5. WoA2. WoB18
Coleshill BRK	BRK	SU2393	14,1. 28,1. 55,1. EW1
Coleshill BRK	WIL		49,1a
Coleshill FLN	CHS	SJ2373	FD2,6
Coleshill	WAR	SP1989	1,5
Coleton	DEV	SX9051	17,31
Coley	STS	SK0122	2,17
Colgrim's Land	SOM	??	21,16
Colham	MDX	TQ0781	7,1;3;5;7–8
Colkirk	NFK	TF9126	10,6;54
Collacombe	DEV	SX4376	28,2
Collaton (in Malborough)	DEV	SX7139	17,35
[Shiphay] Collaton	DEV	SX8965	17,27
Collingbourne [Ducis]	WIL	SU2453	1,19
Collingbourne [Kingston]	WIL	SU2355	10,2
Collingham	NTT	SK8261	S5. 7,5. 8,1. 14,8
Collington	HEF	SO6459	2,50. 10,64
Collingtree	NTH	SP7555	44,1b
Collow: see Calcote LIN			
Collyweston	NTH	SK9902	32,1
Colmworth	BDF	TL1058	23,38. 17,4. 23,24
Coln [Rogers]	GLS	SP0809	1,22 in note
Coln [St Aldwyns]	GLS	SP1405	10,4
Coln [St Dennis]	GLS	SP0810	20,1
Colne	HUN	TL3775	4,1
[Earls, Wakes and White] Colne	ESS	TL8828 TL8628 TL8729	11,5. 20,41. 23,34. 35,8. 42,6. 44,3. 90,68;71;80
Colne [Engaine]	ESS	TL8530	44,4
Colney	NFK	TG1807	9,199. 12,34. 19,38
Colquite	CON	SX0570	5,3,23
Colscott	DEV	SS3614	52,29
Colsterworth	LIN	SK9324	2,39. 68,24
Colston	SFK	TM3167	67,8
Colston [Bassett]	NTT	SK6933	27,2–3
[Car] Colston	NTT	SK7243	1,56. 9,107. 11,24
Colt (=? Littlehay, in Colbon)	STS	??	8,16
Coltishall	NFK	TG2719	8,8;12. 24,4

Colton	NFK	TG1009	8,73
Colton	STS	SK0420	8,15-16. 11,29
Colton (in Temple Newsam) WR	YKS	SE3632	9W1;15 *note*. SW,Sk4;9
Colton (near York) WR	YKS	SE5444	25W3. CW24;27;29;37. SW,An6
Columbjohn	DEV	SX9599	49,2
Colveston	NFK	TL7995	8,40
Colwall	HEF	SO7342	2,31
Colwell	DEV	SY1998	16,170
Colwick	NTT	SK6140	10,1. 12,17. 30,8
Colyton	DEV	SY2494	1,13
Combe (in South Pool)	DEV	SX7640	17,52
Combe BRK	HAM	SU3760	26,1
Combe	OXF	SP4115	7,1
Combe (in Withycombe)	SOM	ST0040	21,62
[Abbas] Combe	SOM	ST7022	14,1
Combe [Baskerville]	GLS	SP2120	45,2
[Castle] Combe	WIL	ST8477	27,23
Combe [Fishacre]	DEV	SX8465	17,23-24
Combe [Hay]	SOM	ST7359	47,20
[Lank] Combe	DEV	SS7845	34,14
Combe [Martin]	DEV	SS5846	20,1
[Monkton] Combe	SOM	ST7761	7,7
Combe [Raleigh]	DEV	ST1502	23,21
Combe [Royal]	DEV	SX7245	29,3
Combe [Sackville]	DEV	SS9702	52,17
Combe [St Nicholas]	SOM	ST3011	6,2
Combe [Sydenham]	SOM	ST0736	25,41
[Temple]combe	SOM	ST7022	4,1
Combebowe	DEV	SX4887	*16,7*
Combeinteignhead	DEV	SX9071	19,28
Comberton	CAM	TL3855	1,6. 32,14. 37,1. 44,1
[Great and Little] Comberton	WOR	SO9542	8,23;27. 9,1a
		SO9642	
Comble	WOR	??	1,1a
Combpyne	DEV	SY2992	16,171
Combs	SFK	TM0456	2,6;8
Combwich	SOM	ST2542	17,2. 32,1
Compton	BRK	SU5179	1,25. 6,1
Compton	HAM	SU3429	53,2
Compton IOW	HAM	SZ3785	1,2
Compton	STS	SO8898	1,2
Compton	SRY	SU9547	22,1
Compton (near Harting) SSX	SRY		18,1
Compton (near Harting) SSX	SSX	SU7714	11,36
Compton (near Laughton)	SSX	TQ4708	10,23
Compton (in Enford)	WIL	SU1352	23,1
Compton WR	YKS	SE3944	CW6 *note*
Compton [Abbas]	DOR	ST8618	19,5
Compton [Abdale]	GLS	SP0616	2,9. EvM100
Compton [Bassett]	WIL	SU0371	27,2. 32,3. 67,63
Compton [Beauchamp]	BRK	SU2887	22,11
[Cassey] Compton	GLS	SP0415	3,5. WoA2
Compton [Chamberlayne]	WIL	SU0230	1,8
Compton [Dando]	SOM	ST6464	5,39
Compton [Dundon]	SOM	ST4932	8,11
Compton [Durville]	SOM	ST4117	1,27. 17,8. 19,3
[Fenny] Compton	WAR	SP4152	16,57. 17,58-59
Compton [Gifford]	DEV	SX4956	17,78
Compton [Greenfield]	GLS	ST5782	3,1. WoA4. WoB15
[Little] Compton WAR	GLS		20,1
[Little] Compton WAR	WAR	SP2630	22,17. EG9

[Long] Compton	WAR	SP2833	30,1
Compton [Martin]	SOM	ST5457	37,10
[Nether and Over] Compton	DOR	ST5917	3,5 *note*. E3 note
		ST5916	
Compton [Pauncefoot]	SOM	ST6426	36,9
Compton [Scorpion]	WAR	SP2140	22,18
Compton [Valence]	DOR	SY5993	51,1
Compton [Verney]	WAR	SP3152	16,11. 17,66
[West] Compton	DOR	SY5694	12,3
Condicote	GLS	SP1528	2,4. 3,6. 36,2. 53,13. WoB20
Condover	SHR	SJ4905	4,1,2
Conersley (in Weaverham)	CHS	SJ6371	1,2
[Great] *Conesby* (in Flixborough)	LIN	SE8913	13,16
[Little] *Conesby* (in Crosby)	LIN	SE8714	32,30
Coney [Weston]	SFK	TL9577	14,76;78;80-81;
Coneysthorpe NR	YKS	SE7171	5N56. SN,B7
Congerstone	LEC	SK3605	14,13. 19,7
Congham	NFK	TF7123	8,26-27. 51,2
Congleton	CHS	SJ8662	14,9
Congresbury	SOM	ST4363	1,21. 6,14
Congreve	STS	SJ9013	1,7
Coningsby	LIN	TF2258	1,96. 13,27. 30,37. 38,4. 68,6.
			CS,34
Conington	CAM	TL3266	21,7. 23,3. 26,46
Conington	HUN	TL1785	20,1. D26
Conisbrough WR	YKS	SK5198	12W1. CW9;11-14. SW, Sf1
Coniston ER	YKS	TA1535	14E6. SE,Hol11
Coniston [Cold] WR	YKS	SD9055	1W73. 13W44. 30W2. SW,Cr5
Conistone WR	YKS	SD9867	29W50
Conkesbury	DBY	SK2165	1,27
Connerton (near Gwithian)	CON	SW5841	1,14
Conningswick	WOR	SO7371	16,4
Conock	WIL	SU0657	20,1
Cononley WR	YKS	SD9846	1W58
Consall	STS	SJ9848	1,56
Constantine	CON	SW7329	4,29
Cook [Hill]: see Cookhill WOR			
Cookbury Wick: see Wick DEV			
Cookham BRK	BRK	SU8985	1,3. EB1
Cookham BRK	BKM		11,1
Cookhill	WOR	SP0558	26,1
Cookley	SFK	TM3475	7,24. 9,3
Cookridge WR	YKS	SE2540	5W3. SW,Sk19
Cooksey [Corner and Green]	WOR	SO9168	1,1c. 26,12
		SO9069	
Cooksland	STS	SJ8626	11,26
Cooling	KEN	TQ7575	5,106;113
Coombe (in Cheriton Fitzpaine)	DEV	SS8908	36,20
Coombe (in Cruwys Morchard)	DEV	SS8511	50,4
Coombe (in Drewsteignton)	DEV	SX7691	52,15
Coombe (in Templeton)	DEV	SS8815	3,75-76;78
Coombe (in Uplowman)	DEV	ST0017	24,10. 25,17
Coombe (in Langton Matravers)	DOR	SZ0078	56,57
Coombe IOW	HAM	SZ4283	7,18
Coombe	SRY	TQ2070	31,1. 36,8
Coombe [Bissett]	WIL	SU1026	1,13
Coombe [Grove]	KEN	TR0746	5,165
Coombe [Keynes]	DOR	SY8484	6,4. 41,4
Coombes	SSX	TQ1908	13,19
Cootham	SSX	TQ0714	11,50-51
Copford	ESS	TL9322	3,10

Copgrove WR	YKS	SE3463	24W12. SW,Bu14
Cople	BDF	TL1048	23,49-55. 53,34
Copmanthorpe WR	YKS	SE5646	24W2. SW,An2
Copnor	HAM	SU6602	28,2
Coppenhall	CHS	SJ7057	8,42
Coppenhall	STS	SJ9019	11,63
Coppingford	HUN	TL1680	11,2
Corburn (in Wigginton) NR	YKS	SE5759	2N30. SN,B21
Corby	NTH	SP8889	1,12;28. 60,3
Corby [Glen]	LIN	TF0025	7,39-41. 68,18
Coreley	SHR	SO6173	6,1
Coresfella	SFK	??	25,44
Corfe Castle: see Wareham Castle DOR			
Corfe [Mullen]	DOR	SY9798	30,1
Corfham (in Diddlebury)	SHR	SO5285	4,1,6
Corfton	SHR	SO4984	4,1,6 note. 4,8,10
Corhampton	HAM	SU6120	23,19
Corley	WAR	SP3085	44,14
[Great and Little] Cornard	SFK	TL8840	1,98-99. 14,29. 25,43.
		TL9039	43,4. 76,4
Cornbrough [House] NR	YKS	SE6267	5N60 *note*. SN,B8
Cornbury	OXF	SP3518	1,10
Corney[bury]	HRT	TL3530	17,4
Cornish [Hall]	ESS	TL6835	90,58
Cornwell	OXF	SP2727	59,26
Cornwood	DEV	SX6059	15,36
Cornworthy	DEV	SX8255	17,48
Corpusty	NFK	TG1129	8,8. 10,17. 19,34
Corringham	ESS	TQ7083	4,9
Corringham	LIN	SK8791	1,39;46;49. 18,6
Corscombe	DOR	ST5105	3,8. 26,65. 56,64
Corsham	WIL	ST8770	1,11
Corsley	WIL	ST8246	67,33
Corston	SOM	ST6965	7,13
Corston	WIL	ST9284	8,6
Cortesley (in Hollington)	SSX	TQ7708	9,16
Corton	DOR	SY6385	13,4 note. 29,1
Corton	SFK	TM5497	1,45. 69,3
Corton	WIL	ST9340	50,4
Corton [Denham]	SOM	ST6322	1,32
Coryton	DEV	SX4583	3,9
Cosawes	CON	SW7637	5,3,1
Cosby	LEC	SP5494	9,4. 17,9. 40,3
Cosford	SHR	SJ7804	4,11,10
Cosgrove	NTH	SP7942	18,12;24. 40,1
Cosham	HAM	SU6605	1,10. 23,60. 68,5
Cossall	NTT	SK4842	10,36. 13,12
Cossington	LEC	SK6013	43,1
Cossington	SOM	ST3540	8,7
Costessy	NFK	TG1712	4,9;11;15;28;34;54;56
Costock	NTT	SK5726	9,94. 10,11;53. 15,5
Coston	LEC	SK8422	14,5
Coston	SHR	SO3880	4,20,13
Coswarth	CON	SW8659	1,15. 4,22
Coteland (in Anwick)	LIN	??	10,5. 64,13
Coten	WAR	SP2865	1,6
Cotes	STS	SJ8434	2,11
Cotes [de Val]	LEC	SP5588	3,5
Cotes [in-Darley]	DBY	SK2863	1,11
[Kipling] Cotes: see Kipling [Cotes] YKS			

Cotesbach	LEC	SP5382	13,48-49
Cotgrave	NTT	SK6435	15,8-10. 16,7
Cotham	NTT	SK7947	6,4. 7,1. 11,4
Cothercott	SHR	SJ4201	4,27,8
Cotheridge	WOR	SO7854	2,14
Cotherstone NR	YKS	NZ0119	6N43 *note.* SN,CtA16
Cotleigh	DEV	ST2002	15,35
Cotness [Hall] ER	YKS	SE7924	3Y4 *note.* SE,How3
Coton	CAM	??	Appx K
Coton (in Keelby)	LIN	TA1511	30,9-11
Coton	NTH	SP6771	35,19a;19h
Coton (in Wem)	SHR	SJ5334	4,14,7
Coton (in Milwich)	STS	SJ9732	1,42
Coton (in Stafford)	STS	SJ9324	8,14
Coton [Clanford]	STS	SJ8723	2,21
Coton [in-the-Elms]	DBY	SK2415	3,4
Cottam	NTT	SK8180	9,18
Cottam ER	YKS	SE9964	2B17 *note.* SE,Th8
Cottenham	CAM	TL4567	5,42. 9,2. 32,40-42. Appx O
Cottered	HRT	TL3129	3,1
Cotterstock	NTH	TL0490	6a,10
Cottesbrooke	NTH	SP7073	39,2. 60,4
Cottesmore	RUT	SK9013	R6
Cottingham	NTH	SP8490	6,2
Cottingham ER	YKS	TA0432	C36. 23E2. SE,Wel3
Cottingley WR	YKS	SE1137	24W1 *note.* 24W21. SW,Sk18
[East] Cottingwith ER	YKS	SE7042	5E10. SE,C9
[West] Cottingwith ER	YKS	SE6941	5E8. 16E2. 24E1. SE, C9. SE,How10
Cottisford OXF	NTH		23,16
Cottisford OXF	OXF	SP5831	EN8
Cotton	HUN	TL2364	2,1. 20,5
Cotton	SHR	SJ6327	4,27,1
Cotton	SFK	TM0766	1,77;79;84;95. 6,61;217. 14,135;148. 25,24. 31,35
Cottons	DBY	SK3532	1,19. 6,89
Cotwalton	STS	SJ9234	1,45. 8,21
Coughton	WAR	SP0860	17,69
Coulby NR	YKS	NZ5013	4N3 *note.* SN,L33
Coulsdon	SRY	TQ3058	8,2
Coulston	WIL	ST9554	67,2
Coulton NR	YKS	SE6374	1N84. 2A4. 5N51. 23N24. SN,Ma22-23
Cound	SHR	SJ5504	4,3,16
Coundon	WAR	SP3181	6,6. 28,9
Counthorpe	LIN	TF0020	30,30. 59,21
Countisbury	DEV	SS7449	19,15
Coupals [Farm]	ESS	TL6844	23,23. 90,40
Court-at-Street: see Street KEN			
Courteenhall	NTH	SP7653	35,6;25
Cove	HAM	SU8555	3,8
[South] Cove	SFK	TM4980	3,12. 6,97
Covehithe (formerly *North Hales*)	SFK	TM5281	1,108. 3,16. 7,12;25. 26,15. 32,20. 76,14
Coven	STS	SJ9006	11,62
Covenham	LIN	TF3394	3,16-19. 22,26-27
Covenhope	HEF	SO4064	9,9
Coventry	WAR	SP3379	15,6
Coverham NR	YKS	SE1086	6N98. SN,CtA30
Covington	HUN	TL0570	17,1
[Little] Cowarne	HEF	SO6051	7,8

[Much] Cowarne	HEF	SO6247	19,10
Cowbridge	ESS	TQ6595	37,18
[Great] Cowden ER	YKS	TA2242	2E36. 14E5 note. SE,No1
[Little] Cowden ER	YKS	TA2442	14E5 note. SE,Hol10
Cowesby NR	YKS	SE4689	1Y2. 23N15. SN,A1
Cowesfield	WIL	SU2523	61,1. 67,10
Cowick	DEV	SX9091	16,106
Cowlam ER	YKS	SE9665	1E60 note. 2B18. 8E1. SE,Th7;9
Cowley	DBY	SK2662	6,3
Cowley	GLS	SO9614	14,1
Cowley	MDX	TQ0582	4,10
Cowley	OXF	SP5404	7,9. 19,1. 35,13. 58,25
Cowley	STS	SJ8219	1,7
Cowling WR	YKS	SD9643	30W18
Cowling: see *Thornton* (= Cowling) YKS			
Cowlinge	SFK	TL7154	3,1
Cowthorpe WR	YKS	SE4252	13W18;37. SW,An17. SW,Bu44
Cowthwaite: see *Cufforth*			
(= Cowthwaite in Aberford) YKS			
[East] Cowton NR	YKS	NZ3003	1Y2. 6N37. SN,A1. SN,CtA15
[North] Cowton NR	YKS	NZ2803	6N1. SN.CtA2
[South] Cowton NR	YKS	NZ2902	6N1 note. SN,CtA2
Coxbench *Herdby*	DBY	SK3743	6,66. 11,5
[High] Coxlease and Foxlease	HAM	SU2906	NF9,28
[Great] Coxwell	BRK	SU2693	1,35
[Little] Coxwell	BRK	SU2893	1,36
Coxwold NR	YKS	SE5377	C36. 23N1
Crachetorp: see *Chrachetorp* YKS			
Crackford	NFK	TG2229	1,195. 8,8
Crackington [Haven] and [Higher and	CON	SX1496	5,8,6
Middle] Crackington		SX1595	
Cradeuuelle: see *Caldeuuelle* YKS			
Cradley	HEF	SO7347	2,30;31
Cradley	WOR	SO9485	23,13
Crafton	BKM	SP8819	6,1. 12,8
[Great] Crakehall NR	YKS	SE2489	6N138. SN,CtA38
Crakehill NR	YKS	SE4273	13N17 note
Crakemarsh	STS	SK0936	1,18
Crambe NR	YKS	SE7364	1N92. 5N62. 31N8. SN,B10
Cranage	CHS	SJ7568	2,31
Cranborne	DOR	SU0513	1,16
Cranbourne [Grange] and [Upper]	HAM	SU4740	6,16
Cranbourne		SU4842	
Crandon	SOM	ST3339	45,17
Cranfield	BDF	SP9542	8,1
Cranford	MDX	TQ1077	19,1
Cranford [St Andrew and St John]	NTH	SP9277	4,18. 6a,31-32. 41,8
		SP9276	
Cranham	ESS	TQ5786	4,1. 18,33
Cranley	SFK	TM1672	43,7
Cranmore and [East] Cranmore	SOM	ST6643	8,32
		ST6843	
Cranoe	LEC	SP7695	1,4. 40,29
Cransford	SFK	TM3164	3,103. 6,44;52;55;128;137. 7,142.
			67,8;33
[Great and Little] Cransley	NTH	SP8376	1,15j. 48,5. 56,13
Cranswick ER	YKS	TA0252	1Y8. 5E39. 23E8. SE, Dr3;5
Crantock	CON	SW7960	4,25
Cranwell	LIN	TF0349	10,5. 24,36;83
Cranwich	NFK	TL7894	8,46
Cranworth	NFK	TF9804	1,85;87

Cratfield	SFK	TM3174	33,10
Crathorne NR	YKS	NZ4407	1N40. 5N29. 31N5. SN,L44–45
[Great] Crawford	DOR	ST9101	1,5 note. 56,12. 57,4–5 notes
Crawle	CON	SW6131	1,1. 5,5,1
Crawley	HAM	SU4234	2,8
[Husborne] Crawley	BDF	SP9536	24,1. 41,1
[North] Crawley	BKM	SP9244	17,30
Crawleybury	ESS	TL4439	20,76
[Foots] Cray	KEN	TQ4771	5,34
[North] Cray	KEN	TQ4972	5,27
[St Mary] Cray	KEN	TQ4767	5,24
[St Paul's] Cray	KEN	TQ4768	5,28
Crayford	KEN	TQ5175	2,7
Crayke NR	YKS	SE5670	3Y10. SN,Bi1
Crays [Hill]	ESS	TQ7192	57,1
Creacombe (in Newton Ferrers)	DEV	SX5949	39,14
Creacombe (near Witheridge)	DEV	SS8119	16,144
[North and South] Creake	NFK	TF8538	1,16. 8,102. 9,83;85;
		TF8536	135. 19,17. 23,3
Crealy	DEV	SY0090	3,94
Creaton and [Little] Creaton	NTH	SP7071	18,7;53. 30,18. 48,8
		SP7171	
Credenhill	HEF	SO4543	2,53. 29,12
Crediton	DEV	SS8300	2,2
Creech	DOR	SY9182	26,54. 28,3. 37,6. 55,37
Creech [St Michael]	SOM	ST2725	1,18
[Lower] Creedy	DEV	SS8402	44 note. 3,72. 34,35;37
Creeksea	ESS	TQ9396	18,18;19. 68,3
Creeting [All Saints, St Mary, and	SFK	TM0856	2,10. 6,5. 16,
St Olave]		TM0956	17. 23,1-2;4. 26,7.
		TM0957	51,2. 74,6
Creeting [St Peter]	SFK	TM0857	2,9. 6,3. 8,52-53. 16,11. 23,1.
			32,1. 51,1-2
Creeton	LIN	TF0119	27,40. 51,7. 59,9-10;21. 68,16
[Long] Crendon	BKM	SP6908	14,5
Crepping	ESS	TL9028	68,5. 90,69
Creslow	BKM	SP8121	24,2;3
Cressage	SHR	SJ5904	4,10,1
[Great] Cressingham	NFK	TF8501	4,7. 10,1;48-49. 22,4
[Little] Cressingham	NFK	TF8700	22,5. 66,69
Cresswell Hundred	HUN	—	26,1
Creswell	STS	SJ8926	8,19
Cretingham	SFK	TM2260	3,47. 4,18. 16,7. 21,98. 31,20.
			52,5;8
Crewe (near Nantwich)	CHS	SJ7055	5,13
Crewe [Hall] (near Farndon)	CHS	SJ4253	2,22
Crewkerne	SOM	ST4409	1,20. 3,1. 12,1. 19,33
Crich	DBY	SK3554	10,11;12-14
[Long] Crichel	DOR	ST9710	34,11. 49,16
[Moor] Crichel	DOR	ST9908	1,3
Crick	NTH	SP5872	47,2
Cricket [Malherbie]	SOM	ST3611	19,34
Cricket [St Thomas]	SOM	ST3708	1,4. 19,1
Cricklade	WIL	SU0993	B4. 1,10. 3,3. 7,6. 8,13. 9,1. 10,5.
			12,5. 26,7. 27,9. 66,6. 67,1.
			68,24
Crigglestone WR	YKS	SE3116	1Y15. SW,Ag9
[Great and Little] Crimbles LAN	YKS	SD4550	1L1 *note*. See also CHS Y2
		SD4650	
Crimplesham	NFK	TF6403	21,3
Cringleford	NFK	TG1905	2,9;12. 4,55. 9,201

Crivelton (near Newton in Yarlside) LAN	YKS	SD2371	1L6 *note.* See also CHS Y7
Crochestrope	BRK	??	17,4
Crockernwell	DEV	SX7592	35,21
Crockington (near Seisdon)	STS	SO8494	1,1. 12,16
Croft	HEF	SO4465	14,5
Croft	LEC	SP5196	10,7. 13,37
Croft	LIN	TF5061	24,74
Croft NR	YKS	NZ2809	6N16. SN,CtA11
Crofton	HAM	SU5504	18,1-2
Crofton	KEN	TQ4465	5,35
Crofton	WIL	SU2662	26,4
Crofton WR	YKS	SE3718	9W98. SW,Ag4
Cromford	DBY	SK2956	1,13
Cromhall *[Abbots]*	GLS	ST6990	1,15
Cromhall *[Lygon]*	GLS	ST6990	1,16
Cromwell	NTT	SK7961	18,2. 30,4
Crondall	HAM	SU7948	3,8
Crook (in Bawdrip)	SOM	ST3239	24,7
Crooke [Burnell]	DEV	SS6800	51,3
Crookham	BRK	SU5464	65,22
Crooks [House] WR	YKS	SD8649	13W39 *note.* 30W4
Crooksby [Barn] NR	YKS	SD9885	6N83 *note.* SN,CtA26
Croom [House] ER	YKS	SE9365	1E58-59 *note.* 2B18. 5E73. 8E1. CE10. SE, Th8
Croome and [Earls] Croome	WOR	SO8044 SO8642	2,32-33
[Hill] Croome	WOR	SO8840	2,34
Cropredy	OXF	SP4646	6,5;13
Cropthorne	WOR	SP0045	2,72
Cropton NR	YKS	SE7589	1N56. SN,D20
Cropwell [Bishop]	NTT	SK6835	5,3
Cropwell [Butler]	NTT	SK6837	11,32. 16,6. 20,7
Crosby	LIN	SE8912	13,16. 32,30
Crosby [Grange] NR	YKS	SE4088	1Y2 *note.* 1N134. SN,A1;9
[Great and Little] Crosby LAN	CHS	SJ3199	R1,2;41
Croscombe	SOM	ST5944	8,20
Croscroft	SFK	??	4,31
[North] Crosland WR	YKS	SE1315	1Y15 *note.* SW,Ag13
[South] Crosland WR	YKS	SE1112	1Y15 note. 9W114. SW,Ag16
[Bucks] Cross	DEV	SS3423	36,2
Cross: see [Bucks] Cross DEV			
Cross [Hills]	SHR	SJ7025	4,14,15
Crostwick	NFK	TG2515	20,25. 26,26
Crostwight	NFK	TG3329	31,3
Croughton	CHS	SJ4172	A8
Croughton	NTH	SP5433	4,29. 18,64. 45,2-3
Crow	HAM	SU1603	NF9,39
Crowcombe	SOM	ST1436	19,7
Crowell	OXF	SU7499	23,1
Crowfield	SFK	TM1457	16,14. 38,4
Crowhurst	SSX	TQ7512	8,13. 9,18
Crowland	LIN	TF2410	11,2
Crowle	LIN	SE7713	14,27. 63,15-16;19;23
Crowle	WOR	SO9255	2,78. 19,14
Crowmarsh [Gifford] OXF	BRK		B9
Crowmarsh [Gifford] OXF	OXF	SU6189	20,3. EBe3
[Preston] Crowmarsh	OXF	SU6190	10,1
Crownthorpe	NFK	TG0803	1,83. 20,13
Croxall STS	DBY		6,14
Croxall STS	STS	SK1913	ED3

Croxby	LIN	TF1998	14,15. 18,10. 32,9-10. 49,2-3. CN,20
Croxden	STS	SK0639	17,18
Croxton	CAM	TL2559	26,43. 39,2. Appx L
Croxton	CHS	SJ7067	19,2
Croxton	LIN	TA0912	1,72. 7,26. 16,45. 25,6;11
Croxton (near Fakenham)	NFK	TF9831	8,104
Croxton (near Thetford)	NFK	TL8786	1,*210*;211 *and note*
Croxton	STS	SJ7831	2,14
Croxton [Kerrial]	LEC	SK8329	1,1a
[South] Croxton	LEC	SK6910	3,13. 15,11
Croyde	DEV	SS4439	15,41
Croydon	CAM	TL3149	13,3. 14,24-25. 25,6. 26,21. 32,11-12
Croydon	SRY	TQ3265	2,1
Crudgington	SHR	SJ6318	4,6,5
Crudwell	WIL	ST9592	8,11
Crunkly [Gill] NR	YKS	NZ7506	23N17;34. 31N10 *note*. SN,L14
Cruttonstall (in Erringden) WR	YKS	SD9826	1Y15 *note*
Cruxton	DOR	SY6096	36,7
Cubbington	STS	??	8,4
Cubbington	WAR	SP3468	6,7. 16,53. 20,1
Cubley	DBY	SK1637	6,54
Cublington	BKM	SP8322	44,3
Cucklington	SOM	ST7527	19,64
Cuckney	NTT	SK5671	9,36. 22,2
Cuddesdon	OXF	SP6003	9,2
Cuddington	CHS	SJ4546	2,16
Cuddington	SRY	TQ2263	5,19
Cudessane	BDF	??	16,8. 23,57
Cudham	KEN	TQ4459	5,36
Cudley	WOR	SO8954	2,54
Cudnor (in Westham)	SSX	TQ6105	10,72;74
Cudworth	SOM	ST3710	22,10
Cufforth (= Cowthwaite in Aberford) WR	YKS	SE4239	9W1 *note*. SW,Sk7
Culbone	SOM	SS8448	5,7
Culeslea (in Alderton)	SFK	TM3343	6,156
Culford	SFK	TL8370	14,53 note;70;88
Culkerton	GLS	ST9395	31,10. 41,4. 44,2 note. 53,4
Culleigh	DEV	SS4519	15,11
Cullingworth WR	YKS	SE0636	24W21 *note*
Cullompton	DEV	ST0207	1,7 note. 9,1
Culm [Davy]	DEV	ST1215	36,18
[Monk] Culm	DEV	??	16,104
Culm [Pyne]	DEV	ST1314	16,122
Culm [Vale]	DEV	SX9397	49,4
Culmington	SHR	SO4982	4,1,29
Culmstock	DEV	ST1013	2,12
Culpho	SFK	TM2149	8,1;3;5. 32,29
Culsworthy	DEV	SS3612	52,3
Culuerdestuna: see *Kuluertestuna*, *Kyluertestuna* SFK			
Culvert's [Farm]	ESS	TL7609	32,36
Culworth	NTH	SP5446	45,9
[Great and Little] Cumberwell	WIL	ST8263 ST8162	27,5
Cumberworth	LIN	TF5073	12,97. 40,20. CS,14
[Lower] Cumberworth WR	YKS	SE2209	1Y15 *note*. SW,Ag12
[Upper] Cumberworth WR	YKS	SE2108	1Y15 note. 9W88. SW, St11
Cumnor	BRK	SP4604	7,1;4;5

Cundall WR	YKS	SE4272	5W38. SW,H8-9
Cuple	HEF	??	10,74
Curdeslege	HEF	??	31,2
Curdworth	WAR	SP1792	17,1
Curling [Tye Green]	ESS	TL8107	33,5
Curridge	BRK	SU4871	13,2. 46,2. 65,9
[East and West] Curry	CON	SX2993	5,7,13
		SX2893	
Curry [Mallet]	SOM	ST3321	21,1-2
[North] Curry	SOM	ST3125	1,19
Curry [Rivel]	SOM	ST3925	1,5. 16,11. 19,*15*;17-18;23-25;27;29. 47,5
Currypool	SOM	ST2238	21,13
Curscombe	DEV	ST1101	15,62
Curtisknowle	DEV	SX7353	17,44
Curworthy	DEV	SX5597	39,6
Cusop	HEF	SO2341	1,3
Custhorpe	NFK	TF7813	22,7
Cusworth WR	YKS	SE5404	10W23. 12W1;14. SW, Sf15
Cutcombe	SOM	SS9339	25,9
Cuton [Hall]	ESS	TL7308	30,17
Cutsdean GLS	GLS	SP0830	E20. EvC24. WoB5
Cutsdean GLS	WOR		2,24
Cutslow: see Cutteslowe OXF			
Cutteslowe (or Cutslow)	OXF	SP5011	14,2. 29,17
Cuxham	OXF	SU6695	35,31
Cuxton	KEN	TQ7066	4,10
Cuxwold	LIN	TA1701	2,9-10. 14,40. 22,9. 25,10. 27,12;13;17. 44,12., 68,44. CN,23-24
Cwybr FLN	CHS	SJ0279	FT1,1
Cwybr Bach FLN	CHS	SJ0280	FT2,1
Cynllaith (Wales)	SHR	??	4,3,42
Cyrchynan FLN	CHS	SJ0475	FT2,5

D

Dacre WR	YKS	SE1960	24W15. SW,Bu28
Dadford	BKM	SP6638	41,3. 57,7
Dadsley WR	YKS	SK5992	10W3 *note*. SW,Sf4
Dagworth	SFK	TM0461	31,43–44;50;52. 41,11
Dalbury	DBY	SK2634	3,1. 6,97
Dalby	LIN	TF4170	13,5
Dalby (near Whenby) NR	YKS	SE6371	1N86. 8N5. 15E16 *note*. SN,D16 note. SN,B2
[Great] Dalby	LEC	SK7414	3,12. 17,25. 32,1
[Little] Dalby	LEC	SK7713	C14. 14,31. 29,19;21
[Low] Dalby (in Thornton Dale) NR	YKS	SE8587	1N50 *note*. SN,D16 *note*
[Old] Dalby	LEC	SK6723	22,1
Dale [Town] NR	YKS	SE5388	1N136 *note*. 11N22. SN,A10
Dalham	SFK	TL7261	25,6
[Field] Dalling NFK	ESS		ENf
[Field] Dalling NFK	NFK	TG0039	1,42. 4,20. 9,86. 38,3
[Wood] Dalling	NFK	TG0827	8,4. 25,4. 34,20
Dallinghoo	SFK	TM2654	3,42;48. 6,265;291. 8,26. 21,99;101. 67,32
Dallington	NTH	SP7361	6a,33
Dallington (in Flawborough)	NTT	SK7843	11,3
Dallington	SSX	TQ6519	9,32
Dalton (near Wigan) LAN	CHS	SD4908	R1,26;41
Dalton WES	YKS	SD5476	1L7 *note*. See also CHS Y8
Dalton (near Huddersfield) WR	YKS	SE1716	9W104;117. SW,Ag7
Dalton (near Ravensworth) NR	YKS	NZ1108	6N47 *note*. SN,CtA17
Dalton (another, near Ravensworth) NR	YKS	NZ1108	6N47 note. 6N48. SN, CtA17
Dalton (near Rotherham) WR	YKS	SK4594	12W1;10. 13W11. SW,Sf26
Dalton (near Topcliffe) NR	YKS	SE4376	13N17 *note*
Dalton [in Furness] LAN	YKS	SD2374	1L6. See also CHS Y7-8
[North] Dalton ER	YKS	SE9352	5E43. 7E1. 29E3. CE8. SE,Wa2
[South] Dalton ER	YKS	SE9645	2E2. SE,Sn8
Damerham HAM	WIL	SU1015	7,1. 11,2
Danbury	ESS	TL7705	30,14
Danby (near Moorsholm) NR	YKS	NZ6906	23N18 *note*. 23N34. 31N10. SN,L14
Danby (in Thornton Steward) NR	YKS	SE1587	6N103. SN,CtA15 note. SN,CtA31
Danby [Wiske] NR	YKS	SE3398	6N36. SN,CtA15 *note*
Danethorpe	NTT	SK8457	14,4
Danfrond FLN	CHS	??	FT2,11
Dankton	SSX	TQ1707	13,42
Dannonchapel	CON	SX0382	5,25,3
Danthorpe ER	YKS	TA2432	2E31 *note*. 14E4. SE,Th13. SE,Mid2. SE,Hol8
Darenth	KEN	TQ5671	2,3. 5,16-17
Darfield WR	YKS	SE4104	29W3. SW,Sf13
Darlaston	STS	SJ8834	4,6
Darley	DBY	SK2763	1,11;15
Darlton	NTT	SK7773	1,1
Darmsden	SFK	TM0953	1,71. 3,57. 21,17. 31,57
Darrington WR	YKS	SE4820	9W51. SW,O9
Darsham	SFK	TM4269	1,13. 3,7. 6,78;94–95;101. 7,36;50

Dart	DEV	??	36,24. 42,20
Dart (in Cadleigh)	DEV	SS9208	21,6
Dart [Raffe]	DEV	SS7915	21,13
Dartford	KEN	TQ5474	1,1
Dartington	DEV	SX7862	20,15
Darton WR	YKS	SE3109	1W24 *note.* 9W73;81. SW,St5;14
[Avon] Dassett	WAR	SP4150	16,5
[Burton] Dassett	WAR	SP3951	38,2
Datchet	BKM	SU9877	51,1
Datchworth	HRT	TL2619	2,1. 9,7. 34,3. 36,1
Dauntsey	WIL	ST9882	8,2
Davenham	CHS	SJ6570	5,10
Davenport	CHS	SJ8066	18,4
Daventry	NTH	SP5762	56,21
Dawley	MDX	TQ0979	7,7
Dawley	SHR	SJ6807	4,1,22. 4,3,28
Dawlish	DEV	SX9676	2,5
Dawna	CON	SX1461	5,5,14
Daylesford GLS	GLS	SP2425	E27;29. EvA121. EvC41. EvN5. WoB7. WoC6
Daylesford GLS	WOR		2,42;44
Deadmans [Well]	SOM	ST2333	1,1
Deal	KEN	TR3752	M14–15;17–19
Dean	BDF	TL0467	3,3. 4,1. 17,1. 57,13–14
Dean	OXF	SP3422	24,5
Dean [Court]	KEN	TQ9848	D24. 5,167
[East] Dean	HAM	SU2726	1,22. 4,1. 45,5. 47,2
[East] Dean	SSX	TV5597	9,44;49;80
Dean [Prior]	DEV	SX7363	20,13
[West] Dean	HAM	SU2527	45,6
[West] Dean (near Eastbourne)	SSX	TV5299	10,33–34
[West] Dean	WIL	SU2527	37,15
Deane	HAM	SU5450	32,2–3
Debach	SFK	TM2454	3,30. 7,125. 8,19. 16,5: 26,18. 32,10. 34,16. 46,10
Debden	ESS	TL5533	34,18
Debden [Green]	ESS	TQ4398	8,8
Debenham	SFK	TM1763	6,11;15–16;18;28;31. 16,33;48. 21,31. 34,12
Deddington	OXF	SP4631	7,2
Dedham	ESS	TM0533	39,5
Dedworth	BRK	SU9476	56,1
Deene	NTH	SP9492	7,1
[High, Middle and Low] Deepdale NR	YKS	TA0485	1Y3 *note.* SN,D5
		TA0485	
		TA0484	
Deeping [St James]: see [East] Deeping LIN			
[East] Deeping	LIN	TF1509	27,39. 51,2–3. CK,1
[East and West] Deeping	LIN		51,11
[West] Deeping	LIN	TF1108	51,1
Deerhurst GLS	GLS	SO8729	19,1. EvK153–4
Deerhurst GLS	WAR		EG8
Deerhurst: see [Deerhurst] Walton GLS			
Defford	WOR	SO9143	8,6
Deighton ER	YKS	SE6244	6E1. SE,P6
Deighton NR	YKS	NZ3801	3Y17. SN,A6
[Kirk and North] Deighton WR	YKS	SE3950	16W5 *note.* 24W20.
		SE3951	SW,Bu43
Deightonby [Fields] WR	YKS	SE4606	5W18 *note.* SW,Sf30
Delabole	CON	SX0684	5,26,2

Delamere	CON	SX0683	5,25,1
[Great] Delce	KEN	TQ7466	5,91
[Little] Delce	KEN	TQ7466	5,90
Delley	DEV	SS5424	42,1
Dembleby	LIN	TF0437	24,89. 26,43. 57,16
Denaby WR	YKS	SK4899	10W12. SW,Sf8
Denbury	DEV	SX8268	5,12
Denby	DBY	SK3946	11,3
[Upper] Denby (in Upper Whitley) WR	YKS	SE2316	9W101 note. SW,St12 note. SW,Ag5
[Upper and Lower] Denby (near Penistone) WR	YKS	SE2207 SE2307	9W87 note. SW,St12 note
Denchworth	BRK	SU3891	21,9. 42,1
[North] Denchworth	BRK	SU3893	23,3
Dendron LAN	YKS	SD2470	1L8. See also CHS Y9
Deneworthy (in Membury)	DEV	??	1,11
Denford	BRK	SU3568	23,2
Denford	NTH	SP9976	4,2
Denge Marsh: see [Denge] Marsh KEN			
Dengie	ESS	TL9801	14,7. 18,22
Denham	BKM	TQ0486	7,1
Denham (near Hargrave)	SFK	TL7561	25,7
Denham (near Hoxne)	SFK	TM1874	1,114. 6,71. 7,4. 19,3
Dennington (in Yarcombe)	DEV	ST2311	11,2
Dennington	SFK	TM2866	6,137;255;257;264;266-269;270 note;289;303
Densham	DEV	SS8109	15,31. 29,9
Denston	SFK	TL7652	25,4;5a. 65,1
Denstone	STS	SK1040	1,55
Denton	HUN	TL1487	2,5
Denton (near Barham)	KEN	TR2146	5,220
Denton (near Gravesend)	KEN	TQ6673	4,11
Denton	LIN	SK8632	1,15;24. 18,25. 59,1
Denton	NFK	TM2788	1,220. 29,6
Denton	NTH	SP8358	9,6. 56,20d;55
Denton WR	YKS	SE1448	2W4. SW,Sk2
Denton(e) (in Low Abbotside) NR	YKS	??	6N76 note. SN,CtA25
Denver	NFK	TF6101	8,18
Deopham	NFK	TG0500	8,79. 20,10
Depden	SFK	TL7756	25,79. 26,9
Deptford	WIL	SU0138	24,36
Derby	DBY	SK3536	B
Derby	LIN	SE8718	1,64
[West] Derby LAN	CHS	SJ3994	R1
[East] Dereham	NFK	TF9813	15,15-16;29. 20,9
[West] Dereham	NFK	TF6602	8,19. 9,232. 13,3. 16,2. 31,28-30. 66,12;44
Derleigh	ESS	TM0728	37,20. 68,8
Dernedale	KEN	TR0747	7,14
Derneford	SFK	??	67,17
Derrington	STS	SJ8922	8,20
Dersingham	NFK	TF6930	29,4. 34,2;13. 66,87
Desborough	NTH	SP8083	1,15f. 18,26. 26,6. 35,12
Desford	LEC	SK4703	C11. 13,5;8
Desning	SFK	TL7363	25,3;35-36;39-41
Detton	SHR	SO6679	4,3,70
Deuxhill	SHR	SO6987	3c,10
Deverill	WIL	??	25,22. 67,52. 68,28
[Brixton] Deverill	WIL	ST8638	17,1
[Hill] Deverill	WIL	ST8640	24,18. 48,8
[Kingston] Deverill	WIL	ST8437	19,1

[Longbridge and Monkton] Deverill	WIL	ST8640 ST8637	7,3;16
Dewdon (in Widecombe in the Moor)	DEV	??	20,10
Dewlish	DOR	SY7798	25,1
Dewsall	HEF	SO4833	1,62
Dewsbury WR	YKS	SE2421	1Y17. SW,M9
Dexthorpe	LIN	TF4071	13,5. 29,27
Dibden	HAM	SU3908	NF9,2
Dic(he) (in Haxby) NR	YKS	??	1N96 *note*. SN,B12
Dickleburgh	NFK	TM1682	14,29
Dickley	ESS	TM1129	32,39
Didderston [Grange] NR	YKS	NZ1807	6N50 *note*. SN,CtA18
Diddington	HUN	TL1965	2,3. 20,9
Didley	HEF	SO4532	2,2
Didlington	DOR	SU0007	20,1
Didlington	NFK	TL7796	8,89 *and note*. 28,2
Didmarton	GLS	ST8287	53,5
Digby	LIN	TF0854	64,4
Digswell	HRT	TL2314	33,5. 36,2. Appx
Dilehurst (in Taplow)	BKM	??	4,14
Dilham	NFK	TG3325	4,37. 7,19. 9,181. 17,47
Dilhorne	STS	SJ9743	11,41
Dillington	HUN	TL1365	6,20
Dilworth [House] LAN	YKS	SD6137	1L1 *note*. See also CHS Y2
Dilwyn and [Little and Sollers] Dilwyn	HEF	SO4154 SO4353 SO4255	1,26;32. 14,8-9
Dimlington ER	YKS	TA3920	14E10
Dimsdale	STS	SJ8448	13,7
Dincolyn FLN	CHS	SJ0679	FT2,16
Dinedor	HEF	SO5336	8,7
Dingley	NTH	SP7787	18,14. 26,9. 30,4. 56,5
Dinham (Wales)	GLS	ST4792	W1;2 note.
Dinnaton (in Cornwood)	DEV	SX6257	1,23. 15,70
Dinnington	SOM	ST4012	8,36. 47,10
Dinnington WR	YKS	SK5285	10W1. 12W1;19. SW,Sf2
[Over] Dinsdale [Grange] NR	YKS	NZ3411	1Y2 *note*. 6N9. SN, A1. SN,CtA9
[Temple] Dinsley	HRT	TL1824	1,9
Dinthill	SHR	SJ4212	3g,11
Dinting	DBY	SK0294	1,30
Dinton	BKM	SP7711	4,2
Dinton	WIL	SU0131	12,6
Dipford	DEV	SS9723	23,6
Diptford	DEV	SX7256	1,15
Dirtham	SRY	TQ1053	19,34-35
Discoed (Wales)	HEF	SO2764	24,3
Discove	SOM	ST6934	47,8
Diseworth	LEC	SK4524	27,1
Dishforth NR	YKS	SE3873	13W38
Dishley	LEC	SK5121	1,9. 43,6
Diss NFK	NFK	TM1180	1,51. 66,62. ESf1
Diss NFK	SFK		1,8;11
Ditchampton	WIL	SU0931	4,4. 13,15
Ditcheat	SOM	ST6236	8,30
Ditchford GLS	GLS	SP2136	E24. EvA118 note. EvC39. WoB7. WoC6
Ditchford GLS	WOR		2,39
Ditchford	WAR	SP2339	22,16
Ditchingham	NFK	TM3292	1,228
Ditchling	SSX	TQ3215	10,102;108. 12,6
Ditteridge	WIL	ST8169	32,11

Dittisham	DEV	SX8655	2,23
Ditton	BKM	SU9977	17,5
Ditton	KEN	TQ7058	5,42
[Earls] Ditton	SHR	SO6275	6,4
[Long] Ditton	SRY	TQ1766	19,21
Ditton [Priors]	SHR	SO6089	4,1,26. 7,2
[Thames] Ditton	SRY	TQ1567	5,27
Dixton	GLS	SO9830	1,43
Dizzard	CON	SX1698	5,7,10. 5,17,3
Docking	NFK	TF7637	2,5. 29,5
Dockworthy	DEV	SS7213	35,25
Dodbrooke	DEV	SX7444	52,53
Doddenham	WOR	SO7556	20,1
Doddinghurst	ESS	TQ5899	41,1
Doddington	CAM	TL4090	5,45
Doddington	LIN	SK9070	9,1-2. 65,1-5. CK,27
[Dry] Doddington	LIN	SK8546	4,76. 26,31-32. 64,16
[Great] Doddington	NTH	SP8864	56,16;53
Doddiscombsleigh	DEV	SX8586	47,5
Dodford	NTH	SP6160	18,58
Dodington	GLS	ST7480	6,9. 42,2
Dodington	SHR	SJ5440	4,7,4
Dodington	SOM	ST1740	47,12
Dodisham (in Cannington)	SOM	??	21,20
Dodleston	CHS	SJ3661	FD6,1
Dodnash	SFK	TM1036	3,72
Dodscott	DEV	SS5419	25,4. 42,6 note
Dodworth WR	YKS	SE3105	9W69. SW,St4
Dogmersfield	HAM	SU7852	68,1
Dolton	DEV	SS5712	16,44. 40,7
Domellick	CON	SW9458	5,24,11
Doncaster WR	YKS	SE5703	5W8;30. 13W9. SW, Sf21;25;34
Done	CHS	??	1,11
Donhead [St Andrew and St Mary]	WIL	ST9124	12,3
		ST9024	
Donington	LIN	TF2035	8,11. 12,61-62;90
Donington	SHR	SJ8004	4,1,25
[Castle] Donington	LEC	SK4427	12,2. 43,1
Donington [le Heath]	LEC	SK4212	39,2
Donington [on Bain]	LIN	TF2382	14,51
Donisthorpe LEC	DBY		14,9. E5
Donisthorpe LEC	LEC	SK3114	14,28. E9
Donnelie (near Wedgnock Park)	WAR	SP2668	16,17
Donningstone	DEV	ST0023	15,57
Donnington	BRK	SU4668	26,1
Donnington	GLS	SP1928	EvE25. EvO6
Donnington	HEF	SO7034	2,19
Donnington	SSX	SU8502	7,2
Donyatt	SOM	ST3314	19,24
[East] Donyland	ESS	TM0120	20,38;42. 68,6. 69,3. 70,2
Dorchester	DOR	SY6890	B1. 1,4. 2,1. 14,1. 24,1
Dorchester OXF	BRK		B9
Dorchester OXF	OXF	SU5794	6,1a;9. EBe3
Dore WR, YKS	DBY	SK3081	16,4-5
Dorking	SRY	TQ1649	1,13
Dormington	HEF	SO5840	6,2. 7,1 note
Dormston	WOR	SO9857	8,14
Dorn	GLS	SP2033	EvA120 note. EvC42. WoB7. WoC6
Dorney	BKM	SU9379	23,2
Dorrington	LIN	TF0852	64,3

Dorrington	SHR	SJ7340	4,15,3
Dorsington WAR	GLS		40,1
Dorsington WAR	WAR	SP1349	EG12
[Little] Dorsington	WAR	SP1250	36,1
Dorslow (near Sugnall)	STS	SJ8031	2,11
Dorstone	HEF	SO3141	23,2
Dorton	BKM	SP6814	14,9
Dosthill	WAR	SP2199	17,13
Dotton	DEV	SY0888	16,135
Doulting	SOM	ST6443	8,23
Dover	KEN	TR3241	D. M3. P9-11. 2,2. 5,188;205. 9,9
Dovercourt	ESS	TM2331	35,10
Doverdale	WOR	SO8666	26,8
Doverhay	SOM	SS8846	21,66
Doveridge DBY	DBY	SK1134	6,25. S
Doveridge DBY	NTT		S5
Dowdeswell	GLS	SP0019	3,5. WoA2. WoB18
Dowdyke	LIN	TF2833	11,5-8
Dowland	DEV	SS5610	24,23;*24*;25
Dowlish [Wake] and [West] Dowlish	SOM	ST3712	5,1
		ST3713	
?Down Court (in Niton) IOW: see *Down*	HAM	SZ4978	
Down, [The] Down (in Bathingbourne or Niton) IOW	HAM	??	1,W1;2
Down, [The] Down (in Bathingbourne or Niton) IOW: see also Down Court (in Niton)			
[East] Down	DEV	SS6041	31,1
Down [Hall]	ESS	TM0006	25,8. 34,23;25
Down [Ralph]: see Rousden DEV			
Down [St Mary]	DEV	SS7404	1,72. 6,4
[The] Down: see *Down* IOW	HAM	??	1,W1;2
Down [Thomas]	DEV	SX5050	17,88
Down [Umfraville]	DEV	??	52,19
[West] Down (near Ilfracombe)	DEV	SS5142	3,26
Downham	CAM	TL5284	5,59. Appx P
Downham [Market]	NFK	TF6103	8,19. 9,231. 15,3. 66,13;47
[Santon] Downham	SFK	TL8187	14,21. 21,8
Downhead	SOM	ST6945	8,35
Downholland LAN	CHS	SD3408	R1,35
Downholme NR	YKS	SE1197	6N70. SN,CtA24
Downicary	DEV	SX3790	17,7
Downinney	CON	SX2090	5,3,20
Downscombe	SOM	SS8439	21,57
Downton	WIL	SU1821	2,1
Downton [on the Rock]	HEF	SO4273	9,2
Dowsby	LIN	TF1129	2,29-31. 57,12. 67,23. CK,49
Dowthorpe [Hall] ER	YKS	TA1538	14E11 *note*. SE, Hol16
Doxey	STS	SJ9023	2,21
Doynton	GLS	ST7274	6,5
Drakelow	DBY	SK2420	14,1
Draughton	NTH	SP7676	1,15d. 54,3. 56,11
Draughton WR	YKS	SE0352	1W73. SW,Cr1
Drax WR	YKS	SE6726	16W1. SW,BA9
Draycot	OXF	SP6506	35,16
Draycot [Cerne]	WIL	ST9278	68,21
Draycot [Fitz Payne]	WIL	SU1462	5,1
Draycot [Foliat]	WIL	SU1877	28,7
Draycott	DBY	SK4433	2,1
Draycott (in Limington)	SOM	ST5421	8,39. 19,12

Draycott (in Rodney Stoke)	SOM	ST4750	47,15
Draycott	STS	SK1528	10,5
Draycott [Moor]	BRK	SU3999	7,26
Drayford	DEV	SS7813	24,6
Draynes	CON	SX2169	5,20,2. 5,24,1
Drayton	BRK	SU4794	18,1. 35,4
Drayton	HAM	SU4243	6,16
Drayton	LIN	TF2439	11,6. 12,59-61;63-68;70-71;73-79.
			57,56. 67,18. CK,66
Drayton	NFK	TG1813	20,26
Drayton (near Wroxton) OXF	OXF	SP4241	28,7. 57,1. ES2
Drayton (near Wroxton) OXF	STS		12,31
Drayton	SHR	SJ6734	4,14,9. 4,19,8
Drayton	SOM	ST4024	9,6. 21,55
Drayton (in Penkridge)	STS	SJ9216	1,7
Drayton [Bassett]	STS	SK1900	1,30
Drayton [Beauchamp]	BKM	SP9011	12,14-15. 43,5
[Dry] Drayton	CAM	TL3762	9,3. 14,60. 26,49. 38,5. 41,15.
			Appx O
[East] Drayton	NTT	SK7775	1,2
[Fen] Drayton	CAM	TL3368	1,21. 7,7. 14,56. 23,6. 32,27
[Fenny] Drayton	LEC	SP3597	10,8
Drayton Hundred	LIN	—	12,58. CK,65
Drayton [Parslow]	BKM	SP8328	4,28. 40,1
[West] Drayton	MDX	TQ0679	3,30
[West] Drayton	NTT	SK7074	9,30-31. 16,11
Drebley WR	YKS	SE0559	25W33
Drewsteignton	DEV	SX7390	16,107
Drewsteignton: see also Teignton DEV			
Drewton ER	YKS	SE9233	11E3 note. SE,C3
Driby	LIN	TF3874	24,73
Driffield	GLS	SU0799	26,2. 45,5 note
[Great] Driffield ER	YKS	TA0257	1Y8-9. 5E22;28;31. CE4-5;7.
			SE,Dr1;4
[Little] Driffield ER	YKS	TA0157	1Y8 note
Drighlington WR	YKS	SE2229	9W128. SW,M5
Drigsell (in Salehurst)	SSX	TQ7523	9,83
Dringhoe ER	YKS	TA1555	14E8
Drinkstone	SFK	TL9561	2,1. 14,56. 21,3
Drointon	STS	SK0226	2,19
Droitwich WOR	BKM		1,3
Droitwich WOR	GLS		1,24;27;47-48. 18,1. 50,1. E18;30.
			EvQ29
Droitwich WOR	HEF		1,4;7;8;10a;40-41. 2,18;20;26-
			28;34. 29,11. E6
Droitwich WOR	OXF		1,6. 58,4
Droitwich WOR	SHR		4,1,25-26. 4,11,4
Droitwich WOR	WAR		28,14. 35,1
Droitwich WOR	WOR	SO8963	1,1a;1c;2;3a;5;7. 2,7;15;48;50;
			68;77-79;82;84. 4,1. 5,1. 7,1.
			8,12-13. 9,1a. 10,10. 12,1. 14,1.
			15,9;13-14. 18,6. 19,12. 22,1.
			24,1. 26,2;8;13;15-16. 27,1.
			28,1. E2-3;10-34
Dromonby [Hall] NR	YKS	NZ5305	29N9 note. SN,L42
Dronfield	DBY	SK3578	1,6
Droxford	HAM	SU6018	3,9
Drypool ER	YKS	TA1028	2E35. 14E49. SE, Mid3.
			SE,Hol25
Duckington	CHS	SJ4951	2,11
Ducklington	OXF	SP3507	28,20. 59,6

Duckmanton	DBY	SK4471	10,6
Duddington	NTH	SK9900	1,14
Dudley	WOR	SO9490	23,10
Dudsbury	DOR	SZ0798	40,5
Dudston	SHR	SO2497	4,1,35
Duffield	DBY	SK3443	6,66
[North] Duffield ER	YKS	SE6836	5E13;26. 21E5. CE19. SE,How 8-9
[South] Duffield ER	YKS	SE6833	5E11-12;26. CE20. SE,How8
Duggleby ER	YKS	SE8767	1Y7. 8E4. SE,Sc6
Dullingham	CAM	TL6357	10,1. 14,75. 26,3. 41,2. Appx D
Dulverton	SOM	SS9127	1,12. 46,2
Dumbleton	GLS	SP0135	13,1. 34,13. 36,3. 53,12
Dummer	HAM	SU5845	23,31. 69,7
Dunbridge	HAM	SU3126	43,2
Dunchideock	DEV	SX8887	32,1
Dunchurch	WAR	SP4871	37,3
Dunclent	WOR	SO8675	12,2
Duncton	SSX	SU9617	11,21
Dundon	SOM	ST4732	8,13
Dundon: see also Compton [Dundon] SOM			
Dungewood IOW	HAM	SZ4680	1,13
Dunham	NTT	SK8174	1,1;8
[Great and Little] Dunham	NFK	TF8714 TF8612	1,212. 22,12. 46,1
Dunham [Massey]	CHS	SJ7488	13,2
Dunham [on the Hill]	CHS	SJ4772	1,3
Dunholme	LIN	TF0279	1,36. 20,1. 35,3. 48,16
Duni	GLS	SO7616	34,12 *in note*
Dunkerton	SOM	ST7159	36,13
Dunkeswell	DEV	ST1407	34,25
Dunkeswick WR	YKS	SE3046	29W36 *note*. SW,Bu35
[Great and Little] Dunmow	ESS	TL6222 TL6521	20,15. 22,9. 23,3. 24,48. 25,14. 28,7. 30,32;36;42. 33,6
Dunnington (near Bewholme) ER	YKS	TA1552	14E24. SE,Hol20
Dunnington (near York) ER	YKS	SE6652	2B8. 13E7. CE26. SE,Sn9-10
Dunningworth	SFK	TM3857	7,149
Dunsbeare	DEV	SS5113	52,5
Dunsby	LIN	TF1026	7,30;33. CK,45
Dunsby	LIN	TF0351	10,3. 64,7
Dunscombe	DEV	SS8805	34,33
Dunsden	OXF	SU7477	4,1
Dunsdon	DEV	SS3008	34,2
Dunsford	DEV	SX8189	23,12. 52,47
[Upper and Lower] Dunsforth WR	YKS	SE4463 SE4464	24W4 *note*. 29W30. 31W3. SW,Bu3-4
Dunsland	DEV	SS4005	16,16
Dunsley	HRT	SP9311	15,9. 39,1
Dunsley NR	YKS	NZ8511	1N20. SN,L6
Dunstall	LIN	SK8993	14,23. 16,24
Dunster	SOM	SS9943	25,2
Dunsthorpe	LIN	SK9235	1,15;21
Dunston	LIN	TF0662	32,34
Dunston	NFK	TG2202	4,53. 9,192. 12,36. 20,35. 65,12
Dunston	STS	SJ9217	1,7
Dunstone (in Widecombe in the Moor)	DEV	SX7175	34,46
Dunstone (in Yealmpton)	DEV	SX5951	29,4. 52,42
Dunterton	DEV	SX3779	16,12
Dunthrop	OXF	SP3528	8,3. 17,4
Duntisbourne	GLS	??	31,7. 32,2. 78,3

Duntisbourne [Abbots]	GLS	SO9707	10,13. 39,7
Duntisbourne *[Hotat]*	GLS	SO9806	68,8;11;13
Duntisbourne [Leer]	GLS	SO9707	17,1
Duntisbourne [Rouse]	GLS	SO9806	53,3
Dunton	BDF	TL2344	16,5. 39,1
Dunton	BKM	SP8224	4,27
Dunton	ESS	TQ6588	18,3. 90,3
Dunton	NFK	TF8730	1,17
Dunton [Bassett]	LEC	SP5490	17,4
Dunwear	SOM	ST3136	24,6
Dunwich	SFK	TM4770	6,84;89. 7,6;26. 21,47
Durborough	SOM	ST1941	8,8
Durleigh	SOM	ST2736	46,15
Durley	HAM	SU3510	69,51
[Great and Little] Durnford	WIL	SU1338	13,3. 32,1
		SU1234	
Durrington	SSX	TQ1104	13,33-34
Durrington	WIL	SU1544	23,2
Dursley	GLS	ST7598	1,15
Durston	SOM	ST2928	22,4
Durton IOW	HAM	SZ5288	9,13
Durweston	DOR	ST8508	49,11. 55,26
Duston	NTH	SP7261	35,4
Dutton	CHS	SJ5779	9,22. 24,7. 26,2
Duxford	BRK	SU3699	65,3
Duxford	CAM	TL4746	14,19. 15,2. 20,1. 21,2. 26,16. Appx E
Dyche	SOM	ST1641	35,13
Dyke	LIN	TF1022	42,3;5-6. 61,2. CK,41
Dykebeck	NFK	TG0901	31,42. 66,39
Dymock	GLS	SO7031	1,53
Dyrham	GLS	ST7475	35,1-2
Dyserth FLN	CHS	SJ0579	FT1,2. FT2,2

E

Each (in Eastry Hundred)	KEN	TR3058	5,216
Each (in *Summerdene* Hundred)	KEN	TR3058	5,212
Eadruneland	KEN	??	*3,22*
Eagle	LIN	SK8767	16,49. 44,18. 48,15. 56,14-16. CK,25
Eakring	NTT	SK6762	1,24. 12,5. 17,7-8
Eanley	CHS	SJ5681	9,21
Earby (near Thornton in Craven) WR	YKS	SD9046	30W20
Earby, another, WR	YKS	SD9046	30W21
Eardington	SHR	SO7290	4,1,32
Eardisland	HEF	SO4158	1,6
Eardisley	HEF	SO3149	1,68. 10,46. 29,17
Eardiston	WOR	SO6968	2,85
Earley	BRK	SU7571	1,21;42. 39,1
Earlham	NFK	TG1908	1,206. 4,53
Earlscourt	WIL	SU2185	66,6
Earlsheaton WR	YKS	SE2521	1Y15 *note*. SW,Ag10
Earlstone: see *Clere* HAM			
Earnshill	SOM	ST3821	21,71. 46,20
Earsham	NFK	TM3188	1,219-220;223;225-226;228– 229;239. 9,63;167. 14,20-21. 29,6. 43,2-3.
Earsham Half Hundred	NFK	—	*15,24*
Earswick NR	YKS	SE6257	2N29. SN,B16
[Gaunts] Earthcott	GLS	ST6384	6,8
Easby (near Ingleby Greenhow) NR	YKS	NZ5708	1N23. SN,L29
Easby (near Richmond) NR	YKS	NZ1800	6N20 *note*. SN,CtA11
Easington	BKM	SP6810	14,8
Easington	OXF	SU6697	58,9
Easington ER	YKS	TA3919	14E9-10. SE,Hol14
Easington NR	YKS	NZ7418	4N2. SN,L13
Easington WR	YKS	SD7150	30W37
Easingwold NR	YKS	SE5269	1Y1. SN,B21
Easole	KEN	TR2552	5,134;217
East Hale (in Eastbourne): see *Easthall* SSX			
Eastbourne	SSX	TV5999	10,2;81-82;84
Eastbourne: see also [East?]Bourne SSX			
Eastbridge	KEN	TR0731	9,10
Eastburn WR	YKS	SE9955	1Y8 *note*. SE,Dr2
Eastburn ER	YKS	SE0244	1W62. 21W15 *note*
Eastbury	WOR	SO8256	2,69
[Good] Easter	ESS	TL6212	12,1
[High] Easter	ESS	TL6214	30,27
Eastergate	SSX	SU9405	11,93
Easthall (later East Hale in Eastbourne)	SSX	TV6198	10,4;9
Eastham	CHS	SJ3580	1,22
Eastham	WOR	SO6568	15,12
Easthampstead	BRK	SU8667	9,1
[Lower] Easthams	SOM	ST4510	1,20. 19,33
Easthope	SHR	SO5695	4,3,11
Easthorpe	ESS	TL9121	20,40
Easthorpe ER	YKS	SE8845	5E19 *note*. 13E2. SE,Wei5

Easthorpe [House] NR	YKS	SE7371	1Y4 *note*. SN,D11
Eastleach [Martin]	GLS	SP2005	54,2. 55,1
Eastleach [Turville]	GLS	SP1905	39,13
Eastleigh	DEV	SS4827	19,6
Eastleigh	HAM	SU4519	56,2
Eastling	KEN	TQ9656	5,158-159
[North] Eastling	KEN	TQ9657	5,156
Eastnor	HEF	SO7337	2,27
Eastoke	HAM	SZ7498	21,8 *in note*
Easton	BDF	TL1371	3,6. 4,2. 17,4-7. 23,24. 35,1. 36,1. 44,1
Easton BDF: see also [Little] Staughton BDF			
Easton	HAM	SU5132	2,5
Easton	HUN	TL1371	D19
Easton	LIN	SK9326	2,38
Easton (near Norwich)	NFK	TG1310	4,9
Easton (near Scottow)	NFK	TG2723	17,24;48
Easton	SFK	TM2858	6,270. 8,23
Easton	WIL	??	49,2
Easton ER	YKS	TA1568	1Y11 *note*. 1E14. SE,Hu5
Easton [Bavents]	SFK	TM5178	1,10. 68,1;3-4
[Crux] Easton	HAM	SU4256	60,2
[Great] Easton	LEC	SP8593	5,2-3
[Great and Little] Easton	ESS	TL6025 TL6023	22,5. 30,37. 42,3. 53,1
Easton [Grey]	WIL	ST8887	45,3
Easton [in-Gordano]	SOM	ST5175	5,24
Easton [Maudit]	NTH	SP8858	35,1h. 40,2 note. 56,52
Easton [Neston]	NTH	SP7049	18,59. 40,6 note. 48,16
Easton [on the Hill]	NTH	TF0104	42,2-3. 46,6
Easton [Piercy] and [Lower] Easton [Piercy]	WIL	ST8877 ST8977	25,26
[Ston] Easton	SOM	ST6253	5,59. 42,3. 46,25
Eastrington ER	YKS	SE7929	3Y4. SE,How2
Eastrip (in Bruton)	SOM	ST6935	36,3. 47,24
Eastrop	HAM	SU6451	36,2
Eastry	KEN	TR3154	3,17
Eastwell	KEN	TR0047	9,1
Eastwell	LEC	SK7728	29,3. 42,7
Eastwick	HRT	TL4311	34,23-24
Eastwick (? in Newby) WR	YKS	SD3467	2W7 *note*. SW,Bu45
Eastwood	ESS	TQ8488	24,20;41
Eastwood	NTT	SK4647	10,32
Eaton	BRK	SP4403	33,7;8
Eaton (near Eccleston)	CHS	SJ4160	1,13
Eaton (near Leominster)	HEF	SO5058	1,22
Eaton	NFK	TG2006	1,104;114;126;184;190;205
Eaton	NTT	SK7178	5,8. 9,9;20-21;25;30
Eaton [Bishop] HEF	GLS		E5
Eaton [Bishop] HEF	HEF	SO4439	2,8
Eaton [Bray]	BDF	SP9720	2,1
[Castle] Eaton	WIL	SU1495	21,1. 66,1
[Church] Eaton	STS	SJ8417	11,65
Eaton [Constantine]	SHR	SJ5906	4,3,21
Eaton [Dovedale]	DBY	SK1037	6,50
Eaton [Hastings]	BRK	SU2596	30,1
[Hill of] Eaton	HEF	SO6027	19,7
Eaton [Leys] BKM: see [Water] Eaton BKM			
[Little] Eaton NTT	DBY	SK3641	B1

[Long] Eaton	DBY	SK4933	2,2
Eaton [Mascott]	SHR	SJ5305	4,3,20
Eaton [Socon]	BDF	TL1658	21,1
[Water] Eaton	BKM	SP8832	5,7
[Water] Eaton	OXF	SP5112	28,5
[Water] Eaton	STS	SJ9011	11,58
[Wood] Eaton	OXF	SP5311	29,7
Eatons	SSX	TQ1816	13,53
Eavestone WR	YKS	SE2268	2W7. SW,Bu47
Ebberston NR	YKS	SE8982	1Y4. SN,D12
Ebbesborne [Wake]	WIL	ST9924	42,10
Ebrige: see Irish Hill BRK			
Ebrington	GLS	SP1840	34,4
Ebsworthy	DEV	SX5090	*16,7*
Ebury	MDX	TQ2878	9,1
Ecchinswell	HAM	SU5059	3,20
Eccles	KEN	TQ7260	5,44
Eccles (near Hempstead)	NFK	TG4128	17,58. 65,4
Eccles (near Wilby)	NFK	TM0189	10,21
Ecclesfield WR	YKS	SK3594	10W16. SW,Sf10
Eccleshall	STS	SJ8329	2,10;13-14;21
Eccleshill WR	YKS	SE1736	SW,M12 *note*
Eccleston	CHS	SJ4162	17,1
[Great] Eccleston LAN	YKS	SD4240	1L1. See also CHS Y2
[Little] Eccleston LAN	YKS	SD4139	1L1. See also CHS Y2
Eccup WR	YKS	SE2842	5W5. SW,Sk20
Eckington	DBY	SK4379	1,1. 10,1
Eckington	SSX	TQ5109	9,41;55;76;97. 10,89-90
Eckington	WOR	SO9241	8,7
Eckweek	SOM	ST7157	19,61. 24,32
Ecton	NTH	SP8263	25,3
Ectone/Estone (in Lindley) WR	YKS	??	2W4 *note*. SW,Sk2 *note*
Edale	DBY	SK1285	1,29
Edderton (Wales)	SHR	SJ2302	4,1,36
Eddington	BRK	SU3469	1,28
Eddintone	KEN	??	5,4
Eddisbury	CHS	SJ5569	1,12
Eddlethorpe ER	YKS	SE7766	1E48 *note*. 31E6. SE,Ac1
Edenham	LIN	TF0621	24,25;29;77. 42,14-15. CK,6
Edenhope	SHR	SO2788	4,1,35
Edensor	DBY	SK2569	1,32. 6,99;101
Edenthorpe: see *Streetthorpe* YKS			
Edeyrnion (Wales)	SHR	??	4,3,42
Edgbaston	WAR	SP0584	27,4
Edgbold	SHR	SJ4511	6,31
Edgcote	NTH	SP5047	4,11
Edgcott	BKM	SP6722	14,35
Edge	CHS	SJ4850	2,8;12
Edgefield	NFK	TG0934	34,14. 36,6
Edgeley	SHR	SJ5540	4,7,3
Edgeworth	GLS	SO9405	28,3. 39,9
Edginswell	DEV	SX8866	32,10
Edgmond	SHR	SJ7219	4,1,23
Edgton	SHR	SO3885	4,20,14
Edingale STS	DBY		6,15. 17,12
Edingale STS	STS	SK2112	ED4;6
Edington	SOM	ST3839	8,5
Edington	WIL	ST9253	15,1. 68,1
Edingworth	SOM	ST3553	8,34
Edlaston	DBY	SK1842	6,59
Edlesborough BKM	BDF		27,1

Edlesborough BKM	BKM	SP9719	E1. 22,1
Edlington	LIN	TF2371	14,63. 24,22. CS,33
[Old] Edlington WR	YKS	SK5397	13W9 note. SW,Sf25
Edmondsham	DOR	SU0611	1,18. 50,1-2
Edmondthorpe	LEC	SK8517	14,6
Edmonton	MDX	TQ3392	9,8
Ednaston DBY	DBY	SK2341	4,2. 9,3. S
Ednaston DBY	NTT		S5
Edritone: see Kinnerton CHS & FLN			
Edstaston	SHR	SJ5131	4,14,6
Edstock	SOM	ST2340	21,32
Edstone	WAR	SP1761	22,8
[Great] Edstone NR	YKS	SE7084	8N22. SN,Ma9
[Little] Edstone NR	YKS	SE7184	8N23 note. SN,Ma9
Eduinestuna	SFK	??	25,69. 36,14
Eduluestuna	SFK	??	39,14
Edvin [Loach] HEF	GLS		1,11. EvK10
Edvin [Loach] HEF	HEF	SO6658	E1. EW2
Edvin [Loach] HEF	WOR		19,11. E35
Edwalton	NTT	SK5935	16,4. 23,1
Edwardestune	HEF	??	10,18
Edwardstone	SFK	TL9442	6,1
Edwinstowe	NTT	SK6266	1,24;28
Edworth	BDF	TL2240	18,4. 57,3iv
Edwyn [Ralph]	HEF	SO6457	1,10a;10c
Effingham	SRY	TQ1153	8,20. 19,44
Efford	DEV	SX5056	29,6
Efford	HAM	SZ2994	NF9,41
Eggbeer	DEV	SX7791	16,130
Eggborough WR	YKS	SE5623	9W61-62. SW,O14
Eggbuckland	DEV	SX4957	17,69
Egginton	DBY	SK2627	9,4
Egglestone [Abbey] NR	YKS	NZ0615	6N1 note. SN,CtA6
Egham	SRY	TQ0171	8,21
Englosroose: see Philleigh CON			
Egmanton	NTT	SK7368	9,14-15
Egmere	NFK	TF8937	1,36. 8,117. 10,11
Egstow	DBY	SK3965	10,7
Egton NR	YKS	NZ8105	5N3. SN,L6
Elberton	GLS	ST6088	1,15
Elborough	SOM	ST3659	5,11. 8,38
Elcombe	WIL	SU1380	23,8
Eldeberge (in Brampton Bierlow) WR	YKS	??	SW,Sf16-17 note
Eldersfield WOR	HEF		1,46
Eldersfield WOR	WOR	SO8031	8,9c note. E6
Eldwick WR	YKS	SE1240	24W1 note. SW,Sk18
Eleigh	SOM	ST3310	21,37
[Brent and Monks] Eleigh	SFK	TL9448	14,27. 15,5. 16,9. 25, 45. 42,1
		TL9647	
Elerkey: see Veryan CON			
Elestolf: see E(le)stolf (in Brigham) YKS			
Elford	STS	SK1810	1,26
Elfordleigh	DEV	SX5458	17,104
Elham	KEN	TR1743	5,129
Eling	BRK	SU5275	44,1
Eling	HAM	SU3612	1,27
Elkesley	NTT	SK6875	1,10. 9,32. 30,41
Elkington	LIN	TF2988	14,84. 22,28
Elkington	NTH	SP6276	18,69. 41,10. 47,1b
Elkstone	GLS	SO9612	68,9
Ella	SFK	??	29,6

[Kirk] Ella ER	YKS	TA0229	5E23. 15E1. 21E1. 23E1. SE,He3-4
Elland WR	YKS	SE1021	9W142. SW,M10
Ellastone	STS	SK1143	2,15. 11,39
Ellbridge	CON	SX4063	5,2,8
Ellel LAN	YKS	SD4856	30W39. See also CHS Y10
Ellenglaze	CON	SW7757	4,18
Ellenhall	STS	SJ8426	2,20
Ellenthorpe WR	YKS	SD8149	13W41. 30W11
Ellenthorpe [Hall] (near Kirby Hill) NR	YKS	SE4167	1Y18 note. SW,H7
Ellerbeck NR	YKS	SE4396	1N130. 23N16. SN,A8
Ellerburn NR	YKS	SE8484	1Y4. 1N49. SN,D16
Ellerby ER	YKS	TA1637	14E43. CE41. SE,Hol24
Ellerby NR	YKS	NZ7914	5N6. SN,L8
Ellerdine	SHR	SJ6020	4,23,7
Ellerker ER	YKS	SE9229	3Y1
Ellerton ER	YKS	SE7039	5E24. CE2. SE,C8
Ellerton [Abbey] NR	YKS	SE0797	6N71 note. SN,CtA24
Ellerton [on Swale] NR	YKS	SE2597	6N29-30;32-5. SN, CtA14
Ellesborough	BKM	SP8306	17,2-3. 43,1
Ellesmere	SHR	SJ4034	4,1,19
Ellingham	HAM	SU1408	69,32
Ellingham (in Clavering Hundred)	NFK	TM3592	1,239
[Great] Ellingham	NFK	TM0196	13,15. 20,5. 66,24
[Little] Ellingham	NFK	TM0099	1,7;136. 8,53
Ellings	GLS	SO8629	19,2
Ellington	HUN	TL1571	6,26
[High] Ellington NR	YKS	SE1983	6N113 note. SN,CtA33
Ellisfield	HAM	SU6346	23,59
Ellough	SFK	TM4486	1,37. 7,44;46
Elloughton ER	YKS	SE9428	2B3. SE,Wel4
[Great] Elm	SOM	ST7449	39,2
Elmbridge	WOR	SO8967	19,13
Elmdon	ESS	TL4639	20,74
Elmdon	WAR	SP1783	17,11
[North] Elmham	NFK	TF9821	10,5
[South] Elmham [All Saints, St Cross, St James, St Margaret, St Michael, St Peter]	SFK	TM3482 TM2984 TM3281 TM3183 TM3483 TM3282 TM3384	3,105. 6,298. 13,6.19,14;16. 18,4
Elmington	NTH	TL0689	11,2-3
Elmley [Lovett]	WOR	SO8669	15;13
Elmore	GLS	SO7815	78,6 in note
[North] Elmsall WR	YKS	SE4712	9W63. SW,Sf37 note. SW,O13
[South] Elmsall WR	YKS	SE4711	9W34. SW,Sf37 note
Elmsett	SFK	TM0546	29,12
Elmstead	ESS	TM0626	24,64. B3m
Elmstone [Hardwicke]	GLS	SO9226	19,2
Elmstone	KEN	TR2660	7,24
Elmswell	SFK	TL9863	14,73
Elmswell ER	YKS	SE9958	1Y8. 29E11. SE,Dr1. SE,Tu8
Elmton	DBY	SK5073	8,5
Elmton	KEN	TR2750	5,214
Elnodestune	HEF	??	10,17
Elsenham	ESS	TL5425	32,44. 65,1
Elsfield	OXF	SP5410	28,15
Elsford	DEV	SX7983	3,8
Elsham	LIN	TA0312	4,16. 7,19. 16,33;34. 64,19

Elsing	NFK	TG0516	8,6
Elslack WR	YKS	SD9349	30W22
Elsted	SSX	SU8119	6,2
Elsthorpe	LIN	TF0524	27,42. 57,57
Elston	NTT	SK7648	6,3;5. 9,1. 20,4-5
Elston	WIL	SU0644	48,1-2
Elstow	BDF	TL0547	53,4. 53,1;3
Elstronwick ER	YKS	TA2332	14E2. SE,Hol5
Elswick LAN	YKS	SD4238	1L1. See also CHS Y2
Elsworth	CAM	TL3163	7,4. 23,2. 26,45
Elsworth (in Norwood) WR	YKS	??	SW,Bu29 *note*
Eltemetone	DEV	??	16,149
Eltham	KEN	TQ4274	5,30
Eltisley	CAM	TL2759	16,1
Elton (near Frodsham)	CHS	SJ4575	1,4
Elton	DBY	SK2261	6,4
Elton	HEF	SO4570	9,5
Elton HUN	HUN	TL0893	6,13
Elton HUN	NTH		6,9. 9,3
Elton	NTT	SK7638	9,110
Elvaston	DBY	SK4132	9,1
Elveden	SFK	TL8279	5,3. 14,20. 25,34. 26,3
Elvedon	BDF	TL0666	44,4
Elvelege	LEC	??	40,10
Elvetham	HAM	SU7856	9,2
Elvington ER	YKS	SE7047	13E14. CE29. SE,P7
Elwicks WR	YKS	SE4459	SW,Bu6
Elworth	DOR	SY5984	34,13
Elworthy	SOM	ST0834	25,33
Ely CAM	CAM	TL5480	5,57. 5,49-50
Ely CAM	SFK		25,36
Ely Hundreds	CAM	—	Appx P
Emanuel [Wood]	ESS	TL5341	21,10. 30,47
Embelle: see Emble SOM			
Ember [Court]: see *Immerworth* SRY			
Emberton	BKM	SP8849	5,21. 53,8
Emble	SOM	ST1133	21,46 (erroneously Embelle)
Embley	HAM	SU3220	39,5
Emborough	SOM	ST6151	5,61
Embsay WR	YKS	SE0053	1W73. SW,Cr1
Emley WR	YKS	SE2413	1Y15. SW,Ag5
Emmington	OXF	SP7402	23,2
Empingham RUT	NTH		35,9. 46,4-5
Empingham RUT	RUT	SK9508	EN12;14-15
Empshott	HAM	SU7531	62,1
Emstrey	SHR	SJ5210	3b,3-4
Enborne	BRK	SU4365	26,2. 27,1. 34,4. 45,1
Enderby	LEC	SP5399	C11. 13,39
[Bag] Enderby	LIN	TF3472	4,66. 28,33;38-39
[Mavis] Enderby	LIN	TF3666	3,21. 14,70. 29,30
[Wood] Enderby	LIN	TF2764	1,103. 38,7
Endon	STS	SJ9253	1,61
Enfield	MDX	TQ3296	9,9
Enford	WIL	SU1351	2,10
Englebi (= Barwick in Ingleby Barwick) NR	YKS	NZ4314	4N3 *note*. SN,L35
Englebi: see also Ingleby [Hill] NR	YKS		
Englebourne	DEV	SX7756	16,175. 20,17
Englefield	BRK	SU6272	22,1;4
Englishcombe	SOM	ST7162	5,44
Enham [Alamein]	HAM	SU3649	69,27-28

Enmore	SOM	ST2335	21,74
Enson	STS	SJ9428	1,43
Enstone	OXF	SP3725	11,1
Enville	STS	SO8286	12,10
Epcombs	HRT	TL3012	42,10
Epperstone	NTT	SK6548	9,73. 14,5
Epping (in Harlow Hundred)	ESS	TL4502	21,1
Epping (in Waltham Hundred)	ESS	TL4502	8,1. 37,9
Eppleby NR	YKS	NZ1713	6N1. SN,CtA4
Epsom	SRY	TQ2060	8,9
Epworth	LIN	SE7803	63,5;9;11
Erbistock FLN	CHS	SJ3542	22,2
[Childs] Ercall	SHR	SJ6625	4,3,23
[High] Ercall	SHR	SJ5917	4,1,21
Erdington	WAR	SP1191	27,3
Eresby	LIN	TF3965	3,22-23
Eriswell	SFK	TL7278	28,1
Ermington	DEV	SX6353	1,23. 15,67
Erpingham	NFK	TG1931	9,176. 17,29. 30,6. 36,1. 66,103
Erringham	SSX	TQ2007	13,4
Eruestuna	SFK	??	31,46
Erwarton	SFK	TM2234	25,63;68
Eryholme NR	YKS	NZ3209	6N1. SN,CtA2
Eschetune	HAM	??	43,6
Escrick ER	YKS	SE6342	6E1. SE,P5
Esher	SRY	TQ1364	5,25. 8,7-8;16. 10,1. 35,1
Eshingtons NR	YKS	SE0187	6N85
Eshton WR	YKS	SD9356	30W33
Eskdaleside NR	YKS	NZ8607	31N10 *note*
Eske ER	YKS	TA0543	2E21 *note*. SE,Th14
Essebeare	DEV	SS8015	42,19
Essella	KEN	??	9,5
Essendine RUT	NTH		5,3
Essendine RUT	RUT	TF0412	EN8
Esseorda	DEV	??	*Note to 44*
Essington STS	STS	SJ9603	12,22
Essington STS	WAR		27,6
E(le)stolf (in Brigham) ER	YKS	??	1Y11 *note*. SE,Tu6
Estolf: see *E(le)stolf* (in Brigham) ER			
YKS			
Eston NR	YKS	NZ5518	5N24. SN,L24
Estone	SHR	??	4,25,4
Estone: see Ectone YKS			
Etchilhampton	WIL	SU0460	24,3. 25,4. 67,49
Etchingwood	SSX	TQ5022	9,54
Eterstorp (in Gristhorpe) NR	YKS	??	1Y3 *note*. SN,D4
Etharin IOW	HAM	??	1,W17
Etherdwick ER	YKS	TA2337	14E2 *note*. SE,Hol6
Ethereg	SFK	??	4,42
Etloe	GLS	SO6705	1,13
Eton	BKM	SU9677	29,2
[Little] Eton (in Pitchford)	SHR	SJ5204	3f,1
Ettingshall	STS	SO9396	12,18
Ettington	WAR	SP2649	17,65. 18,10. 19,4. 44,13
Etton ER	YKS	SE9843	2E6. 5E34. 23E6. SE, Sn5-6
Etwall	DBY	SK2732	6,98. 9,2
Eudon	SHR	SO6888	4,3,61. 4,11,5
Euston	SFK	TL8978	14,98. 68,5
Evebentone	SSX	??	9,108
Evedon (in Ashwardhurne Hundred)	LIN	TF0947	1,2. 7,50. 26,52. 67,4
Evedon (in Flaxwell Hundred)	LIN	TF0947	3,36;38. 64,10

Evegate	KEN	TR0638	9,53
Eveleigh (in Broad Clyst)	DEV	??	49,3
Evenley	NTH	SP5835	18,64-65. 21,5. 39,8;10-11
Evenlode GLS	GLS	SP2229	E28-29. EvA122. EvC41. EvN5. WoB7. WoC6
Evenlode GLS	WOR		2,43-44
Evercreech	SOM	ST6438	6,10
Everdon	NTH	SP5957	2,10
Everingham ER	YKS	SE8042	2B9. SE,P3
Everley NR	YKS	SE9788	13N13. SN,D8
[Great and Little] Eversden	CAM	TL3653	14,46. 26,37. 27,1. 31,7
		TL3753	
Evershaw	BKM	SP6338	57,6
Eversholt	BDF	SP9933	2,2. 23.19. 57,1
Eversley	HAM	SU7762	8,1
Eversy (near Combe Hey)	SOM	ST7059	7,14
Everthorpe ER	YKS	SE9031	SE,C2 *note*
Everton HUN	BDF		53,30
Everton HUN	HUN	TL2051	24,1
Everton	NTT	SK6991	5,8. 9,117;124
Evesbatch	HEF	SO6848	10,34
Evesham	WOR	SP0343	10,1. 26,15-17
Evington	GLS	SO8726	19,2
Evington	LEC	SK6202	13,50. 17,6
Ewell	SRY	TQ2162	1,9
[Temple] Ewell	KEN	TR2844	5,185;192. 9,35-36
Ewelme OXF	BRK		B9
Ewelme OXF	OXF	SU6491	20,9. 31,1. 38,2. 58,8. EBe3
Ewerby	LIN	TF1247	7,45. 24,38. 45,4. 67,1-4. CK,30
Ewhurst	HAM	SU5756	23,21
Ewhurst	SSX	TQ7924	9,120
Ewias Lacy: see Longtown HEF			
Ewyas [Harold]	HEF	SO3828	2,2. 10,1. 13,2. 19,1
Exbourne	DEV	SS6002	16,18. 39,5
Exbury	HAM	SU4200	NF9,8
Exceat	SSX	TV5299	10,24-25;29
[Nether] Exe	DEV	SS9300	3,69
[Up] Exe	DEV	SS9402	3,70
Exelby NR	YKS	SE2987	6N151. SN,CtA41
Exeter	DEV	SX9292	C1-7. 1,40. 2,1;4. 3,1-2. 5,15. 9,2. 15,1. 16,1;58. 17,1;2. 19,1. 23,27. 30,4. 32,6. 34,58. 35,31. 36,27. 39,22. 43,6. 47,15
Exford	SOM	SS8538	21,58-59;68. 25,19-20
Exhall	WAR	SP1055	28,12
Exminster	DEV	SX9487	1,4. 19,8. 22,1
Exning SFK	CAM		1,12. 14,68. Appx A
Exning SFK	SFK	TL6265	EC1-EC2
Exton	HAM	SU6121	3,11
Exton RUT	LIN		56,17
Exton RUT	RUT	SK9211	R12. ELc14
Exton	SOM	SS9233	5,5
Exwick	DEV	SX9094	16,109
Eyam	DBY	SK2176	1,33
Eycot	GLS	SP0010	3,3-4. EvK80. WoA1. WoB16
Eydon	NTH	SP5450	23,14
Eye SFK	NFK		7,21
Eye SFK	SFK	TM1473	6,71;191;204. 18,1. 76,23. ENf3
Eyelid	SSX	TQ7623	9,27-29
Eyeworth	BDF	TL2445	25,10. 55,5
Eyeworth	HAM	SU2214	1,33

Eyford	GLS	SP1424	66,3
Eynesbury HUN	CAM		32,10
Eynesbury HUN	HUN	TL1859	20,5;6. 28,1
Eynsford	KEN	TQ5465	2,29
Eynsford Hundred NFK	SFK	—	56,6
Eynsham	OXF	SP4309	6,6
Eysey	WIL	SU1194	18,2
Eythorne	KEN	TR2749	*3,18*
Eyton FLN	CHS	SJ3545	B6. 16,2
Eyton	HEF	SO4761	1,10c
Eyton (in Alberbury)	SHR	SJ3713	4,4,9. 4,27,16
Eyton (in Baschurch)	SHR	SJ4422	4,6,4
Eyton [on Severn]	SHR	SJ5706	3b,2
Eyton [upon the Weald Moors]	SHR	SJ6514	4,14,18

F

Faccombe	HAM	SU3958	1,46
Faceby NR	YKS	NZ4903	1N38. 31N5 *note*. SN,L44
Facheduna	SFK	??	25,58. 74,2
Fadmoor NR	YKS	SE6789	5N46. SN,Ma17
Faintree	SHR	SO6689	4,16,2
Fairbourne	KEN	TQ8651	5,64;87
Fairburn WR	YKS	SE4727	9W28. SW,BA10
Fairford	GLS	SP1500	1,50
Fairlight (near East Grinstead)	SSX	TQ4138	10,108
Fairoak	SOM	ST8049	21,87
Fairstead	ESS	TL7616	34,7
Fakenham	NFK	TF9129	1,2;15-18;29;40. 8,138. 10,54. 21,22
[Great] Fakenham	SFK	TL8976	14,96. 37,1
[Little] Fakenham	SFK	TL9176	14,97
Faldingworth	LIN	TF0684	26,3;24. 49,1. 53,1
Falkenham	SFK	TM2939	7,76;86;98. 39,3
Falmer	SSX	TQ3508	12,7;16-17
Falsgrave NR	YKS	TA0287	1Y3. 5N32. 13N13. SN,D1
[North] Fambridge	ESS	TQ8597	71,2
[South] Fambridge	ESS	TQ8695	79,1
Fangfoss ER	YKS	SE7653	1Y10. SE,P8
Fanscombe	KEN	TR0647	5,163. 9,51
Fanton [Hall]	ESS	TQ7691	6,2;4. 9,3
Fardel	DEV	SX6157	1,23. 15,67
Fareham	HAM	SU5806	2,15
Farforth	LIN	TF3178	13,31-32
Faringdon	BRK	SU2895	1,34
Farleigh	DEV	SX7553	1,15
Farleigh	SRY	TQ3760	19,8
[East] Farleigh	KEN	TQ7353	3,5
Farleigh [Hungerford]	SOM	ST8057	21,88
[Monkton] Farleigh	WIL	ST8065	67,5;16
Farleigh [Wallop]	HAM	SU6246	69,14
[West] Farleigh	KEN	TQ7153	5,95
Farleton LAN	YKS	SD5767	1L5. See also CHS Y6
Farleton WES	YKS	SD5381	30W40. See also CHS Y13
Farley	DBY	SK2962	1,11
Farley	SHR	SJ3807	4,4,13
Farley	STS	SK0644	1,53
Farley	SFK	TL7353	25,13
Farley [Chamberlayne]	HAM	SU3927	54,1-2
Farlington NR	YKS	SE6167	5N59. SN,B8
Farlow SHR	HEF		1,10a. E9
Farlow SHR	SHR	SO6480	4,28,5. E3
Farmanby (in Thornton Dale) NR	YKS	??	1Y4 *note*. SN,D12
Farmborough	SOM	ST6660	5,18
Farmcote	GLS	SP0629	34,7
Farmington	GLS	SP1315	2,8. EvM3
Farnborough	BRK	SU4381	7,33
Farnborough	HAM	SU8754	3,8
Farnborough	WAR	SP4349	2,1
Farncombe	SRY	SU9745	5,3

Farndish BDF	BDF	SP9263	42,1. 43,1
Farndish BDF	NTH		35,1f
Farndon	CHS	SJ4154	B3. 14,1
Farndon	NTT	SK7651	6,1
[East] Farndon	NTH	SP7185	8,8. 18,18. 56,28. 60,5
[West] Farndon	NTH	SP5251	18,32. 23,1
Farnham	DOR	ST9515	19,11. 49,8;17. 54,11. 55,21
Farnham	ESS	TL4824	28,10. 32,21. 90,25;42
Farnham	SFK	TM3659	6,50;135. 7,139
Farnham	SRY	SU8446	3,1
Farnham WR	YKS	SE3460	1Y19. 28W7. SW,Bu15
Farnham [Royal]	BKM	SU9683	38,1
Farnhill WR	YKS	SE0046	1W60
Farningham	KEN	TQ5466	2,28. 5,10;13;15
Farnley (in Armley) WR	YKS	SE2532	SW,M13 note
Farnley (near Otley) WR	YKS	SE2148	2W4. SW,Sk2
Farnley [Tyas] WR	YKS	SE1612	9W106. SW,Ag7
Farnsfield	NTT	SK6456	1,22. 11,17
Farringdon	DEV	SY0191	15,21. 49,5
[Lower and Upper] Farringdon	HAM	SU7035	5,1
		SU7135	
Farrington [Gurney]	SOM	ST6255	5,58
Farsley WR	YKS	SE2135	9W126 note. SW,M4
Farthinghoe	NTH	SP5339	21,6
Farthingloe	KEN	TR2940	M22
Farthingstone	NTH	SP6154	18,57;75
Farway	DEV	SY1895	3,85. 25,23
Farwood	DEV	SY2095	3,85 note. 21,15
Fastochesfelde	WOR	??	1,2
Fauld	STS	SK1828	10,6-7
Faulkbourne	ESS	TL8016	28,2
Faversham	KEN	TR0161	1,4
Fawkham	KEN	TQ5968	4,3
Fawler	BRK	SU3188	7,38
Fawley	BKM	SU7586	14,4
Fawley	HAM	SU4503	3,19. NF2,1
Fawley	BRK	SU3981	16,3
[South] Fawley	BRK	SU3980	1,30
Fawsley	NTH	SP5656	1,9. 2,5;10. 17,2. 18,30;57-58;75
Fawton	CON	SX1668	5,1,1
Faxton	NTH	SP7875	1,17
Fearby NR	YKS	SE1981	6N116. SN,CtA33
Featherstone	STS	SJ9305	7,16
Featherstone WR	YKS	SE4222	9W54. SW,O11
?Fech	SHR	SJ3425	6,3 note
Feckenham WOR	HEF		1,40;41. E7
Feckenham WOR	WOR	SP0061	X2. E2;3
Feering	ESS	TL8720	6,8. 90,17. B3k
Felbrigg	NFK	TG2039	9,146
Felesmere	SSX	??	10,98
Felixkirk: see Fridebi YKS			
Felliscliffe WR	YKS	SE2356	1Y18 note. SW,Bu30
Felmersham	BDF	SP9957	48,2. 53,11
Felmingham	NFK	TG2529	1,58. 9,179. 17,39
Felpham	SSX	SZ9599	8a,1
Felsham	SFK	TL9457	14,58
Felsted	ESS	TL6720	15,1. 72,2. 73,1
Feltham	MDX	TQ1073	8,3-4
Felthorpe	NFK	TG1617	1,56. 4,34. 20,26. 21,31. 25,9
Felton	HEF	SO5748	6,6
Felton [Butler]	SHR	SJ3917	4,21,10

[West] Felton	SHR	SJ3425	4,3,41
Feltwell	NFK	TL7190	1,210. 8,35;37 and note;39;40.
			15,7;29
Fenacre	DEV	ST0617	25,12
Fenby	LIN	TF2699	12,25
Fencote	HEF	SO5959	1,14
[Great] Fencote NR	YKS	SE2893	6N56 note. SN,CtA21
[Little] Fencote NR	YKS	SE2893	6N56 note. SN,CtA21
Fenemere	SHR	SJ4422	4,28,3
Feniton	DEV	SY1099	15,34
Fenstead	SFK	TL8050	43,1
Fenton	DBY	SK1945	6,56
Fenton	NTT	SK7983	1,33. 9,112-113
Fenton	STS	SJ8944	17,21
[Church and Little] Fenton WR	YKS	SE5136	9W23 note. SW,BA6
		SE5235	
Ferding	DEV	??	39,3
Fernhill (in Shaugh)	DEV	SX5660	17,98
Fernhill	HAM	SZ2496	NF3,16
Fernhill	HEF	SO3949	10,49
Fernworthy	DEV	SX5187	*16,7*
Ferrensby WR	YKS	SE3660	1Y19. SW,Bu16
[North] Ferriby ER	YKS	SE9825	5E3. 15E2. SE,He4
[South] Ferriby	LIN	SE9820	23,1. 24,14. CN,1
Ferring	SSX	TQ0902	3,4
Fersfield	NFK	TM0682	1,175-177;179;181. 66,61
Fetcham	SRY	TQ1455	1,10. 5,22. 36,3
Fewston WR	YKS	SE1954	1Y19. SW,Bu29
Fickenappletree: see *Thickenappletree*			
WOR			
Fiddington	GLS	SO9230	1,24;31
Fiddington	SOM	ST2140	22,8
Fifehead [Magdalen]	DOR	ST7821	27,1
Fifehead [Neville]	DOR	ST7610	40,6
Fifehead [St Quintin]	DOR	ST7710	19,9
Fifield	OXF	SP2318	24,4
Fifield [Bavant]	WIL	SU0125	26,14;23
Figheldean	WIL	SU1547	67,61
Filby	NFK	TG4613	8,13. 9,91. 17,61. 19,37. 55,2.
			66,84
Filey ER	YKS	TA1181	1Y3. SN,D4
Filleigh	DEV	SS6628	1,5. 16,80
Fillingham	LIN	SK9485	16,43. 26,13;23-24. 68,31
Fillongley	WAR	SP2887	5,1. 6,1. 23,2. 44,10
Filsham	SSX	TQ7809	8,10. 9,14
[Great and Little] Finborough	SFK	TM0157	1,64. 5,4. 21,14. 29, 1. 76,16
		TM1849	
Fincham	NFK	TF6806	8,16;19. 13,2. 14,1. 15,2. 21,1.
			31,20. 66,1;35;51
Finchampstead	BRK	SU7963	1,19
Finchingfield	ESS	TL6832	1,12. 20,30-31. 21,4;7.
			23,5;9;13;22. 90,50
Findern	DBY	SK3030	3,1
Findon	SSX	TQ1208	13,7;11
Finedon	NTH	SP9172	1,32. 4,13
Finesford(a)/Finlesford(a)	SFK	TM1849	21,70. 29,14. 32,31. 38,24. 41,18
(in Witnesham)			
Fingall NR	YKS	SE1889	6N132. SN,CtA37
Finglesham	KEN	TR3353	2,39
Fingrith [Hall]	ESS	TL6003	1,21-22
Finley	HAM	SU5757	64,1

Finmere OXF	NTH	4,30
Finmere OXF	OXF	SP6332	7,16. EN1
Finningham	SFK	TM0669	6,59;209;231. 14,131;135. 66,15
Finningley	NTT	SK6799	18,3
Firby ER	YKS	SE7466	31E8 *note*
Firby NR	YKS	SE2686	6N121 *note*. SN, CtA35
[Frog] Firle	SSX	TQ5101	10,44;49. 12,10
[West] Firle	SSX	TQ4707	9,38;56;71;75;91;102. 10,22
[West] Firsby	LIN	SK9985	4,11-12
Fishbourne	SSX	SU8404	11,39
Fisherton [Anger]	WIL	SU1329	22,6
Fisherton [de la Mere]	WIL	SU0038	44,1
Fishlake WR	YKS	SE6513	12W1;23. CW13
Fishley	NFK	TG3911	1,153-154. 17,1. 19,26
Fishtoft: see [Fish] Toft LIN			
Fishwick LAN	YKS	SD5629	1L1 *note*. See also CHS Y2
Fiskerton	LIN	TF0472	8,1-3. 26,6
Fiskerton	NTT	SK7351	11,15;20-21
Fitling ER	YKS	TA2533	14E4. SE,Hol8
Fittleton	WIL	SU1449	42,8
Fitz	SHR	SJ4417	4,20,15
Fivehead	SOM	ST3522	21,70
Fixby WR	YKS	SE1319	SW,M12 *note*
Fladbury	WOR	SO9946	2,15
Flagg	DBY	SK1368	1,28
Flamborough ER	YKS	TA2270	4E1. 29E6. SE,Hu1
Flamstead	HRT	TL0714	22,1
Flasby WR	YKS	SD9456	30W7
Flashbrook	STS	SJ7425	2,11
Flawborough	NTT	SK7842	9,2. 11,1;3;5
Flaxby WR	YKS	SE3957	24W10. SW,Bu11
Flaxton NR	YKS	SE6762	1N102. 2N11. 6N162. 23N33. SN,B17
Fleckney	LEC	SP6493	19,10;12
Flecknoe	WAR	SP5163	3,7. 17,29;32. 44,11-12
Fledborough	NTT	SK8172	6,13
Fleet	DOR	SY6380	1,11. 24,3
Fleet	KEN	TR3060	2,21
Fleet	LIN	TF3823	1,34. 12,83
[Kirkby] Fleetham NR	YKS	SE2894	6N26-27 *note*. 6N31;56. SN,CtA20
Flempton	SFK	TL8169	14,12
Flendish Hundred	CAM	—	Appx E
Fletching	SSX	TQ4223	10,112-113
Flete	DEV	SX6251	28,11
[Old] Fletton	HUN	TL1996	8,1. D28
Flexmore	HRT	TL1522	1,15. 36,17
Flintham	NTT	SK7446	1,61. 9,108-109. 11,25
Flinton ER	YKS	TA2236	2E30. 14E2. SE,Mid1. SE,Hol6
Flitcham	NFK	TF7226	2,4. 8,32. 9,4;6. 66,71
Flitton	BDF	TL0535	30,1
Flitwick	BDF	TL0334	25,2. 41,2
Flixborough	LIN	SE8715	32,17
Flixton (near Bungay)	SFK	TM3187	19,15;17. 53,5
Flixton (near Lowestoft)	SFK	TM5195	1,47;50. 19,21
Flixton ER	YKS	TA0479	1Y11. 1E17. SE,Hu8
Flockthorpe	NFK	TG0304	1,12-13;87. 4,15
Flockton WR	YKS	SE2314	9W100 *note*. SW,Ag4 *note*
Flordon	NFK	TM1897	2,12. 4,54. 9,97;186;190;200;204. 12,38
Flore	NTH	SP6459	18,47. 34,1. 35,3f. 45,6. 48,14

[East and West] Flotmanby ER	YKS	TA0779	2E3 *note.* 20E3. SE,Tu2-3
Flowergate NR	YKS	NZ8911	4N1 *note.* SN,L4
Flowton	SFK	TM0846	7,62. 25,55. 29,4
Floyers Hayes: see *[Floyers] Hayes* DEV			
Fobbing	ESS	TQ7183	20,1
Fockbury	WOR	SO9472	1,1a
Fodderstone	NFK	TF6509	15,2. 21,8. 66,15
Foddington	SOM	ST5829	19,67. 45,13;15
Foggathorpe ER	YKS	SE7537	5E8. 15E6. 21E8. SE,C6-7
Foleshill	WAR	SP3582	15,5
Folkestone	KEN	TR2236	5,128
Folkesworth	HUN	TL1489	12,1
Folkingham	LIN	TF0733	8,9. 18,19. 24,82-84. 57,40
Folkington	SSX	TQ5503	10,42
Folkton ER	YKS	TA0579	1E25. SE,Tu4
Follaton	DEV	SX7860	17,58
Fonaby	LIN	TA1103	1,69
Fonthill [Bishop]	WIL	ST9332	2,2
Fonthill [Gifford]	WIL	ST9231	47,1
Fontmell [Magna]	DOR	ST8616	19,4
Footland	SSX	TQ7720	9,128
Forcett NR	YKS	NZ1712	6N1. SN,CtA3
Ford (in Chivelstone)	DEV	SX7840	17,56
Ford (in Musbury)	DEV	??	16,166
Ford	HEF	SO5155	1,21
Ford	SHR	SJ4113	4,1,16
Ford	SOM	ST1925	2,3. 19,42
Fordbottle (in Yarlside) LAN	YKS	SD2270	1L6 *note.* See also CHS Y7
Forden (Wales)	SHR	SJ2201	4,1,36
Fordham	CAM	TL6370	1,2. 14,71. 22,6. Appx A
Fordham	ESS	TL9228	22,24. 23,35. 47,3. 90,72
Fordham	NFK	TL6199	15,3. 16,2. 31,27. 66,11;46;53
Fordingbridge	HAM	SU1414	28,9
Fordington	DOR	SY6990	1,4
Fordington	LIN	TF4171	13,6
Fordley	SFK	TM4266	6,79;88;106. 7,30;34
Fordon ER	YKS	TA0475	1E22. SE,Tu3
Fordwich	KEN	TR1859	7,10
Foremark	DBY	SK3326	14,4
Forest [Hill]	OXF	SP5807	7,17
[The] Forest	HAM	??	1,23;26-35;37;38. 3,19. 15,5. 17,4. 21,4. 22,1. 23,40;49-52;65. 28,9. 45,1. 51,1. 68,11. 69,32;36;53
Formby LAN	CHS	SD3007	R1,23
Forncett [St Mary and St Peter]	NFK	TM1693 TM1692	9,98;205;223. 11,5. 66,106
Fornetorp (in Cornbrough near Farlington) NR	YKS	??	5N59 *note.* 8N5. NR SN,B8
Fornetorp (in Thwing) ER	YKS	??	1E34-35 *note.* SE,Bt7
Fornham [All Saints]	SFK	TL8367	14,9
Fornham [St Genevieve]	SFK	TL8368	14,53
Fornham [St Martin]	SFK	TL8566	14,50
Fors [Abbey] NR	YKS	SD9390	6N78 *note.* SN,CtA25
Forsbrook	STS	SJ9641	1,60
Forston	DOR	SY6695	26,5;8-11. 53,1
Forthampton GLS	GLS	SO8532	1,35. E1
Forthampton GLS	HEF		1,43. E3
Forton	SHR	SJ4216	4,8,14
Forton LAN	YKS	SD4851	1L1. See CHS Y2
Fosbury	WIL	SU3158	42,2-3
Foscot	OXF	SP2421	32,3

Foscote: see Foxcote BKM			
Fosham ER	YKS	TA2038	14E11. SE,Hol17
Foston	DBY	SK1831	6,26
Foston	LEC	SP6095	25,1
Foston	LIN	SK8542	12,50-51
Foston NR	YKS	SE6965	6N162. SN,B18
Foston [on the Wolds] ER	YKS	TA1055	13E15. SE,Tu6
Fostun(e) (in Humbleton) ER	YKS	??	14E2 note. SE,Hol6
Fotherby	LIN	TF3191	3,20. 18,9. 22,33. CN,29
Fotheringhay	NTH	TL0593	56,7
Fouchers	ESS	TQ6391	37,19
Foulden	NFK	TL7699	4,3. 8,90. 25,14
Foulsham	NFK	TG0324	1,52;185-186. 4,28. 5,4. 17,20. 19,32. 25,1-2;4;6;8. 32,1. 20. 34,20. 39,2
Foulton	ESS	TM2229	24,65. 41,10
Fouswardine (in Sidbury)	SHR	SO6785	4,3,67
Fovant	WIL	SU0029	13,19
Fowlmere	CAM	TL4245	14,20. 21,3. Appx H
Fownhope	HEF	SO5834	29,2
Foxcote	BKM	SP7135	4,32
Foxcote	GLS	SP0118	3,5. WoA2. WoB18
Foxcote	SOM	ST7155	5,42
Foxcotte	HAM	SU3447	45,3
Foxearth	ESS	TL8344	23,17
Foxhall	SFK	TM2243	21,60
Foxholes ER	YKS	TA0173	1Y11. 31E1. SE,Hu8 Hu3
Foxlease: see Coxlease HAM			
Foxley	NFK	TG0321	4,31
Foxley	NTH	SP6451	18,39
Foxley	WIL	ST8985	45,1
Foxton	CAM	TL4148	11,1. 22,4-5
Foxton	LEC	SP7090	1,4. 40,16
Foxton (in Crathorne) NR	YKS	NZ4508	5N28. 31N5. SN,L39
Foxton (in Thimbleby) NR	YKS	SE4296	3Y14. SN,A6
Fradswell	STS	SJ9931	2,8
Fraisthorpe ER	YKS	TA1561	5E48. 23E13. 29E10 SE,Hu4
Framingham [Earl and Pigot]	NFK	TG2702 TG2703	1,49. 2,7. 9,30;33;41; 51;113;161. 12,9
Framlingham	SFK	TM2863	4,12;42. 6,264;264;266;289. 19,11. 43,6
Frampton	DOR	SY6295	1,2. 17,1
Frampton	GLS	SP0133	11,4;5 note
Frampton	LIN	TF3239	12,70. 57,28
Frampton [Cotterell]	GLS	ST6681	58,4
Frampton [Mansell]	GLS	SO9202	46,3
Frampton [on Severn]	GLS	SO7507	54,1
Framsden	SFK	TM2059	4,1
Franche	WOR	SO8278	1.2
Frankley	WOR	SO9980	23,3
Frankton	WAR	SP4270	12,2. 16,29
[English] Frankton	SHR	SJ4529	4,3,49
Frankwell	SSX	TQ6614	9,8
[Great and Little] Fransham	NFK	TF8913 TF9012	8,66;68. 22,11
Frating	ESS	TM0822	20,63. 34,34
Fratton	HAM	SU6500	34,1
Freckenham	SFK	TL6671	20,1
Freckleton LAN	YKS	SD4229	1L1. See also CHS Y2
Freeby	LEC	SK8020	29,3
Freefolk	HAM	SU4948	3,5

Freeford	STS	SK1307	2,22
Freethorpe	NFK	TG4005	1,97. 10,71. 66,101
Fremington	DEV	SS5132	3,6
Fremington NR	YKS	SE0499	6N74. SN,CtA25
Frenze	NFK	TM1380	7,11. 14,28
Freshford	SOM	ST7860	5,35
Freshwater IOW	HAM	SZ3486	1,5. 7,22
Fressingfield	SFK	TM2677	6,207 *note*
Freston	SFK	TM1739	25,76. 27,12
Fretherne	GLS	SO7309	67,7
Frettenham	NFK	TG2418	26,1;4
Frickley WR	YKS	SE4607	9W34 *note*. 10W33. SW,Sf28;37
Fridaythorpe ER	YKS	SE8759	1E55. 2B11. 26E4 *note*. 26E6. SE,Ac10-11
Fridebi (= Felixkirk) NR	YKS	SE4684	23N11-12 *note*
Friesthorpe	LIN	TF0783	26,13
Frieston	LIN	SK9347	37,2
Frieston Hundred	LIN	TF3743	57,39
Frilford	BRK	SU4397	7,18
Frilsham	BRK	SU5373	21,4
Frindsbury	KEN	TQ7469	4,13;15
Fring	NFK	TF7334	5,3. 8,49. 10,20
Fringford	OXF	SP6028	7,14-15
Frinsted	KEN	TQ8957	5,66
Frinton	ESS	TM2319	20,66. 30,19
Frisby	LEC	SK7001	13,54
Frisby [on-the-Wreak]	LEC	SK6917	1,3. 43,1´
Friskney	LIN	TF4655	68,11
Fristling	ESS	TL6700	9,12
Frith	CHS	SJ5948	8,38
Frithelstock	DEV	SS4619	15,10
Fritton	NFK	TM2292	7,20-21. 9,98;161;208. 14,40. 31,9. 35,16. 66,60
Fritton	SFK	TG4700	1,49;58
Fritwell	OXF	SP5229	7,11. 59,17
Frizenham	DEV	SS4718	15,32
Frocester	GLS	SO7803	10,2
Frodesley	SHR	SJ5101	4,27,11
[North] Frodingham ER	YKS	TA0953	14E25. SE,Hol21
Frodsham	CHS	SJ5177	1,8
Frolesworth	LEC	SP5090	9,2. 13,2. 17,3. 40,4
Frome	DOR	??	1,4
Frome	SOM	ST7747	1,8-9;31. 16,1
Frome [Billet]	DOR	SY7290	57,1
[Bishop's] Frome	HEF	SO6648	2,21. 10,67
[Canon] Frome	HEF	SO6543	10,33
[Castle] Frome	HEF	SO6645	10,30
[Halmonds] Frome	HEF	SO6747	10,29
[Priors] Frome	HEF	SO5739	2,58. 13,1. 26,1
Frome [St Quintin]	DOR	ST5902	1,15
Frome [Vauchurch]	DOR	SY5996	34,10
Frome [Whitfield]	DOR	SY6991	55,2
Frostenden	SFK	TM4781	33,6
Frowick [Hall]	ESS	TM1218	20,63
Froxton	CON	SX2599	6,1
[Lower and Upper] Froyle	HAM	SU7644 SU7542	14,2
Frustfield (near Alderstone)	WIL	SU2423	27,26. 46,1. 67,71;93
Fryerning	ESS	TL6300	32,30-31;34
[Ferry] Fryston WR	YKS	SE4824	9W57 *note*. SW,O10
[Water] Fryston WR	YKS	SE4626	9W56 *note*. SW,O12

Fryton NR	YKS	SE6875	5N51. 23N24. SN,Ma24
Fulbeck	LIN	SK9450	12,48
Fulbourn	CAM	TL5256	1,14. 5,12. 14,1. 22,1. 35,1. Appx E
Fulbrook (now Greenfield) FLN	CHS	SJ1977	FT1,7
Fulbrook	OXF	SP2513	29,5
Fulbrook	WAR	SP2560	16,14
Fulford	STS	SJ9538	1,40
[Gate] Fulford ER	YKS	SE6049	C28 note. 6W5 note. SN,Y4
[Great] Fulford	DEV	SX7991	16,132
[Water] Fulford ER	YKS	SE6048	C28 note. 6E1. SE,Wa6-7
Fulham	MDX	TQ2475	3,12-14
Fulking	SSX	TQ2411	12,29
Fullerton	HAM	SU3739	6,14
Fulletby	LIN	TF2973	3,53-54. 13,39-40
Fullready	WAR	SP2846	17,65
Fulmodeston	NFK	TF9930	8,103
Fulnetby	LIN	TF0979	34,20
Fulsby	LIN	TF2460	1,95;98
Fulscot	BRK	SU5488	49,2
Fulstone WR	YKS	SE1709	SW,Ag14 note
Fulstow	LIN	TF3297	3,6. 12,19. 13,21. 38,14. CN,21-22
Fulwell	OXF	SP6234	28,14
Fundenhall	NFK	TM1596	6,6. 9,220;225
Funtley and [Great] Funtley	HAM	SU5608 SU5508	18,2. 28,8. 66,1
Fursham	DEV	SX7193	16,93
Fursnewth	CON	SX2267	4,17
Furtho	NTH	SP7743	18,34;55-56
Furze (in West Buckland)	DEV	SS6433	20,2
Fyfield	BRK	SU4298	21,15;16
Fyfield	ESS	TL5706	20,49-50. 40,6-7
Fyfield	HAM	SU2946	35,9
Fyfield	WIL	SU1468	2,3
Fyling [Old Hall] NR	YKS	NZ9402	4N1 note. 13N1. CN1. SN,L1

Fyling Thorpe: see [Fyling] Thorpe YKS

G

Gaddesby	LEC	SK6813	1,3. 40,34–35. 43,1
[Great] Gaddesden	HRT	TL0211	32,1
[Little] Gaddesden	HRT	SP9913	5,12
[The] Gaer (alias Thornbury, in Wales)	SHR	SO2099	4,1,36
Gailey	STS	SJ9110	11,59
Gainsborough	LIN	SK8190	63,2
Gainsthorpe	LIN	SE9501	14,27
Galby	LEC	SK6901	1,4. 13,53
Galmpton (in Churston Ferrers)	DEV	SX8856	33,2
Galmpton (in South Huish)	DEV	SX6940	17,37
Galowras	CON	SW7944	5,6,10
Galsworthy	DEV	SS3916	15,12
Galton	DOR	SY7785	56,38. 57,17
Gamlingay	CAM	TL2452	25,9. 34,1. 38,4
Gamston (near Elkesley)	NTT	SK7176	9,9. 16,1-2
Gamston (near West Bridgford)	NTT	SK6037	10,14
Gangsdown	OXF	SU6787	35,25
Ganstead ER	YKS	TA1434	14E45. SE,Hol25
Ganthorpe (in Great Ponton)	LIN	SK9229	56,8
Ganthorpe NR	YKS	SE6870	1N88. 5N54. 31N8 note. SN,B4-5
Ganton ER	YKS	SE9977	1Y11. SE,Bt9
Gappah	DEV	SX8677	34,44
Gapton	SFK	TG5105	1,36;55
Gara	KEN	??	D24
?Garah	CON	SW6718	1,1
Garboldisham	NFK	TM0081	1,145. *23,16*
Gardham ER	YKS	SE9441	3Y1 note. SE,Sn8
Gardham: see also *Newton* ER, YKS			
Garford	BRK	SU4296	7,21
Garforth WR	YKS	SE4033	9W1-2. SW,Sk4-5
Gargrave WR	YKS	SD9353	1W73. 30W7;13. SW,Cr3
Garrington	KEN	TR2056	7,6
Garriston NR	YKS	SE1592	6N108. SN,CtA31
Garrowby [Hall] ER	YKS	SE7957	29E19 note. 31E6. SE,Ac4-5
Garsdon	WIL	ST9687	8,10
Garsington	OXF	SP5802	9,7-8. 35,29
Garstang LAN	YKS	SD4945	1L1. See also CHS Y2
[East] Garston	BRK	SU3676	38,3
Garthorpe	LIN	SE8419	63,18-21;23-26
Garton ER	YKS	TA2735	14E9. SE,Hol14
Garton [on the Wolds] ER	YKS	SE9859	2E15. 5N1a. 5E55-56. SE,Tu8
Garveston	NFK	TG0207	13,19
Garway	HEF	SO4522	1,50
Gasthorpe	NFK	TL9881	1,146. 14,9
Gatcombe	DEV	SY2291	51,13
Gatcombe IOW	HAM	SZ4885	6,4
Gategram	WIL	??	67,84
Gatehampton	OXF	SU6079	22,2. 35,1
Gateley	NFK	TF9624	10,53. 23,17. 34,6
Gatenby NR	YKS	SE3287	6N151. SN,CtA42
Gatewood	HAM	SU4301	NF9,7

Gattertop	HEF	SO4853	1,18
Gatton	SRY	TQ2752	5,11
Gawcott	BKM	SP6831	3a,6
Gawsworth	CHS	SJ8869	1,27
Gayhurst	BKM	SP8446	4,42
Gayton	CHS	SJ2680	3,5
Gayton	NFK	TF7319	8,23-24. 18,1. 19,7. 23,13. 66,23
Gayton	NTH	SP7054	49,1 note
Gayton	STS	SJ9728	8,13
Gayton [le Wold]	LIN	TF2385	1,81-90. CS,8
Gayton Thorpe: see [Gayton] Thorpe NFK			
Gaywood	NFK	TF6320	10,2
Gear	CON	SW7224	5,2,33
Geddesduna	ESS	??	6,13
Gedding	SFK	TL9558	14,60. 26,2
Geddington	NTH	SP8983	1,13c. 8,2
Gedgrave	SFK	TM4048	3,49;51. 6,275;286. 7,132
Gedling	NTT	SK6142	9,72. 12,16-17
Gedney	LIN	TF4024	1,31-32. 12,84. CK,71
Gellilyfdy FLN	CHS	SJ1473	FT1,9
Gelston Hundred	LIN	TF9145	12,44
Gembling ER	YKS	TA1057	2E14. SE,Tu6
?Genver (in Tintagel)	CON	SX0888	5,8,10
Georgeham	DEV	SS4639	36,12
Gerlei (Malshanger)	HAM	SU5652	28,1. 32,3. 46,2
Gerleuuorde (= Kirkby Ireleth) LAN	YKS	SD2382	1L6. See also CHS Y7 (Kirkby Ireleth)
Germansweek	DEV	SX4394	16,8
Germansweek: see Week DEV			
Gestingthorpe	ESS	TL8138	23,4. 81,1
Ghigogesmersc: see *Chigogemers* YKS			
Gibsmere	NTT	SK7248	13,13
Gidcott	DEV	SS4009	28,5
[Great, Little and Steeple] Gidding	HUN	TL1183	1,6. 6,21;25. 19,15. 26,1. D22
		TL1281	
		TL1381	
Giddinge	KEN	TR2346	3,17
Gidleigh	DEV	SX6788	15,7
Giggleswick WR	YKS	SD8164	30W1
Gilcott (near Withycombe)	SOM	ST0040	21,64
Gillamoor NR	YKS	SE6890	23N20
Gilling NR	YKS	NZ1805	6N1;8;50. SN,CtA1
Gilling [East] NR	YKS	SE6176	15E17. 23N26. SN,Ma16
Gillingham DOR	DOR	ST8026	1,4. 10,1. 19,10. 33,1. 56,3-5;66. E3
Gillingham DOR	WIL		66,5
Gillingham	KEN	TQ7868	2,12. 5,88
Gillingham NFK	NFK	TM4192	1,60;239. ESf4
Gillingham NFK	SFK		1,38
Gilmorton	LEC	SP5788	16,1
Gimingham	NFK	TG2836	8,119-121
[East] Ginge	BRK	SU4486	65,10
[West] Ginge	BRK	SU4486	7,45-46
Gipton WR	YKS	SE3036	9W1 *note*. 9W15. SW,Sk4;9
Girlington [Hall] NR	YKS	NZ1213	6N1 *note*. SN,CtA5
Girsby	LIN	TF2187	2,5. 34,22
Girsby NR	YKS	NZ3508	3Y16. SN,A3
Girton	CAM	TL4262	12,4-5. 7,10. 32,34. Appx N
Girton	NTT	SK8266	6,4
Gisburn WR	YKS	SD8348	13W41. 30W4

Gisleham	SFK	TM5188	1,23. 4,37. 31,30
Gislingham	SFK	TM0771	1,11;87. 6,194;216;233. 14,44.
			31,38. 35,7-8. 66,13. 68,5
Gissing	NFK	TM1485	1,171. 7,7;13. 9,47. 14,23 *and*
			note;31-32. 66,59
Gittisham	DEV	SY1398	25,15
Givendale WR	YKS	SE3369	2W12 *note*. SW,H1
[Great] Givendale ER	YKS	SE8153	1Y10. SE,Wa5
[Little] Givendale ER	YKS	SE8253	SE,Wa5 *note*
[Nares] Gladley	BDF	SP9127	52,2
Glandford	NFK	TG0441	1,26. 25,19
Glapwell	DBY	SK4766	7,2
Glasshampton	WOR	SO7866	21,3
Glassthorpehill	NTH	SP6760	18,48. 35,3e
Glaston RUT	NTH		1,2e. 56,36
Glaston RUT	RUT	SK8900	EN2;20
Glastonbury	SOM	ST5039	8,1
Glatting	SSX	SU9714	11,24
Glatton	HUN	TL1586	9,1
Glazeley	SHR	SO7088	4,3,64
Gleadthorpe	NTT	SK5970	9,38
Gleaston LAN	YKS	SD2570	1L6. See also CHS Y7
[Great] Glemham	SFK	TM3361	3,95;102. 6,45;49-51;56. 7,144;151.
			8,82. 14,41.
			28,6. 45,2
[Little] Glemham	SFK	TM3458	3,96
Glemsford	SFK	TL8348	21,10. 34,4
[Great] Glen	LEC	SP6597	13,58-59
Glendon	NTH	SP8481	1,15c. 14,3
Glenfield	LEC	SK5306	13,5;40
Glentham	LIN	TF0090	4,7;9. 7,5. 14,17
Glentworth	LIN	SK9488	1,39-40. 4,7. 28,2. 45,1. 50,1
Glevering	SFK	TM2957	67,31
Glinton	NTH	TF1505	6,7. 6a,7
Glooston	LEC	SP7595	40,22
Glossams	SSX	TQ8422	9,111
Glossop	DBY	SK0494	1,30
Glosthorpe	NFK	TF6918	7,1
Gloucester GLS	GLS	SO8318	G1-4. 1,24;47. 3,5. 8,1. 10,14.
			12,4. 20,1. 24,1. 28,1.
			39,2;6;12. 46,1. 50,3. 54,1.
			58,1. 59,1. 60,1. 78,14. E18;30.
			EvK1
Gloucester GLS	WOR		1,7. 7,1
Glusburn WR	YKS	SE0044	13W45. 21W16
Glympton OXF	NTH		4,33
Glympton OXF	OXF	SP4221	EN4
Glynn	CON	SX1165	5,13,5
Gnatingdon	NFK	TF7237	61,3
Gnipe [Howe] NR	YKS	NZ9308	4N1. SN,L2
Gnosall	STS	SJ8220	7,18
Goadby	LEC	SP7598	28,2
Goadby [Marwood]	LEC	SK7826	17,33. 29,3
Goathill DOR	DOR	ST6717	ES3
Goathill DOR	SOM		19,70
Goathurst	SOM	ST2534	35,19
Godalming	SRY	SU9643	1,14
Godesmanescamp	HAM	??	NF9,34
Godington	OXF	SP6427	33,2
Godmanchester	HUN	TL2470	1,10
Godmersham	KEN	TR0650	3,13

Godtorp	LEC	??	29,11
Godwick	NFK	TF9022	22,13
Golborne	CHS	SJ4660	8,2. 24,2
Golcar WR	YKS	SE0915	9W113. SW,Ag15
Golden [Grove] FLN	CHS	SJ0881	FT2,13
Goldhanger	ESS	TL9008	20,58. 27,17. 34,37
Golding	SHR	SJ5403	4,3,17
Goldingham [Hall]	ESS	TL8340	44,2
Goldington	BDF	TL0750	4,5. 23,41-43. 57,8
Goldington [Highfields]	BDF	TL0553	23,7
Goldsborough NR	YKS	NZ8314	5N5. SN,L7
Goldsborough WR	YKS	SE3856	16W3. SW,Bu8
Goldthorpe WR	YKS	SE4604	1W21. 10W28. SW,SF 20;31
Golftyn FLN	CHS	SJ2870	FD2,3
Gomersal WR	YKS	SE2026	9W129 *note*. SW,M5
Gomshall	SRY	TQ0847	1,11
Gonalston	NTT	SK6847	10,3. 14,6. 30,49
Gonerby	LIN	SK8938	1,10. 3,31. 5,3. 31,2. 57,26. 67,24. CK,21
[Little] Gonerby	LIN	SK9036	67,24
Goodcott	DEV	SS6313	25,11
Goodern	CON	SW7843	5,3,14
Gooderstone	NFK	TF7602	12,1;3
Goodleigh	DEV	SS5934	28,7
Goodmanham ER	YKS	SE8843	1Y6. 2B9. 5E18. 13E1. SE,Wei2
Goodrington	DEV	SX8858	23,16
Goodworth [Clatford]	HAM	SU3642	16,3
Goosewell	DEV	SX5252	21,18
Goosey	BRK	SU3591	7,23
Goosnargh LAN	YKS	SD5536	1L1. See also CHS Y2
Goostrey	CHS	SJ7770	9,27. 11,4
Gop FLN	CHS	SJ0880	FT2,16
Gopsall	LEC	SK3506	14,11
Gore	WIL	SU0150	59,2
Gorhuish	DEV	SX5398	16,25
Goring	OXF	SU6080	28,2
Goring	SSX	TQ1102	11,71-73. 13,10;16;38
Gorleston NFK	NFK	TG5204	1,60. ESf2;5-6
Gorleston NFK	SFK		1,32;41-42;54
[North and South] Gorley	HAM	SU1511	68,11
		SU1610	
Gorwell	DEV	ST1609	36,18
Gosberton	LIN	TF2331	7,36. CK,69
Gosberton Hundred	LIN	—	12,76
Goseford	SHR	SJ2400	4,1,35
Goslaches	KEN	??	D18
Gossington	GLS	SO7302	1,15
Gotham	NTT	SK5330	4,3. 30,24
Gothelney	SOM	ST2537	21,15
Gotherington	GLS	SO9629	3,7. WoB19
Gothers	CON	SW9658	5,24,10
Gotten IOW	HAM	SZ4979	6,2
Goulceby	LIN	TF2579	14,47
Goulton [Grange] NR	YKS	NZ4704	1N39 *note*. 5N29. 31N5 *note*. SN,L44
Goviley [Major and Vean]	CON	SW9444	5,3,12
		SW9344	
Gowthorpe ER	YKS	SE7654	2B11. SE,P8
Goxhill	LIN	TA1021	7,23. 27,1. 30,2. 34,6. 68,40. CN,5
Goxhill ER	YKS	TA1844	14E6 *note*

[East] Graby	LIN	TF1029	2,31
[West] Graby	LIN	TF0929	18,17
Graffham	SSX	SU9217	11,17
Grafham	HUN	TL1669	1,9. 19,22. D25
Grafton	OXF	SP2600	17,3
Grafton (near Bromsgrove)	WOR	SO9469	1,1c
Grafton WR	YKS	SE4163	1W33–34. 2W5. 24W5. 29W32. 31W3. SW,Bu5
[Ardens] Grafton	WAR	SP1154	28,13
[East and West] Grafton	WIL	SU2560 SU2460	32,6. 68,5;8-9
Grafton [Flyford]	WOR	SO9655	8,17;20
Grafton [Regis]	NTH	SP7546	18,89
[Temple] Grafton	WAR	SP1254	37,7
Grafton [Underwood]	NTH	SP9280	33,1. 55,5
Grainsby	LIN	TF2799	12,20
Grainthorpe	LIN	TF3896	1,85. 3,18. 22,27
Graizelound: see [Graize]lound LIN			
Granborough	BKM	SP7625	8,1
Granby	NTT	SK7536	S5. 11,26. 27,1
Grandborough	WAR	SP4966	6,2. 44,3
[Great] Gransden	HUN	TL2755	1,5
[Little] Gransden	CAM	TL2755	5,38. 25,9
Gransmoor ER	YKS	TA1259	1Y14. 29E12. 31E1. 31N10 *note*. SE,Bt1
Grantchester	CAM	TL4355	12,3. 14,34. 15,4. 31,4. 32,15. 38,3
Grantham	LIN	SK9135	1,9–11;13–15;23;25. 5,1-3. 18,26. 30,25. 59,1. 67,15. CK,21;24;62;64
[High] Grantley WR	YKS	SE2369	2W7 *note*. SW,Bu48
Grappenhall	CHS	SJ6385	24,9
Grasby	LIN	TA0804	1,74. 4,26-27;41. 68,15
Grassington WR	YKS	SE0064	1W56. 21W15
Grassthorpe	NTT	SK7967	9,62
Graston	DOR	SY5089	55,20
Gratentun (? in Ticehurst) OXF	BRK	??	33,9
Gratton	DBY	SK1960	6,78
Gratton (in High Bray)	DEV	SS6837	3,42
Gratwich	STS	SK0231	11,35
Graveley	CAM	TL2464	7,3
Graveley	HRT	TL2327	5,4. 20,3. 28,1. 35,2. 36,3
Graveney	KEN	TR0562	2,35
Gravenhunger	SHR	SJ7342	4,15,1
Gravenhurst	BDF	TL1135	23,21
Gravesend	ESS	TQ6777	20,5
Gravesend KEN	ESS		20,5 note
Gravesend KEN	KEN	TQ6474	5,54
Grayingham	LIN	SK9396	1,39;45;65. 7,16. 34,27
Greasbrough WR	YKS	SK4195	10W10. 12W1;13. SW,Sf7
Greasby	CHS	SJ2587	25,2
Greasley	NTT	SK4947	10,29-30
Greatford	LIN	TF0811	18,13. 24,28. 51,6
Greatham	HAM	SU7730	1,5
Greatham	SSX	TQ0415	11,56
Greatworth	NTH	SP5542	2,4
Grebby	LIN	TF4368	3,23;46
Greenfield: see Fulbrook FLN			
Greenford	MDX	TQ1482	4,8. 9,4-5. 25,3
Greenhalgh (near Kirkham) LAN	YKS	SD4035	1L1. See also CHS Y2
Greenham	BRK	SU4765	21,5

Greenham	SOM	ST0720	19,21
Greenhill	WOR	SO8258	2,12
Greenslade	DEV	SS6400	16,56
Greenslinch	DEV	SS9603	48,2
Greenstead	ESS	TM0124	B1
Greensted	ESS	TL5302	28,13
Greenway	DEV	ST1605	23,20
Greenwich	KEN	TQ3877	5,29
Greenwick ER	YKS	SE8556	2B11. SE,P9
Greetham	LIN	TF3070	13,1-9. 24,42. CS,1215-16;35
Greetham	RUT	SK9214	R5
Greetland WR	YKS	SE0821	SW,M13 note
Greetwell	LIN	TF0171	17,1
Greinton	SOM	ST4136	8,15
Grendon	HEF	SO5954	10,72
Grendon	NTH	SP8760	56,20b;45
Grendon	WAR	SK2800	19,1
Grendon [Underwood]	BKM	SP6820	27,1
Grenewic	SFK	??	8,14
Grensvill	NFK	TG2600	17,17
Gresford FLN	CHS	SJ3555	22,1. 27,3
Gresham	NFK	TG1638	8,130. 9,146
Gressenhall	NFK	TF9515	8,62
Gressingham LAN	YKS	SD5769	1L3. See also CHS Y4
Gretton	NTH	SP8994	1,11;14
Gretton	SHR	SO5195	4,3,10
Grewelthorpe WR	YKS	SE2376	28W11. 31W5. SW,Bu15 note. SW,Bu23
Greyhurst	DBY	??	1,3
Gribthorpe ER	YKS	SE7635	15E3. 21E5. SE,C7
Griff [Farm] NR	YKS	SE5883	1N78 note. SN,L7 note. SN,Ma17
Grimesbi (in Borrowby) NR	YKS	??	5N10 note. SN,L9
Grimeshou (near Grimesthorpe) WR	YKS	??	10W11 note. SW,Sf7
Grimley	WOR	SO8360	2,66
Grimoldby	LIN	TF3987	1,84. 27,28
Grimpstone	DEV	SX7952	39,12
Grimpstonleigh	DEV	SX7549	39,13;16
Grimsargh LAN	YKS	SD5834	1L1. See also CHS Y2
[Old] Grimsbury OXF	NTH	SP4640	48,11
[Great] Grimsby	LIN	TA2609	4,70-71. 30,14. 36,1. CN,13-14
[Little] Grimsby	LIN	TF3291	3,19. 14,85. 22,25
[East and West] Grimstead	WIL	SU2227 SU2126	37,11. 67,42;59
Grimston	LEC	SK6821	1,3. 17,22
Grimston	NFK	TF7221	2,2. 8,25;27. 9,116. 51,1
Grimston	NTT	SK6865	1,17-18;24;27
Grimston NR	YKS	SE6074	23N24 note
Grimston (in Dunnington) ER	YKS	SE6451	5E38. 13E8. CE27. SE,Sn10
Grimston (in Garton) ER	YKS	TA2935	2E24 note. 14E4. SE,Sc5 note. SE,So2. SE,Hol8
Grimston [Grange] WR	YKS	SE4841	9W29 note. SW,BA5;8
Grimston [Hall]	SFK	TM2636	2,20. 7,99
[Hanging] Grimston ER	YKS	SE8060	26E11. 29E16. SE,Sc5 note. SE,Ac3
[North] Grimston ER	YKS	SE8467	1E53. 2B18. 23E17. 31E8. SE,Sc5-6 note
Grimthorpe [Manor] ER	YKS	SE8152	1Y10 note. SE,Wa6
Grindale ER	YKS	TA1371	1Y11. 2B12. SE, Hu6
Grindleton WR	YKS	SD7545	30W37
Grindon	STS	SK0854	11,3
[Little] Gringley	NTT	SK7381	1,4;43. 5,8

Gringley [on-the-Hill]	NTT	SK7390	9,122
Grinshill	SHR	SJ5223	4,16,1
Grinton NR	YKS	SE0498	6N73. SN,CtA24
Gristhorpe NR	YKS	TA0881	1Y3. SN,D4
Griston	NFK	TL9499	1,4-5;138. 8,71. 9,122. 31,36. 49,4. 66,72
Gritnam	HAM	SU2806	NF9,14
Grittenham	SSX	SU9421	11,20
Grittleton	WIL	ST8580	7,10
Groby	LEC	SK5207	13,6
Gronant FLN	CHS	SJ0983	FT2,13
Groton	SFK	TL9541	1,99. 14,25. 25,50. 76,2
Groundwell	WIL	SU1589	27,13
Grove	BKM	SP9122	44,4
Grove	NTT	SK7379	9,22;24;30
Grovely [Wood]	WIL	SU0534	67,99
Grundisburgh	SFK	TM2251	4,16. 6,122. 8,2;6. 21,55-56. 32,23. 38,23. 67,10
Guarlford: see *Baldenhall* WOR			
Gubblecote	HRT	SP9015	15,6
Guestling	SSX	TQ8514	9,105
Guestwick	NFK	TG0627	10,15. 56,4
Guildford	SRY	SU9949	1,1a. 19,37
Guilsborough	NTH	SP6773	18,80. 35,23
Guiltcross Hundred	NFK	—	15,10 note
Guisborough NR	YKS	NZ6116	1N10. 4N2. 5N19. 11N1. 31N7 note. SN,L18
Guiseley WR	YKS	SE1942	2W4. SW,Sk1
Guist	NFK	TF9925	10,15;34. 25,2. 56,2
Guiting [Power]	GLS	SP0924	34,8
[Temple] Guiting	GLS	SP0928	39,6. 76,1
Gulpher	SFK	TM3036	7,81
Guluesteham	SFK	??	*32,26*
Gulval	CON	SW4831	2,10
Gumley	LEC	SP6890	16,4. 40,17
Gunby (near Candlesby)	LIN	TF4666	29,26
Gunby (near North Witham)	LIN	SK9121	62,1-2
Gunby ER	YKS	SE7035	21E6 note. SE,He9
Gunnerby	LIN	TF2199	12,34
Gunthorpe	NFK	TG0135	1,28;30. 34,15
Gunthorpe	NTT	SK6844	9,74-75
Gunton	NFK	TG2234	4,24. 10,23-24
Gurlyn	CON	SW5632	5,4,18
Guscott	DEV	??	16,13
Gusford	SFK	TM1442	46,5
Gussage [All Saints]	DOR	ST9910	26,44
Gussage [St Michael] DOR	DOR	ST9811	E2
Gussage [St Michael] DOR	WIL		23,10
Guston	KEN	TR3244	M5;*18*
Guthestuna (in Kirton)	SFK	TM2940	7,89
Guton	NFK	TG1320	37,1
Gwaunysgor FLN	CHS	SJ0781	FT2,12
Gwesbyr FLN	CHS	SJ1183	FT2,11
Gwysaney FLN	CHS	SJ2266	FT3,5

H

[High and Low] Habberley	WOR	SO8077	1,2
Habrough	LIN	TA1514	1,77. 13,18. 14,37. 22,3. 27,2;63. 32,23. 34,10-11
[Great and Little] Habton NR	YKS	SE7576 SE7477	1N59. 5N35. SN,Ma2 SE7477
Hacche	DEV	SS7127	42,13
Haccombe	DEV	SX8970	16,152. 19,10
Haceby	LIN	TF0336	24,88. 26,45. 46,1-2. 48,8. 57,18;35
Hacheston	SFK	TM3158	1,94. 3,37. 6,267;283. 14,118
Hackford (near Hingham)	NFK	TG0502	48,1
Hackford (near Reepham)	NFK	TG0722	8,3. 51,10
Hackforth NR	YKS	SE2493	6N60. SN,CtA22
Hackleton	NTH	SP8055	4,15. 56,20e
Hackness NR	YKS	SE9690	13N13. SN,D9
Hackthorn	LIN	SK9982	2,17. 16,21. 26,15-16. 28,12-13. 45,3. 47,2
Hackworthy	DEV	SX8093	44,2
Haconby	LIN	TF1025	7,31. 42,6;14;17-18. 59,17. 61,1-2. CK,41-42;44
Haddenham	BKM	SP7408	2,1
Haddenham: see also Hinton [Hall]	CAM	TL4675	5,54
Haddington	LIN	SK9162	18,30. 65,1. CK,27
Haddiscoe	NFK	TM4396	1,238. 9,103;105;107-108;228. 31,18. 35,17
Haddon	HUN	TL1392	7,4
[East] Haddon	NTH	SP6668	18,5;7;44;87;93
[Nether] Haddon	DBY	SK2366	1,27
[Over] Haddon	DBY	SK2066	1,27
[West] Haddon	NTH	SP6371	12,4. 35,19d. 48,7
Hadfield	DBY	SK0296	1,30
[Little] Hadham	HRT	TL4322	4,6. 8,3
[Much] Hadham	HRT	TL4219	4,2;7;9;21
Hadleigh	SFK	TM0242	15,2
Hadley	SHR	SJ6711	4,3,27
Hadlow	CHS	SJ3377	1,24
Hadlow	KEN	TQ6349	5,60
Hadnall	SHR	SJ5220	4,3,58
Hadstock	ESS	TL5544	10,4
Hadworthy	SOM	ST2934	21,4
Hadzor	WOR	SO9162	20,6
[East] Hagbourne	BRK	SU5388	61,1
[West] Hagbourne	BRK	SU5187	31,5
Haggenby (in Healough) WR	YKS	SE4845	13W16 *note*. CW25;40. SW,An7
Haggerston	MDX	TQ3483	14,1
Hagginton	DEV	SS5547	3,27. 16,70. 23,3
Hagley	WOR	SO9180	23,9
Hagnaby	LIN	TF3462	14,82. 29,12
Hagthorpe ER	YKS	SE7030	SE,How5 *note*. SE,How8
Hagworthingham	LIN	TF3469	12,82;85;96. 13,9. 24,42-44;53. 28,34. 30,33;37
Haighton [Hall] LAN	YKS	SD5735	1L1 *note*. See also CHS Y2
[Low] Hail NR	YKS	NZ3009	6N1. SN,CtA2

Hailes	GLS	SP0430	38,2
Hailey	HRT	TL3710	34,13
Hailsham	SSX	TQ5909	10,68
Hainey	CAM	TL5575	5,58
Hainford	NFK	TG2218	26,2
Hainstone	HRT	??	23,1. 33,8
Hainton	LIN	TF1884	2,23. 4,46-47. 16,12-17. 27,21.
			40,9. CS,24;25
Hainworth WR	YKS	SE0539	24W21 *note*
Haisthorpe ER	YKS	TA1264	1Y14. 2E16. 31E1. SE,Bt4
Halac	WOR	??	15,3
Halas	NFK	??	9,98 *note*;206 *note*
Halberton	DEV	ST0012	1,70 *and note*
Haldley IOW	HAM	??	1,8
Hale	CHS	SJ7786	13,4
Hale IOW	HAM	SZ5484	6,16
Hale	LIN	TF1442	24,41
Halefield	NTH	TL0293	9,1
Hales	NFK	TM3897	9,104. 12,43. 14,42-43. 31,16
[North] Hales: see Covehithe SFK			
[Sheriff] Hales SHR	SHR	SJ7512	ES1;6
[Sheriff] Hales SHR	STS		B4. 8,5
Halesduna	ESS	??	27,8
Halesowen	WOR	SO9683	14,1
Halesworth	SFK	TM3877	3,11. 4,13. 7,17
Halgestou (in Shottisham)	SFK	TM3143	6,176
Halkyn FLN	CHS	SJ2071	FT1,6. FT2,7
Hallam	DBY	SK4540	11,4. 13,1
Hallam WR	YKS	SK3086	10W41 *note*. 10W42. SW,Sf35
Hallaton	LEC	SP7896	28,1
Hallatrow	SOM	ST6357	5,65
Halliggye	CON	SW7123	1,1
Halling	KEN	TQ7063	4,12
[Great and Little] Hallingbury	ESS	TL5119	4,16. 24,46. 26,1. 30,24;26
		TL5017	
Hallington	LIN	TF3085	13,29
Hallow	WOR	SO8258	2,68
Halnaker	SSX	SU9008	11,104;114
Halsall LAN	CHS	SD3710	R1,38;42
Halse	DEV	SS6700	16,50
Halse	NTH	SP5640	21,1
Halse	SOM	ST1427	2,3. 22,1
Halsham ER	YKS	TA2726	2A1. 14E14. SE,Th11. SE,Hol18
Halstead	ESS	TL8130	22,11. 23,26. 90,47;74
Halstead	LEC	SK7505	1,3
Halston	SHR	SJ3431	4,3,32. 4,27,31
Halstow (in Dunsford)	DEV	SX8292	47,12
Halstow (in Woodleigh)	DEV	??	28,14
Halsway	SOM	ST1237	21,41
Halswell	SOM	ST2533	22,17
Haltham	LIN	TF2463	1,97. 38,13
Halton	BKM	SP8710	2,2
Halton	CHS	SJ5381	9,17
Halton	CON	SX4065	5,2,17
Halton (in Bingley) WR	YKS	SE0938	24W1 *note*. 24W21. SW,Sk18
Halton (near Lancaster) LAN	YKS	SD5064	1L2. See also CHS Y3
Halton (in Temple Newsham) WR	YKS	SE3533	9W10. SW,Sk7
[East] Halton	LIN	TA1319	14,37
Halton [East] (near Embsay) WR	YKS	SE0453	1W73. SW,Cr1
Halton [Holegate]	LIN	TF4165	14,73
Halton [Holegate] Hundred	LIN	—	12,40
[West] Halton	LIN	SE9020	13,10-11

Halvana	CON	SX2178	5,24,5
Halvergate	NFK	TG4106	1,152
Halwell	DEV	SX5352	17,107
Halwill	DEV	SX4299	1,58
Halwyn	CON	SW7857	4,8
Ham	KEN	TR3254	5,206
Ham (in Croydon)	SRY	TQ3667	17,4
Ham (near Richmond)	SRY	TQ1772	8,15
Ham	WIL	SU3362	2,5
Ham [Castle]: see Homme [Castle] WOR			
[East] Ham	ESS	TQ4283	6,6. 32,9
[High and Low] Ham	SOM	ST4231	8,17
		ST4329	
[West] Ham	ESS	TQ3983	32,8. 34,8
Hamatethy	CON	SX0978	5,3,22
Hambleden	BKM	SU7886	52,2
Hambledon	HAM	SU6414	21,10. 25,1
Hambledon	SRY	SU9638	27,2
Hambleton RUT	LIN		S13
Hambleton RUT	RUT	SK9007	R19;21. ELc3
Hambleton WR	YKS	SE5531	9W25. SW,BA6
Hambleton LAN	YKS	SD3742	1L1. See also CHS Y2
Hambrook	GLS	ST6478	6,2
Hame	DEV	??	52,7
Hameringham	LIN	TF3167	28,36
Hamerton	HUN	TL1379	15,1
[Green] Hammerton WR	YKS	SE4557	25W24. SW,Bu7
Hammerton [Hall] (in Slaidburn) WR	YKS	SD7153	30W37 *note*
[Kirk] Hammerton WR	YKS	SE4655	25W23. SW,Bu7
Hammerwich	STS	SK0607	2,16
Hammett	CON	SX3265	5,26,4
Hammil	KEN	TR2955	5,184
Hammoon	DOR	ST8114	36,5
Hamnish Clifford and [Upper] Hamnish	HEF	SO5359	1,30
		SO5459	
Hamp	SOM	ST3036	10,4
[Great and Little] Hampden	BKM	SP8402	17,4
		SP8603	
Hampen	GLS	SP0520	2,7. 4,1 note
[Lower] Hampen	GLS	SP0519	2,6 note. 32,13
Hamphall [Stubbs] WR	YKS	SE4911	9W43 *note*. SW,O5
Hampnett	GLS	SP1015	41,1
[East] Hampnett	SSX	SU9106	11,103
[East] Hampnett: see also Westhampnett SSX			
Hampole WR	YKS	SE5010	9W43 note. 10W32. SW,Sf28
Hampreston	DOR	SZ0598	1,19. 49,3. 55,14. 56,19
Hampson	DEV	SS7001	25,8
Hampstead	MDX	TQ2685	4,3–4
Hampstead [Norris]	BRK	SU5276	63,2
Hampton	CHS	SJ4949	2,9
Hampton (in Hope under Dinmore)	HEF	SO5252	1,16;29
Hampton	KEN	TR0743	9,2
Hampton	MDX	TQ1469	12,2
Hampton	WIL	SU1892	27,20. 43,2
Hampton and [Little] Hampton	WOR	SP0243	2,74. 10,11
		SP0342	
Hampton [Bishop]	HEF	SO5638	2,33
Hampton [Gay and Poyle]	OXF	SP4816	B9. 58,16
		SP5015	
Hampton [in-Arden]	WAR	SP2080	31,6

Hampton [Lovett]	WOR	SO8865	26,10;17
Hampton [Lucy]	WAR	SP2557	3,1
[Meysey] Hampton	GLS	SU1199	27,1
Hampton [Wafre]	HEF	SO5757	1,15
Hamsey	SSX	TQ4112	10,109. 12,49
Hamstead IOW	HAM	SZ3991	7,19. 8,10
Hamstead [Marshall]	BRK	SU4165	58,1;3
Hamsworthy	DEV	SS3108	3,10. 34,2 note
Hanbury	WOR	SO9564	2,79
Hanby	LIN	TF4769	14,86;101. CS,20
Hanchet	SFK	TL6445	25,83
Hanchurch	STS	SJ8441	13,5
Handborough	OXF	SP4212	38,1
Handbridge	CHS	SJ4164	9,3. 10,2. 12,1
Handley	CHS	SJ4657	24,1
Handley (near Staveley)	DBY	SK4077	17,6-7
Handley (near Stretton)	DBY	SK3761	10,7
[Sixpenny] Handley	DOR	ST9917	19,1
Handsacre	STS	SK0916	2,22
Handsworth WAR	STS	SK0389	12,29
Handsworth WAR	WAR	SP0590	EBS3
Handsworth WR	YKS	SK4186	5W19. SW,Sf31
Hanechedene	BKM	??	4,20
Hanefelde	BDF	??	17,3. 57,15
Hanford	DOR	ST8411	26,3
Hanford	STS	SJ8642	13,4
Hanger	HAM	SU3313	69,39
Hangleton	SSX	TQ2706	12,23
Hangton NR	YKS	??	31N10 *note*
Hangton [Hill] (in Glaisdale) NR	YKS	NZ7606	31N10 *note*
Hanham	GLS	ST6470	60,7
Hankford	DEV	SS3815	35,19
Hankham	SSX	TQ6105	10,81-82
Hanley [Child and William] WOR	HEF		10,75
Hanley [Child and William] WOR	WOR	SO6565	20,3-4
		SO6766	
Hanley [Castle] WOR	GLS		1,34
Hanley [Castle] WOR	HEF		1,42;44. E2
Hanley [Castle] WOR	WOR	SO8341	E4. EG1. EH1
Hanleys [End] (in Cradley)	HEF	SO6946	23,5
Hanlith WR	YKS	SD9061	1W73. SW,Cr5
[East] Hanney	BRK	SU4193	7,22. 17,8. 36,2
[West] Hanney	BRK	SU4092	20,1-2
[East, South and West] Hanningfield	ESS	TL7701	18,36. 22,15-16. 33,14. 41,6
		TQ7498	
		TQ7399	
Hannington	HAM	SU5455	3,21. 69,44
Hannington	NTH	SP8171	18,42. 56,14
Hannington	WIL	SU1793	7,2
Hanslope	BKM	SP8046	46,1
Hanson [Grange]	DBY	SK1453	1,15
Hanstead	HRT	TL1401	10,1
Hanthorpe	LIN	TF0823	24,77. 42,15. 61,4. CK,42
Hantone	NTH	??	4,14. 40,3
Hanwell	MDX	TQ1580	4,9
Hanwell	OXF	SP4343	58,30
[Great] Hanwood	SHR	SJ4309	4,4,14
Hanworth	MDX	TQ1171	7,2
Hanworth	NFK	TG1935	9,87;142
[Cold] Hanworth	LIN	TF0383	16,50. 26,14. 28,12-13
[Potter] Hanworth Hundred	LIN	—	31,17

[Potter] Hanworth	LIN	TF0566	CK,17
Happisburgh	NFK	TG3731	1,197. 4,51
Hapton	NFK	TM1796	6,6. 9,218. 66,86
Harbilton	KEN	TQ8652	5,84
Harborne WAR	STS	SP0283	2,22
Harborne WAR	WAR	SP0184	EBS1
Harborough	WAR	SP4779	44,1;16
Harbourneford	DEV	SX7162	20,16
Harbridge	HAM	SU1410	NF9,13
Harbury	WAR	SP3760	6,13. 16,7. 17,50. 19,3. 29,2
Harby	LEC	SK7431	15,3. 17,31
Harby	NTT	SK8770	6,4;9
Harcourt (in Stanton upon Hine Heath)	SHR	SJ5625	4,14,10
Harcourt (in Stottesdon)	SHR	SO6982	4,27,35
Hardenhuish	WIL	ST9074	25,25
Hardham	SSX	TQ0317	11,79
Harding	WIL	SU2962	68,6
Hardingstone	NTH	SP7657	1,10. 56,20j
Hardington (near Frome)	SOM	ST7452	5,48. 20,1
Hardington [Mandeville]	SOM	ST5111	1,24
Hardley	HAM	SU4304	NF9,10
Hardley IOW	HAM	SZ6386	6,11
Hardley	NFK	TG3800	17,19
Hardmead	BKM	SP9347	14,44. 17,28-30. 26,10. 53,9
[Lower] Hardres	KEN	TR1553	5,123;133
[Upper] Hardres	KEN	TR1550	5,120
Hardstoft	DBY	SK4463	5,5
Hardwick	BKM	SP8019	12,11. 23,24. 35,2
Hardwick	CAM	TL3759	5,36-37
Hardwick	LIN	SK8675	T2-4
Hardwick	LIN	TF1779	3,9. 34,16
Hardwick NFK	NFK	TM2289	7,21. 9,98. 15,29. 31,9. 65,14
Hardwick NFK	SFK		ENf3
Hardwick	NTH	SP8569	56,47-48
Hardwick (near Stoke Lyne)	OXF	SP5729	28,16
Hardwick RUT	LIN		CK10
Hardwick RUT	NTH		ELc4
Hardwick RUT	RUT	SK9712	ELc19
[Priors] Hardwick	WAR	SP4756	6,14
[West] Hardwick WR	YKS	SE4118	9W54. SW,O11
Hardwicke	GLS	SO9027	19,2
Hare [Street]	HRT	TL3929	16,8. 33,10
Harebeating	SSX	TQ5910	12,8 note
Hareby	LIN	TF3365	14,67
Harefield	MDX	TQ0590	13,1
Harescombe	GLS	SO8310	1,4
Haresfield	GLS	SO8110	1,3
[Sheriffs] Haresfield	GLS	SO8109	53,10
Hareston	DEV	SX5653	15,29;51
Harewood	HEF	SO2642	25,6
Harewood WR	YKS	SE3145	1W9 *note.* SW,Sk13
[Lower and Upper] Harford	GLS	SP1322	52,7
		SP1221	
Harford	HAM	SU3904	NF9,1
Harford (near Cornwood)	DEV	SX6359	15,45
Hargham	NFK	TM0291	20,6. 66,90
Hargrave	CHS	SJ3279	4,2
Hargrave HUN	HUN	TL0370	3,1. 19,13-14
Hargrave HUN	NTH		35,15. EH1;4-5
Hargrave	SFK	TL7660	54,2
Harkstead SFK	ESS		ESf1. 1,26

Harkstead SFK	SFK	TM1935	1,96. 36,13. 46,4. EE1
Harlaston	STS	SK2110	1,32
Harlaxton	LIN	SK8832	1,11
Harlesden	MDX	TQ2183	3,18
Harleston	NFK	TM2483	14,20;22
Harleston	SFK	TM0160	14,36
Harlestone	NTH	SP7064	1,19. 18,22;43. 35,3d
Harley	SHR	SJ5901	4,21,8
[East and West] Harling	NFK	TL9986	1,143. 4,47. 14,11. 19,15. 38,1
		TL9785	
Harlington	BDF	TL0330	24,5
Harlington	MDX	TQ0878	7,4
Harlow	ESS	TL4711	11,2. 20,14. 25,2. 37,3
[East] Harlsey NR	YKS	SE4299	1N125. 31N3. SN,A5
[West] Harlsey NR	YKS	SE4198	1Y2 note. 1N124. SN,A1;5
Harlton	CAM	TL3852	17,4;6. 32,17. Appx K
Harmby NR	YKS	SE1289	6N101. SN,CtA30
Harmondsworth	MDX	TQ0577	5,1. 7,3
Harmston	LIN	SK9762	13,37. 32,36. 36,4
Harnhill	GLS	SP0700	45,4
Harome NR	YKS	SE6482	1N81. 5N42. 8N28. SN,Ma19-20
[Peper] Harow	SRY	SU9344	22,3
Harpham ER	YKS	TA0961	1Y14. 29E12. 31E1 note. 31N10.
			SE,Bt1-2
Harpingden	SSX	TQ4204	12,8
Harpley	NFK	TF7826	2,3. 8,30
Harpole	NTH	SP6960	35,16
Harpole	SFK	TM2956	3,32;44. 6,251;253;259. 7,124.
			21,92;94. 67,22;26
Harpsden	OXF	SU7680	35,26
Harpswell	LIN	SK9389	1,39;42. 2,27. 28,11;13
Harpton (Wales)	HEF	SO2359	9,13. 24,3
[Lower] Harpton	HEF	SO2760	24,3
[East] Harptree	SOM	ST5655	5,9. 19,37
[West] Harptree	SOM	ST5656	5,60. 24,31
Harrietsham	KEN	TQ8753	5,63
Harrington	NTH	SP7780	14,5
Harringworth	NTH	SP9197	56,8
Harrold	BDF	SP9456	53,13
Harrow	MDX	TQ1589	2,2-3
Harrowby	LIN	SK9335	1,15;20. 12,57. 57,23
Harrowden	BDF	TL0647	14,1. 24,27. 53,32
[Great] Harrowden	NTH	SP8870	4,5;19. 41,4
[Little] Harrowden	NTH	SP8771	4,6-7
Harston	CAM	TL4150	5,24. 14,21. 21,4. 32,5
Harston	LEC	SK8331	1,1c
Harswell ER	YKS	SE8240	1Y7. SE,Wei6
Hart [Carrs] LAN	YKS	SD2569	1L6 note. See also CHS Y7
Hartanger	KEN	TR2649	5,202
Hartest	SFK	TL8352	21,11. 25,48
Hartfield	SSX	TQ4735	10,60
Hartford	CHS	SJ6372	17,5
Hartford	HUN	TL2572	1,1
Hartforth NR	YKS	NZ1706	6N1. SN,CtA1
Hartham	WIL	ST8672	22,3. 24,37. 27,22. 67,46;53;87
Harthill	DBY	SK2264	6,75. 10,18
Harthill WR	YKS	SK4980	12W1;9
Harting	SSX	SU7820	11,6-7
Hartington	DBY	SK1260	6,9
Hartland	DEV	SS2624	1,30
Hartlebury	WOR	SO8370	2,82

Hartleigh	DEV	SS5008	3,14
Hartley	BRK	SU7068	46,5
Hartley	KEN	TQ6166	5,3
Hartley [Mauditt]	HAM	SU7436	27,1. 35,2
Hartley [Wespall]	HAM	SU6958	68,9. 69,12
Hartlington WR	YKS	SE0361	29W40;43
Harton NR	YKS	SE7061	1N93. SN,B11
Hartridge	BRK	SU5777	22,3
Hartrow	SOM	ST0934	25,39
Hartshead WR	YKS	SE1822	9W141. SW,M10
Hartshill	WAR	SP3293	15,3
Hartshorne	DBY	SK3220	6,22-23
Hartshurst	SRY	TQ1342	19,48
[Lower] Hartwell	BKM	SP7912	4,3-4. 14,1. 16,1. 28,1. 32,1
Hartwell	NTH	SP7850	2,7
Harty	KEN	TR0166	D18
Harvington	WOR	SP0549	2,65
Harwell .	BRK	SU4989	2,2. 44,1;3;4
Harwell	NTT	SK6891	9,117;124
Harworth	NTT	SK6191	9,55
Haselbech	NTH	SP7177	18,21
Haselbury [Plucknett]	SOM	ST4710	47,17
Haseley (in Thornton) BKM	BKM	??	41,7
Haseley	WAR	SP2367	39,4
[Great] Haseley OXF	BRK		B2
[Great] Haseley OXF	OXF	SP6401	35,2. EBe1
[Little] Haseley	OXF	SP6400	7,7
Haselor	WAR	SP1257	40,2
Hasfield	GLS	SO8227	19,2
Hashundebi (in Sharow) WR	YKS	??	2W13 *note*. SW,H2
Hasingham	ESS	??	90,67
Hasketon	SFK	TM2550	6,118;126. 8,8;12. 21,57. 32,24
Haslingfield	CAM	TL4052	1,7. 14,36-38. 22,8. 31,3. 32,16
Haspley	SFK	TM2841	14,117. 39,9;13
Hassall	CHS	SJ7657	8,11-12
Hassenbrook [Hall]	ESS	TQ6883	18,10. 24,6
Hassingham	NFK	TG3605	1,96
Hassop	DBY	SK2272	1,28
Hasthorpe	LIN	TF4869	24,57
Hastingleigh	KEN	TR0945	5,225. 9,52
Hastings SSX	BRK		21,13
Hastings SSX	ESS		EHu
Hastings SSX	HAM		69,16
Hastings SSX	HUN		D7
Hastings SSX	LIN		CS,39
Hastings SSX	SFK		31,50
Hastings SSX	SSX	TQ8110	5,1. 9,11;107 note
Hatch [Beauchamp]	SOM	ST3020	19,29
Hatch [Warren]	HAM	SU6148	67,1
Hatcham	SRY	TQ3577	5,10
Hatcliffe	LIN	TA2100	12,35
Hatete	WOR	??	26,9
Hatfield	HEF	SO5859	1,11;27
Hatfield	HRT	TL2308	8,1
Hatfield WR	YKS	SE6609	12W1;26
Hatfield [Broad Oak]	ESS	TL5416	1,3. 28,6
[Great] Hatfield ER	YKS	TA1842	14E6;39. SE,Hol23
[Little] Hatfield ER	YKS	TA1743	14E42. SE,Hol24
Hatfield [Peverel]	ESS	TL7811	18,13. 34,4
Hatford	BRK	SU3394	36,4
Hatheburgfelda/Hetheburgafella	SFK	??	4,33. 31,24

Hawton	NTT	SK7851	6,3. 11,7. 14,1-3
Haxby NR	YKS	SE6058	2N22. SN,B23
Haxey	LIN	SK7699	63,7. CW,17
Haxton	DEV	SS6436	2,9
Hay [Street]	SOM	ST6353	46,24
Hayden	GLS	SO9023	19,2
Hayes	GLS	SO7229	68,12
Hayes	MDX	TQ1080	2,1
[Floyers] Hayes (formerly *Shutbrooke*)	DEV	SX9191	*Note to 22*
Hayfield	DBY	SK0386	1,30
Hayling [Island]: see Eastoke HAM			
[North] Hayling	HAM	SU7303	3,25
[South] Hayling	HAM	SU7200	1,12. 10,1
Haynes	BDF	TL0841	23,15
Haythby (in West Halton)	LIN	SE8819	8,10;30. 13,14. 32,16
Hayton ER	YKS	SE8246	1Y10. 13E10. SE,P1
[Great] Haywood	STS	SJ9922	2,5;7-9
Hazard	DEV	SX7559	29,2
Hazelbadge	DBY	SK1780	7,9
Hazelbury	WIL	ST8368	1,23f. 28,13. 56,6. 67,41
Hazelden	SSX	TQ3736	10,103
Hazeleigh	ESS	TL8303	34,13-14
Hazelhanger	HRT	??	5,19. 37,13
Hazelhurst	SSX	TQ6832	9,60
Hazelwood [Castle] WR	YKS	SE4439	13W3 *note*. CW2-3. SW,BA3
Hazle	HEF	SO7036	2,26
Hazleton (near Andoversford)	GLS	SP0718	72,2
Hazleton (in Rodmarton)	GLS	ST9298	41,5
Heacham	NFK	TF6837	8,47
Headingley WR	YKS	SE2836	9W7. SW,Sk11
Headington	OXF	SP5407	1,2
Headley	HAM	SU8236	20,2
Headley	SRY	TQ2054	32,1
Headon	NTT	SK7477	1,6. 9,7;26
Healaugh WR	YKS	SE4947	13W14;16. 18W3. CW25;33-34;40. SW,An7;9
Healing	LIN	TA2110	2,7. 4,31-32. 27,5-6;
Heanor	DBY	SK4346	7,6
[Caffyns] Heanton	DEV	SS6948	34,16
Heanton [Punchardon]	DEV	SS5035	16,69
Heanton [Satchville]	DEV	SS5311	16,35
[West] Heanton	DEV	SS4709	52,8
Heapham	LIN	SK8788	1,39;48. 12,5
Hearthcote	DBY	SK2919	14,1
Heasley IOW	HAM	SZ5485	1,W15
Heath	DBY	SK4567	5,3
[Great and Little] Heath	HEF	SO5562	10,13
Heath and Reach: see Gladley BDF			
Heather	LEC	SK3910	40,7
Heathfield	DEV	SX6850	6,8
Heathfield	SOM	ST1626	2,3. 25,53
Heathfield WR	YKS	SE1367	8E5 *note*. SW,Bu27
?*Heaton* (near Dalton in Furness) LAN	CHS	SD2275	Y7
?*Heaton* (near Dalton in Furness) LAN: see also *Hietun* (?Hawcoat) LAN			
Heaton (near Lancaster) LAN	YKS	SD4460	1L2 *note*. See also CHS Y3
[Hanging] Heaton WR	YKS	SE2523	1Y15 note. SW,M14 *note*
[Kirk]heaton: see Kirk[heaton] YKS			
Heavitree	DEV	SX9392	34,56
Hebden WR	YKS	SE0262	25W32
Heckfield	HAM	SU7260	23,36

Heckingham	NFK	TM3898	9,106;111;229. 12,42. 14,43
Heckington	LIN	TF1444	1,3. 7,47. 24,40. 26,27. 37,7.
			57,31. 67,6. CK,31
Heddington	WIL	ST9966	24,4
Hedenham	NFK	TM3193	6,4-5
[Castle] Hedingham ESS	ESS	TL7835	35,5
[Castle] Hedingham ESS	SFK		EE5
[Sible] Hedingham	ESS	TL7734	39,3. 43,1
Heene	SSX	TQ1303	13,31
Heigham	NFK	TG2108	17,64
[Potter] Heigham	NFK	TG4119	65,7
Heighley	STS	SJ7746	1,36
Heighton (in Beckley)	SSX	TQ8724	9,116-118
[South] Heighton	SSX	TQ4402	10,47
Hela	CON	??	5,1,15
Heldetune (in Clapham or Austwick) WR	YKS	??	1L4 *note*
Hele	CON	SX2197	5,24,3
Hele (in Ilfracombe)	DEV	SS5347	3,44
Hele (in Meeth)	DEV	SS5206	15,47. 39,8. 47,1
Hele (in Petrockstowe)	DEV	SS5106	15,47. 39,8. 47,1
Hele	SOM	ST1824	2,3;5. 19,40
Helescane	DEV	??	16,42
Helhoughton	NFK	TF8627	1,88. 8,108;111;137. 23,6. 34,7
Hellaby WR	YKS	SK5092	10W3 *note*. 10W4. SW,Sf4-5
Helland (near Probus)	CON	SW9049	5,24,20
Hellesdon	NFK	TG2010	61,1
Hellifield WR	YKS	SD8556	1W73. 13W44. 30W4;9. SW,Cr5
Hellington	NFK	TG3103	9,58. 12,18;20-21
Helmdon	NTH	SP5943	18,10
Helmingham	NFK	TG1116	10,16;35. 25,7
Helmingham	SFK	TM1957	2,12. 4,8. 8,74. 16,25-26. 25,61.
			38,18. 52,9
Helmsley NR	YKS	SE6183	1N80. 2A4. 5N50. SN,Ma18
[Gate] Helmsley NR	YKS	SE6955	2N17. SN,B13
[Upper] Helmsley NR	YKS	SE6957	5N61. SN,B12
Helperby NR	YKS	SE4369	2N25-26. SN,B24-25
Helperthorpe ER	YKS	SE9570	2B18. SE,Th4
Helpridge	WOR	SO9166	1,3a
Helpringham	LIN	TF1340	14,96. 24,105. 26,28. 37,1. 51,11
Helsby	CHS	SJ4875	1,7
Helsington WES	YKS	SD4888	1L7 *note*. See also CHS Y8
Helsthorpe	BKM	SP8819	12,10. 43,4
Helston	CON	SW6627	1,2
Helstone	CON	SX0881	5,1,4
Hem (Wales)	SHR	SJ2300	4,1,36
Hemblington	NFK	TG3511	1,159. 10,14;66
Hembury: see Broadhembury,			
Payhembury DEV			
Hemerdon	DEV	SX5657	35,28
Hemingbrough ER	YKS	SE6730	1Y5. SE,How10
Hemingby	LIN	TF2374	13,22-23. 14,48. 25,15
Hemingford HUN	ESS		EHu
Hemingford [Abbots]	HUN	TL2971	16,16-18. 22,2. D7
Hemingford [Grey]	HUN	TL2970	16-18. 19,23. 27,1. D8
Hemingstone	SFK	TM1453	1,7. 3,58;62. 6,8. 7,68. 8,59-
			60;65;67. 16,23. 21,21-22. 56,4.
			62,3-4;6. 67,2. 74,1;5;7. 1;5;7
Hemington	NTH	TL0985	6a,15. 9,4
Hemington	SOM	ST7253	5,48. 20,1
Hemley	SFK	TM2842	7,91. 8,43. 39,5;13. 46,6. 47,1
Hemlington NR	YKS	NZ5014	4N3. SN,L33
Hempnall: see also Schieteshaga	NFK	TM2494	9,101. 31,6;9

Hempshill	NTT	SK5244	10,50
Hempstead	ESS	TL6337	23,41
Hempstead (near Eccles)	NFK	TG4028	1,199
Hempstead (near Holt)	NFK	TG1037	1,20. 10,8
[Hemel] Hempstead	HRT	TL0506	15,10
Hempsted	GLS	SO8116	1,62
Hempton	NFK	TF9129	8,114
Hempton	OXF	SP4431	20,4. 41,2
Hemsby	NFK	TG4917	10,30;43
Hemsted	KEN	TR1441	5,223
Hemswell	LIN	SK9390	1,39;41. 4,8. 45,2
Hemsworth	DOR	ST9605	26,39. 50,3
Hemsworth WR	YKS	SE4213	9W66. SW,St1
Hemyock	DEV	ST1313	1,8
Henbury	CHS	SJ8873	1,31
Henbury	GLS	ST5678	3,1. WoB15
Henderskelfe NR	YKS	SE7170	8N10 *note*. SN,B1
Hendon	MDX	TQ2289	4,12
Hendon (in Hellingly)	SSX	TQ5913	10,52
Hendrebiffa FLN	CHS	SJ2363	FT3,2
[East] Hendred	BRK	SU4588	1,38. 3,2. 17,9-10. 21,17. 44,1. 65,13
[West] Hendred	BRK	SU4488	12,1. 62,1
Henfield	SSX	TQ2116	3,2
Henford	DEV	SX3794	17,20
Hengrave	SFK	TL8268	14,8;12
Henham	ESS	TL5428	33,19. 90,39
Henham	SFK	TM4478	33,8
Henhurst	KEN	TQ6669	5,109
Henley (in Bitterley)	SHR	SO5476	4,3,48
Henley	SFK	TM1551	6,17. 8,72;79. 21,33. 29,11. 41,14. 62,6
Henley	SRY	SU9252	8,30
Henlow	BDF	TL1738	24,29. 32,16. 55,9-10. 56,8
?Hennett	CON	SX1391	5,1,21
Hennock	DEV	SX8280	16,155
[Great and Little] Henny ESS	ESS	TL8637 TL8638	34,21. 40,4. 43,5. 90,13;44;46
[Great and Little] Henny ESS	SFK		EE4;6
Hensall WR	YKS	SE5923	1Y12. 29W25. SW,O16
Henscott	DEV	SS4008	3,12
Hensington	OXF	SP4516	7,23. 29,14. 59,9
Henstead	SFK	TM4886	26,12c
Henstead Hundred	NFK	—	15,28
Henstridge	SOM	ST7219	1,25. 18,4
Hentage	GLS	SP0033	1,43
Henton	OXF	SP7602	35,20
Heppastebe	DEV	??	34,34
Hepworth	SFK	TL9874	14,78;79. 66,7
Hepworth WR	YKS	SE1606	SW,Ag14 *note*
Herdby: see Coxbench DBY			
Hereford HEF	FLN		FT2,19
Hereford HEF	GLS		1,34
Hereford HEF	HEF	SO5139	C1;14-15. 1,3;4;7;39;41;47. 2,1;17;57. 10,7. 13,1. 19,2. E2;4;6-8
Hereford HEF	WOR		1,16. 18,6. X2-3. E1;3;7. EG1
[Little] Hereford	HEF	SO5568	2,51
Hereswode	LEC	??	C18
[Lower and Upper] Hergest	HEF	SO2755 SO2654	1,69
Herleshow (= How Hill) WR	YKS	SE2767	2W7 *note*. SW,Bu48

Herriard	HAM	SU6645	23,29
Herringby	NFK	TG4410	65,8
Herringfleet	SFK	TM4797	1,60
Herringswell	SFK	TL7169	14,18. 25,40. 26,4
Herrison	DOR	SY6794	26,5;8-11. 53,1
Herstanhaia	DEV	??	25,28
Herstmonceux	SSX	TQ6410	9,5
Herston	DOR	SZ0178	47,12. 57,22
Hertford HRT	ESS		1,3
Hertford HRT	HRT	TL3212	B. 34,13
Hertingfordbury	HRT	TL3011	24,3
[East] Heslerton ER	YKS	SE9276	8E1. 23E14. 29E22. 31E2. SE,Th2
[West] Heslerton ER	YKS	SE9175	29E23. 31E2. SE,Th3
Heslington ER	YKS	SE6250	23N29. SE,Wa7
Hessay WR	YKS	SE5253	22W4. 25W17. SW,An13 -14
Hesselton NR	YKS	SE1991	6N136. SN,CtA38
Hesset	SFK	TL9361	12,2. 14,57
Hessle ER	YKS	TA0326	15E2. 21E2. SE,He1
Hessle WR	YKS	SE4317	9W53. SW,O9
Hestley	SFK	TM1468	43,8
Heswall	CHS	SJ2682	3,6
Hetfelle	DEV	??	23,17
Hethe OXF	NTH		4,31
Hethe OXF	OXF	SP5929	EN2
Hetheburgafella: see *Hatheburgfelda* SFK			
Hethel	NFK	TG1700	9,94-95;97. 44,1
Hethersett	NFK	TG1604	4,52. 12,31;35
Hethfelton	DOR	SY8588	11,8. 37,11. 49,14
Hetton WR	YKS	SD9658	30W24
Heuu(o)rde (in Conistone) WR	YKS	??	28W25 *note*. 29W49
Heveningham	SFK	TM3372	7,13;27
Heversham [Head] WES	YKS	SD4983	30W40 *note*. See also CHS Y13
Hevingham	NFK	TG1921	1,195. 10,38. 25,11
Hewelsfield	GLS	SO5602	32,12
[Bridge] Hewick WR	YKS	SE3370	2W10 *note*. SW,H3
[Copt] Hewick WR	YKS	SE3471	2W10 note. 2W11. SW,H2
Hewis	DEV	??	15,28
Hewise	DEV	??	19,22
Heworth NR	YKS	SE6152	C26-27. 23N36. SN,Y4
Hexthorpe WR	YKS	SE5602	5W8. 10W27. CW14;16;21. SW,Sf21
Hexton	HRT	TL1030	1,17. 10,19. 34,11
Heybridge	ESS	TL8507	5,10
Heydon CAM	ESS	TL4339	10,5. 76,1
Heydour	LIN	TF0039	26,51. 57,21
[Nether] Heyford	NTH	SP6658	2,12. 18,41;83-84. 46,2
[Upper] Heyford	NTH	SP6659	18,8
[Lower and Upper] Heyford	OXF	SP4824 SP4926	2,12. 35,19. EN7
[Upper] Heyford OXF	NTH		4,36
Heysham LAN	YKS	SD4161	1L2 *note*. See also CHS Y3
Heytesbury	WIL	ST9242	1,23e
Heythrop	OXF	SP3527	56,3
Hibaldstow	LIN	SE9702	1,39;55;64. 8,22. 14,26-27. 26,19. 68,33
Hickleton WR	YKS	SE4805	27W1. SW,Sf13
Hickling	NFK	TG4124	4,38
Hickling	NTT	SK6929	5,3. 11,30. 20,8
Hidcote [Bartrim]	GLS	SP1742	12,9
Hidcote [Boyce]	GLS	SP1741	11,12
[Cold] Hiendley WR	YKS	SE3714	9W84 note. SW,St16

[South] Hiendley WR	YKS	SE3912	9W67. SW,St3
Hietun (= Hawcoat) LAN	YKS	SD2071	1L6 *note*. See also CHS Y7
			Heaton'
Higford	SHR	SJ7500	4,8,15
Higham	KEN	TQ7174	5,105
Higham	SFK	TM0335	5,6. 16,43. 25,75. 38,21. 58,1
Higham	SSX	TQ8225	9,121
[Cold] Higham	NTH	SP6653	18,28. 39,12
Higham [Ferrers]	NTH	SP9668	35,1a;14–15
Higham [Gobion]	BDF	TL1032	23,23
Higham [Hill]	ESS	TQ3590	36,6
Highampton	DEV	SS4804	16,19
Highclere: see Clere HAM			
Highleigh	DEV	SS9123	34,41
Highley	SHR	SO7483	4,11,11
Highnam	GLS	SO7919	10,8
Highway	WIL	SU0474	8,1. 41,4
Highworth	WIL	SU2092	1,23a. 24,5
Hilborough	NFK	TF8200	8,91
Hilcot	GLS	SO9916	3,5. WoA2. WoB18
Hilcote	STS	SJ8429	1,46
Hildenley [Hall] NR	YKS	SE7470	1N90 *note*. SN,B7
Hildersham	CAM	TL5448	29,9
Hilderstone	STS	SJ9434	1,44. 11,27
Hilderthorpe ER	YKS	TA1765	1Y11 *note*. 29E9. SE,Hu3
Hilgay	NFK	TL6298	1,210. 8,17. 9,230. 14,3. 15,2.
			16,1. 66,7
Hill (in Cruwys Morchard)	DEV	SS8510	50,3
Hill	GLS	ST6495	1,15;18
Hill	WAR	SP4567	7,1
Hill	WOR	SO9848	2,19
[Gold] Hill	DOR	ST8213	44,1
[Higher and Lower] Hill	SOM	ST1542	21,47
		ST1543	
Hill [House]	GLS	SO6912	32,9 *in note*
Hill of Eaton: see [Hill of] Eaton HEF			
Hill [Row]	CAM	TL4475	5,53. Appx P
[West] Hill: see Wast Hills WOR			
Hillam LAN	YKS	SD4552	1L2 *note*. See also CHS Y3
Hillborough	WAR	SP1251	35,1. 37,5
Hillersdon	DEV	SS9907	42,18
Hillesden	BKM	SP6828	12,28. 14,34
Hillesley	GLS	ST7689	67,4
Hillfarrance	SOM	ST1624	2,3;5. 35,22
Hillgrips NR	YKS	SE9986	13N11 *note*. SN,D6
Hillhampton	WOR	SO7765	X1
Hillingdon	MDX	TQ0682	7,6
Hillington	NFK	TF7225	8,28. 29,1. 51,3
Hillmorton	WAR	SP5373	16,35–37. 18,1. 44,5
Hilmarton	WIL	SU0275	25,14. 32,9. 67,19
Hilperton	WIL	ST8759	66,3–4. 67,47;90
Hilston ER	YKS	TA2833	14E3. SE,Hol5
Hilton	CON	SS2303	5,11,1
Hilton	DBY	SK2430	3,1. 6,46
Hilton	DOR	ST7803	13,3
Hilton (in Shenstone)	STS	SK0805	7,10
Hilton (near Wolverhampton)	STS	SJ9505	7,15
Hilton NR	YKS	NZ4611	1N34. 5N28. 31N5. SN,L38
Hilton WR	YKS	??	1Y18 *note*. SW,Bu14
Himbleton	WOR	SO9458	2,70
Himley	STS	SO8891	12,12–13

Hincaster WES	YKS	SD5084	30W40. See also CHS Y13
Hincheslea	HAM	SU2700	NF9,31
Hinchwick	GLS	SP1429	3,6
Hinckley	LEC	SP4293	10,3
Hinderclay	SFK	TM0276	14,74
Hinderwell NR	YKS	NZ7917	4N2. 13N2-3. SN,L11-12
Hindlip	WOR	SO8758	2,52
Hindolveston	NFK	TG0229	10,9;15
Hindrelag(he)/Indrelag(e) (near Richmond) NR	YKS	??	6N19 *note*. 6N69. SN,CtA11;24
Hindringham	NFK	TF9836	1,39. 10,10;13;26;60-61. 11,3. 30,1
Hingham	NFK	TG0202	1,11-12;14. 8,79. 9,81. 20,10-12. 31,41. 66,39
Hinstock	SHR	SJ6926	4,14,14
Hintlesham	SFK	TM0843	1,118. 3,79;80 note
Hinton (in Sharpness)	GLS	ST6803	1,15;18 note
Hinton	HEF	SO5747	6,3
Hinton (near Woodford Halse)	NTH	SP5352	45,4
Hinton	SFK	TM4372	7,5
Hinton and Hinton [Admiral]	HAM	SZ2095 SZ2195	NF3,10;14
Hinton [Ampner]	HAM	SU5927	3,18
Hinton [Blewett]	SOM	ST5956	26,5
[Broad] Hinton	WIL	SU1076	29,7
Hinton [Charterhouse]	SOM	ST7758	40,1
[Cherry] Hinton	CAM	TL4856	14,2-3. Appx E
Hinton [Hall] (in Haddenham)	CAM	TL4675	Appx P
Hinton [in-the-Hedges]	NTH	SP5536	45,8
Hinton [Martell]	DOR	SU0106	1,31
Hinton [on the Green] WOR	GLS		10,7
Hinton [on the Green] WOR	WOR	SP0240	EG6
Hinton [St George]	SOM	ST4112	26,2
Hinton [St Mary]	DOR	ST7816	19,2
Hinton [Waldrist]	BRK	SU3798	65,1;2
Hints	STS	SK1502	2,22
Hinwick	BDF	SP9361	3,12. 25,5. 34,2. 37,1. 47,2. 56.5
Hinworthy	GLS	SO7403	1,18 *in note*
Hinxton	CAM	TL4945	1,10;22. 3,1. 26,14. 32,4. EE1. Appx G
Hinxworth	HRT	TL2340	28,7. 36,15. 37,10
Hipperholme WR	YKS	SE1325	SW,M11 note
Hipswell NR	YKS	SE1898	6N66. SN,CtA23
Hiraddug FLN	CHS	SJ0778	FT2,3
Hiscombe (in West Coker)	SOM	ST5116	5,3. 8,38
Histon	CAM	TL4363	3,3-5. 5,43. 12,5. Appx O
Hitcham	BKM	SU9282	23,3
Hitcham	SFK	TL9851	21,42;44. 25,20;106
Hitchin	BDF	TL1829	E1
Hitchin	HRT	TL1829	1,1-17;19. 34,11-12. 36,17
Hittisleigh	DEV	SX7395	16,114
Hive ER	YKS	SE8231	3Y4. SE,How1
Hiwes	DOR	??	34,3
Hixham [Hall]	HRT	TL4526	4,20
Hixon	STS	SK0025	2,6
Hobbestuna: see *Hopestuna* SFK			
Hoburne DOR	HAM	SZ1993	NF9,11
Hoby	LEC	SK6717	36,2
Hockering	NFK	TG0713	20,14-15
Hockerton	NTT	SK7156	5,17. 9,60. 11,8
Hockham	NFK	TL9592	9,71;126. 66,74
[Little] Hockham	NFK	TL9490	9,72

Hockleton	SHR	SJ2700	4,1,35
Hockley	ESS	TQ8293	9,13. 24,19;33
Hockliffe	BDF	SP9726	55,2
Hockwold	NFK	TL7288	8,35
Hockworthy	DEV	ST0319	16,77. 23,7
Hocsenga	ESS	??	90,66
Hodcott	BRK	SU4781	22,6. 46,7
Hoddesdon HRT	ESS		1,3
Hoddesdon HRT	HRT	TL3708	16,10. 17,14. 32,2. 33,13. 42,7
Hoddington	HAM	SU7047	3,22
Hodenhoe	HRT	TL3433	5,21. 37,15
Hodnell	WAR	SP4257	16,34. 17,30-31. 28,5
Hodnet	SHR	SJ6128	4,1,4
Hodsock	NTT	SK5886	9,46-48
		SK6185	
Hoe	NFK	TF9916	15,15
Hoe	SSX	TQ1906	13,46
[East] Hoe	HAM	SU6315	23,20
Hofinchel	CHS	??	1,31
Hoggeston	BKM	SP8025	17,9
Hognaston	DBY	SK2350	1,14
Hogshaw	BKM	SP7322	16,6
Holbeach	LIN	TF3524	1,32-33. 11,1. 12,83-4. 57,50-51.
			CK,71
Holbeam	DEV	SX8271	48,6
Holborn	MDX	TQ3181	1,3
Holbrook	DBY	SK3645	6,66
Holbrook	DEV	SX9991	15,20. 52,18
Holbrook	SFK	TM1736	3,68
Holcombe (in Dawlish)	DEV	SX9574	34,11
Holcombe (in Aisholt)	SOM	ST1835	21,19
Holcombe [Burnell]	DEV	SX8591	1,69
Holcombe [Rogus]	DEV	ST0518	16,76
Holcot	BDF	SP9438	25,1
Holcot	NTH	SP7969	1,16. 56,43
Holdenby	NTH	SP6967	18,86;92
Holdenhurst DOR	HAM	SZ1295	1,29. 17,1
Holdfast	WOR	SO8537	2,35
Holdgate (formerly Stanton Long)	SHR	SO5689	4,21,5-6
Holdworth WR	YKS	SK2891	10W35. SW,Sf34
Hole (in Clayhidon)	DEV	ST1610	16,124
Hole (in Georgeham)	DEV	SS4539	36,11
[South] Hole (in Hartland)	DEV	SS2220	36,3
Holedene (in Hartlington) WR	YKS	??	29W46-47 *note*
[Rich's and Treble's] Holford	SOM	ST1433	2,3. 21,83-84
		ST1533	
Holford [St Mary]	SOM	ST1541	25,38
Holker LAN	YKS	SD3677	23N22 *note*. See also CHS Y10
Holkham	NFK	TF8743	1,34;41. 4,20. 8,118. 10,13;26.
			34,19. 48,2
Hollacombe (near Holsworthy)	DEV	SS3703	51,15
Hollacombe (in Kentisbury)	DEV	SS6443	23,1
Hollam	DEV	SS5016	35,12
Holland	DEV	SX5656	17,94
[Great and Little] Holland	ESS	TM2119	20,68. 52,3
		TM2016	
Hollesley	SFK	TM3544	6,148-149;154 *note*;156-
			157;160;256;294
Hollin	WOR	SO7270	21,1
Hollingbourne	KEN	TQ8455	2,33. 3,3
Hollingdon	BKM	SP8727	17,11. 23,19. 53,1

Hollington	DBY	SK2239	6,41–42. 9,3
Hollington	SSX	TQ7911	8,15. 9,15
Hollingworth	CHS	SK0096	1,31
Hollow [Court] WOR	HEF		1,41. E7
Hollow [Court] WOR	WOR	SO9758	X2. E3
Hollowcombe (in Ermington)	DEV	SX6252	15,66
Hollowcombe (in Fremington)	DEV	SS5333	36,9
Hollowell	NTH	SP6871	5,1. 18,80;94. 35,19g. 57,3
Hollym ER	YKS	TA3425	14E4. SE,Hol9
Holme	BDF	TL1942	18,5. 23,44. 24,26. 32,11. 51,3. 53,18-19. 57,3v
Holme (near Bakewell)	DBY	SK2169	1,27
Holme (near Chesterfield)	DBY	SK3572	12,3
Holme (in Beckingham)	LIN	SK9053	24,78
Holme (near Bottesford)	LIN	SE9206	8,25
Holme (in Sudbrooke)	LIN	TF0476	8,2. 26,4–6
Holme WES	YKS	SD5278	1L4 *note*. See also CHS Y5
Holme (in Bolton by Bowland) WR	YKS	SD7752	13W40 *note*
Holme (near Holmfirth) WR	YKS	SE1005	1Y15. 1W26. SW,Ag12
Holme (near Swainby) NR	YKS	SE3582	3Y9. SW,H5
Holme: see Biggin WAR			
[East] Holme	DOR	SY8986	41,3. 56,43
Holme [Hale]	NFK	TF8807	1,74. 66,70
Holme [House] (near Gargrave) WR	YKS	SD9454	1W73 *note*. SW,Cr3
Holme [Lacy]	HEF	SO5535	2,12
Holme [next the Sea]	NFK	TF7043	1,134. 19,10
[North] Holme [House] (near Great Edstone) NR	YKS	SE7080	1N72 *note*. 8N18. SN,Ma10 *note*
Holme [on the Wolds] ER	YKS	SE9646	3Y8. SE,Sn9
[Paull] Holme ER	YKS	TA1824	14E1. SE,Hol1;3
Holme [Pierrepont]	NTT	SK6239	9,80-81
[South] Holme (near Hovingham) NR	YKS	SE7077	16N1. 23N24. SN,Ma10 note. SN,Ma22
Holme [upon Spalding Moor] ER	YKS	SE8238	21E9 *note*. SE,Wei2
[Yate]holme: see Yate[holme] YKS			
Holmer	HEF	SO5042	2,41
Holmesfield	DBY	SK3277	8,4
Holmpton ER	YKS	TA3623	14E19. CE49. SE, Holl9
Holne	DEV	SX7069	5 note. 1,34 note. 20,11
Holne (in Holnicote)	SOM	??	21,67
Holnicote	SOM	SS9146	16,13. 21,65
Holsworthy	DEV	SS3403	1,38
Holt	NFK	TG0738	1,19;29;31;42
Holt	WOR	SO8262	2,7
Holt Forest: see *Wimborne Forest* DOR			
Holtby (near York) NR	YKS	SE6754	1N99. SN,B12
Holtby [Hall] (in Kirkby Fleetham) NR	YKS	SE2692	6N62 *note*. SN,CtA22
Holtham (in Legsby)	LIN	TF1586	22,36. 40,13
Holton	DOR	SY9691	37,3
Holton	OXF	SP6006	29,8
Holton	SOM	ST6826	45,4
Holton	SFK	TM4077	6,102. 7,9;23. 13,3
Holton [cum Beckering]	LIN	TF1181	2,14. 28,31
Holton [le Clay]	LIN	TA2802	12,18. 14,2-3. 40,4
Holton [le Moor]	LIN	TF0897	1,80. 14,35. 16,7
Holton St Mary	SFK	TM0536	32,3
Holverston	NFK	TG3003	1,122. 2,7;9. 9,35. 12,11
Holwell (in Radipole)	DOR	SY6583	1,1 note. 26,17
Holwell HRT	BDF		8,8. 9,1
Holwell HRT	HRT	TL1633	EB1-2
Holwell	LEC	SK7323	3,16. 17,30

Holworth	DOR	SY7683	12,12
Holybourne	HAM	SU7340	1,3. NF10,5
Holyoaks	LEC	SP8495	3,11
Holywell	HUN	TL3370	6,6
Holywell	OXF	SP5206	28,28
Homersfield	SFK	TM2885	18,4. 19,13
Homington	WIL	SU1226	57,1
Homme [Castle]	WOR	SO7361	19,8
[Church] Honeybourne	WOR	SP1244	10,9
[Cow] Honeybourne WOR	GLS		11,10
[Cow] Honeybourne WOR	WOR	SP1144	EG7
Honeychurch	DEV	SS6202	16,27
Honibere	SOM	ST1843	46,18
Honicknowle	DEV	SX4658	15,78
Honilega	SFK	??	34,2
Honing	NFK	TG3227	17,51. 36,2
Honingham	NFK	TG1112	4,9;11
Honingham Thorpe: see [Honingham] Thorpe NFK			
Honington	LIN	SK9443	14,89-91. 24,84
Honington	SFK	TL9174	14,85
Honington	WAR	SP2642	6,15
Honington Hundred	LIN	—	CK,63
Honiton (near Axminster)	DEV	ST1600	1,11. 15,23
Honiton (in South Molton)	DEV	SS6824	42,11
Honley WR	YKS	SE1312	9W107. SW,Ag8
Hoo	KEN	TQ7871	5,93
Hoo (near Kettleborough)	SFK	TM2559	21,95
Hoo (in Sutton)	SFK	TM2949	6,158. 21,81
Hooe	DEV	SX5052	17,106
Hooe	SSX	TQ6809	8,9. 9,1
Hooe [Level]	SSX	TQ6806	10,77
Hook (in Ashreigney)	DEV	SS6414	47,2
Hook	HAM	SU5005	23,14
Hook [Norton]	OXF	SP3533	28,6
Hooke	DOR	ST5300	26,59
Hoon	DBY	SK2231	3,1
Hooton	CHS	SJ3679	5,3
Hooton [Levitt] WR	YKS	SK5291	5W12 note. SE,Sf2 note. SW,Sf24
Hooton [Pagnell] WR	YKS	SE4807	5W14. SW,Sf8 note. SW,Sf28
Hooton [Roberts] WR	YKS	SK4897	10W12. SW,Sf8 *note*
[Slade] Hooton WR	YKS	SK5289	10W1. SW,Sf2 *note*
Hope FLN	CHS	SJ3158	17,12
Hope	DBY	SK1783	1,29
Hope [Bowdler]	SHR	SO4792	4,22,3
Hope [Mansell]	HEF	SO6219	15,1
[Miles] Hope	HEF	SO5764	1,10a
[Sollers] Hope	HEF	SO6133	21,4
Hope [under Dinmore]	HEF	SO5152	6,5
Hopesay	SHR	SO3983	4,20,6
Hopestuna/Hobbestuna	SFK	??	6,117. 32,30
Hopleys [Green]	HEF	SO3452	1,5. 10,43
Hopperton WR	YKS	SE4256	1W36. 24W9. 25W25. 29W15. 31W2. SW,Bu10
Hoppetuna/Opituna	SFK	??	6,100. 7,29
Hopsford	WAR	SP4283	31,12
Hopton	DBY	SK2553	1,13
Hopton (in Hodnet)	SHR	SJ5926	4,3,1 note. 4,8,3
Hopton (Wales)	SHR	SO2391	4,1,35
Hopton	STS	SJ9426	11,41
Hopton (near Lowestoft)	SFK	TG5200	1,51

Hopton (in Thelnetham)	SFK	TL9979	14,80
Hopton [Castle]	SHR	SO3678	4,20,12
Hopton [Sollers]	HEF	SO6349	16,2
[Upper] Hopton WR	YKS	SE1918	9W108 note. SW,Ag13
Hopton [Wafers]	SHR	SO6376	7,3
Hopwas	STS	SK1705	1,31
Hopwell	DBY	SK4436	2,1
Horbling	LIN	TF1135	2,33. 12,57. 26,46. 46,2. 57,20
Horbling Hundred	LIN	—	12,56
Horbury WR	YKS	SE2918	1Y15. SW,Ag10
Hordle	HAM	SZ2795	NF5,1
Hordley	SHR	SJ3830	4,18,1
Hore(n)bodebi (in Sessay) NR	YKS	??	3Y12 note. 11N19. SN,Bi4
Horfield	GLS	ST5976	1,15
Horham	SFK	TM2172	6,309;316-317. 7,4. 14,161. 19,4;6. 31,4. 64,2. 75,3
Horkstow	LIN	SE9818	24,15
Horley	OXF	SP4143	16,1. 27,1. 34,2
[Great and Little] Hormead	HRT	TL4029 TL4029	17,11. 24,2. 38,2. Appx
Horn RUT	NTH		3,1. 56,27
Horn RUT	RUT	SK9511	EN6;19
Hornacott	CON	SX3293	5,8,1
Hornblotton	SOM	ST5934	8,30
Hornby LAN	YKS	SD5868	1W70-71. See also CHS Y1
Hornby (near Appleton Wiske) NR	YKS	NZ3605	31N2 note
Hornby (near Hackforth) NR	YKS	SE2293	6N61 note. SN,CtA22
Horncastle	LIN	TF2569	1,91-106
[East and West] Horndon	ESS	TQ6389 TQ6288	18,12. 24,1. 48,1
Horndon [on the-Hill]	ESS	TQ6683	4,10. 20,2. 24,5. 60,1. 61,1. 90,1-2
Hornes	SFK	??	31,31
Horning	NFK	TG3516	17,35
Horninghold	LEC	SP8097	15,1
Horningsea	CAM	TL4962	5,14
Horningsham	WIL	ST8141	19,4. 26,20
Horningtoft	NFK	TF9323	1,77
Hornington [Manor] WR	YKS	SE5141	13W17 note. 25W7. CW31;37. SW,An7
Horns	SSX	TQ6106	10,75-76
Hornsea ER	YKS	TA2047	14E7. SE,Hol12
Horringer	SFK	TL8262	14,2;17. 25,29
Horseham [Hall]	ESS	TL6643	13,2. 35,7. 90,52;75
Horseheath	CAM	TL6147	14,5-6. 19,2. 26,9. 29,8. Appx F
Horsenden	BKM	SP7902	4,8-9. 12,2. 57,14
Horsepool FLN	CHS	??	FT3,2
Horsepool	NTT	SK7047	11,12
Horsewall (Wales)	SHR	SO2098	4,1,36
Horsey	NFK	TG4523	9,88;183. 10,42. 65,1;6
Horsey	SOM	ST3239	24,25
Horsey	SSX	TQ6200	10,73
[Horsey] Pignes: see *Pignes* SOM			
Horsford	NFK	TG1915	7,16
Horsforth WR	YKS	SE2337	1W17 note. 31W4. SW,Sk17
Horsham	NFK	TG2115	7,17
Horsington	LIN	TF1968	13,23. 14,56. 25,17
Horsington	SOM	ST7023	28,1
Horsley	DBY	SK3744	11,2
Horsley	GLS	ST8398	24,1
[East] Horsley	SRY	TQ0952	2,6

[West] Horsley	SRY	TQ0752	22,5
Horspath	OXF	SP5704	29,12
Horstead	NFK	TG2619	1,231-232;235
Horsted [Keynes]	SSX	TQ3828	10,109
[Little] Horsted	SSX	TQ4718	10,66
Horswold	SFK	TM1456	21,19. 29,9
Horton (near Datchet)	BKM	TQ0175	29,1
Horton (in Ivinghoe)	BKM	SP9219	12,23. 22,2. 23,28
Horton	DEV	SS3017	3,11
Horton	DOR	SU0207	14,1
Horton	GLS	ST7684	46,2
Horton	KEN	TR1155	D18. 5,162
Horton	NTH	SP8154	4,28. 39,7. 56,20f;34
Horton (in Hadley)	SHR	SJ6814	4,14,20
Horton (in Wem)	SHR	SJ4929	4,14,3
Horton (near Tamhorn)	STS	??	2,22
Horton	WOR	SO8766	26,11
Horton WR	YKS	SD8550	13W42. 30W4
Horton [in Ribblesdale] WR	YKS	SD8172	30W7
Horton [Kirby]	KEN	TQ5668	5,18
[Monk's] Horton	KEN	TR1240	9,25-26;30
Horwood	DEV	SS5027	3,11;17. 34,8
[Great and Little] Horwood	BKM	SP7731	14,21
Hose	LEC	SK7329	15,13. 20,1-2. 43,9-10
Hoseley FLN	CHS	SJ3755	A19
Hotham ER	YKS	SE8934	1Y7. 3Y1. 5E5-6;16. 11E5-6.
			31E4. SE,C4-5
Hothorpe	NTH	SP6685	8,9
Hotlop	HAM	??	69,23
Hoton	LEC	SK5722	42,5. 43,1
Hottune	NFK	??	10,63
Hougenai (= Millom Castle) CUM	YKS	SD1781	1L6 *note*. See also CHS Y7
Hough [on the Hill]	LIN	SK9246	12,43-46. 24,100
Hougham	KEN	TR2739	M23. 5,138
Hougham	LIN	SK8844	7,54-55. 26,34-35. 56,5
Houghpark	DBY	SK2446	6,47
Houghton	HAM	SU3432	2,20. 21,5. 23,16. 40,1. 68,3
Houghton	HUN	TL2872	6,8
Houghton (in Grantham)	LIN	SK9234	8,12. 31,6. 57,48-49. 67,20-21
Houghton (near West Rudham)	NFK	TF7928	8,108
Houghton	SFK	TL7846	43,1
Houghton ER	YKS	SE8939	1Y6 *note*. 11E7. 21E11. SE,Wei1;3
Houghton [Conquest]	BDF	TL0441	23,14. 53,2. 54,2
[Glass] Houghton WR	YKS	SE4324	9W55. SW,O10
[Great] Houghton WR	YKS	SE4306	5W17. CW20. SW,Sf30
[Great and Little] Houghton	NTH	SP7958	2,2. 35,21. 56,57b;57g;63-64
		SP8059	
[Hanging] Houghton	NTH	SP7573	8,5. 18,31. 39,3. 56,42
[Little] Houghton WR	YKS	SE4205	10W24. SW,Sf18
Houghton [on the Hill]	NFK	TF8605	21,15
Houghton [on-the-Hill]	LEC	SK6703	14,16
Houghton [Regis]	BDF	TL0123	1,3. 1,4
Houghton [St Giles]	NFK	TF9235	1,33
[Stony] Houghton	DBY	SK4966	8,6
Hougon (= Millom) CUM	YKS	SD1780	1L6 *note*. See also CHS Y7
Hound	HAM	SU4708	23,18
Houndsfield	WOR	SP0876	1,1a
Houndstone	SOM	ST5217	19,81
Houndtor	DEV	SX7579	5,11
Housham [Hall]	ESS	TL5011	22,3. 51,1
Hoveringham	NTT	SK6946	11,14

Hoveton (in Welburn) NR	YKS	SE6786	23N20 *note*
Hoveton [St John and St Peter]	NFK	TG3018	1,207. 8,10. 17,21;24;33; 37.
		TG3119	20,31. 26,5
Hovingham NR	YKS	SE6675	23N23
How [Hill]: see *Herleshow* YKS			
Howbridge	ESS	TL8113	4,15. 32,4
Howbury	KEN	TQ5376	5,20
Howden ER	YKS	SE7428	3Y4;6. 5E12;15;25-26. CE16.
			SE,How1;6
Howe	ESS	TL6933	23,15. 90,53
Howe	NFK	TM2799	1,105. 14,17
Howe NR	YKS	SE3580	6N158. SN,CtA44
Howell	LIN	TF1346	1,3. 7,46. 24,39. 26,29. 67,2
Howgrave NR	YKS	SE3179	2W13 *note*. 3Y9. 6N142. SW,H4.
			SN, CtA39
Howle	SHR	SJ6923	4,19,5
Howle [Hill]	HEF	SO6020	1,60
Howsham	LIN	TA0404	1,66. 12,11;13
Howsham ER	YKS	SE7362	5E60;63-65;67. SE,Ac5
Howthorpe [Farm] NR	YKS	SE6772	23N24 *note*
Hoxne	SFK	TM1877	1,92;114. 6,70;308;311-313. 8,36-
			37;42. 14,161. 21,45-46. 44,2.
			64,3. 75,3;5
Hoxton	MDX	TQ3383	3,25-26
[High] Hoyland WR	YKS	SE2710	9W75. SW,St6
Hoyland [Nether] WR	YKS	SE3600	10W18. 12W1;6. SW, Sf11;16
Hoyland [Swaine] WR	YKS	SK2604	9W70;92. SW,St14
Hubberholme WR	YKS	SD9278	30W5
Huby NR	YKS	SE5665	1Y1. 29N13. SN,B17
Hucclecote	GLS	SO8717	2,2
Hucklow	DBY	SK1777	7,10
Hucknall [Torkard]	NTT	SK5349	10,49. 15,4
Huddersfield WR	YKS	SE1416	9W109. SW,Ag13
Huddington	WOR	SO9457	2,57
Hudeston	NFK	TM1193	9,100. 31,8. 50,11
Hudswell NR	YKS	NZ1400	6N68. SN,CtA23
Huffingford IOW	HAM	SZ5086	9,14;20
Huggate ER	YKS	SE8855	1E9. 29E7. SE,Wa3
Huggingehale	SFK	??	*14, 164*
Hughenden	BKM	SU8695	4,16
Huish (near Dolton)	DEV	SS5311	25,2. 42,4
Huish (in Instow)	DEV	SS4829	3,16
Huish (in Tedburn St Mary)	DEV	SX8293	49,7
Huish (in Burnham on Sea)	SOM	ST3147	24,35-36
Huish (in Nettlecombe)	SOM	ST0439	21,43. 31,3
Huish	WIL	SU1463	68,3
Huish [Champflower]	SOM	ST0429	22,2
[North] Huish	DEV	SX7156	17,46
[South] Huish	DEV	SX6941	17,36
Hulcote	NTH	SP7050	2,1. 48,15
Hulland	DBY	SK2447	9,3
Hullasey	GLS	ST9699	1,23
Hullavington	WIL	ST8982	41,1
[Abbey] Hulton	STS	SJ9048	11,21
Humber	HEF	SO5356	1,10c
Humberstone	LEC	SK6206	13,24
Humberstone	LIN	TA3105	14,4
Humbleton ER	YKS	TA2234	14E2. SE,Hol6
Humburton NR	YKS	SE4268	28W33 *note*. 28W36. SW,H6
Humby	LIN	TF0032	31,4
Humet	SHR	??	5,4

Hunchilhuse(s) (in Sherburn in Elmet) WR	YKS	??	9W21 *note.* SW,BA5
Huncoat LAN	CHS	SD7730	R4,2
Huncote	LEC	SP5197	9,3-4
Hunderthwaite NR	YKS	NY9821	6N41. SN,CtA16
Hundesthoft/Hundestuf (in Sutton)	SFK	TM3248	6,250. 21,82
Hundleby	LIN	TF3866	3,24. 14,72
Hundon	LIN	TA1102	1,65. CN,6
Hundon	SFK	TL7348	24,2;12
Hundulfthorpe [Farm] NR	YKS	SE4385	5N75 *note.* SN,Bi8
Hunesworde	OXF	??	21,1 *note*
Hungerton	LEC	SK6907	15,10
Hungerton	LIN	SK8730	18,26
Hunmanby ER	YKS	TA0977	20E1-2;4. SE,Tu1
Hunningham	WAR	SP3768	28,6-7
Hunsdon	HRT	TL4114	25,2. 44,1
Hunshelf [Hall] WR	YKS	SK2799	9W85 *note.* SW,St10
Hunsingore WR	YKS	SE4253	5W36. 24W7-8;20. SW, Bu8
Hunslet WR	YKS	SE3131	9W125. SW,M3
Hunsley ER	YKS	SE9535	3Y1 *note.* 23E4. SE, C3
Hunstanton	NFK	TF6841	1,209. 9,9;118. 10,51. 16,5. 49,2
Hunston	SFK	TL9768	1,89. 14,95
Hunston	SSX	SU8602	11,43
Huntingdon	HUN	TL2371	B. D1
Huntingfield	SFK	TM3374	6,80;82
Huntington	CHS	SJ4262	A4
Huntington (near Hereford)	HEF	SO4841	2,40
Huntington (near Kington)	HEF	SO2553	1,69
Huntington	SHR	SO5371	4,11,2-3
Huntington	STS	SJ9713	13,10
Huntington NR	YKS	SE6156	1N101. 5N66. 6N162. SN,B16
Huntley	GLS	SO7219	32,6
Hunton	KEN	TQ7249	*3,5*
Hunton NR	YKS	SE1892	6N135. SN,CtA38
Hunt's [Hall]	ESS	TL8432	22,13
Huntsham	DEV	ST0020	42,14;23
Huntshaw	DEV	SS5022	19,5
[East and West] Huntspill	SOM	ST3444 ST3044	24,28;34
Huntstile	SOM	ST2633	46,11
Huntworth	SOM	ST3134	35,3
Hunworth	NFK	TG0635	1,23. 4,21. 25,22
Hurcott	WOR	SO8577	1,2
Hurdcott (near Barford St Martin)	WIL	SU0431	27,25
Hurdcott (near Winterbourne Earls)	WIL	SU1733	37,16
Hurley	BRK	SU8283	38,5
Hurlston LAN	CHS	SD4010	R1,32
Hurn DOR	HAM	SZ1296	23,61
Hurpston	DOR	SY9280	55,38-39
Hurst and [Old] Hurst	GLS	SO7102 SO7202	1,17
Hurst (in Chilham)	KEN	TR0651	D18. 5,153
Hurst	SSX	TQ7819	9,129
[Upper] Hurst	DBY	SK2283	10,17
Hurstbourne [Priors]	HAM	SU4346	3,6
Hurstbourne [Tarrant]	HAM	SU3853	1,44
Hurstpierpoint	SSX	TQ2716	12,36. 13,46
Hurtmore	SRY	SU9545	22,2
[Martin] Hussingtree	WOR	SO8860	8,12
Huttoft	LIN	TF5176	13,8. 27,60-61. 68,14
Huttoft Hundred	LIN	—	12,97. CS,16-17

Hutton	ESS	TQ6394	13,1
Hutton	SOM	ST3558	5,10. 8,38
Hutton (in Quernemore) LAN	YKS	SD5163	1L2 *note*. See also CHS Y3
Hutton [Bonville] NR	YKS	NZ3300	1N115 *note*. SN,Bi6 note. SN,A2
Hutton [Buscel] NR	YKS	SE9784	1Y3. SN,L18 note. SN,D7
Hutton [Conyers] NR	YKS	SE3273	2W13 *note*. 3Y9. SW, H3-5
Hutton [Cranswick] ER	YKS	TA0252	5E39 *note*. 23E8. SE,Dr5
Hutton [Hang] NR	YKS	SE1788	6N131. SN,Bi6 note. SN,CtA37
Hutton [le Hole] NR	YKS	SE7090	23N20
[Low] Hutton NR	YKS	SE7667	1N85 *note*. 8N9. 31N8. SN,L18 note. SN,B1
Hutton [Lowcross] NR	YKS	NZ6013	5N19. SN,L18-19 *note*
Hutton [Magna] NR	YKS	NZ1212	6N2. SN,Bi6 note. SN,CtA8
Hutton [Mulgrave] NR	YKS	NZ8310	5N2. SN,L6 *note*
[Old] Hutton WES	YKS	SD5688	1L7. See also CHS Y8
[Priest] Hutton LAN	YKS	SD5373	1L4. See also CHS Y5
Hutton [Roof] WES	YKS	SD5778	1L3. See also CHS Y4
Hutton [Rudby] NR	YKS	NZ4606	5N29. SN,L18 note. SN,L42
[Sand] Hutton (near Thirsk) NR	YKS	SE3882	1Y1. SN,Bi6 note
[Sand] Hutton (near York) NR	YKS	SE6958	1N95. 23N30. CN4 *note*. SNB11
[Sheriff] Hutton NR	YKS	SE6566	1N87. 5N54. CN5 *note*. SN,L6 note. SN,B3
Hutton Wandesley: see [Hutton] Wandesley WR, YKS			
Huxham	DEV	SX9497	34,29
Huxhill	DEV	SS4923	35,11
Huyton LAN	CHS	SJ4491	R1,3
Hyde [Hall]	HRT	TL3432	20,10
[North] Hykeham	LIN	SK9465	12,92. 65,5. CK,29
[South] Hykeham	LIN	SK9364	65,3. CK,27
Hythe	KEN	TR1634	2,26;41

I

Ial (Wales)	SHR	??	4,2,1
Ianulfestorp (in Dunnington) ER	YKS	??	13E6 *note.* CE25-26. SE,Sn9
Iarpestuna: see *Ierp(e)stuna* NFK			
Ibberton	DOR	ST7807	1,10
Ible	DBY	SK2457	1,12
Ibsley	HAM	SU1509	23,52
Ibstock	LEC	SK4009	44,11
Ibstone BKM	BKM	SU7593	48,1. E7-8
Ibstone BKM	OXF		58,11;13
Icheburna	SFK	??	6,297
Ickburgh	NFK	TL8195	8,41. 22,21. 22,15-16, 50,2
Ickenham	MDX	TQ0786	7,8. 9,6. 15,2
Ickford	BKM	SP6407	12,6. 23,8
Ickham	KEN	TR2258	3,8
Ickleton	CAM	TL4943	1,20. 15,1. 26,15;23
Icklingham	SFK	TL7772	1,115. 34,1. 53,1
Ickworth	SFK	TL8161	14,10
[Church] Icomb GLS	GLS	SP2122	E26. EvC40. WoB7. WoC6
[Church] Icomb GLS	WOR		2,41
Icomb *[Place]*	GLS	SP2122	39,4
Icomb *[Proper]*	GLS	SP2022	53,8
Idbury	OXF	SP2320	30,1
Iddesleigh	DEV	SS5608	1,63. 24,22
Iddinshall	CHS	SJ5362	A6
Ide	DEV	SX8990	2,6
Ideford	DEV	SX8977	48,8
Iden	SSX	TQ9123	9,110
Idleigh	KEN	TQ6265	5,7
Idless	CON	SW8247	5,15,6
Idlicote	WAR	SP2844	22,5
Idmiston	WIL	SU1937	7,14
Idson	SOM	ST2244	21,27
Ierp(e)stuna	NFK	??	1,239 *note.* 31,14. 35,18
Iffley	OXF	SP5203	18,1
Ifield	SSX	TQ2537	13,54
Iford	SSX	TQ4007	12,3
Ightfield	SHR	SJ5938	4,23,11
Ilbury	OXF	SP4331	27,7
Ilchester	SOM	ST5222	1,10;31. 24,17
Ildeberga GLS	GLS	??	E34
Ildeberga GLS	WOR		10,12
Ilford	ESS	TQ4486	64,1
Ilfracombe	DEV	SS5147	16,84
Ilkerton	DEV	SS7046	19,16
Ilkeston	DBY	SK4641	13,1. 17,13-14
Ilketshall [St Andrew, St John, St Lawrence, and St Margaret]	SFK	TM3787	4,20;22-24;26;28;32.13,7
		TM3687	
		TM3686	
		TM3485	
Ilkley WR	YKS	SE1147	2W4. 13W5. SW,Sk1;18
?Illand	CON	SX2878	3,7. 5,1,17
Illeigh: see Eleigh SOM			
Illington	NFK	TL9490	8,58

Illston [on-the-Hill]	LEC	SP7099	1,4. 8,3. 13,13. 17,16
Ilmer	BKM	SP7605	4,21
Ilmington	WAR	SP2143	16,20;64. 22,20
Ilminster	SOM	ST3614	9,3
Ilsham	DEV	SX9364	51,9
Ilsington	DEV	SX7876	32,6
Ilsington	DOR	SY7591	27,2
[East] Ilsley	BRK	SU4981	B4. 3,1. 21,2. 22,7. 38,1
[West] Ilsley	BRK	SU4782	38,2
Iltney [Farm]	ESS	TL8804	20,16. 24,42
Ilton	DEV	SX7240	17,39
Ilton	SOM	ST3517	10,1
Ilton NR	YKS	SE1978	6N117. SN,CtA33
Imber	WIL	ST9648	41,6
Immerworth (now Ember [Court])	SRY	TQ1467	19,22
Immingham	LIN	TA1715	22,1. 32,22
Impington	CAM	TL4463	5,41;43. 32,36
Ince	CHS	SJ4476	A16
Ince [Blundell] LAN	CHS	SD3203	R1,10
Indrelag(e): see *Hindrelag(he)* YKS			
Ingardine	SHR	SO6281	4,14,28
Ingarsby	LEC	SK6805	C11. 13,51
Ingatestone	ESS	TQ6599	9,11
Ingbirchworth WR	YKS	SE2205	9W86. SW,St11 *note*
Ingestre	STS	SJ9724	11,32
Ingham	LIN	SK9483	4,5-6. 7,14. 16,41-226,11-13;24. 28,7;9. 40,2-3. 68,30
Ingham	NFK	TG3926	4,39;41. 17,57
Ingham	OXF	SU6794	59,28
Ingham	SFK	TL8570	8,32. 14,64;69
Ingleby	DBY	SK3527	1,26. 10,23. 14,5. 17,23
Ingleby	LIN	SK8977	4,2. 18,1. 22,30
Ingleby [Arncliffe] NR	YKS	NZ4400	1N127. 31N5. SN,A7
Ingleby Barwick NR: see Ingleby Hill, *Englebi* (Barwick), NR, YKS			
Ingleby [Greenhow] NR	YKS	NZ5806	29N9. SN,L35 note. SN,L40
Ingleby [Hill] (in Ingleby Barwick) NR	YKS	NZ4412	4N3 *note*. SN,L35 *note*
Inglecroft FLN	CHS	??	FT2,7
Ingleigh	DEV	SS6007	39,4
Inglethwaite NR	YKS	??	13N15 *note*. SN,B22
Ingleton WR	YKS	SD6972	1L3
Inglewood	BRK	SU3666	40,2. 65,18;20
Ingloss	NFK	TM3496	35,7
Ingmanthorpe [Hall] WR	YKS	SE4250	5W37 *note*. 24W20. SW,Bu44
Ingoldisthorpe	NFK	TF6932	34,4. 50,4
Ingoldmells	LIN	TF5568	38,9
Ingoldsby	LIN	TF0130	24,99. 31,10. 58,3. 67,7-8. CK,35
Ingoluestuna (in Carlford Hundred)	SFK	??	21,65. 32,26. 67,18
Ingoluestuna (in Plomesgate Hundred)	SFK	??	6,146
Ingrave	ESS	TQ6292	18,5. 34,3. 37,1
Ingsdon	DEV	SX8173	32,7. 43,5
Ingthorpe [Grange] WR	YKS	SD8952	30W27 *note*
Ingworth	NFK	TG1929	9,87. 21,33
Inkberrow	WOR	SP0157	2,16. 3,3
Inkersall	NTT	SK6360	17,6
Inkpen	BRK	SU3764	22,10. 65,18
Inskip LAN	YKS	SD4637	1L1. See also CHS Y2
Instaple	DEV	SS3211	19,3
Instead	SFK	TM2380	75,4
Instow	DEV	SS4730	24,26
Intwood	NFK	TG1904	24,7

Inwardleigh	DEV	SX5699	16,23
Inwood	SSX	??	10,116
Iping	SSX	SU8522	14,2
Ipplepen	DEV	SX8366	33,1
Ipsden	OXF	SU6385	58,2
Ipsley WOR	WAR		37,6
Ipsley WOR	WOR	SP0665	EW1
Ipswich SFK	ESS		ESf2
Ipswich SFK	SFK	TM1644	1,116;122a-122d;122f-122g. 3,55;63. 6,4. 16,47. 25,52;60;62. 27,8. 31,55. 32,7. 38,3. 39,12. 41,13. 63,1. 74,9;11
Irby [Manor] NR	YKS	NZ4103	1Y2 *note*. SN,A1
Irby [upon Humber]	LIN	TA1904	13,19. 14,34. 44,9
Irchester	NTH	SP9265	18,81. 35,1e;1j
Ireby LAN	YKS	SD6575	1L3. See also CHS Y4
[Kirk] Ireton	DBY	SK2650	1,13
[Little] Ireton	DBY	SK3141	6,92
Iretone NR	YKS	??	23N1 *note*
Irish Hill (= *Ebrige*)	BRK	SU4066	58,2
Irishcombe	DEV	SS7817	1,66
Irmingland	NFK	TG1229	8,8-9. 25,12
Irnham	LIN	TF0226	27,41. 35,14. CK,9
Irthlingborough	NTH	SP9470	6,15. 6a,30
Irton NR	YKS	TA0184	13N10. SN,D6
Iscoyd FLN	CHS	SJ5042	2,2
Isham	NTH	SP8873	4,8. 41,5. 55,1
Isle [Abbotts]	SOM	ST3520	9,4-5
Isle [Brewers]	SOM	ST3621	19,8. 35,17
Islebeck [Grange] NR	YKS	SE4577	23N8 *note*
Isleham	CAM	TL6474	1,3. 4,1. 14,72. 28,1
Isleton	SFK	TM2143	21,66. 32,27
Isleworth	MDX	TQ1675	12,1
Islington	MDX	TQ3184	3,22-23. 9,3. 23,1
Islington	NFK	TF5716	4,44. 13,13. 14,1;4. 15,4;6. 19,1;3. 23,10. 66,56
Islip	NTH	SP9879	1,13b;13e. 4,27
Islip	OXF	SP5214	55,1
Isombridge	SHR	SJ6113	4,11,18
Isteuertona	SFK	??	31,12
Itchel	HAM	SU7849	3,8
Itchen [Abbas]	HAM	SU5332	44,1
Itchenor	SSX	SU7901	6,1. 11,45
Itchington	GLS	ST6586	3,1. WoA4. WoB15
[Bishop's] Itchington	WAR	SP3857	6,12
[Long] Itchington	WAR	SP4165	42,3
Itford	SSX	TQ4305	10,11
Itterby	LIN	TA3108	4,37;71. 30,16. 47,4
Itteringham	NFK	TG1430	1,195. 8,8
Ivedon	DEV	ST1401	19,42-43. 34,45;47
Iver	BKM	TQ0381	19,1
Ivinghoe	BKM	SP9416	3,2
Ivington	HEF	SO4756	1,10a
Ivonbrook	DBY	SK2458	6,1
Iwerne [Courtney] or [Shroton]	DOR	ST8512	42,1
Iwerne [Minster]	DOR	ST8614	19,7
Iwerne [Stepleton]	DOR	ST8611	36,9
Ixworth	SFK	TL9370	14,100. 66,1;9-10. 75,2
Ixworth Thorpe: see [Ixworth] Thorpe SFK			

J

Jacques [Hall]	ESS	TM1531	39,9
Jaonei	KEN	??	9,39
Jevington	SSX	TQ5602	9,73;10,26

K

Kaldecotes: see *Caldecota(n)* SFK

Kalletuna	SFK	??	21,64
Kalweton	SFK	TM2434	3,78
[Old] Kea	CON	SW8441	5,24,12
[East] Keal	LIN	TF3863	3,23;25;45-46. 14,79. 29,10
[West] Keal	LIN	TF3663	14,80. 29,11;16-17. 68,5-6
Kearby [Town End] WR	YKS	SE3446	13W27 *note*. SW,Bu35
Keddington	LIN	TF3488	3,27-28;30. 40,17. CS,9
Kedington	SFK	TL7047	14,158. 25,15;94. 33,1
Kedleston	DBY	SK3140	6,80
Keelby	LIN	TA1609	1,78. 2,8. 4,28;30. 7,27. 14,45. 30,9. 32,4-5. 47,3. CN,11
Keevil	WIL	ST9258	25,1
Kegworth	LEC	SK4826	C8. 43,6
Keighley WR	YKS	SE0641	1W64 *note*
Keinton [Mandeville]	SOM	ST5430	19,59. 21,92
Keisby	LIN	TF0328	57,41-42. 68,22
Kelbrook WR	YKS	SD9044	13W43. 30W4
Kelby	LIN	TF0041	3,35. 57,34
Keletuna/Cheletuna/Chiletuna	SFK	??	6,41-43 note;288
Kelfield ER	YKS	SE5938	6E1. 23E10. SE,P4
Kelham	NTT	SK7755	9,59. 11,19. 15,3. 18,4. 30,45
[Great] Kelk ER	YKS	TA1058	2E14. SE,Tu4
[Little] Kelk ER	YKS	TA0959	1E28. SE,Tu5
Kellaways: see Tytherton WIL			
[Nether and Over] Kellet LAN	YKS	SD5068 SD5270	1L2 *note*. See also CHS Y3
Kelleythorpe ER	YKS	TA0156	1Y8. 2E10. SE,Dr1-2
Kelling	NFK	TG0841	6,3. 50,9. 57,1. 66,97
Kellington WR	YKS	SE5524	9W60;62. SW,O13-14
Kelly	DEV	SX3981	16,11
Kelmarsh	NTH	SP7379	1,15g. 35,13
Kelsale	SFK	TM3865	6,69;73. 7,3;34-36;72;74;132
[North] Kelsey	LIN	TA0401	1,68. 12,9-12. 22,8
[South] Kelsey	LIN	TF0498	1,79. 16,4
Kelshall	HRT	TL3236	8,2
Kelsit [Grange] NR	YKS	SE5463	1Y1 *note*. SN,B20
Kelstern	LIN	TF2590	13,29. 27,33. 47,10
Kelston FLN	CHS	SJ1081	FT2,11
Kelvedon	ESS	TL8518	6,5. 27,2
Kelvedon [Hatch]	ESS	TQ5698	6,9. 18,25. 28,15
Kelynack	CON	SW3729	5,3,28
Kemberton	SHR	SJ7204	4,9,2
Kemble GLS	GLS	ST9897	E11
Kemble GLS	WIL		8,7
Kembroke	SFK	TM2641	7,92;121. 21,52. 67,9
Kemerton WOR	GLS		1,41. 19,2. 20,1
Kemerton WOR	WOR	SO9437	EG3;9-10
Kempley and Kempley [Green]	GLS	SO6729	39,1
Kempsey	WOR	SO8449	2,2
Kempsford	GLS	SU1696	60,1
Kempshott	HAM	SU5947	23,9
Kempston	BDF	TL0147	53,5. 53,3-4;32-33

Kempston	NFK	TF8816	8,65
Kempton	MDX	TQ1170	8,2;5
Kempton	SHR	SO3683	4,20,5
Kenchester	HEF	SO4342	29,1
Kencot	OXF	SP2504	28,26
Kendal: see Kirkby (in Kendal) WES			
[Great] Kendale ER	YKS	TA0160	1Y8 *note*. SE,Dr2
Kenilworth	WAR	SP2872	1,9
Kenley	SHR	SJ5600	4,3,19
Kenn	DEV	SX9285	16,1;58
Kenn	SOM	ST4169	5,29
Kennett	CAM	TL6968	18,8. Appx A
[East and West] Kennett	WIL	SU1167	26,21. 37,5. 50,5
		SU1168	
Kenninghall NFK	NFK	TM0485	1,76;143-144;146. 4,47. 8,59-60. 9,75;77;132-133. 11,2. 14,9. 15,11-12. 19,14. 39,1. 58,2. 66,76-77;95
Kenninghall NFK	SFK		ENf1
Kenningham	NFK	TM2099	12,39. 48,6-7
Kennington	BRK	SP5202	7,11
Kennington	KEN	TR0245	7,28
Kennington	SRY	TQ3077	36,6
Kenningtons	ESS	TQ5681	22,14. 24,62
Kennythorpe ER	YKS	SE7865	23E14. SE,Sc1
Kensington	MDX	TQ2579	21,1
Kenswick	WOR	SO7958	2,9
Kensworth BDF	BDF	TL0319	E2
Kensworth BDF	HRT		13,1
Kentisbeare	DEV	ST0608	16,100;102
Kentisbury	DEV	SS6243	16,75
Kenton	DEV	SX9583	1,26
Kenton	SFK	TM1965	6,11;271. 14,119. 16,8
Kentwell	SFK	TL8647	12,5
Kepwick NR	YKS	SE4790	1N135. 23N8. SN,A10
Kerdiston	NFK	TG0824	8,2. 31,1
Keresforth [Hall] WR	YKS	SE3304	9W80 *note*. SW,St15
Kermincham	CHS	SJ7967	11,7
Kern IOW	HAM	SZ5786	1,W11
Kersall	NTT	SK7162	17,9
Kersey	SFK	TM0043	24,1. 25,108
Kersford	DEV	SX4986	*16,7*
Kerswell (in Broadhembury)	DEV	ST0806	32,2
Kerswell (in Hockworthy)	DEV	ST0120	23,8
Kesgrave	SFK	TM2145	6,114
Kessingland	SFK	TM5286	1,31. 4,35. 31,27
Keston	KEN	TQ4163	*3,1.* 5,37
Keswick	NFK	TG2104	9,94;198. 12,41
[East] Keswick WR	YKS	SE3644	1W10. SW,Sk14
Ketford	GLS	SO7230	68,12
Ketsby	LIN	TF3676	13,42-43
Kettering	NTH	SP8778	6,17
Ketteringham	NFK	TG1602	9,95;197. 32,5
Kettlebaston	SFK	TL9650	14,114
Kettleburgh	SFK	TM2660	3,31 *note*;34;45 note;52 *note*;53 note;95. 6,261;269. *8,21;22-23*
Kettleby	LIN	TA0307	30,6. 34,8. 64,19
[Ab] Kettleby	LEC	SK7223	17,30
[Eye] Kettleby	LEC	SK7316	29,3
Kettlestone	NFK	TF9631	8,101
Kettlethorpe ER	YKS	SE9133	11E4 *note*. SE,C4 *note*

Kettlethorpe (near Roxby) NR	YKS	??	1N51 *note.* SN,D17
Kettleton	NFK	TM1494	4,56. 9,98;210;223
Kettlewell WR	YKS	SD9772	30W5
Ketton RUT	NTH		1,1
Ketton RUT	RUT	SK9704	EN1
Kewstoke	SOM	ST3363	42,1
Kex [Moor] WR	YKS	SE2075	28W17. SW,Bu25
Kexbrough WR	YKS	SE2909	9W74. SW,St6
Kexby	LIN	SK8785	7,7. 26,22. 68,29
Keyford and [Little] Keyford	SOM	ST7747	5,55. 36,12
		ST7746	
Keyham	LEC	SK6706	1,3
Keyingham ER	YKS	TA2425	14E12. CE44. SE,Holl8
Keymer	SSX	TQ3015	12,18;39
Keynedon	DEV	SX7743	34,55
Keynsham	SOM	ST6568	1,28
Keysoe BDF	BDF	TL0762	23,1. 44,3. 23,2
Keysoe BDF	HUN		13,2. 29,2
Keyston	HUN	TL0475	1,7. D20
Keythorpe	LEC	SK7699	2,6. 28,3
Keyworth	NTT	SP6130	4,7. 9,87-88. 10,10. 13,7
Kibworth [Beauchamp]	LEC	SP6893	19,14-15
Kibworth [Harcourt]	LEC	SP6894	C13. 16,8
Kiddal [Hall] WR	YKS	SE3939	9W1 *note.* 9W9. SW,Sk4;6
Kidderminster	WOR	SO8376	1,2
Kiddington	OXF	SP4122	56,4. 59,15
Kidlington	OXF	SP4914	28,4
Kidsley	DBY	SK4146	1,17
Kidwell	DEV	ST0114	24,8
Kigbeare	DEV	SX5496	16,22
Kilburn NR	YKS	SE5179	23N2
Kilby	LEC	SP6295	38,1
Kilcot	GLS	SO6925	68,12
Kildale NR	YKS	NZ6009	29N5. 31N7. SN,L30
Kildwick WR	YKS	SE0145	1W61
Kilham ER	YKS	TA0664	1Y8. 1E29. 26E12. 29E12. SE,Bt2
Kilkhampton	CON	SS2511	1,5
Killamarsh	DBY	SK4680	12,5. 17,2
Killerby [Hall] (near Catterick) NR	YKS	SE2596	6N52 *note.* SN,CtA19
Killerby [Hall] (in Cayton) NR	YKS	TA0682	13N8 *note.* SN,D5
Killerwick LAN	YKS	SD2274	1L6 *note.* See also CHS Y7
Killigorrick	CON	SX2261	5,2,7
Killinghall WR	YKS	SE2858	1Y18. 2W7. SW,Bu31;46
Killingholme	LIN	TA1417	12,7. 14,31. 30,10. 32,21
Killington	DEV	SS6646	3,37
Kilmarth	CON	SX0078	5,16,2
Kilmersdon	SOM	ST6952	16,14
Kilmeston	HAM	SU5926	2,2;7
Kilmington	DEV	SY2797	1,53
Kilmington WIL	SOM		1,9. 37,7
Kilmington WIL	WIL	ST7736	E4-5
Kilminorth	CON	SX2353	5,4,19
Kilnsea ER	YKS	TA4215	14E2 *note.* SE,Hol4
Kilnsey WR	YKS	SD9767	29W48 *note*
Kilnwick ER	YKS	SE9949	1Y8. 5E30. SE,Sn2-3
Kilnwick [Percy] ER	YKS	SE8249	1Y10 *note.* 31E5. SE,Wa4
Kilpeck	HEF	SO4430	1,53
Kilpin ER	YKS	SE7726	3Y4. SE,How2
Kilsby	NTH	SP5671	12,3
Kilton	SOM	ST1643	25,30
Kilton NR	YKS	NZ7018	1N9. 5N16. SN,L17

Kilve	SOM	ST1442	21,47
Kilverstone NFK	NFK	TL8984	1,142. 7,3. 66,57
?Kilverstone NFK: see			
Kuluertestuna/Kyluertestuna/			
Culuerdestuna SFK			
Kilvington	NTT	SK8042	6,3. 20,2. 22,1
[North] Kilvington NR	YKS	SE4285	1Y2 *note*. 5N72;75. SN,Bi8
[North] Kilworth	LEC	SP6183	44,12-13
[South] Kilworth	LEC	SP6081	16,3. 23,5
Kimber	DEV	SX4998	35,7
Kimberley	NFK	TG0704	1,81. 66,39
Kimberley	NTT	SK4944	10,47-48;63
Kimberworth WR	YKS	SK4093	10W31. SW,Sf27
[Great] Kimble	BKM	SP8205	14,2
[Little] Kimble	BKM	SP8207	35,1
Kimbolton HUN	BDF		17,3
Kimbolton HUN	HUN	TL0967	13,1;5. D10
Kimcote	LEC	SP5886	3,9
Kimmeridge	DOR	SY9179	11,15. 37,5
Kimpton	HAM	SU2846	23,47
Kimpton	HRT	TL1718	5,24
Kimworthy	DEV	SS3112	3,89
Kinder	DBY	SK0888	1,30
Kinderton	CHS	SJ7266	18,3
Kineton	WAR	SP3351	1,2
Kineton [Green]	WAR	SP1281	28,2
Kingcombe	DOR	SY5499	1,2 note. 32,3. 47,7 note. 56,61
Kingerby	LIN	TF0592	4,21. 7,58
Kingham	OXF	SP2523	39,1
King's Lynn: see [King's] Lynn NFK			
Kingsbury	MDX	TQ2088	4,11. 10,2
Kingsbury	WAR	SP2196	15,4
Kingsbury [Episcopi]	SOM	ST4321	6,3
Kingscote	GLS	ST8196	1,15
Kingsey	BKM	SP7406	39,2
Kingsford	DEV	ST0408	16,99
Kingskerswell	DEV	SX8867	1,12
Kingskerswell: see Kerswell DEV			
Kingsland	HEF	SO4461	1,5
Kingsland	SFK	TM2354	39,11
Kingsley	CHS	SJ5474	26,6
Kingsley	STS	SK0147	15,2. 16,2
Kingsnordley SHR	SHR	SO7787	ES4
Kingsnordley SHR	STS		8,2
Kingsteignton	DEV	SX8773	1,10
Kingsteignton: see Teighnton DEV			
Kingsthorpe (near Northampton)	NTH	SP7563	1,18
Kingsthorpe (in Polebrook)	NTH	TL0885	6a,14
Kingston	CAM	TL3455	1,8. 13,12. 14,47. 25,8. 26,38-39. 32,21
Kingston (in Corfe Castle)	DOR	SY9579	19,10
Kingston IOW	HAM	SZ4781	1,14
Kingston	SFK	TM2647	8,6. 21,53
Kingston (upon Thames)	SRY	TQ1869	1,8. 2,3. 5,28. 8,12. 22,4
Kingston [Bagpuize]	BRK	SU4098	21,14. 22,12
Kingston [Blount]	OXF	SU7399	35,4;27
Kingston [By Sea]	SSX	TQ2205	12,23. 13,28-29
Kingston [Lisle]	BRK	SU3287	1,32
Kingston [on-Soar]	NTT	SK5027	3,4. 30,19;21-22
Kingston [Seymour]	SOM	ST4066	5,63-64
Kingstone (in Weston under Penyard) HEF	GLS		1,11. EvK10

Kingstone (in Weston under Penyard) HEF	HEF	SO6324	3,1. E1
Kingstone (near Hereford)	HEF	SO4235	1,3
Kingstone	SOM	ST3713	8,39. 19,10
Kingsweston	GLS	ST5477	1,15
Kingswinford STS	STS	SO8989	1,1
Kingswinford STS	WOR		1,4;5-6
Kingthorpe	LIN	TF1275	14,60;92. 34,23. 40,10-11
Kingthorpe [House] NR	YKS	SE8385	1Y4 note. SN,D12 note
Kington	DOR	ST7623	32,1. 40,2. 56,2
Kington	HEF	SO2956	1,69
Kington	WAR	SP1864	16,19
Kington	WOR	SO9955	18,4
Kington [St Michael]	WIL	ST9077	41,8
Kingweston	SOM	ST5230	17,17
Kinlet	SHR	SO7181	6,9
Kinnerley	SHR	SJ3320	4,27,4
Kinnersley	HEF	SO3449	9,15
?Kinnerton CHS & FLN	CHS	SJ3361	FD5,3 note
		SJ3261	
Kinoulton	NTT	SK6730	11,31. 30,38
Kinsbourne	HRT	TL1016	Appx
Kinsley WR	YKS	SE4114	9W65. SW,St1
Kinson HAM	DOR	SZ0696	31,2
Kintbury	BRK	SU3866	1,26. 16,1. 31,4
Kinvaston	STS	SJ9012	7,14
Kinver STS	STS	SO8483	1,27
Kinver STS	WOR		1,4
Kinwarton	WAR	SP1058	11,4
Kinwick	BDF	TL1947	6,2
Kiplin NR	YKS	SE2897	6N25. SN,CtA12
Kipling [Cotes] ER	YKS	SE9047	2E11 note. 5E20. 13E3. SE,Wei7
Kippax WR	YKS	SE4130	9W1 note. SW,Sk4
Kipton	NFK	TF8423	1,77
Kirby	NTH	SP9292	59,4
Kirby [Bedon]	NFK	TG2705	1,115;119;126. 2,7. 9,29;34. 12,15
Kirby [Bellars]	LEC	SK7117	29,3;16
Kirby [Cane]	NFK	TM3794	6,7. 14,41. 31,12
[Cold] Kirby NR	YKS	SE5384	1Y1. SN,B20
Kirby [Grindalythe] ER	YKS	SE9067	1E57. 5E69-70. SE, A2 note.
			SE,Th6
Kirby [Hall] WR	YKS	SE4561	25W21 note. SW, Sf37 note.
			SW,Bu2
Kirby [Hill] NR	YKS	SE3968	1W54 note. 28W22 note. SW,H6
Kirby [Knowle] NR	YKS	SE4687	23N8 note
Kirby [Misperton] NR	YKS	SE7779	8N1 note. SN,L42 note. SN,Ma1
Kirby [Misperton], another NR	YKS	SE7779	8N1 note. 8N2. SN, L42 note.
			SN,Ma1
[Monks] Kirby	WAR	SP4683	31,1
Kirby [Moorside] NR	YKS	SE6986	23N19 note. 23N20 -21
Kirby [Muxloe]	LEC	SK5204	25,4
Kirby Sigston: see [Kirby] Sigston			
Kirby [Underdale] ER	YKS	SE8058	1E50. 29E17. SE, Ac2 note
Kirby [Wiske] NR	YKS	SE3784	1Y2. 6N30. SN,A1 note.
			SN,CtA13
Kirk Lancaster: see [Kirk] Lancaster LAN			
Kirkburn ER	YKS	SE9855	1Y8 note. 31E3. SE,Dr2
Kirkburton WR	YKS	SE1912	1Y15. SW,Ag13
Kirkby (near Liverpool) LAN	CHS	SJ4198	R1,2
Kirkby (= Kendal) WES	YKS	SD5292	1L7 note. See also CHS Y8
Kirkby (near Stokesley) NR	YKS	NZ5306	29N9 note. SN, L42 note
[East] Kirkby	LIN	TF3362	14,83

Kirkby [Fleetham]: see [Kirkby] Fleetham			
Kirkby [Green]	LIN	TF0857	31,15. 61,6. CK,15
Kirkby [Hall] (in Kirkby Fleetham) NR	YKS	SE2895	6N55 note. SN,A1 note. SN,CtA20
Kirkby [Green] Hundred	LIN	—	31,14. 32,24
Kirkby [in-Ashfield]	NTT	SK4956	13,9. 30,27
Kirkby Ireleth: see *Gerleuuorde* LAN			
Kirkby [la Thorpe]	LIN	TF0946	1,1-3. 3,37-38. 24,101. 26,29;52. CK,34
Kirkby [Lonsdale] WES	YKS	SD6178	1L4. See also CHS Y5
Kirkby [Mallory]	LEC	SK4500	6,7. 13,7;10;42
Kirkby [on Bain]	LIN	TF2462	3,11-15. 4,54. 29,4-7
[South] Kirkby WR	YKS	SE4511	9W34. SW,Sf37 note
Kirkby [Underwood]	LIN	TF0727	12,53-54. 18,16. 27,54-55. CK,47
Kirkby [Wharfe]	YKS	SE5041	9W8 note;30. SW,BA5;9
Kirkdale LAN	CHS	SJ3594	R1,7;41
Kirkham ER	YKS	SE7366	5E62;66 note. SE, Ac9
Kirkham LAN	YKS	SD4232	1L1. See also CHS Y2
Kirkheaton WR	YKS	SE1818	9W103. SW,Ag6
Kirkleatham: see *Weslide* YKS			
Kirkley	SFK	TM5291	1,23;28. 31,33
Kirklington	NTT	SK6757	17,13
Kirklington NR	YKS	SE3181	6N147. SN,CtA40
Kirksanton CUM	YKS	SD1480	1L6. See also CHS Y7
Kirkton	SFK	TM2335	25,67
Kirmington	LIN	TA1011	1,71. 12,8. 25,5. 30,7
Kirmond [le Mire]	LIN	TF1892	22,24
Kirstead	NFK	TM2998	14,38
Kirtling	CAM	TL6857	41,1. Appx B
Kirtling	NFK	TF9415	1,214
Kirtlington	OXF	SP5019	1,3. 14,3. 28,27. 59,8
Kirton	LIN	TF3038	12,88. 57,29
Kirton	NTT	SK6969	1,19;24. 9,13. 12,2. 17,2
Kirton	SFK	TM2839	7,87;114. 38,26
Kirton Hundred	LIN	—	12,71
Kirton [in Lindsey] LIN	LIN	SK9398	1,38-64. CW,19. EN,1;4
Kirton [in Lindsey] LIN	NTT		1,65. 30,44
Kislea	SFK	??	1,25
Kislingbury	NTH	SP6959	18,46. 46,1
Kitchenham	SSX	TQ8825	9,103
Kittisford	SOM	ST0722	22,15
Kiveton WR	YKS	SK4983	12W1
Knaith	LIN	SK8284	7,11
Knapp DOR	HAM	SZ1594	23,62
Knapthorpe	NTT	SK7458	11,9. 12,7;22. 30,3
Knaptoft	LEC	SP6289	10,1
Knapton	NFK	TG3034	8,121
Knapton ER	YKS	SE8875	15E14. SE,Th3
Knapton WR	YKS	SE5652	22W5. 25W18. SW, An14
Knapwell	CAM	TL3362	7,5
Knaresborough WR	YKS	SE3556	1Y19. 1W31. 13W36. 24W8;19. SW,Bu17
Knaresford (in Skelding) WR	YKS	SE2169	2W7 note. 28W41. SW,Bu47;49
Knayton NR	YKS	SE4387	1Y2 note. 3Y13. SN,Bi7. SN,A1
Knebworth	HRT	TL2320	31,1
Knedlington ER	YKS	SE7328	3Y4. SE,How4
Kneesall	NTT	SK7064	17,9
Kneeton	NTT	SK7146	1,62. 2,7-8. 9,102;109
Kneeton [Hall] NR	YKS	NZ2106	6N4 note. SN,CtA8
Knettishall SFK	NFK		1,76

Knettishall SFK	SFK	TL9780	6,208. 14,99. 76,9. ENf1
Knightley	STS	SJ8125	8,6
Knighton	BRK	SU2887	65,4
Knighton	DOR	ST8508	26,45
Knighton IOW	HAM	SZ5686	1,W1. 9,15
Knighton	LEC	SK6001	3,2
Knighton (Wales)	SHR	SO2872	8,1
Knighton (in Adbaston)	STS	SJ7427	2,20
Knighton (in Luggerheads)	STS	SJ7240	17,7
Knighton	WIL	SU1345	67,60
Knighton: see Durweston DOR			
[Chudleigh] Knighton	DEV	SX8477	2,20
Knighton [on Teme]	WOR	SO6369	2,85
[West] Knighton	DOR	SY7387	38,1
Knightwick	WOR	SO7255	2,67
Knill	HEF	SO2960	24,3
Knipton	LEC	SK8231	1,1b. 15,7
Kniveton	DBY	SK2050	4,2
Knodishall	SFK	TM4261	7,21;33;71
Knook	WIL	ST9341	67,14;86
Knossington LEC	LEC	SK8008	1,11. 18,1
Knossington LEC	RUT		ELe1
Knotting	BDF	TL0063	3,1
Knottingley WR	YKS	SE5024	9W58. SW,O12
Knowl	HAM	SU5359	23,23. 29,8
Knowle (in Bristol) GLS	SOM	ST6070	39,1
Knowle (in Timberscombe)	SOM	SS9643	25,26
[Church] Knowle	DOR	SY9481	28,5. 37,8. 40,7. 41,2
Knowle [Park]	SOM	ST6931	45,12
Knowle [St Giles]	SOM	ST3411	21,37
Knowlton	DOR	SU0210	1,6. 26,43. 56,30 note
Knowlton	KEN	TR2853	5,199
Knowsley LAN	CHS	SJ4395	R1,2
Knowstone	DEV	SS8223	23,10-11. 52,41;51
[East] Knoyle	WIL	ST8830	1,20
[West] Knoyle	WIL	ST8532	13,7
Knuston	NTH	SP9366	35,1d. 48,12
Knutsford	CHS	SJ7578	9,13
Knutton	STS	SJ8346	13,8
Kuluertestuna/Kyluertestuna/Culuerdestuna	SFK	??	7,118. 31,11
(? Kilverstone NFK)			
[North] Kyme	LIN	TF1552	18,32. 26,50
[South] Kyme	LIN	TF1749	1,4. 24,76
Kynaston	SHR	SJ3520	4,3,43
Kynnersley	SHR	SJ6716	4,23,1
[Little] Kyre and Kyre [Magna] WOR	GLS		1,11. EvK10
[Little] Kyre and Kyre [Magna] WOR	WOR	SO6463	3,2. 19,4;7. E35
		SO6263	

L

Laceby	LIN	TA2106	4,69. 22,2. 30,15
Lach [Dennis]	CHS	SJ7071	9,29. 26,12
Lache	CHS	SJ3863	A22
Lack	SHR	SO2693	4,27,7
Lackenby NR	YKS	NZ5619	4N2. 5N23. SN,L24
Lackford	SFK	TL7970	14,7;12;71
Lackham	WIL	ST9270	32,12
Lacock	WIL	ST9168	24,33. 26,15
Lacon	SHR	SJ5330	4,10,2
Ladbroke	WAR	SP4158	16,47. 17,18;21;23-24;33. 18,9
Lafham	SFK	??	73,1
Laindon	ESS	TQ6889	3,1. 4,13
Laitone	CHS	??	1,31
Lakenham	NFK	TG2307	1,236
Lakenheath	SFK	TL7182	21,6-7. 25,36. 28,2
Laleham	MDX	TQ0568	8,1. 17,1
Lamarsh	ESS	TL8836	34,22. 90,14;45
Lamas	NFK	TG2423	20,32
Lambert	DEV	SX7592	43,4. 52,12
Lambeth	SRY	TQ3078	14,1. 17,1
Lambley	NTT	SK6345	30,5
Lambourn	BRK	SU3278	1,29. 35,3. 59,1
Lambourne	ESS	TQ4796	20,48
Lambside	DEV	SX5747	17,67
Lamcote	NTT	SK6438	9,96. 15,7. 30,36
Lamellen	CON	SX0577	5,8,9
Lamerton	DEV	SX4577	35,1
Lametton	CON	SX2561	5,7,2
Lampeth	HRT	??	5,3
Lamport	BKM	SP6837	14,25. 43,6
Lamport	NTH	SP7574	8,6. 39,4. 56,9
Lamyatt	SOM	ST6535	8,30
Lancarffe	CON	SX0869	4,22. 5,6,6
Lancaster LAN	YKS	SD4861	1L2. See also CHS Y3
[Kirk] Lancaster LAN	YKS	SD4761	1L2 *note.* See also CHS Y3
Lancing	SSX	TQ1805	13,43-44
Landbeach	CAM	TL4765	14,59. 32,38
Landcross	DEV	SS4624	16,40
Landegea: see [Old] Kea CON			
Landeshers	DEV	??	14,4
Landford	WIL	SU2620	67,92
Landican	CHS	SJ2885	8,7
Landinner CON	CON	SX2383	5,1,14
Landinner CON	DEV		1,25
Landmoth NR	YKS	SE4292	1Y2 *note.* SN,A1
?Landreyne	CON	SX2876	5,2,29
Landulph	CON	SX4361	5,3,26
Landuna	ESS	??	25,9
Laneburc/Laneburh (in Sutton)	SFK	TM3246	6,151;173-174
Laneham NTT	LIN		2,26
Laneham NTT	NTT	SK8076	5,4;8
Lanescot	CON	SX0855	5,3,17
Langage	DEV	SX5756	3,98

136

Langar	NTT	SK7234	10,59. 11,28
Langcliffe WR	YKS	SD8265	30W31
Langdon	DEV	SX5149	17,95-96
Langdon	ESS	TQ6786	24,2
Lang(h)edana/Lang(h)dena	SFK	??	1,68. 7,66. 8,62;64. 29,10. 38,9
Langene	LIN	??	13,6
Langenhoe	ESS	TM0117	20,19
Langer	SFK	TM2832	7,100;102
Langford	BDF	TL1841	32,13. 32,10
Langford (in Cullompton)	DEV	ST0202	16,96
Langford (in Ugborough)	DEV	SX6956	1,55
Langford	DOR	??	10,5
Langford	ESS	TL8309	33,2;22
Langford	NFK	TL8396	23,2
Langford	NTT	SK8259	19,1
Langford	OXF	SP2402	1,8
Langford [Budville]	SOM	ST1122	1,16
[Hanging, Little and Steeple] Langford	WIL	SU0337	7,12-13. 13,13. 20,5. 24,42. 37,7-8
		SU0436	
		SU0337	
Langhale	NFK	TM3096	14,38. 47,4
Langham	ESS	TM0333	23,38
Langham	NFK	TG0041	10,12;22;55
Langham	SOM	SS9836	25,13
Langham	SFK	TL9869	14,94. 66,6
?Langley (in Tilehurst; *Lonchelei*)	BRK	SU6775	33,9
Langley	DBY	??	1,32
Langley (near Heanor)	DBY	SK4446	7,6
Langley (in Yarnscombe and Atherington)	DEV	SS5624	1,40;67
Langley (near Eling)	HAM	SU3410	69,52
Langley (near Fawley)	HAM	SU4401	NF10,2
Langley	HRT	TL2122	34,5
Langley	KEN	TQ8051	5,75
Langley	NFK	TG3500	10,31;33
Langley	SHR	SJ5300	4,27,10
Langley	WAR	SP1962	22,26
[Abbot's] Langley	HRT	TL0902	10,9
Langley [Burrell]	WIL	ST9375	24,31
[King's] Langley	HRT	TL0702	15,11
[Kington] Langley	WIL	ST9277	7,11
[Kirk] Langley	DBY	SK2838	10,21
Langney	SSX	TQ6202	10,80
Langport (in Canterbury)	KEN	TR1557	7,4
Langport (near Romney)	KEN	TR0522	2,43
Langport	SOM	ST4226	1,1;19;31. 19,26
Langridge	SOM	ST7469	5,36
Langstone	DEV	SX7482	16,154
Langthorne NR	YKS	SE2591	6N59. SN,CtA21
Langthorpe NR	YKS	SE3867	28W31. SW,Bu15 note. SW,H6
Langthorpe [Hall] ER	YKS	TA1639	14E41 *note*. CE42. SE,Hol24
Langthwaite WR	YKS	SE5506	5W28 *note*. 5W29-30. SW,Sf34
Langtoft	LIN	TF1212	11,3
Langtoft ER	YKS	TA0067	1Y14. 1E36. 2B16. SE, Bt8
Langton (near Horncastle)	LIN	TF2368	1,94. 4,51. 30,19
Langton (near Spilsby)	LIN	TF3970	13,9
Langton ER	YKS	SE7967	23E14. SE,Sc1
Langton [by Wragby]	LIN	TF1476	3,10. 24,16. 34,19. 38,11. 47,9. CS,22-23
[East] Langton	LEC	SP7292	2,1. 5,1
[Great] Langton NR	YKS	SE2996	6N11. SN,CtA10 note

Langton [Herring]	DOR	SY6182	1,23. 55,31
[Little] Langton NR	YKS	SE3095	6N26 note. SN,CtA10 note. SN,CtA13
[Low] Langton: see *Torp* LIN			
[Thorpe] Langton	LEC	SP7492	13,14;57. 16,6. 17,18
[Tur] Langton	LEC	SP7194	C7. 2,1-2
Langtree	DEV	SS4515	1,62
Langunnett	CON	SX1557	5,2,31
Langwith [Lodge] ER	YKS	SE6548	6E1 note. SE,Wa8
Lanhadron	CON	SW9947	5,2,10
[Lower] Lanherne	CON	SW8767	2,7
Lanow: see St Kew CON			
Lanport	KEN	??	7,27
Lanreath	CON	SX1856	5,3,6
Lansallos	CON	SX1751	5,3,7
Lantivet	CON	SX1651	5,4,4
Lantyan	CON	SX1057	5,13,9
Lanwarnick	CON	SX2057	5,20,1
Lapford	DEV	SS7308	1,66
Lapley STS	NTH		16,1
Lapley STS	STS	SJ8712	EN1
Lapworth	WAR	SP1671	18,7
Larkbeare	DEV	SY0697	16,94. 39,10
Larkton	CHS	SJ5057	2,10
Larling	NFK	TL9889	8,54 *and note.* 58,1
Larpestuna?/Lerp(e)stuna?	NFK	??	1,239 note
Lartington NR	YKS	NZ0117	6N42. SN,CtA16
Lasborough	GLS	ST8294	30,2
Lasham	HAM	SU6742	1,18
Lashbrook	DEV	SS4305	16,20
Lashbrook	OXF	SU7779	20,2
Lashley [Hall]	ESS	TL6426	90,51
Lassington	GLS	SO7921	2,13
Lastingham NR	YKS	SE7290	8N3. SN,D20
Latchingdon	ESS	TL8800	1,6-7. 2,5. 27,5. 84,2
Lathbury	BKM	SP8745	4,41. 5,9. 25,3
Lathom LAN	CHS	SD4609	R1,31
Lattiford	SOM	ST6926	8,19
Latton	ESS	TL4610	11,3. 20,13. 36,2
Latton WIL	GLS		71,1
Latton WIL	WIL	SU0995	18,2
[Temple] Laugherne and [Lower Temple] Laugherne	WOR	SO8256 SO8255	2,11;13
Laughton	LEC	SP6689	15,8
Laughton (in Aveland Hundred)	LIN	TF0731	18,21. 24,96. 42,8-10
Laughton (in Corringham Hundred) LIN	LIN	SK8497	16,28-30. 57,7-9;11. CW,15. EN,2
Laughton (in Corringham Hundred) LIN	NTT		1,66
Laughton	SSX	TQ4913	9,40;50;52;78. 10,23;93. 12,2
Laughton [en le Morthen] WR	YKS	SK5188	10W1. SW,Sf2
Launcells	CON	SS2405	5,11,4
Launceston	CON	SX3384	5,1,22
Launton	OXF	SP6022	1,3
[East, Mid and West] Lavant	SSX	SU8608 SU8508 SU8408	2,7. 10,106. 11,5
Lavendon	BKM	SP9153	5,14-17. 12,35. 14,43. 53,3-5. 57,12
Lavenham	SFK	TL9149	12,6. 35,1. 76,21

[High, Little and Magdalen] Laver	ESS	TL5208	20,45;47. 51,2
		TL5409	
		TL5108	
Laverstock	WIL	SU1530	13,20. 67,96
Laverstoke	HAM	SU4948	6,12
Laverton	SOM	ST7753	26,4
Laverton WR	YKS	SE2273	1W41. 28W9. 29W20. 31W3.
			SW,Bu22
Lavington (= Lenton) LIN	LIN	TF0230	2,42. 8,8. CK,10
Lavington (= Lenton) LIN	NTH		ELc4
Lavington (= Lenton) LIN	RUT		ELc19
[East] Lavington	SSX	SU9416	6,4
[Little] Lavington (in *Lenton*)	LIN	TF0331	24,86. 68,21
[Market and West] Lavington	WIL	SU0154	59,1. 60,1
		SU0052	
Lawford	ESS	TM0831	1,27. 20,69. 23,33. 33,17. 37,20
[Church] Lawford	WAR	SP4476	12,5
[Little] Lawford	WAR	SP4677	17,47
[Long] Lawford	WAR	SP4775	31,4
Lawhitton	CON	SX3582	2,9
Lawley	SHR	SJ6608	4,14,21. 4,19,6
Lawling	ESS	TL9001	2,4. 25,6. 34,24. 41,5. 90,79
Lawn [Hall]	ESS	TL6517	18,38
Lawshall	SFK	TL8654	17,1
Lawton	HEF	SO4459	1,5. 10,40
[Church and Bug-]Lawton	CHS	SJ8255	11,1-2
		SJ8863	
Laxfield	SFK	TM2972	6,305
Laxton	NTH	SP9496	60,2
Laxton	NTT	SK7267	12,1;3
Laxton ER	YKS	SE7925	3Y4. SE,How3
Laycock WR	YKS	SE0341	1W68
Layer [Breton, de la Haye, and Marney]	ESS	TL9418	1,19. 3,6-7. 17,2. 20,21. 27,10.
		TL9691	34,15. 57,3. 68,4. 90,5
		TL9217	
Layham	SFK	TM0340	1,109. 14,110. 28,7. 36,15. 49,1.
			61,2
Laysters	HEF	SO5663	11,2. 22,6. 36,2
Laysthorpe [Lodge] NR	YKS	SE6378	23N25 *note*
Layston: see Buntingford HRT			
Laytham ER	YKS	SE7439	5E8. 21E5. SE,C7-8
Laythorpe (in Kirkby la Thorpe)	LIN	TF0944	7,49. 26,30
Layton LAN	YKS	SD3237	1L1. See also CHS Y2
[East] Layton NR	YKS	NZ1609	6N1;7. SN,CtA7;9
[West] Layton NR	YKS	NZ1409	6N1. SN,CtA7
Lazenby NR	YKS	NZ5719	1N13. 4N2. 29N2. 31N7. SN,L23
Lazenby [Hall] NR	YKS	SE3398	1Y2 *note*. SN,A1
Lazerton	DOR	ST8610	26,3 note. 56,32
Lea (near Backford)	CHS	SJ3872	A9
Lea	DBY	SK3257	10,12
Lea	HEF	SO6521	5,2
Lea	LIN	SK8386	12,4-6
Lea LAN	YKS	SD4830	1L1. See also CHS Y2
Lea [Green]	WOR	SP0975	1,1a
Lea [Marston]	WAR	SP2094	23,3
Lea [Marston]: see also [Lea] Marston			
WAR			
Lea [Newbold]	CHS	SJ4359	1,14;16. 14,2
Lead WR	YKS	SE4636	9W19 *note*. CW3. SW,BA5
Leadbrook FLN	CHS	SJ2571	FD2,4

Leadenham	LIN	SK9552	12,48
Leadon	HEF	SO6846	10,37-38
Leake	LIN	TF4050	12,64
Leake	NTT	SK5526	4,4. 9,89. 24,1. 28,2
Leake NR	YKS	SE4390	1Y2 note. 5N73. SN,A1;9
Lealholm NR	YKS	NZ7607	23N18 note. 23N34. 31N10.
			SN,L14
Leamington [Hastings]	WAR	SP4467	39,1
Leamington [Priors/Spa]	WAR	SP3165	12,1
Leasingham	LIN	TF0548	7,52. 64,12
Leatherhead	SRY	TQ1656	1,9
Leathley WR	YKS	SE2347	1W47. 13W26. 21W6. 31W4.
			SW,Bu33-34
Leaton (near Baschurch)	SHR	SJ4618	4,3,71 note. 4,27,27
Leaveland [Court]	KEN	TR0054	2,34
Leavening ER	YKS	SE7863	29E30. SE,Ac5
Leavening, another ER	YKS	SE7863	SE,Ac5 note
[Castle] Leavington NR	YKS	NZ4610	1N122 note. 31N4 note. SN,A4
[Kirk] Leavington NR	YKS	NZ4309	1N120. 31N4. SN,A4
Lebberston NR	YKS	TA0782	1Y3. SN,D4
Lechlade	GLS	SU2199	59,1
[Lower] Leck LAN	YKS	SD6476	1L3 note. See also CHS Y4
Leckby [Palace] WR	YKS	SE4174	5W38 note. SW,H8
Leckford	HAM	SU3737	6,15. 14,3
Leckhampstead	BRK	SU4376	7,14
Leckhampstead	BKM	SP7237	4,33. 14,30. 21,7
Leckhampton	GLS	SO9419	38,1. 78,9
Leconfield ER	YKS	TA0143	2E13. 5E35. 13E4. SE,Sn6
Ledbury	HEF	SO7137	2,26
Ledemare (in Fordon) ER	YKS	??	1E22 note. SE,Tu4
Ledforda: see Letfort SOM			
Ledicot	HEF	SO4162	9,12. 10,42
Ledsham	CHS	SJ3574	7,3
Ledsham WR	YKS	SE4529	9W28. SW,BA11
Ledston WR	YKS	SE4328	9W1 note. SW,Sk4
Ledwell	OXF	SP4228	1,7b
[Upper] Ledwyche	SHR	SO5579	4,14,22
Lee	CON	SS2212	5,5,3
Lee	GLS	ST5881	6,7
Lee	KEN	TQ3975	5,32
Lee [Brockhurst]	SHR	SJ5427	4,25,2
Lee [Chapel]	ESS	TQ6988	5,1
[Elmdon] Lee	ESS	TL4838	20,75
Leebotwood	SHR	SO4798	4,27,13
Leece LAN	YKS	SD2469	1L6. See also CHS Y7
Leece, another, LAN	YKS	SD2469	1L6 note. See also CHS Y7
Leeds	KEN	TQ8253	5,67
Leeds WR	YKS	SE3033	9W6. SW,Sk11
Leegomery	SHR	SJ6613	4,3,30
Leek	STS	SJ9856	1,21
Leesthorpe	LEC	SK7913	29,10
Leftisford	DOR	SU0712	10,4
Leftwich	CHS	SJ6572	5,7
Lega	ESS	??	32,14
Legbourne	LIN	TF3684	12,87. 13,2. 16,39
Lege	HEF	??	29,19
Legge FLN	CHS	??	FT3,1
[High] Legh	CHS	SJ6984	17,7
Legham	LEC	??	C11
Legsby	LIN	TF1385	22,35-37. CS,26
Leicester	LEC	SK5804	C. 3,1;6. 13,26. 25,2

Leidtorp (in Wilton) NR	YKS	??	8N7 *note.* SN,D16
Leigh	CON	SX3364	5,26,3
Leigh (in Churchstow)	DEV	SX7246	24,21
Leigh (in Coldridge)	DEV	SS6905	16,46
Leigh (in Harberton)	DEV	SX7658	17,50
Leigh (in Loxbeare)	DEV	SS9114	49,6
Leigh (in Milton Abbot)	DEV	SX3977	5,2
Leigh (in Modbury)	DEV	SX6852	17,60
Leigh (in Colehill)	DOR	SZ0299	30,2
Leigh	ESS	TQ8486	34,35
Leigh	GLS	SO8726	20,1
Leigh (in Lydeard St Lawrence)	SOM	ST1229	2,9
Leigh (in Milverton)	SOM	ST0924	25,47
Leigh (in Old Cleeve)	SOM	ST0235	35,14
Leigh (in Winsham)	SOM	ST3506	25,5
Leigh	STS	SK0235	4,7
Leigh	WOR	SO7853	9,5a-5b

Leigh: see also Canonsleigh,
   Challonsleigh, Eastleigh,
   Grimpstonleigh, Inwardleigh,
   Monkleigh, Northleigh,
   Romansleigh, Southleigh, Westleigh
   DEV; Overleigh SOM

[Abbots] Leigh	SOM	ST5473	16,9
[Bessels] Leigh	BRK	SP4501	7,20
[Little] Leigh	CHS	SJ6175	9,23
[North] Leigh	OXF	SP3813	29,10
[Over]leigh	CHS	SJ4065	10,1
[Over]leigh	SOM	ST4835	8,16
[Great and Little] Leighs	ESS	TL7317	25,21. 30,16
		TL7116	
Leighton	CHS	SJ2879	3,3
Leighton (Wales)	SHR	SJ2405	4,4,22
Leighton (near Wellington)	SHR	SJ6105	4,3,22
Leighton [Bromswold]	HUN	TL1175	2,8
Leighton [Buzzard]	BDF	SP9125	1,1. 4,9
Leinthall [Earls and Starkes]	HEF	SO4467	1,10a;10c. 9,6-7
		SO4369	
Leintwardine HEF	HEF	SO4074	ES1-2;4
Leintwardine HEF	SHR		C10. 4,20,20. 6,11
Leire	LEC	SP5290	3,3. 17,2. 19,1
Leiston	SFK	TM4362	6,69-70;83;106;136
Lel	SHR	??	6,3 *note*
Lelley [Dyke] ER	YKS	TA2133	14E1 *note.* SE,Hol3
[Lower] Lemington	GLS	SP2134	1,29
[Upper] Lemington	GLS	SP2233	19,2
Lenborough	BKM	SP6931	4,34. 14,33
[Ab] Lench	WOR	SP0151	2,17
[Atch] Lench	WOR	SP0350	2,76. 10,14
[Church] Lench	WOR	SP0251	10,16
[Rous] Lench	WOR	SP0153	2,18
[Sheriffs] Lench	WOR	SP0149	11,2
Lenchwick	WOR	SP0347	10,3
Lenham	KEN	TQ8952	7,2
[East] Lenham	KEN	TQ9051	2,36
Lenton	NTT	SK5538	1,48. 10,19;24

Lenton: see *Lavington* LIN

Leofstanestuna (in Trimley)	SFK	TM2539	7,93;106;111
Leominster HEF	HEF	SO4959	1,10a;10c;37;70. E9
Leominster HEF	SHR		4,28,5. E3
Leonard	DEV	ST0009	24,16. 51,14

Leopard: see Lyppard WOR
Leppington ER	YKS	SE7661	SE,Ac9 *note*
Lepton WR	YKS	SE2015	9W102. SW,Ag6
Lesnewth	CON	SX1390	5,23,1
Lessingham	NFK	TG3928	1,198
Lessland IOW	HAM	SZ5482	1,W8. 7,8
Lessness	KEN	TQ4978	5,19
Lesteorde	HAM	??	NF3,1
Lestred	HAM	??	23,67
Let(h)a	NFK	??	10,72 *note*;75
Letchworth	HRT	TL2131	20,7. Appx
Letcombe [Bassett]	BRK	SU3785	41,2
Letcombe [Regis]	BRK	SU3886	1,31
Letfort/Ledforda	SOM	??	*1,6*
Letheringham	SFK	TM2658	8,24. 21,97. 32,14
Letheringsett	NFK	TG0638	25,17;21-22;24. 36,7
Letitone	LEC	??	C11
Letton (near Clifford)	HEF	SO3346	10,47
Letton (near Wigmore) HEF	HEF	SO3770	ES11
Letton (near Wigmore) HEF	SHR	SO3870	6,18
Letton	NFK	TF9705	8,81-84 *and note*. 19,16. 66,33
Leueberge	KEN	??	5,189-190;196
Leuetat (in Winterburn) WR	YKS	??	30W7 *note*
Leuricestone	DEV	??	17,72
Levalsa	CON	SW9948	5,12,2
Levedale	STS	SJ8916	11,66
Leven ER	YKS	TA1045	2E41. SE,No2
Levens WES	YKS	SD4886	30W40. See also CHS Y5
Leverage	HRT	TL4316	4,8
Leverton	BRK	SU3370	7,35
Leverton	LIN	TF4047	12,65
Leverton	NTT	SK7882	1,32. 2,10. 5,4. 9,130
Levington	SFK	TM2339	7,94;117. 31,10
Levisham NR	YKS	SE8390	1Y4. SN,D18
Lew	OXF	SP3206	20,6. 58,20
Lewarne	CON	SX1765	5,2,4;20
Lewell	DOR	SY7387	56,11. 57,2
Lewes SSX	NFK		8,2-4;10;12;13;26;56;68-70;80;84;90;112;133
Lewes SSX	SFK		26,1-3;5
Lewes SSX	SSX	TQ4110	2,3-4. 3,2. 7,1. 12,1;3-6;8-9;11;14;19;26-28;31-33;37-44;48;50-51
Lewes, Castellany of, Castle of, SSX	NFK		8,40;45;46;51;58-61
Lewisham	KEN	TQ3875	8,1
Lewknor	OXF	SU7197	9,1. 28,11
Lewtrenchard	DEV	SX4586	16,9
Lexden	ESS	TL9725	1,19. B2
[East and West] Lexham	NFK	TF8517 TF8417	8,63. 20,8
Lexworthy	SOM	ST2535	17,3. 21,75-76
Ley [Green]	HRT	TL1524	1,16
Leybourne	KEN	TQ6858	5,40
Leyburn NR	YKS	SE1190	6N100. SN,CtA30
Leyland LAN	CHS	SD5422	R6,1
Leyton	ESS	TQ3786	6,7. 27,3. 32,10. 36,5. 41,3-4
Leziate	NFK	TF6920	66,58
Libury	HRT	TL3323	2,4. 5,9-12. 30,2-3. 36,8-10. 37,19. 42,3-4
Lichfield STS	STS	SK1209	2,16;22
Lichfield STS	WAR		2,3. EBS1

Liddaton	DEV	SX4582	5,2-3
Liddington	WIL	SU2081	12,5
Lidemore	DEV	??	17,18
Lidgate	SFK	TL7258	54,1. 70,1
Lidham	SSX	TQ8316	9,106;113
Lidlington	BDF	SP9938	11,1
Liedtorp: see *Leidtorp* YKS			
Liffildeuuella	ESS	??	90,43
Lifton	DEV	SX3885	1,25 *and note*
Lighthorne	WAR	SP3355	29,1
Lilbourne	NTH	SP5677	18,70. 21,3-4
Lilford	NTH	TL0384	56,49
Lilinge	LEC	??	29,6
Lilleshall	SHR	SJ7215	3g,3
Lilley	HRT	TL1126	1,12. 34,12
[East] Lilling NR	YKS	SE6664	1N91 note. 1N100. 5N61. 29N11. SN,B9 note. SN,B14-15
[West] Lilling NR	YKS	SE6465	1N91 *note.* 5N61. SN,B9 *note*
Lillingstone [Dayrell]	BKM	SP7039	14,27
Lillingstone [Lovell] BKM	BKM	SP7140	E5-6
Lillingstone [Lovell] BKM	OXF		52,1. 58,1
Lillington	WAR	SP3267	16,50. 17,55
Lilstock	SOM	ST1644	46,16
[Great] Limber	LIN	TA1308	1,67. 2,24-25. 25,3-4. 30,8. 40,1. CN,10
[Little] Limber	LIN	TA1210	1,73. 14,32. 32,28. CN,3
Limington	SOM	ST5422	8,41. 21,93
Limpenhoe	NFK	TG3903	1,95. 19,27. 66,101
Limpsfield	SRY	TQ4053	11,1
Limpwella	ESS	??	18,35
Linburne	SFK	TM2884	14,121
Linby	NTT	SK5350	10,20
Linch	SSX	SU8418	11,12
Lincoln	LIN	SK9771	C. T1;3. 7,8. 51,12. CS,5. CN,6. CW,2-3
Lincoln, High Street	LIN	??	C20
Lincombe	DEV	SS5045	16,83
Lincumbe	HEF	??	29,15
Linden [End]	CAM	TL4674	5,52-53. Appx P
Lindley WR	YKS	SE1118	9W111 note. SW,Ag15
[Old] Lindley WR	YKS	SE0919	1W27 note. SW,M12
Lindon (in Rock)	WOR	SO7571	15,2
Lindsell	ESS	TL6427	14,2. 25,4
Lindsey	SFK	TL9744	14,113. 25,107
Lindsworth (near Birmingham) WAR	WAR	SP0679	EBW1
Lindsworth (near Birmingham) WAR	WOR		1,1a
[Great] Linford	BKM	SP8542	12,33. 14,41. 17,21. 26,9
[Little] Linford	BKM	SP8444	5,8
Lingen HEF	HEF	SO3667	ES7
Lingen HEF	SHR		6,14
Linhou	SFK	??	38,2
Linkenholt	HAM	SU3658	7,1
Linslade BDF	BKM	SP9125	25,1
Linstead [Magna and Parva]	SFK	TM3176 TM3377	6,81;82 note; 104
Linton	CAM	TL5646	14,11. Appx F
Linton DBY	DBY	SK2716	6,19 E6
Linton DBY	LEC		14,34
Linton	HEF	SO6625	1,1. 15,3
Linton ER	YKS	SE9070	SE,Sc8 note
Linton (near Hebden) WR	YKS	SD9962	21W15

Linton (near Wetherby) WR	YKS	SE3946	13W35. SW,Bu42
[Little] Linton	CAM	TL5547	14,13
Linton [upon Ouse] NR	YKS	SE4960	5N67-68
Linwood	LIN	TF1086	27,7-8. 44,10
Lipson	DEV	SX4855	15,79
Liskeard	CON	SX2564	5,1,2
Liss	HAM	SU7827	14,1
Lissett ER	YKS	TA1458	14E23. SE,Hol20
Lissington	LIN	TF1083	2,11-15
Lisson (= Lisson Grove in Marylebone)	MDX	TQ2782	25,1
Liston	ESS	TL8544	47,1. 69,2
Litcham	NFK	TF8817	1,212. 13,16;18
Litchborough	NTH	SP6354	13,1
Litchfield	HAM	SU4653	ˉ23,24
Litchurch	DBY	SK3634	B2-3
[Down] Litherland LAN	CHS	SJ3397	R1,9
[Up] Litherland LAN	CHS	SD3707	R1,28
Litley	HEF	SO5339	22,8
Litlington	CAM	TL3142	1,18-20. 26,20;23
Litnes (near Huish Episcopi)	SOM	ST4126	6,5
Littlebeech	STS	??	2,22
Littleborough	NTT	SK8282	1,34
Littlebourne	KEN	TR2157	7,5
Littlebredy	DOR	SY5889	11,10
Littlebury	ESS	TL5139	10,5
Littlecote	BKM	SP8324	14,17. 17,12. 23,23
Littlecott	WIL	SU0376	28,5
Littlecross	SFK	TM2946	6,163
Littlefield	SRY	??	21,5
Littleham (near Bideford)	DEV	SS4423	1,61
Littleham (near Exmouth)	DEV	SY0281	7,1
Littlehampton	SSX	TQ0202	11,77
Littlehay (in Colton): see *Colt* STS			
Littlehempston	DEV	SX8162	1,47. 17,25
Littlehempston: see Hempston DEV			
Littleover	DBY	SK3334	3,1
Littleport	CAM	TL5686	5,47
Littlestoke	OXF	SU6085	43,1
Littlethorpe	ESS	TQ9187	24,25
Littlethorpe WR	YKS	SE3269	2W7. SW,Bu15 note. SW,Bu45
Littleton	DOR	ST8904	26,28
Littleton	GLS	SP0236	34,13 note. 36,3. 53,12
Littleton	HAM	SU2848	23,45
Littleton (in Compton Dundon)	SOM	ST4930	21,85
Littleton	SRY	SU9847	36,10
Littleton [Drew]	WIL	ST8380	5,6. 7,5
[High] Littleton	SOM	ST6458	5,66
[Middle, North and South] Littleton	WOR	SP0847	10,5;8
		SP0847	
		SP0746	
Littleton [on Severn]	GLS	ST5989	9,1. EvM32
Littleton [Pannell]	WIL	ST9954	32,2
[Stony] Littleton	SOM	ST7356	5,56
Littlewindsor	DOR	ST4404	36,10
Littleworth	BRK	SU3197	1,40
Littleworth: see *Shuttleworth* YKS			
Litton	DBY	SK1674	7,9
Litton	SOM	ST5954	6,17
Litton WR	YKS	SD9074	30W1
Littywood	STS	SJ8918	11,6
[Great] Livermere SFK	NFK		*14,10*

[Great] Livermere SFK	SFK	TL8871	14,22;68. 21,9. 31,40
[Little] Livermere	SFK	TL8772	14,87
Liversedge WR	YKS	SE1923	9W140 *note*. SW,M10
Liverton NR	YKS	NZ7115	4N2. SN,L13
Lizard	CON	SW7012	1,1
Llan Elwy (in St Asaph) FLN	CHS	SJ0374	FT2,5
Llanfair Waterdine: see [Llanfair] Waterdine SHR			
[Castle by] Llantyan	CON	SX0958	5,2,9
Llanvair [Discoed] (Wales)	GLS	ST4492	W1;2 note
Llanwarne	HEF	SO5028	2,12
Llewerllyd FLN	CHS	SJ0479	FT1,1. FT2,1
Llys Edwin FLN	CHS	SJ2370	FD7,2
Llys Y Coed FLN	CHS	SJ1665	FT1,5
Llystyn Hunydd FLN	CHS	SJ1868	FT1,5
Lobb	DEV	SS4737	16,80. 35,20
Lobingeham (in Killingholme)	LIN	??	13,19. 14,44. 22,4. 30,11. 32,3
Lobthorpe	LIN	SK9521	7,44. 68,20
Lockeridge	WIL	SU1467	30,6
Lockerley	HAM	SU2926	4,1. 23,40. 69,18;24
[East] Lockinge	BRK	SU4287	7,44
[West] Lockinge	BRK	SU4287	21,11
Lockington ER	YKS	SE9947	2E5. 5E32. SE,Sn3
Lockton NR	YKS	SE8490	1N52. SN,D17
Lockwood: see [North] Crosland YKS			
Loddington	LEC	SK7802	17,24
Loddington	NTH	SP8178	1,15b
Loddiswell	DEV	SX7248	17,32
Loddon	NFK	TM3698	12,23. 14,35 *and note*;42. 33,3;6. 35,6-11
Loddon Hundred	NFK	—	*15,28*
Loders	DOR	SY4994	1,13. 26,41-42;58. 55,24. 56,51
Loft [Marishes] NR	YKS	SE8779	1N47 *note*. 5N33. SN,D14
Lofthouse (in Harewood) WR	YKS	SE3243	1W14 *note*. SW,Sk15
Lofthouse (near Wakefield) WR	YKS	SE3326	9W119. SW,M2
Loftus NR	YKS	NZ7118	1N5. SN,L14
Loftus [Hill] WR	YKS	SE3761	24W11 *note*. 29W17. SW,Bu12-13
[South] Loftus NR	YKS	NZ7217	4N2. SN,L13
Lohou	ESS	??	62,4
Lollesworth?	SRY	TQ0854	36,9
Lollingdon	BRK	SU5785	43,1
Lolworth	CAM	TL3664	32,32;44
Lomer	HAM	SU5923	6,5
Londesborough ER	YKS	SE8645	2B9. SE,Wei5
London MDX	DEV		C4
London MDX	ESS		7,1. 9,7. 30,18. 31,1
London MDX	LEC		C2
London MDX	MDX	TQ3281	3,12. 4,5 note
London MDX	SRY		1,4. 2,3. 5,8. 14,1. 15,2. 19,1-2;15. 29,1
London MDX	WOR		C1
Londonthorpe	LIN	SK9537	1,15;22. 5,1. 67,17
Long Clawson: see [Long] Clawson LEC			
Longborough	GLS	SP1729	29,1. 69,1
Longborough GLS: see [Upper] Clopton WAR			
Longden	SHR	SJ4406	4,5,9
Longden [upon Tern]	SHR	SJ6215	3g,4
Longdendale CHS and DBY	DBY	??	1,30
Longdon (near Solihull)	WAR	SP1777	17,8

Longdon (in Tredington) WAR	WAR	SP2241	EW3
Longdon (in Tredington) WAR	WOR		2,47
Longdon (near Upton) WOR	GLS		E31. E32 note. EvA41. EvC102;106 note
Longdon (near Upton) WOR	HEF		1,44
Longdon (near Upton) WOR	WOR	SO8336	8,9. E4
Longfield	KEN	TQ6068	4,4
Longfield WR	YKS	SD9323	1Y15 note
Longford (near Newport)	SHR	SJ7218	4,19,1
Longford	WIL	SU1726	67,77
Longham	NFK	TF9415	66,25
Longhope	GLS	SO6819	32,7
Longner	SHR	SJ5211	1,5
Longney	GLS	SO7612	78,12
Longnor	SHR	SJ4800	4,3,15
Longnor	STS	SJ8614	11,6
Longslow	SHR	SJ6535	4,23,10
Longstanton [All Saints and St Michael]	CAM	TL3966	14,58. 21,7. 24,1. 32,30 36,1. Appx L
Longstock: see Stock HAM			
Longstone	DBY	SK2072	1,28. 6,72
Longstow Hundred	CAM	—	Appx L
Longstowe	CAM	TL3155	7,1-2. 14,51. 26,41
Longtown (formerly Ewias Lacy)	HEF	SO3229	10,2
[Cheney] Longville	SHR	SO4284	4,27,32
Longworth	BRK	SU3999	7,39
Lonsdale (near Cockerham) LAN	CHS	SD4354	Y10
Lonsdale LAN	YKS	??	30W38 note
Lonton WR	YKS	NY9524	6N38. SN,CtA15
Loose	KEN	TQ7552	3,5
Loose	SFK	TM0053	25,112. 34,5
Loosebeare	DEV	SS7105	8,1
Loosedon	DEV	SS6008	24,24. 25,6
Lopen	SOM	ST4214	19,6. 21,38. 47,3
[North and South] Lopham	NFK	TM0382 TM0381	9,76-78;132
Loppington	SHR	SJ4729	4,1,18
Lordine	SSX	TQ8022	9,123
Lordington	SSX	SU7809	11,35
Loseley	SRY	SU9747	18,4
Losfield	BRK	SU9374	32,1
Loteland	DEV	??	25,18
Lothersdale WR	YKS	SD9645	30W14
Loton	SHR	SJ3514	4,4,10
Loudham	SFK	TM3054	3,25. 6,188-189;237;247;257. 7,123;127. 21,91. 22,3. 67,24
Loughborough	LEC	SK5319	C8. 43,2-3
Loughton	BKM	SP8337	12,32. 14,39. 43,10
Loughton	ESS	TQ4296	1,4. 8,4-5. 32,11. 36,7;10.
Loughtor	DEV	SX5557	17,103
Lound	LIN	TF0618	8,6;34. 24,32
Lound	NTT	SK6986	1,16. 5,7. 9,51
Lound	SFK	TM5098	1,34;44;46
[East and Graize] Lound	LIN	SK7899 SK7798	63,8-10
Louth	LIN	TF3287	7,56
Louth Hundred	LIN	—	CS,4
Lovacott (in Shebbear)	DEV	SS4508	35,17
Loventor	DEV	SX8462	2,18 note. 17,26
Loversall WR	YKS	SK5798	5W8. CW14;16. SW,Sf21
Loverston IOW	HAM	SZ4983	7,2

Lovington	SOM	ST5930	37,8
Lowdham	NTT	SK6646	5,9. 9,75
Lowe (in Farlow)	SHR	SO6380	6,5
Lowe (in Wem)	SHR	SJ5030	4,8,2. 4,14,4 note
Lowesby	LEC	SK7207	40,24
Lowestoft	SFK	TM5593	1,33
Lowick	NTH	SP9780	4,26. 51,1
Lowley	DEV	SX8387	47,6
[Craze] Lowman	DEV	SS9814	24,8
Lowne: see Heath	DBY	SK4566	5,3
Lowthorpe ER	YKS	TA0760	1E31. 2E16. 29E13. CE31. SE,Bt3
Lowton	DEV	SX7485	47,14
Loxbeare	DEV	SS9116	3,83
Loxhore	DEV	SS6138	16,67-68
Loxley	STS	SK0632	8,18
Loxley	WAR	SP2552	3,5. 16,61. 18,15
Loxton	SOM	ST3755	17,4
Loynton	STS	SJ7724	11,53
Lubbesthorpe	LEC	SK5401	25,3-4
Lubenham	LEC	SP7087	2,3-4. 15,9. 40,15
Luccombe IOW	HAM	SZ5879	1,W9
Luccombe	SOM	SS9144	32,2. 38,1
Luckington	SOM	ST6950	35,23
Luckington	WIL	ST8383	30,7. 41,10
Ludborough	LIN	TF2995	18,8
Ludbrook	DEV	SX6554	1,23. 15,26;72
Luddenham	KEN	TQ9963	5,160
Luddesdown	KEN	TQ6666	5,53
Luddington	LIN	SE8317	63,19-21;23-26
Luddington	WAR	SP1652	16,60
Luddington [in the Brook] NTH	HUN		19,19
Luddington [in the Brook] NTH	NTH	TL1083	6a,16. EH7
Lude	BKM	SU9191	3a,5
Ludford	LIN	TF2089	14,62. 22,21-23. 25,18. 40,16
Ludford SHR	HEF		24,12
Ludford SHR	SHR	SO5173	EH1
Ludgershall	BKM	SP6617	5,2. 34,1
Ludgershall	WIL	SU2650	24,15
Ludgvan	CON	SW5033	5,3,27
Ludham	NFK	TG3818	4,38;51;53;59. 65,3
Ludshott	HAM	SU8434	23,26
Ludwell	DBY	SK1262	6,11
Ludwell	OXF	SP4322	7,48. 28,24. 40,2. 58,5-6
Ludworth	DBY	SJ9991	1,30
Luffenhall	HRT	TL2928	5,13. 13,4. 37,2
[North and South] Luffenham RUT	NTH		1,2f;3. 56,36
[North and South] Luffenham RUT	RUT	SK9303 SK9401	EN2-3;20
Lufton	SOM	ST5116	19,82
Lugwardine	HEF	SO5541	1,2
Lulham	HEF	SO4041	2,4
Lullingstone	KEN	TQ5264	5,8-9;12
Lullington	DBY	SK2513	17,11
Lullington	SOM	ST7851	5,51
[East and West] Lulworth	DOR	SY8682 SY8280	1,6. 26,50-51. 49,15
Lund (near Beverley) ER	YKS	SE9748	3Y2-3 note. SE,He8 note. SE,Wel2
Lund (in Breighton) ER	YKS	SE7033	3Y2 note. 15E5. 21E5. CE14. SE,He8 note

Luntley	HEF	SO3955	1,33
Luppitt	DEV	ST1606	23,19
Lupridge	DEV	SX7153	15,27. 24,20. 25,26
Lupton	DEV	SX9055	17,28
Lupton WES	YKS	SD5581	1L4. See also CHS Y5
Lurkenhope	SHR	SO2874	4,20,23
Lus [Hill]	WIL	SU1693	24,5. 27,6
Lusby	LIN	TF3367	24,24;43-44
Luscombe (in Rattery)	DEV	SX7463	20,15
Luston	HEF	SO4863	1,10a
Lutley	WOR	SO9483	13,1
Luton	BDF	TL0821	1,2. 1,5. 40,1. 57,4
Luton IOW	HAM	SZ4892	1,9. 9,21
Lutterworth	LEC	SP5484	37,1
Lutton	LIN	TF4325	1,29-30
Lutton NTH	HUN		6,14
Lutton NTH	NTH	TL1187	6a,11. 9,2. EH3
[East and West] Lutton ER	YKS	SE9469	2B18. SE,Th4
		SE9369	
Lutwyche	SHR	SO5594	4,3,12
Luuetotholm (in Leven) ER	YKS	??	CE36 *note*
Luxborough	SOM	SS9738	25,27-28
Lychpit	HAM	SU6553	6,7
Lydbury [North]	SHR	SO3586	2,1
Lyddington RUT	NTH		5,2
Lyddington RUT	RUT	SP8797	EN7
[Lower and Upper] Lyde	HEF	SO5144	2,44. 10,25-26. 24,11
		SO4944	
Lyde	SOM	ST5717	22,28
[Bishops] Lydeard	SOM	ST1629	6,8;19
[East] Lydeard	SOM	ST1729	25,50
Lydeard [St Lawrence]	SOM	ST1232	2,9
Lydford	DEV	SX5084	C6. 1,2. 17,1. 34,3
[East] Lydford	SOM	ST5731	8,4
[West] Lydford	SOM	ST5631	47,21
Lydham	SHR	SO3391	4,1,14
Lydiard [Millicent]	WIL	SU0985	1,21
Lydiard [Tregoze]	WIL	SU1084	26,7
Lydiate LAN	CHS	SD3604	R1,34
Lydley [Hayes] (in Cardington)	SHR	SO4998	4,27,12
Lydney GLS	GLS	SO6303	1,55. E5
Lydney GLS	HEF		2,8
[Little] Lydney (alias St Briavels)	GLS	SO5504	32,11
[Lower and Upper] Lye HEF	HEF	SO4066	1,10c. 9,8;14. 24,4. 31,7. ES9
		SO3965	
[Upper] Lye HEF	SHR		6,16
Lyford	BRK	SU3994	7,24;25
Lyme [Regis]	DOR	SY3392	2,5. 8,6. 57,14
[Up] Lyme: see Uplyme DEV			
Lyminge	KEN	TR1640	2,26
Lymington	HAM	SZ3295	NF3,9
Lyminster	SSX	TQ0204	11,59-60. 13,15
Lymm	CHS	SJ6786	17,6. 24,5
Lympne	KEN	TR1134	2,25
Lympstone	DEV	SX9984	26,1
Lyn	DEV	SS7248	19,17;18
Lyncombe	SOM	ST7564	7,9
Lyndhurst	HAM	SU2908	1,31
Lyneham	OXF	SP2720	7,59
Lynford	NFK	TL8194	9,10. 25,15
Lyng	NFK	TG0617	4,29

Lyng	SOM	ST3228	10,5
[King's, North, South, and West] Lynn	NFK	TF6120	22,19. 31,32. 66,17;55
		TF6121	
		TF6119	
		TF6118	
Lynton	DEV	SS7149	19,16
Lyonshall	HEF	SO3355	10,44
Lyppard [Grange]	WOR	SO8755	2,71
Lyscombe	DOR	ST7301	12,9
Lytchett [Matravers]	DOR	SY9495	34,5
Lytham LAN	YKS	SD3727	1L1. See also CHS Y2
Lythe NR	YKS	NZ8413	5N1. SN,L5

M

Mablethorpe	LIN	TF4984	13,7. 24,71. 40,21. CS,15
Macclesfield	CHS	SJ9173	1,25
Mackadown	WAR	SP1686	17,9
Mackham	DEV	ST1509	19,36
Macknade	KEN	TR0259	D18. 5,148
Mackworth	DBY	SK3137	4,2
Maddington	WIL	SU0644	16,7. 63,1
Madeley	SHR	SJ6904	3c,4
Madeley (in Croxden)	STS	SK0638	11,37
[Great] Madeley	STS	SJ7744	11,20
Madgett	GLS	SO5500	1,64. 39,10
Madingley	CAM	TL3960	3,2. 32,33
Madley	HEF	SO4138	2,9
Maen Efa FLN	CHS	SJ0874	FT1,2
Maer	STS	SJ7938	11,17
Maesbrook	SHR	SJ3021	4,3,35
Maesbury	SHR	SJ3025	4,1,11
Maghull LAN	CHS	SD3702	R1,2
Maidenbrooke	SOM	ST2426	2,3
Maidencombe	DEV	SX9268	16,126
Maidenhead	BRK	SU8781	34,2
Maidenwell: see [Maiden] Well LIN			
Maidford	NTH	SP6052	23,8
Maidstone	KEN	TQ7555	2,11
Maidwell	NTH	SP7476	8,12. 15,1. 54,3
Maistana (in Trimley)	SFK	TM3137	7,79
Makeney	DBY	SK3544	6,66
Maker CON	CON	SX4452	5,2,14
Maker CON	DEV		1,22
Makinbrook	KEN	TR1665	*2,14*
[Old] Malden	SRY	TQ2166	8,13. 19,23;25
Maldon (in Maldon Hundred)	ESS	TL8507	1,25. 24,63. 34,31. B6
Maldon (in *Wibertsherne* Hundred)	ESS	TL8507	1,17. 20,34. 34,12
Malham WR	YKS	SD9062	1W73. 13W44. SW,Cr4
[Kirkby] Malham WR	YKS	SD8960	30W1
Malkton (in Tadcaster East) WR	YKS	??	13W15 *note*. SW,An6
[?East] Malling	KEN	TQ7057	2,8
[South] Malling	SSX	TQ4211	2,1;4
[?West] Malling	KEN	TQ6757	4,7
Malmesbury	WIL	ST9387	M. B4-5. 5,4. 7,11. 8,3. 24,20;38. 26,19. 27,10;23. 28,1. 41,1;9. 45,1. 49,1. 67,40
Malpas	CHS	SJ4847	2,4
Malshanger: see *Gerlei* HAM			
Malston	DEV	SX7745	17,55
Maltby	LIN	TF3184	13,29
Maltby NR	YKS	NZ4613	4N3. SN,L35
Maltby WR	YKS	SK5291	10W4;12. SW,Sf5
Maltby [le Marsh]	LIN	TF4681	12,85. 24,64. 25,22. 28,32
[Old] Malton NR	YKS	SE7972	1N65-66. 2N7. 5N37. SN,Ma5-6
[Little] Malvern	WOR	SO7640	2,31
[Kirkby] Malzeard WR	YKS	SE2374	28W10. SW,Bu23
Mamble	WOR	SO6871	16,2

Mamhead	DEV	SX9381	16,63. 52,48
Manadon	DEV	SX4858	17,75
Manaton	DEV	SX7581	16,160. 52,27
Manby	LIN	TF3986	1,83
Manby	LIN	SE9308	44,4
Manchester LAN	CHS	SJ8398	R5,2
Manely	CON	SX1355	5,13,1
Manesfort	SFK	??	36,4
Man(e)uuic/Manewic	SFK	??	4,2-3. 6,19. 16,32
Manfield NR	YKS	NZ2213	6N1. SN,CtA8
Mangotsfield	GLS	ST6576	1,21
Mangreen	NFK	TG2103	9,193
Manley	CHS	SJ5071	1,6
[East] Manley	DEV	SS9811	25,21
[West] Manley	DEV	SS9812	46,1
Manningford [Abbots, Bohune and Bruce]	WIL	SU1458	10,1. 66,2. 67,43
		SU1357	
		SU1358	
Mannington	DOR	SU0605	26,38
Mannington	NFK	TG1431	1,194. 8,8
Mansell: see also Bishopstone HEF			
Mansell [Gamage]	HEF	SO3944	10,56
Mansell [Lacy]	HEF	SO4245	31,4-5
Mansergh WES	YKS	SD5982	1L4 *note*. See also CHS Y5
Mansfield	NTT	SK5361	1,17;23;26;30. 9,47
Manshead Hundred BDF	HRT	—	1,5
Manson	NFK	TG0203	1,87
Manston	DOR	ST8115	40,1
Manston	SFK	TL8356	14,15. 25,31. 27,2
Manston WR	YKS	SE3635	9W1. SW,Sk4
Manthorpe	LIN	TF0716	8,6;34. 24,32. 30,32
Manton	LIN	SE9302	8,20. CW,16
Manton	NTT	SK6178	10,64
Manton	SFK	TL9753	14,114. 34,2
Manton	WIL	SU1768	28,12
Manuden	ESS	TL4926	32,16;22. 33,10. 90,36
Manworthy	SOM	ST0825	25,44
Maperton	SOM	ST6726	36,10
Maplebeck	NTT	SK7160	1,24;29. 17,11
Mapledurham	HAM	SU7321	1,8
Mapledurham	OXF	SU6776	22,1. 35,8
Mapledurwell	HAM	SU6851	24,1
Mapleham	HAM	??	NF9,30
Maplescombe	KEN	TQ5564	5,5;14
[Great] Maplestead	ESS	TL8034	32,23
[Little] Maplestead	ESS	TL8233	40,3. 90,38
Mapperley	DBY	SK4343	1,35
Mapperton (in Almer)	DOR	SY9098	19,13
Mapperton (near Beaminster)	DOR	SY5099	32,5. 36,11
Mappleborough	WAR	SP0866	28,11
Mappleton	DBY	SK1648	1,14
Mappleton ER	YKS	TA2243	14E5-6. SE,Hol9
Mappowder	DOR	ST7306	1,8. 26,23. 34,4. 56,7
Marbury (near Nantwich)	CHS	SJ5545	8,21
March	CAM	TL4196	5,45. 6,1
Marcham	BRK	SU4596	7,17
Marchamley	SHR	SJ5929	4,3,1
Marche	SHR	SJ3310	4,4,17. 4,5,10
Marchington	STS	SK1330	10,4
Marchwood	HAM	SU3810	69,50
[Little] Marcle	HEF	SO6736	10,32. 17,2

[Much] Marcle	HEF	SO6532	1,7;10c. 4,1. 15,4
Marden	HEF	SO5147	C3. 1,4. 10,11. 16,4. 35,1
[East, North, Up and West] Marden	SSX	SU8014	11,31;33–34;38
		SU8016	
		SU7914	
		SU7713	
Marden	WIL	SU0857	51,1
Marderby [Hall] NR	YKS	SE4683	23N10 *note*
Mardley[bury]	HRT	TL2618	20,1. Appx
Mare	LIN	TF4692	CS,39
[North] Marefield	LEC	SK7408	1,3
[South] Marefield	LEC	SK7407	1,3
[Cold] Mareham (in Burton Pedwardine)	LIN	TF0843	57,32
Mareham [le Fen]	LIN	TF2861	1,102
Mareham [on the Hill]	LIN	TF2868	38,6
Marfleet ER	YKS	TA1429	14E6. SE,Th13. SE, Hol11
Margaretting	ESS	TL6600	1,22. 53,2
Margate	KEN	TR3570	7,9
Marham	NFK	TF7009	8,15. 13,1. 15,1. 23,9 *and note*
Marhamchurch	CON	SS2203	5,5,5
Mariansleigh	DEV	SS7422	51,11
[Little] Marish NR	YKS	??	8N14 *note*. SN,D10
Markby	LIN	TF4878	4,66. 13,8. 28,40
Markeaton DBY	DBY	SK3337	4,1. 6,51. S
Markeaton DBY	NTT		S5
Markenfield [Hall] WR	YKS	SE2967	13W20 *note*. SW,Bu19
Markfield	LEC	SK4810	40,9
[East] Markham	NTT	SK7472	1,3. 9,6–11
[West] Markham	NTT	SK7272	9,28–30
Markington WR	YKS	SE2965	2W7;13. SW,Bu48. SW, H3
Marksbury	SOM	ST6662	8,29
Markshall	ESS	TL8425	27,13
Markshall	NFK	TG2205	20,22;35
[Little] Marland	DEV	SS4912	36,6
[Peters] Marland	DEV	SS4713	35,13
Marlborough	WIL	SU1869	B4. 1,23i
Marlesford	SFK	TM3258	1,93–94. 3,43. 6,276. 14,118
Marley	KEN	TQ8853	5,74
Marley WR	YKS	SE0940	24W1 *note*. 24W21. SW,Sk18
Marlingford	NFK	TG1309	4,13
Marlow and [Little] Marlow	BKM	SU8586	4,18. 23,4. 28,2. 52,1
		SU8788	
Marlston	CHS	SJ3963	FD4,1
[High] Marnham	NTT	SK8070	9,64
[Low] Marnham	NTT	SK8069	9,65
Marr WR	YKS	SE5105	5W9;31. 10W27;40. SW,Sf20–21
Marrick NR	YKS	SE0798	6N72. SN,CtA24
Marrington	SHR	SO2796	4,5,15
Marsh	DBY	SK3931	17,21
Marsh Baldon: see [Marsh] Baldon OXF			
[Denge] Marsh	KEN	TR0518	5,177;179
Marsh [Gibbon]	BKM	SP6423	12,29. 17,16
Marsh [Mills]	SOM	ST1938	35,9
Marsham	NFK	TG1923	1,57. 10,40–41. 20,30. 25,10
Marshborough	KEN	TR3057	5,213
[The] Marshes (in Luddington)	LIN	SE8516	63,23–26
Marshfield	GLS	ST7773	1,20
Marske [by the Sea] NR	YKS	NZ6322	4N2 *note*. 5N17. 13N4;6. SN,L21
Marsley	SHR	SJ3902	C3
Marston (in Pembridge)	HEF	SO3657	27,1
Marston	LIN	SK8943	12,45. 26,32–34. 27,50. 54,1–2.
			57,35. CK,19;39;64

Marston (in Diddlebury)	SHR	SO5285	4,14,25
Marston (in Church Eaton) STS	NTH		16,2
Marston (in Church Eaton) STS	STS	SJ8313	EN2
Marston (near Stafford)	STS	SJ9227	8,9
Marston [Bigot]	SOM	ST7544	22,26
[Broad] Marston WOR	GLS		62,2
[Broad] Marston WOR	WOR	SP1446	EG15
[Butlers] Marston	WAR	SP3150	18,2
[Fleet] Marston	BKM	SP7716	28,3
Marston [Green]	WAR	SP1785	17,10
Marston [Jabbett]	WAR	SP3788	16,46
[Lea] Marston	WAR	SP2093	17,48 *note*. 21,1. 23,1;3
[Lea] Marston: see also Lea [Marston] WAR			
[Long] Marston WAR	GLS		15,1
[Long] Marston WAR	WAR	SP1548	EG7
[Long] Marston WR	YKS	SE5051	25W5;11 *note*. SW, An10
Marston [Magna]	SOM	ST5922	19,72-73
Marston [Moretaine]	BDF	SP9941	16,3. 24,8
[North] Marston	BKM	SP7722	4,25. 5,4. 17,7-8. 23,17
Marston [on-Avon]	WAR	SP4176	17,48 note
Marston [on Dove]	DBY	SK2329	6,24
[Potters] Marston	LEC	SP4996	6,2
Marston [St Lawrence]	NTH	SP5342	22,4
Marston [Stannett]	HEF	SO5755	1,10a. 10,71. 14,12. 32,1
Marston [Trussell]	NTH	SP6985	23,2
Marsworth	BKM	SP9214	19,4
Marten	WIL	SU2860	67,83. 68,10;13
Martham	NFK	TG4518	1,45;164. 4,27. 10,30;86. 17,15. 64,9
Martin	DEV	SX6892	16,115
Martin	LIN	TF2366	3,14. 29,5
Martin	NTT	SK6394	9,56
Martin (near Pennington) LAN	YKS	SD2477	1L6 *note*. See also CHS Y7
Martin [Garth] NR	YKS	SE9684	1Y3 *note*. 1N43 *note*. SN,L31 note. SN,D8
Martin Hussingtree: see [Martin] Hussingtree WOR			
Martinhoe	DEV	SS6648	3,23
Martinstown	DOR	SY6488	55,1
Martlesham	SFK	TM2646	39,6
Martley	SFK	TM2858	3,35;52. 6,293. 8,28. 67,27
Martley WOR	HEF		1,39. E8
Martley WOR	WOR	SO7559	18,5. 21,4. X3. E1
Martock	SOM	ST4619	1,27. 35,24
Marton (near Burscough) LAN	CHS	SD4212	R1,32
Marton (near Congleton)	CHS	SJ8468	1,28. 11,6
Marton	LIN	SK8381	12,2
Marton	SHR	SJ2802	3f,2
Marton (near Burton Constable) ER	YKS	TA1839	14E11;51. SE,Hol16;26
Marton (near Grafton) WR	YKS	SE4162	28W1. SW,Bu4
Marton (in Sewerby) ER	YKS	TA2069	1Y11. 2N20. 5E46. 29E8. SE,Hu2
Marton (near Sinnington) NR	YKS	SE7383	8N16. 23N21. SN,L31 note. SN,D21
Marton (near Pennington): see Martin LAN			
[East and West] Marton WR	YKS	SD9051 SD8950	30W26 *note*
[Great and Little] Marton (near Blackpool) LAN	YKS	SD3234 SD3434	1L1. See also CHS Y2
Marton [in Cleveland] NR	YKS	NZ5115	1N25 *note*. 11N6;8. 29N6-7. 31N5. SN, L31 *note*

Marton [in the Forest] NR	YKS	SE6068	5N58. SN,B7
Marwood	DEV	SS5437	16,87. 28,8. 36,16
Marylebone: see Lisson, *Tyburn* MDX			
Marytavy: see Tavy DEV			
Masham NR	YKS	SE2280	6N114;118;123;138. SN,CtA34
Mashbury	ESS	TL6511	12,1 note. 30,13. 90,20
[Great and Little] Massingham	NFK	TF7922	1,1. 5,1. 8,29. 9,5. 19,8. 21,11.
		TF7924	29,2
Matching	ESS	TL5212	14,1. 30,25. 32,6. 61,2
Mateurdin	HEF	??	1,67. 31,1
Matford	DEV	SX9289	1,43 note. 15,55. 19,9
Mathon HEF	HEF	SO7345	10,39. 23,6. E5
Mathon HEF	WOR		9,6
Matlask	NFK	TG1534	1,57;193. 4,22;25
Matlock	DBY	SK2960	1,12. 6,24
Matlock [Bridge]	DBY	SK2960	1,12;15
Mattersey	NTT	SK6989	1,15. 9,132
Mattingley	HAM	SU7357	69,9
Mattishall	NFK	TG0511	8,81. 15,20. 20,16;18 *and note.*
			66,29
Maugersbury	GLS	SP2025	12,1. EvO9
Maulden	BDF	TL0538	16,4. 23,13. 24,12. 53,1. 57,3ii
Maunby NR	YKS	SE3486	1Y2. 6N29. SN,A1. SN,CtA13
Maund Bryan and Rose[maunde]	HEF	SO5650	7,5. 10,6;8. 14,2
		SO5648	
Mautby	NFK	TG4812	1,202. 9,93. 19,37
Mawfield	HEF	SO4536	10,21
Mawgan	CON	SW7025	1,1
Mawley	SHR	SO6875	6,3
Maxudesmares/Maxudesmersc (in Pickering	YKS	??	1Y4 *note.* SN,D12 *note*
Marishes) NR			
Mayfield	STS	SK1545	1,23
Mayfield	SSX	TQ5827	10,118
Mayne	DOR	SY7286	27,4–5
Mayton	NFK	TG2421	26,2
Meadowley	SHR	SO6692	4,21,12
Meaford	STS	SJ8835	5,1. 8,24
Meare	SOM	ST4541	8,1
Measham LEC	DBY		1,24
Measham LEC	LEC	SK3312	E3
Meaux ER	YKS	TA0940	14E11 *note.* SE, Hol15
Meavy	DEV	SX5467	17,79–82. 29,9
Mechlas FLN	CHS	SJ1965	FT1,5
Medbourne	LEC	SP8093	1,4. 15,2
Meddon	DEV	SS2717	52,31
Medehei	SSX	??	9,3
Mederclive	KEN	TR2638	P11
Medland	DEV	SX7795	52,13
Medmenham	BKM	SU8084	26,4
Meering	NTT	SK8165	1,64
Meesden	HRT	TL4332	4,17
Meeth	DEV	SS5408	16,39
Meincatis FLN	CHS	??	FT2,6
Melbourn	CAM	TL3844	5,34. 13,7. 14,33. 26,31
Melbourne	DBY	SK3825	1,19. (10,26)
Melbourne ER	YKS	SE7544	15E8. SE,C10
Melbury	DEV	SX4996	21,5
Melbury [Abbas]	DOR	ST8820	19,6
Melbury [Bubb and Osmund]	DOR	ST5906	26,35. 32,2. 47,2. 56,17
		ST5707	
Melchanestone FLN	CHS	??	FT2,10

Melchbourne	BDF	TL0265	3,2
Melchet [Wood] HAM	WIL	SU2722	13,10;18
Melcombe	SOM	ST2833	24,8. 46,5
Melcombe [Horsey]	DOR	ST7402	1,30. 19,14
Meldreth	CAM	TL3746	5,30-33. 13,6. 14,32. 26,29-30. 31,1-2
Melevsford IOW	HAM	??	9,1
[Long] Melford	SFK	TL8646	14,23
Melhuish	DEV	SX7992	16,116
Meliden FLN	CHS	SJ0681	FT2,15
Melksham	WIL	ST9064	1,12. 67,89
Melling (near Liverpool) LAN	CHS	SD3900	R1,33
Melling (near Lancaster) LAN	YKS	SD5971	1W70-71. See also CHS Y1
Mellington (Wales)	SHR	SO2592	4,1,35
Mellis	SFK	TM1074	6,195;227. 14,140. 35,7
Mells	SOM	ST7249	8,25
Mells	SFK	TM4076	44,3
Melmerby (near Hutton Conyers) NR	YKS	SE3377	6N145. SN,CtA40
Melmerby (near Middleham) NR	YKS	SE0785	6N95. SN,CtA29
Melsonby NR	YKS	NZ2008	6N50. SN,CtA18
Meltham WR	YKS	SE1010	9W107. SW,Ag8
Melton	SFK	TM2850	3,24. 6,175. 8,17. 21,80;*83*;93. 32,13
Melton [Constable]	NFK	TG0331	10,58
[Great] Melton	NFK	TG1406	12,30;32-33. 32,4;6. 66,105
[High] Melton WR	YKS	SE5001	10W20 *note*. SW,Sf11 note. SW,Sf14
[Little] Melton	NFK	TG1506	12,32-33
Melton [Mowbray]	LEC	SK7519	29,3-4;18
Melton [Ross]	LIN	TA0710	34,1
[West] Melton WR	YKS	SE4200	10W19. 19W2. 29W4-5;7. SW,Sf11 *note*. SW,Sf16
Meltonby ER	YKS	SE7952	1Y10. SE,Wa4
Melverley	SHR	SJ3316	4,3,37
Membland	DEV	SX5648	17,68
Membury	DEV	ST2703	1,11 *note*. 19,44
Mendham SFK	NFK		10,32. 14,19;22;*35*
Mendham SFK	SFK	TM2682	6,72;313. 8,37;42. 13,1. 14,106. 19,2
Mendlesham	SFK	TM1065	1,65-66;76-8082;85;87. 8,55. 14,146
Menethorpe ER	YKS	SE7667	1E47. 5E61. 8E2. SE,Ac1
Menston WR	YKS	SE1643	2W4. SW,Sk1
Mentmore	BKM	SP9019	13,1
Menutton	SHR	SO3077	4,20,22
Meole	SHR	SJ4810	1,3. 3d,3. 6,33
[Great and Little] Meols	CHS	SJ2390	3,9-10
[North] Meols LAN	CHS	SD3419	R1,42
[Raven] Meols LAN	CHS	SD2705	R1,12;30
Meon	HAM	SU5303	2,17
Meon and [Lower] Meon WAR	GLS		1,12
Meon and [Lower] Meon WAR	WAR	SP1845	EG1
[East] Meon	HAM	SU6822	1,16. 2,13
[West] Meon	HAM	SU6424	2,11
Meonstoke	HAM	SU6119	1,15;45. 2,12
Meopham	KEN	TQ6466	3,4
Meppershall BDF	BDF	TL1336	48,1
Meppershall BDF	HRT		40,1
Mercaston	DBY	SK2642	6,96
Merclesham	KEN	??	P20
Mere	CHS	SJ7281	17,9

Mere	WIL	ST8132	67,45;68;76
Merestone/Merestun (= Wigmore Castle)	HEF	SO4069	1,5. 9,1
Meretown	STS	SJ7520	1,24
Mereworth	KEN	TQ6653	12,3
Merridge	SOM	ST2034	35,20
Merrington	SHR	SJ4720	4,20,16
Merriott	SOM	ST4412	19,32. 47,6
[East] Mersea	ESS	TM0514	24,49
[West] Mersea	ESS	TM0112	2,2. 17,1
Mersham	KEN	TR0539	2,22
Merstham and [South] Merstham	SRY	TQ2953	2,5
		TQ2952	
Merston IOW	HAM	SZ5285	6,18;21
Merston	KEN	TQ6971	5,114
Merston	SSX	SU8903	11,110
Merton	DEV	SS5212	3,5
Merton	NFK	TL9198	31,35
Merton	OXF	SP5717	53,1
Merton	SRY	TQ2569	1,5
Mertyn FLN	CHS	SJ1577	FT1,8
Meshaw	DEV	SS7519	16,141
Messing	ESS	TL8918	33,9. 39,4
Messingham	LIN	SE8904	7,17. 8,31-32. 34,3
Metcombe	DEV	SS5339	3,29
Metheringham	LIN	TF0761	13,35. 31,18. 59,19. 68,4
Methleigh	CON	SW6226	2,2
Methley WR	YKS	SE3927	9W94 *note*. SW,Ag1
Methwold	NFK	TL7394	1,210;*211*. 8,38
Mettingham	SFK	TM3689	4,21;23
Metton	NFK	TG1937	9,143;146
Mexborough WR	YKS	SK4799	10W13. SW,Sf8
Meyseyhampton: see [Meysey] Hampton GLS			
Michaelstow	ESS	TM2131	33,17
Micheldever	HAM	SU5139	6,16
Michelton (= Roake)	HAM	SU3131	69,20
Mickfield	SFK	TM1361	14,38. 34,10
Mickleby NR	YKS	NZ8012	5N7. SN,L8
Mickleham	SRY	TQ1753	5,23. 19,19
Mickleover	DBY	SK3034	3,1. 6,53
Micklethwaite WR	YKS	SE1041	24W1 *note*. SW,Sk18
Mickleton	GLS	SP1643	18,1
Mickleton NR	YKS	NY9623	6N39. SN,CtA15
Middelham (in Muscoates) NR	YKS	??	23N21 *note*
Middlecote (in Mells)	SOM	ST7048	5,50 ˎ
Middlecott (in Broadwood Kelly)	DEV	SS6106	16,28;30
Middlecott (in Chagford)	DEV	SX7186	52,37
Middleham (near Leyburn) NR	YKS	SE1287	6N99. SN,CtA30
Middlehope	SHR	SO4988	4,8,11
Middlethorpe WR	YKS	SE6048	1W29 note. 11W2. 22W1. SW,Sf37 note. SW,An1
Middleton	DBY	SK2756	1,13. 6,77
Middleton	DEV	SS6445	3,52
Middleton	ESS	TL8739	23,20. 82,1. 90,84
Middleton	HAM	SU4244	16,5
Middleton (in Lower Harpton)	HEF	SO2759	9,13
Middleton (near Forncett St Peter)	NFK	TM1592	4,56
Middleton (near King's Lynn)	NFK	TF6616	4,45. 14,5. 19,4;6. 23,11
Middleton (in Bitterley)	SHR	SO5477	4,14,23
Middleton (in Chirbury)	SHR	SO2999	4,5,13. 4,27,22
Middleton	SFK	TM4367	3,6. 4,15. 6,86. 7,31;39. 26,13

Middleton	SSX	SU9700	11,83
Middleton	WAR	SP1798	18,4. 45,1
Middleton	WIL	ST9044	24,29. 48,5
Middleton LAN	YKS	SD4258	1L2. See also CHS Y3
Middleton (in Appleton Wiske) NR	YKS	??	28W39 *note*
Middleton (in Guisborough) NR	YKS	??	5N19 *note*. SN,L18
Middleton (near Ilkley) WR	YKS	SE1249	2W4. SW,Sk2
Middleton (near Leeds) WR	YKS	SE3028	9W119 *note*. SW,M2
Middleton (near Pickering) NR	YKS	SE7885	1Y4. SN,L39 note. SN,D18
Middleton [by-Youlgrave]	DBY	SK1963	1,13
Middleton [Cheney]	NTH	SP5041	18,37. 22,6. 23,10
Middleton [Hall] WES	YKS	SD6287	1L4 *note*. See also CHS Y5
Middleton [on the Hill]	HEF	SO5464	1,31
Middleton [on the Wolds] ER	YKS	SE9449	2E12. 5E21-22;27-28. CE3-7. SE,Sn1
Middleton [Quernhow] NR	YKS	SE3378	6N146. SN,CtA40
Middleton [Scriven]	SHR	SO6887	4,3,65
Middleton [Stoney]	OXF	SP5323	33,1
[Stony] Middleton	DBY	SK2375	1,34. 10,16-17
Middleton [Tyas] NR	YKS	NZ2205	6N3. SN,CtA8
Middleton [upon Leven] NR	YKS	NZ4609	5N28. SN,L39 *note*
Middlewich	CHS	SJ7066	S2
Middlewich (in Droitwich)	WOR	SO8963	1,3a
Middlewick	DEV	SS8214	3,80
Middlewood (in Clifford)	HEF	SO2844	25,5
Middlewood (in Winforton)	HEF	SO3045	6,9
Middlezoy SOM: see Zoy			
[Little] Middop WR	YKS	SD8445	13W39 *note*
Midebroc	ESS	??	90,9
Mideham	SRY	??	19,41-42
Midelney	SOM	ST4122	9,1
Midgell	SOM	ST4668	5,68
Midgham	BRK	SU5567	34,1
Midgham	HAM	SU1312	69,31;34
Midgley WR	YKS	SE0226	1Y15
Midley	KEN	TR0123	5,208
Milborne [Port] SOM	DOR		2,6
Milborne [Port] SOM	SOM	ST6718	1,10;31. 14,1. 19,70;71. EDo1
Milborne [St Andrew]	DOR	SY8097	46,1
Milborne [Stileham]	DOR	SY8097	54,12. 56,53
Milby NR	YKS	SE4067	1Y18. SW,H7
Milcombe	OXF	SP4134	17,5. 58,35
Milcote	WAR	SP1952	36,2
Milden	SFK	TL9546	14,34. 41,10
Mildenhall SFK	NFK		42,1
Mildenhall SFK	SFK	TL7174	1,115. 25,39. ENf5
Mildenhall	WIL	SU2069	7,7
Mildon	DEV	SS8822	19,37
Mileham	NFK	TF9219	1,79-80;212;214;217;232. 4,8. 8,69-70. 9,80. 10,5;53. 13,17. 15,15. 20,7-9. 21,19. 31,39-40. 34,5-6. 66,25;38
Milford	DBY	SK3445	6,66
Milford (in Hartland)	DEV	SS2322	36,4
Milford (in Stowford)	DEV	SX4086	3,87
Milford	WIL	SU1529	27,27. 67,79
Milford [on Sea]	HAM	SZ2891	NF9,35;40
[North] Milford [Hall] WR	YKS	SE5039	9W33 *note*. CW3. SW,BA9
Millbrook	BDF	TL0138	24,9
Millbrook	HAM	SU3813	3,17
Millichope	SHR	SO5289	4,21,3

Millington	CHS	SJ7284	9,12
Millington ER	YKS	SE8351	1Y10. 2B13. 31E5. SE,Wa6
Millmeece	STS	SJ8333	1,37
Millmeece: see also Coldmeece STS			
Millom [Castle]: see *Hougenai* CUM			
Millom: see *Hougon* CUM			
Millow	BDF	TL2343	5,1. 16,6. 18,3
[Marsh] Mills: see Mills SOM			
Milson	SHR	SO6472	5,9
Milston	WIL	SU1645	21,2. 42,6
Milton	BRK	SU4892	7,27
Milton	CAM	TL4762	32,37
Milton	CON	SS2414	5,5,2
Milton	DBY	SK3226	1,20
Milton	ESS	TQ8785	2,7
Milton	HEF	SO3860	24,1
Milton (near Gravesend)	KEN	TQ6573	5,52
Milton	NTH	TL1499	6a,2
Milton	NTT	SK7173	10,3
Milton (in Skilgate)	SOM	SS9727	22,12
Milton (in Weston Super Mare)	SOM	ST3462	24,2. 46,19
Milton	SRY	TQ1549	21,4
Milton [Abbas]	DOR	ST8001	12,2
Milton [Abbot]	DEV	SX4079	5,2
Milton [Bryan]	BDF	SP9730	2,3. 23,20
Milton [Clevedon]	SOM	ST6637	44,3
Milton [Damerel]	DEV	SS3711	28,1
Milton [Ernest]	BDF	TL0156	19,2. 23,26. 24,19. 32,2. 54,4. 57,17
[Great] Milton	OXF	SP6202	6,3;11
Milton [Keynes]	BKM	SP8839	14,47. 17,31. 57,13
Milton [Malsor] (near Northampton)	NTH	SP7355	44,1a;1c
[Old] Milton	HAM	SZ2394	NF10,1
Milton [on Stour]	DOR	ST8028	35,1. 56,1
Milton [Regis]	KEN	TQ9065	1,3. 13,1
[South] Milton	DEV	SX6942	39,15
Milton [under-Wychwood]	OXF	SP2618	14,6. 59,21
[West] Milton	DOR	SY5096	11,14
Milverton	SOM	ST1225	1,11;26. 6,18. 16,4. 21,81
Milverton	WAR	SP2967	16,2
Milwich	STS	SJ9732	1,41. 11,30
[North] Mimms	HRT	TL2204	7,1
[South] Mimms	MDX	TL2201	9,8
Minchinhampton	GLS	SO8700	23,2
Minchins	GLS	ST8689	28,6 *in note*
Minehead	SOM	SS9646	25,10
Miningsby	LIN	TF3264	14,68
Minley	HAM	SU8258	69,10
Minsden	HRT	TL1924	1,2
[Church] Minshull	CHS	SJ6660	8,14
Minshull [Vernon]	CHS	SJ6760	8,13
Minskip WR	YKS	SE3864	1W39. SW,Bu13
Minsmere	SFK	TM4665	6,107. 7,32
Minstead	HAM	SU2811	NF9,37
Minster	CON	SX1190	5,4,9
[Little] Minster and Minster [Lovell]	OXF	SP3111 SP3211	18,2. 58,33
Minster [in Thanet]	KEN	TR3164	*2.14.* 7,8
Minsterley	SHR	SJ3705	4,1,7
Minsterworth	GLS	SO7717	53,1 *in note*
Minsthorpe WR	YKS	SE4712	9W64. SW,O16

Mint [House] (near Kendal) WES	YKS	SD5294	1L7. See also CHS Y8
Minting	LIN	TF1873	14,54. 56,23
[Little] Minting	LIN	TF1673	14,54
Mintlyn	NFK	TF6519	10,50
Minton	SHR	SO4390	4,28,4
Minworth	WAR	SP1592	17,4
Mirfield WR	YKS	SE2019	9W108 note. 9W138. SW,M9
Miserden	GLS	SO9308	66,6
Misperton NR	YKS	SE7779	8N1-2 note. 23N21
[Great] Missenden	BKM	SP8901	14,3
[Little] Missenden	BKM	SU9298	12,1. 26,1. 36,1
Misson	NTT	SK6995	1,65-66. 9,21. 30,43-44
Misterton	LEC	SP5584	3,7. 23,3. 37,2
Misterton	NTT	SK7694	1,38. 9,121;123
Mistley	ESS	TM1031	39,10
Miswell	HRT	SP9112	15,7. 21,1
Mitcham	SRY	TQ2868	5,6. 21,2
Mitcheldean	GLS	SO6618	37,3
Mitton	GLS	SO9033	E19. EvA104. EvC23. WoB5. WoC4
Mitton	STS	SJ8815	11,6
Mitton (in Bredon)	WOR	SO9033	2,23
[Great] Mitton WR	YKS	SD7138	30W37
[Lower] Mitton	WOR	SO8171	1,2
Mixbury	OXF	SP6034	29,1
Mobberley	CHS	SJ7880	14,4
Moccas	HEF	SO3542	6,7. 7,7
Mockham	DEV	SS6735	16,72
Modbury	DEV	SX6551	15,49;64
Moddershall	STS	SJ9236	8,21
Molescroft ER	YKS	TA0140	2E9. SE,Sn8
[East] Molesey	SRY	TQ1467	19,29;31
[West] Molesey	SRY	TQ1368	35,2
Molesworth	HUN	TL0775	20,4
Molland (in North Molton)	DEV	SS7033	36,17
Molland (near West Anstey)	DEV	SS8028	1,41. 3,61
Mollington	CHS	SJ3970	3,1-2
Mollington OXF	NTH		35,26
Mollington OXF	OXF	SP4447	17,7. EN12. EW2
Mollington OXF	WAR		37,9
[North] Molton	DEV	SS7329	1,27
[South] Molton	DEV	SS7125	1,6. 13a,1
Monetvile (in Castle Church)	STS	??	11,68
Monewden	SFK	TM2358	6,262. 8,20;22;28. 21,104. 46,12
[Great and Little] Mongeham	KEN	TR3451 TR3350	7,20
Mongewell	OXF	SU6187	59,23
Monk [Hay Stile] WR	YKS	SE4140	5W7 *note*. SW,BA3
Monkhide	HEF	SO6143	10,35
Monkland	HEF	SO4657	8,2
Monkleigh	DEV	SS4520	15,9
Monkokehampton	DEV	SS5805	16,17
Monksilver	SOM	ST0737	1,6. 21,39-40. 35,10
Monkswell	DEV	SX5271	35,30
Monkton	KEN	TR2765	3,7
[Bishop] Monkton WR	YKS	SE3266	2W7. SW,Bu46
[Moor] Monkton WR	YKS	SE5056	22W3. SW,An13
[Nun] Monkton WR	YKS	SE5057	25W20. CW38. SW,Bu1
[West] Monkton	SOM	ST2628	8,28
Monkwith ER	YKS	TA3032	2E25 *note*. SE,So2
Monmouth (Wales)	GLS		E35

Monmouth (Wales)	HEF	SO5012	1,48
Monnington (in Vowchurch)	HEF	SO3836	19,1;4
Monnington [on Wye]	HEF	SO3743	8,6
Montacute	SOM	ST4916	19,38;86
Montacute: see also *Bishopstone* SOM			
Montford	SHR	SJ4114	4,4,23
Montgomery [Castle] (Wales)	SHR	SO2198	4,1,15;35
Monxton *[Anne]*	HAM	SU3144	1,39
Monyash	DBY	SK1566	1,27
Moor (in Broadwoodwidger)	DEV	SX4294	17,10
Moor IOW	HAM	SZ5382	7,14
Moor	NFK	TG3707	55,1
Moor [in Rock]: see Rockmoor WOR			
[Lower and Upper] Moor	WOR	SO9847	2,19
		SO9747	
[The] Moor	HEF	SO5040	2,54
Moorbath	DOR	SY4395	54,4
Moorby	LIN	TF2964	1,101
Moorcroft and [Upper] Moorcroft	GLS	SO7917	37,1
		SO7918	
Moorsholm NR	YKS	NZ6814	1N7. 5N13. 31N8. SN,L15
[Little] Moorsholm NR	YKS	NZ6816	5N14. SN,L16
Moorthorpe WR	YKS	SE4611	9W34. SW,Sf37 *note*
Moortown	SOM	ST3723	21,55
Morborne	HUN	TL1391	5,1
Morchard [Bishop]	DEV	SS7707	1,68
[Cruwys] Morchard	DEV	SS8712	3,72;73. 19,35
Morcott RUT	NTH		1,2d
Morcott RUT	RUT	SK9200	EN2
Morden	DOR	SY9195	26,24. 41,5. 49,2. 55,10. 56,13
Morden	SRY	TQ2567	6,2
[Guilden] Morden	CAM	TL2744	13,2. 22,7. 26,20. 32,8;10;13.
			Appx J
[Steeple] Morden	CAM	TL2842	2,1. 13,1. 26,19
Morebath	DEV	SS9524	1,42
Moreby [Hall] ER	YKS	SE5943	6E1 *note*. 23E12. SE,P6
Moredon	WIL	SU1387	26,9. 29,6. 43,1
Moreleigh	DEV	SX7652	39,16
Moresk	CON	SW8543	5,1,9
Moreton	DOR	SY8089	26,56. 56,37
Moreton	ESS	TL5307	45,1
Moreton	SOM	ST5759	37,11
Moreton (in Colwich)	STS	SK0222	2,18. 16,3
Moreton (in Gnosall)	STS	SJ7817	8,7
Moreton (near Marchington)	STS	SK1429	10,8
Moreton [Corbet]	SHR	SJ5523	4,19,9
[Great] Moreton	CON	SS2707	5,7,4
Moreton [in Marsh]	GLS	SP2032	19,2
Moreton [Jeffries]	HEF	SO6048	2,20
[Maids] Moreton	BKM	SP7035	14,28-29. 57,3
Moreton [Morrell]	WAR	SP3155	16,8
[North] Moreton	BRK	SU5689	27,2
Moreton [on Lugg]	HEF	SO5045	2,42
Moreton [Pinkney]	NTH	SP5749	43,2
Moreton [Say]	SHR	SJ6334	4,8,1
[South] Moreton	BRK	SU5688	26,3. 54,4
Moreton [Valence]	GLS	SO7809	53,11
Moretonhampstead	DEV	SX7586	1,45
Morfe	STS	SO8287	12,2
Morley	DBY	SK3941	6,70;100
Morley	SSX	TQ2317	13,26

Morley WR	YKS	SE2628	9W118 note. CW23 note. SW,M1
Morley [St Botolph and St Peter]	NFK	TG0600	8,78. 20,11
		TM0698	
Morningthorpe: see [Morning] Thorpe NFK			
Morston	NFK	TG0043	1,29;148. 9,141
Morston	SFK	TM2538	2,17. 7,90;115. 21,48. 39,2;4
Mortehoe	DEV	SS4545	31,4
Mortham [Tower] NR	YKS	NZ0814	6N1 note. SN,CtA6
Mortimer [West End]: see Stratfield Mortimer HAM			
Mortlake	SRY	TQ2075	2,3. 13,1
Mortoft	NFK	TG1128	8,8
Morton	DBY	SK4060	8,1. S
Morton	GLS	SO7017	10,11
Morton	LIN	TF0924	24,77. 42,15-19. 61,3. CK,42-43
Morton	LIN	SK8091	1,39. 14,24
Morton (near Babworth)	NTT	SK6780	1,11
Morton (near Lenton)	NTT	SK5638	10,17
Morton	SHR	SJ3023	4,3,34
Morton WR	YKS	SE1042	1W5. 1W6 note. 1W8 note. SW,Sk11 *note*
[? North] Morton [Hall]	NTT	SK6580	9,34. 30,42
[Abbots] Morton	WOR	SP0254	10,13
Morton [Bagot]	WAR	SP1164	22,19
Morton Grange (in East Harlsey) NR	YKS	SE4299	1N126 note. 31N4 note. SN,B19 note. SN,A7
Morton [Grange] (near Guisborough) NR	YKS	NZ5514	1N19 note. 31N4 note. 31N6. SN,L28
Morton [in-Fiskerton]	NTT	SK7251	11,16. 13,13
[Little] Morton	NTT	SK6778	1,11 *note*
Morton [Underhill]	WOR	SP0159	17,1
Morton [upon Swale] NR	YKS	SE3292	6N27;31. SN,B19 note. SN,CtA14
Mortun (in Overton or Skelton) NR	YKS	??	C34 note. SN,Y2 note. SN,Y8
Mortune (in Harewood) WR	YKS	??	1W8 note. SW,Sk11 note
Morville	SHR	SO6694	4,1,5
Morwents [End]	GLS	SO7922	10,1
Mosborough	DBY	SK4281	10,2
Moseley	STS	SJ9304	12,21
Moseley WAR	WAR	SP0883	EBW1
Moseley WAR	WOR		1,1a
Mosterton	DOR	ST4505	54,5
Moston	SHR	SJ5626	4,26,6
Mostyn FLN	CHS	SJ1580	FT2,9
Mottisfont	HAM	SU3226	4,1. 69,25
Mottistone IOW	HAM	SZ4083	7,17
Mottram [St Andrew]	CHS	SJ8879	26,10
Moulham	DOR	SZ0180	57,21
Moulsham [Hall]	ESS	TL7218	18,41-42
Moulsham [Lodge]	ESS	TL7105	6,14
Moulsoe	BKM	SP9041	14,45
Moulstone	SSX	TQ3408	12,53
Moulton	CHS	SJ6569	5,8
Moulton	LIN	TF3024	14,100. 57,53
Moulton	NTH	SP7866	1,18. 30,14. 56,29;33;44
Moulton	SFK	TL6964	15,1
Moulton NR	YKS	NZ2303	6N1. SN,CtA4
Moulton [St Mary]	NFK	TG4007	1,43;150;160;163
Moulton [St Michael]	NFK	TM1690	4,56. 9,98;212;223.,65,13
Mount [Grace]: see *Bordelby* YKS			

Mountfield	SSX	TQ7320	9,22
Mountnessing	ESS	TQ6496	37,16-17
Mowlish	DEV	SX9581	34,13. 52,49
Mowsley	LEC	SP6489	31,1. 34,2
[Low] Mowthorpe ER	YKS	SE8967	2B18 *note*. 5E71. SE,Th6-7
[Low] Mowthorpe [Farm] NR	YKS	SE6869	SN,B27 *note*
Moxby [Hall] NR	YKS	SE5966	1Y1 *note*. SN,B19
Moze ESS	ESS	TM2026	30,18. ESf2
Moze ESS	SFK		32,7
Muchedeswelle	DBY	??	1,29. 6,79
Muchelney	SOM	ST4224	9,1
Muchlarnick	CON	SX2156	5,2,3
Mucking	ESS	TQ6881	9,1;4
Mucklestone	STS	SJ7237	17,8
Mucknell	WOR	SO9051	2,3
Muckton	LIN	TF3781	55,3
Mudford and [Up and West] Mudford	SOM	ST5719	1,35. 19,87. 37,12
		ST5718	
		ST5620	
Mugginton	DBY	SK2843	6,95
Mulbarton	NFK	TG1901	9,196. 20,34
Mul(h)ede/Mulehale	YKS	??	29W11 *note*. CW30. SW,An16
(in Bishopthorpe) WR			
Mulgrave [Castle] NR	YKS	NZ8311	5N4 *note*. SN,L7 *note*
Mulintone FLN	CHS	??	FT3,1-2
Mullacott	DEV	SS5145	47,7
Mumby	LIN	TF5174	12,93-96. 24,55-56. 29,32. CS,18
[Great] Munden	HRT	TL3523	16,2-3. Appx
[Little] Munden	HRT	TL3321	30,1-2
Mundesley	NFK	TG3136	8,123;129
Mundford	NFK	TL8093	8,40. 9,119. 15,9
Mundham NFK	NFK	TM3298	1,183;229. 9,49-50;55;60;67;170.
			14,36. 35,8-10. 47,6. 50,10.
			57,2
Mundham NFK	SFK		ENf4
Mundham	SSX	SU8702	11,41
Mundon	ESS	TL8702	25,5
Munentone FLN	CHS	??	FT3,2
Munsley	HEF	SO6640	10,31. 15,10. 16,1. 28,2
Munslow [Aston]	SHR	SO5186	4,3,45
Muntham	SSX	TQ1109	13,50
Munton	SHR	??	4,27,23
Murlai	NFK	??	10,11
Murley	DEV	ST0216	24,9
Murrells [End]	GLS	SO7822	1,2
Mursley	BKM	SP8128	12,26. 14,24. 57,2
Murton (near Cold Kirby) NR	YKS	SE5388	11N21. SN,B19 *note*. SN,A10
Murton (near York) NR	YKS	SE6452	C23. SN,Y2 *note*
Murton [Farm] NR	YKS	SE6064	1Y1 *note*. 2N12. SN,B19 *note*
Musbury	DEV	SY2794	16,164
Muscott	NTH	SP6263	18,45
Musden	STS	SK1250	1,50
Muskham NTT	LIN		CW,16
[North] Muskham NTT	NTT	SK7958	5,2. 8,2. 12,11-13. 30,7
[South] Muskham NTT	NTT	SK7957	5,5. 30,46
Muston ER	YKS	TA0979	1E19. 20E3. SE,Tu1;3
Mutford	SFK	TM4888	1,23-24. 7,46
Mutley	DEV	SX4855	17,70-71
Muxbere	DEV	ST0311	40,5
Mycelegata (in Trimley)	SFK	TM2638	6,111. 7,110
Myddle	SHR	SJ4623	4,3,53

Myndtown	SHR	SO3989	4,20,2
[East and West] Myne	SOM	SS9248	25,24
Mynyddbrydd	HEF	SO2841	23,4
Mythop LAN	YKS	SD3634	1L1. See also CHS Y2
Myton	WAR	SP3064	16,1. 17,60;63
Myton (in Hull) ER	YKS	??	15E2 *note*. SE,He5
Myton [on Swale] NR	YKS	SE4366	1N104. 2N25. 5N69. SN,B23;25
Mytton	SHR	SJ4417	3d,5

N

Naas: see Nass GLS

Naburn ER	YKS	SE5945	1E8. 7E2. CE9. SE, Wa1

Nachededorne: see *Barethorn* BRK

Nackington	KEN	TR1554	*2,16.* 5,126
Nacton	SFK	TM2139	31,8;13a;55
Nafferton ER	YKS	TA0559	1E27. 13E16. SE,Tu7
Nafford	WOR	SO9441	8,25
Nancekuke	CON	SW6645	4,6
Nantwich	CHS	SJ6552	S1. 1,1;8. 8,16
Nappa WR	YKS	SD8553	13W42
Napsbury	HRT	TL1604	10,11
Napsted	ESS	TL8132	18,21
Napton	WAR	SP4661	16,31. 17,28;38
Narborough	NFK	TF7412	9,70
Narford	NFK	TF7613	4,2
Naruestuna	NFK	??	33,4
Naseby	NTH	SP6877	35,2;5;25
Nash	HEF	SO3062	24,3
Nashenden	KEN	TQ7366	5,48
Nashway	BKM	SP6413	41,1
Nass	GLS	SO6402	1,54
Nassington	NTH	TL0696	1,20:23
Nately [Scures]	HAM	SU7053	23,8
Natson	DEV	SS7100	52,9
Natsworthy	DEV	SX7279	30,2
Natton	GLS	SO9232	1,24;32
Naunton (near Bourton-on-the-Water)	GLS	SP1123	48,3. 78,8
Naunton (in Toddington)	GLS	SP0133	11,6
Naunton [Beauchamp]	WOR	SO9652	8,16
Navenby	LIN	SK9857	44,16-18. CK,15
Navestock	ESS	TQ5498	5,7-8. 28,14
Nawton NR	YKS	SE6584	2N6. 8N24. 23N21. SN,Ma11
Nayland	ESS	TL9634	24,57
Nayland	NFK	TM1598	5,5. 6,6. 9,187;191
Nayland	SFK	TL9734	27,6
[The] Naze	ESS	TM2323	5,11
Nazeing	ESS	TL4106	8,2. 37,8-9
Neadon	DEV	SX7581	16,156
Neatham	HAM	SU7440	1,2
Neatishead	NFK	TG3420	17,36
Nec(c)hemara/Neckemara	SFK	??	6,113. 32,25. 67,13
Nechendune	WIL	??	20,2
Necton	NFK	TF8709	22,1 *and note*;10-16;18;20-23
Nedging	SFK	TL9948	21,43
Neen [Savage]	SHR	SO6777	6,6-7
Neen [Sollars]	SHR	SO6672	5,8
Neenton	SHR	SO6387	4,11,8
Nesfield WR	YKS	SE0949	13W24. SW,Bu32
Ness	CHS	SJ3075	7,2
Ness	NFK	TG4821	9,92
Ness	SHR	SJ3918	4,1,17. 4,3,52
[East] Ness NR	YKS	SE6978	16N1 *note*. 23N24. SN,Ma21
[Great] Neston	CHS	SJ2977	A13. 9,6

[Little] Neston	CHS	SJ3077	4,1
Neswick [Hall] ER	YKS	SE9752	5E40 *note*. SE,Dr4
Netheravon	WIL	SU1448	1,18. 56,3. 68,2
Netherbury	DOR	SY4799	3,11
Nethercote	OXF	SU7098	35,5;28
Nethercott	OXF	SP4820	7,35
Netherfield	SSX	TQ7118	8,7. 9,23
Netheridge	GLS	SO8115	1,6 *in note*
Netherleigh	CHS	SJ4165	9,2
Netherpool: see [Nether] Pool CHS			
Netherton	WOR	SO9941	2,72
Netley	HAM	SU4508	42,1
Netley	SHR	SJ4601	4,28,2
Nettlecombe	DOR	SY5195	11,13
Nettlecombe	SOM	ST0537	1,14. 5,5
Nettleham	LIN	TF0075	1,35-37. 24,8. 48,16. CW,7
Nettlestead	KEN	TQ6852	5,96
Nettlestead	SFK	TM0849	3,56;59 note62. 76,13
Nettlestone IOW	HAM	SZ6290	1,W18. 9,10;11
Nettleton	LIN	TA1100	4,23-24. 16,44. 34,7. 44,5. 68,48
Nettleton	WIL	ST8178	7,9
Neuhuse/Niuuehusum (in Ulleskelfe) WR	YKS	??	9W31 *note*. CW3. SW,BA8
Neuson (in Leconfield) ER	YKS	??	5E41 *note*. SE,Sn6
Neutone (in Scorton) NR	YKS	??	6N23 *note*. SN,CtA12
Neutuna (near Holt)	NFK	??	1,27
Nevendon	ESS	TQ7391	62,1. 70,1
Nevlebi	LEC	SK4107	13,45
Newark	NTT	SK7954	6,1. 21,3
Newarne GLS	GLS	SO6011	E2
Newarne GLS	HEF	SO6212	1,72
[North and South] Newbald ER	YKS	SE9136	2B6. SE,C4
		SE9135	
Newball	LIN	TF0776	13,45
Newbold	DBY	SK3772	1,1
Newbold	NTT	SK6831	1,58
Newbold [Astbury]	CHS	SJ8461	18,1
Newbold [Comyn]	WAR	SP3365	9,1. 16,59
Newbold [Folville]	LEC	SK7012	40,33
Newbold [on-Avon]	WAR	SP4877	31,2
Newbold [Pacey]	WAR	SP2957	39,3
Newbold [Revel]	WAR	SP4580	31,3
Newbold [Saucey]	LEC	SK7608	14,33
Newbold [Verdon]	LEC	SK4403	13,11;74
Newbottle (near Brackley)	NTH	SP5236	23,9
Newbottle (in Harrington)	NTH	SP7781	14,1
Newbound	NTT	SK4963	10,18-19
Newbourn	SFK	TM2743	8,15. 14,117. 21,54. 39,10
Newbury	BRK	SU4767	50,1
Newenden	KEN	TQ8327	2,27
Newent	GLS	SO7225	1,11. 16,1. EvK10
Newetone	SHR	??	4,27,34
Newhall	SOM	ST1740	31,5
Newhall (in Harewood) WR	YKS	??	1W12 *note*. SW,Sk13-14
Newhall [Grange] WR	YKS	SK5091	10W1 *note*. SW,Sf2 *and note*
Newham [Hall] NR	YKS	NZ5113	1N26 *note*. 11N7. 31N5. SN,L5
			note. SN,L31-32
Newhill WR	YKS	SK4399	10W12. SW,Sf2 note. SW,Sf8
Newholm NR	YKS	NZ8610	4N1 *note*. SN,L5 *note*
Newington (near Folkestone)	KEN	TR1836	5,204. 9,37-38
Newington (near Milton Regis)	KEN	TQ8665	13,1
Newington (near Brookhampton) OXF	BRK		B9

Newington (near Brookhampton) OXF	OXF	SU6096	2,1. EBe3
Newington [Bagpath]	GLS	ST8194	1,17
[South] Newington	OXF	SP4033	7,39–42. 59,19
[Stoke] Newington	MDX	TQ3386	3,24
Newland [Hall]	ESS	TL6309	20,51
Newnham	GLS	SO6911	32,10
Newnham	HRT	TL2437	10,18
Newnham	WAR	SP1560	6,19
Newnham [Hall]	ESS	TL5842	20,78
Newnham [Murren] OXF	BRK		B2
Newnham [Murren] OXF	OXF	SU6188	35,11. EBe1
Newnham [Paddox]	WAR	SP4783	31,11. 37,9
[Long] Newnton GLS	GLS	ST9092	E12
[Long] Newnton GLS	WIL		8,8
[North] Newnton	WIL	SU1257	13,2
Newport ESS	CAM		1,17
Newport ESS	ESS	TL5234	1,28
Newport [Pagnell]	BKM	SP8743	17,17
[Temple] Newsam WR	YKS	SE3630	9W16 *note.* SW,Sk10
Newsells	HRT	TL3837	31,3–4;7
Newsham	LIN	TA1213	1,77. 14,33. 27,63–64. 34,10–11
Newsham WR	YKS	??	9W41 *note.* SW,O5
Newsham (in Amotherby) NR	YKS	SE7476	1N61. 5N36 *note.* 23N24. 29N12. 31N8. SN,Ma3
Newsham (near Hutton Magna) NR	YKS	NZ1010	6N46. SN,CtA17
Newsham (near Kirby Wiske) NR	YKS	SE3784	1N110 *note.* 23N6. SN,Bi7 *note*
Newsham (near Preston) LAN	YKS	SD5136	1L1. See also CHS Y2
Newsham (in Skerton) LAN	YKS	SD4866	1L2 *note.* See also CHS Y3
Newsham [Grange] NR	YKS	SE3895	1Y2 *note.* SN,Bi7 note. SN,A1
Newsholme ER	YKS	SE7129	15E3. SE,He7
Newsholme (near Gisburn) WR	YKS	SD8451	13W41. 30W4
Newsholme (in Keighley) WR	YKS	SE0239	1W67 *note*
Newsome [Farm] WR	YKS	SE3751	24W18 *note.* SW, Bu42
[Great and Little] Newsome ER	YKS	TA3026	14E15 *note.* SE, Hol19
Newthorpe	NTT	SK4846	4,8. 10,33;62–63
Newtimber	HAM	??	21,9
Newtimber	SSX	TQ2713	12,34
Newton	BRK	SU3698	36,5
Newton (in Middlewich)	CHS	SJ7065	19,1
Newton	DBY	SK4459	10,10
Newton (in Chittlehampton)	DEV	SS6625	16,81
Newton (in Zeal Monachorum)	DEV	SS6904	25,10. 47,4
Newton (near Leominster)	HEF	SO5053	1,25. 14,4
Newton (near Weobley)	HEF	SO3953	24,7
Newton	LIN	TF0436	3,32;55–56. 26,40–4148,5–7. 67,10
Newton (near Castle Acre)	NFK	TF8315	1,72. 27,1
Newton (near Norwich)	NFK	TG2508	1,123
Newton (near Geddington)	NTH	SP8883	48,2. 56,30;37
Newton	NTT	SK6841	9,97. 12,20
Newton (in Bicknoller)	SOM	ST1038	25,31
Newton (in Blithfield)	STS	SK0325	14,2
Newton (in Draycott in the Moors)	STS	SJ9839	1,58
Newton (near Lowestoft)	SFK	TM5498	1,57
Newton (near Sudbury)	SFK	TL9141	14,32. 43,3
Newton (near Swilland)	SFK	TM1951	38,16;23–24
Newton	WAR	SP5378	17,41–43
Newton (near Gardham) ER	YKS	??	3Y1 *note.* 3Y7. CE24. SE,Sn8
Newton (near Gardham): see also Gardham ER, YKS			
Newton (near Guisborough) NR	YKS	NZ5613	1N18. 31N6 *note.* SN,L28
Newton (in Lancaster) LAN	YKS	??	1L2 *note.* See also CHS Y3

Newton (near Levisham) NR	YKS	SE8190	1Y4. 8N12. SN,D10-11
Newton (on Hodder) WR	YKS	SD6950	30W37 note
Newton (near Preston) LAN	YKS	SD4430	1L1. See also CHS Y2
Newton (in West Ayton) NR	YKS	??	1Y3 note. SN,D7
Newton (in Whittington) LAN	YKS	SD5974	1L3. See also CHS Y4
Newton (in Wintringham) ER	YKS	SE8872	16E4 note. SE,Tu2-3 note. SE,Th1
[Bank] Newton WR	YKS	SD9153	8W3. 30W23
Newton [Bromswold] NTH	BDF		3,9
Newton [Bromswold] NTH	NTH	SP9965	4,20. EB1
Newton [Burgoland]	LEC	SK3709	14,24-25
Newton [by Chester]	CHS	SJ4168	C1. 9,1
Newton [by Toft]	LIN	TF0587	4,12;18. 40,3. 68,41
[Cold] Newton	LEC	SK7106	29,15. 42,2-3
[East] Newton ER	YKS	TA2637	14E11. SE,Hol15;17
[East] Newton NR	YKS	SE6479	1N76. 2N5. 23N24. SN,Ma15
Newton [Ferrers]	CON	SX3466	5,2,24;28
Newton [Ferrers]	DEV	SX5448	15,37
Newton [Flotman]	NFK	TM2198	9,97;203. 48,5
Newton [Garth] ER	YKS	TA1827	14E1. SE,Hol2 note
Newton [Grange]	DBY	SK1653	6,8
Newton [Hall]	ESS	TL6122	30,28
Newton [Harcourt]	LEC	SP6496	C13. 16,9
[High] Newton (in Cartmel) LAN	YKS	SD4083	1L6 note. See also CHS Y7
Newton [Kyme] WR	YKS	SE4644	5W7. 25W29-30. CW3. SW,BA3;8;13
Newton [le-Willows] LAN	CHS	SJ5995	R2,1
Newton [le-Willows] NR	YKS	SE2189	6N134. SN,B22 note. SN,CtA37
[Little] Newton WR	YKS	SD8557	30W7
Newton [Longville]	BKM	SP8431	14,38
[Maiden] Newton	DOR	SY5997	40,8
Newton [Morrell] NR	YKS	NZ2309	6N1. SN,B22 note. SN,CtA1
Newton [Mulgrave] NR	YKS	NZ7815	5N8. SN,L8
[North and West] Newton	SOM	ST3031 ST2829	17,1. 21,3. 22,7. 46,8;17
[Old] Newton (near Stowmarket)	SFK	TM0562	8,50. 16,12. 23,3;5. 31,35;51
Newton [on Trent]	LIN	SK8374	2,26
[Out] Newton ER	YKS	TA3821	14E20. SE,Hol12 note. SE,Hol20
Newton [Picot] NR	YKS	SE3189	6N151 note. SN,CtA42
Newton [St Cyres]	DEV	SX8898	2,2. 52,34
Newton [St Loe]	SOM	ST7064	5,57
Newton [St Petrock]	DEV	SS4112	51,16
Newton [Solney]	DBY	SK2825	1,18
[South] Newton	WIL	SU0834	13,10
Newton [Stacey]	HAM	SU4140	48,1
[Sturminster] Newton	DOR	ST7813	8,1
Newton [Tony]	WIL	SU2140	26,5
Newton [Tracey]	DEV	SS5226	25,3
Newton [upon Ouse] NR	YKS	SE5159	16N2. 16W6. SN,B22 note
Newton [Valence]	HAM	SU7232	38,1
Newton [Wallis] WR	YKS	SE4427	9W27 note. SW,BA8
[Water] Newton	HUN	TL1097	7,5
[West] Newton	NFK	TF6927	2,4
[West] Newton ER	YKS	TA1937	2E29. SE,Mid1
[West] Newton [Grange] NR	YKS	SE6380	1N75 note. SN,Ma16
[Wold] Newton	LIN	TF2496	3,7. 12,30-31. CN,25
[Wold] Newton ER	YKS	TA0473	1E20-21. 20E4. SE, Tu2-3 note
[Wood]newton	NTH	TL0394	55,2
Nidd WR	YKS	SE3060	2W7. SW,Bu45
Nimete	DEV	??	1,41
Ninfield	SSX	TQ7012	9,4

Ningwood IOW	HAM	SZ4088	9,18
Niton IOW	HAM	SZ5076	1,W21
Niuetuna	ESS	??	49,2
Niuetuna	SFK	??	6,32
Niuuehusum: see *Neuhuse* YKS			
Noakes	HEF	SO6355	2,3. 33,1
Nobottle	NTH	SP6763	35,3a-b
Nocton	LIN	TF0664	32,32-33
Noctorum	CHS	SJ2987	8,10
Noke	OXF	SP5413	59,7;18
Nomansland	MDX	??	1,1
Nongetune/Nongtune	LIN	??	1,13. 5,2
Norbury (near Marbury)	CHS	SJ5547	8,21
Norbury (near Stockport)	CHS	SJ9185	14,5
Norbury	DBY	SK1242	6,53;57
Norbury	STS	SJ7823	8,10
Norcote	GLS	SP0402	26,3. 69,4
Nordberia	SFK	??	8,81
Nordley: see Kingsnordley SHR			
Normacot	STS	SJ9242	13,3
Normanby	LIN	SE8816	30,3-4. 57,5. CW,20
Normanby (near Eston) NR	YKS	NZ5418	5N25. 11N2. 13N6. SN,L3 note. SN,L25
Normanby (in Fylingdales) NR	YKS	NZ9206	1N1. SN,L3 *note*
Normanby (near Thornton Riseborough) NR	YKS	SE7381	1N74. 23N21. SN,L3 note. SN,Ma14
Normanby [-by-Spital]	LIN	TF0088	4,10. 14,18;19. 28,3-4
Normanby [by Stow]	LIN	SK8883	7,7
Normanby [le Wold]	LIN	TF1294	14,8-10. 28,23. 30,36
Normancross	HUN	TL1690	1,3. 19,4;7
Normanebi (in Carthorpe) NR	YKS	??	6N149 note. SN, CtA41
Normanton WR	YKS	SE3822	1Y16. 1W25. SW,Ag3
Normanton [by-Clumber]	NTT	SK6574	1,8
Normanton [by-Derby]	DBY	SK3433	1,19. 6,91
Normanton [by-Southwell]	NTT	SK7054	17,14. 30,11
Normanton Hundred	LIN	SK9446	37,2
Normanton [on-Soar]	NTT	SK5123	3,2. 4,1. 9,78. 30,14;16
Normanton [on-the-Wolds]	NTT	SK6232	9,84-85. 10,10
Normanton [on-Trent]	NTT	SK7969	6,14. 9,68-69
[South] Normanton	DBY	SK4456	7,4
[Temple] Normanton	DBY	SK4167	1,4;9
North Cray: see [North] Cray KEN			
North Eastling: see [North] Eastling KEN			
Northallerton NR	YKS	SE3693	1Y2. 6N9. SN,A1
Northam	DEV	SS4429	12,1
Northam	HAM	??	68,4
Northampton	NTH	SP7561	B1;37
Northborough	KEN	??	D24
Northbourne	KEN	TR3352	7,19
Northbrook	OXF	SP4922	27,8. 29,9;20
Northcote (in East Down)	DEV	SS6042	3,46;49
Northenden	CHS	SJ8389	27,1
Northey [Island]	ESS	TL8706	28,12. 90,32
Northfield WAR	WAR	SP0279	EBW4
Northfield WAR	WOR		23,2
Northfield [Farm] NR	YKS	SE9890	1Y3 note. SN,D1
Northfleet	KEN	TQ6274	2,9
Northgate	KEN	TR1558	3,9
Northill	BDF	TL1446	21,15-16. 23,56. 25,15
Northleach	GLS	SP1114	2,8. EvK103;230. EvM3;6;99

Northleigh	DEV	SY1995	15,25. 48,12
Northlew	DEV	SX5099	1,57 *and note*
Northolt	MDX	TQ1384	9,7
Northorpe (lost off Easington) ER	YKS	??	14E22 *note*. CE51. SE,B4 note. SE,Hol20
Northover: see Ilchester SOM			
Northowram WR	YKS	SE1126	9W143 note. SW,M11
Northrepps	NFK	TG2439	8,126;128
Northrepps: see also Repps, Southrepps NFK			
Northstow Hundred	CAM	—	Appx N
Northwich	CHS	SJ6573	S3. 9,17. 17,5;8. 20,3
Northwick	WOR	SO8457	2,48
Northwold	NFK	TL7597	8,39. 15,8;29
Nortoft	NTH	SP6773	18,80. 35,19f
Norton	CHS	SJ5581	9,20
Norton	CON	SS2508	5,7,3
Norton YKS	DBY	SK3582	1,8. 16,6
Norton (in Broadwoodwidger)	DEV	SX4092	17,6
Norton (in Churchstow)	DEV	SX7245	6,9
Norton (in Selbourne)	HAM	SU7335	23,55. 29,12
Norton (in Wonston)	HAM	SU4741	69,2
Norton	HRT	TL2334	10,7
Norton	KEN	TQ9661	5,143
Norton (near Daventry)	NTH	SP6063	19,1
Norton (in Aston Botterell)	SHR	SO6382	4,3,69
Norton (in Condover)	SHR	SJ4907	4,14,13
Norton (Wales)	SHR	SO3067	8,2
Norton (near Bury St Edmund's)	SFK	TL9666	1,61-65;67;73;88
Norton (near Trimley)	SFK	TM2538	7,84;107;122
Norton	WIL	ST8884	8,5
Norton (near Evesham)	WOR	SP0447	10,3
Norton ER	YKS	SE7971	1E38-39. 15E11. 23E15. SE,Sc3-4
Norton WR	YKS	SE5415	9W35. SW,O2
Norton [Bavant]	WIL	ST9043	26,12
[Bishop] Norton	LIN	SK9892	7,4
[Bishops] Norton	GLS	SO8424	2,3
[Blo] Norton	NFK	TM0179	8,59. 9,78. 14,8. 15,13
[Bredons] Norton	WOR	SO9339	2,29
[Brize] Norton	OXF	SP2907	29,4. 58,17;26
[Burnt] Norton	GLS	SP1441	68,3
Norton [Canes]	STS	SK0107	2,16
Norton [Canon]	HEF	SO3847	2,45
[Chipping] Norton	OXF	SP3127	40,3
[Cold] Norton	ESS	TQ8599	33,3
Norton [Conyers] NR	YKS	SE3176	3Y9 *note*. SW,H4
Norton [Disney]	LIN	SK8959	56,10
[East] Norton	LEC	SK7800	19,18. 29,2
Norton [Fitzwarren]	SOM	ST1925	2,3. 19,41
[Greens] Norton	NTH	SP6649	1,6. 18,95. 22,7
Norton [in Hales]	SHR	SJ7038	4,21,1
Norton [in-the-Moors]	STS	SJ8951	11,19
Norton [juxta Twycross]	LEC	SK3207	11,1
[King's] Norton	LEC	SK6800	1,4
[King's] Norton WAR	WAR	SP0478	EBW1
[King's] Norton WAR	WOR		1,1a
Norton [le Clay] NR	YKS	SE4071	5W38. SW,H8
Norton [Lindsey]	WAR	SP2263	22,23
Norton [Malreward]	SOM	ST6065	5,16
Norton [Mandeville]	ESS	TL5804	5,6. 28,16

O

Oadby	LEC	SK6200	13,31. 40,1;25
Oak	DEV	SX5399	16,24
Oake	SOM	ST1525	2,3. 21,81
Oaken	STS	SJ8502	11,45
Oakford	DEV	SS9121	19,37
Oakham RUT	LEC		1,11
Oakham RUT	RUT	SK8509	R17-18;21. ELe1
Oakhanger	HAM	SU7635	69,4
Oakington	CAM	TL4164	5,40. 9,1. 32,35. 41,13. 43,1
Oakleigh	KEN	TQ7274	5,108
Oakley	BDF	TL0153	26,2. 53,7
Oakley	BKM	SP6312	19,3
Oakley	GLS	SO9802	39,19. 52,1. 67,3
Oakley	HAM	SU5650	23,27. 28,1. 44,2
Oakley	SOM	ST5320	*1*,27. 35,24
Oakley (in Edingale)	STS	SK1913	11,47
Oakley (in Loggerheads)	STS	SJ7036	1,35
Oakley	SFK	TM1577	6,65. 7,75. 14,129;137-138. 19,12
[Great] Oakley	ESS	TM2028	32,38
[Great] Oakley	NTH	SP8785	56,38
[Little] Oakley	ESS	TM2128	33,15
Oaks	SHR	SJ4204	4,5,4
Oaksey	WIL	ST9993	67,6
Oakthorpe LEC	DBY	SK3212	14,10
Oakthorpe LEC	LEC	SK3213	E10
Oaktrow	SOM	SS9440	25,22
Oakworth WR	YKS	SE0338	1W66 *note*. 21W17
Oare	KEN	TR0063	D18. 5,141;154
Oare	SOM	SS8047	30,2
Oasby	LIN	TF0039	24,85
Obley	SHR	SO3277	4,20,11
Oborne	DOR	ST6518	3,2
Obthorpe	LIN	TF0915	14,94. 24,31
Oby	NFK	TG4114	9,14;22. 17,13;15
Occleston	CHS	SJ6962	1,33
Occold	SFK	TM1570	1,82. 6,193;224. 14,144. 31,6;60. 43,9. 77,1-2.
Ockbrook	DBY	SK4235	9,6
[North and South] Ockendon	ESS	TQ5884 TQ6083	1,21-21a. 6,10-11. 30,4
Ockham	SRY	TQ0756	19,45
Ockley	SRY	TQ1439	19,46
Ocle [Pychard]	HEF	SO5946	10,5
Ocselea	NFK	??	1,14
Octon ER	YKS	TA0369	1E35 *note*. SE,Bt7
Odcombe	SOM	ST5015	19,46
Oddingley	WOR	SO9159	2,56
[Lower and Upper] Oddington	GLS	SP2325 SP2225	2,4
Oddington	OXF	SP5514	55,2
Odell	BDF	SP9658	15,6. 32,4
Odenham	DOR	??	7,1
Odiham HAM	HAM	SU7451	1,1. 69,6
Odiham HAM	SFK		77,4

Odsthorpe	NTT	??	1,12. 9,42;71. 30,12
Odstock	WIL	SU1426	67,9
Odstone	BRK	SU2786	28,3
Odstone	LEC	SK3907	19,9
Odulfesmare/Ouduluesmersc (in Pickering Marishes) NR	YKS	??	1Y4 *note*. SN,D12, *note*
Offcote	DBY	SK1948	1,14
Offenham	WOR	SP0546	10,5
Offerton	DBY	SK2181	1,29. 10,17
Offerton	WOR	SO8958	2,52
Offham	KEN	TQ6557	5,47;56
Offham	SSX	TQ0208	11,92
Offington	SSX	TQ1305	13,21
[Bishops] Offley	STS	SJ7729	2,11
[Great] Offley	HRT	TL1427	1,10-11. 28,8
[High] Offley	STS	SJ7826	11,14
[Little] Offley	HRT	TL1328	1,11
Offord (in Wootton Wawen)	WAR	SP1562	22,7;28
Offord [Cluny]	HUN	TL2167	18,1
Offord [d'Arcy]	HUN	TL2166	6,19. 19,25. 20,7
Offton	SFK	TM0649	1,69. 7,60. 29,7. 62,1
Offwell	DEV	SY1999	16,172
Ogbourne [Maizey, St Andrew and St George]	WIL	SU1871 SU1872 SU1974	1,22. 28,11. 67,62;85
Oglethorpe [Hall] WR	YKS	SE4444	5W7 *note*. 25W29. CW2. SW,BA3;8
Ogley [Hay]	STS	SK0506	7,11
Ogston	DBY	SK3759	8,1. 10,14
[East and West] Ogwell	DEV	SX8370 SX8170	34,27-28. 48,5. 52,14
[Child] Okeford	DOR	ST8312	1,7. 26,4. 42,1 note
Okeford [Fitzpaine]	DOR	ST8010	8,2
Okehampton	DEV	SX5895	16,3
[Monk] Okehampton: see Monkokehampton DEV			
Okenbury	DEV	SX6447	17,65
Okeover	STS	SK1548	4,8
Old	NTH	SP7873	1,17
Old [Hall]	ESS	TM1032	54,2
Oldberrow WAR	WAR	SP1265	EW6
Oldberrow WAR	WOR		10,4
Oldbury	GLS	SO9812	50,4
Oldbury	SHR	SO7192	4,3,68
Oldbury [on the Hill]	GLS	ST8188	60,4
Olden (in Coddenham)	SFK	TM1256	1,5. 6,7. 8,61. 16,16;21. 21,23. 23,6. 51,2. 53,2. 56,3. 74,4
Oldington	WOR	SO8173	1,2
Oldland	GLS	ST6671	5,1
Oldridge	DEV	SX8296	16,118
Ollerton	CHS	SJ7776	1,9. 20,8. 26,11
Ollerton	NTT	SK6567	9,17. 17,3
Olney	BKM	SP8851	5,13
Olveston	GLS	ST6087	7,1
Ombersley	WOR	SO8463	10,10
Ompton	NTT	SK6865	1,24. 12,6. 15,2. 17,10
Onehouse	SFK	TM0159	2,7. 14,37. 34,6. 56,1
Onesacre WR	YKS	SK2993	1W22
[Chipping and High] Ongar	ESS	TL5503 TL5603	20,46. 40,8. 90,87
Onibury	SHR	SO4579	2,2

[High] Onn	STS	SJ8216	8,8
[Little] Onn	STS	SJ8416	17,16
Onneley	SHR	SJ7542	4,15,4
Onslow	SHR	SJ4312	3f,7. 4,5,7
Opetone	CHS	??	1,18
Opetone/Opetune (in Snape) NR	YKS	??	6N120 *note*. SN, CtA35
Opituna: see *Hoppetuna* SFK			
Orby	LIN	TF4967	3,46
Orchard	DOR	SY9480	55,47
[Cann] Orchard	CON	SS2204	5,11,5
[Week] Orchard	CON	SS2300	5,5,6
Orchardleigh	SOM	ST7751	5,52
Orcheston	WIL	SU0545	24,11-12. 48,3;7
Orcheton	DEV	SX6349	15,65
Ordsall	NTT	SK7079	1,5;12. 9,19;23. 30,56
[South] Ordsall	NTT	SK7079	1,13
Orford (in Stainton le Vale)	LIN	TF2094	57,6
Orgarswick	KEN	TR0930	*3,22*
Orgrave LAN	YKS	SD2375	1L6 *note*. See also CHS Y7
Orgreave WR	YKS	SK4286	10W9
Orham IOW	HAM	??	6,12
Oridge [Street]	GLS	SO7827	19,2
Orlestone	KEN	TR0034	9,28
Orleswick (in Piddinghoe)	SSX	TQ4303	12,9
Orleton	HEF	SO4967	9,19
Orleton	WOR	SO6967	20,5
Orlingbury	NTH	SP8672	18,78
Ormesby NR	YKS	NZ5316	29N3-4. 31N7. SN,L26
Ormesby [St Margaret and St Michael]	NFK	TG4914 TG4814	1,45-46;48;59. 9,16. 10,44. 65,10
[North] Ormsby	LIN	TF2893	7,25. 14,65. 30,20-21
[South] Ormsby	LIN	TF3775	2,22. 13,51. 32,31
Orpington	KEN	TQ4666	2,30, 3,1
Orsett	ESS	TQ6481	3,2. 20,4
Orston	NTT	SK7641	1,51
Orton	NTH	SP8079	1,15a
Orton	STS	SO8695	12,7
Orton [Longueville]	HUN	TL1696	2,6. 19,4;6-7
Orton [on-the-Hill]	LEC	SK3004	14,9
Orton [Waterville]	HUN	TL1596	1,4. 8,3-4
Ortone	BRK	??	31,1
Orway	DEV	ST0807	19,21 note. 38,2
Orwell	CAM	TL3650	11,5. 13,8. 14,41. 17,6. 21,6. 22,10. 26,34. 31,5. Appx K
Orwell	HRT	TL3236	5,15. 37,6. Appx
Osbaldwick NR	YKS	SE6351	C23. 2W1. SN,Y2
Osbaston	LEC	SK4204	21,1
Osbaston (in Kinnerley)	SHR	SJ3222	4,3,43
Osberton	NTT	SK6279	30,1
Osbournby	LIN	TF0738	24,90. 57,15;16-17;21. CK,53
Osea [Island]	ESS	TL9106	28,18
Oselei	HAM	??	NF3,5-6
Osfran	LIN	??	24,26
Osgathorpe	LEC	SK4319	14,27
Osgodby (in Bardney)	LIN	TF1372	24,18
Osgodby (near Lenton)	LIN	TF0128	8,8
Osgodby (near West Rasen)	LIN	TF0792	4,19;22. 14,10-11. 16,9;11. 28,22;24. 35,10. 68,22;43;46. CN,17
Osgodby ER	YKS	SE6433	5E15;17. CE21. SE, How9
Osgodby NR	YKS	TA0584	1Y3. SN,D1

Osgoodby [Hall] NR	YKS	SE4980	23N1 *note*
Oslachintone	KEN	??	D18
Osleston	DBY	SK2437	6,63
Osmanthorpe	NTT	SK6756	5,14
Osmaston	DBY	SK1944	6,58-59
Osmaston [by-Derby]	DBY	SK3734	1,19. 6,88-89
Osmerley	WOR	SP0470	26,2
Osmington	DOR	SY7282	12,7
Osmondiston (= Scole)	NFK	TM1579	9,48. 41,1. 66,83
Osmotherley NR	YKS	SE4597	1N131. SN,A8
Ospringe	KEN	TR0060	D18. 5,145
Ossaborough	DEV	SS4843	36,14
Ossett WR	YKS	SE2720	1Y15. SW,Ag11
Ossington	NTT	SK7565	15,1
Oswaldkirk NR	YKS	SE6278	5N38. 8N19. SN,Ma15
Oswestry [Castle]	SHR	SJ2929	4,1,11
Otby	LIN	TF1393	14,13. 16,11
Otford	KEN	TQ5259	2,4
Otham	KEN	TQ7854	5,83
Otherton	STS	SJ9312	11,60
Othorpe	LEC	SP7795	40,19
Otley	SFK	TM2054	8,11. 38,25. 41,19. 52,1;3;7;9
Otley WR	YKS	SE2045	2W4 *note*. SW,Sk1-2
Otterbourne	HAM	SU4623	29,1
Otterburn WR	YKS	SD8857	1W73. 30W12. SW,Cr4
Otterden	KEN	TQ9454	5,76
Otterham	CON	SX1690	5,3,21
Otterhampton	SOM	ST2443	21,17. 35,6. 47,25
Ottering [Hithe]	NFK	TL7194	8,43;45
[North] Otterington NR	YKS	SE3689	1Y2 *note*. SN,A1 *note*
[South] Otterington NR	YKS	SE3787	1N113. 31N3. SN,A1 note. SN,A2
Otterpool	KEN	TR1036	9,49
Otterton	DEV	SY0885	11,1
Otterwood	HAM	SU4102	NF9,4;6
Ottery (in Lamerton)	DEV	SX4475	5 note. 5,3 note. 28,2
[Mohuns] Ottery	DEV	ST1805	23,18
Ottery [St Mary]	DEV	SY0995	10,1
Ottringham ER	YKS	TA2624	2E26. 14E11;13. SE,So2. SE,Hol18
Oubrough ER	YKS	TA1536	14E44. SE,Hol24
Ouduluesmersc: see *Odulfesmare* YKS			
Oulston NR	YKS	SE5474	1N107-108 note. 28W35. SN,Bi3
Oulton	CHS	SJ5964	25,1
Oulton	NFK	TG1328	1,57
Oundle	NTH	TL0388	6,10a. 6a,11;15-17
Ounesbi (in Gatenby) NR	YKS	??	6N151 note. SN, CtA42
Ousden	SFK	TL7359	5,1. 72,1
[Great] Ouseburn WR	YKS	SE4461	1W30. 31W2. SW,Bu3
[Little] Ouseburn WR	YKS	SE4460	1W31. 25W21 note. 29W14. SW,Bu3
Ouseby (in Birthorpe)	LIN	TF1034	26,37;41. 48,6. 67,22
Ousethorpe [Farm] ER	YKS	SE8151	1Y10 note. SE,C4 note. SE,Wa4
Ouston [Farm] WR	YKS	SE5042	13W14 note. CW40. SW,An6
Outwell	NFK	TF5103	8,20. 16,2
Outwick	HAM	SU1417	45,2
Over	CAM	TL3770	7,8. 11,6. 26,48. 32,28. 41,14
Over	CHS	SJ6466	1,21
Over WAR	NTH	??	36,4
Over WAR	WAR	??	EN6 *note*

Over: see also Brownsover, Cestersover,
  Churchover WAR

[Kirkby] Overblow WR	YKS	SE3249	13W28-29. SW,Bu36
Overbury	WOR	SO9537	2,62
Overleigh: see [Over]leigh CHS, SOM			
Overs	SHR	SO3996	4,1,34. 4,27,14
Oversley	WAR	SP0956	16,63
Overstrand	NFK	TG2440	51,8
Overton	CHS	SJ4748	2,15
Overton	HAM	SU5149	2,10
Overton (in Stottesdon)	SHR	SO6686	4,11,16
Overton NR	YKS	SE5555	C32-33. 6W2. SN,Y6
Overton LAN	YKS	SD4357	1L2. See also CHS Y3
[Cold] Overton	LEC	SK8110	36,1
[East] Overton	WIL	SU1366	2,11
[Market] Overton RUT	LIN		56,11;20
[Market] Overton RUT	RUT	SK8816	R7. ELc11;16
[West] Overton	WIL	SU1367	13,8
Oving	BKM	SP7821	5,3
Ovingdean	SSX	TQ3503	12,11-12;53
Ovington	ESS	TL7642	43,3. 90,63
Ovington NR	YKS	NZ1314	6N1. SN,CtA5
Ovretone	WOR	??	2,84
Owdeswell	GLS	SP0218	3,5 note. WoA2
Ower	DOR	SY9985	12,13
Ower	HAM	SU3216	11,1
Owermoigne	DOR	SY7685	46,2
Owersby	LIN	TF0694	4,74. 7,28. 16,8. 22,6-7. 32,6.
			68,42. CN,16
Owlacombe	DEV	SS5716	36,7
Owlcotes	DBY	SK4467	8,3
Owmby	LIN	TA0704	1,75. 12,12. 22,31
Owmby [by-Spital]	LIN	TF0087	4,81. 7,6. 14,20-21. 28,3-4;13.
			CW,13
[North]Owram: see Northowram YKS			
[South]Owram: see Southowram YKS			
Owsthorpe ER	YKS	SE8030	3Y4 note. SE,How1
Owston	LEC	SK7707	40,26
Owston WR	YKS	SE5511	9W40. SW,O4
Owston [Ferry]	LIN	SE8000	63,6;22
Owstwick ER	YKS	TA2732	14E2-3. SE,Hol5
Owthorne ER	YKS	TA3428	14E4 note. SE,Hol9
Owthorpe	NTT	SK6733	9,111. 12,21. 26,1
Oxborough	NFK	TF7300	12,3. 28,1
Oxcliffe [Hall] LAN	YKS	SD4561	1L2 *note*. See also CHS Y3
Oxcombe	LIN	TF3177	3,54. 13,32
Oxelanda (in Trimley)	SFK	TM3236	7,120
Oxelei	HAM	??	NF9,33
Oxenbold	SHR	SO5992	4,21,4
[Great and Little] Oxendon	NTH	SP7383	1,15h. 18,20. 56,32
		SP7284	
Oxenhall	GLS	SO7126	39,2
Oxenton	GLS	SO9531	1,25
Oxford OXF	BRK		B2. 1,39. 38,6
Oxford OXF	BKM		1,3
Oxford OXF	OXF	SP5106	B. 14,1. 28,8. EBe1
Oxhill	WAR	SP3145	18,5
Oxley	STS	SJ9001	12,9
Oxnead	NFK	TG2224	61,2
Oxspring WR	YKS	SE2702	9W91. SW,St13

Oxted	SRY	TQ3852	15,1
Oxton	NTT	SK6351	5,11. 9,76. 11,11
Oxton WR	YKS	SE5043	25W5. CW37. SW,An5
Oxwick	HRT	??	10,6
Oxwick	NFK	TF9125	15,14 *and note*
Ozleworth	GLS	ST7993	1,15

P

Pachesham (near Leatherhead)	SRY	TQ1558	5,15 (erroneously Pachevesham)
Pachetuna	SFK	??	16,19
Pachevesham: see Pachesham SRY			
Packington	LEC	SK3614	6,6
Packington	STS	SK1606	2,16;22
Packington	WAR	SP2384	17,7
Padbury	BKM	SP7230	19,1. 43,8
Paddington	SRY	TQ1047	21,7
Paddlesworth (near Snodland)	KEN	TQ6862	5,45
Padfield	DBY	SK0296	1,30
Padinc	DBY	??	1,3
Padstow	CON	SW9175	4,4
Padworth	BRK	SU6266	23,1. 64,1
Pagham	SSX	SZ8897	2,5
Paglesham	ESS	TQ9293	6,15. 22,22. 33,21. 41,11. 90,8
Paignton	DEV	SX8860	2,18
Painley WR	YKS	SD8450	13W41. 30W4
Painsthorpe ER	YKS	SE8158	1E52. 29E18. SE,Ac2
Painswick	GLS	SO8609	39,8
Pakefield	SFK	TM5388	1,23;27. 4,41
Pakenham	SFK	TL9267	14,49
Palgrave	NFK	TF8311	1,71. 4,5. 8,94
Palgrave	SFK	TM1178	14,45
Pallathorpe WR	YKS	SE5142	5W35 *note*. 13W13. 25W4. CW30;37. SW, Sf37 note. SW,An5
Palling	NFK	TG4226	1,200. 4,51. 9,182
Palstre [Court]	KEN	TQ8828	5,172-173
Palterton	DBY	SK4768	10,5
Pamington	GLS	SO9433	1,24
Pampisford	CAM	TL4948	5,18-19. 14,17. 25,2. 26,12;55. 32,3. 41,6
Pan IOW	HAM	SZ5088	9,5
[Black] Pan IOW	HAM	SZ5883	7,9
Panborough	SOM	ST4745	8,1
Panfield	ESS	TL7325	16,1. 23,6
Pangbourne	BRK	SU6376	1,43. 33,1
Pangdean	SSX	TQ2911	12,31-32
Pannington	SFK	TM1440	3,76. 27,10
Panshanger	HRT	TL2913	34,22
Panson	DEV	SX3692	5 note. 1,50 note. 35,4
Panton	LIN	TF1778	2,3-4. 34,15
Panworth	NFK	TF8904	21,16
Panxworth	NFK	TG3413	1,156-157. 4,37. 19,25
Papplewick	NTT	SK5451	10,21. 30,29
Papworth [Everard and St Agnes] CAM	CAM	TL2862 TL2664	14,53. 19,1. 23,1. 26,44. 30,1-3. 32,26. EHu
Papworth [Everard and St Agnes] CAM	HUN		19,24
Papworth Hundred	CAM	—	Appx M
Pardlestone	SOM	ST1441	21,47
Parford	DEV	SX7189	43,1
Parham	SFK	TM3060	1,75;94. 3,88;90. 4,9. 6,32;35
Parham	SSX	TQ0614	4,1. 11,52

Parkham	DEV	SS3821	16,33. 52,33
[West] Parley	DOR	SZ0997	54,10
Parlington WR	YKS	SE4236	9W1 *note*. 9W9. SW,Sk4;6
[Great and Little] Parndon	ESS	TL4308	9,6. 20,12. 36,3. 37,4–6
		TL4411	
Parracombe	DEV	SS6644	20,3
Parrock	SSX	TQ4535	10,63
Partney	LIN	TF4168	24,45. 38,9
Parwich	DBY	SK1854	1,15
Paslow [Hall]	ESS	TL5703	8,6
Passenham	NTH	SP7839	1,30. 17,4. 18,24
Paston	NFK	TG3234	8,11. 17,40. 19,35
Patcham	SSX	TQ3009	12,5
Patching	SSX	TQ0806	2,8
Patching [Hall]	ESS	TL6908	18,40. 30,8. 32,35
Patchole	DEV	SS6142	3,36
Patmore	HRT	TL4525	4,10
Patrieda	CON	SX3073	5,1,18
Patrington ER	YKS	TA3122	2A1. SE,Th10
Patrixbourne	KEN	TR1855	5,119
Patshull	STS	SJ8000	11,44
Pattesley	NFK	TF8924	34,5
Pattingham	STS	SO8299	1,28
Pattishall	NTH	SP6754	39,12;18
Patton	SHR	SO5894	4,8,4
Patton [Hall] WES	YKS	SD5496	1L7 *note*. See also CHS Y8
Paulerspury	NTH	SP7145	35,22
Paull ER	YKS	TA1626	14E1. SE,Hol1
Pauntley	GLS	SO7429	68,12
Pavenham	BDF	SP9855	15,4. 29,1. 47,1
Pawlett	SOM	ST2942	24,26
Pawthorne	SSX	TQ2309	12,26
Pawton	CON	SW9570	2,4
[Great] Paxton	HUN	TL2164	10,1. 20,8. D23
Pay: see Hembury DEV			
Payhembury	DEV	ST0801	16,95. 52,22
Paynsley	STS	SJ9838	1,59
Paythorne WR	YKS	SD8351	13W41. 30W11 *note*
Peadhill	DEV	SS9714	3,84
Peak's Arse	DBY	SK1482	7,7
Peamore	DEV	SX9188	34,12
Peasemore	BRK	SU4577	17,2. 36,6. 46,6
Peasenhall	SFK	TM3569	6,92;103. 7,10;12;20;72. 7,12
Peatling [Magna]	LEC	SP5992	8,1. 17,1. 40,2. 44,5
Peatling [Parva]	LEC	SP5889	13,32. 41,2
Pebmarsh	ESS	TL8533	23,18. 43,2. 90,38;59
Pebworth WOR	GLS		34,1;2. 62,1. EvN14
Pebworth WOR	WOR	SP1346	EG11;14
Peckforton	CHS	SJ5356	2,28
Peckham	SRY	TQ3476	5,13. 6,1 note
[East] Peckham	KEN	TQ6649	3,2
[West] Peckham	KEN	TQ6452	5,59
Peckleton	LEC	SK4700	13,12
Pedley	DEV	SS7712	21,10;11
Pedmore	WOR	SO9182	23,12
Pedwardine HEF	HEF	SO3670	ES16–18
Pedwardine HEF	SHR		6,24–26
Pedwell	SOM	ST4236	8,11
Peek (in Ugborough)	DEV	SX6858	15,71
Peeke (in Luffincott)	DEV	SX3493	35,6
Peelings	SSX	TQ6104	10,71;79

Pegglesworth	GLS	SO9818	3,5. WoA2. WoB18
Pegsdon	BDF	TL1130	8,3
Peldon	ESS	TL9816	24,50. 66,1
[Brent, Furneaux, Stocking] Pelham	HRT	TL4330	4,12-16;18-19
		TL4327	
		TL4429	
Pelsall	STS	SK0203	7,9
Pelynt	CON	SX2055	5,15,3
Pembridge	HEF	SO3958	19,8
Pemscott	OXF	SP2707	27,3
Pen Y Gors FLN	CHS	??	FT2,1
Pen y Lan (alias *Woodluston*, Wales)	SHR	SJ2201	4,1,35
Pencarrow	CON	SX0371	5,4,2
Pendavey	CON	SX0071	1,6
Pendeford	STS	SJ8903	12,20
Pendleton LAN	CHS	SD7539	R4,2
Pendley	HRT	SP9411	15,4
Pendock WOR	GLS		WoC4
Pendock WOR	WOR	SO7832	2,26;62
Pendomer	SOM	ST5210	19,51
Pendrim	CON	SX2655	1,7
Penebecdoc	HEF	??	1,59
Penenden	KEN	TQ7657	D23
Penfound	CON	SX2299	5,9,3
Pengdeslion FLN	CHS	??	FT2,3
Pengelly	CON	SX3174	5,18,1
Pengest	SSX	??	10,50
Pengold	CON	SX1394	5,24,17
Penhallym	CON	SX2197	5,3,19
Penhalt	CON	SS1900	5,13,7
Penharget	CON	SX2970	3,5
Penhawger	CON	SX2866	5,2,13
Penheale	CON	SX2688	1,12
Penhole	CON	SX2876	5,24,7
Penhurst	SSX	TQ6916	8,8
Penistone WR	YKS	SE2403	1W23 *note.* 9W71. SW,St5
Penkhull	STS	SJ8644	1,16
Penkridge	STS	SJ9214	1,7. 7,17
[Lower] Penn	STS	SO8796	12,5
[Upper] Penn	STS	SO8995	B8. 12,6
[East] Pennard	SOM	ST5937	8,21
Pennington LAN	YKS	SD2677	1L6. See also CHS Y7
Penpell	CON	SW9144	5,5,15
Penpoll	CON	SX3363	5,2,22
Penpont	CON	SX2281	5,13,8
Penselwood	SOM	ST7531	22,27
Pensham	WOR	SO9444	8,3
Pensthorpe	NFK	TF9429	21,21
Pentewan	CON	SX0147	5,15,4
Pentlow	ESS	TL8146	33,11
Pentney	NFK	TF7213	9,2
Penton [Grafton]	HAM	SU3247	13,1
Penton [Mewsey]	HAM	SU3347	21,3
Pentre FLN	CHS	SJ0380	FT1,1
Pentrich	DBY	SK3952	10,15;25
Pentridge	DOR	SU0317	8,5
Penventinue	CON	SX1153	5,5,19
Penwortham LAN	CHS	SD5128	R6,5
Peopleton	WOR	SO9350	8,21-22
[Nether and Over] Peover	CHS	SJ7474	9,16. 17,10. 20,4;6
Peplow	SHR	SJ6324	4,11,19

Perching	SSX	TQ2411	12,27-28;35
Pereio	OXF	??	7,24
Perkley	SHR	SO6198	3c,7
Perlethorpe	NTT	SK6470	1,24;26;30. 9,37
Perranuthnoe	CON	SW5329	5,23,5
Perranzabuloe	CON	SW7656	4,26
[North] Perrott	SOM	ST4709	19,45
[South] Perrott	DOR	ST4706	27,9
Perry	SOM	ST2739	21,5-6. 22,6. 46,7
Perry (in St Martin's, Worcester)	WOR	SO8654	2,61
Perry [Barr] STS	STS	SP0691	12,27
Perry [Barr] STS	WAR		EBS2
Perry [Court] (in Preston near Faversham)	KEN	TR0160	D18. 5,151
[West] Perry	HUN	TL1466	19,30
Perry [Wood] (in Selling)	KEN	TR0355	D18. 5,150
Persene (in Scorborough) ER	YKS	??	3Y3 *note*. SE,Sn4
Pershore	WOR	SO9445	8,1;28. 9,1a
Pertenhall BDF	BDF	TL0865	E5;9
Pertenhall BDF	HUN		2,9 D16
Perton	STS	SO8598	3,1
[Higher] Pertwood	WIL	ST8835	5,5
Petecote	DEV	??	16,139
Peterborough	NTH	TL1999	4,23. 6,1. 6a,30. 42,2. ELc2-3
Petersham	DOR	SU0204	54,14. 55a,1
Petersham	SRY	TQ1873	8,14
Petham	KEN	TR1351	2,15
Petherham (in Otterhampton)	SOM	ST2342	21,21
[North] Petherton	SOM	ST2933	1,3;5;13. 16,7. 35,1-2
[South] Petherton	SOM	ST4316	1,4-5. 16,5. 19,2
Pethill	DEV	SX5360	17,99
Petrockstowe	DEV	SS5109	6,1
Pett	KEN	TQ9648	*3,15*
Pettaugh	SFK	TM1659	16,39. 21,30. 67,3
Petton	SHR	SJ4326	4,6,3
Petworth	SSX	SU9721	11,18
Pevensey	SSX	TQ6404	10,1
Pewsey	WIL	SU1660	1,23c. 10,3. 25,6. 67,50
Peyton	SFK	TM3141	27,13
Peyton [Hall]	ESS	TL4828	22,10
Phepson	WOR	SO9459	2,77
Philleigh	CON	SW8739	5,4,17
Pickburn WR	YKS	SE5107	5W15. SW,Sf29
[North and South] Pickenham	NFK	TF8606	1,71;75. 4,6-7. 8,97. 21,14-15.
		TF8504	22,3. 51,9. 66,52
Pickering NR	YKS	SE7984	1Y4. SN,D11
Pickhill NR	YKS	SE3483	6N155;161. SN,CtA42
Pickthorn	SHR	SO6684	3c,11
Pickwell	DEV	SS4540	3,39
Pickwell	LEC	SK7811	C14. 29,10-12;21
Pickworth	LIN	TF0433	3,33-34. 24,87. 26,53-54. CK,54
Picton FLN	CHS	SJ1182	FT2,10
Picton (near Chester)	CHS	SJ4371	5,2
Piddington	NTH	SP8054	56,65
Piddington	OXF	SP6417	53,2
Piddle	DOR	??	19,14. 26,21-22
[North] Piddle	WOR	SO9654	8,14 note;15;18
[Wyre] Piddle	WOR	SO9647	2,19. 9,1a
Piddlehinton	DOR	SY7197	26,20
Piddletrenthide	DOR	SY7000	9,1
Pightley	SOM	ST2235	21,14

Pignes (in Horsey Pignes)	SOM	ST3139	46,6
[Higher and Lower] Pigsdon	CON	SS2809	7,1
Pileberga	SFK	??	29,3
Pilham	LIN	SK8693	1,39;52
Pilland	DEV	SS5435	3,24;38
Pillaton	CON	SX3664	5,2,18
Pillaton	STS	SJ9413	4,10
Pillerton [Hersey]	WAR	SP2948	18,3
Pillerton [Priors]	WAR	SP2947	B2. 13,1. 18,11
Pilleth (Wales)	HEF	SO2568	9,13
Pilley	HAM	SZ3398	NF6,1. NF9,17;27
Pilley WR	YKS	SE3300	5W32. SW,St8
Pillocks [Orchard] (in Cannington)	SOM	ST2639	21,25
Pillwoods [Farm] ER	YKS	TA0434	23E2 *note*. SE,Wel7
Pilsbury	DBY	SK1163	6,11
Pilsdon	DOR	SY4199	56,46
Pilsgate	NTH	TF0605	6,6
Pilsley (near Bakewell) DBY	DBY	SK2471	6,71
Pilsley (near North Wingfield) DBY	DBY	SK4262	8,3. S
Pilsley (near North Wingfield) DBY	NTT		S5
Pilton	DEV	SS5534	3,25
Pilton	NTH	TL0284	6a,20
Pilton	SOM	ST5840	8,20
Pimperne	DOR	ST9009	1,5
Pimp's [Court]	KEN	TQ7552	5,94-95
Pinbury	GLS	SO9504	23,1
Pinchbeck	LIN	TF2425	14,99. 57,52
Pinchinthorpe [Hall] NR	YKS	NZ5714	1N15 *note*. 11N3. 31N6. SN,L16
			note. SN,L27
Pinchpools	ESS	TL4927	57,4
Pinden	KEN	TQ5969	5,11
Pineham	KEN	TR3145	5,174
Pinhoe	DEV	SX9694	1,52
Pinnock	GLS	SP0728	78,10
Pipe	HEF	SO5044	2,43
Pipe and Lyde: see Pipe, Lyde HEF			
Pipewell	NTH	SP8485	18,16. 26,7. 39,1
Pirnhow	NFK	TM3391	9,63
Pirtochesworda	SOM	??	*25,33*
Pirton	HRT	TL1431	23,3
Pirton	WOR	SO8847	8,19
Pirzwell	DEV	ST0709	19,21
Pising	KEN	TR3245	5,174
Pitchford	SHR	SJ5303	4,19,12
Pitchingworth	SRY	TQ1250	36,1
Pitcombe	SOM	ST6733	36,1
Pitcote	SOM	ST6549	5,43. 46,22
Pitminster	SOM	ST2219	2,10
Pitney	SOM	ST4428	1,34
Pitsea	ESS	TQ7387	84,1
Pitsford	NTH	SP7568	18,25. 39,6
Pitstone	BKM	SP9414	12,16-19. 14,19. 23,26-27
Pittleworth	HAM	SU3229	4,1. 57,1
Pivington	KEN	TQ9146	5,168
Pixley	HEF	SO6638	21,2. 28,1
Pixton	SOM	SS9227	21,53
Plainsfield	SOM	ST1936	35,8
Plaish	SHR	SO5296	4,8,12
Plaistow	DEV	SS5738	3,58
Plaitford HAM	WIL	SU2719	67,56
Playden	SSX	TQ9121	9,109

Playford	SFK	TM2148	6,112
Pledgdon [Hall]	ESS	TL5527	25,16. 30,49
Plesingho	ESS	TL5908	20,18. 90,30
Plompton [Hall] WR	YKS	SE3554	13W31 *note.* 21W13. SW,Bu40
Plotelei	LEC	??	44,9
Pluckley	KEN	TQ9245	2,20
Plumber	DOR	ST7711	56,29
Plumberow	ESS	TQ8393	22,23. 24,31
Plumgeard (in Trimley)	SFK	TM2836	7,85. 21,51
Plumpton	NTH	SP5948	39,13
Plumpton	SSX	TQ3613	12,42
[Field] Plumpton LAN: see [Great and Little] Plumpton			
[Great and Little] Plumpton LAN	YKS	SD3833 SD3832	1L1 *note.* See also CHS Y2
[Wood] Plumpton LAN	YKS	SD5034	1L1 note. See also CHS Y2
Plumstead	KEN	TQ4578	5,21. 7,1
Plumstead (near Matlask)	NFK	TG1334	8,134
[Great and Little] Plumstead	NFK	TG3009 TG3112	1,100;102;104. 10, 29;67;69;70. 19,28. 20,20. 53,1
Plumtree	NTT	SK6133	9,82;85-87
Plumtree Hundred	NTT	—	24,1
Plunker's [Green]	ESS	TQ5897	34,28
Plympton	DEV	SX5356	1,17
Plymstock	DEV	SX5153	5,14
Plymtree	DEV	ST0502	42,17
Pockley NR	YKS	SE6386	2N9. 5N40. SN,Ma19
Pocklington ER	YKS	SE8048	1Y10. 11E9. 21E12. 26E3. 29E4. CE20. SE,P1
Pockthorpe ER	YKS	TA0463	13E16 *note.* SE,Tu7
Podimore	SOM	ST5424	8,3
Podington BDF	BDF	SP9462	32,5. 34,1
Podington BDF	NTH		35,1g
Podmore	STS	SJ7835	2,20
Pointon	LIN	TF1131	24,98. 26,38. 52,2. 57,13
Pointon Hundred	LIN	—	12,54
Polebrook	NTH	TL0687	6a,13. 55,3
Polehanger BDF	BDF	TL1337	E3
Polehanger BDF	HRT		19,2
Poleshill	SOM	ST0823	25,46
Polhampton	HAM	SU5250	3,10. 31,1
[Lower and Upper] Pollicot(t)	BKM	SP7012 SP7013	14,10
Polmere	SHR	SJ4109	4,27,19
Polroad	CON	SX0578	4,15
Polscoe	CON	SX1160	5,3,2. 5,24,22
Polsloe	DEV	SX9393	3,99. 16,91
Polstead	SFK	TL9838	27,5
Polsue	CON	SW8546	5,3,13
Poltimore	DEV	SX9696	16,90;92. 50,1
Polyphant	CON	SX2682	5,6,9
Pomeroy	WIL	ST8156	66,8
Ponsford	DEV	ST0007	16,97-98
[North] Ponshall	KEN	TR2847	5,136
[South] Ponshall	KEN	TR2846	5,137
Pontesbury	SHR	SJ3906	4,4,12
Ponteside (near Banwell)	SOM	ST4159	21,80
[Great] Ponton	LIN	SK9230	1,14. 30,23. 56,6. CK,19
[Little] Ponton	LIN	SK9232	30,23-24. 56,7. CK,19
Pontrilas	HEF	SO3927	1,56
Pontshill	HEF	SO6321	22,2

Pool (near Kingsbridge)	DEV	SX7740	17,51. 24,19. 34,55
Pool WR	YKS	SE2445	2W4. SW,Sk1
[Nether- and Over-] Pool	CHS	SJ3978	8,5
		SJ3877	
Poole	CHS	SJ6456	8,36-37;43
Poole [Keynes] GLS	GLS	SU0095	E14
Poole [Keynes] GLS	WIL		24,27
Poorton	DOR	SY5198	13,7. 16,2. 32,4. 47,8. 54,7
Popham	HAM	SU5543	6,16
Popletone (in Fountains Earth) WR	YKS	??	1W42 *note*. 28W19. SW,Bu25
[Nether] Poppleton WR	YKS	SE5655	25W14. CW32. SW,An12
[Upper] Poppleton WR	YKS	SE5554	2W2. 25W13. CW32. SW,An11
Poringland	NFK	TG2701	1,112. 2,8. 9,37;115-116. 12,8.
			14,17. 66,82
Porlock	SOM	SS8846	20,3
Portbury	SOM	ST5075	5,33
Portchester	HAM	SU6204	1,11. 35,4
Portesham	DOR	SY6085	13,4
?Porthallow	CON	SX2251	5,14,6
Portington ER	YKS	SE7830	3Y4. SE,How1
Portishead	SOM	ST4676	5,25
Portland	DOR	SY6972	1,1
Portland RUT	NTH		1,5
Portland RUT	RUT		EN5
Portland RUT	LIN		ENt1
[West] Portlemouth	DEV	SX7139	17,38
Porton	WIL	SU1936	24,40. 67,72
Portskewett (Wales)	GLS	ST4988	W1;2 note
Portslade	SSX	TQ2506	12,24-25
Poslingford	SFK	TL7648	14,154. 25,87;98. 33,2
Possefelda	SFK	??	6,277
Postling	KEN	TR1439	5,169. 9,16
Postlip	GLS	SO9926	68,5
Poston	HEF	SO3637	14,6
Poston	SHR	SO5482	3e,1. 4,21,17
Postwick	NFK	TG2907	24,6. 66,100
Potheridge	DEV	SS5114	16,36
Potlock	DBY	SK3128	3,1
Potsford	SFK	TM2957	67,30
Potsgrove	BDF	SP9529	40,1. 52,1. 57,1-2
Potterne	WIL	ST9958	3,1. 25,2. 67,11
Potterspury	NTH	SP7543	25,1. 56,66
Potterton WR	YKS	SE4038	9W1. SW,Sk4
Potton	BDF	TL2249	53,16. 53,20. 53,29-30. 54,3
Poughill	CON	SS2207	5,10,1
Poughill	DEV	SS8508	15,19. 35,24
Poulshot	WIL	ST9659	1,11
Poulston	DEV	SX7754	1,34 note. 17,43
Poultney	LEC	SP5885	3,6
Poulton (near Pulford)	CHS	SJ4059	6,1
Poulton (in Awre)	GLS	SO6906	1,54
Poulton (near Cirencester) GLS	GLS	SP1000	E13
Poulton (near Cirencester) GLS	WIL		21,3
Poulton	KEN	TR2741	9,41
Poulton (in Mildenhall)	WIL	SU1969	27,19
Poulton [Hall] (in Poulton le Sands) LAN	YKS	SD4364	1L2 *note*. See also CHS Y3
Poulton [Lancelyn]	CHS	SJ3381	24,3
Poulton [le Fylde] LAN	YKS	SD3439	1L1. See also CHS Y2
Poundstock	CON	SX2099	1,4. 5,7,6
Povington	DOR	SY8882	30,4

Powderham	DEV	SX9684	22,1
Powerstock	DOR	SY5196	47,6
Powick	WOR	SO8351	8,10
Poxwell	DOR	SY7484	11,6
Poynings	SSX	TQ2612	12,30
Poyntington DOR	DOR	ST6520	ES6
Poyntington DOR	SOM		19,76
Poynton	SHR	SJ5717	4,27,29
Praunsley	DEV	SS7630	35,22
[West] Prawle	DEV	SX7637	16,176
Preen	SHR	SO5498	4,21,7
Prees	SHR	SJ5533	1,8
Preesall LAN	YKS	SD3647	1L1. See also CHS Y2
Preese [Hall] LAN	YKS	SD3736	1L1 note. See also CHS Y2
Prenton	CHS	SJ3184	7,4
Prestatyn FLN	CHS	SJ0682	FT2,15
Prestbury	GLS	SO9723	4,1
Prestby (in Whitby) NR	YKS	NZ9011	4N1 note. SN,L2
Prested	ESS	TL8819	34,27
Prestetuna (in Plomesgate Hundred)	SFK	??	6,147
Prestgrave (DB Abegrave)	LEC	SP8692	1,5
Preston (in Tarrant Rushton)	DOR	ST9304	6,2
Preston (near Cirencester)	GLS	SP0400	26,4. 69,3
Preston (in Dymock)	GLS	SO6734	10,9
Preston IOW	HAM	SZ5991	6,19
Preston (near Fordwich)	KEN	TR2460	7,23
Preston (near Lavenham)	SFK	TL9450	8,47. 14,26
Preston (near Martlesham)	SFK	TM2446	8,1. 39,8
Preston (in Beddingham)	SSX	TQ4507	9,57. 10,12
Preston (in Binderton)	SSX	SU8511	6,3
Preston (near Brighton)	SSX	TQ3006	3,9
Preston ER	YKS	TA1830	14E1;48. CE45. SE, Hol3;25
Preston LAN	YKS	SD5329	1L1. See also CHS Y2
Preston [Bagot]	WAR	SP1765	16,18;62
Preston [Bissett]	BKM	SP6529	4,35
Preston [Bowyer]	SOM	ST1326	1,11. 19.35. 35,18
Preston [Brockhurst]	SHR	SJ5324	4,19,10. 4,23,15
Preston [Capes]	NTH	SP5754	18,74;85;90. 39,14 note
Preston [Deanery]	NTH	SP7855	4,16. 56,57c
[East] Preston	SSX	TQ0702	11,69
[Great and Little] Preston WR	YKS	SE4029	9W1 note. SW,Sk4
		SE3830	
Preston [Gubbals]	SHR	SJ4919	3g,8
Preston [Hill] NR	YKS	SE9784	1Y3 note. SN,D7
[Long] Preston WR	YKS	SD8358	30W4
Preston [Montford]	SHR	SJ4314	3g,10. 4,4,24
Preston [on Stour] WAR	GLS		20,1
Preston [on Stour] WAR	WAR	SP2049	EG9
Preston [on Wye]	HEF	SO3842	2,5
Preston [Patrick] WES	YKS	SD5483	1L4 note. See also CHS Y5
Preston [Plucknett]	SOM	ST5316	45,18
Preston [Richard] WES	YKS	SD5384	1L4 note. 30W40. See also CHS Y13
[South] Preston	KEN	TR0260	3,11
Preston [under Scar] NR	YKS	SE0791	6N91 note. SN,CtA28
Preston [upon the Weald Moors]	SHR	SJ6815	4,11,17
[West] Preston (?Nunminster)	SSX	TQ0602	11,63–64
Preston [Wynne]	HEF	SO5547	2,16
Prestwold	LEC	SK5721	35,1. 43,1
Priestcliffe	DBY	SK1372	1,28
Priestley	BDF	TL0133	24,4. 57,3i

Priestweston	SHR	SO2997	4,5,14
Primethorpe	LEC	SP5293	19,3
Priston	SOM	ST6960	7,2
Prittlewell	ESS	TQ8786	24,22
Probus	CON	SW8947	4,24
Puckington	SOM	ST3718	21,54
Pucklechurch	GLS	ST6976	8,1
Puckpool IOW	HAM	SZ6191	1,W17
Puddington	CHS	SJ3273	13,1
Puddington	DEV	SS8310	19,39
[Little] Puddle	DOR	SY7196	1,14. 11,2. 12,15. 26,21-22 notes
[Turners] Puddle	DOR	SY8393	55,16
Puddletown	DOR	SY7594	1,8. 24,3
Pudleston	HEF	SO5659	10,14
Pudsey WR	YKS	SE2233	9W122. SW,M4
Pudsey [Hall]	ESS	TQ8895	24,32;34;36-37
Pulborough	SSX	TQ0418	11,55
Puleston	SHR	SJ7322	4,19,3
Pulford	CHS	SJ3859	A20. 12,3
Pulham	DEV	SS7729	35,22
Pulham	DOR	ST7008	24,4. 36,4
Pulham [St Mary Magdalene and St Mary the Virgin]	NFK	TM1986 TM2185	1,226. 15,24;27;29
Pull [Court] WOR	HEF		1,44
Pull [Court] WOR	WOR	SO8636	E4
Pullabrook	DEV	SX7979	3,8
Pulley	SHR	SJ4809	4,27,6. 6,30
Pulloxhill	BDF	TL0634	24,17
Pulston	DOR	SY6695	26,5;8-11. 53,1
Pulverbatch	SHR	SJ4302	4,26,4
Puncknowle	DOR	SY5388	55,22
Purbeck	DOR	??	1,8. 17,1 note
Puriton	SOM	ST3241	11,1
Purleigh	ESS	TL8402	20,17. 27,4;6-7. 32,12. 42,2;4
Purley	BRK	SU6676	49,3. 63,4
Purslow	SHR	SO3680	4,20,9
[Great and Little] Purston	NTH	SP5139	18,61. 28,3
Purston [Jaglin] WR	YKS	SE4219	9W54. SW,O11
Purtepyt	SFK	??	25,66
Purton	GLS	SO6704	1,13;54
Purton	WIL	SU0987	8,13
Pusey	BRK	SU3596	7,43. 13,1. 21,19. 44,5
[East] Putford	DEV	SS3616	15,13
[West] Putford	DEV	SS3515	1,37. 19,4. 34,7. 35,9
Putley	HEF	SO6437	10,4
Putney	SRY	TQ2475	2,3
Putnoe	BDF	TL0651	23,3. 23,6-7
Puttenham	HRT	SP8814	5,1
Puxley	NTH	SP7542	1,30. 2,8
Pylle	SOM	ST6038	8,20
[Canon] Pyon	HEF	SO4648	2,39
[Kings] Pyon	HEF	SO4350	10,50
Pyrford	SRY	TQ0458	6,5
Pyrleston: see Billingford NFK			
Pyrton OXF	BRK		B9
Pyrton OXF	OXF	SU6895	15,2. EBe3
Pytchley	NTH	SP8574	6a,25. 18,77. 60,1
Pyworthy	DEV	SS3102	17,16

Q

Quadring	LIN	TF2233	7,35;37. 12,90. CK,68
Quainton	BKM	SP7420	23,12. 49,1
Quantock	SOM	ST2335	35,21
[East] Quantoxhead	SOM	ST1343	31,2
[West] Quantoxhead	SOM	ST1141	25,29
Quarles	NFK	TF8838	1,35. 9,85
Quarleston see *Winterborne* (Eastern Winterborne) DOR			
Quarley	HAM	SU2743	1,40
Quarmby WR	YKS	SE1117	9W112 *note*. SW,Ag15
[North and South] Quarme	SOM	SS9236	25,14. 43,1
Quarndon NTT	DBY	SK3341	B1
Quarrendon	BKM	SP7915	21,4
Quarrington	LIN	TF0544	1,3. 7,48. 10,1-3. 42,19. CK,32-33
Quatford	SHR	SO7390	4,1,32
Quatt SHR	SHR	SO7588	EW1
Quatt SHR	STS		EW1
Quatt SHR	WAR		12,8
Queenhill WOR	HEF		1,45
Queenhill WOR	WOR	SO8636	2,36. E5
Quenby	LEC	SK7006	15,11
Quendon	ESS	TL5131	25,23
Queniborough	LEC	SK6512	29,13
Quenington	GLS	SP1404	39,12
Querentune	HEF	??	24,3
Quicksbury [Farm]	ESS	TL4914	22,4
Quidenham	NFK	TM0287	1,144. 9,133. 14,7
Quinton	NTH	SP7754	56,20i;57d-e
[Lower] Quinton WAR	GLS		62,4. EvN11
[Lower] Quinton WAR	WAR	SP1847	EG14
[Upper] Quinton WAR	GLS		62,3
[Upper] Quinton WAR	WAR	SP1746	EG13
Quintone	WIL	??	1,3
Quy	CAM	TL5161	5,11. 29,6. 32,1-2

R

Raby	CHS	SJ3179	A14. 9,7
Rackenford	DEV	SS8518	16,148
[Little] Rackenford	DEV	SS8618	23,13
Rackheath	NFK	TG2714	1,191. 17,22. 20,25
Racton	SSX	SU7809	11,32
Radbourn	WAR	SP4558	17,21
Radbourne	DBY	SK2836	6,99
Radcliffe LAN	CHS	SD7807	R5,2
Radcliffe [on-Trent]	NTT	SK6439	10,55. 11,33
Radclive	BKM	SP6733	41,4
Raddington	SOM	ST0225	22,13
Raddon (in Marystowe)	DEV	SX4585	17,4
Raddon (in Thorverton)	DEV	SS9002	5,9. 51,6
[West] Raddon	DEV	SS8902	15,5. 24,4
Radfield Hundred	CAM	—	Appx D
Radford	NTT	SK5540	10,15
Radford	OXF	SP4023	59,14
Radford [Semele]	WAR	SP3464	17,56
Radholme [Laund] WR	YKS	SD6645	30W37
Radington (near Flint) FLN	CHS	SJ2473	FD1,2
Radipole	DOR	SY6681	11,3
Radish	DEV	SY1891	34,54. 35,4
Radlet	SOM	ST2038	21,28. 35,7
Radley (near Whittington)	WOR	SO8553	2,58
Radnor (near Gresford) FLN	CHS	SJ3656	27,3
[Old] Radnor (Wales)	HEF	SO2559	1,65
Radstock	SOM	ST6854	5,47
Radstone	NTH	SP5840	22,5
Radway	WAR	SP3648	6,20. 14,6. 44,6
Radwell	BDF	TL0057	24,22. 53,12
Radwell	HRT	TL2335	5,17. 36,16
Radwinter	ESS	TL6037	25,24. 35,13. 38,3. 56,1
Radworthy (in Challacombe)	DEV	SS6942	21,1
Radworthy (in North Molton)	DEV	SS7534	19,19
Ragdale	LEC	SK6619	17,26;33
Ragnall	NTT	SK8073	1,1
Rainham	ESS	TQ5282	18,30. 32,28. 52,2. 70,3
Rainthorpe	NFK	TM2097	9,202. 43,4
Rainton NR	YKS	SE3675	6N161. 13N18 *note*. SN,Bi5. SN,CtA44
Raisthorpe ER	YKS	SE8561	1E56 *note*. 23E14. 26E7. SE,Ac12
Raithby	LIN	TF3767	3,21. 14,71. 29,31
Raithby	LIN	TF3184	13,29
Raleigh	DEV	SS5634	3,28
Rame	CON	SX4249	3,3
Rampisham	DOR	ST5602	4,1
Rampton	CAM	TL4268	32,31
Rampton	NTT	SK7978	9,131
Ramsbury	WIL	SU2771	3,3
Ramsden [Bellhouse and Crays]	ESS	TQ7194 TQ7093	3,3. 4,12. 18,6. 27, 1. 32,1-2. 37,2
Ramsey	ESS	TM2130	33,16
Ramsholt	SFK	TM3042	6,177. 11,3

187

Ranby	LIN	TF2378	4,44. 43,1-4
Ranby	NTT	SK6581	1,13-14;30. 9,24-25
Rand	LIN	TF1079	34,21
Ranskill	NTT	SK6587	5,12
Ranston	DOR	ST8612	30,3
Ranton	STS	SJ8524	11,25
Ranworth	NFK	TG3514	1,157
Raphael	CON	SX1950	5,2,6
Rapps	SOM	ST3317	32,7
Rapshays	DEV	SY1498	19,34. 25,15 note. 34,32
[Market] Rasen	LIN	TF1089	16,11. 27,9
[Middle] Rasen	LIN	TF0889	4,39. 16,3. 27,8. 28,19. 35,7. 44,19
[West] Rasen	LIN	TF0689	4,38. 35,6;17
Raskelf NR	YKS	SE4870	1N103. SN,B21
Rastrick WR	YKS	SE1321	1W28. SW,M12
Ratby	LEC	SK5106	13,5
Ratcliffe	NTT	SK4928	30,20
Ratcliffe [Culey]	LEC	SP3299	19,5
Ratcliffe [on-the-Wreak]	LEC	SK6314	17,29
Ratfyn	WIL	SU1642	24,6. 68,15
Rathmell WR	YKS	SD8059	30W1;9
Ratley	WAR	SP3847	17,57
Ratlinghope	SHR	SO4096	4,5,2
Rattery	DEV	SX7461	20,14
Rattlesden	SFK	TL9759	2,2. 5,2. 14,61. 21,1-2. 25,26. 26,1
Ratton	SSX	TQ5801	9,48;64;68;72;91. 10,31;35-37
Rauceby Hundred	LIN	—	3,37. CK,12-13
[North and South] Rauceby	LIN	TF0246 TF0245	37,4. 59,12-15. 64,8-9
Raunds	NTH	SP9972	4,1. 35,1i-j
[West] Ravendale	LIN	TF2299	3,40. 4,68. 12,26. 47,6. 57,2
Ravenfield WR	YKS	SK4895	12W1-2
Raveningham	NFK	TM3996	1,208;240. 6,7. 9,108. 10,47. 20,36. 31,10;15. 50,12. 65,17. 66,98
Ravensholm	DBY	??	1,7
Ravensthorpe	NTH	SP6770	18,6. 35,17. 57,4
Ravensthorpe [Manor] NR	YKS	SE4985	1Y2 note. 23N12;14. SN,A1
Ravenstone	BKM	SP8450	14,42
Ravenstone LEC	DBY		14,8. E7
Ravenstone LEC	LEC	SK4013	26,1. E8
Ravensworth NR	YKS	NZ1407	6N49. SN,CtA17
Raventhorpe	LIN	SE9308	8,23;25-26. CW,16
Raventhorpe ER	YKS	TA0042	2E7 note. 5E36. SE,Sn7
Rawcliff [Banks] NR	YKS	NZ6316	4N2 note. SN,L19
Rawcliffe NR	YKS	SE5855	C31. 1W1 note. SN,Y6
Rawcliffe [Hall] (= Middle Rawcliffe) LAN	YKS	SD4141	1L1 note. See also CHS Y2
[Out] Rawcliffe LAN	YKS	SD4041	1L1 note. See also CHS Y2
[Upper] Rawcliffe LAN	YKS	SD4341	1L1 note. See also CHS Y2
Rawdon WR	YKS	SE2139	1W18. 31W4. SW,Sk17
Rawmarsh WR	YKS	SK4396	19W3. SW,Sf12
Rawridge	DEV	ST2006	1,11. 10,2
Raydon	SFK	TM0438	5,8. 16,37;41. 25,74. 28,5. 32,4;8. 61,1
Raygill [Moss] WR	YKS	SD8049	13W40 note
Rayleigh	ESS	TQ8090	24,17-18
Rayne	ESS	TL7322	3,8. 27,11. 28,4. 39,1-2
[East and West] Raynham	NFK	TF8725 TF8825	1,88. 9,139. 21,22. 23,5

[South] Raynham	NFK	TF8824	9,140. 23,5-6
Rayton	NTT	SK6179	1,24;30
Reading	BRK	SU7173	B1. 1,41;42. 15,2
Rearsby	LEC	SK6514	17,21. 40,12. 43,1
Reasby	LIN	TF0679	1,37. 13,25. 22,13. 28,26
Reculver	KEN	TR2269	2,13
Redbourn	HRT	TL1012	6,1. 10,10;14. 15,13
Redbourne	LIN	SK9799	1,39;57. 7,57. 14,41-42. 26,18.
			28,15. 41,2. 48,3. 61,10
Redbridge	HAM	SU3713	23,66
[Lower] Redbrook GLS	GLS	SO5309	E3
[Lower] Redbrook GLS	HEF		1,73
[Upper] Redbrook GLS	GLS	SO5310	E4 in note
[Upper] Redbrook GLS	HEF		1,74
Redcliff	CHS	SJ4166	C1. B10. 10,3
Rede	SFK	TL8055	14,16. 21,4. 25,32. 27,1
Redenhall NFK	NFK	TM2684	1,128;131;222;226
Redenhall NFK	SFK		1,92
Redgrave	SFK	TM0578	14,42
Redisham	SFK	TM4086	7,51
Redles	SFK	??	62,7
Redlingfield	SFK	TM1870	6,192
Redlynch	SOM	ST7033	*1,9.* 19,58
Redmarley (in Great Witley)	WOR	SO7566	15,10. 20,2
Redmarley [d'Abitot] GLS	GLS	SO7531	E21. EvA105. EvC25. WoB5.
			WoC4
Redmarley [d'Abitot] GLS	WOR		2,25
Redmere (in Owthorne) ER	YKS	??	14E4 *note.* 14E18. CE48.
			SE,Hol9;19
Redmile	LEC	SK7935	15,6
Redmire NR	YKS	SE0491	6N90. SN,CtA28
Rednal WAR	WAR	SP0076	EBW1
Rednal WAR	WOR		1,1a
Redwick	GLS	ST5485	3,1. WoB15
Reed	HRT	TL3636	5,16. 16,5-6. 17,2. 31,2. 37,8
Reedham	NFK	TG4202	1,162. 17,3. 19,24
Reepham	LIN	TF0373	8,3. 26,9. 43,5-6. CW,8
Reepham	NFK	TG1022	31,1
Reestones WR	YKS	SE2732	9W121 *note.* SW,M3
Reeth NR	YKS	SE0399	6N75. SN,CtA25
Reigate	SRY	TQ2649	1,7
Reighton ER	YKS	TA1375	1E16. 2E14. SE,Hu6
Remenham	BRK	SU7784	1,16
Rempstone	NTT	SK5724	9,94. 10,54. 15,6
Renching (in Westham)	SSX	TQ6404	10,78
Rendcomb	GLS	SP0109	52,4-5
Rendham	SFK	TM3464	3,99. 6,43. 7,135;141;146;148
Rendlesham	SFK	TM3252	3,39. 6,268;270;272;281. 7,131.
			21,102. 67,29
Renscombe	DOR	SY9677	11,16
Repps (near Acle)	NFK	TG4216	4,27. 9,13;20;23. 17,15. 19,30.
			64,3
Repps: see also Northrepps, Southrepps	NFK		8,125. 17,7. 19,20
Repton	DBY	SK3027	1,20;26. 3,3. 14,6
[North] Reston	LIN	TF3883	22,29
Retford	NTT	SK7081	5,8. 9,42;71
Retmore	WIL	??	22,1
Rettendon	ESS	TQ7698	10,3. 25,20. 34,30
Revesby	LIN	TF2961	14,83
Rewe	DEV	SX9499	3,68
Rexworthy	SOM	ST2536	21,11
Reydon	SFK	TM4978	33,4

Reymerston	NFK	TG0106	*13,19.* 66,27
Rhiston	SHR	SO2595	4,27,24
Rhiwargor FLN	CHS	??	FT2,2
Rhode	HAM	SU7534	55,1
Rhos Ithel FLN	CHS	SJ2361	FT3,4
Rhuddlan FLN	CHS	SJ0277	FT1,1. FT2,1;17-20
Rhyd Orddwy FLN	CHS	SJ0381	FT2,1
Rialton	CON	SW8461	4,5
Ribbesford	WOR	SO7874	1,2
Ribby LAN	YKS	SD4031	1L1. See also CHS Y2
Ribchester LAN	YKS	SD6435	1L1. See also CHS Y2
[Great and Little] Ribston WR	YKS	SE3953	1W35 *note.* 13W19. 16W2. 24W9.
		SE3853	SW,Bu9
Riby	LIN	TA1807	13,19-20. 16,1
Riccal [House] NR	YKS	SE6780	1N82 *note.* SN,Ma20
Riccall ER	YKS	SE6237	2B7. 3Y6. SE,How6;11
Richards [Castle]	HEF	SO4870	12,2. 24,13
Riche (in Wigtoft)	LIN	??	12,74
Richmond: see *Hindrelag(he)* YKS			
Rickerscote	STS	SJ9320	11,67
Rickinghall [Inferior]	SFK	TM0375	6,302. 14,75;79
Rickinghall [Superior]	SFK	TM0475	6,62. 14,46;136 *note.* 35,7
Rickling	ESS	TL4931	1,29
Rickmansworth	HRT	TQ0593	10,15
Ricstorp (in Muston) ER	YKS	??	20E3 *note.* SE,Tu1
Riddlecombe	DEV	SS6013	25,5
Riddlesden WR	YKS	SE0742	1W6 *note.* SW,Sk13
Riddlesworth	NFK	TL9681	39,1
Ridgehill	SOM	ST5362	16,10. 37,6
Ridgewell	ESS	TL7340	20,23
Ridley	KEN	TQ6163	5,6
Ridley [Hall]	ESS	TL7515	30,23
Ridlington	NFK	TG3431	36,4
Ridlington	RUT	SK8402	R20
[Hamstall] Ridware	STS	SK1019	5,2. 8,26. 11,50
[Mavesyn] Ridware	STS	SK0816	8,17
[Pipe] Ridware	STS	SK0917	2,22
Rifton	DEV	SS8917	36,25
Rigneseta	SFK	??	25,57
Rigsby	LIN	TF4375	2,18-20. 4,61-64
Rigton WR	YKS	SE2849	21W8. 29W37. SW,Bu37
[East] Rigton WR	YKS	SE3743	29W24 *note.* CW6. SW,Sk3
Rillaton	CON	SX2973	5,1,13
Rillington ER	YKS	SE8574	1E43;46. 5E62. SE, Sc9-10
Rime (in North Petherton Hundred)	SOM	??	21,9
Rimington WR	YKS	SD8045	13W39
Rimpton	SOM	ST6021	2,12
Rimswell ER	YKS	TA3128	14E16. SE,Hol19
Ringbrough ER	YKS	TA2737	14E2 *note.* 14E9;11. SE,Hol6;14;17
Ringcombe	DEV	SS8328	16,79
Ringedone	DEV	??	1,6
Ringland	NFK	TG1314	25,8
Ringlestone	KEN	TQ8855	5,161
Ringlethorpe	LEC	SK7723	40,11. 42,8
Ringleton	KEN	TR2957	5,183
Ringmore (near Bigbury)	DEV	SX6546	17,64
Ringmore (in St Nicholas)	DEV	SX9271	16,112
Ringsfield	SFK	TM4088	1,16-17;20. 4,29. 7,41.
Ringshall	SFK	TM0452	2,11. 7,56. 30,1-2
Ringstead	DOR	SY7581	52,2. 55,34;36. 56,39
Ringstead	NFK	TF7040	9,8. 16,5. 19,10. 20,3. 49,1-2

Ringstone (in Rippingale)	LIN	TF0926	7,32-33. 18,15. 42,11-12
Ringwood	HAM	SU1405	1,30
Rinsey	CON	SW5927	1,1. 5,24,6
Ripe	KEN	TR0319	P6;17
Ripe	SSX	TQ5010	9,42;59;69;74. 10,86
Ripley	DBY	SK3950	10,25
Ripley	HAM	SZ1698	23,65. 69,36
Ripley WR	YKS	SE2860	16W4. 29W35. SW,Bu27
Riplingham ER	YKS	SE9632	15E2 *note*. SE,He5
Ripon WR	YKS	SE3171	2W7-9. SW,Bu45
Rippingale	LIN	TF0927	27,53. 42,11;13. 57,10-11. CK,46;48-49
Ripple	WOR	SO8737	2,31
Rippon	NFK	TG2122	25,11
Ripton	KEN	TQ9944	7,17
[Abbots] Ripton	HUN	TL2377	6,2
[Monks] Risborough	BKM	SP8004	2,3
[Princes] Risborough BKM	OXF	SP8003	B5
Risbury	HEF	SO5455	1,23
Risby	LIN	SE9214	4,20. 8,27. 17,2. 24,10;23
Risby	LIN	TF1491	4,20
Risby	SFK	TL8066	8,44. 14,1;12
Risby ER	YKS	TA0034	2E4. CE33. SE,Wel5
Rise ER	YKS	TA1441	2E37. 14E37. CE39 SE,No1 *note*. SE,Hol23
Riseburc	SFK	??	1,12
Riseholme	LIN	SK9875	8,13. 24,2. 26,2;20. 68,47. CW,2
Riseley	BDF	TL0462	3,7. 4,3. 23,2;25. 44,2. 50,1
Risgby Hundred	LIN	—	CS,13-14
Rishangles	SFK	TM1668	6,222
Rising (near Feltwell)	NFK	TL7090	8,35-36
[Castle] Rising	NFK	TF6624	2,4
[Wood] Rising	NFK	TF9803	1,14. 8,87
Riskenton Hundred	LIN	TF3038	12,72
Risley	DBY	SK4635	16,2. 17,20
[Great] Rissington	GLS	SP1917	46,1
[Little] Rissington	GLS	SP1919	48,1
[Wyck] Rissington	GLS	SP1921	39,5
[Long] Riston ER	YKS	TA1242	14E7;36. SE,Hol13;23
Rivenhall	ESS	TL8217	20,8-9. 24,44. 32,5. 72,1
Roade	NTH	SP7551	2,9. 48,17
Roadway	DEV	SS4742	31,3. 39,9
Roake: see *Michelton* HAM			
Roall [Hall] WR	YKS	SE5725	9W61 *note*. SW,O14
Roborough (near Great Torrington)	DEV	SS5717	3,19. 5,8 note
Roby LAN	CHS	SJ4391	R1;2
Rocestre STS	DBY		6,57-59
Rocester	STS	SK1139	1,17
Rochdale LAN	CHS	SD8913	R5,3
Rochester	KEN	TQ7468	R. 1,2. 2,3. 4,15. 5,44;53;56;70;93;97;104. 13,1
Rochford	ESS	TQ8790	24,26
Rochford and [Upper] Rochford WOR	HEF		22,5. 23,1
Rochford and [Upper] Rochford WOR	WOR	SO6268 SO6267	EH2-3
Rockbeare	DEV	SY0295	15,22. 16,133-134;138
Rockbourne	HAM	SU1118	1,36-37. 69,30;33
Rockell's [Farm]	ESS	TL4636	90,22-23
Rockford	HAM	SU1508	23,51
Rockhampton	GLS	ST6593	50,1
Rockingham	NTH	SP8691	1,27

Rockland [All Saints and St Andrew]	NFK	TL9996	8,55. 9,130. 24,1. 50,8
		TL9996	
Rockland [St Mary]	NFK	TG3104	1,109;116;120. 9,27;41;44;161.
			10,31. 12,12;16
Rockland [St Peter]	NFK	TL9997	8,52
Rockley	WIL	SU1671	24,34. 26,13
Rockmoor	WOR	SO7271	15,5;7
Rockstead	HAM	SU1217	23,50
Rocombe	DEV	SX9069	16,127. 19,29. 48,4
Rodbaston	STS	SJ9212	13,9
Rodbourne	WIL	SU1386	28,9
Rodden	SOM	ST7947	41,3
Rode	SOM	ST8053	5,54. 45,14
[North] Rode	CHS	SJ8866	14,7
[Odd] Rode	CHS	SJ8056	27,4
Rodebestorp/Roudeluestorp (in Gristhorpe)	YKS	??	1Y3 *note.* SN,D4
NR			
Rodeham	SFK	??	16,13
Rodenhala	SFK	??	4,36. 31,28
Rodhanger	HRT	TL2334	34,8. 42,13
Rodhuish	SOM	ST0139	35,15
[Abbess] Roding	ESS	TL5711	25,19. 30,3
[Aythorpe, Berners, High, Leaden,	ESS	TL5815	1,8. 10,2. 22,7-8. 26,2. 28,8.
Margaret and White] Roding ESS		TL6009	30,30; 35;39-40;43. ENf
		TL6017	
		TL5913	
		TL5912	
		TL5613	
[Aythorpe, High, Leaden, Margaret, and	NFK		38,́3
White] Roding ESS			
[Beauchamp] Roding	ESS	TL5709	21,8
[Morrell] Roding	ESS	TL5615	23,30. 25,3. 30,41
Rodington	SHR	SJ5814	4,3,31
Rodmarton	GLS	ST9497	30,1. 78,4
Rodmell	SSX	TQ4105	10,61. 12,4. 13,2
Rodouuelle WR	YKS	??	25W3 *note*
Rodsall	SRY	SU9245	5,2-3
Rodsley	DBY	SK2040	3,1. 6,62
Roel	GLS	SP0724	22,1
Rofford	OXF	SU6298	58,31
Rogerthorpe [Manor] WR	YKS	SE4615	9W45 *note.* SW,O7
Rokeby [Hall] NR	YKS	NZ0814	6N44 *note.* SN,CtA16
Rollesby	NFK	TG4415	1,167. 9,13. 10,87. 17,10;15. 64,2
Rolleston	LEC	SK7300	28,5
Rolleston	NTT	SK7452	5,6. 7,5. 11,18
Rolleston	STS	SK2327	10,3
Rollington	DOR	SY9682	47,10
[Great] Rollright	OXF	SP3231	27,2. 56,56 note 58,4;10
[Little] Rollright	OXF	SP2930	6,8
Rollstone	HAM	SU4302	NF9,9
Rolston ER	YKS	TA2145	14E5 *note.* SE,Hol10
Romaldkirk NR	YKS	NY9922	6N40. SN,CtA15
Romanby NR	YKS	SE3693	1Y2. 1N114. SN,A1-2
Romansleigh	DEV	SS7220	5,10
Romiley	CHS	SJ9390	1,31
Romney	KEN	TR0325	2,25;43. 5,178
Romsey	HAM	SU3521	15,1
Romsley SHR	SHR	SO7882	EW2
Romsley SHR	STS		EW2
Romsley SHR	WAR		12,9
Rookwith NR	YKS	SE2086	6N130. SN,CtA37

Roolton	NTT	SK6281	9,44
Roos ER	YKS	TA2933	14E2;53. SE,Hol4;26
Roose LAN	YKS	SD2269	1L6. See also CHS Y7
Rooting	KEN	TQ9445	7,16
Ropsley	LIN	SK9934	18,24
Ropsley Hundred	LIN	—	CK,56
Rorrington	SHR	SJ3000	4,4,21. 4,5,12
Roscarnon	CON	SW7721	1,1. 5,7,1
?Roscarrock	CON	SW9880	5,6,5. 5,11,7
Rosebenault	CON	SX1784	5,6,4
Rosecare	CON	SX1695	5,8,4
Rosecraddoc	CON	SX2667	5,5,9
Rosemaund: see Maund HEF			
Roseworthy	CON	SW6139	1,11
Roskelthorpe (in Loftus) NR	YKS	??	4N2 *note*. SN,L10
Rosliston	DBY	SK2416	1,16
Ross [on-Wye]	HEF	SO6024	2,24;25
Rossall	SHR	SJ4615	3f,6. 4,3,56
Rossall LAN	YKS	SD3144	1L1 *note*. See also CHS Y2
Rossett [Green] WR	YKS	SE2952	1W52 *note*. 21W10. SW,Bu38
Rostherne	CHS	SJ7483	17,11
Roston	DBY	SK1241	6,57
Rothend	ESS	TL5939	21,11
Rotherby	LEC	SK6716	43,1
Rotherfield	SSX	TQ5529	1,2
Rotherfield [Greys]	OXF	SU7282	59,5
Rotherfield [Peppard]	OXF	SU7181	35,7
Rotherham WR	YKS	SK4292	5W13. SW,Sf26
Rothersthorpe	NTH	SP7156	44,1c;2. 48,9
Rotherwas	HEF	SO5338	25,1
Rothley	LEC	SK5812	1,3
Rothwell	LIN	TF1599	4,25. 27,14-16. 44,6;11-14
Rothwell	NTH	SP8181	1,15a;15l
Rothwell WR	YKS	SE3428	9W119. 25W3 note. SW,M2
Rotsea ER	YKS	TA0651	SE,Dr4 *note*
Rottingdean	SSX	TQ3602	12,10
Roud IOW	HAM	SZ5180	8,3
Roudeluestorp: see *Rodebestorp* YKS			
Roudham	NFK	TL9587	1,141. 8,57. 15,10. 24,3
Rougham	NFK	TF8320	1,78. 8,68. 13,17
Rougham	SFK	TL9162	14,51;57;67
Roughbirchworth WR	YKS	SE2601	9W91. SW,St11 note. SW,St13
Roughton	LIN	TF2464	1,99. 38,2
Roughton	NFK	TG2136	3,1. 9,87;148. 23,7
Roundshill	WAR	SP2670	16,4
[East] Rounton NR	YKS	NZ4203	1N41. SN,L45
[West] Rounton NR	YKS	NZ4103	1Y2. SN,A1
Rousdon (alias Down Ralph)	DEV	SY2990	52,25
Rousham	OXF	SP4724	28,23. 29,19
Routh ER	YKS	TA0942	2E33. 14E6. SE,Mid2. SE,Hol12
Rowborough IOW	HAM	SZ6088	7,13
Rowde	WIL	ST9762	26,2
Rowden	HEF	SO6356	1,71. 34,2
Rowden WR	YKS	SE2557	1W44. SW,Bu30
Rowington	WAR	SP2069	18,13
Rowland	DBY	SK2172	1,28
Rowley	DEV	SS6543	3,64
Rowley	STS	SK1221	2,16
Rownall	STS	SJ9549	1,62
Rowner	HAM	SU5801	35,1
[Great] Rowsley	DBY	SK2565	1,27

Rowston	LIN	TF0856	64,5
Rowthorn	DBY	SK4764	16,8
Rowton (in Alberbury)	SHR	SJ3712	4,27,18
Rowton (in Ercall Magna)	SHR	SJ6119	4,27,26
Rowton [Farm] ER	YKS	TA1340	14E11 *note*. SE,Hol16
Roxby	LIN	SE9217	24,11. 32,14. 35,4
Roxby (near Loftus) NR	YKS	NZ7616	1N2. 5N8;11. SN,L9 *note*
Roxby [Hill] (in Thornton Dale) NR	YKS	SE8282	1Y4 *note*. SN,L9 note. SN,D12
Roxford	HRT	TL3010	34,21
Roxham	NFK	TL6399	66,45
Roxholm	LIN	TF0649	27,44. 64,11
Roxton	BDF	TL1554	23,35. 25,9
Roydon	ESS	TL4010	37,3
Roydon (near Diss)	NFK	TM0980	7,12. *14,23*;26;34. 20,23
Roydon (near King's Lynn)	NFK	TF6923	2,4. *14,23*
Royston WR	YKS	SE3611	9W68. SW,St3
Ruardean GLS	GLS	SO6117	E7
Ruardean GLS	HEF		15,2
Ruckham	DEV	SS8711	50,2
Ruckinge	KEN	TR0233	*3,8*. 9,29
Ruckland	LIN	TF3378	13,30
Rudby NR	YKS	NZ4706	5N29
Ruddington	NTT	SK5733	2,6. 9,83. 17,15. 25,2
Ruddle (in Awre)	GLS	SO6608	58,3 note
Ruddle (in Newnham)	GLS	SO6811	58,2
Rudfarlington WR	YKS	SE3454	13W30. 21W12. SW, Bu39-40
Rudford	GLS	SO7721	78,17
Rudge SHR	SHR	SO8197	EW3
Rudge SHR	STS		EW3
Rudge SHR	WAR		12,10
[The] Rudge	STS	SJ7634	11,15
[East and West] Rudham	NFK	TF8228	4,17. 8,107-109. 34,11
		TF8127	
Rudston ER	YKS	TA0967	5E54. 16E5. 29E14. 31E2. SE,Bt6
Rudyard	STS	SJ9659	1,63
Rufford	NTT	SK6464	17,4
Rufforth WR	YKS	SE5251	25W19. CW41. SW,An15
Rug [Moor] (= Camden Town)	MDX	TQ2983	3,19
Rugby	WAR	SP5075	17,25
Rugeley	STS	SK0417	1,22
Ruislip	MDX	TQ1087	10,1
Rumboldswhyke	SSX	SU8603	11,40
Rumburgh SFK	NFK		9,49
Rumburgh SFK	SFK	TM3481	ENf2;4. 3,2;105
Runcton	SSX	SU8802	11,111
Runcton [Holme] and [South] Runcton	NFK	TF6109	14,1;3. 66,40
		TF6308	
[North] Runcton	NFK	TF6415	13,14. 19,5
Runhall	NFK	TG0506	1,84. 4,11
Runham	NFK	TG4510	1,59;203. 9,90. 65,9
Runnington	SOM	ST1121	25,45
Runton	NFK	TG1742	9,147. 19,22
Runwell	ESS	TQ7594	5,9. 20,53-54
Rushall	NFK	TM1982	1,224. 32,7. 35,4
Rushall	STS	SK0201	12,26
Rushall	WIL	SU1255	1,9
Rushbrooke (near Bury St Edmund's)	SFK	TL8961	14,67
Rushbrooke (near Thorpe Morieux)	SFK	TL9452	14,115. 25,110
Rushbury	SHR	SO5191	4,8,5
Rushden HRT	CAM		32,10;25
Rushden HRT	HRT	TL3031	41,1. EC1-2. Appx

Rushden NTH	BDF		3,17. 22,2
Rushden NTH	NTH	SP9566	35,1b;1j. EB2;4
Rushford	DEV	SX7089	16,113
Rushford	NFK	TL9281	15,12. 58,2
Rushford	SFK	TL9281	37,6
Rushmere (near Gisleham)	SFK	TM4987	1,23–24;26. 4,40. 31,34
Rushmere (near Snape)	SFK	TM4259	6,139
Rushmere [St Andrew] (near Ipswich)	SFK	TM1946	1,15. 3,17;19. 6,13;116;125. 8,16. 21,62;69. 67,14
Rushock	HEF	SO3058	1,69. 14,7
Rushock	WOR	SO8871	26,6
Rushton	CHS	SJ5863	1,17
Rushton	DOR	SY8786	37,9. 54,13. 55,32. 56,25;42
Rushton	NTH	SP8482	1,22. 14,4. 26,5. 30,13. 56,46
Rushton	STS	SJ9361	1,64
Rushton [Grange]	STS	SJ8848	11,21
Ruskington	LIN	TF0851	30,35. 64,1-11
Ruston	DEV	SS7612	3,95
Ruston NR	YKS	SE9583	1Y3. SN,D8
[East] Ruston	NFK	TG3427	31,5
Ruston [Parva] ER	YKS	TA0661	1E30. 2E16. SE,Bt3
[Sco] Ruston	NFK	TG2821	8,12. 17,45. 26,5
Ruswick NR	YKS	SE1989	6N133. SN,CtA37
Ruthall	SHR	SO5989	4,23,13
Rutleigh	DEV	SS5101	35,8
Ruxley	KEN	TQ4870	5,22
Ruyton [Eleven Towns]	SHR	SJ3922	4,18,2
Ryarsh	KEN	TQ6759	5,46
[Great] Ryburgh	NFK	TF9627	8,113. 34,9
[Little] Ryburgh	NFK	TF9627	8,106. 34,8
Rycote	OXF	SP6604	25,1. 39,2. 58,28
Rye	GLS	SO8430	19,2
Rye	SSX	TQ9220	5,1
Rye [House]	HRT	TL3809	5,25
Ryes	ESS	TL5216	28,6
Ryhall RUT	NTH		56,1
Ryhall RUT	RUT	TF0310	EN16
Ryhill WR	YKS	SE3814	9W93. SW,St16
Rylstone WR	YKS	SD9758	29W39;44
Rysome [Garth] ER	YKS	TA3622	14E21. CE50. SE,No1 note. SE,Hol20
Ryston	NFK	TF6201	13,9. 66,10;54
Ryther WR	YKS	SE5539	9W24. CW3. SW,BA6
Ryton	SHR	SJ7602	4,17,3. 4,25,6 note
Ryton NR	YKS	SE7975	1N60. 23N21. SN,Ma3
Ryton [on-Dunsmore]	WAR	SP3874	17,6

S

Sacombe	HRT	TL3319	2,5. 36,11. 37,1. 42,5;14
Sactun/Santone WR	YKS	??	1Y13 *note*. SW,St7
Saddington	LEC	SP6591	C15. 1,6
Saddlescombe	SSX	TQ2711	12,33
Saham [Toney]	NFK	TF8902	1,3;7;9-10;135-136. 9,124. 21,17. 49,5. 66,67
Saibamus	SFK	??	76,5
Saighton	CHS	SJ4462	A2
St Albans HRT	BRK		B6
St Albans HRT	HRT	TL1407	10,5
St Andrew's Church (Northover, in Ilchester)	SOM	ST5223	8,37. 15,1
St Andrew's Church: see Ilchester SOM			
St Asaph: see Llan Elwy FLN			
St Briavels: see [Little] Lydney GLS			
St Buryan	CON	SW4025	4,27
St Clair's: see *Binstead* HAM			
St Enoder	CON	SW8956	4,12
St Gennys	CON	SX1497	1,4. 5,7,9
St Germans	CON	SX3557	2,6
St Ives	HUN	TL3072	6,7
St James Church	DEV	SX9390	52,50
St Juliot	CON	SX1291	5,4,6
St Keverne	CON	SW7921	4,23
St Kew	CON	SX0276	1,4. 5,7,6. 5,24,4
St Lawrence	ESS	TL9604	2,6. 37,14
St Leonards: see Losfield BRK			
St Margaret's [at Cliffe]	KEN	TR3544	M6-13;14;21. P8
St Martin's	KEN	TR1557	2,*16*;24
St Marychurch	DEV	SX9165	2,8. 15,42
St Michael Church	SOM	ST3030	46,13
St Michael's Church: see Ashton-under-Lyne LAN			
St Michael's [on Wyre] LAN	YKS	SD4641	1L1 *note*. See also CHS Y2
St Neot	CON	SX1867	4,28. 5,14,2
St Neot's	HUN	TL1860	28,1
St Osyth	ESS	TM1215	3,14. 20,63. 34,33
St Pancras	MDX	TQ3083	3,21;29
St Peter's [Chapel]	ESS	TM0308	14,6. 27,12
St Stephens	CON	SX3285	4,2
St Tudy	CON	SX0676	*4,21*
St Winnow	CON	SX1157	2,11
Saintbury	GLS	SP1139	66,1
Sakeham	SSX	TQ2219	13,27
Salcombe [Regis]	DEV	SY1488	2,16
Salden	BKM	SP8229	12,25. 57,1
Saleby	LIN	TF4578	24,65. 25,23
Salehurst	SSX	TQ7424	9,82
Salescale (in Ryton) NR	YKS	??	SN,Ma2 *note*
Salford	BDF	SP9339	23,18
Salford LAN	CHS	SJ8298	R5. R6,2
Salford	OXF	SP2828	59,27
[Abbot's] Salford	WAR	SP0650	11,3

Salford [Priors]	WAR	SP0751	43,1
[Great] Saling	ESS	TL7025	40,2. 90,62
Salisbury WIL	SOM		2,9
Salisbury WIL	WIL	SU1332	B3–4. 3,4
Sall	NFK	TG1124	1,185. 8,5. 20,28. 56,8. 57,3
Salmonby	LIN	TF3273	13,9
Salperton	GLS	SP0720	63,3
Salph	BDF	TL0752	23,16
Salt	STS	SJ9527	11,12
Saltby	LEC	SK8526	18,3
Salterford	NTT	SK6052	27,3
Saltfleet	LIN	TF4591	CS,39–40
Saltfleetby	LIN	TF4590	1,82. 3,28–29. 27,29. 40,19. 49,6
Saltford	SOM	ST6867	5,23
Salthouse	NFK	TG0743	8,130. 19,19. 66,97
Salthrop	WIL	SU1180	27,8
Saltmarshe ER	YKS	SE7824	3Y4. SE,How3
Salton NR	YKS	SE7180	2N2. SN,Ma7
Saltwood	KEN	TR1535	2,41
Salwarpe	WOR	SO8761	5,1. 14,2
Salwick [Hall] LAN	YKS	SD4632	1L1 note. See also CHS Y2
Sambourne	WAR	SP0661	11,2
Sambrook	SHR	SJ7124	4,19,4
Sampford [Arundel]	SOM	ST1018	21,72
Sampford [Brett]	SOM	ST0840	18,2
Sampford [Courtenay]	DEV	SS6301	16,14
[Great] Sampford	ESS	TL6435	1,30
[Little] Sampford	ESS	TL6533	23,40
Sampford [Peverell]	DEV	ST0314	27,1
Sampford [Spiney]	DEV	SX5372	21,21
Sampson's [Farm]	ESS	TL9915	18,20
Sancton ER	YKS	SE9039	11E8. 21E10. CE22. SE,Wei3
Sandal [Magna] WR	YKS	SE3418	1Y15. SW,Ag4
[Kirk] Sandall WR	YKS	SE6108	5W30. 12W1;12. CW11. SW,Sf34
[Long] Sandall WR	YKS	SE6006	5W11. 12W1;28. SW, Sf24
Sandbach	CHS	SJ7560	1,33. 14,10
Sandburn [House] NR	YKS	SE6659	C25 note. SN,Y3
Sanderstead	SRY	TQ3461	7,1
Sandford IOW	HAM	SZ5481	1,W3
Sandford (in Prees)	SHR	SJ5834	4,23,6
Sandford (in Wembdon)	SOM	ST2737	22,5
[Dry] Sandford	BRK	SP4600	7,9
Sandford [on Thames]	OXF	SP5301	9,3–5
Sandford [Orcas] DOR	DOR	ST6220	ES8
Sandford [Orcas] DOR	SOM		45,5
Sandford [St Martin]	OXF	SP4226	7,53
Sandhurst	GLS	SO8223	1,3
Sandiacre DBY	DBY	SK4736	17,14;15–17
Sandiacre DBY	NTT		23,2
Sandlings	KEN	TQ4666	5,38
Sandon	HRT	TL3234	13,5. Appx
Sandon	STS	SJ9528	1,13
[Little] Sandon (in Sandon)	STS	SJ9529	11,10
Sandown IOW	HAM	SZ5984	1,W13
Sandridge	HRT	TL1710	10,3
Sandringham	NFK	TF6928	35,1
Sandwich	KEN	TR3358	D22;24. 2,2. 3,23. 5,198
Sandy	BDF	TL1749	21,6
Sanhest	HAM	??	NF9,25
Santon	LIN	SE9412	17,3. 24,23. 57,5
Santon	NFK	TL8287	8,42

Santone: see *Sactun* YKS			
Sapcote	LEC	SP4893	10,2. 13,2;34
Sapeham	HRT	??	20,11
[Lower] Sapey	WOR	SO6960	19,9
Sapiston	SFK	TL9274	14,83. 37,3. 59,2. 66,5
Sapperton	DBY	SK1834	6,29
Sapperton (in Bishops Cleeve)	GLS	SO9626	3,7. WoB19
Sapperton (near Cirencester)	GLS	SO9403	46,3
Sapperton	LIN	TF0133	1,15;17. 14,88
[Great] Saredon	STS	SJ9508	11,61
[Little] Saredon	STS	SJ9407	17,2
Sarnesfield and [Little] Sarnesfield	HEF	SO3750	1,17;21
		SO3852	
Sarsden	OXF	SP2822	32,2
Satterleigh	DEV	SS6622	47,8
[Great and Little] Saughall	CHS	SJ3670	A11. 8,6
Saundby	NTT	SK7888	1,44. 5,4. 9,118
Saunderton	BKM	SP7901	4,19. 23,5
Saunton	DEV	SS4537	36,10
Sawbridge WAR	NTH		10,3
Sawbridge WAR	WAR	SP5065	EN1
Sawbridgeworth	HRT	TL4814	33,17
Sawbury [Hill]	HEF	SO6255	2,3. 10,65
Sawcliffe	LIN	SE9114	8,27. 17,2. 24,10
Sawley	DBY	SK4731	2,1
Sawley WR	YKS	SE2467	2W7. SW,Bu47
Sawston	CAM	TL4849	12,1. 22,2. 25,3. Appx G
Sawtry	HUN	TL1683	6,12. 19,1. 20,2. 29,6. D27
Saxby	LEC	SK8220	14,4. 40,40
Saxby	LIN	TF0086	1,39;44. 29,29
Saxby [All Saints]	LIN	SE9916	14,30
Saxelby	LEC	SK7021	1,3
Sax(e)hale/Saxhalla (in Tadcaster) WR	YKS	SE4942	13W4 *note*. CW3. SW,BA4
[Great and Little] Saxham	SFK	TL7862	1,63. 14,6;11. 25,28 TL7963
Saxilby LIN	LIN	SK8976	EN,3
Saxilby LIN	NTT		21,3
Saxlingham (near Holt)	NFK	TG0239	10,7-8;55. 34,12
Saxlingham [Nethergate]	NFK	TM2397	1,118;127. 7,4. 9,164. 17,18. 25,26. 30,4. 35,2. 49,7
Saxlingham [Thorpe]	NFK	TM2197	1,118;127. 7,4. 9,164. 17,18. 25,26. 30,4. 35,2. 49,7
Saxmundham	SFK	TM3862	7,20-21;70-71;74
Saxon [Street]	CAM	TL6759	29,2
Saxondale	NTT	SK6839	9,103
Saxtead	SFK	TM2665	4,12
Saxthorpe	NFK	TG1130	1,193. 4,21-22;35
Saxton WR	YKS	SE4736	9W8 *note*. SW,BA5
Scackleton NR	YKS	SE6472	1N86. 5N44. 23N24. SN,B2
Scaftworth	NTT	SK6691	5,8
Scagglethorpe ER	YKS	SE8372	5E61. SE,Sc10
Scagglethorpe WR	YKS	SE5455	25W16 *note*. CW32. SW,An12. SE.Sc10
Scalby NR	YKS	TA0090	1Y3. SN,D2
Scaldeford IOW	HAM	SZ5783	1,W7. 7,10. 8,1
Scaldwell	NTH	SP7672	4,3. 8,4. 56,41
Scalford	LEC	SK7624	17,33. 40,23
Scamblesby	LIN	TF2778	14,49
Scampston ER	YKS	SE8675	1E43-44. 15E13. 31E2. SE,Sc8-9
Scampton	LIN	SK9479	24,1-2;6-9. 60,1. CW,4
Scarcliffe	DBY	SK4968	10,5
Scardiztorp/Scradiztorp (in Skirpenbeck) ER	YKS	??	26E8 *note*. CE32. SE,Ac8

Scargill NR	YKS	NZ0510	6N1. SN,CtA6
[South] Scarle	NTT	SK8464	6,4
Scarning	NFK	TF9512	8,62;67. 31,40. 66,38
Scarrington	NTT	SK7341	1,52
Scartho	LIN	TA2606	4,69
Scawby	LIN	SE9605	14,28. 26,17;19. 28,16. 35,16. 41,1-2. 44,2-3. 48,2-3
Scawsby WR	YKS	SE5404	10W43 note. SW,O3
Scawthorpe (near Gristhorpe) NR	YKS	TA0983	1Y3 note. SN,D4
Scawton NR	YKS	SE5483	5N39. 11N14. SN,Ma17
Scepeworde	SOM	??	47,22
Scetre	DOR	??	1,27
Schemin	LIN	??	CN,28
Schieteshaga (in Hempnall)	NFK	??	31,6
Schildricheham: see *Cildresham* KEN			
Sciddeham/Scilcheham	ESS	??	59,1. 90,82
Scinestorp (in Sprotbrough) WR	YKS	??	5W30 note. SW,Sf34
Sclive	HAM	??	NF2,3
Scloftone/Scolfstona (in Muston) ER	YKS	??	20E3 note. SE,Tu2
Sco	NFK	TG4518	10,30;89
Sco Ruston: see [Sco] Ruston NFK			
Scobitor	DEV	SX7275	3,8
Scoca: see also Stoke [Talmage]	BRK	??	B9
Scofton	NTT	SK6280	1,24;30
Scole: see Osmondiston NFK			
Scopwick	LIN	TF0758	31,15. 61,6;8. CK,15
Scopwick Hundred	LIN	—	31,14. 32,24
Scorborough ER	YKS	TA0145	3Y1 note. SE,Sn4-5
Scoreby [Manor] ER	YKS	SE6952	13E5 note. CE26. SE,Sn9
Scortebroc	KEN	??	P14
Scorton NR	YKS	NZ2500	6N51. SN,CtA18
Scosthrop WR	YKS	SD9059	1W73. 30W29. SW,Cr4
Scotforth LAN	YKS	SD4859	30W39. See also CHS Y10
Scothern	LIN	TF0377	8,2. 20,2. 26,4-6. 32,29. 43,6
Scothern Hundred	LIN	—	CW,5-6
Scotter	LIN	SE8800	8,17-18. CW,16
Scotterthorpe	LIN	SE8702	8,18
Scottlethorpe	LIN	TF0520	18,18. 57,14
Scotton	LIN	SK8999	8,15-16. 14,25. 16,29. 57,9. CW,16
Scotton NR	YKS	SE1995	6N67. SN,CtA23
Scotton WR	YKS	SE3259	21W3. 29W18. 31W3. SW,Bu17
Scotton Thorpe: see *[Scotton] Thorpe* YKS			
Scottow	NFK	TG2623	1,194. 4,36. 17,23;45. 20,31-32. 21,32;36
Scoulton	NFK	TF9700	8,53. 50,5. 51,6
Scradiztorp: see *Scardiztorp* YKS			
[West] Scrafton NR	YKS	SE0783	6N94. SN,CtA28
Scraptoft	LEC	SK6405	6,5
Scratby	NFK	TG5015	10,43. 17,62. 65,10
Scrayingham ER	YKS	SE7360	23N31;33. 23E18. SE,Ac7
Scredington	LIN	TF0940	24,104. 59,16
Scremby	LIN	TF4467	3,43-45;47. 24,47. 29,13. CS,36-37
Screveton	NTT	SK7343	1,55. 7,6. 9,106
Scrivelsby	LIN	TF2665	1,100. 38,3;6
Scriven WR	YKS	SE3458	1Y19. SW,Bu16
Scrooby	NTT	SK6590	5,7
Scropton	DBY	SK1930	6,27-28;48
Scruton NR	YKS	SE3092	6N58. SN,CtA21
Sculthorp (in North Luffenham) RUT	NTH		1,3
Sculthorp (in North Luffenham) RUT	RUT	SK9302	EN3

Sculthorpe	NFK	TF8931	4,4;98
Scunthorpe	LIN	SE8911	1,39;63. 8,32
Seaberton (in Stogursey)	SOM	ST2045	25,1
Seaborough DOR	DOR	ST4206	3,10 note. ES1
Seaborough DOR	SOM		3,1
Seacourt	BRK	SP4807	7,2
Seacroft WR	YKS	SE3535	9W11. SW,Sk7
Seagrave	LEC	SK6217	1,3. 14,7. 17,23. (43,1)
[Lower and Upper] Seagry	WIL	ST9580	30,4. 49,1
		ST9480	
Seal	KEN	TQ5556	5,26
[Nether] Seal DBY	DBY	SK2813	E3
[Nether] Seal DBY	LEC		14,19
[Over] Seal DBY	DBY	SK2915	E2
[Over] Seal DBY	LEC		14,20, 39,1
Seamer (near Scarborough) NR	YKS	TA0183	13N9. SN,L38 note. SN,D6
Seamer (near Stokesley) NR	YKS	NZ4910	5N28. SN,L38 *note*
Searby	LIN	TA0705	1,76. 12,10. 44,7. CN,7
Seasalter	KEN	TR0964	3,10
Seaton	DEV	SY2490	7,3
Seaton RUT	NTH		1,2b;2g. 26,3. 56,36
Seaton RUT	RUT	SP9098	EN2;11;20
Seaton ER	YKS	TA1646	14E32. SE,Hol22
Seaton [Hall] NR	YKS	NZ7817	5N11 *note*. SN,L12
Seaton [Ross] ER	YKS	SE7841	1Y7. 5E4. SE,C6
Seavington [Abbots, St Mary and	SOM	ST4015	10,3. 19,2. 47,2
St Michael]		ST3914	
		ST4115	
Seawell	NTH	SP6252	26,4
Seckford	SFK	TM2548	16,2
Seckington	WAR	SK2607	16,25. 28,3
Sedbergh WR	YKS	SD6592	1L3
Sedborough	DEV	SS3621	16,33. 52,33
Sedgeberrow	WOR	SP0238	2,63
Sedgebrook	LIN	SK8538	58,6-7
Sedgeford	NFK	TF7036	10,20. 66,88
Sedgley	STS	SO9193	12,1;4
Sedlescombe	SSX	TQ7718	9,122;125-127
Sedsall	DBY	SK1137	6,50
Seething	NFK	TM3197	1,230. 6,5. 9,25;51;62;69;169;171.
			47,5;7
Sefton LAN	CHS	SD3501	R1,16
Segenhoe	BDF	SP9835	33,1
Segensworth	HAM	SU5407	23,13
Segnescombe	SSX	??	9,98
Seighford	STS	SJ8825	2,21
Seisdon	STS	SO8394	12,17
Selavestune	DOR	??	49,4
Selborne	HAM	SU7433	1,7. 47,3
Sele [House]	HRT	TL3112	34,20
Selham	SSX	SU9320	11,14
Sellake	DEV	ST0014	16,161
Selley	SHR	SO2676	4,20,27
Sellindge	KEN	TR0938	9,24
Selling	KEN	TR0356	7,15
Selly [Oak] WAR	WAR	SP0382	EBW3;5
Selly [Oak] WAR	WOR		23,1;5
Selmeston	SSX	TQ5007	9,92. 10,53
Selsey	SSX	SZ8593	3,7
Selside WR	YKS	SD7875	30W7-8 *note*
Selston	NTT	SK4553	10,65

Selworthy	SOM	SS9146	32,3
Semer	SFK	TL9946	14,108
Semere	NFK	TM1884	7,13. 14,23;30
Sempringham	LIN	TF1032	18,23. 24,97. 27,57
Send	SRY	TQ0255	33,1
Serlby	NTT	SK6389	9,52
Sessay NR	YKS	SE4575	3Y11-12. SN,Bi4
Sessingham	SSX	TQ5408	9,47. 10,56
Settle WR	YKS	SD8263	30W6
Settrington ER	YKS	SE8370	8E3. SE,Sc4
Seuenetorp (in Swainby) NR	YKS	??	6N154 *note.* SN, CtA43
Sevenhampton	GLS	SP0321	4,1
Sevington	KEN	TR0340	9,3
Sevington	WIL	ST8678	32,13
Sewell	BDF	SP9922	1,4
Sewerby ER	YKS	TA1968	4E1 *note.* 5E45. 29E27.
			SE,Hu1-2
Sewstern	LEC	SK8821	27,3
Sexintone	OXF	??	7,12-13
Sezincote	GLS	SP1730	53,7. 57,1. 65,1. 66,2. 70,2
Shabbington	BKM	SP6607	23,7
Shackerstone	LEC	SK3706	19,6
Shadingfield	SFK	TM4383	1,112. 7,47;52. 32,16. 33,11
Shadwell WR	YKS	SE3439	1W7. SW,Sk10
Shaftesbury	DOR	ST8622	B4
Shafton WR	YKS	SE3911	5W18. 9W76;93. SW,St7
Shalbourne WIL	BRK		1,27
Shalbourne WIL	WIL	SU3163	50,1. 67,65;82. 68,7. E1
Shalcombe IOW	HAM	SZ3985	3,1
Shalden	HAM	SU6942	35,8
Shalfleet IOW	HAM	SZ4189	8,9
Shalford	ESS	TL7229	1,11. 66,2. 67,1. B3j
Shalford	SRY	TQ0046	19,37
Shalmsford [Street]	KEN	TR0954	5,170
Shalstone	BKM	SP6436	4,30. 19,6
Shangton	LEC	SP7196	1,4. 13,55. 16,5
Shanklin IOW	HAM	SZ5881	7,6. 8,4
Shapcombe	DEV	ST1504	23,20. 42,16
Shapley (in Chagford)	DEV	SX6884	16,61-62;64. 45,1
Shapley (in North Bovey)	DEV	SX7183	52,44
Shapwick	DOR	ST9301	1,3
Shapwick	SOM	ST4138	8,5
Shardlow	DBY	SK4330	1,38
Shareshill	STS	SJ9406	11,64
Sharnbrook	BDF	SP9959	3,13-16. 15,7. 23,31. 34,3. 46,1.
			49,4. 53,14. 56,6
Sharnford	LEC	SP4891	3,4. 8,5. 13,3. 40,5. 42,10
Sharpness	GLS	SO6702	1,19
Sharpstone	SFK	TM1251	1,72. 3,62. 16,24;27. 21,27;33
Sharrington	NFK	TG0336	1,29;31
Shate IOW	HAM	SZ4282	9,17
Shatton	DBY	SK2082	1,29
Shaugh [Prior]	DEV	SX5463	17,100-101
Shavington	CHS	SJ6951	8,23
Shavington	SHR	SJ6338	4,24,2
Shaw	BRK	SU4868	51,1
Shaw (in Chute)	WIL	SU2854	42,9
Shaw (near East Overton)	WIL	SU1365	33,1
Shawbury	SHR	SJ5521	4,23,3
Shawell	LEC	SP5479	44,8
Shearsby	LEC	SP6291	8,2. 10,6. 13,33

Shearston	SOM	ST2830	21,8
Sheat IOW	HAM	SZ4984	9,3
Shebbear	DEV	SS4409	1,39
Sheen	STS	SK1161	1,51
Sheepy [Magna and Parva]	LEC	SK3201	13,47. 14,12
		SK3301	
Sheering	ESS	TL5013	36,1
[The] Sheet	SHR	SO5374	6,10
Sheffield [Bottom]	BRK	SU6469	17,1
Sheffield	SSX	TQ4124	10,111
Sheffield WR	YKS	SK3487	10W42. SW,Sf35
[East] Shefford	BRK	SU3974	57,1
[Great] Shefford	BRK	SU3875	41,3. 44,2. 52,1
Sheinton	SHR	SJ6103	4,11,1. 6,32
Shelborough	KEN	TQ8852	5,65
Sheldon	DBY	SK1768	1,28
Sheldon	DEV	ST1208	34,19
Shelf WR	YKS	SE1228	SW,M11 *note*
Shelfhanger	NFK	TM1083	1,174. 4,49-50. 14,27;32. 63,1.
			66,41
Shelfield	STS	SK0302	1,6
Shelford	NTT	SK6642	9,99. 12,19
[Great and Little] Shelford CAM	CAM	TL4652	1,17. 5,25-27. 14,22. 26,18. EE2
		TL4551	
Shelford CAM	ESS		1,28
Shell	WOR	SO9559	18,3
Shelland	SFK	TL9959	25,51
Shelley	ESS	TL5505	30,2
Shelley	SFK	TM0338	1,100;104
Shelley WR	YKS	SE2011	1Y15. SW,Ag8
Shellingford	BRK	SU3193	7,42
Shellow [Bowells]	ESS	TL6007	1,5. 25,13. 30,33-34;41
Shelsley [Beauchamp]	WOR	SO7362	15,11
Shelsley [Walsh]	WOR	SO7263	19,6
Shelswell OXF	NTH		4,32
Shelswell OXF	OXF	SP6030	EN3
Shelton	BDF	TL0368	3,5
Shelton	BDF	SP9943	24,6-7. 49,3. 54,1
Shelton	NFK	TM2291	9,98;216.́ 35,13
Shelton	NTT	SK7844	9,2. 14,8. 20,2
Shelton	SHR	SJ4513	1,4
Shelton [-under-Harley]	STS	SJ8139	1,38
[New] Shelve	KEN	TQ9151	5,78
[Old] Shelve	KEN	TQ9251	5,77;82
Shelving	KEN	TR2954	5,135;219
Shelwick	HEF	SO5243	2,35-36
Shenfield	ESS	TQ6095	20,3
Shenington OXF	GLS		1,36
Shenington OXF	OXF	SP3742	EG1
Shenley (in Cashio Hundred)	HRT	TL1801	10,2
Shenley (in Dacorum Hundred)	HRT	TL1900	15,2. 33,3
Shenley [Brook End]	BKM	SP8335	42,1. 45,1
Shenley [Church End]	BKM	SP8336	13,2-3
Shenstone	STS	SK1004	8,32
Shenton	LEC	SK3800	10,5. 14,15. 16,2
Shephall	HRT	TL2522	2,3. 10,8. Appx
Shepley WR	YKS	SE1909	1Y15. SW,Ag8 *note*
Shepperton	MDX	TQ0767	4,7
Sheppey	KEN	TQ9272	2,37
Shepreth	CAM	TL3947	5,35. 11,4. 14,40. 22,9. 26,32-33
Shepshed	LEC	SK4719	C15. 1,10. 14,3

Shepton [Beauchamp]	SOM	ST4017	19,5
Shepton [Mallet]	SOM	ST6143	8,20
Shepton [Montague]	SOM	ST6731	19,57
Sherborne	DOR	ST6316	2,6. 3,1;9. 34,14
Sherborne	GLS	SP1714	11,1
[Monk] Sherborne	HAM	SU6056	23,57
Sherborne [St John]	HAM	SU6255	23,4
Sherbourne	WAR	SP2661	16,13
Sherburn ER	YKS	SE9677	2B18 note. 23E13-14. SE,Th1
Sherburn [in Elmet] WR	YKS	SE4833	2B1. SW,BA1
Shere	SRY	TQ0747	1,12
Shereford	NFK	TF8829	8,112
Sherfield [English]	HAM	SU2922	23,42
Sherford (in Brixton)	DEV	SX5453	17,83
Sherford (near Kingsbridge)	DEV	SS7744	1,34
Sheriffhales: see [Sheriff] Hales SHR			
Sheringham	NFK	TG1543	19,18-19
Sherington	BKM	SP8846	5,20
Shermanbury	SSX	TQ2119	13,25
Shernborne	NFK	TF7132	2,4. 8,86. 27,2. 51,4. 66,88
Sherrington	SSX	TQ5007	9,62;77. 10,18
Sherrington	WIL	ST9639	48,10-11
Sherston	WIL	ST8585	1,23g. 27,24
Sheviock	CON	SX3755	3,1
Shide IOW	HAM	SZ5088	1,10. 7,21. 8,6
Shifford	OXF	SP3701	6,7
Shifnal	SHR	SJ7407	4,9,1
Shillingford	DEV	SX9087	19,7. 49,1
Shillingham	KEN	TR0554	7,18
Shillingstone	DOR	ST8211	54,6
Shillingstone: see Okeford DOR			
Shillington	BDF	TL1234	8,7
Shillingham	KEN	TR0753	7,18
Shilston	DEV	SX6753	15,76
Shilstone	DEV	SX7090	1,26 note. 43,3
Shilton	WAR	SP4084	16,45
[Earl] Shilton	LEC	SP4798	C11. 13,4
Shilvinghampton	DOR	SY6284	13,5. 26,68. 56,33
Shimpling	NFK	TM1582	1,172;180. 7,13. 9,46. 14,23 and note;33
Shimpling	SFK	TL8551	33,13. 46,1
Shinfield	BRK	SU7368	1,18
Shingay	CAM	TL3047	13,2;4-5
Shingham	NFK	TF7605	22,14
Shipbrook	CHS	SJ6771	5,5
Shipden (lost off Cromer)	NFK	TG2242	9,153. 10,24. 17,6
Shipdham	NFK	TF9507	1,87;192. 8,81-83;84 and note. 13,20. 66,67
Shipham	SOM	ST4457	21,79
Shipley	DBY	SK4344	13,2
Shipley	DOR	??	3,14
Shipley SHR	SHR	SO8095	EW4
Shipley SHR	STS		EW4
Shipley SHR	WAR		12,11
Shipley	SSX	TQ1421	12,29
Shipley	WIL	SU2278	3,5
Shipley WR	YKS	SE1437	9W133. SW,Ag8 note. SW,M8
Shipmeadow	SFK	TM3889	4,23;27. 7,48
Shippen [House] WR	YKS	SE3834	9W4 note. SW,Sk6
Shippon	BRK	SU4898	7,7-8
Shipston [on Stour] WAR	WAR	SP2540	EW4

Shipston [on Stour] WAR	WOR		2,64
Shipton	SHR	SO5691	3c,6
Shipton NR	YKS	SE5558	SN,B27 note
Shipton [Bellinger]	HAM	SU2345	28,4. 36,1
Shipton *[Chamflurs]*	GLS	SP0318	63,2
Shipton *[Dovel]*	GLS	ST8991	31,9
Shipton [Gorge]	DOR	SY4991	1,2
Shipton [Lee]	BKM	SP7321	16,4. 27,2. 56,3
Shipton [Moyne]	GLS	ST8989	73,1-3
Shipton [Oliffe]	GLS	SP0318	38,4. 68,6
Shipton [on-Cherwell] OXF	NTH		23,18
Shipton [on-Cherwell] OXF	OXF	SP4816	7,26. EN10
Shipton *[Pelye]*	GLS	SP0418	53,9
Shipton [Solers]	GLS	SP0318	2,6
Shipton [under-Wychwood]	OXF	SP2717	B5. 1,5;9. 58,15;29
Shiptonthorpe ER	YKS	SE8543	1Y6 note. SE,Wei1
Shirburn OXF	BRK		B9
Shirburn OXF	OXF	SU6995	28,9. 29,6. EBe3
Shirdon	BDF	TL0964	35,2
Shirland	DBY	SK3958	7,5
Shirley	DBY	SK2141	6,41;43
Shirley	HAM	SU3914	29,5
Shirley HEF	HEF	SO3865	ES8
Shirley HEF	SHR		6,15
Shirwell	DEV	SS5937	16,65. 21,2. 42,9
Shitlington WR	YKS	SE2617	1Y15 note. SW,Ag11
Shobdon	HEF	SO4062	9,10
Shobrooke (near Crediton)	DEV	SS8601	15,4
Shobrooke (in Morchard Bishop)	DEV	SS7504	24,29
Shoby	LEC	SK6820	10,16
Shocklach	CHS	SJ4348	2,17
Shoddesden	HAM	SU2748	69,26
[North and South] Shoebury	ESS	TQ9286	18,17. 24,23;28
		TQ9384	
Shoflet IOW	HAM	SZ5394	1,W20
Shopland	ESS	TQ8988	20,80
Shopnoller	SOM	ST1632	2,3
Shoreham	SSX	TQ2105	13,5;55
Shorncote GLS	GLS	SU0296	E17
Shorncote GLS	WIL		52,1
Shortgrove	ESS	TL5235	20,22;24. 32,42
Shortley (in Quainton)	BKM	??	23,11. 56,2
Shortmansford (near Durborough)	SOM	??	25,42
Shorwell IOW	HAM	SZ4582	1,12. 8,8
Shotesham [All Saints and St Mary]	NFK	TM2499	1,106;110;113;184. 2,8. 7,5.
		TM2398	9,24;38;159;163. 14,16. 17,16.
			25,25;28
Shotford	NFK	TM2582	7,6. 26,6
Shotley	SFK	TM2336	1,102-104. 25,64
Shotover	OXF	SP5806	1,10
Shottesbrook	BRK	SU8478	65,5
Shottisham	SFK	TM3244	6,167;186;238. 21,73;89
Shottle	DBY	SK3149	6,12
Shotwick	CHS	SJ3371	A12
Shouldham [All Saints and St Margaret]	NFK	TF6808	21,7. 31,32
		TF6809	
Shouldham Thorpe: see [Shouldham] Thorpe NFK			
Shovel	SOM	ST2832	46,14
Shovelstrode	SSX	TQ4237	10,96-97
Showell	OXF	SP3529	7,51. 17,8

Shrawardine	SHR	SJ4015	4,3,50
Shrewley	WAR	SP2167	18,6
Shrewsbury	SHR	SJ4912	C1;14. 1,1-2. 3b,1. 3g,1-2. 4,1,37. 6,33
Shrewton	WIL	SU0643	24,7;10;35
Shrivenham	BRK	SU2489	1,33
Shropham	NFK	TL9892	6,1. 9,126-128. 24,2. 52,1. 66,43
Shroton: see Iwerne Courtney DOR			
Shuckburgh	WAR	SP4862	16,32. 17,39. 44,4
Shuckstonfield	DBY	SK3457	10,11
Shurlach	CHS	SJ6773	5,6
Shurvenhill (in Bromsgrove)	WOR	SO9373	1,1a
Shushions	STS	SJ8414	17,20
Shustoke	WAR	SP2290	31,7
Shutbrooke: see *[Floyers] Hayes* DEV			
Shuttington	WAR	SK2505	16,22-23
Shuttleworth (= Littleworth) WR	YKS	??	5W8 *note*. SW,Sf21
Sibbertoft	NTH	SP6882	18,17
Sibdon [Carwood]	SHR	SO4183	4,20,7
Sibertswold	KEN	TR2647	M15-16;20. P12. 7,21
Sibford [Ferris]	OXF	SP3537	24,3
Sibford [Ferris and Gower] OXF	NTH		23,19
Sibford [Ferris and Gower] OXF	STS		12,30
Sibford [Gower]	OXF	SP3537	EN11. ES1
Siborne	KEN	??	9,45
Sibsey	LIN	TF3550	14,77
Sibson	HUN	TL0997	7,6;7. 9,3;4
Sibson	LEC	SK3500	10,4
Sibthorpe	NTT	SK7645	2,1-2. 10,2. 20,1
Sibton	SFK	TM3669	3,9. 6,90;93
Sicklinghall WR	YKS	SE3648	1W50. SW,Bu36
Sidbury	DEV	SY1391	2,15
Sidbury	SHR	SO6885	4,11,7
Siddington	CHS	SJ8470	14,7
Siddington	GLS	SU0299	39,18. 66,5. 69,5
Siddington [House]	GLS	SP0400	32,3
Sidestrand	NFK	TG2539	8,120-121. 8,127
Sidlesham	SSX	SZ8598	3,6
Sidmouth	DEV	SY1287	10,1. 11,1 note
Sidnor (in Selmeston)	SSX	TQ5008	10,53-54
Siefton	SHR	SO4883	4,1,28
Siffleton	KEN	TQ7158	5,43
Sigford	DEV	SX7773	35,23
Sigglesthorne ER	YKS	TA1545	2E38. SE,No1
[Kirby] Sigston NR	YKS	SE4194	1Y2 *note*. SN,A1
Silchester	HAM	SU6262	29,14. 32,4
Sileby	LEC	SK6015	C11. 1,3. 13,64. 43,1
Silkmore	STS	SJ9321	11,6
Silkstone WR	YKS	SE2905	9W64;70. SW,St2;4
Silsden WR	YKS	SE0446	25W31
Silsoe	BDF	TL0835	24,16. 33,2
Silton	DOR	ST7829	35,1
[Nether] Silton NR	YKS	SE4592	SN,A8 *note*
[Over] Silton NR	YKS	SE4593	1N132. SN,A8
Silverley	CAM	TL7060	29,3. Appx B
Silverstone	NTH	SP6644	18,52. 43,3. 45,7
Silverton	DEV	SS9502	*Note to 44*. 1,7. 3,68 note
Simenton(e)	NTT	??	1,42. 5,8
Simpson	BKM	SP8835	5,6. 57,9
Sinderby NR	YKS	SE3481	6N156. SN,CtA43
Sinfin	DBY	SK3431	6,90

Singleborough	BKM	SP7632	14,22
Singleton	SSX	SU8713	11,3
Singleton LAN	YKS	SD3838	1L1. See also CHS Y2
Sinnington NR	YKS	SE7485	8N8;25. SN,D21. SN,Ma10
Sisland	NFK	TM3498	1,183. 12,25
Siston	GLS	ST6875	42,3
Sitlington: see Shitlington YKS			
Siuuarbi (in Wressle) ER	YKS	??	21E5 *note*
Sixhills	LIN	TF1787	4,56. 16,16. 40,12;14
Skeckling ER	YKS	TA2228	14E1 *note*. SE,Hol2
Skeeby NR	YKS	NZ2002	6N22. SN,CtA12
Skeffington	LEC	SK7402	1,3
Skegby (near Marnham)	NTT	SK7870	9,66
Skegby (near Sutton in Ashfield)	NTT	SK5060	1,23
Skegness: see *Tric* LIN			
Skelbrooke WR	YKS	SE5112	9W42. SW,O5
Skellingthorpe	LIN	SK9272	65,4. CK,27
Skellow WR	YKS	SE5310	9W39 *note*. SW,O4
Skelmanthorpe WR	YKS	SE2310	9W86 *note*. SW,St12
Skelmersdale LAN	CHS	SD4606	R1,27
Skelton (near Boroughbridge) WR	YKS	SE3667	2W12 *note*. 28W24. SW,H2;6
Skelton (near Kilpin) ER	YKS	SE7625	3Y4. SE,How3
Skelton (near Saltburn) NR	YKS	NZ6518	5N18. SN,L17
Skelton (near York) NR	YKS	SE5656	C33 *note*. 1W2 *note*. 6W2 *note*. SN,Y7
Skelton [Grange] (near Leeds) WR	YKS	SE3331	9W1 *note*. SW,Sk4
Skendleby	LIN	TF4369	24,46
Skerne ER	YKS	TA0455	1Y8. 23E8. SE,Dr3-4
Skerraton	DEV	SX7064	52,45
Skerton LAN	YKS	SD4763	1L2. See also CHS Y3
Skewes	CON	SW6921	1,1
Skewsby NR	YKS	SE6270	5N57. SN,B9
Skeyton	NFK	TG2425	20,31. 31,2
Skibeden WR	YKS	SE0152	1W73 *note*. SW,Cr2
Skidbrooke	LIN	TF4493	1,89. 3,17. 49,6. CS,39
Skidbrooke Hundred	LIN	—	CS,10
Skidby ER	YKS	TA0133	2E1. SE,We14
Skilgate	SOM	SS9827	22,11
Skillington LIN	LIN	SK8925	1,25. 2,37-39. 57,46. 68,23. CK,8;10
Skillington LIN	NTH		ELc4
Skillington LIN	RUT		ELc19
Skinnand	LIN	SK9456	59,18
Skipton WR	YKS	SD9851	1W73. SW,Cr2
Skipton [on Swale] NR	YKS	SE3679	13N17
Skipwith ER	YKS	SE6638	23E5. SE,How9
Skirbeck	LIN	TF3343	12,67. 29,33
[North] Skirlaw [Skirlaugh] ER	YKS	TA1440	14E7. SE,Th13. SE,Hol13 *note*
[South] Skirlaw [Skirlaugh] ER	YKS	TA1439	14E11. SE,Hol13 note. SE,Hol15-16
[High] Skirlington ER	YKS	TA1852	14E7 *note*. SE,Hol13
Skirpenbeck ER	YKS	SE7457	26E10. CE32. SE,Ac7
Skutterskelfe [Hall] NR	YKS	NZ4807	1N32 *note*. 5N29. 29N9
Slacham	HAM	??	1,32
Slackbury	SHR	??	4,26,1
Slaidburn WR	YKS	SD7152	30W37
Slampseys	ESS	TL7319	3,4
Slapton	BKM	SP9320	9,1
Slapton	DEV	SX8244	2,24
Slapton	NTH	SP6446	22,9
[Lower] Slaughter	GLS	SP1622	1,10

[Upper] Slaughter	GLS	SP1523	39,20. EvN11
Slawston	LEC	SP7894	17,17;20
[New] Sleaford	LIN	TF0645	7,43
[Old] Sleaford	LIN	TF0745	7,45–46. 10,2
Sleap (in Wem)	SHR	SJ4826	4,14,26
Sledmere ER	YKS	SE9364	5E72. 28W40. SE,Th7
Sleningford WR	YKS	SE2777	2W8 *note*. SW,Bu48
Slimbridge	GLS	ST7303	1,17
Slindon	STS	SJ8232	2,11
Slindon	SSX	SU9608	11,88
Slingsby NR	YKS	SE6974	5N48. 23N24. SN,Ma23
Slipton	NTH	SP9579	6,14
Sloley	NFK	TG2924	17,48. 20,33. 21,36
Sloothby	LIN	TF4970	3,52. 14,86. 24,58;62. 25,25
Slyne LAN	YKS	SD4765	1L2. See also CHS Y3
Smallands	ESS	TL8110	41,2
Smallbrook	WIL	ST8844	68,27
Smallburgh	NFK	TG3323	9,180. 17,49
Smalley	DBY	SK4044	1,17
Smallicombe	DEV	SY2097	16,168
Smallridge	DEV	ST3000	1,11. 34,51
Smalton	ESS	TL7834	90,37
[Great] Smeaton NR	YKS	NZ4304	1Y2. 6N10. SN,A1. SN,CtA10
[Kirk and Little] Smeaton WR	YKS	SE5216	9W47 *note*. 9W48. SW,O8
[Little] Smeaton NR	YKS	NZ3403	1Y2 *note*. 1N116. SN,A1;3
Smedmore	DOR	SY9278	37,12
Smeetham [Hall]	ESS	TL8441	20,32
Smeeton	WAR	SP4180	14,3
Smeeton [Westerby]	LEC	SP6892	1,4. 13,26;29. 19,11
Smercote	WAR	SP3285	16,43
Smethcott	SHR	SO4499	4,27,15
Smethwick	STS	SP0288	2,22
Smisby	DBY	SK3419	14,7
[Great and Little] Smithcot	WIL	SU0082	27,11
		SU9982	
Smithdown LAN	CHS	SJ3888	R1,14
Smithycote	DBY	SK4349	7,6
Smockington	LEC	SP4589	14,14
Smytham	DEV	SS4816	15,15
Snailwell	CAM	TL6467	28,2. Appx A
Snainton NR	YKS	SE9182	1Y4. 8N13. 13N14.˙28W27. SN,D13
Snaith WR	YKS	SE6422	9W26. 29W10;25
Snape	SFK	TM3959	6,129;133
[Great] Snarehill	NFK	TL8983	9,74. 14,10 *and note*. 66,76–77
[Little] Snarehill	NFK	TL8881	9,75
Snarestone	LEC	SK3409	19,8
Snarford	LIN	TF0582	3,2. 16,20–21;50. 35,17
[Low] Snaygill WR	YKS	SD9949	1W73 *note*. SW,Cr2
Sneaton NR	YKS	NZ8907	4N1. SN,L3
Sneinton	NTT	SK5839	1,63
Snelland	LIN	TF0780	2,13. 22,14–15. 28,25–26
Snelson	CHS	SJ8073	20,9
Snelston	DBY	SK1543	3,1. 6,53
Snelston (near Stoke Dry) RUT	NTH		5,2
Snelston (near Stoke Dry) RUT	RUT	SP8695	EN7
Snetterton	NFK	TL9991	6,1. 9,73. 66,75
Snettisham	NFK	TF6934	2,1;3–5;10. 8,48
Snitertun WR	YKS	??	9W18 *note*. SW,Sk12
Snitterby	LIN	SK9894	1,39;43. 14,19. 28,10. 61,9
Snitterfield	WAR	SP2160	16,15

Snitterton	DBY	SK2860	1,12
Snoddington	HAM	SU2545	23,39
Snodeswick	DBY	??	7,3
Snodland	KEN	TQ7061	4,9
[Upton] Snodsbury	WOR	SO9454	8,11
Snore	NFK	TL6299	16,2
[Great] Snoring	NFK	TF9434	1,92. 34,17
[Great] Snoring	NFK	TF9434	1,92. 34,17
[Little] Snoring	NFK	TF9532	1,16. 8,101. 34,7
[Little] Snoring	NFK	TF9532	1,16. 8,101. 34,7
Snorscomb	NTH	SP5956	18,60;97
Snowshill	GLS	SP0933	11,9
Snydale WR	YKS	SE4021	9W97. SW,Ag3
Snydles	DEV	SS6619	16,88
Soar	DEV	SX7037	17,41
Soberton	HAM	SU6116	1,13-14. 55,2. 56,1
Soberton	HAM	??	2,1
Sock [Dennis]	SOM	ST5121	19,85
[Mudford] Sock	SOM	ST5519	21,95
[Little] Sodbury	GLS	ST7583	30,3
[Old] Sodbury	GLS	ST7581	1,48
Sodington	WOR	SO6971	16,1
Sogenhoe	SFK	TM2852	6,242
Soham	CAM	TL5973	1,1;13. 5,8. 6,3. 14,73;74.
			Appx A
Soham	DBY	SK0866	6,10
[Earl] Soham	SFK	TM2363	3,20;33 *note*;46;48 *note*. 6,285.
			31,59
[Monk] Soham	SFK	TM2165	14,102. 21,46. 31,3
Solberge NR	YKS	SE3589	6N28 *note*. SN, CtA13
Sole (in Astley)	WAR	SP3287	16,43
Soles [Court]	KEN	TR2550	5,201
Solihull: see Longdon, Ulverley WAR			
Solton	KEN	TR3345	5,187
Somborne: see Stockbridge HAM			
[King's] Somborne	HAM	SU3631	1,47. 45,8-9
[Little] Somborne	HAM	SU3832	39,2
Somerby	LEC	SK7710	1,3. 14,31. 19,19. 29,11
Somerby	LIN	SK8489	1,39;50. 12,6. 14,22. 63,3
Somerby	LIN	TA0606	13,18. 22,28
[Old] Somerby	LIN	SK9633	1,15-16. 31,3-4. 57,43;55. 67,12.
			CK,55
Somercotes	LIN	TF4295	1,86. 16,40. 40,24
Somercotes Hundred	LIN	—	CS,8-9
Somerford	CHS	SJ8165	11,8
Somerford [Booths]	CHS	SJ8566	26,1
[Great and Little] Somerford	WIL	ST9682	8,3. 24,20. 26,18. 27,10. 67,22-25
		ST9684	
Somerford [Keynes] GLS	GLS	SU0195	E10
Somerford [Keynes] GLS	WIL		6,2
Somerley	SSX	SZ8198	11,46
Somerleyton	SFK	TM4997	1,41;48;52. 69,4
Somersal [Herbert]	DBY	SK1335	6,32
[Potter] Somersal	DBY	SK1435	6,33
Somersby	LIN	TF3472	28,36-37
Somersham	HUN	TL3677	4,3
Somersham	SFK	TM0948	1,4. 7,59. 29,2;6. 62,2. 76,13
Somerton	LIN	SK9558	27,59
Somerton	OXF	SP4928	7,10. 35,14;34
Somerton	SOM	ST4928	1,1-2. 46,11
Somerton	SFK	TL8153	14,28;33. 40,2

[East and West] Somerton	NFK	TG4819 TG4719	1,217. 4,26-27. 9,23. 10,83. 64,7. 66,79
Sompting	SSX	TQ1605	13,37-40
Sonning	BRK	SU7575	3,1
Sonnings (in Horton Kirby)	KEN	TQ5868	5,7 *note*
Sophis	KEN	??	D24
Sopley	HAM	SZ1597	51,1
Sopworth	WIL	ST8286	32,15
Soresdene	HAM	??	45,4
Sorley	DEV	SX7246	17,42
Sotby	LIN	TF2078	4,50;52
Sotherton	SFK	TM4479	48,1
Sotleie (in Bowland Forest) WR	YKS	??	30W37 *note*
Sotterley	SFK	TM4585	4,30-31
Sotwell	BRK	SU5890	10,2
Soughton FLN	CHS	SJ2466	FD8,2
Soulbury	BKM	SP8827	17,10. 23,18. 25,2. 44,2. 54,1. 57,18
Soulton	SHR	SJ5430	3e,2
Sourton	DEV	SX5390	3,86
South Mimms: see [South] Mimms MDX			
South Runcton: see [South] Runcton NFK			
Southam	GLS	SO9725	3,7. WoB19
Southam	WAR	SP4161	6,8
Southampton	HAM	SU4211	3,16. 29,5. 39,4. S1-3
Southburgh: see [South] Burgh NFK			
Southburn ER	YKS	SE9854	1Y8. SE,Dr3
Southchurch	ESS	TQ9086	2,8
Southcoates ER	YKS	TA1230	2E35 *note*. 14E49. CE52. SE,Mid3. SE,Hol25
Southcote	BRK	SU6871	25,1
Southcote	BKM	SP7911	33,1
Southease	SSX	TQ4205	7,1
Southery	NFK	TL6294	14,2
Southfleet	KEN	TQ6171	4,1
Southill	BDF	TL1442	21,8. 23,8. 25,11. 32,14-15. 39,3. 53,31
Southleigh	DEV	SY2093	19,46
Southmere	NFK	TF7537	1,2
Southminster	ESS	TQ9699	3,9
Southoe	HUN	TL1864	19,29. 25,2
Southorpe (in Edenham)	LIN	TF0622	57,45
Southorpe	NTH	TF0803	6a,6
Southorpe ER	YKS	TA1946	14E7 *note*. SE,Bt4 note. SE,Hol12
Southowram WR	YKS	SE1123	9W143 *note*. SW,M10
Southrepps	NFK	TG2536	8,128
Southrepps: see also Northrepps, Repps NFK			
Southrey	LIN	TF1366	4,47. 7,29. 16,17. 24,19
Southwark	SRY	TQ3280	1,5. 2,3. 5,8;28. 6,1. 15,1-2. 19,1- 2;17;21. 29,1
Southweek	DEV	SX4393	34,1
Southweek: see Week DEV			
Southwell	NTT	SK6953	5,1;18. 11,15-17. 13,13. 17,13-14
Southwell Hundred	NTT	—	11,17
Southwick	GLS	SO8830	1,24
Southwold	SFK	TM5076	14,162-163
Southwood	NFK	TG3905	12,45. 19,29. 31,11. 66,102
Sowerby WR	YKS	SE0423	1Y15

Sowerby (near Thirsk) NR	YKS	SE4381	1Y1. 1N111. SN,Bi7
Sowerby (in Whitby) NR	YKS	NZ8909	4N1 *note.* SN,L4
Sowerby [Hall] (in Dalton in Furness) LAN	YKS	SD1972	1L6 *note.* See also CHS Y7
Sowerby [Hall] (near Preston) LAN	YKS	SD4738	1L1 *note.* See also CHS Y2
Sowerby [under Cotcliffe] NR	YKS	SE4193	1Y2 *note.* 1N133. SN,A1;9
Sowton (formerly Clyst Fomison)	DEV	SX9792	3,93
Spalding	LIN	TF2422	11,2. 14,97-98. 57,54
Spaldington ER	YKS	SE7533	5E8. 15E3. 21E5. SE,He7
Spaldwick	HUN	TL1272	4,4;5. D19
Spalford	NTT	SK8369	6,4. 9,4
Spanby	LIN	TF0938	26,39. 42,7
Sparham	NFK	TG0719	12,27. 33,1. 56,6
Sparkford	SOM	ST6026	24,18
Sparkwell	DEV	SX7865	2,7-8 notes. 16,162
Sparsholt	BRK	SU3487	1,10. 21,12. 35,5. 55,4
Spaunton NR	YKS	SE7289	8N4. SN,Ma13
Spaxton	SOM	ST2237	35,5
Speccott	DEV	SS5014	36,5
Speen	BRK	SU4668	54,1
Speeton ER	YKS	TA1574	1Y11. 5E50. SE,Hu7
Speke LAN	CHS	SJ4283	R1,16
Spelsbury OXF	OXF	SP3421	EW1
Spelsbury OXF	WAR		3,6
Spennithorne NR	YKS	SE1388	6N102. SN,CtA31
Sperchedene	SSX	??	10,101
Spernall	WAR	SP0862	29,4
Spetchley	WOR	SO8953	2,70
Spettisbury	DOR	ST9102	1,5 note. 26,25. 36,2
Spilsby	LIN	TF4066	3,22-23;26. 14,72
Spitchwick	DEV	SX7072	1,48
Spixworth	NFK	TG2415	26,3
Spofforth WR	YKS	SE3651	13W33. SW,Bu41
Spondon	DBY	SK3935	1,35. 6,67
Spoonley	SHR	SJ6636	4,24,3
Sporle	NFK	TF8411	1,71;79;132;137-138;188;234. 7,17
Spratton	NTH	SP7170	18,88. 30,16. 56,50
Spreacombe	DEV	SS4841	36,13
Spreyton	DEV	SX6996	16,108
Spriddlescombe	DEV	SX6854	15,77
Spriddlestone	DEV	SX5351	15,52
Spridlington	LIN	TF0084	12,42. 26,24-25
Springfield	ESS	TL7108	32,33. 34,29
Springthorpe	LIN	SK8789	1,39;49;64
Sproatley ER	YKS	TA1934	14E1;4;52. CE43. SE,Th13. SE,Hol3;8;26
Sproston	CHS	SJ7367	8,15
Sprotbrough WR	YKS	SE5302	1W20. 10W23. SW,Sf15
Sprowston	NFK	TG2411	1,188. 7,17
Sproxton	LEC	SK8524	24,3. 30,1. 40,41
Sproxton NR	YKS	SE6181	1N77. SN,Ma16
Sprytown	DEV	SX4185	39,2
Spurstow	CHS	SJ5556	2,27
Spurway	DEV	SS8921	3,74. 23,14
Stackhouse WR	YKS	SD8165	30W32
Stadbury	DEV	SX6845	17,63
Staddiscombe	DEV	SX5151	17,89
Staddon (in Plymstock)	DEV	SX4951	17,90
Stafford	DEV	SS5811	40,1
Stafford	DOR	SY7289	26,7. 27,4-5 notes. 55,8. 57,1 note
Stafford STS	BRK		42,1

Stafford STS	STS	SJ9223	B. 4,1. 6,1. 8,9;19. 10,911,7
Stagenhoe	HRT	TL1822	25,1
Stagsden	BDF	SP9849	2,6. 15,3. 23,4. 53,10
Stainborough [Castle] WR	YKS	SE3103	9W79 note. SW,St10
Stainburn WR	YKS	SE2448	1W51. SW,Bu38
Stainby	LIN	SK9022	27,43
Staine Hundred	CAM	—	Appx C
Staines MDX	BKM		7,2
Staines MDX	MDX	TQ0371	4,5. 8,1-2. 17,1. 18,1
Stainfield	LIN	TF0725	42,14. 61,1-2
Stainfield	LIN	TF1173	22,16-17. CS,30
Stainforth (near Settle) WR	YKS	SD8267	30W1;4
Stainforth (near Thorne) WR	YKS	SE6411	12W1;21. CW13
Staining LAN	YKS	SD3436	1L1. See also CHS Y2
Stainland WR	YKS	SE0719	SW,M11 note
[East] Stainley WR	YKS	??	2W8 note. SW,Bu48 note
[North] Stainley WR	YKS	SE2877	2W8. 5W38. SW,Bul4 note. SW,Bu48. SW,H9
[South] Stainley WR	YKS	SE3063	1Y18-19. 2W13. SW, Bu14 note. SW,Bu18. SW,Bu48 note. SW,H3
Stainsby	DBY	SK4565	5,4
Stainsby [Hall] NR	YKS	NZ4615	4N3 note. SN,L37
Stainton (near Lincoln)	LIN	SK9896	1,39;56. 4,15. 16,32. 28,14. 61,10
Stainton WR	YKS	SK5593	10W3;5. SW,Sf3;4
Stainton LAN	YKS	SD2472	1L6. See also CHS Y7
Stainton WES	YKS	SD5285	1L7. See also CHS Y8
Stainton (in Stanghow) NR	YKS	NZ7414	1N6 note. 5N12. 31N8. SN,L15 note
Stainton (near Thornaby on Tees) NR	YKS	NZ4814	4N3. 11N10;12. SN, L15 note. SN,L34
Stainton [by Langworth]	LIN	TF0677	13,24-25
Stainton [le Vale]	LIN	TF1794	22,32. 25,8. 30,17. 40,5
[Little] Stainton WR	YKS	SD8953	1W73 note. 30W25. SW,Cr4
[Market] Stainton	LIN	TF2279	43,3
Staintondale NR	YKS	SE9998	1Y3 note. SN,L15 note. SN,D2
[High] Stakesby NR	YKS	NZ8810	4N1 note. SN,L5
Stalbridge	DOR	ST7317	3,6
Stalham	NFK	TG3725	4,38-39. 9,88;183. 17,56. 65,2
Stalisfield	KEN	TQ9652	5,142
Stallenge [Thorne]	DEV	ST0220	42,14
Stallingborough	LIN	TA1911	2,6-7;25. 4,30. 25,7. 32,1. CN,9-10
Stalmine LAN	YKS	SD3745	1L1. See also CHS Y2
Stambourne	ESS	TL7238	28,11. 90,26;33
[Great] Stambridge	ESS	TQ8990	18,14. 24,27
[Little] Stambridge	ESS	TQ8891	2,9. 90,7
Stamford LIN	LIN	TF0207	S. 27,35. ER1. ENt1
Stamford LIN	NTH		ELc1
Stamford LIN	RUT		R21. ELc1
Stanage (Wales)	SHR	SO3371	5,5
Stancil WR	YKS	SK6095	CW18 note
Stancombe (in Sherford)	DEV	SX7845	17,54
Standen	SSX	TQ3835	10,107
Standen BRK	WIL	SU3266	39,1
Standen (in Chute)	WIL	SU3053	25,7
[Great East and Little East] Standen IOW	HAM	SZ5287	6,20
[West] Standen IOW	HAM	SZ5087	7,3
Standerwick	SOM	ST8150	21,86
Standish	GLS	SO8008	2,10. EvM4

Standlynch	WIL	SU1924	35,1. 37,4. 67,26
Standon	HRT	TL3922	42a,1
Standon	STS	SJ8134	11,15
Standone	DEV	??	34,17
Stane	HEF	??	2,2
Stanestaple	MDX	??	3,28
Stanfelda	SFK	??	5,7;8 note
Stanfield	NFK	TF9320	4,8. 8,70
Stanford	BDF	TL1641	21,9-10. 23,9;48. 25,12. 55,7. 57,9-10
Stanford	NFK	TL8594	9,121. 10,52. 21,12. 23,14. 50,1
Stanford	NTT	SK5422	9,77. 28,1-2
Stanford [Bishop and Regis]	HEF	SO6851	1,9;10c. 10,73
		SO6650	
Stanford [Dingley]	BRK	SU5771	22,9
Stanford [in the Vale]	BRK	SU3493	21,18
Stanford [on Avon] NTH	LEC		23,2;4-6
Stanford [on Avon] NTH	NTH	SP5878	41,3;7.ELe2
Stanford [on Teme]	WOR	SO7065	18,2. 19,5
Stanford [Rivers]	ESS	TL5300	20,43-44
Stanground	HUN	TL2096	7,2
Stanhoe	NFK	TF8036	1,2;16. 2,5. 8,85
Stanion	NTH	SP9186	1,13d. 4,25
Stanley	DBY	SK4140	15,1
Stanley	WIL	ST9572	37,6
Stanley WR	YKS	SE3422	1Y15 note. SW,Ag11
[Kings] Stanley	GLS	SO8103	67,6
[Leonard] Stanley	GLS	SO8003	43,2
Stanley [Pontlarge]	GLS	SO9930	1,33
Stanmer	ESS	TQ7293	57,1
Stanmer	SSX	TQ3409	2,3
Stanmore	WIL	SU1567	29,9
[Great and Little] Stanmore	MDX	TQ1692	8,6. 18,2
		TQ1890	
Stanney	CHS	SJ4174	1,35
Stanningfield	SFK	TL8756	2,5. 14,66. 33,12
Stanninghall	NFK	TG2517	1,232
Stanpit DOR	HAM	SZ1792	23,63-64
Stansfield	SFK	TL7852	14,155. 25,11;78
Stansfield WR	YKS	SD9424	1Y15 note
Stansgate	ESS	TL9305	34,26. 90,12
Stanshope	STS	SK1254	1,52
Stanstead	SFK	TL8449	31,41
Stanstead [Abbots]	HRT	TL3811	25,2. 33,16. 34,23. 42,15. 44,1
Stanstead [Hall]	ESS	TL8228	44,1;4
Stansted (in Bircholt Hundred)	KEN	TR0637	P4
Stansted (in Street Hundred)	KEN	TR0637	P3
Stansted [Mountfitchet]	ESS	TL5124	32,16
Stanswood	HAM	SU4600	1,26
Stanton (near Newhall)	DBY	SK2719	6,21
Stanton	GLS	SP0634	11,7
Stanton	STS	SK1246	1,49
Stanton	SFK	TL9673	6,301. 14,72;78. 76,8
Stanton [by-Bridge]	DBY	SK3727	17,22-23
Stanton [by-Dale]	DBY	SK4638	13,1
Stanton [Drew]	SOM	ST5963	1,28
[Fen]stanton HUN	CAM		23,1;4
[Fen]stanton HUN	HUN	TL3168	21,1
Stanton [Fitzwarren]	WIL	SU1790	67,44
Stanton [Harcourt]	OXF	SP4105	7,3
Stanton [in-Peak]	DBY	SK2464	6,73

Stanton [Lacy]	SHR	SO4978	7,4
Stanton [Long]	SHR	SO5790	4,8,6
Stanton [Long]: see also Holdgate SHR			
Stanton [on–the–Wolds]	NTT	SK6330	4,5-6. 9,86. 10,10. 28,2
Stanton [Prior]	SOM	ST6762	7,3
Stanton [St Bernard]	WIL	SU0962	13,1
Stanton [St Gabriel]	DOR	SY4092	26,62
Stanton [St John]	OXF	SP5709	7,20;30;63
Stanton [St Quintin] and [Lower]	WIL	ST9079	7,5. 48,4
Stanton [St Quintin]		ST9180	
Stanton [under–Bardon]	LEC	SK4610	29,1
Stanton [upon Hine Heath]	SHR	SJ5623	4,3,3
Stantonbury	BKM	SP8441	23,32
Stantune	SHR	SO3194	4,1,35
Stanwardine [in the Fields]	SHR	SJ4124	4,6,2
Stanway	ESS	TL9324	1,19
Stanway and [Wood] Stanway	GLS	SP0632	1,27
		SP0631	
Stanway HEF	HEF	SO4070	ES5
Stanway HEF	SHR		6,12
Stanway (in Rushbury)	SHR	SO5391	4,3,9
Stanwell	MDX	TQ0574	11,1-2
Stanwick NTH	BDF	SP9871	7,1
Stanwick NTH	NTH	SP9871	6,16. EB3
Stanwick NR	YKS	NZ1811	6N1 *note*. 6N8. SN, CtA7;9 *note*
Stanwick, another NR	YKS	NZ1811	6N1 *note*. SN,CtA7;9 *note*
Stapeley	CHS	SJ6749	8,34
Stapenhill STS	DBY		3,5. 14,2
Stapenhill STS	STS	SK2522	ED2;5
Staple [Fitzpaine]	SOM	ST2618	19,26
Stapleford	CAM	TL4751	5,28
Stapleford	CHS	SJ4864	21,1
Stapleford	LEC	SK8118	14,1;4
Stapleford	LIN	SK8857	4,79. 56,9
Stapleford	NTT	SK4837	10,16
Stapleford	WIL	SU0737	67,94
Stapleford [Abbotts]	ESS	TQ5095	11,6. 32,27
Stapleford [Tawney]	ESS	TQ5099	24,59
Staplehill	DEV	SX8273	48,9
Stapleton	LEC	SP4398	6,4. 7,1. 13,9
Stapleton (near Church Pulverbatch)	SHR	SJ4704	4,4,2. 4,27,9
Stapleton NR	YKS	NZ2612	6N1;5. SN,CtA3;8
Stapleton WR	YKS	SE5119	9W50 *note*. SW,O9
Stapleton [Terne] (in Slyne	YKS	??	1L2 *note*. See also CHS Y3
with Hest) LAN			
Staploe Hundred	CAM	—	Appx A
Starbotton WR	YKS	SD9574	30W5
Starcote (Wales)	SHR	SO2198	4,1,36
Starston	NFK	TM2384	1,130;223. 9,167. 14,21. 35,5. 43,3
Startforth NR	YKS	NZ0415	6N18. SN,CtA11
Statenborough	KEN	TR3155	2,39
Stathern	LEC	SK7731	15,16. 29,18
[Great] Staughton	HUN	TL1264	2,2
[Little] Staughton: see Easton BDF			
Staunton (in Corse)	GLS	SO7829	E33 note. EvA53. EvC108
Staunton GLS	GLS	SO5512	E4
Staunton GLS	HEF		1,74
Staunton	NTT	SK8043	1,53. 11,2
Staunton	SOM	SS9744	25,18
Staunton [Harold]	LEC	SK3820	13,67
Staunton [on Arrow]	HEF	SO3760	9,11. 24,8

Staunton [on Wye]	HEF	SO3645	10,55;56 note;57
Staveley	DBY	SK4374	12,2
Staveley WR	YKS	SE3662	28W6. SW,Bu14 *note*
Staverton	DEV	SX7964	2,7
Staverton	GLS	SO8923	20,1
Staverton	NTH	SP5361	18,30. 23,6
Staverton	SFK	TM3550	6,31;187;235;260;273;280
Staverton	WIL	ST8560	67,8
Stawell	SOM	ST3638	8,10
Stawley	SOM	ST0622	35,16
Staxton ER	YKS	TA0179	1Y11. 1E18. SE,Hu8
Staythorpe	NTT	SK7554	18,7
Steane	NTH	SP5539	43,5
Stears	GLS	SO6812	32,8
Stearsby NR	YKS	SE6171	23N27. SN,B26
Steart	SOM	ST5627	19,38
Stebbing	ESS	TL6624	29,2. 34,20
Stebbingford [House]	ESS	TL6722	63,2
Stedcombe	DEV	SY2691	16,169
Stedham	SSX	SU8622	11,10
Steel	SHR	SJ5436	4,7,5
[Great] Steeping	LIN	TF4464	24,48. 38,9
[Little] Steeping	LIN	TF4363	12,40. 14,73
Steeple	DOR	SY9181	28,4
Steeple	ESS	TL9303	1,15. 25,7. 29,3. 90,81
Steeton WR	YKS	SE0344	21W15 *note*
Steeton [Hall] WR	YKS	SE5344	13W7 *note*. 25W1. CW24;27;37. SW,An4-5
Stei(n)torp (in Etton) ER	YKS	??	5E34 *note*. SE,Sn5
Stelling	KEN	TR1448	5,121
Stema(i)nesbi (in Scalby) NR	YKS	??	5N32 *note*. 29N10. SN,D3
Stenbury IOW	HAM	SZ5279	1,W19
Stenigot	LIN	TF2581	14,52
Stenning (in Swineshead)	LIN	TF2340	12,89. 37,6. CK,67
Stenson	DBY	SK3230	6,86-87
Stenwith	LIN	SK8336	58,5. CK,22
Stepney	MDX	TQ3581	3,1-11. 15,1. 16,1
Steppingley	BDF	TL0135	25,2
Stepple	SHR	SO6678	6,8
Sternfield	SFK	TM3961	3,97. 6,131;141. 7,138;143
Stert	WIL	SU0259	27,3
Stetchworth	CAM	TL6458	5,1-2. 14,76. 26,50
Stetchworth	HRT	??	33,12
Stevenage	HRT	TL2426	9,5-6. 28,1
Steventon	BRK	SU4691	1,39
Steventon	HAM	SU5448	69,48
Steventon	SHR	SO5273	4,21,16
Stevington	BDF	SP9853	15,2. 2,8
Stevington [End]	ESS	TL5942	21,12. 35,14. 38,2. 90,85
Stewkley	BKM	SP8526	5,5. 23,29
Stewton	LIN	TF3686	4,73. 27,26. CS,10
Steyning	SSX	TQ1711	5,2. 13,10
Stibbard	NFK	TF9828	1,16. 8,106
Stibbington HUN	HUN	TL0998	7,7. 9,4
Stibbington HUN	NTH		59,1
Stickford	LIN	TF3560	14,78
Stickney	LIN	TF3457	14,76
Stiffkey	NFK	TF9743	1,38;89;91;148. 21,25
Stifford	ESS	TQ6080	9,10. 18,32;34. 75,2
Stildon	WOR	SO7169	21,2
Stillingfleet ER	YKS	SE5940	1E11a. 6W5. 23E11. 24E2. SE,P5

Stillington NR	YKS	SE5867	2N21. SN,B18
Stilton	HUN	TL1689	1,3. 2,7. 19,5
Stiltons [Farm] NR	YKS	SE5984	1N79 *note*. 5N49. SN,Ma18
Stinsford	DOR	SY7191	26,6;12 notes. 52,1. 56,40
Stinton	NFK	TG1125	8,1
Stisted	ESS	TL7924	2,3
Stitchcombe	WIL	SU2269	67,48
Stittenham NR	YKS	SE6767	5N53 *note*. SN,B3
Stixwould	LIN	TF1765	14,55. 27,19. 46,4
Stoborough	DOR	SY9286	26,53
Stoche	HAM	??	68,2
Stochelie	DEV	??	15,2
Stoches	HAM	??	2,14
Stock WR	YKS	SD8649	30W16
Stock [Gaylard]	DOR	ST7212	34,14
[Long]stock	HAM	SU3537	14,4. ?68,2
Stockbridge	HAM	SU3535	32,1
Stockbury	KEN	TQ8461	5,69
Stockerston LEC	LEC	SP8397	C11. 13,15. 40,21
Stockerston LEC	NTT		23,1
Stockingham (in Laughton)	SSX	TQ4912	9,53. 10,94
Stockland DEV	DEV	ST2404	ED2
Stockland DEV	DOR		2 note. 3 note. 12,14
Stockland [Bristol]	SOM	ST2443	21,26. 25,1. 31,1
Stockleigh	DEV	??	15,17-18
Stockleigh (in Highampton)	DEV	SS5104	15,6
Stockleigh (in Meeth)	DEV	SS5409	15,54. 16,37
Stockleigh [English]	DEV	SS8506	15,48
Stockleigh [Pomeroy]	DEV	SS8703	34,31
Stockley	OXF	SP2913	1,6
Stocklinch [Ottersey and St Magdalen]	SOM	ST3817	25,48. 47,14
Stockton	HEF	SO5161	1,10a
Stockton	NFK	TM3894	1,239
Stockton (in Sutton Maddock)	SHR	SO7299	4,23,18
Stockton	WIL	ST9838	2,12
Stockton WR	YKS	SE3345	1W11 *note*. SW,Sk14
Stockton [on Teme]	WOR	SO7167	18,1
Stockton [on the Forest] NR	YKS	SE6556	C24. 6W4. SN,Y3
Stody	NFK	TG0535	1,24. 36,7
Stofalde	LEC	??	27,4
Stogumber	SOM	ST0937	16,2
Stogursey	SOM	ST2042	27,1
Stoke	DBY	SK2179	1,29
Stoke (in Devonport)	DEV	SX4655	28,15
Stoke (in Guildford)	SRY	SU9950	1,3˙
Stoke (in Hartland)	DEV	SS2324	45,3
Stoke (in Holne)	DEV	SX6970	20,12
Stoke	KEN	TQ8275	4,16. 5,92
Stoke	SFK	TM1643	21,15
Stoke [Abbot]	DOR	ST4500	3,9
Stoke [Albany]	NTH	SP8088	1,28. 26,1
Stoke [Ash]	SFK	TM1170	1,86. 6,213;220. 14,122;125;146
Stoke [Bardolph]	NTT	SK6441	12,16
Stoke [Bishop]	GLS	ST5675	3,1. WoA4. WoB15
[Bishop]stoke: see Bishopstoke HAM			
Stoke [Bliss] WOR	HEF		31,6
Stoke [Bliss] WOR	WOR	SO6562	EH4
Stoke [Bruerne]	NTH	SP7449	B29. 50,1
Stoke [by Clare]	SFK	TL7443	25,17;97
Stoke [by Nayland]	SFK	TL9836	27,3

Stoke [by-Stone]	STS	SJ9133	11,9
Stoke [Canon]	DEV	SX9398	2,13
[Chew] Stoke	SOM	ST5561	37,3-4. 47,16
Stoke [d'Abernon]	SRY	TQ1259	19,32-33
Stoke [Doyle]	NTH	TL0286	6a,19
Stoke [Dry] RUT	NTH		5,2. 6,10c
Stoke [Dry] RUT	RUT	SP8596	EN7;9
[East] Stoke	DOR	SY8786	26,52
[East] Stoke	NTT	SK7450	6,3. 11,6. 20,3-4. 21,1
Stoke [Edith]	HEF	SO6040	8,10
Stoke [Ferry]	NFK	TL7099	4,43. 21,4. 31,26;28. 66,37
Stoke [Fleming]	DEV	SX8648	23,22
Stoke [Gifford]	GLS	ST6279	3,1 note. 50,2. WoB15 note
Stoke [Goldington]	BKM	SP8348	5,11. 16,10
Stoke half Hundred	LIN	—	30,25. CK,23
Stoke [Hammond]	BKM	SP8829	43,9
[Harry] Stoke	GLS	ST6278	6,4
Stoke [Holy Cross]	NFK	TG2300	1,107;117;125;205. 9,25;39;160. 12,7. 25,27. 35,3. 48,3-4
[Itchen] Stoke	HAM	SU5532	15,2
Stoke [Lacy]	HEF	SO6249	10,63
[Lark and Lower Lark] Stoke WAR	GLS		12,8. EvO1 note;3;5 note
[Lark and Lower Lark] Stoke WAR	WAR	SP1943	EG6
Stoke [Lyne]	OXF	SP5628	20,5;10.. 29,21
Stoke [Mandeville]	BKM	SP8310	3a,1
Stoke Newington: see [Stoke] Newington MDX			
[North] Stoke	LIN	SK9128	1,12. 30,26
[North] Stoke OXF	BRK		B2
[North] Stoke OXF	OXF	SU6186	35,10. EBe1
[North] Stoke	SSX	TQ0210	11,67
Stoke [on Tern]	SHR	SJ6428	4,8,3;7-8
Stoke [on-Trent]	STS	SJ8745	11,36
Stoke [Orchard]	GLS	SO9228	1,45. 3,7. WoB19
Stoke [Pero]	SOM	SS8743	21,60
Stoke [Poges]	BKM	SU9883	17,6
Stoke [Prior]	HEF	SO5256	1,10a
Stoke [Prior]	WOR	SO9467	2,81
Stoke [Rivers]	DEV	SS6335	21,3
[Rodney] Stoke	SOM	ST4849	5,4
Stoke [St Mary]	SOM	ST2622	2,3. 25,52
Stoke [St Milborough]	SHR	SO5682	3c,9
[Severn] Stoke	WOR	SO8544	8,26 .
[South] Stoke	LIN	SK9227	1,12. 12,91
[South] Stoke	OXF	SU6083	6,1c
[South] Stoke	SSX	TQ0209	11,84
Stoke [Rochford]: see [South] Stoke LIN			
[Stoney] Stoke	SOM	ST7032	19,57
Stoke [Sub Hamdon]	SOM	ST4717	8,39. 19,11;13-14
Stoke [Talmage] OXF: for Scoca, doubtful	BRK	??	B9
Stoke [Trister]	SOM	ST7328	19,63
Stoke [Wake]	DOR	ST7606	19,12
Stoke [Wallis]	DOR	SY3896	33,5-6. 56,44
Stokeham	NTT	SK7876	6,15
Stokeinteignhead	DEV	SX9170	48,3
Stokenbury (in East Peckham)	KEN	TQ6749	3,2. 5,61
Stokerland	SFK	TM3248	6,236
Stokesay	SHR	SO4381	7,5
Stokesby	NFK	TG4310	19,23;28;30;36
Stokesley NR	YKS	NZ5208	29N8. SN,L40

Ston Easton: see Easton SOM

Stondon	BDF	TL1535	8,9. 55,13
Stone	BKM	SP7812	4,1. 18,1
Stone	HAM	SZ4599	69,54
Stone	KEN	TQ5774	4,2
Stone (in Exford)	SOM	SS8638	21,69
Stone (in Mudford)	SOM	ST5518	37,12
Stone	WOR	SO8575	26,7
Stone[bury]	HRT	TL3828	36,13
Stone [Street] (in Hadleigh)	SFK	TM0143	25,112
Stone [Street] (in Rumburgh)	SFK	TM3882	3,2
Stonegrave NR	YKS	SE6577	2N15. 16N1. CN2. SN,Ma21
[North] Stoneham	HAM	SU4317	6,8
[South] Stoneham	HAM	SU4315	3,16
Stonehouse	DEV	SX4654	29,7
Stonehouse	GLS	SO8005	31,1
Stoneleigh	WAR	SP3372	1,4;9. 16,49
Stoneley	CHS	SJ6151	8,41
Stonesby	LEC	SK8224	24,1
Stonesfield	OXF	SP3917	27,4
Stoneton WAR	NTH		27,1
Stoneton WAR	WAR	SP4654	EN4
Stoney [Stanton]	LEC	SP4994	19,2
Stonham [Aspal]	SFK	TM1359	38,6-7;19. 38,25
[Earl and Little] Stonham	SFK	TM1058	1,6;66. 3,59. 6,9. 7,63-64. 8,52;54–
		TM1160	55;63. 14,39. 16,15;22. 25,54.
			34,11. 64,1-2
Stonton [Wyville]	LEC	SP7395	13,56. 40,28
Stoodleigh (near Oakford)	DEV	SS9218	3,77. 34,40
Stoodleigh (in West Buckland)	DEV	SS6532	3,53. 23,4
Stopham	SSX	TQ0218	11,25
Storeton	CHS	SJ3084	25,3
Storkhill ER	YKS	TA0442	2E22 note. SE,Th14
Stormesworth	LEC	SP5880	23,2. 29,8
Storrington	SSX	TQ0814	11,48-49. 13,52
[Bishop's] Stortford	HRT	TL4921	4,22
Stotfold	BDF	TL2136	23,12. 55,9
Stotfold WR	YKS	SE4706	5W18 note. 10W33. SW,Sf28;30
Stottesdon	SHR	SO6782	4,1,30
Stoughton	LEC	SK6402	13,52
Stoughton	SSX	SU8011	11,37
Stoulton	WOR	SO9049	2,3
Stour	DOR	ST7922	19,3;14. 28,1
Stourmouth	KEN	TR2562	2,14
Stourpaine	DOR	ST8609	50,4. 57,19
Stourton	WIL	ST7734	36,2
Stoven	SFK	TM4481	7,22. 31,7
Stow	CAM	TL5260	5,11. 14,66. 29,6. 32,1
Stow	LIN	TF0934	24,92
Stow [Bardolph]	NFK	TF6205	13,7-8. 66,6;8
Stow [Bedon]	NFK	TL9695	1,10;135-136. 8,37;71. 47,1
Stow [Maries]	ESS	TQ8399	30,44;50. 42,5
Stow [on-the-Wold]	GLS	SP1925	12,1. EvO9
Stow [St Mary]	LIN	SK8881	T4. 7,1-5;7;10;13;55;57. 12,41.
			20,3. 24,9. 28,6. 36,5. CN,27.
			CW,10
[West] Stow	SFK	TL8170	14,71
Stowe	BKM	SP6737	4,31
Stowe	LIN	TF1010	8,35-38. 24,34. 27,36. 51,5
[Church] Stowe	NTH	SP6357	46,3
Stowell	GLS	SP0813	2,8

Stowell	SOM	ST6822	5,70
Stowey (in Oare)	SOM	SS8145	30,1
[Nether] Stowey	SOM	ST1839	35,11-12
[Old] Stowey	SOM	SS9538	25,21
Stowford (in Colaton Raleigh)	DEV	SY0687	14,3
Stowford (near Lifton)	DEV	SX4386	42,2
Stowford (in West Down)	DEV	SS5342	3,41
Stowford	OXF	SP5508	1,10
Stowlangtoft	SFK	TL9568	14,77. 25,22
Stowmarket	SFK	TM0458	2,8. 34,6
Stowting	KEN	TR1241	2,25
Stradbroke	SFK	TM2373	6,308. 8,39
Stradishall	SFK	TL7452	25,100
Stradsett	NFK	TF6605	9,232. 13,10
Stramshall	STS	SK0835	17,17
Strangford	HEF	SO5828	29,20
Stratesergum (in Gisburn) WR	YKS	??	13W39 *note*
Stratfield [Mortimer] BRK	BRK	SU6363	46,3. EH1
Stratfield [Mortimer] BRK	HAM		29,16
Stratfield [Saye]	HAM	SU6861	43,5. 44,3. 69,11
Stratfield [Turgis]	HAM	SU6959	23,38
Stratford [St Andrew]	SFK	TM3560	6,48. 45,3
Stratford [St Mary]	SFK	TM0534	27,9
Stratford [Tony]	WIL	SU0926	23,9
Stratford [upon Avon]	WAR	SP2054	3,2
[Water] Stratford	BKM	SP6534	19,7
Stratton	BDF	TL2044	16,7. 32,10. 51,1. 53,17
Stratton	CON	SS2306	5,1,3
Stratton	GLS	SP0103	39,17
Stratton	SFK	TM2438	6,110. 7,119
Stratton [Audley]	OXF	SP6026	28,17
[East and West] Stratton	HAM	SU5439	6,16
		SU5240	
[Lower and Over] Stratton	SOM	ST4415	1,4
		ST4315	
Stratton [on-the-Fosse]	SOM	ST6550	5,43. 8,38
Stratton [St Margaret]	WIL	SU1787	56,1
Stratton [St Mary and St Michael]	NFK	TM1992	4,56. 9,98(5);215; 223. 10,19;46.
		TM2093	14,40. 15,29. 35,15
Stratton [Strawless]	NFK	TG2220	1,57. 10,41. 25,10. 26,2
Streat	SSX	TQ3515	12,40
Streatham	SRY	TQ3071	5,14. 19,11
Streatley	BDF	TL0728	18,2. 23,22. 24,18. 25,3. 57,4
Streatley	BRK	SU5980	38,6
Street	HEF	SO4260	1,5. 10,41
Street	SOM	ST3507	25,6
[Court-at] Street	KEN	TR0935	9,31
Streetly	CAM	TL6148	5,15
Streetthorpe (= Edenthorpe) WR	YKS	??	12W1 *note.* 12W27. CW14
Strefford	SHR	SO4485	4,3,47
Strelley	NTT	SK5042	10,27-28. 30,31
Strensall NR	YKS	SE6360	2N27. SN,B15
Stretcholt	SOM	ST2944	24,3-4
Strete [Ralegh]	DEV	SY0595	34,38
Stretford	HEF	SO4455	19,9
Strethall	ESS	TL4839	10,5
Stretham	CAM	TL5174	5,50. Appx P
Strettington	SSX	SU8807	11,107-109
Stretton	DBY	SK3961	10,7
Stretton (in Stretton Sugwas)	HEF	SO4642	10,24. 29,13
Stretton RUT	LIN		56,11

Stretton RUT	RUT	SK9415	R7. ELc11
Stretton	SHR	SO4593	4,1,27. 4,28,4
Stretton (near Burton)	STS	SK2526	4,4
Stretton (in Penkridge)	STS	SJ8811	11,57
Stretton [Baskerville]	WAR	SP4291	25,1
Stretton [en-le-Field] DBY	DBY	SK3011	6,16. E5
Stretton [en-le-Field] DBY	LEC		14,28. E6
Stretton [Grandison]	HEF	SO6344	15,6;8 note
[Great] Stretton	LEC	SK6500	1,4
Stretton [Hall]	DBY	SK3762	10,8
[Little] Stretton	LEC	SK6600	1,4
Stretton [on-Dunsmore]	WAR	SP4072	12,3
Stretton [on-Fosse]	WAR	SP2238	33,1. 37,8
Stretton Sugwas: see Stretton, Sugwas HEF			
Strickland	SFK	TM3869	1,14. 6,87;98. 7,35;37
Strickland [Roger] WES	YKS	SD4997	1L7 note. See also CHS Y8
Stringston	SOM	ST1742	21,34. 35,4
Stroxton	LIN	SK9031	30,22-23
Strubby (near Langton by Wragby)	LIN	TF1677	4,48. 14,61. 16,13. 40,11
Strubby (near Maltby le Marsh)	LIN	TF4582	4,60. 12,87. 24,67. 25,22
Struestuna/Struustuna	SFK	TM2540	7,88;103;105
Strumpshaw	NFK	TG3407	1,98
Stub [House] WR	YKS	SE3043	1W15 note. SW,Sk15
Stubbington	HAM	SU5503	23,15
Stubham WR	YKS	SE1148	2W4 note. SW,Sk2
Stubhampton	DOR	ST9113	49,6
Stubton	LIN	SK8748	32,26-27. 64,14
Stuchbury	NTH	SP5644	43,8
Studham	BDF	TL0115	26,1
Studland	DOR	SZ0382	26,61
Studley	DOR	SY4094	56,45;47
Studley	WAR	SP0763	28,16. 29,5
Studley [Roger] WR	YKS	SE2970	2W8. SW,Bu47
Studley [Royal] WR	YKS	SE2770	13W22. 28W12. 29W33. SW,Bu21
Studly	ESS	TL8100	1,6. 27,9
[Great and Little] Stukeley	HUN	TL2174	6,1. 19,10. 20,3
		TL2075	
Stuntney	CAM	TL5578	5,48
Stuppington	KEN	TQ9659	5,117
Sturden	GLS	ST6480	6,3 in note
Sturmer	ESS	TL6943	38,6-7
Sturminster [Marshall]	DOR	ST9400	28,2
Sturry	KEN	TR1760	7,7
Sturston	DBY	SK1946	6,56
Sturston	NFK	TL8794	9,120. 22,9. 31,33
Sturthill	DOR	SY5291	16,1 note. 55,19
Sturton	LIN	SE9704	14,28. 26,17. 28,16. 35,16. 41,1. 44,2-3
Sturton [by Stow]	LIN	SK8980	4,3
Sturton [by Stow] Hundred	LIN	—	CW,9
Sturton [Grange] WR	YKS	SE4233	9W4-5. SW,Sk5-6
[Great] Sturton	LIN	TF2176	4,43-44. 43,2-3
Sturton [le Steeple]	NTT	SK7883	1,35. 9,114
[Little] Sturton	LIN	TF2175	3,10-12. 29,1;6-7;15
Sturtune	KEN	??	3,22
Stuston	SFK	TM1377	14,137. 50,1
Stutton	SFK	TM1634	3,83. 32,6. 36,2;10
Stutton WR	YKS	SE4741	13W2. 25W28. CW3. SW,BA4-5
Styrrup	NTT	SK6090	9,57-58
Stytchbrook	STS	SK1111	2,16

Suckley WOR	HEF		1,47. E4;8
Suckley WOR	WOR	SO7251	1,1b. X3. E7
Sudberie	HAM	??	69,13
Sudborough	NTH	SP9682	7,2
Sudbourne	SFK	TM4153	6,143. 21,37;38;*81*. 8,25
Sudbrooke	LIN	TF0375	8,2. 26,4-6
Sudbury	BDF	TL1761	38,1
Sudbury	DBY	SK1632	3,1. 6,30
Sudbury SFK	ESS		23,27. 34,21. 35,5. 40,4
Sudbury SFK	SFK	TL8741	1,97. EE2;4-6
Sudcniton/Sudnicton (in Wistow) ER	YKS	??	5E65 *note*. SE,Ac9
Sudeley	GLS	SP0327	61,1
Sudfelle FLN	CHS	??	FT3,1
Sudtelch	SHR	??	4,14,27
Sudtone (near Little Sturton)	LIN	??	24,21. 29,2-3;15
Suduuale	WOR	??	1,2
Suduuelle (in Swayfield)	LIN	??	31,7-8
Suestone	KEN	??	9,54
Suffield	NFK	TG2331	4,23. 9,149;179;181
Suffield NR	YKS	SE9890	13N13. SN,D8
Sugnall	STS	SJ7930	2,20
Sugwas (in Stretton Sugwas)	HEF	SO4542	2,37
Sugworth	BRK	SP5100	7,11
Sulby	NTH	SP6682	41,7. 47,1c
Sulgrave	NTH	SP5545	43,11
Sulham	BRK	SU6474	29,1. 33,2. 63,3
Sullington	SSX	TQ0913	11,58. 13,12
Sumerlede/Summerlede	LIN	??	4,19. 28,22
Sunbury	MDX	TQ1068	4,6
Sunderland	CHS	SJ7390	27,2
[Old] Sunderlandwick ER	YKS	TA0154	1E5 *note*. 28W26. SE,Dr6
Sundon	BDF	TL0426	18,1
Sundridge	KEN	TQ4854	2,5
Sunningwell	BRK	SP4900	7,11
Suntun (in Barrow in Furness) LAN	YKS	??	1L6 *note*. See also CHS Y7
Sunwood	HAM	SU7519	21,7
Surfleet	LIN	TF2528	61,5
Surland	WAR	??	6,3
Surlingham	NFK	TG3006	1,108. 9,26;40;43;161. 10,31;92. 12,14
Surrendell	WIL	ST8782	41,7
Susacres WR	YKS	SE3061	1Y19. 25W26. 31W3 *note*. SW,Bu18
Sustead	NFK	TG1837	8,131. 9,87;144;146
Sutcombe	DEV	SS3411	3,91
Suthauuic/Sutheuuic (? near Bridge Hewick) WR	YKS	??	2W8 *note*. SW,H1
Sutreworde	DEV	??	23,15
Sutterby	LIN	TF3872	13,5
Sutton	BDF	TL2147	21,7. 53,21-28. 57,3vi;5
Sutton (? in Sutton Courtenay)	BRK		1,13
Sutton	CAM	TL4478	5,63. Appx P
Sutton FLN	CHS	SJ4148	16,2
Sutton (near Middlewich)	CHS	SJ7064	1,33. 14,11
Sutton (in Halberton)	DEV	ST0109	40,6. 41,1
Sutton (in Plymouth)	DEV	SX4854	1,20
Sutton (in Widworthy)	DEV	SY2098	51,10
Sutton	ESS	TQ8889	24,30;35;39. 71,4
Sutton (near Mileham)	NFK	TF9218	21,19
Sutton (near Stalham)	NFK	TG3823	9,13;88
Sutton (in Diddlebury)	SHR	SO5183	4,14,24. 4,21,15

Sutton (near Shrewsbury)	SHR	SJ5010	3c,12
Sutton	SFK	TM3046	3,22. 6,149;155;165;170;178; 184;248;252;254. 21,71. 67,21
Sutton (near Cheam)	SRY	TQ2564	8,3
Sutton (in Shere)	SRY	TQ1045	5,29
Sutton (in Woking)	SRY	TQ0153	28,1
Sutton	SSX	SU9715	11,22
Sutton	WOR	SO8276	1,2
Sutton (near Burghwallis) WR	YKS	SE5512	9W41 *note.* SW,O5
Sutton (near Keighley) WR	YKS	SE0044	1W69
Sutton [Bassett]	NTH	SP7790	30,3. 56,3
Sutton [Bingham]	SOM	ST5411	22,23
[Bishops] Sutton	HAM	SU6031	20,1-2
Sutton [Bonington]	NTT	SK5025	3,1;3. 4,2. 24,2. 30,15;17-18
Sutton [by-Retford]	NTT	SK6884	5,7-8
Sutton [Cheney]	LEC	SK4100	7,1. 13,43
Sutton [Coldfield]	WAR	SP1296	1,7
Sutton [Courtenay]	BRK	SU5093	B1-2. 1,13;37. 7,29
[East] Sutton	KEN	TQ8249	5,73
Sutton [Grange] ER	YKS	SE7970	1E37-38 *note.* 2B18. 15E11. 29E15. SE, Sc1-3
Sutton [Grange] WR	YKS	SE2873	2W8. SW,Bu48
[Great and Little] Sutton	CHS	SJ3775 SJ3777	A10
[Guilden] Sutton	CHS	SJ4468	B5. 2,29
[High] Sutton NR	YKS	SE2082	6N115;118. SN,CtA33 *note.* SN,CtA34
Sutton [Howgrave] NR	YKS	SE3179	3Y9. 6N143. SW,H2;4. SN,CtA33 note. SN, CtA39
Sutton [in-Ashfield]	NTT	SK4959	1,23
Sutton [in-the-Elms]	LEC	SP5293	8,2. 10,7. 19,4
[Kings] Sutton	NTH	SP5036	1,8. 2,6;11. 17,3. 18,37;61-63. 22,6. 23,11
Sutton [le Marsh]	LIN	TF5280	2,19. 12,97. 13,8. 29,14. 68,13-14. CS,17
[Long] Sutton	HAM	SU7347	3,8
[Long] Sutton	LIN	TF4322	CK,70
[Long] Sutton	SOM	ST4625	10,2;6. 21,98
Sutton [Maddock]	SHR	SJ7201	4,23,16
Sutton [Mallet]	SOM	ST3736	8,5
Sutton [Mandeville]	WIL	ST9828	40,1
Sutton [Montis]	SOM	ST6224	19,56
Sutton [on Hull] ER	YKS	TA1132	2E34. 14E1;46. SE, Mid2. SE,Hol1;25
Sutton [on the Forest] NR	YKS	SE5864	1Y1. 1N97-98. SN, B12;20
Sutton [on-the-Hill]	DBY	SK2334	3,1. 6,39
Sutton [on-Trent]	NTT	SK8065	2,4. 9,63;67
Sutton [Passeys]	NTT	SK5339	10,38. 30,55
Sutton [Poyntz]	DOR	SY7083	1,4
Sutton [St Michael and St Nicholas]	HEF	SO5246 SO5345	7,3-4. 29,5
Sutton [Scarsdale]	DBY	SK4468	5,1
Sutton [Scotney]	HAM	SU4639	28,7. 69,1
Sutton [under-Brailes] WAR	GLS		19,2
Sutton [under-Brailes] WAR	WAR	SP2937	EG8
Sutton [under Whitestone Cliffe] NR	YKS	SE4882	23N8 *note.* 23N9
Sutton [upon Derwent] ER	YKS	SE7047	5E44. 13E12. SE,P3-4
Sutton [upon Tern]	SHR	SJ6631	4,7,1
Sutton [Valence]	KEN	TQ8149	5,71
Sutton [Veny]	WIL	ST9041	34,1. 38,1. 56,4
Sutton [Waldron]	DOR	ST8615	40,3

Swaby	LIN	TF3877	13,3
Swaby Hundred	LIN	—	13,8. CS,12
Swadlincote	DBY	SK3019	14,3
Swaffham	NFK	TF8208	4,1;3. 66,63
Swaffham [Bulbeck and Prior]	CAM	TL5562	5,9-10. 14,63-64. 17,2-3. 26,1;53.
		TL5663	29,4. Appx C
Swafield	NFK	TG2833	10,18. 19,35. 36,3
[Low] Swainby NR	YKS	SE3385	6N152 note. SN, CtA42
Swainseat (Swainshead in Over Wyresdale) LAN	YKS	SD5353	1L1 note. See also CHS Y2
Swainsthorpe	NFK	TG2100	9,195. 12,40. 24,7. 48,4
Swainswick	SOM	ST7568	5,38. 47,18
Swalecliffe	KEN	TR1367	5,139
Swallow	LIN	TA1703	2,10. 4,27. 12,15;17. 16,2. 27,6. 36,1. CN,13
Swallowcliffe	WIL	ST9626	13,4. 67,3;13
Swallowfield BRK	BRK	SU7264	1,17;46. 64,2
Swallowfield BRK	HAM		43,4-5
Swampton	HAM	SU4150	29,9
Swanage	DOR	SZ0278	17,1 note. 55,42. 58,3
Swanbourne	BKM	SP8027	1,4. 12,24. 14,20. 17,14. 21,6
Swang	SOM	ST2338	21,29
Swannington	NFK	TG1319	4,32. 25,6
Swanscombe	KEN	TQ6073	5,2
Swanston	NTT	SK8074	1,1
Swanstone	HEF	SO4453	10,53
Swanton (in Bilsington)	KEN	TR0235	9,46
Swanton (in Lydden)	KEN	TR2444	5,193
Swanton	NFK	TM1694	4,56. 9,98;102;213;221;223
Swanton [Abbot]	NFK	TG2626	17,25
Swanton [Morley]	NFK	TG0117	20,7
Swanton [Novers]	NFK	TG0132	10,9
Swarby	LIN	TF0440	48,12. 57,33-34
Swardeston	NFK	TG1902	9,185;194. 12,37. 20,34. 66,85
Swarkeston	DBY	SK3728	1,19. 6,83
Swarling	KEN	TR1252	*2,15*
Swarthorpe (in Ellington in Mashamsire) NR	YKS	SE2083	6N114 note. SN,CtA33
Swathing	NFK	TF9804	1,84;86
Swaton	LIN	TF1337	26,44-45. 37,5. 57,19
Swavesey	CAM	TL3669	14,37;48;55. 21,9. 23,5. 14,37;
Sway	HAM	SZ2798	15,5. NF3,2-3. NF9,45
Swayfield	LIN	SK9922	7,41
Swaythorpe ER	YKS	TA0369	26E9 note. SE,Bt7
Swefling	SFK	TM3463	3,100;104. 6,46. 7,147
Swell	SOM	ST3623	19,15
[Lower] Swell	GLS	SP1725	31,12. 45,6. EvN12
[Upper] Swell	GLS	SP1726	12,5. EvK133. EvM65
Swepstone	LEC	SK3610	14,23
Swerford	OXF	SP3731	59,20
Swetton WR	YKS	SE1973	28W18. SW,Bu24
Swilland	SFK	TM1852	41,2
Swillington WR	YKS	SE3830	9W1 note. 9W3. SW, Sk4-5
Swimbridge	DEV	SS6229	13a,2
Swinbrook	OXF	SP2812	58,15
Swinden WR	YKS	SD8654	13W44
Swinderby	LIN	SK8663	56,16. 67,25
Swindon	GLS	SO9324	2,5
Swindon	WIL	SU1584	1,3. 4,3. 26,8. 67,69;74. 68,25
Swine	LIN	TF3998	CS,39
Swine ER	YKS	TA1335	2A2. SE,Th12

Swineshead BDF	BDF	TL0565	E6-8
Swineshead BDF	HUN		13,3. 19,11. D14
Swinford	LEC	SP5779	3,10. 8,4. 10,10. 13,25. 17,7;11. 29,9
[Kings] Swinford: see Kingswinford WOR			
[Old] Swinford	WOR	SO9083	23,11
Swinhope	LIN	TF2196	12,33. 32,10. 48,4
Swinstead	LIN	TF0122	7,42. 31,8. 35,12. 56,3. 68,17
Swinthorpe (near Snelland)	LIN	TF0680	1,37. 2,12. 28,27
Swinton WR	YKS	SK4599	10W17. 21W2. SW,Sf10;27
Swinton (near Malton) NR	YKS	SE7573	1N68. SN,Ma7
Swinton (near Masham) NR	YKS	SE2179	6N118. SN,CtA34
Swynchurch	STS	SJ8037	2,20
Swyncombe	OXF	SU6890	35,33
Swynnerton	STS	SJ8535	11,18
Swyre	DOR	SY5288	34,8
Syde	GLS	SO9410	68,10
Sydeham	DEV	SS8719	24,7
Sydenham (in Marystowe)	DEV	SX4283	17,8
Sydenham	OXF	SP7301	59,2
Sydenham	SOM	ST3137	22,16
Sydenham [Damerel]	DEV	SX4076	17,14
Syderstone	NFK	TF8332	4,17. 8,108-109
Sydling [St Nicholas]	DOR	SY6399	12,1. 17,1 note. 26,26-27
Sydmonton	HAM	SU4857	15,3
Syerscote	STS	SK2207	11,48
Syerston	NTT	SK7447	2,3. 6,3. 21,2. 30,40
Syleham	SFK	TM2078	19,1. 44,2
Symonds [Hall]	GLS	ST7996	1,15
Symondsbury	DOR	SY4493	11,17
Syndercombe	SOM	ST0330	36,4
Syresham	NTH	SP6241	18,40. 21,1. 43,10
Sysonby	LEC	SK7319	29,3;17. 40,14
Syston	LEC	SK6211	13,60
Syston	LIN	SK9340	14,91. 39,3. CK,57
Sywell	NTH	SP8267	18,1

T

[Nether] Tabley	CHS	SJ7278	19,3
[Over] Tabley	CHS	SJ7280	9,14
[Bishop's] Tachbrook	WAR	SP3161	2,3
Tachbrook [Mallory]	WAR	SP3162	16,58
Tackbear DEV	CON		5,24,18
Tackbear DEV	DEV	SS2501	EC2
Tackley	OXF	SP4720	15,3
Tacolneston	NFK	TM1495	1,237. 9,224
Tadcaster WR	YKS	SE4843	13W1. CW3;5. SW,BA12
Taddington	DBY	SK1471	1,28
Taddington	GLS	SP0831	1,28
Tadlow	CAM	TL2847	32,7. 41,9. 42,1
Tadmarton	OXF	SP3937	9,9a
Tadwick	SOM	ST7470	45,7-8
Tadworth	SRY	TQ2356	5,21. 20,1
Takeley	ESS	TL5521	14,3. 25,15. 32,17
Talaton	DEV	SY0699	2,14
Tale	DEV	ST0601	34,21-22
Talke	STS	SJ8253	17,14
Tallington	LIN	TF0907	18,12. 27,38-39. CK,1
Tamerlande	DEV	??	35,5
Tamerton [Foliot]	DEV	SX4760	39,19
[Kings] Tamerton	DEV	SX4558	1,21
Tamhorn	STS	SK1807	2,22
Tamworth STS	STS	SK2004	1,9;30
Tamworth STS	WAR		1,5
Tandridge	SRY	TQ3750	19,4
[East] Tanfield NR	YKS	SE2877	5W38 *note*. 6N139 SW,H9. SN,CtA38
[West] Tanfield NR	YKS	SE2678	6N140. SN,CtA39
Tangmere	SSX	SU9006	2,6
Tankersley WR	YKS	SK3499	5W33. SW,St9
Tannington	SFK	TM2467	6,304
Tanshelf WR	YKS	SE4522	9W64 *note*. 9W78-84;96. SW,O15
Tansley	DBY	SK3259	1,12. 10,12
Tansor	NTH	TL0591	1,24-25
Tansterne ER	YKS	TA2237	14E2 *note*. ŚE,Hol5
Tanton NR	YKS	NZ5210	1N30. 5N28. 29N9. 31N5. SN,L37-38
Tapeley	DEV	SS4729	3,92
Taplow	BKM	SU9182	4,15
Tapps	DEV	SS8923	16,150
Tapton	DBY	SK3972	1,1. 17,8
Tarbock LAN	CHS	SJ4687	R1,13
Tardebigge	WOR	SO9969	1,4-5
Tarlton	GLS	ST9599	31,8. 44,1
Tarnock	SOM	ST3752	24,12-13
Tarporley	CHS	SJ5562	17,3
Tarrant [Crawford]	DOR	ST9203	6,1
Tarrant [Gunville, Rawston and Rushton]	DOR	ST9212 ST9306 ST9305	1,24-26 *note*;31. 49,5 *note*. 54,9 *note*. 55,25 *note*;29-30
Tarrant [Hinton]	DOR	ST9311	19,8

Tarrant [Keyneston]	DOR	ST9204	6,3
Tarrant [Launceston]	DOR	ST9409	21,1
Tarrant [Monkton]	DOR	ST9408	10,6
Tarring [Neville]	SSX	TQ4403	10,43;107
[West] Tarring	SSX	TQ1304	2,9-10
Tarrington and [Little] Tarrington	HEF	SO6140	10,36. 21,1
		SO6241	
Tarvin	CHS	SJ4867	B4
Tasburgh	NFK	TM2095	4,56. 9,219;227. 11,4-5. 19,39
Tatchbury	HAM	SU3314	6,10
Tatebi (in Ulceby)	LIN	??	2,20
Tatham LAN	YKS	SD6069	1L5. See also CHS Y6
Tathwell	LIN	TF3282	13,28-29. 38,12
Tathwell Hundred	LIN	—	CS,1-3
Tatsfield	SRY	TQ4157	5,4
Tattenhall	CHS	SJ4858	8,1
Tatterford	NFK	TF8628	40,1
Tattersett	NFK	TF8529	8,110
Tattershall	LIN	TF2157	29,33
Tattingstone	SFK	TM1337	16,46. 36,9;12
Tattiscombe	DEV	SS6346	15,56
Tatton	CHS	SJ7481	9,11. 20,3
Tatton	DOR	SY6382	49,10. 55,23
Taunton	SOM	ST2224	2,1-5;8-9. 19,40
Taverham	NFK	TG1613	1,55. 4,33. 8,7. 10,36. 10a,1. 20,27
Tavistock	DEV	SX4874	5,1
[Mary] Tavy	DEV	SX5079	17,13
[Peter] Tavy	DEV	SX5177	39,21
Taw [Green]	DEV	SX6597	51,2
Tawstock	DEV	SS5529	1,40;67
[Bishops] Tawton	DEV	SS5630	2,11
[North] Tawton	DEV	SS6601	1,3. 16,56
[South] Tawton	DEV	SX6594	1,29. 43,1. 45,1. 51,2
Taynton	GLS	SO7321	34,10
Taynton	OXF	SP2313	B8. 13,1
[Little] Taynton	GLS	SO7423	37,4
Tealby	LIN	TF1590	4,41. 14,10. 16,10-11. 27,11. 28,20-21. 35,9-10. 40,14
Tealby Hundred	LIN	—	CN,18
Tean	STS	SK0139	11,2
Tedburn [St Mary]	DEV	SX8194	16,119-120. 19,30
Teddington GLS	GLS	SO9633	E19. EvA104. EvC23. WoB5. WoC4
Teddington GLS	WOR		2,23
Tedstone [Delamere and Wafre]	HEF	SO6958	2,3. 10,68
		SO6759	
Teeton	NTH	SP6970	35,18
Teffont [Evias]	WIL	ST9931	26,3
Tehidy	CON	SW6444	5,1,12
Teigh	RUT	SK8616	R10
[George] Teign	DEV	SX8583	16,59
Teigncombe	DEV	SX6787	3,66
Teigngrace	DEV	SX8473	16,153
Teignharvey	DEV	SX9172	16,117
Teignton: see Bishopsteignton, Drewsteignton, Kingsteignton DEV			
Tellisford	SOM	ST8055	5,53
Tempsford	BDF	TL1653	4,6. 21,4-5. 39,2. 57,3iii
Tenbury [Wells]	WOR	SO5968	6,1. 19,2
Tendring	ESS	TM1424	4,5. 20,64;70. 32,38a. 34,32. 68,7

Terling	ESS	TL7714	1,2 note. 34,6. 90,10. B3q
Termentuna	NFK	??	49,8 note
Terrington NR	YKS	SE6770	5N54-55. 6N162. 8N20. SN,B5-6
Terrington [St Clement and St John]	NFK	TF5520	13,12. 31,31
		TF5315	
Tessall (in Kings Norton) WAR	WAR	SP0078	EBW1
Tessall (in Kings Norton) WAR	WOR		1,1a
Testerton	NFK	TF9326	34,10
Teston	KEN	TQ7053	5,99
Tetbury	GLS	ST8993	41,2
Tetchwick	BKM	SP6718	16,3
Tetcott	DEV	SX3396	17,17
Tetford	LIN	TF3374	2,21-22. 13,9. 28,35
Tetney	LIN	TA3101	14,1-4
Tetstill	SHR	SO6671	5,2
Tettenhall	STS	SJ8900	1,2-3. 7,5
Tetton	CHS	SJ7163	20,12
Tetton	SOM	ST2030	18,1
Teulesberge	WOR	??	1,2
Teversal	NTT	SK4861	13,8
Teversham	CAM	TL4958	5,13. 14,3-4. 35,2. Appx E
[Duns] Tew	OXF	SP4528	7,43. 8,2. 27,5. 28,29
[Great] Tew	OXF	SP3929	7,4
[Little] Tew	OXF	SP3828	7,38;44;62. 8,1
Tewin	HRT	TL2714	36,19. Appx
Tewin (= Queen's Hoo)	HRT	TL2716	9,6
Tewkesbury GLS	GLS	SO8932	1,24-6;34-5;37-9
Tewkesbury GLS	WAR		EG2
[Great and Little] Tey	ESS	TL8925	20,36
		TL8923	
[Marks] Tey	ESS	TL9123	30,1
Teynham	KEN	TQ9663	*2,37*
Thakeham	SSX	TQ1117	13,49
Thame	OXF	SP7006	6,2;10
Thanington	KEN	TR1356	*2,16*
Tharlesthorpe (lost off Patrington) ER	YKS	??	2A1 *note*. SE,Th12
Tharston	NFK	TM1994	9,98(5);99. 35,14
Thatcham	BRK	SU5167	1,2
Thaxted	ESS	TL6131	23,2
Theakston NR	YKS	SE3085	6N151. SN,CtA41
Thealby	LIN	SE8918	1,64. 13,15. 30,4-5. 32,18
Thealby Hundred	LIN	—	CW,19
Theberton	SFK	TM4365	6,109
Theddingworth	LEC	SP6685	10,12-13. 27,2. 40,31. 43,5
Theddlethorpe	LIN	TF4688	12,95. 13,7. 27,62. 68,12
Theddlethorpe Hundred	LIN	—	CS,15
Thelbridge	DEV	SS7812	3,80
Thelnetham	SFK	TM0178	6,300. 12,1. 14,90
Thelveton	NFK	TM1681	7,9;13. 15,26. 52,4
Thenford	NTH	SP5141	28,2. 54,1
Theobald [Street]	HRT	TQ1897	5,2. 9,2-3. 10,13. 33,1. 34,2
Theodoric's Land	SOM	??	21,30
Therfield	HRT	TL3337	11,1. 37,7. Appx
Thetford	NFK	TL8782	1,69;70;210-211. 9,1
[Little] Thetford	CAM	TL5376	5,49
Theydon [Bois, Garnon and Mount]	ESS	TQ4499	24,60. 25,18. 36,11. 74,1
		TQ4799	
		TQ4799	
Thiccebrom	SFK	??	6,295
Thickenappletree/Fickenappletree	WOR	??	27,1
Thickwood	WIL	ST8272	24,30

Thimbleby	LIN	TF2470	1,92. 4,52. 30,18
Thimbleby NR	YKS	SE4595	1Y2. SN,A1
Thinghill	HEF	SO5644	6,4. 7,6
Thingwall	CHS	SJ2784	8,9
Thirkleby NR	YKS	SE4778	23N1
Thirkleby [Manor] ER	YKS	SE9268	2B18 note. 15E15. SE,Th5 note
Thirkleby [Manor], another ER	YKS	SE9268	2B18 note. 5E68. SE,Th5 note
Thirley [Cotes] NR	YKS	SE9795	1Y3. SN,D2
Thirn NR	YKS	SE2185	6N129. SN,CtA37
Thirnby [Wood] LAN	YKS	SD6177	1L3 note. See also CHS Y4
Thirsk NR	YKS	SE4282	1N112. 23N5. SN,Bi6
Thirtleby ER	YKS	TA1734	14E6. SE,Hol11
Thistleton RUT	LIN		27,47-49. 51,10. 56,12;21
Thistleton RUT	RUT	SK9118	R8-9. ELc6-9;12;17
Thistleton	SFK	TM2352	8,9. 21,58. 67,16
Thixendale ER	YKS	SE8461	5E67. 26E5-6. SE, Ac11
Tholthorpe NR	YKS	SE4766	2N25. SN,B24
Thomley	OXF	SP6308	7,31. 35,15
Thompson	NFK	TL9296	8,53. 9,125. 47,1. 51,7. 66,73
[Upper]thong: see Upperthong YKS			
Thonock (near Gainsborough)	LIN	SK8292	16,23
Thoralby NR	YKS	SE0086	6N84. SN,CtA26
Thoralby [Hall] ER	YKS	SE7758	29E20 note. SE,Ac6
Thoraldby [Farm] NR	YKS	NZ4907	1N33 note. 29N9. SN,L39
Thorent (in Henstridge)	SOM	ST7019	4,1
Thoresby	NTT	SK6371	1,24
Thoresby NR	YKS	SE0390	6N89 note. 6N92. SN,B22 note. SN,CtA27-28
[North] Thoresby	LIN	TF2998	4,24;42. 12,38. 25,12. 27,16. 44,6
[South] Thoresby	LIN	TF4077	13,3
Thoresthorpe	LIN	TF4677	25,24
Thoresway	LIN	TF1696	14,14. 27,10
Thorganby	LIN	TF2097	3,7. 4,75. 14,12. 18,9. 32,7. 47,5. 48,9. 49,3
Thorganby ER	YKS	SE6841	16E1-2. SE,How11
Thorington (near Dunwich)	SFK	TM4274	3,5. 7,38. 26,14. 32,19
Thorington (near Stoke by Nayland)	SFK	TM0135	40,6
Thorlby WR	YKS	SD9652	1W73. SW,Cr2
Thorley IOW	HAM	SZ3788	9,2
Thorley	HRT	TL4719	4,23. 33,18-19
Thorley	LIN	TF1573	14,57
Thormanby NR	YKS	SE4974	1Y1. 11N11 note. 11N16. SN,Bi1
Thorn [Hill]	DOR	SU0304	56,18
Thornaby NR	YKS	NZ4517	1N21. 4N3. 11N11 note. 31N5. SN,L36
Thornage	NFK	TG0436	10,7-8
Thornborough	BKM	SP7433	43,7
Thornborough WR	YKS	SE4258	28W5. SW,Bu5
Thornbury (in Drewsteignton)	DEV	SX7093	15,59
Thornbury (near Holsworthy)	DEV	SS4008	5,5
Thornbury	GLS	ST6390	1,47
Thornbury	HEF	SO6259	20,1-2
Thornbury (Wales): see [The] Gaer SHR			
Thornby	NTH	SP6675	35,19b;20
Thorncombe DOR	DEV		16,165
Thorncombe DOR	DOR	ST3703	ED1
Thorncroft	SRY	TQ1655	19,39
Thorndon	SFK	TM1469	6,223. 14,128;143
Thorne	CON	SX2799	5,5,8
Thorne (in Holsworthy Hamlets)	DEV	SS3005	3,88
Thorne	DOR	SY9978	55,44-45

Thorne WR	YKS	SE6813	12W1;24
Thorne: see Stallenge [Thorne] DEV			
Thorne [Coffin]	SOM	ST5217	19,77-78
Thorne [St Margaret]	SOM	ST0921	21,73
Thorner WR	YKS	SE3740	9W12. CW1. SW,Sk8
Thorney	CAM	TF2604	8,1
Thorney	NTT	SK8572	6,4
Thorney	SOM	ST4223	9,1
Thorney	SFK	TM0558	1,1;65. 8,51;54. 29,1. 31,44;49;53. 67,1
[West] Thorney	SSX	SU7602	6,1
Thornfalcon	SOM	ST2823	19,31
Thornford	DOR	ST6013	3,3
Thorngumbald ER	YKS	TA2026	14E1. SE,Hol3
Thornham	NFK	TF7343	10,3
Thornham [Magna]	SFK	TM1071	1,81. 6,200;214– 21514,127;130;147. 35,7. 62,5
Thornham [Parva]	SFK	TM1072	6,199;218
Thornhill	WIL	SU0778	29,5. 68,22
Thornhill WR	YKS	SE2518	9W115. SW,Ag5
Thornholme ER	YKS	TA1163	1Y14. 31E1. SE,Bt4
Thornicombe	DOR	ST8703	56,15
Thornsett	DBY	SK0187	1,30
Thornthorpe ER	YKS	SE7867	31E7 note
Thornton	BKM	SP7535	41,6
Thornton (near Liverpool) LAN	CHS	SD3442	R1,11
Thornton	DOR	ST8018	34,1
Thornton (near Horncastle)	LIN	TF2467	38,1
Thornton ER	YKS	SE7545	15E9. SE,C10
Thornton NR	YKS	NZ4713	4N3. 11N12. SN,L34 note
Thornton WR	YKS	SE1032	9W131;144. SW,M7
Thornton (in Cowling) NR	YKS	??	6N128 note. SN, CtA36
[Bishop] Thornton WR·	YKS	SE2663	2W7. SW,Bu46
Thornton [Bridge] NR	YKS	SE4371	28W32 note. SW,H6
Thornton [Curtis]	LIN	TA0817	34,5. 36,2
Thornton [Dale] NR	YKS	SE8383	1Y4. 1N48. 8N15. 31N8. SN,L34 note. SN,D15-16
Thornton [Fields] NR	YKS	NZ6118	1N11. SN,L20
Thornton [Hough]	CHS	SJ3080	3,4
Thornton [in Craven] WR	YKS	SD9048	13W43. 30W19
Thornton [in Lonsdale] WR	YKS	SD6873	1W72
Thornton [le-Beans] NR	YKS	SE3990	1Y2. SN,A1
Thornton [le-Clay] NR	YKS	SE6865	5N61. 6N162. 11N15. SN,B9-10 note
Thornton [le Fylde] LAN	YKS	SD3342	1L1. See also CHS Y2
Thornton [le Moor]	LIN	TF0596	16,5-6. 22,5-6
Thornton [le-Moor] NR	YKS	SE3888	11N20. SN,A9
Thornton [le-Moors]	CHS	SJ4474	14;3
Thornton [le Street] NR	YKS	SE4186	1Y2. SN,B9 note. SN, A1
Thornton [Riseborough] NR	YKS	SE7482	1N58 note. SN,Ma1
Thornton [Rust] NR	YKS	SD9788	6N81. SN,CtA26
Thornton [Steward] NR	YKS	SE1787	6N110;112. SN,CtA32
Thornton [Watlass] NR	YKS	SE2385	6N125 note. SN, CtA36
Thornton [Watlass]: see also [Thornton] Watlass YKS			
[Old] Thornville [Hall]: see *[Little] Cattal* YKS			
Thoroton	NTT	SK7642	1,54. 20,2
Thorp [Arch] WR	YKS	SE4346	25W8. SW,Sf37 note. SW,An8
Thorp [Perrow] NR	YKS	SE2685	6N127 note. SN,B20 note. SN,CtA36

Thorpe	DBY	SK1550	1,14
Thorpe (in Shipdham)	NFK	TF9708	15,17;21
Thorpe NTH: see Long[thorpe] NTH			
Thorpe (in Aldringham)	SFK	TM4560	6,136
Thorpe (in Dallinghoo)	SFK	TM2755	32,21
Thorpe (near Heveningham)	SFK	TM3473	3,8. 7,16;26
Thorpe (in Trimley)	SFK	TM2537	2,18. 7,104;116
Thorpe	SRY	TQ0268	8,19
Thorpe (near Hebden) WR	YKS	SE0161	25W32. 29W42 *note*
Thorpe: see also *Torp, Torpe* SFK			
Thorpe [Abbots]	NFK	TM2079	1,225-226, 14,18
Thorpe [Acre]	LEC	SK5120	C15. 1,8
Thorpe [Arnold]	LEC	SK7720	13,70-71
[Ashwell]thorpe	NFK	TM1497	5,6
Thorpe [Audlin] WR	YKS	SE4815	9W46. SW,Sf37 note. SW,O6
[Bacons]thorpe (near Holt)	NFK	TG1236	9,177. 33,12
Thorpe [Bassett] ER	YKS	SE8573	1E45. SE,Bt4 note. SE,Sc9
[Bassing]thorpe	LIN	SK9628	14,95
[Busling]thorpe	LIN	TF0885	18,3
Thorpe [by Water] RUT	NTH		1,2c. 56,36
Thorpe [by Water] RUT	RUT	SP8996	EN2;20
Thorpe [by-Newark]	NTT	SK7650	14,7
[Calce]thorpe	LIN	TF2488	27,30-31
[Cock] Thorpe	NFK	TF9842	10,12;62
Thorpe [Constantine]	STS	SK2608	16,1
[Culver]thorpe	LIN	TF0240	24,37-38
[East] Thorpe	LIN	TF1347	1,3. 24,38. 26,26. 45,4. CK,30
[Ewerby] Thorpe: see [East] Thorpe LIN			
[Fyling] Thorpe NR	YKS	NZ9405	4N1 *note*. SN,L1
[Gayton] Thorpe	NFK	TF7418	2,1. 9,3. 13,16. 22,17. 66,22
Thorpe [Hall] (in Ashfield)	SFK	TM2062	4,6-7. 6,12;21;23;25. 14,40. 21,34
Thorpe [Hall] (near Rudston) ER	YKS	TA1168	SE,Bt4 *note*
Thorpe [Hall] (near Wycliffe) NR	YKS	NZ1014	6N1 *note*. SN,B20 note. SN,CtA5
Thorpe [Hesley] WR	YKS	SK3796	SW,Sk10 note. SW, Sf16-17 *note*
Thorpe [Hill] WR	YKS	SE4559	28W4. SW,Sf37 note. SW,Bu1-2
Thorpe [Hill] (in Sand Hutton near York) NR	YKS	SE7159	23N29
Thorpe [Hill] (in Sutton on the Forest) NR	ẎKS	SE5964	1Y1 *note*. SN,B20 *note*
Thorpe [Hill]: see Welwick [Thorpe] YKS			
[Honingham] Thorpe	NFK	TG1111	4,9
[Nor]thorpe Hundred	LIN	—	CW,14-15
[Ingoldis] Thorpe: see Ingoldisthorpe NFK			
Thorpe [in-the-Glebe]	NTT	SK6025	1,60. 9,91. 30,26
[Ixworth] Thorpe	SFK	TL9172	9,2. 14,91;101. 37,2. 59,1. 75,1
[Kettle]thorpe: see Kettlethorpe YKS			
[Kettleby] *Thorpe*	LIN	TA0407	25,13
[Kilton] Thorpe NR	YKS	NZ6917	1N8. 5N15. SN,L16 *note*
[Lang]thorpe: see Langthorpe YKS			
Thorpe [le Fallows]	LIN	SK9180	24,6-7. 68,27-28
Thorpe [le Street] ER	YKS	SE8344	1Y7 note. 21E12. CE28. SE,P3
Thorpe [le Willows] NR	YKS	SE5776	1N108 *note*. SN,B20 note. SN,Bi2
Thorpe [Lidget] ER	YKS	SE7629	3Y4. SE,C4 note. SE, How4
[Little] Thorpe	LEC	SP5496	10,14
[Long]thorpe	NTH	TL1698	6,3
Thorpe [Lubenham]	NTH	SP7086	23,2
Thorpe [Malsor]	NTH	SP8379	18,76
Thorpe [Mandeville]	NTH	SP5344	43,7

Thorpe [Market]	NFK	TG2435	8,122;128. 33,5
[Middle]thorpe: see Middlethorpe YKS			
[Mins]thorpe: see Minsthorpe YKS			
[Moor]thorpe: see Moorthorpe YKS			
Thorpe [Morieux]	SFK	TL9453	8,35. 14,115-116
[Morning] Thorpe	NFK	TM2192	4,56. 14,40
[Nor]thorpe	LIN	SK8997	1,39;53. 4,13. 8,16. 16,22;25;27
[Nor]thorpe: see Northorpe YKS			
[Nun]thorpe: see Nunthorpe YKS			
Thorpe [on the Hill]	LIN	SK9065	1,27. 9,2. CK,28
Thorpe [on the Hill] WR	YKS	SE3126	9W119. SW,Sf37 note. SW,M2
[Ouse]thorpe [Farm]: see Ousethorpe [Farm] YKS			
[Pains]thorpe: see Painsthorpe YKS			
[Palla]thorpe: see Pallathorpe YKS			
Thorpe [Parva]	NFK	TM1679	7,9
[Pinchin]thorpe [Hall]: see Pinchinthorpe [Hall] YKS			
[Pock]thorpe: see Pockthorpe YKS			
[Rais]thorpe: see Raisthorpe YKS			
Thorpe [St Andrew]	NFK	TG2709	1,63;216;218;233-234;236. 66,94
Thorpe [St Peter]	LIN	TF4860	3,22-23. 14,74
Thorpe [Salvin] WR	YKS	SK5281	10W1. SW,Sk10 note. SW,Sf2
[Scaggle]thorpe: see Scagglethorpe YKS			
[Scaw]thorpe: see Scawthorpe YKS			
[Scotton] Thorpe (in Scotton) WR	YKS	??	29W19 note. 31W3. SW,Bu15 note
[Shipton]thorpe: see Shiptonthorpe YKS			
[Shouldham] Thorpe	NFK	TF6607	21,8. 31,23 note. 66,14
[Sou]thorpe: see Southorpe YKS			
[South]thorpe	LIN	SK8895	16,25
Thorpe [Stapleton] WR	YKS	SE3430	9W17 note. SW,Sk10 note
[Tattershall] Thorpe	LIN	TF2159	3,15;42. 4,55. 29,8;28;34
[Thol]thorpe: see Tholthorpe YKS			
[Thorn]thorpe: see Thornthorpe YKS			
[Tib]thorpe: see Tibthorpe YKS			
[Tow]thorpe: see Towthorpe YKS			
Thorpe [Underwood] WR	YKS	SE4659	16W6 note. SW,Bu1
[Welwick] Thorpe (near Thorpe Hill) ER	YKS	??	2A1 note. SE,Bt4 note. SE,Th11
Thorpe [Willoughby] WR	YKS	SE5731	9W20. SW,Sk10 note. SW,BA5
[Wood]thorpe	LIN	TF4380	25,21
Thorpefield (in Irton) NR	YKS	??	13N10 note. SN,L16 note. SN,D6
Thorpefield (in Sowerby) NR	YKS	SE4279	23N6 note
Thorpehall	ESS	TQ9185	37,10
Thorpland	NFK	TF6108	13,6. 14,3. 66,5
Thorpland	NFK	TF9332	1,16
Thorrington	ESS	TM0919	18,43
Thorstanestuna: see Turstanestuna SFK			
Thrandeston	SFK	TM1176	6,66-67;202;204. 8,30. 14,139;150. 18,6. 19,19. 35,7. 50,2
Thrapston	NTH	SP9978	4,24. 52,1
Threekingham	LIN	TF0836	3,55-56. 10,4. 24,91. 26,42. 48,7. 57,40. 67,11
Threlfall (in Goosnargh) LAN	CHS	SD5541	Y2. See also YKS 1L1 note
Threfall (in Goosnargh): see also Threfall's [Farm] LAN			
Threlfall's [Farm] (in Broughton) LAN for Threlfall (in Goosnargh) LAN	CHS	SD5335	Y2. See also 1L1 note
Threshfield WR	YKS	SD9863	1W57. 21W15
Threxton	NFK	TF8800	8,50. 21,18
Thrigby	NFK	TG4612	1,204. 9,89. 10,45. 19,37

Thringstone	DBY	SK4217	1,22. 14,11
Thringstone	LEC	SK4217	E2;11
Thrintoft NR	YKS	SE3293	6N27. SN,CtA13
Thriplow	CAM	TL4446	5,20-22. 22,3. 26,56-57. Appx H
Thriplow Hundred	CAM	—	Appx H
Throapham WR	YKS	SK5286	10W1. SW,Sf2
Throcking	HRT	TL3330	4,1. 5,22. 17,5. 37,16
Througham	GLS	SO9207	28,2
Througham	HAM	SZ3997	NF2,2. NF3,7. NF6,2. NF9,21-22
Throwleigh	DEV	SX6690	32,4
Throwley	KEN	TQ9955	D18. 5,155
Thrumpton	NTT	SK5131	9,79. 10,4. 23,2
Thrunscoe	LIN	TA3107	2,7. 4,33;71. 14,6
Thrupp	OXF	SP4715	29,16
Thrupp [Grounds]	NTH	SP6065	18,67. 23,7. 48,10. 56,35
Thrushelton	DEV	SX4487	17,3
Thrussington	LEC	SK6415	23,1
Thruxton	HEF	SO4334	22,7
Thruxton *[Anne]*	HAM	SU2945	61,1
Thrybergh WR	YKS	SK4695	13W10. SW,Sf26
Thuborough	DEV	SS3410	28,4
Thulston	DBY	SK4132	6,81. 9,1
Thunderley [Hall]	ESS	TL5536	35,3
Thundersley	ESS	TQ7888	24,16
Thundridge	HRT	TL3617	5,26
Thurcaston	LEC	SK5610	C11. 13,19. 29,1;15;20
Thur(e)stuna	NFK	??	1,86 *note*. 8,84. 9,134. 15,12
Thurgarton	NFK	TG1835	9,87;152. 17,5
Thurgarton	NTT	SK6949	11,12
Thurgoland WR	YKS	SE2900	9W78. SW,St10
Thurketeliart (in Aldeby)	NFK	??	20,36
Thurlaston	LEC	SP5099	13,27-28
Thurlaston	WAR	SP4671	16,33. 18,8
Thurlbear	SOM	ST2621	19,30
Thurlby (near Cumberworth)	LIN	TF4975	13,8
Thurlby (near Norton Disney)	LIN	SK9061	48,14. 56,15. CK,25-26
Thurlby (near Obthorpe)	LIN	TF1016	8,4;39. 27,52. 59,8
Thurleigh	BDF	TL0558	19,3. 23,32. 28,1-2. 32,8-9
Thurleston	SFK	TM1548	1,122e. 3,64;66. 8,69-70;75. 9,4. 25,60;62. 41,3. 74,8;12;15
Thurlestone	DEV	SX6742	17,33
Thurlibeer	CON	SS2504	5,11,2
[Great and Little] Thurlow	SFK	TL6850 TL6751	1,90. 14,156. 25, 93;104
Thurlstone WR	YKS	SE2303	9W86. SW,St11
Thurlton	NFK	TM4198	1,241. 4,57. 9,110. 19,40. 31,19. 50,13. 65,16. 66,26 *note*
Thurmaston	LEC	SK6109	13,23;62
Thurne	NFK	TG4015	9,17. 17,12. 66,78
Thurnham	KEN	TQ8057	5,86
[Upper and Lower] Thurnham LAN	YKS	SD4554	1L2 *note*. See also CHS Y3
Thurning	NFK	TG0829	1,186. 8,4. 10,34. 56,9
Thurning NTH	HUN		5,2. 19,18
Thurning NTH	NTH	TL0883	6,10b. EH2;6
Thurnscoe WR	YKS	SE4505	5W18. 10W28. 13W7. SW,Sf20;30
[Grays and West] Thurrock	ESS	TQ6177 TQ5977	18,28-29;31;34. 31,1. 48,2
[Little] Thurrock	ESS	TQ6277	4,6. 90,4
Thursfield	STS	SJ8655	13,1
Thursford	NFK	TF9833	1,93

Thurstanestuna: see *Turstanestuna* SFK

Thurstaston	CHS	SJ2483	3,7
Thurston (near Bury St Edmund's)	SFK	TL9265	1,62. 14,54
Thurston (near Hawkedon)	SFK	TL7951	8,33
Thurstonland WR	YKS	SE1610	SW,Ag14 *note*
Thurstuna: see *Thur(e)stuna* NFK			
Thurton	NFK	TG1021	19,34. 21,34
Thurton	NFK	TG3200	9,64;68. 15,28. 49,8 *note*
Thurvaston	DBY	SK2437	6,60;64
Thustuna: see *Thur(e)stuna* NFK			
Thuxton	NFK	TG0307	1,86 *note*. 8,81 *note*. 66,26 *note*
Thwaite	NFK	TG1932	17,27
Thwing ER	YKS	TA0470	1Y14. 1E33;35. 31E1-2. SE,Bt6
Tibberton	GLS	SO7521	32,5
Tibberton	SHR	SJ6820	4,7,2
Tibberton	WOR	SO9057	2,48
Tibenham	NFK	TM1389	4,56. 9,98;217;223;226. 14,39. 17,65. 29,7;10. 66,107
Tibeton	SHR	??	4,3,36
Tibshelf	DBY	SK4360	1,36
Tibthorpe ER	YKS	SE9655	1Y8. 1E6. 29E2. 31E3. SE,Dr3;6
Tickencote RUT	NTH		56,26
Tickencote RUT	RUT	SK9809	EN18
Tickenham	SOM	ST4571	26,8. 41,2
Tickenhurst	KEN	TR2954	5,210
Tickford	BKM	SP9042	17,27
Ticklerton	SHR	SO4890	3c,3
Ticknall	DBY	SK3524	1,22;26. 3,7. 14,6
Tickton ER	YKS	TA0641	2E20. SE,Th14
Tidcombe	WIL	SU2958	67,80
Tiddington	OXF	SP6404	58,32
Tidenham	GLS	ST5595	1,56. 31,6. 39,11
Tideswell	DBY	SK1575	1,29
Tidgrove	HAM	SU5254	23,68
Tidmington WAR	WAR	SP2538	EW1
Tidmington WAR	WOR		2,45
Tidover (in Kirkby Overblow) WR	YKS	SE3349	13W28 *note*. SW,Bu36
[North] Tidworth	WIL	SU2349	4,1. 24,13-14. 68,14
[South] Tidworth	HAM	SU2347	28,3;6. 60,1
Tiffenden	KEN	TQ9136	9,44
Tiffield	NTH	SP6951	18,33;54
Tilbrook HUN	BDF	TL0769	17,2-3
[East and West] Tilbury	ESS	TQ6877	22,2. 24,3. 30,21. 71,1
		TQ6677	
Tilbury [juxta-Clare]	ESS	TL7540	38,8
Tillingdown	SRY	TQ3455	19,5
Tillingham	ESS	TL9903	5,5
Tillington	STS	SJ9125	11,1
Tillington	SSX	SU9621	11,19
Tillislow	DEV	SX3893	17,12
Tilmanstone	KEN	TR3051	2,40
Tiln	NTT	SK7084	1,31;41. 5,8
Tilshead	WIL	SU0347	1,7. 67,12;18;29-30
Tilston	CHS	SJ4551	2,5
Tilstone [Fearnall]	CHS	SJ5660	2,23
Tilsworth	BDF	SP9724	22,1
Tilton	LEC	SK7405	1,3. 2,7. 19,17
Tilton	SSX	TQ4906	9,43. 10,17;20
Tilty	ESS	TL5926	29,1
Timberhanger	WOR	SO9270	1,1a
Timberland	LIN	TF1258	13,36. 32,25. 61,7
Timberland Hundred	LIN	—	31,13

Timberscombe	SOM	SS9542	22,14
Timble WR	YKS	SE1852	1Y18 *note*. SW,Bu29
[Nether] Timble WR	YKS	SE1852	2W4 *note*. SW,Sk2
Timsbury	HAM	SU3424	14,5
Timsbury	SOM	ST6658	5,15. 45,6
Timworth	SFK	TL8669	14,63. 25,25
Tincleton	DOR	SY7791	27,3
Tingewick	BKM	SP6532	4,38
Tingrith	BDF	TL0032	24,3
Tinsley WR	YKS	SK4090	10W8. SW,Sf6-7
Tinten	CON	SX0675	2,8
Tintinhull	SOM	ST4919	8,31. 19,9
Tinton	KEN	TQ9831	5,182. 9,8;22
Tintwistle	CHS	SK0297	1,31
Tinwell RUT	NTH		6,13
Tinwell RUT	RUT	TF0006	EN10
Tipton	STS	SO9592	2,22
Tisbury	WIL	ST9429	12,2
Tiscott	HRT	SP8818	19,1
Tissington	DBY	SK1752	6,7
[West] Tisted	HAM	SU6529	2,22
Titchfield	HAM	SU5305	1,45
Titchmarsh	NTH	TL0279	6a,23. 25,2
Titchwell	NFK	TF7643	1,2. 9,117. 16,5
Tithby	NTT	SK6936	10,57. 11,13
Titley	HEF	SO3360	24,3;6
Titsey	SRY	TQ4054	30,1
Tittenley SHR	CHS		8,33
Tittenley SHR	SHR	SJ6437	EC1
Tittensor	STS	SJ8738	11,33
Tittleshall	NFK	TF8920	8,69. 31,38
Tiverton	CHS	SJ5560	2,26
Tiverton	DEV	SS9512	1,35. 32,8
Tivetshall [St Margaret and St Mary]	NFK	TM1687	1,173. 10,93. 14,23. 15,27
		TM1686	
Tixall	STS	SJ9722	8,23. 11,31
Tixover RUT	NTH		1,1
Tixover RUT	RUT	SK9700	EN1
Tochestorp/Toke(s)torp	NFK	??	4,14. 8,74;76. 12,5
Tockenham and Tockenham [Court]	WIL	SU0379	30,2. 41,2. 67,20;27;31
		SU3078	
Tocketts [Farm] NR	YKS	NZ6117	5N20 *note*. SN,L20
Tockington	GLS	ST6086	1,61
Tockwith WR	YKS	SE4652	25W11
Todber	DOR	ST7920	36,1
Toddington	BDF	TL0028	20,1. 25,1;4
Toddington	GLS	SP0333	61,2
Toddington	SSX	TQ0303	11,61
Todenham	GLS	SP2436	19,2
Todham	SSX	SU9020	11,16
Todwick WR	YKS	SK4984	5W16. SW,Sf30
Toft	CAM	TL3655	14,48. 32,22. 44,2
Toft	LIN	TF0617	8,6;34. 24,32
Toft	SFK	??	16,47. 25,73
[Fish]toft	LIN	TF3642	12,66. 57,37
Toft [Monks]	NFK	TM4295	1,230;238;240. 20,36
Toftes (in Wombwell) WR	YKS	??	10W19 *note*. 19W2. SW,Sf11-12
Toft [next Newton]	LIN	TF0488	4,40
Toftrees	NFK	TF8927	8,98. 34,9
[West] Tofts	NFK	TL8392	10,4

Toke(s)torp: see *Tochestorp* NFK

Tolcarne (near Newquay)	CON	SW8865	4,22
Tolcarne (near North Hill)	CON	SX2478	3,6
Tolethorpe RUT	NTH		36,1
Tolethorpe RUT	RUT	TF0210	EN13
Tolgullow	CON	SW7343	5,17,1
Tolland	SOM	ST1032	2,3. 21,82
Tollard [Royal]	WIL	ST9417	24,39. 32,16. 55,1
Toller [Fratrum and Porcorum]	DOR	SY5797	40,9
		SY5697	
Toller [Whelme]	DOR	ST5101	26,66
Tollerton	NTT	SK6134	9,95
Tollerton NR	YKS	SE5064	2N23. SN,B23
Tollesbury	ESS	TL9510	9,14. 20,62
Tollesby NR	YKS	NZ5116	1N27 note. 11N8. 29N7. 31N5.
			SN,L32
Tolleshunt [d'Arcy, Knights and Major]	ESS	TL9211	18,45. 20,57;59-60. 24,66. 27,18.
		TL9214	32,37; 45. 33,23. 34,36. 41,12.
		TL9011	80,1. B3r
Tollington	MDX	TQ3086	22,1
Tolpuddle	DOR	SY7994	13,2
Tolworth	SRY	TQ1965	19,20;38
Tonbridge	KEN	TQ5946	4,1
Tong	SHR	SJ7907	4,1,24
Tong WR	YKS	SE2130	9W127. SW,M4
Tonge	KEN	TQ9364	5,118
Tonge	LEC	SK4123	14,2
Tonge (in Alvechurch)	WOR	??	2,84
Toombers	NFK	TF6506	21,3
Toot Baldon: see [Toot] Baldon OXF			
Tooting [Bec]	SRY	TQ2972	19,10
Tooting [Graveney] and [Upper]	SRY	TQ2771	6,4. 8,25-26
Tooting		TQ2772	
Topcliffe NR	YKS	SE4076	13N17. SN,Bi4
Topcroft	NFK	TM2692	14,37. 29,8
Toppesfield	ESS	TL7337	20,33. 28,11. 90,56-57
Toppesfield	SFK	TM0241	15,3-4
Topsham	DEV	SX9688	1,44
Torbryan	DEV	SX8266	52,52
Toredone	DEV	??	19,40
Toresbi (in Newton upon Ouse) NR	YKS	??	16N2 note. SN,B22 note
Torksey	LIN	SK8378	T
Tormarton	GLS	ST7678	49,1
Tormoham	DEV	SX9264	51,12
Torp (=? Low Langton)	LIN	??	2,23 note. CS,22
Torp (near Langton near Horncastle)	LIN	??	1,94. 4,51
Torp (in Lodden Hundred)	NFK	??	12,26. 15,28;29
Torp	SFK	??	25,65
Torp (in Croft) NR	YKS	??	6N17 note. SN,B20 note.
			SN,CtA11
Torp (in Etton) ER	YKS	??	23E7 note. SE,C4 note. SE,Sn5
Torp(i) (in Thorpe le Street) ER	YKS	??	1Y7 note. SE,Wei6
Torp (in Pickhill) NR	YKS	??	3Y9 note. SW,Bu15 note. SW,H5
Torp (in Tibthorpe) ER	YKS	??	1E7 note. SE,C4 note. SE,Dr6
Torpe	SFK	??	31,47
Torridge	DEV	SX5456	15,50. 17,102
Torrington	LIN	TF1483	27,20-21. 34,18
[Black] Torrington	DEV	SS4605	1,37
[Great] Torrington	DEV	SS4919	34,9. 40,2, 42.5-6
[Little] Torrington	DEV	SS4916	1,31. 15,16. 16,34
[West] Torrington	LIN	TF1382	16,19
Torrisholme LAN	YKS	SD4563	1L2. See also CHS Y3

Torstanestuna: see *Turstanestuna* SFK			
Torstuna	SFK	??	31,49
Tortington	SSX	TQ0005	11,85
Tortworth	GLS	ST7093	67,5
Torvestuna (perhaps Thurlton)	NFK	??	66,26 note
Torweston	SOM	ST0940	25,37
Torworth	NTT	SK6586	9,53
Toschetorp (in Brantingham) ER	YKS	??	5E9 *note*
Tostock	SFK	TL9663	1,61. 14,65
Totfled (in Hull) ER	YKS	??	15E2 *note*. SE,He6
[Great and Little] Totham	ESS	TL8613	4,2-3. 24,67. 27,16. 28,17
		TL8811	
Tothby	LIN	TF4476	4,64
Tothill	LIN	TF4181	13,3
Totley YKS	DBY	SK3079	17,4
Totleys [Farm] ER	YKS	TA2327	14E11 *note*. SE,Hol5;18
Totnes	DEV	SX8060	C6. 1,2;55. 17,1
Toton	NTT	SK5034	10,25. 13,5
Tottenham	MDX	TQ3390	24,1
Tottenham [Court]	MDX	TQ2982	3,20
Tottenhill	NFK	TF6411	31,23
Totternhoe	BDF	SP9921	32,1. 40,3
Tottington	KEN	TQ7359	5,49-50
Tottington	NFK	TL8995	9,12. 43,1
Tottington	SSX	TQ2111	13,7
Totton	HAM	SU3613	15,4. 69,37
Toulston WR	YKS	SE4544	5W7 *note*. 25W29-30. CW3.
			SW,BA3;8
Towan	CON	SX0149	1,3
Towcester	NTH	SP6948	1,7. 18,54
Towersey OXF: see Kingsey BKM			
Townstall	DEV	SX8651	23,26
Towthorpe (in Londonthorpe)	LIN	SK9238	57,24-25;49. 67,14. CK,60
Towthorpe NR	YKS	SE6258	2N28. SN,B15
Towthorpe (near Fimber) ER	YKS	SE9062	1E40-41 *note*. 5E60. SE,Sc7
Towthorpe (in Londesborough) ER	YKS	SE8643	2B9 *note*. SE,Wei6
Towton WR	YKS	SE4839	SW,BA5 *note*
Toxteth LAN	CHS	SJ3788	R1,4-5
Toynton	LIN	TF2770	1,93;106. 13,27
Toynton [All Saints]	LIN	TF3963	3,26. 14,75
Toynton [St Peter]	LIN	TF4063	3,26. 14,81
Trafford	NTH	SP5248	22,3
[Bridge] Trafford	CHS	SJ4571	A15
[Mickle] Trafford	CHS	SJ4469	1,23
[Wimbolds] Trafford	CHS	SJ4472	1,5
Train	DEV	SX5250	35,27
Treal	CON	SW7116	1,1
Treales LAN	YKS	SD4332	1L1 *note*. See also CHS Y2
Trebarfoot	CON	SX1899	5,4,8
Trebartha	CON	SX2677	5,4,20
Trebeigh CON	CON	SX3067	3,7. 5,1,20
Trebeigh CON	DEV		1,25
Treblary	CON	SX1587	5,7,8 (erroneously Tremblary)
Treborough	SOM	ST0136	32,6
Trecan	CON	SX1658	5,2,30
Tredaule	CON	SX2381	5,6,7
Tredington	GLS	SO9029	1,24
Tredington WAR	WAR	SP2543	EW1
Tredington WAR	WOR		2,45
?Tredinnick	CON	SX3559	5,2,15
Tredower	CON	SW7423	1,1

Tredveng FLN	CHS	??	FT2,1
Tredwen	CON	SX1785	5,24,25
Treeton WR	YKS	SK4387	5W20. SW,Sf32
Trefraith FLN	CHS	SJ1372	FT2,6
Trefreock	CON	SW9979	5,25,2
?Trefrize	CON	SX3076	5,2,23
Tregaire	CON	SW8637	2,3
Tregal	CON	??	5,23,2
Tregamellyn	CON	SX1853	5,5,12
[Higher and Lower] Tregantle	CON	SX3952	5,2,16
		SX3953	
Tregardock	CON	SX0483	5,16,1
?Tregarland	CON	SX2557	5,2,1
Tregavethan	CON	SW7847	5,5,18
?Tregeagle	CON	SW8647	5,23,3
Treglasta	CON	SX1886	5,1,5
Tregole	CON	SX1998	4,16
Tregona	CON	SW8569	4,22
Tregony	CON	SW9244	5,24,21
Tregoose	CON	SW6824	1,1
Tregrenna	CON	SX2379	3,4
Tregrill	CON	SX2863	5,13,12
Tregunnick	CON	SX1754	5,24,16
Trehaverne	CON	SW8245	5,5,21
Trehawke	CON	SX3162	5,2,21
Trehudreth	CON	SX1172	5,17,4
Treknow	CON	SX0586	4,20
Trelamar	CON	??	5,21,1
Trelan	CON	SW7418	1,1. 5,4,1
Trelaske	CON	SX2880	5,13,11
Trelawne	CON	SX2154	5,2,2
Trelawnyd FLN	CHS	SJ0879	FT2,4
Treliever	CON	SW7635	2,1
Treligga	CON	SX0584	5,14,3
Trellyniau FLN	CHS	SJ1869	FT1,4
Trelowarren	CON	SW7223	1,1
Trelowia	CON	SX2956	5,5,11
Trelowth	CON	SW9951	5,4,14
Treloy	CON	SW8562	4,11
Trelystan (alias *Wolston Mynd*, Wales)	SHR	SJ2603	4,1,35
Tremadart	CON	SX2158	5,13,3
Tremail	CON	SX1686	4,14
Trematon	CON	SX3959	5,2,11
Tremblary (mistake for Treblary)			
Trembraze	CON	SW7821	1,1
Tremeirchion FLN	CHS	SJ0873	FT1,3
?Tremoan	CON	SX3965	5,2,19
Tremoddrett	CON	SX0061	5,5,16
Tremore	CON	SX0164	4,22
Trenance (near Mullion)	CON	SW6718	1,1
?Trenance (in St Austell)	CON	SX0054	5,5,20
?*Trenance* (near St Austell)	CON	SX0152	5,9,4
Trenance (near St Keverne)	CON	SW8022	5,15,1
Trenant and [Little] Trenant	CON	SX2455	5,13,4
?Trenderway	CON	SX2153	5,4,5
?Trenewen	CON	SX1753	5,4,3
Trenhale	CON	SW8258	4,22
Treninnick	CON	SW8160	4,22
Trenowth	CON	SW9350	5,1,7
Trent DOR	DOR	ST5918	ES5
Trent DOR	SOM		19,75

Trentham	STS	SJ8641	1,8
Trentishoe	DEV	SS6448	3,48
?Trenuth	CON	SX1284	5,6,3
Trerice	CON	SW9357	5,7,11
Treroosel	CON	SX0580	5,24,14
Trescott	STS	SO8497	7,4
Trescowe	CON	SW5730	5,17,2
Treslay	CON	SX1388	5,8,7
Tresparrett	CON	SX1491	5,7,7
Treswell	NTT	SK7879	2,9. 9,129
Trethake	CON	SX1552	5,5,13
Tretheake	CON	SW9341	5,4,15
Trethevy	CON	SX0373	5,3,25
Trevague	CON	SX2379	5,6,8
Treval	CON	SX4255	5,14,5
Trevalga	CON	SX0890	1,17
?Treveador	CON	SW7425	1,1 (erroneously Trevedor)
?Trevedor: see Treveador CON			
?Trevell	CON	SX2581	5,1,19
?Trevelyan	.CON	SX1554	5,2,32
Treveniel	CON	SX2677	5,14,4
Treverbyn	CON	SX0257	5,3,15
Treverras	CON	SW8438	5,23,4
?Trevesson	CON	SW9941	5,15,5
Trevigue	CON	SX1395	5,8,5
Treville [Wood]	HEF	SO4232	1,3
Trevillis	CON	SX1861	5,24,19
Trevillyn	CON	SX0461	5,13,10
?Trevilveth	CON	SW9442	5,24,2
Trevisquite	CON	SX0474	5,3,24
Trevornick	CON	SW9265	4,22
Trewanta	CON	SX2680	3,7. ?5,1,16
Trewarnevas	CON	SW7824	1,1
?Trewen	CON	SX0577	5,8,8
Trewern (Wales)	SHR	SJ2811	4,1,8
Trewethart	CON	SX0180	5,25,4
?Trewidland	CON	SX2559	5,2,1
Trewince	CON	SW7322	5,15,2
Trewint	CON	SX2280	5,26,1
Trewirgie	CON	SW8845	5,1,10
Trewolland	CON	SX2665	5,5,10
Trewoon	CON	SW9952	5,5,17
?Treworder	CON	SW7215	1,1
Treworrick	CON	SW9744	5,4,16
Treworyan	CON	SW8950	5,7,12
Trewsbury	GLS	ST9899	52,1 note;2
Treyford	SSX	SU8218	11,8
Trezance	CON	SX1269	5,3,3
Tric	LIN	TF5563	12,77. 29,21;24. 38,9
Trill	DOR	ST5912	27,6
Trimley [St Martin and St Mary]	SFK	TM2737	7,97;112. 21,49. 39,1
		TM2836	
Trimpley	WOR	SO7978	1,2
Trimworth	KEN	TR0649	*12,1*
Tring	HRT	SP9211	15,4–6;9. 17,1. 39,1
Troston	SFK	TL9072	14,86
Trottiscliffe	KEN	TQ6460	4,8
Trotton	SSX	SU8322	11,7
Troutsdale NR	YKS	SE9389	1N45 *note*. SN,D13
Trow	WIL	ST9622	58,2
Trowbridge	WIL	ST8558	67,7

Trowell	NTT	SK4839	29,2. 30,30;50-51
Trowle	WIL	ST8258	67,4
Trowse	NFK	TG2406	1,49;121;124. 9,162
Truleigh	SSX	TQ2211	12,28. 13,6
Trumpington	CAM	TL4454	15,3. 18,7. 32,6. 38,2. 41,8. B
Trunch	NFK	TG2834	8,124;129
Trusham	DEV	SX8582	6,5
Trusley	DBY	SK2535	6,38
Trusthorpe	LIN	TF5183	2,19. 13,8
Truthall	CON	SW6530	1,1
Truthwall	CON	SW5232	4,1. 5,25,5
Trysull	STS	SO8594	12,15
Tubney	BRK	SU4398	7,19
Tucoyse (near Constantine)	CON	SW7129	5,24,13
Tucoyse (near St Ewe)	CON	SW9645	5,3,11
Tuddenham (near Culpho)	SFK	TM1948	3,18. 6,120. 8,4. 21,63. 38.13;15;22. 67,15
Tuddenham (near Mildenhall)	SFK	TL7371	12,4. 25,37. 28,3
[East] Tuddenham	NFK	TG0811	4,15;29. 13,23. 20,17. 66,68
[North] Tuddenham	NFK	TG0512	15,19. 20,15. 62,2. 66,30;32
Tudeley	KEN	TQ6245	5,62
Tudworth [Green] WR	YKS	SE6810	12W1 note. 12W25. CW13
Tuesley	SRY	SU9642	1,15
Tuffley and [Lower] Tuffley	GLS	SO8315 SO8115	10,1
Tufton	HAM	SU4546	16,2
Tugby	LEC	SK7601	1,3
Tugford	SHR	SO5587	4,3,8
Tumbelawe HEF or SHR	HEF	??	ES10
Tumbelawe HEF or SHR	SHR	??	6,17
Tumby	LIN	TF2360	29,9
Tunestan	SHR	??	4,27,29
Tunstall	DBY	??	5,4. 10,5
Tunstall	KEN	TQ8961	5,115
Tunstall	NFK	TG4108	20,19. 24,5. 38,4. 52,2
Tunstall	STS	SJ7727	2,20
Tunstall (near Nettlestead)	SFK	TM0849	8,55;58. 26,5.
Tunstall (near Wantisden)	SFK	TM3655	6,36
Tunstall LAN	YKS	SD6173	1L5. See also CHS Y6
Tunstall (near Catterick) NR	YKS	SE2195	6N52;54. SN,CtA19-20
Tunstall (near Roos) ER	YKS	TA3031	14E2;4. SE,Hol4;9
Tunstall [Farm] (in Nunthorpe) NR	YKS	NZ5212	1N29 note. SN,L37
Tunstead	NFK	TG3022	26,5
Tunworth	HAM	SU6748	23,7
Tupsley	HEF	SO5340	2,34
Tupton	DBY	SK3965	1,8. 8,3. 17,3
Turchetlestuna	SFK	??	36,6
[Lower] Turkdean	GLS	SP1017	38,5
[Upper] Turkdean	GLS	SP1017	48,2
Turlestane	HEF	??	1,7
Turnworth	DOR	ST8207	45,1
Turodebi (in Kirby Grindalythe) ER	YKS	??	1Y7 note. SE,Th5
Turstanestuna (in Trimley)	SFK	TM2838	7,83
Turstanestuna/Thorstanestuna'/ Thurstanestuna/Torstanestuna (in Bromeswell)	SFK	TM3050	6,153. 11,2. 26,19
Turvey	BDF	SP9452	2,8. 3,11. 15,5. 23,30. 24,23. 26,3. 32,3. 57,19
Turville	BKM	SU7691	39,1
Turweston	BKM	SP6037	31,1
Tusemera	SFK	??	34,17

Tushingham	CHS	SJ5246	2,18
Tusmore	OXF	SP5630	20,10
Tutbury	STS	SK2129	10,1
Tutnall	WOR	SO9870	1,1a
Tuttington	NFK	TG2227	8,8. 17,30
Tuxford	NTT	SK7371	9,12;29
Tuxwell	SOM	ST2037	22,9. 47,9
Twerton	SOM	ST7264	5,45-46
Twigbeare	DEV	SS4712	35,14;18
Twinstead	ESS	TL8636	23,24
Twinyeo	DEV	SX8476	52,46
Twislebrook (in Swinton) NR	YKS	SE2179	6N118 *note*. SN,CtA34
Twitchen (in Arlington)	DEV	SS6440	38,1
Twycross	LEC	SK3304	14,10
Twyford BKM	BKM	SP6626	37,1
Twyford BKM	OXF		B5
Twyford	DBY	SK3228	6,86-87;91
Twyford	HAM	SU4824	2,3-4
Twyford	LEC	SK7310	1,3. 13,30
Twyford	LIN	SK9222	2,35. 56,2
Twyford	MDX	TQ1883	3,15-16
Twynham (= Christchurch) DOR	HAM	SZ1592	1,28. 17,1-2
Twyning	GLS	SO8936	1,44. 11,3
Twywell	NTH	SP9578	10,1. 56,22
Tyberton	HEF	SO3839	2,6
Tybesta	CON	SW9448	5,1,6
Tyburn (= Marylebone)	MDX	TQ2882	6,1
Tyby	NFK	TG0828	56,7
Tydd [St Mary]	LIN	TF4418	1,28;30. 14,98. 57,51. CK,70
Tymmore	STS	SK1808	2,22
Tyneham	DOR	SY8880	26,55. 27,8. 54,8. 56,49
Tynsall (in Tardebigge)	WOR	SP0069	1,1a
Tyringham	BKM	SP8547	5,10. 17,22
Tyrley STS	SHR		4,14,5
Tyrley STS	STS	SJ7134	ES1
Tysoe	WAR	SP3344	22,4
Tytherington	GLS	ST6688	5,2
Tytherington	WIL	ST9141	23,6
Tytherley HAM	WIL		67,66
[East] Tytherley HAM	HAM	SU2929	4,1. 43,3. 69,17
[West] Tytherley HAM	HAM	SU2729	4,1. 45,7. 69,16. EW2
Tytherton [Kellaways]	WIL	ST9575	48,9
[East and West] Tytherton	WIL	ST9674	24,32. 26,22
		ST9474	
Tythorp BKM	BKM	SP7307	E2-3
Tythorp BKM	OXF		7,5-6
Tyting	SRY	TQ0248	4,2
Tywardreath	CON	SX0854	5,3,8
Tywarnhayle	CON	SW7554	4,7

U

Ubbeston	SFK	TM3272	33,9
Ubley	SOM	ST5258	42,2
Uckham	SSX	TQ7516	8,3
Uckington	GLS	SO9124	20,1
Uckington	SHR	SJ5709	3g,5
Udecheshale	ESS	??	35,2
Udeford	SHR	??	4,18,2
Udeham (in Sutton)	SFK	TM3044	22,1
Udimore	SSX	TQ8618	9,104
Uffcott	WIL	SU1277	30,3. 67,67
Uffculme	DEV	ST0612	23,9
Uffington	BRK	SU3089	7,37
Uffington LIN	LIN	TF0607	8,33. 18,11. 27,34–36. 56,4. CK,1-2
Uffington LIN	NTH		ELc2-3
Uffington LIN	RUT		ELc10;18
Uffington	SHR	SJ5213	4,21,14
Ufford	SFK	TM2952	6,239;243;255. 7,127. 14,166. 21,90
Ufton	WAR	SP3762	6,11
Ufton [Nervet]	BRK	SU6367	34,3
Ufton [Robert]	BRK	SU6268	22,5
Uftonfields	DBY	SK3956	7,5. 10,15
Ugborough	DEV	SX6755	39,17
Ugford	WIL	SU0831	13,14. 48,12
Uggeshall	SFK	TM4580	4,14. 7,8. 14,164. 68,2. 76,19
Ugglebarnby NR	YKS	NZ8807	4N1. SN,L3
Ughill WR	YKS	SK2590	10W36. SW,Sf36
Ugley	ESS	TL5128	35,4
Ugthorpe NR	YKS	NZ7911	1N3. SN,L10
Ulceby (near Well)	LIN	TF4272	24,69. 40,22. CS,14
Ulceby (near Wootton)	LIN	TA1014	7,22. 32,20. 34,2. 68,39. CN,4
Ulchenol FLN	CHS	??	FT1,6
Ulchiltorp (in West Lutton) ER	YKS	??	2B18 *note*
Ulcombe	KEN	TQ8449	2,32
Uleham's [Farm]	ESS	TQ8798	4,17. 20,35
Ulestanecote	DEV	??	25,27
Uley	GLS	ST7998	1,15
Ullenhall	WAR	SP1267	22,6
Ulleskelf WR	YKS	SE5140	2W6 *note*. SW,BA2
Ullesthorpe	LEC	SP5087	29,5
Ulley WR	YKS	SK4687	5W24. SW,Sf33
Ullingswick	HEF	SO5949	2,18
Ullington WOR	GLS		34,2
Ullington WOR	WOR	SP1047	EG12
Ulrome ER	YKS	TA1656	14E27. SE,Hol21
Ulting	ESS	TL8008	33,1
Ultuna	SFK	??	31,48
Ulure	CHS	??	8,3
Uluritune	DBY	??	17,19
Uluuinescherham	ESS	??	1,16
Ulverley (near Solihull)	WAR	SP1381	42,1
Ulverston	SFK	TM1463	16,29–30;38. 34,10;13;18

Ulverston LAN	YKS	SD2878	1L8. See also CHS Y9
Umberleigh	DEV	SS6023	13,1
Uncleby ER	YKS	SE8159	1E51. 8E1. SE,Ac3
Undercleave	DEV	ST2901	1,11
Undley	SFK	TL6981	21,7
Unstone	DBY	SK3777	1,5;9
Upavon	WIL	SU1355	1,23g
Upchurch	KEN	TQ8467	5,116
Upcote	GLS	SP0216	3,5 note. WoA2
Upham	ESS	??	22,1
Uphill	SOM	ST3158	37,2
Upholland LAN	CHS	SD5205	R1,25
Upleadon	GLS	SO7526	10,10
Upleadon	HEF	SO6642	18,1
Upleatham NR	YKS	NZ6319	4N2. SN,L20
Uplowman	DEV	ST0115	25,16;19. 34,43
Uplowman: see Lowman DEV			
Uplyme	DEV	SY3293	4,1
Upminster	ESS	TQ5687	8,10. 18,26. 52,1
Upottery	DEV	ST2007	34,50
Uppacott (in Tedburn St Mary)	DEV	SX8193	16,131
Upperthong WR	YKS	SE1208	1Y15 *note.* SW,Ag12
Upperthorpe	LIN	SE7500	63,15
Uppington	SHR	SJ5909	4,23,2
Upsall (near Kirkby Knowle) NR	YKS	SE4587	5N75-76. SN,Bi8 *note*
Upsall [Hall] (in Upsall) NR	YKS	NZ5616	1N14 *note.* 29N4. 31N6. SN,L26
Upsland NR	YKS	SE3079	6N141. SN,Bi8 note. SN,CtA39
Upton	BRK	SU5186	55,2
Upton (in Dinton)	BKM	SP7711	16,2. 23,1
Upton (in Slough)	BKM	SU9879	1,5
Upton	DBY	??	1,7
Upton	HAM	SU3655	1,24
Upton	HUN	TL1778	11,1
Upton	LIN	SK8687	7,7
Upton	NFK	TG3912	1,154. 12,6. 17,1. 66,92
Upton (near Northampton)	NTH	SP7160	1,19
Upton (near Headon)	NTT	SK7476	1,7. 7,5. 9,8;27
Upton	WAR	SP1257	1,8. 29,3
Upton ER	YKS	TA1454	14E8
Upton WR	YKS	SE4713	9W45. SW,O7
Upton [Bishop]	HEF	SO6527	2,25
Upton [by Chester]	CHS	SJ4069	1,34
Upton [Cressett]	SHR	SO6592	4,3,63
Upton [in Wirral]	CHS	SJ2687	8,8
Upton [Lovell]	WIL	ST9440	18,1
[Lower and Nun] Upton	HEF	SO5466	1,10a. 11,1
Upton [Magna]	SHR	SJ5512	4,3,24
Upton [Noble]	SOM	ST7139	5,67
Upton [St Leonards]	GLS	SO8614	1,2. 70,1
Upton [Scudamore]	WIL	ST8647	25,23. 26,11. 32,17
Upton Snodsbury: see [Upton] Snodsbury WOR			
[Tetbury] Upton	GLS	ST8895	41,3
Upton [upon Severn]	WOR	SO8540	2,31
Upton [Warren]	WOR	SO9367	26,15
[Waters] Upton	SHR	SJ6319	4,8,9
Upwell	NFK	TF5002	1,210. 13,11. 21,5;8. 66,49
Upwey	DOR	SY6685	
Upwey: see *Wey* DOR			
Upwich (in Droitwich)	WOR	SO9063	1,3a
Upwood	HUN	TL2582	6,5

Urchfont	WIL	SU0457	14,1
Utefel	HAM	??	NF9,42
Utley WR	YKS	SE0542	1W63
Uttoxeter	STS	SK0933	1,19
UUarle	SFK	??	13,4
UUilmundestun	SFK	??	*14,16*

UUilmundestuna: see also *Wimundestuna*
  SFK

V

Vange	ESS	TQ7287	18,1. 34,2
Varley (in Marwood)	DEV	SS5436	3,59
Varleys (in Petrockstowe)	DEV	SS5010	52,32
Venn (in Ugborough)	DEV	SX6856	15,68
Venns [Green]	HEF	SO5348	16,3
[The] Vern	HEF	SO5150	16,4
Verneveld	OXF	??	1,11
Veryan	CON	SW9139	5,24,4
[Lower and Higher] Vexford	SOM	ST1035	21,44-45
		ST1135	
Villavin	DEV	SS5816	25,1
Virley	ESS	TL9413	32,15
Virworthy	DEV	SS3110	19,2. 24,32

W

Wacton	NFK	TM1791	4,56. 9,98;214;216;223
Wadborough	WOR	SO9047	9,1a;1d-e
Waddesdon	BKM	SP7416	23,14
Waddingham	LIN	SK9896	1,56. 4,15. 28,10;14. 61,10. 68,34-36
Waddington	LIN	SK9764	13,34-37. 36,4
Waddington	SRY	TQ3258	8,1
Waddington WR	YKS	SD7243	30W37
Waddingworth	LIN	TF1871	3,12. 29,6
Waddon	DOR	SY6185	23,1. 56,36
Wadenhoe	NTH	TL0183	4,3-4. 6a,21
Wadetune	HEF	??	10,16
Wadfast	CON	SX2697	5,5,7
Wadgate	SFK	TM2933	7,82;109
Wadham	DEV	SS8123	52,40
Wadholt	KEN	TR2946	7,22
Wadshelf	DBY	SK3170	8,2. 12,3-4
Wadsley WR	YKS	SK3290	10W36. SW,Sf36
Wadsworth WR	YKS	SD9928	1Y15 *note*
Wadworth WR	YKS	SK5697	10W2. CW18-19. SW,Sf3
Wain [Wood]	HRT	TL1725	1,4;13-14. Appx
Wainfleet	LIN	TF4958	3,47. 13,7. 24,52;75. 28,41. 29,16;20
Wainhill	OXF	SP7701	35,12. 59,16
Waithe	LIN	TA2800	4,68. 12,22. 14,36. 57,4
Wakefield	NTH	SP7342	20,1
Wakefield WR	YKS	SE3320	1Y15-f7;25-26. CW23. SW,Ag9. SW,M14
Wakeley	HRT	TL3426	16,7. 17,9. 37,18
[Great] Wakering	ESS	TQ9487	24,21
[Little] Wakering	ESS	TQ9388	24,29
Wakerley	NTH	SP9599	42,1
Walberton	SSX	SU9705	11,81
Walcot (near Alkborough)	LIN	SE8721	8,28-30. 13,11
Walcot (near Billinghay)	LIN	TF1356	2,4132,15-16. 34,25
Walcot (near Folkingham)	LIN	TF0635	8,9-10. 24,93
Walcot (in Chirbury)	SHR	SO2699	4,1,35
Walcot	WIL	SU1684	28,6
Walcot Hundred	LIN	—	31,12. CK,52
Walcote	LEC	SP5683	3,8. 17,8
Walcote (in Grandborough)	WAR	SP5068	17,37
Walcott	NFK	TG3631	36,5. 66,104
[King's] Walden	HRT	TL1623	1,6
[Saffron] Walden	ESS	TL5338	30,45
[St Paul's] Walden	HRT	TL1922	10,4
Walden [Stubbs] WR	YKS	SE5516	9W44. SW,O6
Waldershare	KEN	TR2948	5,215
Waldershelf (near Westnall) WR	YKS	SK2696	1W22 *note*. SW,Sf36
[Great and Little] Waldingfield	SFK	TL9143 TL9245	8,48. 14,31. 25, 46;49. 34,2. 35,2. 39,16
Walditch	DOR	SY4892	57,11
Waldridge	BKM	SP7807	4,22. 21,2
Waldringfield	SFK	TM2844	6,115. 14,117. 39,7

Waldron	SOM	ST2840	21,6
Waldron	SSX	TQ5419	9,58. 10,92
Wales WR	YKS	SK4782	5W23. 10W1. SW,Sf2;32
Walesby	LIN	TF1392	14,13. 16,11. 40,6
Walesby	NTT	SK6870	1,20. 9,13. 12,4. 16,10
Walesby Hundred	LIN	—	30,36
Waletone	NTH	??	56,24
Walford	DEV	??	17,93
Walford	DOR	SU0000	56,24
Walford (near Ross)	HEF	SO5820	2,23;25
Walford (near Leintwardine) HEF	HEF	SO3972	ES12-13
Walford (near Leintwardine) HEF	SHR		6,19-20
Walford (in Baschurch)	SHR	SJ4320	4,6,1
Walgherton	CHS	SJ6948	8,22
Walgrave	NTH	SP8072	1,17. 18,79. 56,40
Walhampton	HAM	SZ3395	NF3,8
Walkeringham	NTT	SK7792	1,37. 9,120
Walkern	HRT	TL2826	42,2
Walkhampton	DEV	SX5369	1,19;22
Walkingham [Hill] WR	YKS	SE3461	1Y19 *note*. SW,Bu16
Walkingstead	SRY	TQ3651	15,2
Walkington ER	YKS	SE9937	2B4. 3Y1. 29E24. CE33. SE,Wel1;5;7
Wall [Town]	SHR	SO6978	4,11,14
Wallasey	CHS	SJ3192	3,11
Wallbury	ESS	TL4917	23,1
Wallingford BRK	BRK	SU6089	B. 1,37. 2,3. 3,1. 15,1. 20,3. 27,2
Wallingford BRK	OXF		EBe1
Wallington	HRT	TL2933	16,4. 20,9. 33,6. 35,3. 37,4
Wallington	NFK	TF6207	9,230. 66,16
Wallington	SRY	TQ2864	1,6
[Nether] Wallop	HAM	SU3036	1,19;?23. 69,21
[Over] Wallop	HAM	SU2838	1,20. 23,41;43-44. 69,19
Wallover	DEV	SS6838	3,50
Wallstone	DBY	SK2949	6,12
Walmsgate	LIN	TF3677	13,43
Walpan IOW	HAM	SZ4778	1,13
Walpole [St Andrew and St Peter]	NFK	TF5017 TF5016	49,9
Walpole	SOM	ST3041	24,5
Walpole	SFK	TM3674	3,4
Walsgrave [on-Sow]	WAR	SP3781	6,10. 44,7
Walsham [le Willows]	SFK	TL9971	6,299. 14,92; 66,2. 13;15
[North] Walsham	NFK	TG2830	8,12. 17,38;52
[South] Walsham	NFK	TG3613	1,103;150;155;168;204. 10,27. 12,6. 17,1
Walsingham (near East Carleton)	NFK	TG1701	9,188.32,2-3
[Great and Little] Walsingham	NFK	TF9337 TF9336	1,40. 21,24. 34,18
Walsoken	NFK	TF4710	16,3
Walson	DEV	SS7300	16,52
Walsopthorne	HEF	SO6542	15,9
Walter [Hall]	ESS	TL7310	8,11. 18,39. 86,1
Waltham	LIN	TA2603	12,21-28;32-36;38-39
[Bishops] Waltham	HAM	SU5517	2,9
[Great and Little] Waltham	ESS	TL6913 TL7112	11,7. 20,55. 30,5- 6. 41,7-8
Waltham [Holy Cross]	ESS	TL3800	7,1. 32,7. 37,9
Waltham [on-the-Wolds]	LEC	SK8025	13,69. 24,2
Waltham [St Lawrence]	BRK	SU8277	1,4 *note*
[Up] Waltham	SSX	SU9413	11,112-113

[White] Waltham	BRK	SU8577	4,1. 11,1
Walthamstow	ESS	TQ3789	55,1
Walton	DBY	SK3569	1,10
Walton	LEC	SP5987	10,11
Walton	OXF	SP5007	29,22
Walton (in Stottesdon)	SHR	SO6781	4,11,12
Walton (near Glastonbury)	SOM	ST4636	8,11;14
Walton (in Kilmersdon)	SOM	ST6951	46,23
Walton (in Eccleshall)	STS	SJ8627	2,20
Walton (in Stone)	STS	SJ9033	11,8
Walton	SFK	TM2935	7,76;81;122. 21,50. 31,13
Walton	WAR	SP2853	16,9-10
Walton (near Wakefield) WR	YKS	SE3517	SW,Ag3 note
Walton (in Welburn) NR	YKS	??	8N27 note. 23N20. SN,Ma13
Walton (near Wetherby) WR	YKS	SE4447	25W9. CW34;41. SW, An9
Walton [Cardiff]	GLS	SO9032	1,24
[Deerhurst] Walton	GLS	SO8828	20,1
[East] Walton	NFK	TF7416	4,45. 9,2. 22,15
Walton [Grange]	STS	SJ8017	8,11
Walton [Grounds]	NTH	SP5034	2,6. 18,35;62
Walton [Hall] (near Holker) LAN	YKS	SD3678	1L6 note. See also CHS Y7
Walton [Head] WR	YKS	SE3149	13W28 note. SW,Bu36
Walton [in Gordano]	SOM	ST4273	29,1
Walton [le-Dale] LAN	CHS	SD5528	R4,2
Walton [on-Thames]	SRY	TQ1066	19,26;27;30. 27,1
Walton [on the Hill] LAN	CHS	SJ3695	R1,8
Walton [on-the-Hill]	STS	SJ9521	2,2
Walton [on-the-Hill]	SRY	TQ2255	19,17
Walton [on-the-Wolds]	LEC	SK5919	10,17
Walton [upon-Trent]	DBY	SK2118	1,16
[West] Walton	NFK	TF4713	8,21. 15,4;*29*. 20,4. 66,21
[Wood] Walton	HUN	TL2180	14,1
Walworth	SRY	TQ3278	2,4
Wanborough	SRY	SU9348	25,3
Wanborough	WIL	SU2082	2,9
Wanden	BKM	??	57,10
[Hutton] Wandesley WR	YKS	SE5148	25W12 note. SW,An11
Wandon [End]	HRT	TL1420	1,7
Wandsworth	SRY	TQ2575	6,1. 9,1. 21,3
Wangford (near Bramdon)	SFK	TL7583	14,19. *21,5;9*. 25,41
Wangford (near Southwold)	SFK	TM4679	33,7
Wanlip	LEC	SK6011	10,15
Wannerton	WOR	SO8678	1,2
Wannock	SSX	TQ5703	10,38
Wansley	NTT	SK4651	13,10
Wanstead	ESS	TQ4088	3,5
Wanstrow	SOM	ST7141	6,16. 36,11
Wantage	BRK	SU4087	1,9
Wantisden	SFK	TM3653	3,86;91. 6,30-31;38;40. 7,137. 8,80. 21,37
Wantley	SSX	TQ2116	13,23
Wapleford	HEF	??	1,3
Wapley	GLS	ST7179	1,9. 43,1
Wapley	HEF	SO3462	1,12
Wapley *[Rectory]*	GLS	ST7179	6,6
Waplington [Hall] ER	YKS	SE7746	1Y10 note. SE,P2
Wappenbury	WAR	SP3769	31,5
Wappenham	NTH	SP6245	43,4
Wappingthorne	SSX	TQ1613	13,14
Warabetuna: see *Wrabetuna* SFK			
Warbleton	SSX	TQ6018	9,34

Washbourne	DEV	SX7954	1,34 note. 25,24
[Great] Washbourne	GLS	SO9834	1,30
[Little] Washbourne GLS	GLS	SO9933	E22. EvA107. EvC27. WoB5. WoC4
[Little] Washbourne GLS	WOR		2,27
Washern	WIL	SU0930	13,18
Washfield	DEV	SS9315	34,39
[Little] Washfield	DEV	??	32,9
Washford [Pyne]	DEV	SS8111	20,6. 24,5. 36,21-23
Washingborough	LIN	TF0170	1,7-8
Washingford	NFK	TG3101	12,24
Washingley	HUN	TL1389	19,3. 29,1
Washington	SSX	TQ1212	13,9;47;51
Wasing	BRK	SU5764	60,1
Wasperton	WAR	SP2658	6,18
Waspley	DEV	SS8819	28,10-11 notes. 52,43
Wassand [Hall] ER	YKS	TA1746	14E38 *note.* SE, Hol23
Wast [Hills]	WOR	SP0376	2,84
Watchet	SOM	ST0743	25,36
Watchfield	BRK	SU2490	7,36
[Lower and Upper] Watchingwell IOW	HAM	SZ4489 SZ4488	5,1
Watcombe	OXF	SU6894	35,30. 59,4
Waterbeach	CAM	TL4965	32,39. 40,1
Watercombe	DOR	SY7584	1,29. 55,34;36 notes
Waterden	NFK	TF8835	8,102
[Llanfair] Waterdine	SHR	SO2476	6,22
Waterfield	DBY	SK1779	7,12
Wateringbury	KEN	TQ6853	5,97-98
Waterperry OXF	BRK		B9
Waterperry OXF	OXF	SP6206	28,22. EBe3
Waterstock	OXF	SP6305	6,16
Waterston	DOR	SY7395	26,21-22 notes. 48,1
Waterton	LIN	SE8518	63,23-24
Watford NTH	LEC		C12
Watford NTH	NTH	SP6068	23,3. 57,2. ELe1
Wath (near East Tanfield) NR	YKS	SE3277	6N144. SN,CtA39
Wath (near Hovingham) NR	YKS	SE6775	23N24 *note*
Wath [upon Dearne] WR	YKS	SE4300	10W17. 29W6. SW, Sf10;16
[Thornton] Watlass NR	YKS	SE2483	6N126 *note.* SN,CtA36
[Thornton] Watlass: see also Thornton [Watlass] YKS			
Watlingeseta (in Diss)	NFK	??	1,50
Watlington OXF	BRK		B9
Watlington OXF	OXF	SU6894	12,1. 28,1. 59,3. EBe3
Watnall	NTT	SK5046	10,42-46;50
Wattisfield	SFK	TM0174	4,11. 14,79. 31,2
Wattisham	SFK	TM0051	25,19. 53,7
Wattlesborough	SHR	SJ3512	4,4,16
Watton	HRT	TL3018	2,2. 9,8. 16,1. 42,1;3
Watton	NFK	TF9200	9,11
Watton ER	YKS	TA0249	5E29. 29E26. SE,Sn2
Wauldby ER	YKS	SE9629	2B3 *note.* 15E2. SE,He5. SE,Wel4
Wavendon	BKM	SP9037	12,36-38. 26,11. 57,5;8
Waverton	CHS	SJ4663	23,1
Wavertree LAN	CHS	SJ3789	R1,20
Wawne ER	YKS	TA0936	2E18. 14E11. SE,Th14. SE,Hol15
Waxham	NFK	TG4426	4,40;42. 9,182. 17,54. 65,5
Waxholme ER	YKS	TA3229	14E4;11;17. CE47. SE,Hol8;17;19
Way	DEV	SX4989	*16,7*
Weacombe	SOM	ST1140	21,48
Weald	OXF	SP3002	58,18 *note*

[North] Weald [Bassett]	ESS	TL4905	36,4;12. 37,7
[South] Weald	ESS	TQ5793	8,9. 32,29
Weardley WR	YKS	SE2944	28W30 note. CW6. SW,Sk3
Weare and [Lower] Weare	SOM	ST4152	24,9
		ST4053	
Weare [Giffard]	DEV	SS4721	35,10
[Little] Weare	DEV	SS4823	15,39 note. 42,5
Wearne	SOM	ST4228	46,1
Weasenham [All Saints and St Peter]	NFK	TF8421	1,79. 8,64
		TF8522	
Weathergrove DOR	DOR	ST6121	ES2
Weathergrove DOR	SOM		5,69
Weaver	CHS	SJ6664	1,33. 14,13
Weaverham	CHS	SJ6173	1,1
Weaverthorpe ER	YKS	SE9671	2B18. SE,Th4
Webbery	DEV	SS4926	48,1
Webton	HEF	SO4236	10,22-23
Weddington	WAR	SP3693	16,26
Wederige	DEV	??	15,53
Wedfield	DEV	SS3517	15,33
Wedgnock: see *Donnelie* WAR			
Wedmore	SOM	ST4347	1,2. 6,15
Wednesbury	STS	SO9894	1,6
Wednesfield	STS	SJ9400	7,7
Weedon [Bec]	NTH	SP6259	18,20. 23,3
Weedon [Lois]	NTH	SP6047	43,1
Weeford	STS	SK1403	2,22
Week (in Thornbury)	DEV	SS3807	52,26
Week IOW	HAM	SZ5377	1,W3
Week [St Mary]	CON	SX2397	5,3,18
Weekley	NTH	SP8880	1,31
Weel ER	YKS	TA0639	2E19. SE,Th14
Weeley	ESS	TM1521	25,22
Weelsby	LIN	TA2708	30,12-13
Weethley	WAR	SP0555	11,5
Weeting	NFK	TL7789	1,210. 8,44 *and note*
Weeton ER	YKS	TA3520	2E23. SE,So1
Weeton WR	YKS	SE2846	1W48. 28W29. 29W22. SW,Bu34
Weeton LAN	YKS	SD3834	1L1. See also CHS Y2
[Little] Weighton ER	YKS	SE9833	23E3-4. SE,Wel3
[Market] Weighton ER	YKS	SE8741	1Y6. 11E6-8. SE,Wei1
Welbatch	SHR	SJ4508	4,4,1
Welborne	NFK	TF0610	8,75
Welbourn	LIN	SK9654	58,1
Welburn (near Bulmer) NR	YKS	SE7168	5N54. SN,Ma12 note. SN,B4
Welburn (near Kirby Moorside) NR	YKS	SE6884	1N73. 8N26. 23N21. SN,Ma12 note
Welbury NR	YKS	NZ3902	1N123. 31N3. SN,A5
Welby	LEC	SK7221	29,4. 40,13;37-38
Welby	LIN	SK9738	1,15;18. 57,22. CK,58
Welcombe	DEV	SS2218	3,90
Weldon	NTH	SP9289	26,5. 30,6-8;13. 60,3
[Little] Weldon	NTH	SP9289	24,1
Weledana	SFK	??	41,11
Welford	BRK	SU4073	7,13
Welford	NTH	SP6480	47,1a
Welford [on-Avon] WAR	GLS		20,1
Welford [on-Avon] WAR	WAR	SP1452	EG9
Welham	LEC	SP7692	2,5. 17,19. 40,30
Welham	NTT	SK7282	1,42. 5,8
Welham ER	YKS	SE7869	15E10-11. 23E15. SE,Sc2

Well	LIN	TF4473	4,62. 24,68. CS,13
Well	NFK	TF7220	18,1
Well NR	YKS	SE2682	6N120;127. SN,CtA35
Well: see Edginswell, Coffinswell DEV			
Well[bury]	HRT	TL1329	1,12
Well [Farm]	ESS	TQ6791	4,7
[Maiden]well	LIN	TF3279	13,33. CS,6
Welledene	DBY	??	1,13
Wellesbourne	WAR	SP2755	1,2
Wellhead	SSX	TQ7723	9,130
Wellingborough	NTH	SP8967	4,19. 11,5. 56,23;53
Wellingham	NFK	TF8722	31,39
Wellingore	LIN	SK9856	1,6. 44,17
Wellington	HEF	SO4948	29,11;14
Wellington	SHR	SJ6511	4,1,22
Wellington	SOM	ST1420	6,7
Wellisford	SOM	ST0921	46,4
Wellow IOW	HAM	SZ3888	1,4
Wellow	NTT	SK6766	17,12
[East] Wellow	HAM	SU3020	45,2. 69,22
Wells	SOM	ST5445	6,1
Wells [next the Sea]	NFK	TF9143	1,37;90. 4,20. 10,10. 34,16. 60,1
Wellwood	DOR	ST4703	3,18
[Great and Little] Welnetham	SFK	TL8759	2,4. 14,62
		TL8860	
Welshampton	SHR	SJ4335	4,3,54. 4,26,2
[Lower and Upper] Welson	HEF	SO2950	1,69
		SO2951	
Welton	LIN	TF0179	7,8-9
Welton	NTH	SP5866	18,98. 23,5. 56,35
Welton ER	YKS	SE9527	3Y1-2;8. 5E6;16;32-33;37. 11E6.
			CE11;24;33. SE,Wel1
Welton [le Marsh]	LIN	TF4768	14,101. 24,60. 28,43
Welton [le Wold]	LIN	TF2787	1,90. 3,49. 12,37. 16,38. 55,4
Weltune FLN	CHS	??	FT3,2
Welwick ER	YKS	TA3421	2E23. SE,So1
Welwyn	HRT	TL2316	7,4. 20,8. 28,2-3. 34,4. 36,4.
			42,11
Wem	SHR	SJ5128	4,14,4
Wembdon	SOM	ST2837	24,22
Wemberham	SOM	ST4065	6,14
Wembworthy	DEV	SS6609	16,57
Wendens [Ambo and Lofts]	ESS	TL5136	22,19. 32,18. 33,18. 90,24
		TL4638	
Wendlebury	OXF	SP5619	39,3
Wendling	NFK	TF9313	14,12
Wendover	BKM	SP8608	1,2. 57,10-11
Wendy	CAM	TL3247	14,26. 26,22
Wenechetone IOW	HAM	??	1,W20
Wenesuuic	ESS	??	30,51
Wenfesne FLN	CHS	??	FT2,14
Wenfleet	LIN	??	4,29
[Great and Little] Wenham	SFK	TM0738	3,67;84. 16,36;40. 40,3-4
		TM0839	
Wenhaston	SFK	TM4275	3,5
[Little] Wenlock	SHR	SJ6406	3c,5
[Much] Wenlock	SHR	SO6299	3c,2
Wennington	ESS	TQ5380	6,12
Wennington LAN	YKS	SD6170	1W70-71. 1L5. See also CHS Y1;6
Wensley	DBY	SK2661	1,12
Wensley NR	YKS	SE0989	6N92 *note*. SN,CtA29

Wensley, another NR	YKS	SE0989	6N92 *note*. SN,CtA29
Wentnor	SHR	SO3892	4,4,4
Wentworth	CAM	TL4878	5,61
Wentworth WR	YKS	SK3898	10W17. SW,Sf10;16;18
Weobley	HEF	SO4051	10,48
Wepham	SSX	TQ0408	11,74
Wepre FLN	CHS	SJ2969	A21. FD3,2
Wereham	NFK	TF6801	21,4
Weristetone IOW	HAM	??	8,5
Werlavescote	WAR	??	16,28
Werneth	CHS	SJ9592	1,31
Werredune	DBY	??	10,27
Werrington DEV	CON		*4,21*
Werrington DEV	DEV	SX3287	*Note to 5*. 1,50 *and note*. *5,5*
Werrington	NTH	TF1703	6,8. 6a,8
Wervin	CHS	SJ4171	A7. 8,4
Weslide/Westlid(um)/Westlidun/Westude (= Kirkleatham) NR	YKS	NZ5921	1N12 *note*. 4N2. 5N21. 13N5. SN,L21-22
Wessington	DBY	SK3757	8,1. 10,13
Wessuunic	ESS	??	90,27
West Bromwich: see [West] Bromwich STS			
Westborough	LIN	SK8544	64,14-16
Westbourne	SSX	SU7507	11,30;37
Westbrook	HRT	TL0205	Appx
Westbury (near Brackley)	BKM	SP6235	4,29
Westbury (in Shenley)	BKM	SP8235	41,2
Westbury	HAM	SU6523	23,17
Westbury	SHR	SJ3509	4,4,15
Westbury	WIL	ST8751	1,16. 68,20
Westbury [on-Severn]	GLS	SO7114	1,11. 32,9. 34,12 EvK10
Westbury [on Trym]	GLS	ST5777	3,1. EvM8. WoA4. WoB15
Westbury [sub Mendip]	SOM	ST5048	6,11
Westby	LIN	SK9728	12,52. 26,51. 59,11. 68,19
Westby LAN	YKS	SD3831	1L1. See also CHS Y2
Westcombe	SOM	ST6739	8,24
?Westcott	CON	SX2895	5,8,3
Westcott	SRY	TQ1448	32,2
Westcotts	BDF	TL0743	24,13. 57,12.
Westelet	HEF	??	6,11
Westerby (near Altofts) WR	YKS	SE3723	9W96 *note*. SW,Ag2
Westerfield	SFK	TM1747	3,61;63-64. 6,13;24. 8,73;76. 21,29. 31,58. 32,2. 38,12;14. 14,4;6. 74,11;14
Westerham	KEN	TQ4454	10,1
Westfield	NFK	TF9909	4,16
Westfield	SSX	TQ8116	9,17
Westgate (in Canterbury)	KEN	TR1457	2,16;24
Westhampnett	SSX	SU8806	11,105
Westhampnett	SSX	SU8806	11,105
Westhide	HEF	SO5844	8,8. 29,4 note
Westhope	SHR	SO4786	4,20,17
Westhorpe	LIN	SK9633	31,5-6. CK,62
Westhorpe	SFK	TM0469	6,58;59 note;60;210. 14,132;142. 37,7. 41,9. 53,6. 66,14
Westhouse (near Northallerton) NR	YKS	??	1Y2 *note*. SN,A1
Westlaby	LIN	TF0981	14,43. 22,11
Westlecott	WIL	SU1482	50,2
Westleigh (near Bideford)	DEV	SS4728	28,6
Westleigh (near Burlescombe)	DEV	ST0617	41,2
Westleton	SFK	TM4469	6,85;96;105. 66,12

Westley	SFK	TL8264	14,17. 25,27
Westley [Waterless]	CAM	TL6156	5,3. 14,77. 26,4. 41,3
Westmancote and [Lower] Westmancote WOR	GLS		WoC4
Westmancote and [Lower] Westmancote WOR	WOR	SO3437 SO3337	2,28
Westmeston	SSX	TQ3313	12,41
Westmill	HRT	TL3627	20,13. 22,2
Westminster	MDX	TQ3079	4,1-2
Westnanetuna	ESS	??	77,1
Weston	BRK	SU3973	7,14
Weston (near Runcorn)	CHS	SJ5080	9,18
Weston	DEV	ST1400	19,27
Weston	HRT	TL2530	28,1-4;6. Appx
Weston	LEC	SK3002	21,2
Weston	LIN	TF2925	14,100. 57,53
Weston	NTT	SK7768	9,70
Weston (near Bath)	SOM	ST7266	7,5. 41,1
Weston	SFK	TM4287	1,18;21;113. 7,43;49;53. 31,22. 32,17
Weston (in Standon)	STS	SJ8036	11,16
Weston WR	YKS	SE1747	8W1. SW,Bu33
Weston [Bampfylde]	SOM	ST6124	19,69. 36,5-6
Weston [Beggard]	HEF	SO5841	10,27
[Buckhorn] Weston	DOR	ST7524	26,1
Weston [by Welland]	NTH	SP7791	30,2. 56,4
Weston *[Cantilupe]* (in Weston on Avon) WAR	GLS	SP1651	12,7. EvE10. EvK 135. EvM67. EvO25-6
Weston [Colville] CAM	CAM	TL6153	14,80. 18,3-4. 26,6-7. ESf. Appx D
Weston [Colville] CAM	SFK		3,1
Weston [Coton]	SHR	SJ2928	4,3,38
Weston [Coyney]	STS	SJ9343	11,34
Weston [Dovel]	GLS	ST8689	32,4
Weston [Favell]	NTH	SP7962	1,18. 14,6. 18,4;82. 48,13
Weston [Green]	SRY	TQ1566	12,1
[Hail] Weston	HUN	TL1662	19,27-28. 25,1. D10;13
Weston [Hall]	ESS	TL8345	20,29. 43,6
Weston [in Gordano]	SOM	ST4474	5,22;26
Weston [in-Arden]	WAR	SP3887	16,38
Weston [Longville]	NFK	TG1115	2,10. 4,28. 19,32. 56,5
[Lower and Upper] Weston (Wales)	HEF	SO2169 SO2170	9,13
Weston [Madoc] (Wales)	SHR	SO2394	4,1,36
[Market] Weston	SFK	TL9978	9,2. 14,84. 60,1
Weston *[Maudit]* (in Weston on Avon) WAR	GLS	SP1651	62,5
[Old] Weston	HUN	TL0977	6,24. 19,20
Weston [on-Avon] WAR	WAR	SP1551	EG5;15
Weston [on-Avon] WAR: see also Weston *[Cantilupe* and *Maudit]* WAR			
Weston [on-the-Green]	OXF	SP5318	28,18
Weston [Patrick]	HAM	SU6847	37,2
Weston [Peverell]	DEV	SX4757	17,73
[Priest] Weston: see Priestweston SHR			
Weston [Rhyn]	SHR	SJ2835	4,3,33
[South] Weston OXF	BRK		B9
[South] Weston OXF	OXF	SU7098	15,1. EBe3
[Stalbridge] Weston	DOR	ST7116	3,7
Weston [sub-Edge]	GLS	SP1241	68,2
Weston [Turville]	BKM	SP8510	4,5

Weston [under Lizard]	STS	SJ8010	14,1
Weston [under Penyard]	HEF	SO6223	22,3
Weston [under Redcastle]	SHR	SJ5628	4,10,3
Weston [under Wetherley]	WAR	SP3669	16,52. 17,53. 28,8
Weston [Underwood]	BKM	SP8650	5,12. 12,34. 53,2
Weston [Underwood]	DBY	SK2942	11,1
Weston [upon-Trent]	DBY	SK4027	1,17;37
Weston [upon-Trent]	STS	SJ9727	17,15
Westonbirt	GLS	ST8689	28,5. EvK159. EvM108;112
Westoning BDF	BDF	TL0232	E1
Westoning BDF	HRT		1,5
Westowe	SOM	ST1232	1,6. 21,49
Westude (= Kirkleatham): see *Weslide* etc. NR, YKS			
Westwell	KEN	TQ9947	3,16
Westwell	OXF	SP2210	45,2
Westwick	CAM	TL4265	32,43. 39,3
Westwick	NFK	TG2825	26,5
Westwick WR	YKS	SE3566	2W7 *note*. SW,Bu46
Westwood	HEF	??	1,61
Westwood	WIL	ST8059	2,6
Westwood[side]	LIN	SK7499	63,17
Wetherby WR	YKS	SE4048	13W36. 24W19. SW, Bu43
Wetherden	SFK	TM0062	14,35. 31,45. 41,12
Wetheringsett	SFK	TM1266	1,80. 6,234. 14,124153. 21,39
Wetherley Hundred	CAM	—	Appx K
Wethersfield	ESS	TL7131	1,13. 23,28. 87,1
Wetmore	STS	SK2524	4,3
Wettenhall	CHS	SJ6261	17,4
Wetwang ER	YKS	SE9359	2B10. SE,Wa3
Wey	DOR	??	1,22. 26,14–16. 54,3. 55,5–6. 56,9
Wey: see also Broadwey, Upwey and Weymouth DOR			
Weybourne	NFK	TG1143	6,2. 66,97
Weybread	SFK	TM2480	1,92. 6,312;314–3158,37–38;41. 14,107. 18,2
Weybridge	SRY	TQ0764	5,26. 8,10–11
Weycroft	DEV	SY3099	34,52;57
Weymouth	DOR	SY6779	
Weymouth: see also *Wey* DOR			
Whaddon (near Bletchley)	BKM	SP8034	14,23
Whaddon (in Slapton)	BKM	SP9221	4,26. 26,7
Whaddon	CAM	TL3446	5,29. 14,28–31. 19,4. 26,26–28
Whaddon	GLS	SO8313	53,6
Whaddon (near Alderbury)	WIL	SU1926	37,12–13
Whaddon (near Staverton)	WIL	ST8761	67,17
Whalesbeech	SSX	TQ3934	10,106
Whalesborough	CON	SS2103	5,9,2
Whalley LAN	CHS	SD7336	R4,1
Whaplode	LIN	TF3224	1,33. 11,1. 12,83–84. 57,50–51
Wharram [le Street] ER	YKS	SE8665	5E59. SE,Sc4
Wharram [Percy] ER	YKS	SE8564	1E54 *note*. 29E21. SE,Ac10
Wharton	CHS	SJ6666	5,9
Wharton	HEF	SO5055	1,24
Wharton	LIN	SK8493	16,23
Whatborough	LEC	SK7705	1,7
Whatcombe	BRK	SU3978	38,4
Whatcote	WAR	SP2944	18,12
Whatfield	SFK	TM0246	2,15. 7,2. 14,111–112. 25,111. 29,13. 34,14. 40,5. 66,11
Whatley (near Frome)	SOM	ST7347	8,26

Whatley (in Winsham)	SOM	ST3606	26,1
Whatlington	SSX	TQ7618	9,21
Whatton	NTT	SK7439	17,16
Wheatacre	NFK	TM4693	31,17
Wheatcroft (in Thorner) WR	YKS	SE3437	9W13 *note*. SW,Sk8
Wheatenhurst	GLS	SO7609	78,15
Wheatfield	OXF	SU6899	28,10
Wheathampstead	HRT	TL1714	9,1
Wheathill	SHR	SO6282	4,8,16
Wheathill	SOM	ST5830	37,9
Wheatley	ESS	TQ7990	18,7. 24,14–15
Wheatley	NTT	SK7685	1,36. 5,4. 9,115
Wheatley	OXF	SP5905	9,8 note
Wheatley WR	YKS	SE5804	5W26–27;30. SW,Sf34
Wheatley LAN	YKS	SD6239	1L1. See also CHS Y2
Wheelock	CHS	SJ7458	20,11
Wheldale WR	YKS	SE4526	9W56 *note*. SW,O12
Wheldrake ER	YKS	SE6844	13E13. CE30. SE,P7
Whenby NR	YKS	SE6369	SN,B18 *note*
Whepstead	SFK	TL8358	14,3
Wherstead	SFK	TM1640	3,70;77. 27,11
Wherwell	HAM	SU3840	16,1
Whetstone	LEC	SP5597	44,4
Whicham CUM	YKS	SD1382	1L6. See also CHS Y7
Whichford WAR	NTH		46,7
Whichford WAR	WAR	SP3134	EN7
Whiddon	DEV	SS5538	42,8
Whilton	NTH	SP6364	18,27
Whimple	DEV	SY0497	16,94. 19,20. 39,10
Whimpwell	NFK	TG3829	17,55;60
Whinburgh	NFK	TG0008	13,19;21
Whipley [Hall] WR	YKS	SE2660	1Y18 *note*. 24W14. 29W34. SW,Bu25
Whippingham IOW	HAM	SZ5193	1,W19. 6,13. 9,9
Whippington GLS	GLS	SO5614	E6
Whippington GLS	HEF		2,22
Whipton	DEV	SX9593	19,38
Whisby	LIN	SK9067	65,2. CK,27
Whissendine RUT	LIN		56,13
Whissendine RUT	RUT	SK8214	R11. ELc13
Whissonsett	NFK	TF9123	9,80
Whistley [Green]	BRK	SU7974	7,32
Whiston	NTH	SP8460	9,6. 56,20c
Whiston	STS	SJ8914	4,9
Whiston WR	YKS	SK4490	5W19. 12W1;17. SW, Sf31
[Nether] Whitacre WAR	WAR	SP2392	17,14. 24,2
[Over] Whitacre WAR	NTH		19,3
[Over] Whitacre WAR	WAR	SP2591	18,16. EN3
Whitby NR	YKS	NZ9011	4N1. CN1. SN,L2
Whitchurch	BKM	SP8020	14,16
Whitchurch	DEV	SX4972	35,29
Whitchurch	HAM	SU4648	3,5
Whitchurch	OXF	SU6377	35,9
Whitchurch SHR	CHS		8,21;41
Whitchurch SHR	SHR	SJ5441	4,13,1. E1–2
Whitchurch	WAR	SP2248	16,21;65
Whitchurch [Canonicorum]	DOR	SY3995	18,1
Whitcomb	SOM	ST6323	1,33
Whitcombe	DOR	SY7188	12,8
[Great] Whitcombe IOW	HAM	SZ4886	6,5
White [Ox Mead]	SOM	ST7158	21,89

Whitecliff	DOR	SZ0380	48,2
Whitecliff	WIL	ST8538	68,29
Whitefield (in Challacombe)	DEV	SS6741	3,34
Whitefield (in High Bray)	DEV	SS7036	3,30
Whitefield (in Marwood)	DEV	SS5539	28,9
Whitefield IOW	HAM	SZ5989	6,14
[Little] Whitefield IOW	HAM	SZ5889	6,15
Whitehill	OXF	SP4819	7,25. 29,15
Whitelackington	SOM	ST3715	22,3
Whitestaunton	SOM	ST2810	19,4
Whitestone (near Exeter)	DEV	SX8693	16,125;137. 22,2
Whiteway	DEV	SX8875	16,157
Whitfield	DBY	SK0393	1,30
Whitfield	NTH	SP6039	1,8
Whitford FLN	CHS	SJ1478	FT1,8. FT2,8
Whitford	DEV	SY2595	1,54
Whitford	SRY	TQ2768	5,7. 21,1
Whitleigh	DEV	SX4759	17,76. 28,16
Whitley	BRK	SU7170	63,5
Whitley	CHS	SJ6178	9,26
Whitley	DEV	SY1797	*Note to 44*
Whitley	WAR	SP1666	22,25
Whitley	WIL	ST8866	53,2
Whitley WR	YKS	SE5621	29W10. SW,O16
[Lower] Whitley WR	YKS	SE2217	9W116 *note*. SW,Ag6
Whitlingham	NFK	TG2707	1,114;120. 9,31
[Great] Whitmans	ESS	TL8300	32,13
Whitmore	STS	SJ8140	13,2
Whitnage	DEV	ST0215	25,22
Whitnal	HAM	SU4851	3,5
Whitnash	WAR	SP3263	39,2
Whitney	HEF	SO2647	1,66. 6,10
[West] Whitnole	DEV	SS8818	47,13
Whitstable	KEN	TR1066	2,14
Whitstone	CON	SX2698	5,24,24
Whitstone	DEV	SS6526	16,82
Whittingham	SFK	TM2778	8,36
Whittingham [Hall] LAN	YKS	SD5436	1L1 *note*. See also CHS Y2
Whittingslow	SHR	SO4389	4,28,4
Whittington	DBY	SK3875	1,1
Whittington	GLS	SP0120	38,3
Whittington	SHR	SJ3231	4,1,12
Whittington	WOR	SO8752	2,5;58
Whittington LAN	YKS	SD6076	1L3. See also CHS Y4
Whittlesey	CAM	TL2797	5,44. 8,1
Whittlesey Mere CAM	HUN	TL2290	7,8
Whittlesford	CAM	TL4748	14,18. 26,13;18. 41,7. Appx G
Whittlesford Hundred	CAM	—	Appx G
Whitton	LIN	SE9024	21,1
Whitton (in Westbury)	SHR	SJ3308	4,4,19
Whitton	SFK	TM1347	74,13
Whitwell	CAM	TL4058	13,10. 14,43. 26,36. 32,20
Whitwell	DBY	SK5276	10,4
Whitwell	NFK	TG1022	1,53. 21,27
Whitwell RUT	LIN		56,18
Whitwell RUT	RUT	SK9208	R13. ELc15
Whitwell [on the Hill] NR	YKS	SE7265	5N65. SN,B14
Whitwick	HEF	SO6145	15,7
Whitwick	LEC	SK4316	13,68
Whitwood WR	YKS	SE4024	9W32;99. SW,Ag2
Whixall	SHR	SJ5134	4,10,4

Whixley WR	YKS	SE4458	13W18;37. 25W22. SW,Bu6
Whorlton NR	YKS	NZ4802	5N29 note. SN,L44
Whyle	HEF	SO5560	24,10
Wibaldslei (in Much Woolton) LAN	CHS	??	R1,18
Wibsey WR	YKS	SE1530	9W131 note. 9W144. SW,M7
Wibtoft	WAR	SP4787	16,39-40
Wiburgestoke	WOR	??	2,65
Wic	KEN	??	2,16
Wich: see Nantwich, Northwich, Middlewich CHS			
Wichedis	SFK	??	32,18
Wichling	KEN	TQ9155	5,81
Wichnor	STS	SK1716	11,49
Wick	NFK	TM0182	8,60. 11,2. 23,16. 66,95
Wick (in Garboldisham)	NFK	??	23,16
Wick (near Pershore)	WOR	SO9645	8,2. 9,1a
[Cookbury] Wick	DEV	SS3805	28,3
Wick [Episcopi]	WOR	SO8353	2,6
Wick Rissington: see Rissington GLS			
Wicken	CAM	TL5770	14,74
Wicken	NTH	SP7439	28,1. 54,2
[Ash] Wicken	NFK	TF6918	4,45. 21,10
Wicken [Bonhunt]	ESS	TL4933	58,1
Wickenby	LIN	TF0881	1,37. 22,10-15;34. 28,28
Wickersley WR	YKS	SK4791	10W6. SW,Sf4
Wickford	ESS	TQ7493	18,7-9. 24,9-12. 68,1. 69,1
Wickham	HAM	SU5711	23,12
Wickham	HRT	TL4723	4,24-25. 33,19-20. 34,25
Wickham	SSX	TQ2916	12,38
Wickham [Bishops]	ESS	TL8312	3,13 .
Wickham [Market]	SFK	TM3055	3,29. 6,241;251. 7,130. 16,4. 22,2. 32,12. 67,20
Wickham [St Paul's]	ESS	TL8237	5,4. 23,8
Wickham [Skeith]	SFK	TM0969	1,78;85. 6,230. 8,31. 14,126;152
[West] Wickham	CAM	TL6149	5,15. 14,7. 18,6. 19,3. 26,10
[West] Wickham	KEN	TQ3864	5,25
Wickhambreux	KEN	TR2258	5,67;124
Wickhambrook	SFK	TL7554	25,99
Wickhamford WOR	GLS		12,6. EvK133
Wickhamford WOR	WOR	SP0641	10,6. EG8
Wickhampton	NFK	TG4205	1,161;163
Wicklewood	NFK	TG0702	8,77. 31,41178. 17,34
Wickmere	NFK	TG1733	1,57. 2,11. 8,8. 9,
Wickwar	GLS	ST7288	69,7
Wicton	HEF	SO6255	30,1
Widdington	ESS	TL5331	14,5. 32,41. 90,11
Widdington [Hall] WR	YKS	SE4959	29W21 note. 31W2. SW,Bu2
Wide [Open Farm] (in Skelton) NR	YKS	SE5757	2N25 note. SN,B24
Widefield (in Inwardleigh)	DEV	SX5596	39,6
Widemouth	CON	SS2001	5,9,1
Widey	DEV	SX4858	28,16
Widford	HRT	TL4115	4,3-4
Widford OXF	GLS		2,11
Widford OXF	OXF	SP2712	EG2
[Lower and Upper] Widhill	WIL	SU1291 SU1390	26,10. 68,16
Widhulde FLN	CHS	??	FT1,3
Widmerpool	NTT	SK6328	13,14. 30,47-48
[Lower and Upper] Wield	HAM	SU6340 SU6238	2,21
Wiganthorpe [Hall] NR	YKS	SE6672	1N89 note. 5N55. 8N21. SN,B6

Wigarestun	HAM	??	NF9,18
Wigborough	SOM	ST4415	46,10
[Great and Little] Wigborough	ESS	TL9615	9,8. 28,9. 34,17. 60,2. 90,31
		TL9814	
Wiggenhall [St Germans, St Mary	NFK	TF5914	31,24. 66,19
Magdalen, St Mary the Virgin, and		TF5911	
St Peter]		TF5814	
		TF6013	
Wiggins [Hill]	WAR	SP1693	17,12
Wigginton	HRT	SP9310	15,5
Wigginton	OXF	SP3833	44,1
Wigginton	STS	SK2006	1,9
Wigginton NR	YKS	SE5958	C35. SN,Y8
Wigglesworth WR	YKS	SD8056	30W4;9-10
Wighill WR	YKS	SE4746	18W3 *note*. SW,An9
Wighill [Park] WR	YKS	SE4648	18W3 *note*. SW,An9
[Isle of] Wight HAM	HAM		1,26-27;29-30;37. 17,1. NF1,1.
			See also EL;EW1
[Isle of] Wight HAM	LEC		1,10
Wightfield	GLS	SO8628	19,2
Wighton	NFK	TF9439	1,32;41-42
Wightwick	STS	SO8798	1,3
Wigmore	HEF	SO4169	1,19. 9,1
Wigmore	SHR	SJ3411	4,5,11
Wigmore Castle: see *Merestone/ Merestun*			
HEF			
Wigsley	NTT	SK8670	6,4
Wigston [Magna]	LEC	SP6099	C11. 13,1. 40,25
Wigston [Parva]	LEC	SP4689	8,5
Wigwig	SHR	SJ6001	4,19,13
Wike WR	YKS	SE3342	1W13 *note*. SW,Sk16
Wilbarston	NTH	SP8188	1,29. 26,2
[Great and Little] Wilbraham	CAM	TL5457	1,5. 14,65. 29,5. Appx C
		TL5458	
Wilbrighton	STS	SJ7918	11,54
Wilburton	CAM	TL4774	5,51
Wilby	NFK	TM0389	9,126. 19,11. 31,37
Wilby	NTH	SP8666	56,17
Wilby	SFK	TM2472	6,310. 18,3. 19,5;7
Wilcot	WIL	SU1460	24,1
Wilcote	OXF	SP3715	7,21
Wilden	BDF	TL0955	2,9
Wildene	SSX	??	10,59
Wilderley	SHR	SJ4301	4,22,2
Wilderton	KEN	TQ9956	7,12
Wildetone	SSX	??	10,101
Wildon [Grange] NR	YKS	SE5178	23N3 *note*
Wildthorpe WR	YKS	SE5101	10W21 *note*. Sw,Sf14
Wilford	NTT	SK5637	10,8
Wilford	SFK	TM2950	6,171;256. 7,128
Wilkesley	CHS	SJ6241	8,32
Wilksby	LIN	TF2862	1,104. 38,5
Wilkswood	DOR	SY9979	55,40;48
Wilksworth	DOR	SU0001	56,21;23
Will [Hall]	HAM	SU7039	46,1
Willand	DEV	ST0310	42,24
Willaston (near Nantwich)	CHS	SJ6752	8,18
Willenhall	STS	SO9698	1,10. 7,8
Willerby (near Hull) ER	YKS	TA0230	SE,He11 *note*
Willerby (near Hunmanby) ER	YKS	TA0079	1Y11. SE,Bt9
Willersey	GLS	SP1039	12,6. EvK134. EvM66

Willersley	HEF	SO3147	8,3-4
Willesden	MDX	TQ2284	3,17
Willesley LEC	DBY		1,21. 6,20
Willesley LEC	LEC	SK3414	E1;7
Willestrew	DEV	SX4378	28,2
Willett	SOM	ST1033	25,34
Willey (near Much Wenlock)	SHR	SO6799	4,19,11
Willey	WAR	SP4984	16,39-40
Williamthorpe	DBY	SK4265	8,3
Willian	HRT	TL2230	34,7
Willicote and [Little] Willicote WAR	GLS		62,6
Willicote and [Little] Willicote WAR	WAR	SP1749	EG16
		SP1848	
Willingale [Doe and Spain]	ESS	TL5907	21,2. 24,47. 34,10. 63,1
		TL5806	
Willingdon	SSX	TQ5802	9,45;67;70;91;96;101. 10,8;27;70
Willingham	CAM	TL4070	5,39. 14,57. 32,29
Willingham	SFK	TM4586	1,37. 7,42-43. 31,21;23
Willingham [by Stow]	LIN	SK8784	4,4. 7,2. 12,3. 20,4. 28,5-6
[Cherry] Willingham	LIN	TF0372	7,29;59. 24,5;8;19
[North] Willingham	LIN	TF1688	14,7. 28,21. 35,8
[South] Willingham	LIN	TF1983	2,1-2. 4,53. 40,8. CS,28-29
Willingthorpe	LIN	??	C11
Willington	BDF	TL1149	23,11. 23,52
Willington	BRK	SU5491	21,8
Willington	CHS	SJ5367	7,1
Willington	DBY	SK2928	10,20
Willington	WAR	SP2639	22,15. 32,1
Willingwick (in Bromsgrove)	WOR	SO9675	1,1c-1d. 23,4
Willisham	SFK	TM0750	8,56
Willitoft ER	YKS	SE7434	5E8. 15E6. 21E5. SE,He10-11
Williton	SOM	ST0741	1,6;13. 25,33
Willoughby	LIN	TF4772	24,54;59-60
Willoughby (near Norwell)	NTT	SK7862	5,15. 12,15
Willoughby (near Walesby)	NTT	SK6870	1,20;24. 12,3. 16,12
Willoughby	WAR	SP5167	17,34;37;40. 18,1
Willoughby Hundred	LIN	—	CS,19-20
[West] Willoughby Hundred	LIN	SK9643	37,2
Willoughby [on-the-Wolds]	NTT	SK6325	9,92-93. 10,10. 16,5. 24,3. 30,26;35
[Scott] Willoughby	LIN	TF0537	24,79. 39,1-2. 57,17
[Silk] Willoughby	LIN	TF0543	3,37. 7,53. 24,102. 46,3. 48,13. 59,20
Willoughby [Waterless]	LEC	SP5792	13,35-36. 40,6
Willoughton	LIN	SK9393	47,1. 48,1
Willows	LEC	SK6618	17,27
Willsworthy	CON	SX2896	5,4,7
Willsworthy	DEV	SX5381	39,1
Wilmastone	HEF	SO3440	29,8
Wilmcote	WAR	SP1658	37,2
Wilmersham	SOM	SS8743	5,6
Wilmingham IOW	HAM	SZ3687	1,6
Wilmington	DEV	SY2199	16,173. 36,26
Wilmington	SOM	ST6962	7,4
Wilmington	SSX	TQ5404	8,6. 10,39
Wilnecote	WAR	SK2201	16,24
Wilsden WR	YKS	SE0936	1W65
Wilsford	LIN	TF0043	51,12. 58,7
Wilsford (near Amesbury)	WIL	SU1339	22,2. 42,7
Wilsford (near Pewsey)	WIL	SU1057	67,15
Wilshamstead	BDF	TL0643	53,3

Wilsic [Hall] WR	YKS	SK5695	12W1 *note*. 12W8. CW10
Wilsill WR	YKS	SE1864	2W7 *note*. SW,Bu47
Wilson (in Witheridge)	DEV	SS8317	16,146
Wilsthorpe	LIN	TF0913	14,93-94;96
Wilsthorpe ER	YKS	TA1764	1Y11 *note*. 14E54. SE,Hu3-4
Wilstrop [Hall] WR	YKS	SE4855	25W11 *note*. SW,An10
Wilting	SSX	TQ7711	8,14. 9,19
Wilton	HEF	SO5824	1,8 *note*
Wilton	NFK	TL7388	8,34. 66,66
Wilton	WIL	SU0931	B1. 1,3. 1,18. 3,4. 13,22. 23,9. 26,14. 27,23. 32,1. 48,11. 51,1. 67,9
Wilton (near Eston) NR	YKS	NZ5819	5N22. 29N1-2. SN,L22-23 *note*
Wilton (near Pickering) NR	YKS	SE8682	1Y4. SN,L22 note. SN,D12
[Bishop] Wilton ER	YKS	SE7955	2B11. SE,P6
Wimbish	ESS	TL5836	33,7
Wimboldsley	CHS	SJ6862	1,33. 14,12
Wimborne	DOR	??	26,32
Wimborne Forest (now Holt Forest)	DOR	SU0305	14,1
Wimborne [Minster]	DOR	SZ0099	1,3;21;31. 14,1. 31,1
Wimborne [St Giles]	DOR	SU0312	1,3. 10,3. 20,2. 55,13. 56,16. 57,9
[Up] Wimborne: see Wimborne [St Giles] DOR			
Wimbotsham	NFK	TF6204	8,17. 13,8. 16,1. 66,8
Wimpole	CAM	TL3350	14,44. 25,7
Wimpton	NTT	SK7973	1,1
Wimundahala	SFK	??	7,53. 31,29
Wimundestuna	SFK	??	14,16 note . 25,18;105
Wimundestuna: see also *UUilmundestuna* SFK			
Wincanton	SOM	ST7128	24,16
Winceby	LIN	TF3268	13,9. 28,42
[East] Winch	NFK	TF6916	1,132. 9,3;234. 22,20. 66,20;108
[West] Winch	NFK	TF6315	13,14. 21,9. 66,18;50
Wincham	CHS	SJ6775	17,8
Winchcombe GLS	GLS	SP0228	B1. 1,25;43. 3,5. 4,1. 12,4;10. 20,1. 34,3;8. 39,6. 41,1. 47,1. 59,1. 78,10. EvK116
Winchcombe GLS	WAR		EG11
[Lower] Winchendon	BKM	SP7312	14,13
[Upper] Winchendon	BKM	SP7414	10,1
Winchester HAM	DEV		C4
Winchester HAM	HAM	SU4829	1,19;25;42;46. 2,11;20 note. 4,1. 6,1;9 notes. 8,1. 15,1. 16,7. 21,2. 23,5 note;19. 29,3. 32,1 note. 39,3. 44,3. 68,7. 69,2;7. NF9,37
Winchfield	HAM	SU7654	9,1
Wincot WAR	GLS		1,42. 33,1
Wincot WAR	WAR	SP1849	EG3;10
Windesers	LEC	??	14,30
Windridge	HRT	TL1205	10,12. 34,1
Windrush	GLS	SP1913	11,14. 39,15-16. 78,1-2
Windsor BRK	BRK	SU9777	1,1;3. 41,6. 49,1
Windsor BRK	BKM		40,1
Windsor BRK	SRY		6,1
Windsor: see Broadwindsor, Littlewindsor			
Winestead ER	YKS	TA2923	2A1. 14E2. SE,Th10. SE,Hol7
Winetune	HEF	??	2,52

Winfarthing	NFK	TM1085	1,169;174;181. 66,41-42
Winford	SOM	ST5465	5,41
Winforton	HEF	SO2947	8,3-4
Winfrith [Newburgh]	DOR	SY8084	1,6. 24,2
Wing	BKM	SP8822	12,7
Wingerworth	DBY	SK3867	1,2
Wingfield	SFK	TM2276	6,308. 19,8. 21,45
Wingfield	WIL	ST8256	5,3
[North] Wingfield	DBY	SK4165	8,3
[South] Wingfield	DBY	SK3755	7,13
Winghale	LIN	TF0296	16,8. CN,15
Wingham	KEN	TR2457	2,21
Wingrave	BKM	SP8618	12,9. 23,20-22. 50,1
Winkburn	NTT	SK7158	18,5
Winkfield	BRK	SU9072	7,31
Winkleigh	DEV	SS6308	1,64 *and note*
Winksley WR	YKS	SE2571	28W13. SW,Bu22
Winkton DOR	HAM	SZ1696	45,1
Winkton (lost off Barmston) ER	YKS	TA1559	14E24 *note.* SE,Hol21
Winnall	HEF	SO4534	25,3
Winnianton	CON	SW6620	1,1
Winnington	CHS	SJ6474	20,2. 24,4
Winnington	STS	SJ7238	17,9
Winscombe	SOM	ST4257	8,2
Winscott (in Peters Marland)	DEV	SS4912	35,15
Winsford	SOM	SS9034	1,17. 46,3
Winsham	DEV	SS4938	3,43
Winsham	SOM	ST3706	6,12
Winshill STS	DBY		3,3
Winshill STS	STS	SK2623	ED1
Winslade	HAM	SU6548	23,11
Winsley	SHR	SJ3507	4,4,5
Winslow	BKM	SP7627	8,3
Winson	GLS	SP0908	68,7
Winster	DBY	SK2460	6,2
Winston	DEV	SX5551	15,30
Winston	SFK	TM1861	4,4-5. 6,14. 16,33. 21,28
Winstone	GLS	SO9609	68,1;13
Winswell	DEV	SS4913	35,16
Winterborne (on the Eastern or the South Winterborne)	DOR		1,6 *and note*. 5,1-2. 39,1
Winterborne (on the Eastern Winterborne)	DOR		26,30-31;33-34;36; 48. 40,4. 55,11-12;27-28. 56,6;26;60. 57,6;10
Winterborne (on the South Winterborne)	DOR		26,13;18-19. 55,7;9. 56,10
Winterborne [Belet]	DOR	SY7086	57,3
Winterborne [Came]: see *Winterborne* (South Winterborne)	DOR	SY7088	
Winterborne [Clenston]: see *Winterborne* (Eastern Winterborne)	DOR	ST8303	
Winterborne [Farringdon]: see *Winterborne* (South Winterborne)	DOR	SY6988	
Winterborne [Herringston]: see *Winterborne* (South Winterborne)	DOR	SY6888	
Winterborne [Houghton]	DOR	ST8204	36,3. 55,17. 56,28
Winterborne [Kingston]: see *Winterborne* (Eastern Winterborne)	DOR	SY8697	
Winterborne [Monkton]	DOR	SY6787	58,2
Winterborne [Muston]: see *Winterborne* (Eastern Winterborne)	DOR	SY8797	

Winterborne [Quarlestone]: see	DOR	ST8505	
Winterborne (Eastern Winterborne)			
Winterborne [Stickland]	DOR	ST8304	22,1
Winterborne [Tomson]: see *Winterborne*	DOR	SY8897	
(Eastern Winterborne)			
Winterborne [Whitechurch]	DOR	ST8300	12,11
Winterborne [Zelston]: see *Winterborne*	DOR	SY8997	
(Eastern Winterborne)			
Winterbourne	BRK	SU4572	1,47. 3,3. 35,1;2
Winterbourne	GLS	ST6580	1,9
Winterbourne	SSX	TQ3908	12,19
Winterbourne	WIL	??	25,24. 26,6
Winterbourne (on River Bourne)	WIL	??	5,7. 7,15. 65,1. 67,36;95
Winterbourne (on River Till)	WIL	??	67,39
Winterbourne (on River Till): see also			
Adestone, Elston, Maddington,			
Shrewton WIL			
Winterbourne [Abbas]	DOR	SY6190	11.11
Winterbourne [Bassett]	WIL	SU1074	16,6. 27,18
Winterbourne [Earls]	WIL	SU1734	24,41
Winterbourne [Monkton]	WIL	SU0971	7,8
Winterbourne [Steepleton]: see	DOR	SY62889	
Winterborne (Eastern Winterborne)			
Winterbourne [Stoke]	WIL	SU0741	1,17. 24,8-9
Winterburn WR	YKS	SD9358	30W7
Winterhead	SOM	ST4357	5,12
Winteringham	LIN	SE9222	24,12. CW,18
[East and West] Winterslow	WIL	SU2433	20,6. 23,3. 67,66;73
		SU2332	
Winterton	LIN	SE9218	1,39;62. 13,12. 21,2. 32,13. 34,26.
			35,5. 44,3. 68,38
Winterton	NFK	TG4919	1,48;168. 9,158. 10,30;82;85. 17,9.
			19,30. 64,8
Winthorpe	NTT	SK8156	6,3
Winton	SSX	TQ5203	9,66
Winton NR	YKS	SE4196	3Y18 *note.* SN,A6
Wintringham ER	YKS	SE8873	15E12. SE,Sc8
Winwick LAN	CHS	SJ6092	R2,1
Winwick HUN	HUN	TL1080	19,16-17
Winwick HUN	NTH		6a,17. 55,4
Winwick NTH	NTH	SP6273	12,1-2;4. 35,19c
Wirksworth	DBY	SK2854	1,13;15. 10,12
Wirswall	CHS	SJ5444	8,21
Wisbech	CAM	TF4609	5,55-56. 6,2. 7,12. 9,4. 18,9
Wiselei FLN	CHS	??	FT3,1
Wiseton	NTT	SK7189	1,39
Wishaw	WAR	SP1794	28,4
[Great and Little] Wishford	WIL	SU0735	13,12. 37,10. 68,32
		SU0736	
Wisley	SRY	TQ0659	36,5
Wispington	LIN	TF2071	3,11. 29,7
Wissett	SFK	TM3679	3,10;13 note ;14;16. 76,17
Wistanstow	SHR	SO4385	9,1
Wistaston	CHS	SJ6853	8,26
Wisterson (in Willaston near Nantwich)	CHS	SJ6653	8,35
Wiston	SSX	TQ1512	13,13
Wistow	HUN	TL2780	6,4
Wistow	LEC	SP6495	19,13;16
Witcham	CAM	TL4680	5,62. Appx P
Witchampton	DOR	ST9806	1,20. 26,40
Witchford	CAM	TL5078	5,44;60. Appx P

[Great and Little] Witchingham	NFK	TG1020	1,187. 5,4. 17,20. 19,32-34. 21,28.
		TG1120	25,5
Witcomb	WIL	SU0275	25,13
Witelebroc	ESS	??	33,17
Witestan FLN	CHS	??	FT2,16
Witestone IOW	HAM	??	7,11
Witesuuorda	ESS	??	23,37
Witham	ESS	TL8114	1,2. 20,11. 32,3. 68,2
Witham [Friary]	SOM	ST7441	21,90. 36,2
Witham [on the Hill] Hundred	LIN	—	30,32. CK,6
[North] Witham	LIN	SK9221	2,34-36. 56,22. 62,2
Witham [on the Hill]	LIN	TF0516	8,6;34-35;37. 24,32. 35,11
[South] Witham LIN	LIN	SK9219	27,47-48. 56,1;20-21. 68,25
[South] Witham LIN	RUT		ELc6-7;16-17
Withcall	LIN	TF2883	4,72. 40,26. 49,4
Withcall Hundred	LIN	—	CS,11
Withcote	LEC	SK7905	19,20. 29,20
Witheridge	DEV	SS8014	1,32
Witherington	WIL	SU1824	67,54
Withermarsh	SFK	TM0037	27,4
Withern	LIN	TF4282	13,4. 24,66. 25,20
Withernsea ER	YKS	TA3427	14E4. SE,Hol7
Withernwick ER	YKS	TA1940	2E32. 14E5;40. SE, Mid2.
			SE,Hol11;24
Withersdale	SFK	TM2880	6,104
Withersfield	SFK	TL6547	25,84;96. 26,10
Withiel	CON	SW9965	4,19
Withiel	SOM	ST2439	21,33
Withington	GLS	SP0315	3,5. WoA2. WoB18
Withington	HEF	SO5643	2,17
Withington	SHR	SJ5713	4,27,2
[Lower] Withington	CHS	SJ8168	1,29
Withycombe	SOM	ST0141	5,8
Withycombe [Raleigh]	DEV	SY0282	24,3
Withypool	SOM	SS8435	46,3
Witley	SRY	SU9439	24,1
[Little] Witley	WOR	SO7863	2,8
Witnesham	SFK	TM1750	41,17
Witney	OXF	SP3509	3,1
Wittenham (in Wingfield)	WIL	ST8058	5,2
[Little] Wittenham	BRK	SU5693	7,30
[Long] Wittenham	BRK	SU5493	B1. 20,3
Wittering	NTH	TF0502	6a,4;9
[East] Wittering	SSX	SZ7997	3,8
[West] Wittering	SSX	SZ7898	11,47
Witton	CHS	SJ6673	18,5
Witton (near North Walsham)	NFK	TG3331	1,196. 8,12. 17,41
Witton (near Norwich)	NFK	TG3109	1,101. 10,81. 58,3
Witton	WAR	SP0891	27,2
Witton (in Droitwich)	WOR	SO8962	24,1. 26,16
[East] Witton NR	YKS	SE1486	6N92 *note.* 6N111;124. SN,CtA28
[West] Witton NR	YKS	SE0688	6N92 *note.* SN,CtA28
Wiveliscombe	SOM	ST0827	6,6
Wivenhoe	ESS	TM0321	32,25
Wiverton	NTT	SK7136	10,58;60. 11,29;32. 27,2
Wiveton	NFK	TG0442	8,115. 21,23
Wix	ESS	TM1628	27,15. 42,7
Wixford	WAR	SP0954	11,1
Wixoe	SFK	TL7142	33,3
Wlferesforde	SHR	??	4,28,6

Wltune	SOM	??	36,2
Wluetone	HEF	??	29,7
Woburn	BDF	SP9433	16,1. 57,1
Wokefield	BRK	SU6765	1,44;45. 31,6
Woking	SRY	TQ0058	1,2. 4,1
Wolborough	DEV	SX8570	16,163
Woldingham	SRY	TQ3755	19,9
Wolferlow	HEF	SO6661	9,18. 10,66
Wolfhall	WIL	SU2461	68,12
Wolfhampcote	WAR	SP5265	17,5;17
Wolfin	DEV	SS7504	24,28
Wolford	WAR	SP2534	4,4. 16,66. 22,2;13–14
Wolfreton ER	YKS	TA0329	15E2. SE,He6
Wolgarston	STS	SJ9413	1,7
Wollaston	NTH	SP9063	48,4. 56,20g;51
Wollaston	SHR	SJ3212	4,1,8 note. 4,4,7 *note*
Wollaton	DEV	SX5552	17,85
Wollaton	NTT	SK5239	1,47. 10,35. 30,55
Wollerton	SHR	SJ6230	4,23,12
Wolseley	STS	SK0220	2,7
Wolstanton	STS	SJ8548	1,15
Wolston	WAR	SP4175	12,4;7
Wolston [Mynd] (Wales): see Trelystan SHR			
Wolterton	NFK	TG1632	8,135. 17,32. 20,32
Wolvercote	OXF	SP4909	29,23
Wolverhampton	STS	SO9198	7,1;5
Wolverley	SHR	SJ4731	4,14,1
Wolverley	WOR	SO8379	2,83
Wolverton	BKM	SP8140	43,11
Wolverton	HAM	SU5558	64,1–2
Wolverton IOW	HAM	SZ4582	6,7. 8,11
Wolverton	WAR	SP2062	22,24. 28,17
[Lower and Upper] Wolverton	WOR	SO9250 SO9150	2,3;4
Wolvey	WAR	SP4387	24,1
Womberford	DEV	??	15,24
Wombleton NR	YKS	SE6683	2N8. SN,Ma12
Wombourn	STS	SO8793	12,8
Wombwell WR	YKS	SE3903	10W19. 19W1. 29W4. SW,Sf11
Womersley WR	YKS	SE5319	9W49. SW,O8
Womerton	SHR	SO4597	4,5,3
Wonford (in Heavitree)	DEV	SX9491	1,28
Wonford (in Thornbury)	DEV	SS3709	35,3
Wonston	HAM	SU4739	3,14
Wooburn	BKM	SU9087	3a,4
Woodadvent	SOM	ST0337	*1,6*
Woodbeare	DEV	ST0504	25,13
Woodborough	NTT	SK6347	5,18–19. 9,73. 14,5. 30,6;9–10
Woodborough	SOM	ST6956	39,3
Woodborough	WIL	SU1159	42,1
Woodbridge	SFK	TM2749	3,45. 6,263;287;294. 7,134. 8,27. 21,100;103. 32,15. 38,27
Woodburn	DEV	SS8623	16,151
Woodbury	DEV	SY0087	1,33
Woodchester	GLS	SO8402	1,63. 78,14
Woodcombe	DEV	SX7837	23,24
Woodcote	LEC	SK3518	14,26
Woodcote (Newport)	SHR	SJ7615	4,9,3
Woodcote (in Shrewsbury St Chad)	SHR	SJ4511	4,5,8
Woodcote	WAR	SP2869	16,3;51

Woodcote and Woodcote [Green]	WOR	SO9272	1,1a. 26,5
		SO9172	
Woodcott	HAM	SU4354	52,1
Woodcroft Hundred	BDF	—	1,4
Woodditton	CAM	TL6559	1,11. 14,61
Woodend: see *[Little] Blakesley* NTH			
Woodford	DEV	SX5256	17,105
Woodford	ESS	TQ4092	8,3
Woodford (near Denford)	NTH	SP9676	4,23. 6a,28
Woodford [Halse]	NTH	SP5452	23,13
Woodham [Ferrers]	ESS	TQ7999	29,4
Woodham [Mortimer]	ESS	TL8104	34,11
Woodham [Walter]	ESS	TL8006	33,4
Woodhill	WIL	SU0676	4,2
Woodhuish	DEV	SX9152	30,1
Woodleigh	DEV	SX7348	28,13
Woodleys	OXF	SP4219	59,24
Woodluston (Wales): see Pen y Lan	SSX	TQ2315	13,22
Woodmancote			
Woodmancott	HAM	SU5642	6,13
Woodmansterne	SRY	TQ2759	19,16
Woodnesborough (in Eastry Hundred)	KEN	TR3056	5,197
Woodnesborough (in *Summerdene* Hundred)	KEN	TR3056	5,211
Woodperry	OXF	SP5710	7,18
Woodplumpton LAN	YKS	SD4934	1L1
Woodsford	DOR	SY7690	11,7. 57,13
Woodspring	SOM	ST3466	27,3
Woodstock	OXF	SP4417	1,10
Woodstone	HUN	TL1897	7,3
Woodstreet	DOR	SY8585	57,18
Woodton	NFK	TM2894	1,182;184. 6,5. 7,15. 9,54. 29,9. 47,3
Woodwick (in Freshford)	SOM	ST7760	7,12
Woodyates	DOR	SU0219	8,4
Wool	DOR	SY8486	26,60. 56,62-63
Woolacombe	DEV	SS4543	19,11. 36,15
Woolaston	GLS	ST5899	31,5
Woolavington	SOM	ST3441	8,5
Woolbeding	SSX	SU8722	14,1
Woolcombe (in Melbury Bubb)	DOR	ST6005	34,7
Woolcombe (in Toller Porcorum)	DOR	SY5595	56,50. 57,8
Wooldale WR	YKS	SE1508	SW,Ag14 *note*
Woolfardisworthy (in Hartland)	DEV	SS3321	52,4
Woolfardisworthy (near Witheridge)	DEV	SS8208	21,12
Woolfly	SSX	TQ2217	13,24
Woolgarston	DOR	SY9881	37,14
Woolhampton	BRK	SU5766	21,22
Woolhope	HEF	SO6135	2,13
Woolladon	DEV	SS5207	16,38
Woolland	DOR	ST7706	12,10
Woollaston	STS	SJ8615	11,6
Woolleigh (in Beaford)	DEV	SS5316	16,41
Woolleigh (in Bovey Tracey)	DEV	SX8080	3,8
Woolley	BRK	SU4180	24,1
Woolley	HUN	TL1574	19,21. 29,5
Woolley	SOM	ST7468	5,37
Woolley WR	YKS	SE3113	1Y13
Woolmersdon	SOM	ST2833	35,1
Woolpit	SFK	TL9762	14,55
Woolstaston	SHR	SO4598	4,5,1

Woolsthorpe	LIN	SK8333	18,27-28. CK,20
Woolston (near St Ives)	CON	SX2968	5,19,1
Woolston	DEV	SX7141	5 note. 17,47
Woolston	HAM	SU4310	59,1
Woolston (in West Felton)	SHR	SJ3224	4,3,40
Woolston (in Wistanstow)	SHR	SO4287	4,20,18
Woolston (in Bicknoller)	SOM	ST0939	25,32
Woolston (in South Cadbury)	SOM	ST6427	19,55. 36,7
Woolston (in Stogursey)	SOM	ST2344	21,18
Woolston [Hall]	ESS	TQ4495	1,20
Woolstone	BRK	SU2987	2,1
Woolstone (near Poundstock)	CON	SS2202	5,6,1
Woolstone	GLS	SO9630	20,1
[Great] Woolstone	BKM	SP8738	14,37
[Little] Woolstone	BKM	SP8739	14,36. 17,19
[Little] Woolton LAN	CHS	SJ4387	R1,13
[Much] Woolton LAN	CHS	SJ4286	R1,19
Woolverstone	SFK	TM1838	3,74. 36,8
Woolverton IOW	HAM	SZ6286	1,W12
Woolwich	KEN	TQ4378	12,2
Woolwicks	HRT	TL2225	20,5. 36,5
Woonton (in Almeley)	HEF	SO3552	1,70. 10,45
Woonton (in Laysters)	HEF	SO5462	10,12
Woore	SHR	SJ7342	4,15,2
Wootton	BDF	TL0045	49,2. 49,3
Wootton	HAM	SZ2498	NF9,32
Wootton IOW	HAM	SZ5392	1,W22
Wootton	LIN	TA0816	7,21. 32,19. 36,2
Wootton	NTH	SP7656	39,16. 56,57f
Wootton OXF	NTH		4,34
Wootton OXF	OXF	SP4319	'1,4. EN5
Wootton (in Oswestry)	SHR	SJ3427	4,3,39
Wootton (in Eccleshall)	STS	SJ8327	2,20
Wootton (in East Chiltington)	SSX	TQ3715	2,2. 10,99. 12,45
Wootton (near Folkington)	SSX	TQ5605	10,67;85
[Abbotts] Wootton	DOR	SY3796	13,6
Wootton [Bassett]	WIL	SU0682	28,1
Wootton [Courtenay]	SOM	SS9343	27,2
Wootton [Fitzpaine]	DOR	SY3795	26,63;69. 49,12
[Glanvilles] Wootton	DOR	ST6708	37,1-2
[North] Wootton	SOM	ST5641	8,20
[North and South] Wootton	NFK	TF6324	1,133
		TF6422	
Wootton [Rivers]	WIL	SU1963	1,15
Wootton [St Lawrence]	HAM	SU5953	3,24. 23,58
Wootton [under-Weaver]	STS	SK1045	1,48
Wootton [Wawen]	WAR	SP1563	22,9
Worcester WOR	HEF		1,39;41;44;47. 2,32
Worcester WOR	WOR	SO8555	C1. 1,2. 2,49;51. 10,2;17. 14,1. 15,9. 23,12. 24,1. 26,2;15. 28,1. E1;3-4;7;9
Wordwell	SFK	TL8272	14,88
Worfield SHR	SHR	SO7595	ES2;7
Worfield SHR	STS		B5. 9,1
Worgret	DOR	SY9086	11,9. 37,10. 57,7
Worksop	NTT	SK5879	S5. 9,43
Worlaby (near Elsham)	LIN	TA0114	7,20. 13,18. 25,2
Worlaby (near Tetford)	LIN	TF3476	2,28. 3,54
[East] Worldham	HAM	SU7438	62,2
[West] Worldham	HAM	SU7436	NF10,5
Worle	SOM	ST3562	24,1

Worleston	CHS	SJ6856	8,29
Worlingham	SFK	TM4489	1,19;22. 4,34. 14,121. 31,25
Worlington (in Instow)	DEV	SS4830	3,18
Worlington (near Witheridge)	DEV	SS7713	3,81. 20,7. 42,21
Worlington	SFK	TL6973	12,3
Worlingworth	SFK	TM2368	14,103
Wormegay	NFK	TF6611	13,4. 66,3
Wormelow [Tump]	HEF	SO4930	C3
Wormhill	DBY	SK1274	6,79
Wormingford	ESS	TL9332	32,24
Worminghall	BKM	SP6408	5,1
Wormington	GLS	SP0336	39,21
Wormleighton	WAR	SP4453	16,54. 17,61. 30,2
Wormley	HRT	TL3605	14,1. 16,11. 42,6
Wormshill	KEN	TQ8857	5,80
Wormsley	HEF	SO4247	2,47. 10,61-62
Worplesdon	SRY	SU9753	18,3
Worrall WR	YKS	SK3092	10W36. SW,Sf36
[High] Worsall NR	YKS	NZ3809	1N117. SN,A3
[Low] Worsall NR	YKS	NZ3910	1N118. 31N2. SN,A3
Worsborough WR	YKS	SE3503	9W77. SW,St8
Worsley	WOR	SO7569	15,1
Worstead	NFK	TG3026	4,37. 17,43. 21,36
Worth	DEV	SS9414	21,14
Worth (in Cudworth)	SOM	ST3710	21,36
?Worth (near Crawley) SSX	SRY		19,13
Worth (near Crawley) SSX	SSX	TQ3036	E1
Worth (near Little Horsted)	SSX	TQ4618	10,65
Worth [Matravers]	DOR	SY9777	47,9;11. 55,43
Wortham	SFK	TM0877	6,197;219. 11,4-5. 14,43. 35,7
Worthele	DEV	SX6254	17,59
Worthen	SHR	SJ3204	4,4,20
Worthenbury FLN	CHS	SJ4246	2,3
Worthing	SSX	TQ1402	13,35-37
Worthington	LEC	SK4020	14,3
Worthy (?in Rackenford)	DEV	SS8419	16,145
[Abbots] Worthy	HAM	SU4932	6,17
[Headbourne] Worthy	HAM	SU4832	29,3-4. 39,3
[Kings] Worthy	HAM	SU4933	1,17
[Martyr] Worthy	HAM	SU5132	3,13
Worthygate	DEV	SS3623	5,7
Worthyvale	CON	SX1086	5,6,2
Worting	HAM	SU6051	6,2
Wortley WR	YKS	SK3099	5W34. 29W26. SW,St8-9
Worton	OXF	SP4611	59,29
Worton NR	YKS	SD9590	6N80. SN,CtA26
[Nether and Over] Worton OXF	NTH		4,35
[Nether and Over] Worton OXF	OXF	SP4230	7,52. 58,37. EN6
		SP4329	
Wothersome WR	YKS	SE4042	1W3 *note*. SW,Sk12
Wotherton	SHR	SJ2800	4,27,21
Wothorpe	NTH	TF0205	6a,9. 11,1. 56,59
Wotton	SRY	TQ1247	36,4
Wotton [St Mary]	GLS	SO8520	36,1
Wotton [under-Edge]	GLS	ST7692	1,15
Wotton [Underwood]	BKM	SP6815	14,14
Woughton [on the Green]	BKM	SP8737	12,31. 47,1
Wouldham	KEN	TQ7164	4,6
Wrabetuna/Warabetuna/UUrab(r)etuna	SFK	??	3,15. 6,91;99;108. 7,11;28
Wrabbatuna			
Wrabness	ESS	TM1731	11,8

Wragby	LIN	TF1377	22,37. 34,12-23. 47,8-9. CS,24
Wramplingham	NFK	TG1106	4,10;12. 12,4-5
Wrangle	LIN	TF4250	12,63. 57,36
[Great and Little] Wratting	SFK	TL6848	14,159. 25,10;81;85
		TL6497	
[West] Wratting	CAM	TL6052	5,4-5. 14,81. 18,5. 26,8;51.
			Appx D
Wratworth	CAM	TL3448	13,9. 14,42. 26,35. 31,6. 32,19
Wrawby	LIN	TA0208	64,18-19
Wraxall	DOR	ST5601	47,7
Wraxall	SOM	ST4971	5,40
[North] Wraxall	WIL	ST8175	24,38
Wray	DEV	SX7784	52,16
Wraysbury	BKM	TQ0074	20,1
Wrelton NR	YKS	SE7686	1N54. SN,D19
Wrenbury	CHS	SJ5947	8,19
Wreningham	NFK	TM1698	9,187. 13,24
Wrentham	SFK	TM4882	26,12
Wrentnall	SHR	SJ4203	4,26,3
Wressle ER	YKS	SE7031	15E3 note. 21E5. SE,He6-7
[East] Wretham	NFK	TL9190	22,23
[West] Wretham	NFK	TL8991	22,23
Wribbenhall	WOR	SO7975	1,2
Wricklesmarsh	KEN	TQ4176	5,31
Wringhala	ESS	??	25,5
Wrington	SOM	ST4662	8,27
Wringworthy	DEV	SX5077	*17,13*
Writhlington	SOM	ST7055	47,23
Writtle	ESS	TL6706	1,24. 19,1. 20,51
Wrockwardine	SHR	SJ6212	4,1,1
Wropton (Wales)	SHR	SJ2300	4,1,36
Wrotham	KEN	TQ6159	2,10
Wrotham [Heath]	KEN	TQ6358	5,103
Wrottesley	STS	SJ8501	11,46
Wroughton	WIL	SU1480	2,7. 27,7. 67,38
Wroxall IOW	HAM	SZ5579	1,W14
Wroxeter	SHR	SJ5608	4,3,26
Wroxham	NFK	TG2917	1,190. 17,21. 20,19-21;24-25
Wroxton	OXF	SP4141	36,1
Wyaston	DBY	SK1842	6,59
Wyberton	LIN	TF3240	12,68-69. 57,27
Wyboston	BDF	TL1656	8,4. 21,2. 23,33. 24,24. 38,2. 55,4
Wybunbury	CHS	SJ6949	B8
Wychbold	WOR	SO9265	19,12
Wychwood	OXF	SP3317	1,10
Wycliffe NR	YKS	NZ1114	6N1 note. SN,CtA5
Wycomb	LEC	SK7724	1,3
[High] Wycombe	BKM	SU8693	19,2
[West] Wycombe	BKM	SU8294	3,1. 4,17. 12,5
Wyddial	HRT	TL3731	37,14
Wye	KEN	TR0546	D24. 6,1
[The River] Wye	HEF	??	10,7
Wyegate	GLS	SO5506	31,4
Wyfordby	LEC	SK7918	14,8. 18,4. 29,3
Wyham	LIN	TF2795	7,24-25. 14,64
Wyke (in Shobrooke)	DEV	SX8799	15,3
Wyke	SRY	SU9251	18,2
Wyke WR	YKS	SE1527	9W135. SW,M8
Wyke [Green] (in Axminster)	DEV	SY2996	52,24
Wykeham (in Nettleton)	LIN	TF1297	44,15
Wykeham (in Old Malton) NR	YKS	SE8175	1N63. SN,Ma3

Wykeham (near Scarborough) NR	YKS	SE9683	1Y3. 1N43. 31N9. SN,D8
[East] Wykeham	LIN	TF2288	16,37. 27,31-32
Wykeham [Hill] NR	YKS	SE8175	1N64. 2N1. SN,Ma4-5
[West] Wykeham (in Ludford Magna)	LIN	TF2189	25,18. 40,15-16
Wyken	SFK	TL9671	37,5. 66,4;8
Wykey	SHR	SJ3924	4,18,3
Wykham	OXF	SP4437	6,15
Wyld	BRK	SU5475	36,1
Wylye	WIL	SU0037	13,11
Wymering	HAM	SU6506	1,9
Wymeswold	LEC	SK6023	13,63. 18,2. 35,2. 42,6
Wymington	BDF	SP9564	25,6. 31,1. 32,6-7. 57,7;21
Wymondham	LEC	SK8518	14,6. 17,32
Wymondham	NFK	TG1101	1,215;237. 8,72;80. 66,39
[Great] Wymondley	HRT	TL2128	1,1. 5,6. 35,1. Appx
[Little] Wymondley	HRT	TL2127	20,6
Wyndlam	DOR	ST7829	47,1
Wynford [Eagle]˙	DOR	SY5895	34,9
Wyrley	STS	SK0105	2,16
Wysall	NTT	SK6027	9,90-91
Wythall	WOR	SP0774	1,1a
Wytham	BRK	SP4708	7,3
[Great] Wytheford	SHR	SJ5719	4,3,4-5. 4,14,2
[Little] Wytheford	SHR	SJ5619	4,8,8. 4,27,3
Wythemail	NTH	SP8471	39,5
Wythwood	WOR	SP0775	1,1a
Wyton	HUN	TL2772	6,9
Wyton ER	YKS	TA1733	14E6. SE,Hol11
Wyverstone	SFK	TM0467	1,83. 6,57;211. 14,123;134;151. 31,36. 57,1. 66,16
Wyville	LIN	SK8829	18,25 ˙

Y

Yaddlethorpe	LIN	SE8807	1,39;61. 68,37
Yafford IOW	HAM	SZ4481	9,23
Yafforth NR	YKS	SE3494	1Y2. 6N33. SN,A1. SN,CtA14
Yagdons (= Leaton near Baschurch)	SHR	SJ4619	4,27,28
Yalding	KEN	TQ6950	11,1
Yale: see Ial SHR			
Yanworth	GLS	SP0713	72,3
Yapham ER	YKS	SE7852	1E11. SE,Wa5
Yarburgh	LIN	TF3593	1,87. CS,8
Yarcombe	DEV	ST2408	11,3
Yard (in Ilfracombe)	DEV	SS4645	16,83
Yard (in Rose Ash)	DEV	SS7721	16,142
Yard (in Silverton)	DEV	SS9701	47,10
Yardley	ESS	TL5932	38,1
Yardley WAR	WAR	SP1385	EBW2
Yardley WAR	WOR		9,2
Yardley [Hastings]	NTH	SP8656	56,20a;57a
Yarkhill	HEF	SO6042	10,28
Yarlet	STS	SJ9129	8,12
Yarlington	SOM	ST6529	19,54
Yarm NR	YKS	NZ4112	1N121. 31N2. SN,A5
Yarmouth IOW	HAM	SZ3589	9,16
Yarmouth NFK	NFK	TG5207	1,67. ESf3
Yarmouth NFK	SFK		1,32. 14,162
Yarnfield WIL	SOM		23,1
Yarnfield WIL	WIL	ST7637	E3
Yarnscombe	DEV	SS5623	16,32. 36,1
Yarnton	OXF	SP4711	6,14. 7,34
Yarnwick NR	YKS	SE3181	6N148 *note*. SN, CtA40
Yarpole	HEF	SO4764	1,10a;36. 12,1
Yarsop	HEF	SO4047	2,3. 10,59. 14,10-11. 34,1
Yate	GLS	ST7182	3,1. WoB15
Yateholme WR	YKS	SE1104	1Y15 *note*. SW,Ag12
Yatesbury	WIL	SU0671	54,1
Yattendon	BRK	SU5574	22,8
Yatton	HEF	SO6330	1,75
Yatton	SOM	ST4365	6,14
Yatton [Keynell]	WIL	ST8676	6,1. 25,27. 32,14
Yaverland IOW	HAM	SZ6185	1,W5. 7,5
Yavington	HAM	SU5432	2,18. 14,6
Yawthorpe	LIN	SK8991	8,14. 16,26. 63,4
Yaxham	NFK	TG0010	4,15. 9,82. 13,22. 15,21-22. 21,20. 66,28
Yaxley	HUN	TL1892	7,1
Yaxley	SFK	TM1273	6,196;229. 18,6;19
Yazor	HEF	SO4046	10,58
Yeadbury	DEV	SS8610	34,36
Yeadon WR	YKS	SE2041	1W19 *note*. CW2. SW,Sk17
Yealand [Conyers and Redmayne] LAN	YKS	SD5074 SD5075	30W40 *note*. See also CHS
Yealmpton	DEV	SX5751	1,18
Yearsley NR	YKS	SE5874	23N1
Yeaton	SHR	SJ4319	4,3,55

Yeaveley	DBY	SK1840	6,61
Yelden	BDF	TL0166	3,4
Yeldersley	DBY	SK2144	6,45
[Great and Little] Yeldham	ESS	TL7538	20,25. 21,6. 23,7. 37,13. 90,54
		TL7739	
Yelford	OXF	SP3604	45,1
Yelling HUN	ESS		EHu
Yelling HUN	HUN	TL2662	6,15. 22,1. D7
Yelvertoft	NTH	SP6075	18,49;71. 22,8
Yelverton	NFK	TG2902	1,111. 2,7. 8,88. 9,36;161;165-166. 12,10
?[Hunt] Yelverton	NFK	TG2902	9,166 note
Yeovil	SOM	ST5516	19,83-84. 26,6
Yeovilton	SOM	ST5422	26,3
Yetminster	DOR	ST5910	2,4
Yeverington	SSX	TQ6102	10,7
Yockleton	SHR	SJ3910	4,4,11
Yokefleet ER	YKS	SE8132	3Y4 note. SE,C10 note. SE,How2
Yokefleet [Grange] (in Gilberdyke) ER	YKS	SE8224	3Y1 note. 11E5. SE, C10 note
York(shire) YKS	ESS		6,15. 30,16
York YKS	DEV		C4
York YKS	LIN		T1
York YKS	NTT		B20
York NR	YKS	SE6052	C1-22;29;37;40. 2B2. 22W6. CE20. CW35. SN,Y1;8
Yorton	SHR	SJ5023	3f,4
Youlgrave	DBY	SK2164	6,76
Youlthorpe ER	YKS	SE7655	2B11. 26E3. SE,P8
Youlton NR	YKS	SE4963	2N25. SN,B23
Yowlestone	DEV	SS8410	19,33
Yoxall	STS	SK1419	2,22
Yoxford	SFK	TM3968	7,18. 44,4
Ysceifiog FLN	CHS	SJ1869	FT1,4

Z

Zeal [Monachorum]	DEV	SS7204	6,3
Zeals	WIL	ST7831	64,1. 67,32
[Middle]zoy and [Weston]zoyland	SOM	ST3733	8,6
		ST3534	

PART TWO

Supplementary Index

A

Abbey Foregate: see Foregate			
Abcott	SHR	SO3978	4,20,24
Accott	DEV	SS6432	2,11
Acton (in Lydbury North)	SHR	SO3184	4,20,8
Adcote	SHR	SJ4119	4,3,52
Addiscott	DEV	SX6693	1,29
Adeney	SHR	SJ7018	4,1,23
Admaston	SHR	SJ6313	4,1,1
Affcot	SHR	SO4486	3g
Affeton	DEV	SS7513	1,3. 21,9-12
Aggborough	WOR	??	8,10a
Aldenham	SHR	SO6795	4,1,5
Alfardisworthy	DEV	SS2911	19,2
Alfordon	DEV	SX6196	16,3
Alkmond Park	SHR	SJ4815	3g,2
All Hallows	DOR	SU0212	1,3. 10,3
Allaleigh	DEV	SX8153	17,48
Allaston	GLS	SO6304	37,5
Allecot	SHR	??	4,3,19
Allen Wood	DEV	??	14,3-4
North Aller	DEV	SS6928	42,12-13
Allerford	DEV	SX4285	17,4
Allewston	DOR	ST6614	2,6
Allhallows	DEV	ST0910	34,20
Allscott	SHR	SJ6113	4,1,1
Almer	DOR	??	19,13
Als	DEV	??	40,2
Alscott	DEV	SS5225	15,39
Alston (in Holbeton)	DEV	SX5848	17,67
Alstone	GLS	SO9832	E19
Ampney *Mareys*	GLS	SP0704	67,2
Anderson	DOR	SY8897	26,13
Annery	DEV	SS4522	5. 5,6
Apley (in Stockton)	SHR	SO7199	4,8,15
Apley (in Wellington)	SHR	SJ6512	4,1,22
Applethorn Slade	DEV	??	1,7
Arkstone	HEF	SO4336	10,20
Arlescott	SHR	SJ6400	3c,2
Arleston	SHR	SJ6110	4,1,22
Armswell	DOR	ST7203	8,3
Arne	DOR	SY9788	19,10
Arscott	SHR	SJ4307	4,1,16
Arwystli (Wales)	SHR	??	4,1,15
Ash (? in Cullompton)	DEV	??	9,1
Ash (in Iddesleigh)	DEV	SS5706	1,63
Ash (in Netherbury)	DOR	SY4695	3,11
Ash Magna	SHR	SJ5739	4,13,1
Ash Parva	SHR	SJ5739	4,13,1
Seven Ash	DEV	SS6044	3,36
Chapel Ashe	DEV	ST2795	16,164
Ashfield	SHR	SO5889	4,1,26
Ashford (in Mamhead)	DEV	??	52,48

Ashford(near Bromfield)	SHR	??	3d,6
Ashford Bowdler	SHR	SO5170	EH1
Ashford Jones	SHR	SO5271	4,11,2-3
Ashforde (? in Kentisbeare)	DEV	??	51,7
Ashlees	SHR	SJ4010	4,1,16
Ashridge	DEV	SS4424	12,1
Ashton	DOR	SY6687	55,1
Ashton (in Hinton Parva)	DOR	SU0004	1,31
Ashwell	DEV	SX7655	1,15
Asmacun: see *Villa Asmacun*			
Asselonde	DEV	??	16,140
Assh	DEV	??	40,2
Assh: see *Choldasshe*			
Asterley	SHR	SJ3707	4,4,12
Asterton	SHR	SO3991	2,1
Astley (in Alveley)	SHR	SO7885	ES4-5
Astley Abbots	SHR	SO7096	4,1,5
Astley Nook	SHR	??	4,1,16
Astley Parva	SHR	??	4,1,5
Astol	SHR	SJ7300	4,8,15
Aston	SHR	SJ6109	3b,2. 4,1,22
Chetwynd Aston	SHR	SJ7417	4,1,23. 4,8,12
Church Aston	SHR	SJ7517	4,1,23. 4,8,12
Aston on Clun	SHR	SO3981	4,20,6
Aston Pigott	SHR	SJ3305	4,4,20
Aston Rogers	SHR	SJ3406	4,4,20
Astwick	NTH	SP5734	39,11
Astwood	WOR	SO9365	2,79
Atterley	SHR	SO6497	3c,2
Atworthy	DEV	SS3117	34,6
Audley Brow	SHR	SJ6335	4,8,1;7
Axnoller Farms	DOR	ST4803	3,10
		ST4904	
Aylton	HEF	SO6537	17,2
Ayneshill	DEV	??	15,44
Azores	DEV	SX4877	5,1

B

Babcombe	DEV	SX8677	34,44
Bache	SHR	SO4681	4,1,6
Bagber	DOR	ST7615	8,1
Baggeridge	DOR	??	56,30
Bagley	SHR	SJ4027	4,1,3
Balderton	SHR	SJ4823	4,3,53
Ballingham	HEF	SO5731	1,51
Banks Fee	GLS	SP1728	29,1
Bardley	SHR	SO6980	4,1,30
Barn Down: see *Down*			
Barnsley	DOR	SZ9903	1,3
Barnston	DOR	SY9381	41,2
Barrow	SHR	SO6599	3c,2
Beales Place	GLS	SP0828	76,1
Beaples Barton	DEV	??	23,10-11
East Barton (in Horwood)	DEV	SS5127	34,8
West Barton (in Horwood)	DEV	SS5027	3,17
Batchcott	SHR	SO4970	EH1
Batcombe	DOR	ST6104	47,2

Batshorne	DEV	SY1599	15,23
Batsworthy	DEV	SS8219	42,21
Bealy	DEV	SS7415	16,140
Beamish	SHR	SJ8204	4,1,25
Beara (in Rose Ash)	DEV	SS7720	16,142
Beardon	DEV	SX5184	39,1
Beare (in Broad Clyst)	DEV	SS9800	1,56
Bearscombe	DEV	SX7544	24,18
Beckett	DEV	SX4196	17,12
Beckjay	SHR	SO3977	4,20,25
Beden	DEV	??	25,16
Beer Hackett	DOR	ST5911	2,6
Belchalwell	DOR	ST7909	19,9
Belhuish	DOR	SY8282	26,50-51
Bellamarsh	DEV	SX8577	34,44
Benley	DEV	SS7315	16,140
Benthall (near Much Wenlock)	SHR	SJ6602	3c,2
Benville	DOR	ST5303	17,1
Beobridge	SHR	SO7991	ES3
Berrow	WOR	SO7934	2,62
Berwick	DOR	SY5289	34,8
Bestedon	DOR	??	12,4
Betchcott	SHR	SO4398	4,27,13
Bettiscombe	DOR	SY3999	17,1
Bickington (near Ashburton)	DEV	SX7972	2,19
Welsh Bicknor HEF	GLS	SO5917	E35
Bicton (in Clun)	SHR	SO2882	4,20,8
Billingsley	SHR	SO7085	4,1,5
Billington	BDF	SP9422	1,1
Binghams	DOR	SY4796	3,11
Binnegar	DOR	SY8787	37,9
Binweston	SHR	SJ3004	4,4,20
Birch	DEV	SS7005	1,64
Bishops Castle: see Castle			
Bishops Down: see Down			
Bishopsleigh	DEV	SS7809	2,2
Bishton	GLS	ST3887	W2;5;13
Bitton Prebend	GLS	ST6869	78,13
Blackaton	DEV	SX6977	16,163
Blackberry	DEV	SY0686	1,9
Blackmore	DOR	ST6709	12,1
Blagdon	DEV	SX3696	17,15
Blakemoor	SHR	SO4288	3g
Blandford Forum	DOR	??	1,5
Blashenwell	DOR	SY9580	19,10
Blatchworthy	DEV	SS8817	47,13
Bletchley	SHR	SJ6233	4,8,1;7
Blinsham	DEV	SS5116	36,7
Blodwell	SHR	SJ2622	4,3,36
Bobbington STS	SHR	??	ES. ES3
Bockleton	SHR	SO5783	3c,9
Great Bolas	SHR	SJ6421	4,11,18
Little Bolas	SHR	SJ6421	4,1,4. 4,11,19
The Bold	SHR	SO6484	4,21,13
Bolealler	DEV	ST0204	32,3
Boningale	SHR	SJ8102	4,8,15
Boohay	DEV	SX8952	23,16
Booley	SHR	SJ5725	4,25,2
Boraston	SHR	SO6170	5,1
Borcombe	DEV	SY1991	34,54
Boringdon	DEV	SX5358	1,17

Borough (in Chivelstone)	DEV	SX7937	17,53
Borough (in Mortehoe)	DEV	SS4844	31,3-4
Bosomzeal	DEV	SX8554	1,34
Bothenhampton	DOR	SY4791	1,13
Bottreaux Mill	DEV	SS8226	1,41
Botvyle	SHR	SO4796	4,27,12
Boulsdon	GLS	SO7024	16,1
Boveria	SHR	??	4,5,2. 4,22,2. 4,27,8;13;15
Bovystok	DEV	??	2,11
Bow	SHR	SO3689	2,1
Bowden (in Cheriton Bishop)	DEV	SX7492	16,130
Bowden (in Totnes)	DEV	SX8058	1,34
Bowerhayes	DEV	ST1408	34,25
Bowerswain	DOR	SU0009	26,44
Bowley	GLS	SU0199	69,5
Bradeley	SHR	SO5994	3c,2
Bradham	DEV	SY0181	9. 1,9
Bradiford	DEV	SS7306	24,28
Bradley	SHR	SJ6301	3c,2
Little Bray (in Charles)	DEV	SS6835	3,30
South Bray (in Chittlehampton)	DEV	SS6624	1,41
Brenton	DEV	SX9086	1,4
Brerlawe	SHR	??	4,5,11
Bretchel	SHR	SJ3311	4,4,16
Brewood Forest	SHR	??	4,25,6
Bridge (in North Tawton)	DEV	SS6502	16,56
Bridgnorth	SHR	SO7193	4,1,5
Bridgwalton	SHR	SO6892	4,1,5
Brightlycott	DEV	SS5835	16,65
Brightston	DEV	??	1,56. 43,2
Brisworthy	DEV	SX5565	17,79-82
Broadridge	DEV	SS8508	1,9. 35,24
Broadstone	SHR	SO5489	4,3,9
Broadward	SHR	SO3876	4,20,12
Broadwell (in Leckhampton)	GLS	SO9419	38,1
Brockhampton	DOR	ST7106	8,3
Brockhill	DEV	SX9895	1,56
Brockton (in Lydbury North)	SHR	SO3285	2,1
Little Bromfield	SHR	??	3d,6
Bromlow	SHR	SJ3101	4,27,23
Brompton	SHR	SJ5407	4,27,24
Little Brompton	SHR	SO3681	4,20,4
Bromwich	SHR	SJ3225	4,6,6
Broncroft	SHR	SO5386	4,1,6
Broomcroft	SHR	SJ5601	4,3,19
Broome (in Sibdon Carwood)	SHR	SO4080	4,20,7
Broomford	DEV	SS5701	5,4
Broomscott	DEV	SS6231	2,11
Broseley	SHR	SJ6701	3c,2
Broughall	SHR	SJ5641	4,13,1
Broughton (in Claverley)	SHR	SO8091	ES3
Broughton (in Lydham)	SHR	SO3090	2,1
Brownstone (in Brixham)	DEV	SX9050	23,16
Brownstone (? in Newton Ferrers)	DEV	SX5949	15,37
Brunslow	SHR	SO3684	4,20,14
La Brunthuchene	DEV	??	34,16
Buckerell	DEV	ST1200	34,23
Buckfastleigh	DEV	SX7366	6,13
Bucknell	WOR	??	8,8
Budbrooke	DEV	SX7592	1,28
Budleigh Salterton	DEV	??	1,9

Little Buildwas	SHR	SJ6404	4,3,26
Bunson	DEV	SS6917	16,140
Buntingsdale	SHR	SJ6532	4,14,15
Burcot	SHR	SJ6211	4,1,1
Burdon	DEV	SS4703	16,19
Burghope	HEF	SO5050	1,4. 10,11
Burhulla	SHR	??	4,8,7
Burley	HAM	SU2103	1,30
Burley	SHR	SO4781	4,1,29
Burlton	SHR	SJ4626	4,1,18
Burrough	DEV	SX7491	52,15
Burstow SRY	SSX	TQ3141	2,9
Burton (in Charminster)	DOR	SY6891	1,4
Burton (in Marnhull)	DOR	ST7819	8,1
Burton (in Winfrith)	DOR	SY8386	1,6
Burton: see Longburton			
Burway	SHR	SO5075	3d,6
Bushmoor	SHR	SO4387	3g. 4,28,4
Buskin	DEV	SS5901	16,18
Buston: see Buskin			
Buttington (Wales)	SHR	SJ2408	4,1,8
Bystock	DEV	SY0283	1,46

C

Cadbury (in Chulmleigh)	DEV	SS6917	16,140
Cadover	DEV	SX5564	17,79-82
Calchurch	DEV	??	16,137
Caldicott (The Heath)	SHR	SJ3522	4,27,34
Callaughton	SHR	SO6197	3c,2
Calvington	SHR	SJ7022	4,11,18
Campscott	DEV	SS4944	3,46
Canworthy	DEV	SS8419	16,148
Carey	DEV	SX3691	1,50
Casehayes	DEV	??	1,11
Castell Coch	GLS	ST4188	W18
Bishops Castle	SHR	SO3288	2,1
Castle Foregate: see Foregate			
Castleton	DOR	ST6417	3,4
Catshayes	DEV	SY1397	16,97-100;102
Caughley	SHR	SJ6900	3c. 3c,2. 4,8,4
Caulston	DEV	SX5647	17,68
Bishops Caundle	DOR	ST6913	2,6
Caundle Marsh	DOR	ST6812	2,6
Cause	SHR	SJ3307	4,4,20
Causeway	DOR	SY6581	26,14-16
Caynton	SHR	SJ6921	4,11,18
Cedewain (Wales)	SHR	??	4,1,15
Ceri (Wales)	SHR	??	4,1,15
Nether Cerne	DOR	SY6698	11,1
Chaceley GLS	WOR	SO8530	8,9a
Chalmington	DOR	ST5900	12. 12,1
Chamberlains	GLS	ST9497	78,4
Champson	DEV	SS8028	3,61
Chantmarle	DOR	ST5802	12,4
Chapel Marsh	DOR	ST4804	3,10
Chapner	DEV	SS8113	3,80
Charlecombe	DEV	SX9070	48,4;10

Charlham	GLS	SU0999	67,1
Charlton	DOR	SY6895	1,4. 26,5;8-11
Charlton	GLS	ST5880	3,1
Charlton (near Preston Gubbals)	SHR	??	3g. 3g,8
Charlton (in Wrockwardine)	SHR	SJ5911	4,1,1
Charlton	WOR	SP0045	2,73
Chatwall	SHR	SO5097	4,3,44
Chawleigh Week: see Week			
Chawlmoor	DEV	SS9123	3,74
Cheddington	DOR	ST4805	3,10
Chelsdon	DEV	SS4810	52,5-6
Chenson	DEV	SS7009	16,43
Chesewaldesleye	SHR	??	5,4
Chesterton	GLS	SP0100	32,1
Cheswardine Hall	SHR	SJ7230	ES8
Cheswell	SHR	SJ7116	4,19,1
Chetnole	DOR	ST6008	2,4
Chieflowman	DEV	ST0015	1,70
Chillaton	DEV	SX4381	5,2
Chilton (in Thorverton)	DEV	SS9205	1,7. 44,2
Chirbury (in Hodnet)	SHR	SJ5928	4,10,3
Chittlehamholt	DEV	SS6421	52,10
Chochele	DEV	??	15,44
Choldasshe	DEV	??	25,8-9
Chollaton	DEV	SS3714	35,9
Christchurch	GLS	ST3389	W2;19
Christow	DEV	SX8384	16,106;128
Churchstowe	DEV	SX7145	6,9
Cilcewydd (Wales)	SHR	SJ2203	4,1,35;36
Clapley	GLS	SP1530	57,1
Clayfelton	SHR	SO5076	3d,6
Cleedowntown	SHR	SO5880	3c,9
Cleeton St Mary	SHR	SO6178	4,14,22
Cleeve	DEV	SX6355	1,23
Clevelode	WOR	SO8247	8,10a
Cliff	SHR	SJ6532	4,7,1
Clifton	DEV	SX8850	23,22
Clive	SHR	SJ5124	3d,1
Clotley	SHR	SJ6310	4,1,1
Clotworthy	DEV	SS6828	3,56-57
Cluddley	SHR	SJ6310	4,1,1
Bishops Clyst	DEV	??	3,7
Clyst Honiton	DEV	SX9893	2,15-17
La Clyve	DEV	??	1,44
Coates *Cockerell*	GLS	SO9800	67,3
Coates *Randulf*	GLS	SO9800	39,19
Coates	SHR	SO5890	4,8,6
Coats	SHR	SO5292	4,8,5
Cobden	DEV	??	19,20
Cobintone	SHR	??	ES
Cockesputt	DEV	ST0801	16,95
Cocktree	DEV	SX6698	51,2
Codrington	GLS	ST7278	1,9. 43,1
Cofflete	DEV	SX5451	1,18
Colbrook	DEV	ST0006	9,1
Colcombe	DEV	SY2494	1,13
Coldethorn	DEV	??	52,20
Coldra	GLS	ST3490	W19
Colebatch	SHR	SO3187	2,1
Colebrook (in Plympton St Mary)	DEV	SX5457	1,17
Colebrooke (near Crediton)	DEV	SS7700	2,2

Colewilhilt	DEV	??	15,44
Colhays	DEV	ST1299	25,14;21
Collacott	DEV	SS6511	1,64
Collaton (in Halwell)	DEV	SX7952	1,34
Collaton St Mary	DEV	SX8660	2,18
Colleton	DEV	SS6614	16,140
Colley	DEV	SX8194	16,119-120
Colmer	DEV	SX7053	24,20
Colston	DEV	SS8614	3,73
Coltleigh	DOR	SY5199	3,10
Colway	DOR	??	8,6
Colyford	DEV	SY2592	1,13
Challons Combe	DEV	SX6748	35,26
Combe (in Aveton Giffard)	DEV	SX6748	35,26
Combe (in Bigbury)	DEV	SX6748	15,44
Combe (in Cornwood)	DEV	SX6261	15,36
Combe Deverel	DOR	??	26,21-22
Combe Lancey	DEV	SS8101	2,2
Combe Pafford	DEV	SX9166	2,7-8
Combend	GLS	SO9811	68,9
Comberoy	DEV	ST0100	49,3
Comley	SHR	SO4896	4,27,12
Compton Pool	DEV	SX8665	2,18
Cookbury	DEV	SS4005	28,3
Coombe (in Puddington)	DEV	SS8411	19,39. 50,4
Coombe (in Witheridge)	DEV	??	50,4
Coombe (in Castleton)	DOR	ST6218	2,6
Coombeland	DEV	SS9010	36,20
Cornwood	SHR	??	5,1
Corscombe	DEV	SX6296	16,14
Corstone	DEV	SS6104	16,26;28;30
Corve	SHR	SO5993	3c,6. 4,3,13
Cotwall	SHR	SJ6017	4,1,21
Countess Wear: see Wear			
Cove	DEV	SS9519	1,35
Cowley	DEV	SX9095	3,67. 24,2
Cowsden	WOR	SO9453	8,11
Coxall HEF	SHR	SO3774	6,27-28
Coxleigh	DEV	SS5835	16,65
Coxwell	DEV	SS6003	39,5.
Crackaway	DEV	SS5341	3,40-41
Crannaford	DEV	SS0196	1,56
Crebor	DEV	SX4572	5,1;4
Creketway	DOR	??	26,14-16
Little Crichel	DOR	??	1,3
Crick	GLS	ST4890	W16
Criddon	SHR	SO6691	4,3,61
Cripton	DOR	??	57,3
Crockadon	DEV	SX7753	1,34
Croft	SHR	SO6894	4,1,5
Crossworthy	DEV	??	17,15
Cruckmeole	SHR	SJ4209	4,1,16
Cruckton	SHR	SJ4310	4,1,16
Cruft	DEV	SX5296	16,22
Cudliptown	DEV	SX5279	5,1
Culmayre	SHR	??	4,19,1
Cutland	DEV	SS6817	16,140
Cutton	DEV	SX9798	16,90
Cwmcarvan	GLS	SO4707	W2

D

Daccombe	DEV	SX9068	5. 5,12-13
Daglingworth	GLS	SO9905	31,7. 32,2
Dainton	DEV	??	7,2. 33,1
Dalditch	DEV	SY0483	1,9
Dalwood DEV	DOR	ST2400	1,4. 12,14
Darliston	SHR	SJ5833	1,8
Dartmoor	DEV	??	1,2
Dartmouth	DEV	SX8751	23,22
Dene (in West Down)	DEV	SS5042	3,26
Dennington (in Swimbridge)	DEV	SS6228	2,11
Deptford (in Cruwys Morchard)	DEV	SS8412	36,21-23
Deptford (in Hartland)	DEV	SS2618	52,31
Deverel	DOR	SY8098	46,1
Dewelepole	DOR	ST6812	2,6
Dewstow	GLS	ST4688	W6
Dexbeer	DEV	SS2909	34,2
Didcot	GLS	SP0035	1,59
Diddlebury	SHR	SO5085	4,1,6
Dimworthy	DEV	SS3115	34,6
Lower and Upper Dinchope	SHR	SO4584	3d,6. 4,20,21
		SO4583	
Dingestow	GLS	SO4510	E35
Dinnaton (in Swimbridge)	DEV	SS6228	2,11
The Ditches	SHR	SJ4929	4,14,4
Dixton	GLS	SO5113	E35
Doddiscombe	DEV	SS9823	23,5
Dodecote	SHR	SJ6723	4,3,23
Donnington (near Oakengates)	SHR	SJ7012	3g,3
Donnington (in Wroxeter)	SHR	SJ5707	3b,2
Dorn GLS	WOR	SP2034	2,38
Dornaford and Dornaford Park	DEV	SS5900	16,18
		SX6099	
Dorsley	DEV	SX7760	1,34
Dorweeke	DEV	SS9506	47,9
Dothill	SHR	SJ6412	4,1,22
Doune: see Stevenedon			
Dovaston	SHR	SJ3421	4,3,43
Dowles WOR	SHR	SO7776	4,1,30
Barn Down	DOR	??	55,25
Bishops Down	DOR	ST6712	2,6
Guilden Down	SHR	SO3082	4,20,8
West Down (in Bradworthy)	DEV	SS2914	34,6
Downing	GLS	SO9228	1,45
Downton (in Stanton Lacy)	SHR	SO5279	7,4
Downton (in Upton Magna)	SHR	SJ5412	4,3,24
Downton on the Rock HEF	SHR	??	6
Dowrich	DEV	SS8205	2,2
Drascombe	DEV	SX7092	1,28
Draycott	HEF	SO5053	1,10b
Druce	DOR	SY7495	26,21-22
Dryton	SHR	SJ5805	3b,2
Duddlewick	SHR	SO6583	4,1,30
Dudley Moor	DOR	??	12,4
Dudmaston	SHR	SO7488	EW1
Dunhampstead	WOR	SO9160	2,68
Dunstable	BDF	TL0121	1,2
Duntish	DOR	ST6907	8,3
Duvale	DEV	SS9420	23,5

E

Earlscombe	DEV	SX6555	15,75
Earnwood	SHR	SO7380	6,2
Eastacombe	DEV	SX5599	16,23
Eastbrook	DEV	ST0817	24,30
Eastdown	DEV	SX3499	17,15
Easton	DEV	SX7293	52,11
Eaton (in Lydbury North)	SHR	SO3789	4,5,6
Eaton upon Tern	SHR	SJ6523	4,8,7
Ebberly	DEV	SS5618	3,19
Edgbolton	SHR	SJ5721	4,3,4-5
Edge	SHR	SJ3908	4,1,16
Mount Edgecumbe	DEV	??	1,20-22
Edgerley	SHR	SJ3518	4,27,4
Edmeston	DEV	SX6452	15,26;28;64
Eggardon	DOR	SY5393	53,2
Eggesford	DEV	SS6811	16,57
Eggington	BDF	SP9525	1,1b
Ellerton	SHR	SJ7125	4,19,2;4
Ellston	DOR	ST6302	12,1
Elmley Castle	WOR	SO9841	2,73
Enchmarsh	SHR	SO5096	4,3,44
Encombe	DOR	SY9478	19,10
Ensdon	SHR	SJ4016	4,3,50
Ernly: see Benville			
Ernsborough: see Irishborough			
Eseberge	SHR	??	EW2
Espley	SHR	SJ6026	4,3,1
Estcourt	GLS	ST8991	73,3
Estelleia	DEV	??	11,1
Estwere	DEV	??	3,39. 36,11
Eton under Heywood	SHR	SO5090	3c,3;4
Evelith	SHR	SJ7405	4,9,1. 4,19,9
Everards	DOR	??	57,1
Exbridge	DEV	SS9320	23,5
Exton	DEV	SX9886	34,34
Eye	SHR	SJ6005	4,9,3-4
Eyton (in Lydbury North)	SHR	SO3787	2,1

F

Fair Oak: see Oak			
Fairfield	WOR	SO9475	26,13
Great Fairwood	DEV	SX8194	19,30
Felhampton	SHR	SO4487	4,3,47. 9,1
Felton	SHR	SO5076	3d,6
La Fenne	DEV	??	19,18
Fernhill (in Clawton)	DEV	SX3398	17,15
Fertecota	SHR	??	4,1,5. 4,3,8
Finelegh	DOR	??	13,1
Fishleigh	DEV	SS5505	5,4
Flyford Flavell	WOR	SO9854	8,15

Fludda	DEV	SX8479	16,155
Foghanger	DEV	SX4278	5,2
Foldhay	DEV	SS7004	47,2-4
Folk	DOR	ST6513	2,6
Ford (in Crediton Hamlets)	DEV	SX7997	2,2
Ford and Ford Farm (in Coryton)	DEV	SX4784	3,9
		SX4683	
The Ford	SHR	SO6584	4,3,66
Forde	DEV	ST3604	16,165
Forde	DEV	??	15,31
Fordesham	SHR	??	4,1,16
Foregate	SHR	??	3b,1
La Forsen	DEV	??	15,52
Four Shire Stone(s)	WAR	SP2332	3,4
Foxcote	SHR	SO7181	6,9
Frampton Court	GLS	SP0132	11,4
France	DEV	ST0808	16,101
France	DOR	??	1,28
Freemancott	DEV	??	24,6
Frieland	DEV	??	32,3
Frodetone	DEV	??	16,78
Frome Whitwell	DOR	SY6791	1,4
Fromemouth	DOR	??	12
Fulcume	DOR	??	1,27
Fursdon	DEV	SS9204	19,24
Furze (in Shobrooke)	DEV	SS8800	36,19
Furzehill	DEV	SS7244	19,16
Fytelecoth'	DEV	??	42,9

G

Gabwell	DEV	SX9269	16,117. 48,3
Ganarew HEF	GLS	SO5216	E35
Garland	DEV	SS7118	16,140
Garmston	SHR	SJ6006	4,3,22
Garth	GLS	SO5213	E35
Gatacre	SHR	SO7990	ES3
Gatemerston	DOR	SY8481	26,50-51
Gatsford	HEF	SO6126	1,1. 6,1
Godford	DEV	ST1302	19,26;32
Godlingston	DOR	SZ0280	8,3
Godmanstone	DOR	SY6697	11,1. 24,5
Godwynescoth	DEV	??	52,9
Goldcliff	GLS	ST3683	W2;19
Goldstone	SHR	SJ7028	4,3,23
Goodameavy	DEV	SX5364	17,79-82
Gorewell	DOR	SY5787	53,2
Gorlofen	DEV	SX5652	17,86-87
Grafton	SHR	SJ4318	4,20,15
Gratton (in Meavy)	DEV	SX5267	17,79-82
Green Island	DOR	??	12. 12,13
Greendale	DEV	SY8809	1,33
Greendown (in Northlew)	DEV	SX4899	35,7
Greendown (in Warkleigh)	DEV	SS6524	1,41
Greete	SHR	SO5770	5,1
Grendon	DEV	SS8017	42,19
Grilstone	DEV	SS7324	2,21
Grimstone	DOR	SY6494	2,1

Grindle	SHR	SJ7503	4,9,1
Grindle Brook	DEV	??	1,33
Grosmont	GLS	SO4024	W4
Grove Court	GLS	SO8514	1,2
Guildborough	WAR	SP2332	3,4
Guilden Down: see Down			
Gussage St Andrew	DOR	??	19,1

H

Habberley	SHR	SJ3903	4,4,20
Great Hagley	SHR	SO3476	4,20,12
Little Hales	SHR	SJ7416	4,1,23
Halesowen WOR	SHR	??	E
Halfhide	DOR	??	12,1
Halford	DEV	SX6497	16,14
Halford	SHR	SO4383	3d,6. 4,20,21
Hallows: see All Hallows			
Halmpstone	DEV	SS5928	2,11
Halsdon (in Cookbury)	DEV	SS3805	28,3
Halsdon (in Dolton)	DEV	SS5512	42,7
Halsford	DEV	SX8793	1,28
Halstock	DOR	ST5307	2-3. 3,8
Halswill	DEV	??	1,23
Lady, Hill and Priors Halton	SHR	SO4775	3d,6
		SO4875	
		SO4975	
Hamelton	DOR	??	11,15
Hamworthy	DOR	??	31,1
Handsford (in Bondleigh)	DEV	SS6404	3,20
Handsford (in Chawleigh)	DEV	SS7210	16,140
Hannaborough	DEV	SS5202	5,4
Little Hanwood	SHR	SJ4407	4,1,16
Harberton	DEV	SX7758	1,34
Harbertonford	DEV	SX7856	1,34
Hardingsleigh	DEV	SS7212	16,43
Hardisworthy	DEV	SS2220	36,3-4
Hardness	DEV	??	23,22
Hardwick	GLS	ST5393	W16
Hardwick	SHR	SO3690	2,1
Hardwicke	SHR	SJ5121	4,3,58
Harewood	HEF	SO5226	1,52
Harford (in Landkey)	DEV	SS6031	2,11
Hargreaves	SHR	SJ3110	4,1,8
Harlescott	SHR	SJ5015	4,3,51;57
Harnage	SHR	SO5604	4,3,16
Harpford	DEV	SY0990	1,9. 11,1. 52,35
Harpsford	SHR	SO6991	4,1,5
Harrington	SHR	SJ7402	4,26,5
Harrowbeer	DEV	SX5168	21
Harthall	SHR	SO5970	5,1
Hartley	DOR	ST6406	1,4
Harton	SHR	SO4888	3c,3
Haske	DEV	SS8502	3,72
Haston	SHR	SJ5120	4,3,58
Hatch	DEV	SX7146	17,32
Hatton (in Eaton under Heywood)	SHR	SO4690	3c,3
Haughton (in Morville)	SHR	SO6795	4,1,5

Haughton (in Shifnal)	SHR	SJ7408	4,9,1
Haukadon	DEV	SX3689	1,50
Haw	GLS	SO8427	20,1
Hawkchurch DEV	DOR	??	11,1
Hawkerland	DEV	SY0588	23,5
Hawkhurst	SHR	SO4288	4,28,4
Hawkstone	SHR	SJ5829	4,10,3
Hawson	DEV	SX7168	1,34
Haydon	DOR	ST6715	2,6
Hayes	SHR	SJ3515	4,4,10
Haylake	DEV	SX7892	16,130
Hayne (in Bishops Nympton)	DEV	SS7725	2,21
Hayne (in Brushford)	DEV	SS6709	16,53-54
Hayne (in Whitestone)	DEV	SX8693	16,125
Moss Hayne	DEV	SX9895	16,92
Lower Hayton	SHR	SO5080	7,4
Upper Hayton	SHR	SO5181	7,4
Heane?	KEN	TQ1535	9,47
Heath	SHR	SO5585	3c,9
Heath Barton	DEV	SX8494	16,137
The Heath: see Caldicott			
Heazille	DEV	SS9500	3,68
La Heghland	DEV	??	15,22
Hele (in Bickleigh)	DEV	SX5262	21,21
Hele (in Bradninch)	DEV	SY9902	16,104
Hele (in Clayhanger)	DEV	ST0222	23,5
Helshaw	SHR	SJ6329	1,9. 4,8,7
The Hem	SHR	SJ7305	4,9,1
Henceford	DEV	SS8211	1,32
Hencott	SHR	SJ4815	3g. 3g,2
Hendrew	GLS	ST3991	W18
Henland	DEV	ST0807	9,1
Henley (in Acton Scott)	SHR	SO4588	4,27,33
Henstill	DEV	SS8003	2,2
Hermitage	DOR	ST6407	1,4
Hernaford	DEV	SX7855	20,17
Hetherland	DEV	??	11,1
Hethley	SHR	??	4,13,1
Hewstock: see Yewstock			
Heywood	SHR	SO6282	4,3,66
Highweek	DEV	SX8471	1,10
Hilfield	DOR	ST6305	12. 12,1
Hill(? in Colyton)	DEV	??	21,15. 51,10
Hill (in Farringdon)	DEV	SY0090	34,34
Hill (in Iddesleigh)	DEV	SS5806	1,63
Hill(? in Merton)	DEV	??	24,6
Hill (in Withycombe Raleigh).	DEV	SY0081	1,9
Hill	SHR	??	EH1
Court of Hill	SHR	SO6072	5,1
Hill Hall	SHR	SJ7230	ES8
Hill House	SHR	SJ6529	4,8,7
Hinnington	SHR	SJ7404	4,9,1
Hinton	DEV	??	1,44
Hinton (in Dyrham)	GLS	ST7376	35,2
Hinton (in Stottesdon)	SHR	SO6582	4,1,30
Hinton (in Whitchurch)	SHR	SJ5343	4,13,1
Hinton Parva	DOR	SU0004	1,31
Hints	SHR	SO6175	4,11,4
Hiscott	DEV	SS5426	1,40. 25,3. 40,2
Hisland	SHR	SJ3127	4,6,6
Hockford Waters	DEV	ST0220	23,7

Hodenac	HEF	SO5314	10,7
Holbeton	DEV	SX6150	1,23
Holcombe (in Dawlish)	DEV	SX9574	2. 2,4-6. 16,131
Holditch	DEV	ST3402	23,17
Eight Holes	DOR	??	58,3
Holleham	DEV	??	1,4
Hollocombe	DEV	SS6311	1,64
Holnest	DOR	ST6509	2,6
Holt	SHR	SO5396	4,21,7
Holwell	DEV	SX6647	15,44
Nether Holwells	DEV	SS0297	1,56
Clyst Honiton: see Clyst			
Hoo Meavy: see Meavy			
Hood	DEV	SX7763	20,15
Hoodown	DEV	SX8852	17,29
Hook (in Okehampton)	DEV	SX5896	16,3
Hookedrise	DEV	ST1207	19,27
Hookney	DEV	SX7182	52,44
Hookway	DEV	SX8598	2,2
Hope (Wales)	SHR	SJ2507	4,1,8
Hope (near Worthen)	SHR	SJ3401	4,4,20
Hope Bagot	SHR	SO5874	4,11,4
Hopton (in Great Ness)	SHR	SJ3820	4,1,17
Hopton Cangeford	SHR	SO5480	7,4
Horner	DEV	SX7654	1,15
Horridge	DEV	SX7674	19,29. 32,6-7
Horswell	DEV	SX6942	39,15
Hortonlane	SHR	SJ4411	4,4,12
Houghton	DEV	SX6546	15,44
Houndbeare Farms	DEV	SY0493	14,3-4. 16,136
		SY0593	
Howton	DEV	SX7487	1,45
Hudson	DEV	SS2909	34,2
Hughley	SHR	SO5698	3c,14
Humphreston	SHR	SJ8105	4,25,6
Hundeslawa	HEF	??	15,10
Hunecroft	DOR	??	26,44
Hungerford	GLS	SP1913	39,15
Hungerstone	HEF	SO4435	1,3
Hungryhatton	SHR	SJ6726	4,3,23
Hunkington	SHR	SJ5613	4,3,24
Hurdwick	DEV	SX4775	5,1
Hyde	DOR	ST9109	19,8
Hyde	GLS	SO6812	32,10
Hyssington (Wales)	SHR	SO3194	4,1,35

I

Iddlecott	DEV	SS5712	40,7
Ieclescombe	DEV	??	15,44
Ifton	GLS	ST4688	W2;18
Incledon	DEV	SS4738	3,43. 19,12-13
Innerstone	GLS	SO7529	E21. EvA105. EvC25. WoB5. WoC4
Irishborough	DEV	SS6328	2,11
Itton	GLS	ST4995	W2;16

J

Jacobstowe	DEV	SS5701	4. 5,4
Jay HEF	SHR	SO3974	4,20,25
Jewelscombe	DEV	??	15,44
Julian	DEV	SS3614	35,9
Jurston	DEV	SX6984	16,61–62;64

K

Kemeys Commander	GLS	SO3404	W2
Kemeys Inferior	GLS	ST3892	W2;18
The Kempley	SHR	SJ5936	4,13,1
Kempthorne	DEV	SX3497	17,15
Kenbury	DEV	SX9287	1,4
Kendon	DEV	SX7181	52,44
Kennerleigh	DEV	SS8107	2,2
Kennicott	DEV	SX3598	17,15
Kenstone	SHR	SJ5928	4,10,3
Kentleworth	DOR	??	8,1
Kerscott	DEV	SS7925	2,21
Kerswell (in Hatherleigh)	DEV	SS5203	5,4
Ketley	SHR	SJ6710	4,3,30
Keysett	SHR	SO2782	4,20,8
Kilbury	DEV	SX7566	1,23. 6,13
Kilgwrrwg	GLS	ST4698	W2
Killatree	DEV	SS3203	17,15
Killerton	DEV	SS9701	1,56
Kilsall	SHR	SJ7906	4,1,25
Kingsbridge	DEV	SX7344	6,9
Kingsford	DEV	SX8391	1,69
Kingsland (in Netherbury)	DOR	SY4597	1,2
Kingsley	SHR	SO6995	4,1,5
Kingston	DEV	SX6347	1,23
Kingston Lacy	DOR	SZ9701	1,3
Kingston Maurward	DOR	SY7191	1,4
Kingston Russell	DOR	SY5891	1,2
Kingswear	DEV	SX8851	23,22
Kingswell	DEV	SX8592	1,69
Kingswood	GLS	ST7491	E16
Kinnerton	SHR	SO3796	4,4,4
Kinseys HEF	SHR	SO3269	5,4
Lower and Upper Kinsham HEF	SHR	SO3564	5,5
		SO3664	
Kinson	SHR	SO5782	3c,9
Kinton (in Great Ness)	SHR	SJ3719	4,1,17
Kinton (in Leintwardine)	SHR	SO4074	6,11
Kinton (in Middleton in Chirbury)	SHR	SO2899	4,5,13
Kipscott	DEV	SS8026	2,21
Kismeldon	DEV	SS3416	28,4
East Knighton	DOR	SY8185	1,6
South Knighton	DEV	SX8172	2,20
Knightstone	DEV	SS7806	2,2
Knightstreet	DOR	ST7719	8,1
Knockin	SHR	SJ3322	4,3,43
Knoll	DOR	ST7004	8,3
Knowle	DEV	SS7801	2,2

Knowle (in Woodlands)	DOR	SU0309	56,30
Knowle	SHR	SJ7208	4,9,1
Kynetete	DEV	??	34,16
Kynewardesbergh'	DEV	??	1,56

L

Lamsede	DEV	??	52,53
Landkey	DEV	SS5931	2,11
Lane	DEV	SS3420	36,2. 42,3
Langabeare	DEV	SS5501	5,4
Langdon	DOR	ST5001	3,10
Langham	DEV	SX6256	15,70
Langley (in Cadeleigh)	DEV	SS9109	1,9
Langston	DEV	SX6448	17,65
Langstone	GLS	ST3789	W2;9
Langton Matravers	DOR	SY9978	37,13
Langton Wallis	DOR	??	37,13
Lapland	DEV	??	1,15;55
Larcombe	DEV	SX7457	28,12
Larden	SHR	SO5693	3c,6
Lawton	SHR	SO5183	4,1,6
Lea	DEV	??	23,5;7
Lea (in Lydham)	SHR	SO3589	2,1
Lea (near Pontesbury)	SHR	SJ4108	4,1,16
Lea (in Preston Gubbals)	SHR	SJ4921	3g. 3g,8
Leaton (in Wrockwardine)	SHR	SJ6111	4,1,1
Lower Ledwyche	SHR	SO5374	3d,4;6
Lee	DEV	SS4846	16,83
Lee (in Ellesmere)	SHR	SJ4032	4,1,19
La Lee	DOR	ST8301	12,11
Malins Lee	SHR	SJ6909	4,3,30
The Lee	SHR	SJ6626	4,3,23
The Lees	SHR	SJ6638	4,23,9
Leeson	DOR	SZ0078	1,8
Leeton	SHR	??	1,8
Leigh	DOR	ST6108	2,4
Leigh	SHR	SJ3303	4,4,20
Leigh	WOR	??	2,52
Leigham	DEV	SX5158	17,69;75
Leweston	DOR	ST6312	2,6
Leworthy	DEV	SS3201	17,15
Ley (in Bere Ferrers)	DEV	SX4564	15,46
Ley (in North Huish)	DEV	SX7154	15,27
Lillington	DOR	ST6212	2,6
Lindridge	WOR	SO6769	2,85
Linley (in More)	SHR	SO3592	2,1
Linley (near Much Wenlock)	SHR	SO6898	3c,2. 4,19,11
Liswerry	GLS	ST3487	W19
Littlecombe	DEV	??	15,36
Litton Cheney	DOR	SY5590	1,2. 53,2
Lizard	SHR	SJ7709	4,9,1
Llanbadoc	GLS	SO3700	W2
Llanddewi Fach	GLS	ST3395	W2;4
Llandegveth	GLS	ST3395	W2
Llandenny	GLS	SO4103	W2
Llandevenny	GLS	ST4186	W2;18
Llandogo	GLS	SO5204	W2;4;16
Llanfihangel Rogiet	GLS	ST4587	W2;6

Llanfrechfa	GLS	ST3193	W2
Llangattock	GLS	ST3390	W2;18. E36
Llangattock Vibon Avel	GLS	SO4515	E35
Llangeview	GLS	SP3900	W2
Llangovan	GLS	SO4505	W2
Llangua	GLS	SO3925	W4
Llangwm	GLS	ST4299	W2
Llangybi	GLS	ST3796	W2
Llanhedrick	SHR	SO2884	4,20,8
Llanhennock	GLS	ST3592	W2;18. E36
Llanishen	GLS	SO4703	W2
Llanllwydd	GLS	SO4117	E35
Llanllywel *alias* Llanlowell	GLS	ST3998	W2
Llanlowell *alias* Llanllywel	GLS	ST3998	W2
Llanmartin	GLS	ST3989	W2;5;18
Llanrothal HEF	GLS	SO4618	E35
Llansoy	GLS	SO4402	W2
Llantarnam	GLS	ST3093	W2;18. E36
Llantilio Crossenny	GLS	SO3914	W4
Llantrisant	GLS	ST3996	W2
Llanvaches	GLS	ST4391	W16
Llanvihangel Pontymoel	GLS	SO3001	W2
Llanvihangel Tormynydd	GLS	SO4601	W2
Llanwern	GLS	ST3787	W2;18
Longacre	DEV	??	1,56
Longburton	DOR	ST6412	2,6
Longfleet	DOR	??	31,1
Longford (in Moreton Say)	SHR	SJ6433	4,1,4
Longville in the Dale	SHR	SO5493	3c,3
Longworth	HEF	SO5639	1,2
Look	DOR	SY5488	47,5
Loops	DOR	??	1,4
Lostford	SHR	SJ6231	4,3,1
Lovacott (in Fremington)	DEV	SS5227	34,8
Lovard	DOR	??	26,21-22
Lovaton	DEV	SX5466	29,9
Loverley	DOR	SU0008	26,44
Lovistone	DEV	SS5410	25,2
Lowbrook	DOR	ST7809	8,2
Luckley	SHR	SJ3201	4,27,23
Lucton	SHR	??	ES3
Ludlow	SHR	SO5174	7,4
Ludstone	SHR	SO8094	ES3
Luffincott	DEV	SX3394	35,5
Lurcombe	DEV	SX8073	2,19
Lurley	DEV	SS9214	1,35
Luscombe (in Harberton)	DEV	SX7957	20,17
Lushcott	SHR	SO5595	3c,3
Lustleigh	DEV	SX7881	23,15
Luton	DEV	SX9076	2,4-6
Lutton	DEV	SX5959	15,36
Lydcott	DEV	SX6297	16,14
Lydlinch	DOR	SY7413	2,6
Lymbury	DEV	SX9898	1,56
Lymscott	DEV	SS2912	34,6
Lyneham	DEV	SX5753	1,18
Lytchett Minster	DOR	SY9693	34,5
Great Lyth	SHR	SJ4507	4,1,2
Little Lyth	SHR	SJ4706	4,1,2
Lythe Wood Hall Farm and Lythe Wood Hall View	SHR	SJ4607 SJ4708	4,27,6

M

Maddaford	DEV	SX5494	16,22
Madford	DEV	ST1411	1,8. 19,36
Madjeston	DOR	ST8025	40,2
Madresfield	WOR	SO8047	8,10a
Maesgwenith	GLS	ST4493	W7
Magdalene	DEV	SS4919	34,9
Magor	GLS	ST4287	W2;10;18
Maidenford	DEV	SS5833	3,3
Malehurst	SHR	SJ3806	4,4,12
Malpas	GLS	ST3090	W18. E37
Mangerton	DOR	SY4895	3,11
Mansley	DEV	SS2221	36,3-4
Mappercombe	DOR	SY5099	11,13-14
Maristow	DEV	SX4764	39,19-20
Marlbrook	SHR	SO6670	5,2
Marlcombe	DEV	ST1103	25,14;16
Marley	DEV	SX7261	20,14
Marnhull	DOR	ST7818	8,1
Marsh	SHR	SO4488	3g. 4,3,47. 4,20,4. 9,1
Marsh: see Chapel Marsh			
Marshall	DEV	SX8888	2. 2,4-6
Marshford	DEV	SS5301	5,4
Marshwood	DOR	SY3899	26,63
Marston-on-Avon	WAR	SP4176	17,48
Martinstown	DOR	SY6488	26,13. 55,1
Marton	WAR	SP4068	16,35
Marwell	DEV	SX6547	17,65
Le Mary	GLS	SP1913	78,2
Mathern	GLS	ST5290	W2;13
Matravers	DOR	??	26,41-42. 55,24
Matson	GLS	SO8415	1,2
Meadwell	DEV	SX4081	16,11
Meaton	SHR	SO7177	6,9
Hoo Meavy	DEV	SX5365	17,79-82
Medlicott	SHR	SO4094	4,4,4
Meeson	SHR	SJ6520	4,11,18
Melbury Sampford	DOR	??	36,8
Melcombe Regis	DOR	SY6880	1,1;22
Meldon	DEV	SX5692	16,3
Melplash	DOR	SY4898	3,11
East and West Mere	DEV	SS9516	1,35
		SS9915	
Metherell	DEV	??	2,7-8
Mickley	SHR	SJ6132	1,8
Middlecott (in Virginstow)	DEV	SX3893	17,5
Middleton Priors	SHR	SO6290	4,1,26
Milford	SHR	SJ4120	4,3,52
Mill	DEV	SX7694	52,11
Millenheath	SHR	SJ5735	1,8
Millsome	DEV	SS6605	47,2-4
Milton	GLS	ST3688	W18
Minchingdown	DEV	SS8210	20,8-9
Minterne	DOR	ST6504	11. 11,1. 12,16
Mitchel Troy	GLS	SO4910	W2
Mocktree	SHR	SO4276	6,11
Monk Foregate: see Foregate			
Monkerton	DEV	SX9693	1,52

Monkhall	SHR	SO6194	3c,2. 4,3,6
Monkhopton	SHR	SO6293	3c,2
Monkmoor	SHR	SJ5113	4,21,14
Monkton (near Honiton)	DEV	ST1803	1,13
Monkton (in Shobrooke and Thorveton)	DEV	??	2,2
Monkton Up Wimborne: see Wimborne			
Monyeston	DEV	??	16,78
Moor (? in Clyst Honiton)	DEV	??	15,20
Moor (? in Pyworthy)	DEV	??	17,15;18
Moor Park	SHR	SO5071	Eh1
Moorstone	DEV	ST0109	51,14
Moortown	SHR	SJ6117	4,1,21
Morden	DOR	SY9195	34,5
More	SHR	SO3491	4,1,14
Morwell	DEV	SX4470	5,1
Morwellham	DEV	SX4469	5,1
Mose	SHR	SO7590	EW1
Mounton	GLS	ST5192	W16
Mowley	HEF	SO3360	24,8
Moynes Court	GLS	ST5190	W16
Muckleton	SHR	SJ5921	4,3,4-5
Mucklewick	SHR	SO3397	4,1,35
Muckley	SHR	SO6495	4,3,6
Munslow	SHR	SO5288	4,3,45
Muston	DOR	SY7295	11,2. 26,21-22
Muxton	SHR	SJ7114	3g,3
Mythe	GLS	SO8934	1,44

N

Naginton	SHR	SJ6725	4,3,23
Nanheudwy (Wales)	SHR	??	4,1,13
Narracott	DEV	SS7619	5,10
Nash	DOR	ST7819	8,1
Nash	GLS	ST3483	W2;10;19
Nash	SHR	SO6071	5,1
Nene Monell	SHR	??	6,6-7
Nethercote	DEV	??	19,10
Netherton (in Farway)	DEV	SX1895	24,17
Netherton (in Haccombe with Combe)	DEV	SX8971	19,10
Newarch	SHR	??	4,1,36
Newcastle	GLS	SO4417	E35
Newcastle	SHR	SO2482	4,20,8
Newcott	DEV	ST1610	16,124
Newenham	DEV	SY2897	1,11
Newland (in Bradworthy)	DEV	SS3012	3,86-87;89
Newland (in Cullompton)	DEV	ST0407	1,7
Newland (in Landkey and Swimbridge)	DEV	SS6030	2,11
Newland (in North Tawton)	DEV	SS6500	16,56
Newnham	DEV	SS6617	16,140
Newnham	SHR	SJ4110	4,1,16
Newport	SHR	SJ7419	4,1,23
Newton (in Zeal Monachorum)	DEV	SS7004	16,48-49
Newton (in Ellesmere)	SHR	SJ4234	4,1,19
Newton (in Stoke St Milborough)	SHR	SO5882	3c,9
Newton (in Stokesay)	SHR	SO4482	7,5
Newton (in Stottesdon)	SHR	SO6585	4,1,30. 4,3,66
Newton Abbot	DEV	SX8671	1,10. 16,163

Osborne Newton	DEV	SX6945	39,15
Newton Poppleford	DEV	SY0889	16,136
Noddon	DEV	SX6547	15,44
Noneley	SHR	SJ4728	4,1,3
Norbury	SHR	SO3692	2,1
Nordley	SHR	SO6996	4,1,5
Normandy	DOR	??	22,1
Norncott	SHR	SO5686	3c,9
Northcombe	DEV	SX4595	16,5
Northcote (in Burrington)	DEV	SS6218	5,8
Northcote (in Cruwys Morchard)	DEV	SS8613	3,73. 19,35
Northcott (in Ashreigney)	DEV	SS5914	25,5
Northcott (in Luffincott)	DEV	SX3492	35,5
Northslepe	SHR	??	4,3,43
Northwill	DEV	??	48,2
Northwood	SHR	SO6784	4,1,30
Norton (in.Dartmouth)	DEV	SX8551	23,22
Norton (in Newton St Cyres)	DEV	SX8899	2. 2,2
Norton (in Culmington)	SHR	SO4681	4,1,6
Norton (in Stockton)	SHR	SJ7200	4,8,15
Norton (in Wroxeter)	SHR	SJ5609	4,3,24;26
Tong Norton	SHR	SJ7908	4,1,24
Notintone	DOR	SY6682	47,5
Nutbeam	GLS	SO9707	78,3
Nutley	DEV	SX5075	5,1

O

Fair Oak	DEV	ST1808	34,50
Oakeley	SHR	SO3388	2,1
Oakhill	SHR	SO3673	5,7
Oakly	SHR	SO4876	3d,6
Oar Stone: see Stone			
Obreton	SHR	??	4,1,17
Oburnford	DEV	SS9809	1,70
Livers Ocle	HEF	SO5746	29,3
Odham	DEV	SS7419	5,10
Ogbere	DEV	SX4474	5,1
Oldfields	SHR	SJ6236	4,8,1;7
Ollerton	SHR	SJ6525	4,8,7
Omouskerigge	DOR	??	17,1
Orchard	DEV	??	16,9-10
Orleigh	DEV	SS4222	5. 5,6
Orleton	SHR	SJ6311	4,11,18
Osbaston (in Ercall Magna)	SHR	SJ5918	4,1,21
Osborne Newton: see Newton			
Othull	DOR	??	8,3
Venn Ottery	DEV	SY0791	1,9
Overton	SHR	SO5072	EH1
Oxen: see White Oxen			

P

Padbrook	DEV	ST0106	1,7
Pafford: see Combe Pafford			
Pallington	DOR	SY7891	11,5

Palstone	DEV	SX7060	6,11-12
Pancrasweek	DEV	SS2905	34,2
Panteg	GLS	ST3199	W2
Park	SHR	SJ3910	4,4,11
Stoke Park	SHR	SJ6526	4,8,7
Parkstone	DOR	??	31,1
Partridge	DEV	SX7393	52,11
Partridge Walls	DEV	SS6708	16,53-54
Paschoe	DEV	SS7501	2,2
Patsford	DEV	SS5339	36,16
Paygrove	GLS	SO8520	36,1
Peaton	SHR	SO5384	4,1,6
Pen-y-Clawdd	GLS	SO4507	W2
Penallt	GLS	SO5210	W2
Pencombe	HEF	SO5952	19,6
Penhorwood	DEV	SS5028	34,8
Penhow	GLS	ST4290	W2;18
Penson	DEV	SX7254	15,27
Penstone	DEV	SS7700	2,2
Penterry	GLS	ST5299	W2;16
Perendon	SHR	??	4,4,17. 4,5,10
Perry Moor	GLS	SO9901	1,8
Perth Hir	GLS	SO4815	E35
Peterhayes	DEV	ST2406	11,2-3
North Petherwin	DEV	??	1,50
Petsey	SHR	SJ6327	4,8,7
Petton	DEV	ST0024	15,57
Philipston	DOR	SU0311	20,2
Philleyholme DEV	DOR	ST3500	17,1
Picket	DOR	ST4705	3,10
Picklescott	SHR	SO4399	4,27,15
Pickstock	SHR	SJ7223	4,1,23
Piddle: see Combe Deverel, *Lovard,*			
Muston, Little Puddle, Waterston			
Pidsley	DEV	SS8105	2,2
Pierston	DOR	ST7928	35,1
Pimley	SHR	SJ5214	4,3,24
Pinchpool	GLS	SP1913	39,16
Pinford	DOR	ST6617	2,6
Pippacott	DEV	SS5237	3,31
Pixham	WOR	SO8348	8,10a
Pixley	SHR	SJ6825	4,19,2;4
Plealey	SHR	SJ4206	4,1,16
Plowden	SHR	SO3786	2,1
Plush	DOR	ST7102	8,3
Poflet	DEV	SX4379	5,2
Pomeroy	DEV	SY1398	34,32
Pontesford	SHR	SJ4106	4,1,16
Pool (? in Stokeinteignhead)	DEV	??	16,126
Pool Anthony	DEV	SS9712	1,35. 46,1
Poole	DOR	??	31,1
Pools	SHR	SO4879	7,4
Port	DEV	SS7725	2,21
Porthcasseg	GLS	ST5298	W16
East Portlemouth	DEV	??	52,53
Porton	GLS	ST3883	W11
Posenhall	SHR	SJ6501	3c,2
Potford	SHR	SJ6321	4,23,8
Prescott (in Baschurch)	SHR	SJ4221	4,1,3
Prescott (in Stottesdon)	SHR	SO6681	4,1,30
Presteigne (Wales)	SHR	SO3164	5,4

Presthope	SHR	SO5897	3c,2;14
Preston	DEV	SS6522	1,41
Preston (in Sutton Poyntz)	DOR	SY7083	1,4
Preston (in Upton Magna)	SHR	SJ5211	4,3,3;24;31
Prinsley	DOR	??	2,6
Priors Court	GLS	SP0204	78,5
Priorslee	SHR	SJ7109	4,9,1
Priorton	DEV	SS8304	2,2
Pudford	WOR	SO7461	21,4
Pugsley	DEV	SS6423	1,41
Pulworthy	DEV	SS5104	5,4. 16,19
Purlogue	SHR	SO2876	4,20,22
Puslinch	DEV	SX5650	15,37
Putton	DOR	SY6580	1,4
Pwllmeyric	GLS	ST5192	W16
Pwllpan	GLS	ST3587	S2. W19
Pymore	DOR	SY4694	1,13
Pynamead	DEV	SS6716	16,140
Pynes	DEV	SX9196	16,129

Q

Quarleston	DOR	ST8303	55,1
Quither	DEV	SX4481	5,2

R

Raddicombe	DEV	SX9053	30,1-2
Radford	DEV	SX5052	1,17
Radsbury	DEV	SS7145	19,16
Radway	DEV	SY0986	11,1
Ragdon	SHR	SO4591	4,22,3
Raglan	GLS	SO4107	W2
Rake	DEV	SX7247	17,40;42
Ravensden	BDF	TL0754	23,5
Ravenshill	WOR	SO9056	2,68
Rawstone	DEV	SS7426	2,21
Rea	SHR	SJ5612	4,3,24
Rea	SHR	??	4,4,6
Reabrook	SHR	SO3604	4,4,6
Redcastle	SHR	SJ5729	4,10,3
Reddaway	DEV	SX6295	16,14
Redland	GLS	ST5875	3,1
Redwick	GLS	ST4184	W2;11
Rew	DOR	SY6389	26,13
Ridgeway	DEV	SX5356	1,17
Ridgeway	GLS	ST6275	1,21
Ridgwardyne	SHR	SJ6838	4,23,9
Ringmoor	DEV	SX5566	21,21
Ringwell	DEV	SX9692	19,38
Ritton	SHR	SO3497	4,4,4
Lower Rixtail	DEV	SX9477	2,4-6
Roborough (near Tavistock)	DEV	??	5. 5,1
Rock	SHR	SO5275	7,4
Rockfield	GLS	SO4814	E35

Rocknell	DEV	ST0516	24,30
Rodden	DOR	SY6184	13,1
Roden	SHR	SJ5716	4,3,3;31
Rodenhurst	SHR	SJ5815	4,3,31
Rogerstone	GLS	ST5096	W14
Rogiet	GLS	ST4587	W2;18
Rokewrth'	DEV	??	16,14
Rollstone	DEV	SX9099	16,123
Rolstone	DEV	SS7905	2,2
Rosamondford	DEV	SY0291	49,5
Rose Court	GLS	SP1022	34,6
Roughton	SHR	SO7594	ES2;7
Rowaldsway	DOR	??	26,14-16. 55,5-6
Rowden	DEV	SS8016	42,19
Rowhorne	DEV	SX8794	1,44
Rowton (in Clungunford)	SHR	SO4180	4,20,24
Ruckley	SHR	SJ7706	4,1,24
Rudge (in Crediton Hamlets)	DEV	SS7407	2,2
Rudge (in Morchard Bishop)	DEV	SX8597	2,2
Rushton	SHR	SJ6008	3b,2
North Russell	DEV	SX5092	3,86-87
Lower and Upper Rye	GLS	SP1930	65,1. 66,2
		SP1831	
Ryme Intrinseca	DOR	ST5810	2,4

S

St Andrews	DOR	SY8380	26,50-51
St Arvans	GLS	ST5196	W2;16
St Brides Netherwent	GLS	ST4289	W2;18
St Giles in the Heath	DEV	??	1,50
St Hill	DEV	ST0908	16,101
St Maughans	GLS	SO4617	E35
St Sidwells	DEV	??	2
St Wormets	GLS	ST5095	W16
Sakynton	DEV	??	2,2
Salcombe	DEV	SX7339	15,74
Salisbury	GLS	ST4288	W18
Sandford	DEV	SS8202	2,2
Sandford (in West Felton)	SHR	SJ3423	4,3,40
Sandridge	DEV	SX8656	2,18
Sansaw	SHR	SJ5023	3d,1
Sarson	HAM	SU3042	
Sascott	SHR	SJ4211	4,1,16
Scobchester	DEV	SX5196	39,7
Scorriton	DEV	SX7068	1,34
Scotworthy	DEV	??	19,2
Sedge	DEV	??	1,44
Sepscott	DEV	SS5936	16,65
Sessacott	DEV	SS3516	19,2
Shackerley	SHR	SJ8106	4,1,25
Shaftsboro	DEV	SS4845	31,3-4
Sharpham	DEV	SX8158	1,34
Sheafhayne	DEV	ST2509	11,3
Sheepsbyre	DEV	SS7215	16,140
Sheepstor	DEV	SS5567	21,21
Sheepwash (in Bishops Nympton)	DEV	SS7927	2,21
Sheepwash (near Shebbear)	DEV	SS4806	1,39

Shelderton	SHR	SO4077	4,3,46. 4,20,12
Shelve	SHR	SO3399	4,4,20
Shelvock	SHR	SO3724	4,18,3
Shirenewton	GLS	ST4793	W2;15
Shirlowe	SHR	SJ6016	4,1,21
Shotton	SHR	SJ4922	4,3,58
Little Shrawardine	SHR	SJ3915	4,1,16
Shute	DEV	SS8900	16,139
Sibberscote	SHR	SJ4207	4,1,16
Silkland	DEV	SS4116	15,12
Silvington	SHR	SO6279	3a,1
Simons Bromfield	SHR	??	3d,6
Sitterton	DOR	SY8495	1,27
Siwaldeton	SHR	??	3b,2
Skenfrith	GLS	SO4520	W4
Skimblescott	SHR	SO5892	3c,6
Skyborry	SHR	SO2674	4,20,18-27
Slade	DEV	SS6701	1,3
Slade: see Applethorn Slade			
Sleap (in Ercall Magna)	SHR	SJ6317	4,1,21. 4,6,5
Sleap Parva (in Wem)	SHR	SJ4826	4,3,53
Smallbrook	DEV	SY8698	2,2
Smethcote	SHR	SJ5020	4,3,58
Smythapark	DEV	SS6238	16,67-68
Snakescroft	SHR	SO3387	2,1
Snead	SHR	SO3291	4,1,35
Snitton	SHR	SO5575	4,11,4
Somerton	DEV	??	52,11
Great and Little Soudley	SHR	SJ7128	ES8
		SJ7228	
Southbrook	DEV	SY0296	1,56
Southbrook	DOR	SY8494	1,27
Southcombe	DEV	??	16,5
Southcott (in Morchard Bishop)	DEV	SS7505	2,2
Southcott (in Winkleigh)	DEV	SS6306	1,64
Southgarston	DOR	??	8,2
Southrop	GLS	SP2003	55,1
Southteign	DEV	??	1,26
Southwey	DOR	??	1,4
Southwood	DEV	??	1,7
Southwood (in Dawlish)	DEV	SX9375	1,4. 2. 2,4-6
Sowden	DEV	SX9983	26,1
Sowton (in Dunsford)	DEV	SX8388	23,12. 52,47
Sparchford	SHR	SO4983	4,1,6
Sparhanger	DEV	SS7146	19,17
Spittle	DEV	SS6817	16,140
Staddon (in Cheriton Bishop)	DEV	SX7594	52,11
Staddon (in North Tawton)	DEV	SS6702	1,3
Stallen	DOR	ST6016	3,5
Stanbridge	BDF	SP9624	1,1b
Stancombe (in Harberton)	DEV	??	1,34
Standon	DEV	SX5481	39,1
Stanlowe	SHR	??	4,1,35
Stanton (in Shifnal)	SHR	SJ7707	4,9,1
Stantor	DEV	SX8863	2,18
Stanwardine in the Wood	SHR	SJ4227	4,18,2
Stapledon	DEV	SS3804	28,3
Stapleford	DOR	??	47,7
Stapleton HEF	SHR	SO3265	5,4;5
Staunton GLS	WOR	SO7829	8,9a
Stenhill	DEV	ST0610	23,9

Stentwood	DEV	??	34,35
Stevenedon	DEV	??	1,41
Stevenstone (in St Giles in the Wood)	DEV	SS5219	40,2
Stevenstone (in Upton Pyne)	DEV	SX9199	24,2
Stinchcombe	GLS	ST7298	1,15
Stirchley	SHR	SJ6906	4,19,1
Stitt	SHR	SO4098	4,5,2
Stock Castle and South Stock	DEV	SS7146	19,16
		SS7145	
Stockett	SHR	SJ4329	4,1,19
Stockey	DEV	SS5407	16,39
Stockley	DEV	SX6095	16,3
Stockton (in Marton)	SHR	SJ2601	4,1,10
Stockton (in Woodcote)	SHR	SJ7716	4,19,2
Stoke (in Greete)	SHR	SO5770	5,1
Stoke Aubrey	SHR	??	4,8,7
Stoke Grange	SHR	SJ6331	1,9
Stoke Park: see Park			
Stokenham	DEV	SX8042	1,24;34
Stone	DEV	SS7113	16,140
Stone: see *Stevenedon*			
Oar Stone	DEV	SX9562	15,42
Stoneacton	SHR	SO5093	4,3,9
Storridge	DEV	SX7453	39,16
Stottingway	DOR	SY6684	56,9
Stourton	DEV	SS8012	3,39. 36,11-13;21-23
Stow	SHR	SO3173	4,20,18-27
Stowford (in Bradworthy)	DEV	SS2913	34,6
Stowford (in Swimbridge)	DEV	SS6226	2,11
Stratton	DOR	SY6593	2,1
Strensham	WOR	SO9039	8,23
Stretch	DEV	SS8113	36,21-23
Strigoil	GLS	ST5393	W14;16-17
Strixton	NTH	SP9061	40,2
Stroat	GLS	ST5797	31,6. 39,11
Stroxworthy	DEV	SS3419	16,31
Styche	SHR	SJ6435	4,8,1;7
Sudbrook	GLS	ST5087	W16
Sugdon	SHR	SJ6014	4,3,31. 4,11,18
Sutton (in Stockleigh English)	DEV	SS8605	15,17-18
Sutton (in Claverley)	SHR	SO7994	EW2
Swainstone	DEV	SX6054	1,23

T

Taddiport	DEV	SS4818	1,31
Tare	DEV	??	25,13
Tasley	SHR	SO6994	4,1,5
Tately	SHR	SO4278	4,20,12;24
Taviton	DEV	SX5074	5,1
Venny Tedburn	DEV	SX8297	2,2
Tedsmore	SHR	SJ3625	4,3,41
Teignmouth	DEV	SX9373	2,4-6
Teignwick: see Highweek			
Tennaton	DEV	SX7455	1,15
Tern	SHR	SJ6216	4,1,21
Tern Hill	SHR	SJ6332	1,9
Thonglands	SHR	SO5489	4,3,7;8

Thongsleigh	DEV	SS9011	36,20
Thoredoghes	DEV	??	15,12
Thorn (? in St Budeaux)	DEV	??	17,76
Thorndon	DEV	SX4095	17,12
Thorne (in Clannaborough)	DEV	SS7300	16,52
North Thorne (in Broadwoodwidger)	DEV	SX4095	17,12
Thornworthy	DEV	SS7145	19,16
Thorverton	DEV	SS9202	1,7
Three Shire Ash	WAR	SP2351	40,1
Three Shire Elms	WAR	SP1048	43,2
Tideford	DEV	SX8254	17,48
Tilley	SHR	SJ5027	4,14,4
Tilsop	SHR	SO6172	5,1
Tilstock	SHR	SJ5437	4,13,1
Timberth	SHR	SO2596	4,1,10
Tinacre	DEV	SS3600	17,15
Tintern	GLS	SO5300	W2
Titterton	DEV	SS6605	1,64. 25,7;13
Titwell	DEV	SX6849	35,26
Tongeslond	DEV	??	15,79
Torkridge	DEV	??	2,21
Torpeek	DEV	SX6656	15,71
Tortysfenne	DEV	??	17,48
Toteneye	SHR	??	4,3,66
Totterton	SHR	SO3687	2,1
Tower	DEV	SS2225	1,30
Towersey OXF	BKM	SP7305	39,2
West Town	DEV	SX8593	16,125
Towsington	DEV	SX9387	19,8
Traston	GLS	ST3385	W19
Treable	DEV	SX7192	52,11
Treasbeare	DEV	SY0094	2,15-17
Tredunnock	GLS	ST3794	W2;18. E35
Trefnant	SHR	SJ3010	4,1,8
Tregate HEF	GLS	SO4817	E35
Trelleck	GLS	SO5005	W2
Treprenal	SHR	SJ2821	4,3,36
Trilbehegh	DEV	??	34,24
Trill	DEV	SY2995	16,168
Trilwardyne	SHR	??	4,9,1
Trippleton	SHR	SO4173	6,11
Trobridge	DEV	SX8397	2,2
Trostrey	GLS	SO3604	W2
Trotshill	WOR	SO8855	2,53
Tunstall	SHR	SJ6935	4,23,9
Turford	SHR	??	EH1
Turnham	DEV	ST0419	16,77
Twyford	SHR	SJ3426	4,6,6
Tythecott	DEV	SS4117	15,12

U

Uddens	DOR	SO0402	20,1
Uggaton	DEV	ST0903	52,22
Lower and Upper Underley	HEF	SO6561	9,18. 10,66
		SO6562	
Undy	GLS	ST4386	W2;18
Upcott (in Cheriton Fitzpaine)	DEV	SS8608	15,17-18

Upcott (in Cookbury)	DEV	SS3804	28,3
Upcott (in Dowland)	DEV	SS5709	1,63
Upcott (in Thelbridge)	DEV	SS8212	36,21-23
Upcott	HEF	SO3250	6,8
Uppacott (in Mariansleigh)	DEV	SS7521	2,21
Upsydling	DOR	ST6201	11,1. 12,1. 26,26-27
Upton (in Cullompton)	DEV	ST0306	9,1
Upton (in South Milton)	DEV	SX7043	17,36
Upton	DOR	SY7483	11,6. 52,2
Upton (in Shifnal)	SHR	SJ7506	4,9,1
North Upton (in Thurlestone)	DEV	SX6844	17,36
Upton Pyne	DEV	SX9197	16,129
Usk	GLS	SO3700	W2
Uton	DEV	SX8298	2,2

V

Vaglefield	DEV	SS3606	28,3
Valeridge	DEV	SS9122	3,74
Venn (in Brixton)	DEV	SX5552	15,52
Venn (in Chagford)	DEV	SX6984	16,61-62;64
Venn (in Morchard Bishop)	DEV	SS7705	2,2
Venn (in Teignmouth)	DEV	SX9275	2,4-6
Venn Channing	DEV	??	44
Venn Ottery: see Ottery			
Venny Tedburn: see Tedburn			
Venton	DEV	SX7560	20,15
Veraby	DEV	SS7726	2,21
View Edge	SHR	SO4280	4,3,46. 7,6
Villa Asmacun	HEF	??	1,61

W

Waddeton	DEV	SX8756	2,18
Waddon	DEV	SX8879	2,2;4-6
Wagland	DEV	SX7654	1,15;55
Walcot (in Lydbury North)	SHR	SO3485	2,1
Walcot (in Wrockwardine)	SHR	SJ5911	4,1,1;22
Waldons	DEV	SS5706	42,4
Walkerslow	SHR	SO6586	4,1,30
Wall	GLS	SP1510	78,11
Wall Bank	SHR	SO5092	4,8,5
East Wall	SHR	SO5293	4,8,5
Wall under Heywood	SHR	SO5192	4,8,5
Wallaford	DEV	SX7265	5. 20,13
Walland	DEV	SS3522	42,3-4
Wallon	DEV	SX7790	16,110
Wallop	SHR	SJ3207	4,4,14;19
Wallstone	GLS	ST5189	W17
Walton (in Ercall Magna)	SHR	SJ5918	4,1,21
Walton (in Onibury)	SHR	SO4679	2,2
Walton (in Worthen)	SHR	SJ2905	4,4,20
Wambrook SOM	DOR	ST2907	3,13
Wansley	DEV	SS5617	3,19
Wappenshall	SHR	SJ6614	4,3,30

Wardale	SHR	SJ6729	4,8,7
Wardeslegh'	DEV	??	28,10-11
Waresley	WOR	SO8470	2,82
Warkleigh	DEV	SS6522	1,41
Warran	SHR	SJ6530	4,8,7
Watercombe	DEV	SX6261	15,36
Waterhouse	DEV	ST2603	1,11
Watmore	SHR	SO6171	5,1
Wayhoughton	DOR	??	55,5-6
Countess Wear	DEV	SX9490	1,44
Weaver	DEV	ST0404	9,1
Webscott	SHR	SJ4722	4,3,53
Week (in Chillaton)	DEV	SX4581	5,2
Week (in Chulmleigh)	DEV	SS7316	16,140
Week (in North Tawton)	DEV	SS6501	1,3
Chawleigh Week	DEV	SS6813	16,43
East Week (in South Tawton)	DEV	SX6692	1,29
Great Weeke	DEV	SX7187	1,26
Welsbeare	DEV	??	44,2
Wembury	DEV	SX5148	1,17
Wenlock Walton	SHR	SO6398	3c,2
Weo	SHR	SO4180	4,3,46. 7,6
Westacombe (in Dunsford)	DEV	SX7990	16,110
Westacombe (in Inwardleigh)	DEV	SX5598	16,23-24
Westacott (in Inwardleigh)	DEV	SS5300	16,23
Westacott (in Landkey)	DEV	SS5832	2,11
Westacott (in Sampford Courtenay)	DEV	SS6103	16,14
Westbrook	DOR	SY6684	26,14-16. 27,4-5
Westcott (in Marwood)	DEV	SS5338	36,16
Westcott (in Thelbridge)	DEV	SS8011	36,21-23
Westcott	SHR	SJ7028	ES8
Westecot	DEV	??	16,78
Westley	SHR	SJ4606	4,1,2
Westmyngton	DOR	??	1,27
Weston (? in Staverton)	DEV	SX7564	52,52
Weston (in Clun)	SHR	SO2781	4,20,8
Weston (in Monkhopton)	SHR	SO5992	3c,2
Weston (in Nash)	SHR	SO5871	5,1
Weston (in Stowe)	SHR	SO3273	4,20,18-27
Cold Weston	SHR	SO5583	4,1,5. 7,4
Little Weston	SHR	SO2998	4,5,14
Weston Lullingfields	SHR	SJ4224	4,1,17
Westport	DOR	SY9287	37,10
Westwood	GLS	SO9205	28,3
Wey: see Causeway, *Creketway,*			
Rowaldsway, Stottingway,			
Southwey, Wayhoughton, Westbrook,			
Weymouth			
Weymouth	DOR	SY6779	1,1
Whatcombe	DOR	ST8301	26,13. 55,1
Whelmstone	DEV	SS7500	2,2
Whettleton	SHR	SO4482	7,5
South Whimple	DEV	SY0094	1,56
Whiston	SHR	SJ7902	4,25,6
Whitcot	SHR	SO3791	2,1
Whitcott	SHR	SO2782	4,20,8
White Oxen	DEV	SX7261	20,14
Whitebroc	SHR	??	EH1
Whitechapel	DEV	SS7527	2,21
Whiteheathfield	DEV	ST0103	32,3. 49,4
Higher Whiteleigh	DEV	SS4202	1,37

Whitham	DEV	SX4874	5,1
Whitsburn	SHR	SJ3302	4,27,23
Whitsleigh	DEV	SS5517	40,2
Whitson	GLS	ST3883	W2-3
Whittimere	SHR	SO8292	ES. ES3
Whitton	SHR	SO5772	5,1
Whitwell	DEV	SY2392	1,13
Whympston	DEV	SX6650	15,64
Widcombe	DEV	SY1894	44. 48,12
Widecombe in the Moor	DEV	??	34,46
Wigley	SHR	SO5276	7,4
Wilcott	SHR	SJ3718	4,1,17
Wilcrick	GLS	ST4088	W2;18
Wilderhope	SHR	SO5492	4,8,5
Wildislond	SHR	??	4,1,21
Wilfrescota	SHR	??	3g
Willaston	SHR	SJ5935	1,8
Willeswell	DEV	??	35,16
Willey	DEV	SX6495	16,14
Willey HEF	SHR	SO3267	5,4-5
Williamstrip	GLS	SP1505	39,14
Willstone	SHR	SO4995	4,3,44
Wilmington	SHR	SJ2901	4,1,35
Wilson (in Cheriton Bishop)	DEV	SX7595	52,11
Wilson (in East Worlington)	DEV	SS7814	42,21
Wimborne: see All Hallows, *Philipston*			
Monkton Up Wimborne	DOR	SU0113	1,3. 10,3
Windbow	DEV	SS9116	11,1
Winnington	SHR	SJ3110	4,1,8
Winsbury	SHR	SO2498	4,1,35
Winscott (in Pyworthy)	DEV	SS3301	17,15
Winterborne Belet	DOR	SY7086	56,10. 57,3
Winterborne Came	DOR	SY7088	17,1
Winterborne Clenston	DOR	ST8303	5,1-2. 26,13
Winterborne Farringdon	DOR	SY6988	26,13
Winterborne Herringston	DOR	SY6888	26,13
Winterborne Houghton	DOR	ST8204	36,3. 55,17. 56,28
Winterborne Huntingdon	DOR	??	17,1. 57,3
Winterborne Kingston	DOR	SY8697	55,1. 56,6;60
Winterborne Monkton	DOR	SY6787	58,2
Winterborne Muston	DOR	SY8797	26,13. 40,4
Winterborne Nicholston	DOR	??	26,13
Winterborne Phelpston	DOR	??	26,13
Winterborne Stickland	DOR	ST8304	22,1
Winterborne Tomson	DOR	SY8897	40,4
Winterborne Whitechurch	DOR	ST8300	12,11. 26,13. 46,1. 55,1
Winterborne Zelston	DOR	SY8997	1,6
Winterbourne Abbas	DOR	SY6190	11,11
Winterbourne Steepleton	DOR	SY6289	56,10
Wiscombe	DEV	SY1893	11,1
Wistanswick	SHR	SJ6629	4,8,7
Witcham	DOR	ST5702	12,4
Witchcot	SHR	SO5381	4,21,15
Within	DEV	SY0290	49,5
Within Furze	DEV	SY0290	49,5
Withymore	DEV	SX7040	17,10;36
Wittery	SHR	SO2798	4,1,10
Wolfeton	DOR	SY6792	1,4. 3,14. 26,5;8-11
Wolfgar	DEV	SX7595	52,11
Wolverstone	DEV	ST1204	25,14
Wolverton	SHR	SO4787	3c,3

Wolvesnewton	GLS	ST4599	W2
Wombridge	SHR	??	4,3,27
Wonastow	GLS	SO4810	E35
Wood	DEV	??	42,7
Woodbatch	SHR	SO3088	2,1
Woodbury Salterton	DEV	SY0189	1,33. 11,1
Woodcourt	DEV	SX7755	20,17
Woodhouse (in Stoke upon Tern)	SHR	SJ6426	4,8,7
New and Old Woodhouse (in Ash)	SHR	SJ5941	4,13,1
		SJ5842	
The Woodhouse (in Shifnal)	SHR	SJ7210	4,9,1
Woodington	DEV	SS8112	1,32
Woodland (in Crediton Hamlets)	DEV	SX7797	2,2
Woodland (in Swimbridge)	DEV	SS6126	2,11
Woodlands	DOR	??	26,43
Woodmanstone	DEV	SX7544	24,18
Woodscombe	DEV	SS8312	50,4
Woofferton	SHR	SO5268	EH1
Wool Bridge	DOR	SY8487	11,8
Woolhanger	DEV	SS6945	19,16
Woollashill	WOR	SO9440	8,7
Wooton	SHR	SO5773	5,1
Wootton (in Onibury)	SHR	SO4578	7,4
Wootton (in Quatt)	SHR	SO7689	EW1
North Wootton	DOR	ST6514	2,6
Worden	DEV	SS3013	34,6
Wormington	HEF	??	1,61
La Worth	DEV	??	34,16
Worthy(? in Chulmleigh)	DEV	??	16,140
Wotenhull	SHR	??	1,8
Wrangaton	DEV	SX6757	1,15;55
Wricton	SHR	SO6485	4,1,30
Wryngoldon	DEV	??	15,44
Wyesham	GLS	SO5112	E35
Wyke (in Castleton)	DOR	ST6014	3,4
Wyke	SHR	SJ6402	3c,2
Wyke Regis	DOR	SY6577	1,1
The Wyke	SHR	SJ7306	4,9,1
West Wyke (in South Tawton)	DEV	SX6592	1,29
Wyneslegh	DEV	??	35,15
Wytefeld	DEV	??	40,2
Wytherston	DOR	SY5397	47,6

Y

Yalberton	DEV	SX8659	2,18
Yales	DEV	??	3,65–66
Yarcombe	DOR	ST2408	12
Yarde	DEV	SX7140	17,40
Yardgrove	DOR	ST7717	8,1
Yarnscombe	DEV	??	34,55
Yendacott	DEV	SS8900	24,2;4
Yenne Park	DEV	SS6207	39,4
Yeo	DEV	??	2,2
Yeoford	DEV	SX7899	2,2
Yettington	DEV	SY0585	1,9
Yewstock	DOR	ST7915	8,1
Yondercott	DEV	ST0712	23,9
Youngcott	DEV	SX4076	5,2

CONCORDANCE OF SYSTEMS OF REFERENCE TO THE TWO VOLUMES OF DOMESDAY BOOK

This concordance serves two main purposes. Firstly, to enable readers of the Phillimore Edition of Domesday Book, who are consulting the extensive literature on Domesday, to narrow down the folio references usually quoted to the corresponding Phillimore reference quoted in this Index. It will also enable those readers to follow up any related entries which the Index reveals.

Secondly, it will enable those readers who are using this Index as a guide to their researches in the folios of the Farley or Facsimile Editions, or who are using the Victoria County History translations, to trace references in the Index and to find other folios in which related references may be found.

I. The various systems

The manuscript of the larger volume (here referred to as DB) is divided into numbered chapters, and the chapters into sections, usually marked by large initials and red ink. Farley did not number the sections and later historians, using his edition, have referred to the text of DB by folio numbers, which cannot be closer than an entire page or column. Moreover, several different ways of referring to the same column have been devised. In 1816 Ellis used three separate systems in his indices: (i) on pages i–cvii, 435-518, 537-570; (ii) on pages 1–144; (iii) on pages 145–433 and 519–535. Other systems have since come into use, notably that used by Vinogradoff, here followed. The present edition numbers the sections, the normal practicable form of close reference; but since all discussion of DB for two hundred years has been obliged to refer to folio or column, a comparative table will help to locate references given. The five columns below give Vinogradoff's notation, Ellis's three systems, and that used by Weldon Finn and others. Maitland, Stenton, Darby and others have usually followed Ellis (i).

Vinogradoff	Ellis (i)	Ellis (ii)	Ellis (iii)	Finn
152a	152	152a	152	152ai
152b	152	152a	152.2	152a2
152c	152b	152b	152b	152bi
152d	152b	152b	152b2	152b2

The manuscript of Little Domesday Book (here referred to as LDB) has one column per page but is again divided into numbered chapters and the chapters into sections, usually distinguished by paragraph-marks. Modern users of LDB have referred to its text by folio number, e.g. 152(a) 15 Section III, p. 00.

II. Key to the relation between Vinogradoff's notation of the folios and columns of the MS text of DB and the numbered chapters and sections of the Phillimore edition

KENT (KEN)

1a	D1	- D10
b	D11	- D24
c	D25	- M10
d	M11	- M24
2a	C1	- R1
b	P1	- Landholders
c	1,1	- 1,3
d	1,3	- 1,4
3a	2,1	- 2,7
b	2,7	- 2,11
c	2,12	- 2,16
d	2,16	- 2,22
4a	2,22	- 2,27
b	2,28	- 2,35
c	2,36	- 2,43
d	3,1	- 3,7
5a	3,7	- 3,15
b	3,16	- 3,23
c	4,1	- 4,9
d	4,10	- 4,16
6a	5,1	- 5,8
b	5,9	- 5,18
c	5,18	- 5,25
d	5,25	- 5,34
7a	5,34	- 5,43
b	5,43	- 5,51
c	5,52	- 5,59
d	5,59	- 5,70
8a	5,70	- 5,78
b	5,79	- 5,88
c	5,88	- 5,95
d	5,95	- 5,104
9a	5,104	- 5,115
b	5,115	- 5,124
c	5,124	- 5,128
d	5,129	- 5,138
10a	5,139	- 5,146
b	5,147	- 5,156
c	5,157	- 5,166
d	5,167	- 5,178
11a	5,178	- 5,192
b	5,192	- 5,203
c	5,204	- 5,217
d	5,218	- 6,1
12a	7,1	- 7,8
b	7,8	- 7,17

c	7,18	- 7,23
d	7,23	- 8,1
13a	9,1	- 9,12
b	9,12	- 9,23
c	9,24	- 9,35
d	9,36	- 9,48
14a	9,48	- 10,2
b	11,1	- 12,4
c	13,1	
d	blank	
15a-d	blank	

SUSSEX (SSX)

16a	Landholders	
b	1,1	- 2,1e
c	2,1f	- 2,8
d	2,8	- 3,4
17a	3,4	- 4,1
b	5,1	- 6,1
c	6,1	- 7,2
d	8,1	- 8a,1
18a	9,1	- 9,6
b	9,7	- 9,14
c	9,14	- 9,19
d	9,20	- 9,35
19a	9,35	- 9,55
b	9,56	- 9,74
c	9,75	- 9,91
d	9,91	- 9,109
20a	9,109	- 9,123
b	9,123	- 9,131
c	10,1	- 10,4
d	10,4	- 10,18
21a	10,19	- 10,28
b	10,29	- 10,38
c	10,39	- 10,51
d	10,52	- 10,65
22a	10,65	- 10,80
b	10,80	- 10,93
c	10,93	- 10,105
d	10,106	- 10,118
23a	11,1	- 11,5
b	11,6	- 11,12
c	11,13	- 11,21
d	11,21	- 11,30
24a	11,30	- 11,38
b	11,38	- 11,49

c	11,49	- 11,60
d	11,61	- 11,71
25a	11,71	- 11,81
b	11,82	- 11,92
c	11,93	- 11,105
d	11,106	- 11, 116
26a	12,1	- 12,4
b	12,4	- 12,9
c	12,9	- 12,18
d	12,18	- 12,29
27a	12,29	- 12,37
b	12,37	- 12,44
c	12,44	- 12,53
d	12,54	- 12,56
28a	13,1	- 13,9
b	13,9	- 13,17
c	13,18	- 13,28
d	13,28	- 13,38
29a	13,38	- 13,46
b	13,46	- 13,57
c	14,1	- 14,2
d	blank	

SURREY (SRY)

30a	Landholders	- 1,2
b	1,2	- 1,7
c	1,8	- 1,13
d	1,13	- 2,3
31a	2,3	- 4,1
b	4,1	- 5,3
c	5,3	- 5,11
d	5,11	- 5,22
32a	5,22	- 5,30
b	6,1	- 7,1
c	7,1	- 8,11
d	8,12	- 8,22
33a,b	8,23	- 8,27
c,d	blank	
34a	8,28	- 14,1. 8,22
b	14,1	- 18,1
c	18,2	- 19,4
d	19,4	- 19,15
35a	19,15	- 19,24
b	19,24	- 19,34
c	19,35	- 19,43
d	19,44	- 21,3
36a	21,3	- 22,4. 23,1
b	24,1	- 27,3. 22,5
c	28,1	- 32,2
d	33,1	- 36,10

HAMPSHIRE (HAM)

37a-c	blank	
d	Landholders	
38a	1,1	- 1,8
b	1,8	- 1,16
c	1,17	- 1,21
d	1,22	- 1,28
39a	1,28	- 1,37
b	1,37	- 1,45
c	1,45	- 1W7
d	1,W7	- 1,W20
40a	1,W20	- 2,5
b	2,5	- 2,10
c	2,11	- 2,17
d	2,17	- 2,25
41a	3,1	- 3,5
b	3,5	- 3,8
c	3,8	- 3,14
d	3,14	- 3,24
42ab	4,1. 6,13	- 6,15
cd	6,16	- 6,17
43a	3,24	- 3,27. 5,1-6,5
b	6,5	- 6,12. 7,1
c	8,1	- 13,1
d	13,1	- 15,2
44a	15,2	- 16,7
b	17,1	- 18,3
c	19,1	- 21,5
d	21,6	- 23,3
45a	23,4	- 23,15
b	23,15	- 23,23
c	23,23	- 23,35
d	23,35	- 23,46
46a	23,46	- 23,55
b	23,56	- 23,67
c	23,68	- 28,2
d	28,3	- 29,6
47a	29,6	- 29,16
b	30,1	- 34,1
c	35,1	- 35,9
d	36,1	- 39,5
48a	40,1	- 43,6
b	44,1	- 45,5
c	45,6	- 50,2
d	50,2	- 55,2
49a	55,2	- 60,2
b	61,1	- 67,1
c	68,1	- 68,11
d	69,1	- 69,11
50a	69,12	- 69,22
b	69,23	- 69,33

76a,b	1,31	
c,d	blank	
77a	2,6	- 3,9
b	3,9	- 5,2
c	6,1	- 8,6
d	9,1	- 11,5
78a	11,6	- 12,1
b	12,2	- 13,1
c	13,2	- 18,2
d	19,1	- 19,14
79a	20,1	- 25,1
b	26,1	- 26,21
c	26,22	- 26,40
d	26,41	- 26,61
80a	26,61	- 27,6
b	27,6	- 29,1
c	30,1	- 33,4
d	33,4	- 34,13
81a,b	42,1	
c,d	36,4	- 36,11
82a	34,13	- 36,3. 37,1-7
b	37,8	- 40,7
c	40,8	- 41,5. 43,1- 47,4
d	47,5	- 49,6
83a	49,7	- 50,4. 52,1-2
b	52,2	- 54,14. 51,1
c	55,1	- 55,17
d	55,18	- 55,36
84a	55,37	- 56,9
b	56,10	- 56,32
c	56,32	- 56,55
d	56,56	- 57,8
85a	57,9	- 58,3
b-d	blank	

SOMERSET (SOM)

86a	Landholders	
b	1,1	- 1,5
c	1,6	- 1,10
d	1,11	- 1,20
87a	1,20	- 1,28
b	1,28	- 1,35
c	2,1	- 2,10
d	2,11	- 5,5
88a	5,6	- 5,18
b	5,18	- 5,32
c	5,33	- 5,43
d	5,43	- 5,55
89a	5,56	- 5,70
b	6,1	- 6,8

c	6,9	- 6,17
d	6,18	- 7,15
90a	8,1	- 8,10
b	8,11	- 8,20
c	8,20	- 8,26
d	8,27	- 8,36
91a	8,37	- 10,1
b	10,2	- 16,2
c	16,3	- 17,6
d	17,7	- 19,9
92a	19,10	- 19,24. 19.25
b	19,24	- 19,39
c	19,39	- 19,54. 19,70
d	19,54	- 19,69
93a	19,71	- 20,3
b	21,1	- 21,17
c	21,18	- 21,35
d	21,36	- 21,54
94a	21,54	- 21,75
b	21,76	- 21,94
c	21,95	- 22,13
d	22,13	- 22,28
95a	23,1	- 24,15
b	24,16	- 24,29
c	24,29	- 25,7
d	25,7	- 25,20
96a	25,21	- 25,37
b	25,38	- 25,53
c	25,54	- 27,1
d	27,2	- 31,5
97a	32,1	- 35,2
b	35,3	- 35,18
c	35,19	- 36,7
d	36,7	- 37,5
98a	37,6	- 39,3
b	40,1	- 44,3
c	45,1-2	- 46,1-16
d	46,17	- 47,7
99a	47,7	- 47,23
b	47,24	- 47,25. 45,3-18
c,d	blank	

DEVON (DEV)

100a	C	- Landholders
b	1,1	- 1,11
c	1,11	- 1,23
d	1,23	- 1,35
101a	1,35	- 1,47
b	1,48	- 1,62
c	1,62	- 1,72
d	2,1	- 2,13

102a	2,14	- 3,4
b	3,5	- 3,20
c	3,21	- 3,37
d	3,38	- 3,59
103a	3,59	- 3,76
b	3,77	- 3,94
c	3,95	- 5,5
d	5,5	- 6,4
104a	6,4	- 9,1
b	9,2	- 13a,3
c	14,1	- 15,14
d	15,15	- 15,31
105a	15,32	- 15,44
b	15,44	- 15,58
c	15,59	- 15,74
d	15,75	- 16,7
106a	16,8	- 16,22
b	16,23	- 16,38
c	16,39	- 16,56
d	16,56	- 16,73
107a	16,74	- 16,88
b	16,89	- 16,104
c	16,105	- 16,120
d	16,120	- 16,135
108a	16,136	- 16,149
b	16,150	- 16,166
c	16,167	- 17,5
d	17,5	- 17,17
109a	17,18	- 17,34
b	17,35	- 17,53
c	17,53	- 17,70
d	17,71	- 17,89
110a	17,89	- 17,105
b	17,105	- 19,12
c	19,13	- 19,28
d	19,29	- 19,44
111a	19,44	- 20,14
b	20,14	- 21,11
c	21,12	- 23,2
d	23,2	- 23,15
112a	23,16	- 24,2
b	24,3	- 24,18
c	24,19	- 25,3
d	25,3	- 25,20
113a	25,21	- 28,4
b	28,4	- 29,2
c	29,2	- 31,4
d	32,1	- 34,1
114a	34,2	- 34,17
b	34,18	- 34,32
c	34,33	- 34,49
d	34,49	- 35,5

115a	35,5	- 35,19
b	35,20	- 36,5
c	36,6	- 36,21
d	36,22	- 39,3
116a	39,4	- 39,17
b	39,18	- 41,2
c	42,1	- 42,14
d	42,15	- 43,3
117a	43,3	- 47,5
b	47,5	- 48,8
c	48,8	- 51,2
d	51,2	- 51,16
118a	52,1	- 52,19
b	52,20	- 52,36
c	52,37	- 52,53
d	blank	
119a-d	blank	

CORNWALL (CON)

120a	Landholders	- 1,3
b	1,4	- 1,14
c	1,14	- 2,6
d	2,7	- 2,15. 4,1-6
121a	4,7	- 4,22
b	4,22	- 4,29. 3,1-8
c	3,4	- 3,7. 5,1,1-7
d	5,1,8,	- 5,1,22
122a	5,2,1	- 5,2,18
b	5,2,19	- 5,3,4
c	5,3,5	- 5,3,21
d	5,3,21	- 5,4,10
123a	5,4,11	- 5,4,18. 5,5,1-8
b	5,5,8	- 5,6,2. 5,4,19-20
c	5,6,2	- 5,6,6. 5,6,8- 5,7,8
d	5,7,9	- 5,8,10. 5,6,7
124a	5,9,1	- 5,12,3
b	5,13,1	- 5,14,4
c	5,14,5	- 5,21,1
d	5,21,1	- 5,24,12
125a	5,24,13	- 5,25,5
b	5,25,5	- 7,1
c,d	blank	

MIDDLESEX (MDX)

126a-c	blank	
d	Landholders	
127a	1,1	- 2,2
b	2,3	- 3,4
c	3,4	- 3,12
d	3,13	- 3,19

128a	3,20	- 3,29
b	3,29	- 4,5
c	4,5	- 4,10
d	4,10	- 6,1
129a	7,1	- 7,7
b	7,8	- 8.5
c	8,6	- 9,6
d	9,6	- 10,2
130a	10,2	- 12,1
b	12,1	- 15,2
c	15,2	- 20,1
d	20,1	- 25,3
131a-d	blank	

HERTFORDSHIRE (HRT)

132a	B1	- B11
b	Landholders	- 1,2
c	1,3	- 1,7
d	1,7	- 1,11
133a	1,11	- 1,18
b	1,18	- 3,1
c	4,1	- 4,8
d	4,8	- 4,17
134a	4,17	- 4,25
b	5,1	- 5,10
c	5,10	- 5,18
d	5,18	- 6,1
135a	7,1	- 8,3
b	9,1	- 9,10
c	9,10	- 10,6
d	10,6	- 10,13
136a	10,14	- 10,20
b	11,1	- 13,5
c	14,1	- 15,5
d	15,5	- 16,1
137a	16,1	- 16,11
b	16,12	- 17,8
c	17,8	- 18,1
d	19,1	- 20,7
138a	20,7	- 22,1
b	22,1	- 24,1
c	24,2	- 26,1
d	26,1	- 28,7
139a	28,8	- 31,6
b	31,6	- 33,1
c	33,1	- 33,8
d	33,9	- 33,17
140a	33,17	- 34,5
b	34,6	- 34,13
c	34,13	- 34,21
d	34,22	- 36,1

141a	36,2	- 36,11
b	36,11	- 36,19
c	39,19	- 37,9
d	37,10	- 37,19
142a	37,19	- 41,1
b	41,1	- 42,11
c	42,11	- 42,15
d	42a,1	- 44,1

BUCKINGHAMSHIRE (BKM)

143a	B1	- B13
b	Landholders	- 1,1
c	1,2	- 1,7
d	2,1	- 3a,1
144a	3a,2	- 4,5
b	4,5	- 4,15
c	4,16	- 4,26
d	4,27	- 4,35
145a	4,36	- 4,43
b	5,1	- 5,10
c	5,10	- 5,19
d	5,20	- 8,2
146a	8,3	- 12,5
b	12,6	- 12,18
c	12,19	- 12,31
d	12,31	- 13,2
147a	13,3	- 14,9
b	14,9	- 14,20
c	14,20	- 14,30
d	14,30	- 14,39
148a	14,40	- 14,49
b	15,1	- 16,10
c	17,1	- 17,10
d	17,11	- 17,22
149a	17,22	- 17,31
b	18,1	- 19,3
c	19,4	- 21,4
d	21,4	- 23,3
150a	23,3	- 23,14
b	23,14	- 23,28
c	23,28	- 25,2
d	25,3	- 26,11
151a	26,11	- 29,3
b	29,4	- 35,3
c	36,1	- 40,1
d	40,1	- 43,2
152a	43,2	- 43,11
b	43,11	- 47,1
c	47,1	- 52,1
d	52,2	- 53,10

178a	28,1	- X3
b-d	blank	

HEREFORDSHIRE (HEF)

179a	C1	- C15
b	A1	- Landholders
c	1,1	- 1,4
d	1,5	- 1,8
180a	1,8	- 1,10c
b	1,11	- 1,32
c	1,33	- 1,41
d	1.42	- 1,48
181a	1,49	- 1,61
b	1,61	- 1,75
c	2,1	- 2,11
d	2,12	- 2,21
182a	2,21	- 2,31
b	2,31	- 2,42
c	2,43	- 2,56
d	2,57	- 6,11
183a	7,1	- 7,9
b	8,1	- 8,8
c	8,9	- 9,10
d	9,10	- 9,19
184a	10,1	- 10,15
b	10,16	- 10,30
c	10,31	- 10,44
d	10,45	- 10,57
185a	10,57	- 10,70
a	10,71	- 13,2
c	14,1	- 15,3
d	15,4	- 17,2
186a	18,1	- 19,8
b	19,8	- 21,6
c	21,7	- 23,6
d	24,1	- 25,2
187a	25,3	- 29,1
b	29,1	- 29,20
c	30,1	- 36,3
d	blank	
188a-d	blank	

CAMBRIDGESHIRE (CAM)

189a	B1	- B14
b	Landholders	- 1,1
c	1,1	- 1,6
d	1,6	- 1,13
190a	1,14	- 1,23
b	2,1	- 3,3
c	3,3	- 5,2
d	5,3	- 5,11

191a	5,11	- 5,22
b	5,22	- 5,32
c	5,33	- 5,42
d	5,43	- 5,50
192a	5,50	- 5,58
b	5,58	- 6,3
c	7,1	- 7,8
d	7,8	- 9,2
193a	9,3	- 11,6
b	12,1	- 13,5
c	13,6	- 13,12
d	14,1	- 14,9
194a	14,9	- 14,19
b	14,19	- 14,27
c	14,28	- 14,38
d	14,39	- 14,48
195a	14,49	- 14,57
b	14,57	- 14,64
c	14,64	- 14,72
d	14,72	- 14,82
196a	15,1	- 17,1
b	17,2	- 18,3
c	18,3	- 19,3
d	19,4	- 21,5
197a	21,5	- 22,5
b	22,6	- 23,2
c	23,2	- 25,5
d	25,5	- 26,5
198a	26,6	- 26,17
b	26,17	- 26,24
c	26,24	- 26,33
d	26,34	- 26,42
199a	26,42	- 26,49
b	26,49	- 28,2
c	28,2	- 29,7
d	29,8	- 31,1
200a	31,1	- 31,7
b	32,1	- 32,8
c	32,8	- 32,16
d	32,17	- 32,23
201a	32,23	- 32,31
b	32,31	- 32,36
c	32,37	- 32,44
d	33,1	- 38,1
202a	38,1	- 40,1
b	41,1	- 41,12
c	41,13	- 44,2
d	blank	

HUNTINGDONSHIRE (HUN)

203a	B1	- B14
b	B15	- B21. Landholders

228a	49,1	- 55,6
b	56,1	- 56,20a
c	56,20a	- 56,31
d	56,32	- 56,46
229a	56,46	- 56,64
b	56,65	- 60,5
c,d	blank	

LEICESTERSHIRE (LEC)

230a	C1	- C18
b	Landholders	- 1,3
c	1,3	- 1,7
d	1,7	- 3,1
231a	3,2	- 4,1
b	5,1	- 8,5
c	9,1	- 10,7
d	10,8	- 12,2
232a	13,1	- 13,15
b	13,16	- 13,29
c	13,30	- 13,46
d	13,47	- 13,63
233a	13,63	- 13,74
b	14,1	- 14,17
c	14,18	- 14,34
d	15,1	- 15,13
234a	15,14	- 16,9
b	17,1	- 17,20
c	17,21	- 18,2
d	18,2	- 19,14
235a	19,15	- 23,2
b	23,2	- 26,1
c	27,1	- 29,3
d	29,4	- 31,1
236a	32,1	- 39,2
b	40,1	- 40,19
c	40,19	- 40,37
d	40,38	- 42,10
237a	43,1	- 43,11
b	44,1	- 44,13
c,d	blank	

WARWICKSHIRE (WAR)

238a	B1	- Landholders
b	1,1	- 1,9
c	2,1	- 3,4
d	4,1	- 6,9
239a	6,10	- 10,1
b	11,1	- 13,1
c	14,1	- 15,6
d	16,1	- 16,14

240a	16,15	- 16,26
b	16,27	- 16,42
c	16,42	- 16,57
d	16,58	- 17,6
241a	17,7	- 17,22
b	17,23	- 17,44
c	17,45	- 17,59
d	17,60	- 17,70
242a	18,1	- 18,14
b	18,14	- 21,1
c	22,1	- 22,17
d	22,17	- 24,2
243a	25,1	- 28,5
b	28,6	- 29,1
c	29,2	- 31,7
d	31,7	- 36,2
244a	37,1	- 39,1
b	39,2	- 43,2
c	44,1	- 44,14. 45,1
d	44,15	- 44,16
245a-d	blank	

STAFFORDSHIRE (STS)

246a	B1	- Landholders
b	1,1	- 1,13
c	1,14	- 1,28
d	1,29	- 1,64
247a	2,1	- 2,16
b	2,16	- 2,22
c	3,1	- 5,2
d	6,1	- 7,18
248a	8,1	- 8,12
b	8,13	- 8,30
c	8,30	- 10,10
d	11,1	- 11,16
249a	11,17	- 11,33
b	11,34	- 11,49
c	11,50	- 11,65
d	11,66	- 12,14
250a	12,15	- 12,28
b	12,29	- 12,31
c	13,1	- 16,1
d	17,1	- 17,21. 16,2-3
251a-d	blank	

SHROPSHIRE (SHR)

252a	C1	- Landholders
b	1,1	- 3a,1
c	3b,1	- 3c,7
d	3c,8	- 3e,2

280a	(Nottingham)	
b	B1	- B16
c	S1	- S6

NOTTINGHAMSHIRE (NTT)

280a	B1	- B20
b	(Derby)	
c	S1	- S6
d	Landholders (also for RUT)	
281a	1,1	- 1,13
b	1,14	- 1,31
c	1,32	- 1,50
d	1,51	- 1,66
282a,b	blank	
c	2,1	- 3,4
d	4,1	- 4,8
283a	5,1	- 5,6
b	5,7	- 5,19
c	blank	
d	6,1	- 6,11
284a	6,11	- 6,15
b	7,1	- 8,2
c	9,1	- 9,15. 9,21
d	9,15	- 9,20. 9,22-28
285a	9,29	- 9,40
b	9,40	- 9,53
c	9,54	- 9,65
d	9,66	- 9,76
286a	9,76	- 9,80. 9,82-93
b	9,94	- 9,106. 9,81
c	9,107	- 9,118
d	9,118	- 9,127
287a	9,128	- 9,132
b	10,1	- 10,15
c	10,15	- 10,28
d	10,29	- 10,46
288a	10,46	- 10,60
b	10,61	- 10,66
c	11,1	- 11,12. 11,13
d	11,12	- 11,25
289a	11,26	- 11,33
b	12,1	- 12,19
c	12,19	- 13,11
d	13,11	- 14,8
290a	15,1	- 15,10
b	16,1	- 16,12
c	17,1	- 17,12
d	17,13	- 17,18
291a	18,1	- 19,1
b	20,1	- 20,8
c	21,1	- 23,2
d	24,1	- 26,1

292a	27,1	- 29,2
b	blank	
c	30,1	- 30,13
d	30,14	- 30,31
293a	30,31	- 30,46
b	30,46	- 30,56

RUTLAND (RUT)

280d	Landholders (with NTT)	
293c	R1	- 12
d	R12	- 20
294a	R21	
b-d	blank	
295a-296d blank		

YORKSHIRE (YKS)

297a-d	blank	
298a	C1a	- C10
b	C11	- C28
c	C28	- C37
d	C38	- Landholders
299a	1Y1	- 1Y3
b	1Y3	- 1Y7
c	1Y8	- 1Y13
d	1Y14	- 1Y18
300a	1Y18	- 1N20
b	1N21	- 1N61
c	1N62	- 1N94
d	1N95	- 1N132
301a	1N133	- 1E44
b	1E45	- 1W28
c	1W29	- 1W72
d	1W73	- 1L6
302a	1L7	- 1L8
b	2A1	- 2A4
c	2B1	- 2B5
d	2B6	- 2B14
303a	2B15	- 2N7
b	2N8	- 2N25
c	2N26	- 2W5
d	2W6	- 2W13
304a	2E1	- 2E14
b	2E15	- 2E41
c	3Y1	- 3Y7
d	3Y7	- 3Y18
305a	4N1	- 4E2
b	5N1	- 5N12
c	5N13	- 5N27
d	5N28	- 5N48

306a	5N49	- 5N61		c	10W17	- 10W27
b	5N62	- 5E4		d	10W27	- 10W37
c	5E5	- 5E22		320a	10W38	- 10W43
d	5E23	- 5E36		b	blank	
307a	5E37	- 5E58		c	11E1	- 11N6
b	5E59	- 5E71		d	11N7	- 11W1
c	5E72	- 5W7		321a	11W2	- 11W4. 12W21-28
d	5W7	- 5W14		b	12W1	- 12W20
308a	5W15	- 5W21		c	13W1	- 13W9
b	5W21	- 5W32		d	13W9	- 13W18
c	5W32	- 5W38		322a	13W19	- 13W31
d	blank			b	13W32	- 13W45
309a	6N1	- 6N2		c	13E1	- 13E12
b	6N3	- 6N11		d	13E12	- 13N5
c	6N12	- 6N23		323a	13N5	- 13N16
d	6N24	- 6N31		b	13N17	- 13N19
310a	6N31	- 6N40		c	14E1	- 14E4
b	6N41	- 6N51		d	14E4	- 14E9
c	6N52	- 6N57		324a	14E9	- 14E15
d	6N58	- 6N67		b	14E16	- 14E26
311a	6N68	- 6N80		c	14E26	- 14E36
b	6N80	- 6N92		d	14E37	- 14E47
c	6N92	- 6N101		325a	14E47	- 14E54
d	6N102	- 6N113		b	15E1	- 15E12
312a	6N113	- 6N120		c	15E12	- 15E17
b	6N121	- 6N132		d	16E1	- 16W3
c	6N133	- 6N139		326a	16W3	- 18W3
d	6N139	- 6N150		b	19W1	- 20E4
313a	6N151	- 6N161. 6W1-5		c	21E1	- 21E8
b	6W6	- 6E1. 6N162		d	21E9	- 21W11
c,d	blank			327a	21W12	- 22W6
314a	7E1	- 8N5		b	23N1	- 23N10
b	8N6	- 8N23		c	23N10	- 23N22
c	8N24	- 8E6		d	23N23	- 23N33
d	blank			328a	23N33	- 23N33. 23E1-11
315a	9W1	- 9W8		b	23E11	- 23E19. 23N34-36
b	9W9	- 9W19		c	24W1	- 24W12
c	9W20	- 9W31		d	24W12	- 24E2
d	9W32	- 9W41		329a	25W1	- 25W11
316a	9W42	- 9W50		b	25W11	- 25W20
b	9W50	- 9W60		c	25W21	- 25W33
c	9W60	- 9W67		d	26E1	- 27W2
d	9W67	- 9W76		330a	28W1	- 28W22
317a	9W77	- 9W87		b	28W23	- 28W41
b	9W87	- 9W98		c	29W1	- 29W11
c	9W99	- 9W112		d	29W12	- 29W24. 29E1-7
d	9W112	- 9W122		331a	29E8	- 29E26
318a	9W123	- 9W135		b	29N1	- 29N13. 29E27-28
b	9W136	- 9W144		c	29E29	- 29E30. 29W25-38
c,d	blank			d	29W39	- 29W51
319a	10W1	- 10W6		332a	30W1	- 30W33
b	10W6	- 10W16		b	30W34	- 30W40

c	31E1	- 31W3
d	31W4	- 31N8
333a	31N8	- 31N10
b-d	blank	

334a-335d blank

(336a-372d Lincolnshire)

373a	CN1	- CE15
b	CE15	- CE27
c	CE28	- CE33. CW1-4
d	CW5	- CW24
374a	CW25	- CW39
b	CE34	- CE52. CW40-42
c,d	blank	

(375a-37d Lincolnshire)

379a	SN,Y	- SW,Sk. SW,BA1-3
b	SW,BA4	- SW,BA13. SW,Sf1-34
c	SW,Sf35	- Sf37. SW,O. SW,St. SW, Ag1-8
d	SW,Ag9	- SW,Ag16. SW,M. SW, An. SW,Bu1-5
380a	SW,Bu6	- SW,Bu49
b	SW,H1	- SW,Cr5
c	SN,L1	- SN,D4
d	SN,D5	- SN,D21. SN,Ma. SN, B1-6
381a	SN,B7	- SN,B27. SN,Bi. SN,A
b	SN,CtA1	- SN,CtA45
c	SE,He1	- SE,He11. SE,Wel. SE, C. SE,How. SE,Wei1-14
d	SE,Wei5	- SE,Wei7. SE,Sn. SE, Dr. SE,Wa. SE,P. SE, Hu1-6
382a	SE,Hu7	- SE,Hu8. SE,Tu. SE, Bt. SE,Sc. SE,Ac
b	SE,Th1	- SE,Th14. SE,So. SE, Mid. SE,No. SE,Hol-26
c,d	blank	

LINCOLNSHIRE (LIN)

336a	C1	- C11
b	C12	- C21
c	C21	- C33
d	S1	- S16
337a	T1	- T5
b	Landholders	
c	1,1	- 1,7
d	1,8	- 1,15
338a	1,16	- 1,31
b	1.32	- 1,39
c	1,40	- 1,66
d	1,67	- 1,87

339a	1,88	- 1,105
b	1,105	- 1,106
c	2,1	- 2,11
d	2,12	- 2,22
340a	2,23	- 2,35
b	2,35	- 2,42
c	3,1	- 3,11
d	3,12	- 3,26
341a	3,27	- 3,28. 3,30-36
b	3,37	- 3,48. 3,29
c	3,48	- 3,56
d	blank	
342a	4,1	- 4,5. 4,7-11
b	4,11	- 4,25. 4,6
c	4,26	- 4,39
d	4,40	- 4,51
343a	4,51	- 4,63
b	4,63	- 4,75
c	4,75	- 4,81
d	5,1	- 6,1
344a	7,1	- 7,13
b	7,14	- 7,26
c	7,27	- 7,39
d	7,39	- 7,52
345a	7,52	- 7,59
b	blank	
c	8,1	- 8,8
d	8,8	- 8,18
346a	8,18	- 8,32
b	8,33	- 9,2
c	10,1	- 10,4
d	11,1	- 11,9
347a	12,1	- 12,11
b	12,11	- 12,24
c	12,24	- 12,38
d	12,38	- 12,48
348a	12,49	- 12,58
b	12,59	- 12,71
c	12,71	- 12,84
d	12,85	- 12,97
349a	13,1	- 13,9
b	13,9	- 13,21
c	13,22	- 13,33
d	13,34	- 13,45
350a	14,1	- 14,13
b	14,13	- 14,25
c	14,26	- 14,38
d	14,39	- 14,52
351a	14,52	- 14,64
b	14,65	- 14,79
c	14,79	- 14,92
d	14,93	- 15,2

III. Key to the relation between the folio notation of the MS. Text of LDB and the Numbered Chapters and Sections of the Present Edition. See section I, above.

ESSEX (ESS)

1a	Landholders	
b	1,1	- 1,2
2a	1,2	- 1,3
b	1,3	- 1,4
3a	1,4	- 1,8
b	1,9	- 1,11
4a	1,12	- 1,14
b	1,15	- 1,19
5a	1,19	- 1,24
b	1,24	- 1,25
6a	1,25	- 1,27
b	1,27	
7a	1,28	- 1,29
b	1,29	- 1,31
8a	2,1	- 2,6
b	2,6	- 2,9
9a	Landholders	
b	3,1	- 3,5
10a	3,6	- 3,9
b	3,9	- 3,13
11a	3,13	- 4,2
b	4,3	- 4,9
12a	4,9	- 4,15
b	4,16	- 5,3
13a	5,3	- 5,8
b5,8	- 5,12	
14a	5,12	- 6,5
b	6,6	- 6,9
15a	6,9	- 6,15
b	7,1	- 8,1
16a	8,1	- 8,8
b	8,8	- 8,11
17a	Landholders	
b	9,1	- 9,7
18a	9,7	- 9,12
b	9,13	- 10,1
19a	10,2	- 10,5
b	10,5	- 11,3
20a	11,3	- 11,8
b	12,1	- 14,2
21a	14,2	- 14,7
b	14,7	- 15,2
22a	15,2	- 17,2
b	18,1	- 18,5
23a	18,5	- 18,11
b	18,11	- 18,19
24a	18,20	- 18,25
b	18,25	- 18,34
25a	18,34	- 18,38

b	18,39	- 18,45
26a	18,45	- 20,2
b	20,2	- 20,7
27a	20,7	- 20,13
b	20,13	- 20,19
28a	20,19	- 20,23
b	20,24	- 20,27
29a	20,28	- 20,34
b	20,34	- 20,37
30a	20,37	- 20,42
b	20,43	- 20,46
31a	20,46	- 20,52
b	20,52	- 20,56
32a	20,56	- 20,62
b	20,63	- 20,67
33a	20,67	- 20,71
b	20,71	- 20,75
34a	20,75	- 20,79
b	20,79	- 20,80
35a	21,1	- 21,6
b	21,6	- 21,12
36a	22,1	- 22,5
b	22,6	- 22,9
37a	22,10	- 22,13
b	22,13	- 22,18
38a	22,19	- 22,24
b	23,1	- 23,3
39a	23,3	- 23,8
b	23,8	- 23,16
40a	23,16	- 23,28
b	23,28	- 23,34
41a	23,34	- 23,40
b	23,40	- 23,43
42a	24,1	- 24,5
b	24,5	- 24,10
43a	24,10	- 24,16
b	24,17	- 24,20
44a	24,20	- 24,24
b	24,24	- 24,28
45a	24,28	- 24,33
b	24,33	- 24,42
46a	24,42	- 24,46
b	24,46	- 24,53
47a	24,53	- 24,57
b	24,57	- 24,61
48a	24,61	- 24,66
b	24,66	- 24,67
49a	25,1	- 25,4
b	25,4	- 25,10
50a	25,10	- 25,15
b	25,15	- 25,19

51a	25,19	- 25,23	79a	36,6	- 36,11
b	25,23	- 25,26	b	36,11	- 37,2
52a	26,1	- 26,4	80a	37,2	- 37,7
b	26,5	- 27,3	b	37,7	- 37,11
53a	27,3	- 27,7	81a	37,11	- 37,17
b	27,8	- 27,13	b	37,17	- 38,1
54a	27,13	- 27,17	82a	38,2	- 38,6
b	27,17	- 28,2	b	38,6	- 39,1
55a	28,3	- 28,8	83a'	39,2	- 39,6
b	28,8	- 28,12	b	39,6	- 39,12
56a	28,13	- 28,17	84a	40,1	- 40,4
b	28,17	- 29,2	b	40,4	- 40,9
57a	29,2	- 29,5	85a	40,9	- 41,5
b	30,1	- 30,4	b	41,5	- 41,10
58a	30,4	- 30,7	86a	41,10	- 42,1
b	30,7	- 30,13	b	42,1	- 42,6
59a	30,14	- 30,18	87a	42,7	- 42,9
b	30,18	- 30,22	b	43,1	- 43,5
60a	30,22	- 30,27	88a	43,5	- 44,2
b	30,27	- 30,30	b	44,2	- 45,1
61a	30,30	- 30,34	89a	45,1	- 46,3
b	30,35	- 30,40	b	46,3	- 47,3
62a	30,40	- 30,45	90a	48,1	- 49,1
b	30,45	- 30,49	b	49,1	- 50,1
63a	30,49	- 31,1	91a	51,1	- 52,3
b	32,1	- 32,5	b	52,3	- 54,2
64a	32,6	- 32,9	92a	54,2	- 56,1
b	32,9	- 32,14	b	57,1	- 57,5
65a	32,14	- 32,19	93a	57,5	- 60,2
b	32,19	- 32,23	b	60,2	- 61,2
66a	32,23	- 32,26	94a	61,2	- 64,1
b	32,26	- 32,30	b	64,1	- 66,2
67a	32,30	- 32,36	95a	66,2	- 68,4
b	32,36	- 32,40	b	68,4	- 69,2
68a	32,40	- 32,45	96a	69,3	- 71,3
b	32,45	- 33,2	b	71,4	- 73,1
69a	32,2	- 33,6	97a	73,1	- 77,1
b	33,6	- 33,11	b	77,1	- 81,1
70a	33,11	- 33,13	98a	81,1	- 84,1
b	33,13	- 33,17	b	84,1	- 88,2
71a	33,17	- 33,22	99a	89,1	- 90,4
b	33,22	- 34,2	b	90,5	- 90,14
72a	34,2	- 34,6	100a	90,15	- 90,22
b	34,6	- 34,9	b	90,23	- 90,34
73a	34,9	- 34,13	101a	90,35	- 90,44
b	34,14	- 34,19	b	90,45	- 90,53
74a	34,19	- 34,22	102a	90,53	- 90,63
b	34,22	- 34,27	b	90,64	- 90,73
75a	34,27	- 34,32	103a	90,74	- 90,83
b	34,32	- 34,36	b	90,84	- 90,87
76a	34,36	- 35,2	104a	B1	- B3a
b	35,2	- 35,5	b	B3a	
77a	35,5	- 35,8	105a	B3a	
b	35,9	- 35,12	b	B3a	
78a	35,13	- 36,2	106a	B3a	- B3d
b	36,2	- 36,6	b	B3d	- B3p

107a	B3p	- B6		b	1,196	- 1,198
b	B6	- B7		134a	1,198	- 1,201
108a	blank			b	1,201	- 1,203
b	blank			135a	1,203	- 1,206
				b	1,206	- 1,209
NORFOLK (NFK)				136a	1,209	- 1,210
				b	1,210	- 1,212
109a	Landholders			137a	1,212	- 1,214
b	1,1	- 1,2		b	1,215	- 1,216
110a	1,2	- 1,6		138a	1,216	- 1,218
b	1,6	- 1,11		b	1,218	- 1,221
111a	1,11	- 1,16		139a	1,221	- 1,226
b	1,16	- 1,19		b	1,226	- 1,228
112a	1,19	- 1,26		140a	1,228	- 1,231
b	1,26	- 1,32		b	1,231	- 1,236
113a	1,32	- 1,41		141a	1,237	- 1,239
b	1,41	- 1,48		b	1,239	- 1,241
114a	1,48	- 1,52		142a	2,1	- 2,4
b	1,52	- 1,57		b	2,4	
115a	1,57			143a	2,5	- 2,8
b	1,57	- 1,59		b	2,8	- 3,1
116a	1,59	- 1,61		144a	3,1	- 4,2
b	1,61			b	4,2	- 4,9
117a	1,61			145a	4,9	- 4,11
b	1,61	- 1,64		b	4,11	- 4,17
118a	1,65	- 1,67		146a	4,17	- 4,22
b	1,67	- 1,70		b	4,22	- 4,27
119a	1,70			147a	4,28	- 4,31
b	1,71			b	4,31	- 4,34
120a	1,71	- 1,76		148a	4,35	- 4,39
b	1,76	- 1,78		b	4,39	- 4,41
121a	1,78	- 1,82		149a	4,41	- 4,45
b	1,82	- 1,86		b	4,45	- 4,50
122a	1,87	- 1,89		150a	4,50	- 4,53
b	1,89	- 1,94		b	4,53	- 4,56
123a	1,94	- 1,99		151a	4,56	- 5,2
b	1,99	- 1,106		b	5.2	- 5,6
124a	1,106	- 1,116		152a	5,6	- 6,3
b	1,116	- 1,122		b	6,3	- 6,6
125a	1,122	- 1,128		153a	6,6	- 6,7
b	1,128	- 1,132		b	7,1	- 7,3
126a	1,132	- 1,136		154a	7,3	- 7,8
b	1,136	- 1,139		b	7,8	- 7,13
127a	1,139	- 1,143		155a	7,13	- 7,16
b	1.143	- 1,146		b	7,16	- 7,18
128a	1,146	- 1,150		156a	7,18	- 7,21
b	1,150	- 1,152		b	blank	
129a	1,152	- 1,159		157a	8,1	- 8,2
b	1,159	- 1,169		b	8,3	- 8,7
130a	1,169	- 1,176		158a	8,7	- 8,8
b	1,176	- 1,182		b	8,8	- 8,11
131a	1,182	- 1,185		159a	8,11	- 8,13
b	1,185	- 1,188		b	8,14	- 8,17
132a	1,189	- 1,192		160a	8,17	- 8,21
b	1,192	- 1,194		b	8,21	- 8,25
133a	1,194	- 1,196		161a	8,25	- 8,29

b	8,29	- 8,34
162a	8,34	- 8,39
b	8,39	- 8,45
163a	8,45	- 8,47
b	8,47	- 8,52
164a	8,53	- 8,56
b	8,57	- 8,61
165a	8,61	- 8,64
b	8,64	- 8,69
166a	8,69	- 8,77
b	8,78	- 8,84
167a	8,84	- 8,90
b	8,90	- 8,95
168a	8,95	- 8,99
b	8,99	- 8,103
169a	8,103	- 8,107
b	8,108	- 8,110
170a	8,110	- 8,116
b	8,117	- 8,121
171a	8,121	- 8,126
b	8,127	- 8,132
172a	8,132	- 8,137
b	8,137	- 8,138
173a	9,1	- 9,6
b	9,6	- 9,9
174a	9,9	- 9,13
b	9,13	- 9,24
175a	9,24	- 9,28
b	9,28	- 9,31
176a	9,32	- 9,42
b	9,42	- 9,49
177a	9,49	- 9,59
b	9,59	- 9,70
178a	9,70	- 9,75
b	9,75	- 9,80
179a	9,80	- 9,86
b	9,86	- 9,88
180a	9,88	- 9,94
b	9,94	- 9,98
181a	9,98	- 9,99
b	9,99	- 9,104
182a	9,104	- 9,108
b	9,109	- 9,115
183a	9,115	- 9,126
b	9,126	- 9,136
184a	9,136	- 9,146
b	9,146	- 9,150
185a	9,150	- 9,157
b	9,157	- 9,164
186a	9,164	- 9,169
b	9,169	- 9,177
187a	9,177	- 9,182
b	9,183	- 9,190
188a	9,190	- 9,196
b	9,196	- 9,200
189a	9,200	- 9,212
b	9,212	- 9,223
190a	9,223	- 9,232
b	9,232	- 9,234
191a	10,1	- 10,4
	10,4	- 10,7
192a	10,7	- 10,10
b	10,11	- 10,15
193a	10,15	- 10,19
b	10,20	
194a	10,21	- 10,23
b	10,24	- 10,28
195a	10,28	- 10,30
b	10,30	- 10,33
196a	10,33	- 10,38
b	10,38	- 10,42
197a	10,42	- 10,47
b	10,48	- 10,55
198a	10,55	- 10,59
b	10,60	- 10,65
199a	10,66	- 10,71
b	10,71	- 10,74
200a	10,74	- 10,80
b	10,80	- 10,86
201a	10,86	- 10,90
b	10,91	- 11,1
202a	11,1	- 12,1
b	12,1	- 12,6
203a	12,7	- 12,17
b	12,17	- 12,24
204a	12,25	- 12,30
b	12,30	- 12,34
205a	12,34	- 12,42
b	12,42	- 13,3
206a	13,3	- 13,7
b	13,7	- 13,12
207a	13,12	- 13,16
b	13,16	- 13,19
208a	13,19	- 13,24
b	13,24	
209a	14,1	- 14,6
b	14,6	- 14,14
210a	14,14	- 14,17
b	14,17	- 14,23
211a	14,23	- 14,29
b	14,29	- 14,37
212a	14,37	- 14,42
b	14,42	- 15,2
213a	15,2	- 15,7
b	15,7	- 15,11
214a	15,11	- 15,17
b	15,17	- 15,25
215a	15,25	- 16,1
b	16,1	- 16,6
216a	17,1	- 17,8
b	17,8	- 17,13
217a	17,14	- 17,18

b	17,18	- 17,24		b	29,1	- 29,5
218a	17,24	- 17,31		246a	29,5	- 29,8
b	17,32	- 17,38		b	29,8	- 29,11
219a	17,38	- 17,43		247a	30,1	- 30,4
b	17,44	- 17,52		b	30,4	- 31,1
220a	17,52	- 17,55		248a	31,2	- 31,5
b	17,56	- 17,62		b	31,5	- 31,6
221a	17,62	- 17,65		249a	31,6	- 31,10
b	18,1	- 19,2		b	31,10	- 31,15
222a	19,3	- 19,9		250a	31,15	- 31,17
b	19,9	- 19,11		b	31,17	- 31,22
223a	19,11	- 19,15		251a	31,22	- 31,28
b	19,16	- 19,21		b	31,28	- 31,33
224a	19,21	- 19,25		252a	31,34	- 31,37
b	19,26	- 19,32		b	31,38	- 31,41
225a	19,32	- 19,36		253a	31,41	- 31,44
b	19,36	- 20,1		b	31,44	- 31,45
226a	20,1	- 20,6		254a	32,1	- 32,3
b	20,6	- 20,8		b	32,3	- 32,7
227a	20,8	- 20,10		255a	32,7	- 33,2
b	20,10	- 20,14		b	33,2	- 33,6
228a	20,14	- 20,19		256a	34,1	- 34,3
b	20,19	- 20,24		b	34,3	- 34,6
229a	20,24	- 20,29		257a	34,6	- 34,9
b	20,29	- 20,34		b	34,9	- 34,15
230a	20,35	- 21,2		258a	34,15	- 34,19
b	21,2	- 21,5		b	34,20	- 35,3
231a	21,5	- 21,8		259a	35,3	- 35,8
b	21,8	- 21,13		b	35,8	- 35,13
232a	21,13	- 21,16		260a	35,13	- 35,18
b	21,17	- 21,21		b	35,18	- 36,5
233a	21,22	- 21,25		261a	36,5	- 36,7
b	21,25	- 21,28		b	37,1	- 37,3
234a	21,28	- 21,32		262a	38,1	- 39,1
b	21,32	- 21,37		b	39,1	- 40,1
235a	22,1	- 22,6		263a	41,1	- 43,2
b	22,6	- 22,13		b	43,2	- 45,1
236a	22,13	- 22,21		264a	46,1	- 47,6
b	22,21	- 22,23		b	47,6	- 48,3
237a	23,1	- 23,4		265a	48,3	- 48,8
b	23,4	- 23,8		b	49,1	- 49,5
238a	23,8	- 23,12		266a	49,5	- 49,9
b	23,12	- 23,16		b	50,1	- 50,5
239a	23,16	- 23,18		267a	50,6	- 50,10
b	24,1	- 24,5		b	50,10	- 51,3
240a	24,5	- 24,7		268a	51,3	- 51,8
b	24,7	- 25,1		b	51,8	- 52,3
241a	25,2	- 25,7		269a	52,3	- 54,1
b	25,7	- 25,12		b	54,1	- 56,2
242a	25,12	- 25,17		270a	56,3	- 57,3
b	25,17	- 25,25		b	58,1	- 59,1
243a	25,25	- 26,1		271a	59,1	- 61,1
b	26,1	- 26,3		b	61,1	- 62,2
244a	26,3	- 26,5		272a	62,2	- 64,4
b	26,5	- 27,2		b	64,5	- 65,7
245a	27,2	- 28,2		273a	65,8	- 65,16

328a	6,301	- 6,304		356a	13,3	- 13,7
b	6,305	- 6,308		b	14,1	- 14,3
329a	6,308	- 6,311		357a	14,3	- 14,7
b	6,311	- 6,317		b	14,8	- 14,12
330a	6,317	- 6,319		358a	14,12	- 14,16
b	7,1	- 7,3		b	14,16	- 14,20
331a	7,3	- 7,6		359a	14,21	- 14,24
b	7,6	- 7,10		b	14,24	- 14,28
332a	7,10	- 7,15		360a	14,28	- 14,36
b	7,15			b	14,36	- 14,42
333a	7,16	- 7,20		361a	14,42	- 14,47
b	7,20	- 7,26		b	14,48	- 14,50
334a	7,26	- 7,33		362a	14,50	- 14,53
b	7,33	- 7,37		b	14,53	- 14,59
335a	7,37	- 7,42		363a	14,59	- 14,64
b	7,42	- 7,49		b	14,64	- 14,68
336a	7,49	- 7,56		364a	14,69	- 14,72
b	7,56	- 7,58		b	14,72	- 14,75
337a	7,58	- 7,61		365a	14,75	- 14,77
b	7,61	- 7,65		b	14,78	- 14,81
338a	7,65	- 7,68		366a	14,81	- 14,85
b	7,68	- 7,72		b	14,85	- 14,90
339a	7,72	- 7,75		367a	14,90	- 14,95
b	7,76	- 7,79		b	14,96	- 14,101
340a	7,79	- 7,85		368a	14,102	- 14,106
b	7,85	- 7,92		b	14,106	- 14,110
341a	7,92	- 7,98		369a	14,111	- 14,115
b	7,98	- 7,105		b	14,115	- 14,120
342a	7,105	- 7,111		370a	14,120	- 14,128
b	7,111	- 7,119		b	14,129	- 14,138
343a	7,119	- 7,122		371a	14,138	- 14,153
b	7,122	- 7,133		b	14,154	- 14,166
344a	7,133	- 7,138		372a	14,167.	Landholders
b	7,138	- 7,143		b	15,1	- 15,4
345a	7,143	- 7,148		373a	15,5	- 16,3
b	7,149	- 7,151		b	16,4	- 16,10
346a	8,1	- 8,6		374a	16,10	- 16,14
b	8,6	- 8,9		b	16,14	- 16,17
347a	8,9	- 8,14		375a	16,17	- 16,20
b	8,14	- 8,23		b	16,21	- 16,25
348a	8,23	- 8,32		376a	16,25	- 16,27
b	8,32	- 8,35		b	16,28	- 16,31
349a	8,35	- 8,42		377a	16,32	- 16,35
b	8,42	- 8,46		b	16,36	- 16,40
350a	8,46	- 8,49		378a	16,40	- 16,45
b	8,49	- 8,55		b	16,45	- 17,1
351a	8,55	- 8,56		379a	18,1	- 18,5
b	8,56	- 8,59		b	18,6	- 19,10
352a	8,59	- 8,66		380a	19,11	- 19,16
b	8,66	- 8,78		b	19,16	- 19,18
353a	8,78	- 9,1		381a	19,18	- 20,1
b	9,1	- 9,3		b	21,1	- 21,5
354a	9,3	- 11,2		382a	21,5	- 21,11
b	11,2	- 12,1		b	21,11	- 21,16
355a	12,1	- 12,6		383a	21,16	- 21,25
b	12,6	- 13,3		b	21,25	- 21,29

440a	66,10	- 66,17	
b	67,1	- 67,3	
441a	67,3	- 67,8	
b	67,8	- 67,11	
442a	67,11	- 67,15	
b	67,15	- 67,19	
443a	67,19	- 67,27	
b	67,27	- 67,30	
444a	67,30	- 68,1	
b	68,1	- 68,5	
445a	69,1	- 70,1	

b	71,1	- 73,1	
446a	74,1	- 74,9	
b	74,9	- 74,15	
447a	74,16	- 75,4	
b	75,5	- 76,3	
448a	76,3	- 76,7	
b	76,8	- 76,16	
449a	76,16	- 76,22	
b	76,22	- 76,23	
450a	77,1	- 4. Colophon	